Praise for Paul Goldberger's

Building Art

"Terrifically readable. . . . Satisfying detail on Gehry's career path and hugely complex personality." —*Los Angeles Times*

"Convey[s] the architect's personality and process with deft strokes that have an artistic ease of their own. . . . If you're intrigued by Frank Gehry . . . I can't recommend this expansive survey of his life and work too highly." —John King, *San Francisco Chronicle*

"Fascinating. . . . Agilely balances the disparate subjects of art and biography. Goldberger's critical assessments of Gehry's designs are insightful and often riveting." —*Richmond Times-Dispatch*

"Critically fluent, socially and psychologically acute. . . . An involving work of significant architectural history and a discerning and affecting portrait of a daring and original master builder." —*Booklist* (starred review)

"This full-length critical study of an important contemporary architect is by one of our finest architectural critics. . . . [An] outstanding volume. . . . Highly recommended." —*Library Journal* (starred review)

"Richly researched, intelligent, and graceful." —*Kirkus Reviews*

"[Goldberger] contextualizes Gehry's work with smart discussions of trends in Modernism and the Los Angeles art scene that inspired such trends, and offers his usual shrewd, evocative insights into the look and feel of buildings." —*Publishers Weekly*

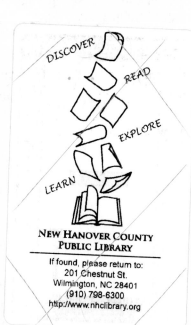

Paul Goldberger

Building Art

Paul Goldberger, a contributing editor at *Vanity Fair*, spent fifteen years as the architecture critic for *The New Yorker* and began his career at *The New York Times*, where he was awarded the Pulitzer Prize for distinguished criticism for his writing on architecture. He is the author of many books, including *Why Architecture Matters, Building Up and Tearing Down: Reflections on the Age of Architecture*, and *Up from Zero*. He teaches at The New School and lectures widely around the country on architecture, design, historic preservation, and cities. He and his wife, Susan Solomon, live in New York City.

www.paulgoldberger.com

ALSO BY PAUL GOLDBERGER

The City Observed

The Skyscraper

On the Rise

The Houses of the Hamptons

Up from Zero

Building Up and Tearing Down:
    Reflections on the Age of Architecture

Why Architecture Matters

Christo and Jeanne-Claude

Building with History

New York Mid-Century, 1945–1965

    (with Robert Gottlieb and Anne Cohen-Solal)

Building Art

The Life and Work of Frank Gehry

Paul Goldberger

VINTAGE BOOKS
A Division of Penguin Random House LLC
New York

FIRST VINTAGE BOOKS EDITION, NOVEMBER 2017

Copyright © 2015 by Paul Goldberger

All rights reserved. Published in the United States by Vintage Books, a division
of Penguin Random House LLC, New York, and distributed in Canada by
Random House of Canada, a division of Penguin Random House Canada Limited,
Toronto. Originally published in hardcover in the United States by Alfred A. Knopf,
a division of Penguin Random House LLC, New York, in 2015.

Vintage and colophon are registered trademarks of Penguin Random House LLC.

The Library of Congress has cataloged the Knopf edition as follows:
Goldberger, Paul.
Building art : the life and work of Frank Gehry / by Paul Goldberger.—First Edition.
pages cm
1. Gehry, Frank O., 1929–   2. Architects—United States—Biography.   I. Title.
NA737.G44G65 2015
720.92—dc23
[B] 2015026562

Vintage Books Trade Paperback ISBN: 978-0-307-94639-3
eBook ISBN: 978-1-101-87580-3

Author photograph © Michael Lionstar
Book design by Iris Weinstein

www.vintagebooks.com

Printed in the United States of America
10 9 8 7 6 5 4 3 2 1

For Susan

Rationalists, wearing square hats,

Think, in square rooms,

Looking at the floor,

Looking at the ceiling.

They confine themselves

To right-angled triangles.

If they tried rhomboids,

Cones, waving lines, ellipses—

As, for example, the ellipse of the half-moon—

Rationalists would wear sombreros.

WALLACE STEVENS, "SIX SIGNIFICANT LANDSCAPES," VI

Contents

Preface

In the spring of 1974, as a young writer for *The New York Times*, I went to Washington, D.C., for the annual convention of the American Institute of Architects. I didn't normally go to conventions, but I had just become the newspaper's junior architecture critic, and I had the thought that attending the largest gathering of architects in the country might be a source of a few good stories, or at least a chance to meet some people and have them meet me. The AIA had just opened its new national headquarters building and wanted to show it off, and as a consequence the big party of the convention was held not in a hotel ballroom but on the grounds of the AIA building on New York Avenue. I was standing at the edge of the party, which spilled out to the sidewalk, talking to my colleague Ada Louise Huxtable, when a pleasant man with a mustache who looked to be in his forties—I was then in my twenties—recognized her and came up to say hello.

He, too, seemed an unlikely convention-goer, a bit more casually dressed than most architects, who in the early 1970s tended to look either like insurance salesmen or college professors. This guy had a quiet, eager freshness to his manner. He told Ada Louise that his name was Frank Gehry, and that he was an architect from Los Angeles. His name did not ring a bell; he told us we might have heard of some cardboard furniture he had designed that was sold at Bloomingdale's a few years ago, which did seem vaguely familiar, but I certainly didn't know of any buildings he had done. He had a curiosity about our work as journalists, and was interested in criticism and ideas. He told us he was more involved with artists in Los Angeles than with his fellow architects. He did not seem to know many people at the party, and it did not take long to see that he was something of an outlier. But he was not a typical outlier, or he would not have been there at all. He was an outlier who wanted in, but, as I discovered as time went by, on his own terms.

Ada Louise excused herself to return to her hotel, and Frank and I kept talking. That evening began a conversation that has lasted for more than four decades, and this book is one result of it. Gehry invited me to talk further if I ever came to Los Angeles, which I was beginning to do more frequently—I sensed, more than most New Yorkers, that the city needed to be taken seriously as a laboratory of architecture and urbanism, although I didn't understand at that point how central Frank Gehry would be to what was happening there. But I was happy to come and see some of his work for myself. In 1976 I wrote "Studied Slapdash," an essay in *The New York Times Magazine* about the house Gehry designed for the painter Ron Davis in Malibu, which turned out to be the first time one of his buildings was written about in a national general-interest publication. So I have been documenting his work from a very early point in his career, and an even earlier point in my own.

Over the years, as I came to know and admire his work more fully, and as it grew in both scale and complexity, I wrote about it frequently in *The New York Times*, *The New Yorker*, and *Vanity Fair*, my three professional homes as a journalist and critic. Gehry and I discussed my writing an essay for a monograph on his work at several points; none of these projects came to fruition, but when Alfred A. Knopf proposed to me that I write a full-length biography of him—by then he was the most famous architect in the world—I asked if he would be willing to cooperate with me on that project instead of proceeding with the monograph. I said that if he agreed to work with me, it would be necessary to open his archives to me, to discuss the difficult times in his personal and professional life as well as the happy and triumphant ones, and, most important, to agree that he could have no editorial control over the text. He graciously agreed to all of these conditions, and this book is the result.

Building Art

I

Night of the Supermoon

The guest list for the party that Bruce Ratner, a New York City real estate developer, gave in the unfinished seventy-second-floor penthouse of his new apartment tower in Lower Manhattan on the night of March 19, 2011, was unusual for an event celebrating the opening of a new real estate project. The singer and activist Bono showed up; so did several artists, including Chuck Close and Claes Oldenburg. There were actors like Ben Gazzara and Candice Bergen; the art dealer Larry Gagosian; Harvey Lichtenstein, the longtime head of the Brooklyn Academy of Music; the hotelier Ian Schrager; and celebrated journalists like Morley Safer, Tom Brokaw, and Carl Bernstein. These and other famous names had not come to get a preview of the steel-clad building, even though it was then the tallest residential tower in the city and the question of what its apartments would be like had been the subject of much speculative talk around town. Neither were most of the guests friends of Bruce Ratner. The celebrities—and about three hundred other somewhat less recognizable people—were friends and acquaintances of a short, somewhat stocky, gray-haired man with glasses, dressed in a black T-shirt and black suit jacket, who spent much of his time standing near the windows on the north side of the penthouse, which had a spectacular view of the Manhattan skyline and the towers of the Brooklyn Bridge. He had designed the building, and he was arguably the most famous architect in the world.

Frank Gehry had turned eighty-two two and a half weeks earlier, and Bruce Ratner decided that a birthday party for the architect would be the perfect way to mark the tower's completion. It would also encourage everyone to forget that twenty-one months earlier Ratner had abruptly fired Gehry from another job, even bigger than the apartment tower: designing

Left to right: Ben Gazzara, Bruce Ratner, Bono, Carl Bernstein, and Frank Gehry in the penthouse of Ratner's tower at 8 Spruce Street

the master plan and the buildings for Atlantic Yards, a huge real estate project his company, Forest City Ratner, was preparing to erect over railyards in downtown Brooklyn that was to contain seventeen buildings, including a new arena for the Nets basketball team, which was moving to Brooklyn from New Jersey. Gehry had produced an arena design and schemes for several skyscrapers as well as an overall plan, and his involvement gave Atlantic Yards the air of a more serious enterprise than the usual large commercial real estate project. But after winning preliminary approval for the project based on Gehry's plans, Ratner replaced him with another firm and ordered up buildings that were simpler and presumably less expensive than the ones Gehry had designed. Gehry was shaken and angry about the decision, which required him to lay off many of the architects who were working on the project in his office back home in Los Angeles. His frustration was compounded by the fact that he could only express his unhappiness in private, since he was continuing to work on Bruce Ratner's tall apartment building for Lower Manhattan, and he could hardly get into a public spat with him. He seethed inwardly, as he usually did when something did not go as he had hoped. He was not fond of confrontation, and he had generally managed to get his way by being friendly and easygoing, not by acting the role of the temperamental artist.

That suited Ratner just fine, since he did not want to be remembered as the developer who had fired Frank Gehry. He much preferred to be known as the developer who had given Gehry the opportunity to build the tallest apartment tower in New York. After firing him from Atlantic Yards, Ratner was doing all he could to connect his name to Gehry's in a different way. He had called the new Lower Manhattan tower "New York by Gehry," agreeing with his marketing advisers that he was selling Frank Gehry as much as anything else at 8 Spruce Street—that Gehry's reputation was such that his name could mean as much as views, closets, fancy kitchens, big windows, or even the ultimate factor in real estate, location. There had never been a Frank Gehry apartment tower in New York before. There had never been a Frank Gehry skyscraper anywhere before, for that matter. Gehry was known for museums, concert halls, houses, academic buildings, and smaller commercial buildings, and his Los Angeles–based firm, while large—it employed about 150 people at the time of the birthday party— was not the sort of place that churned out office towers by the dozen. It was more of a gigantic artist's atelier, a big workshop centered on the creative imagination of its founder, who in the years leading up to the opening of the New York tower had designed two of the most acclaimed buildings of the last generation, the Guggenheim Museum in Bilbao, Spain, which opened in 1997, and Walt Disney Concert Hall in Los Angeles, finished in 2003. When *Vanity Fair* polled ninety of the world's leading architects and critics in 2010 and asked them to name the five most important build- ings erected since 1980, the museum in Bilbao was the overwhelming win- ner, with three times as many votes as any other building anywhere in the world. "Therefore it seems fair to conclude," the magazine pronounced, "that the 81-year old, Canadian-born Gehry is the most important architect of our age."

The extraordinary shape Gehry had conceived for Bilbao, a swirling, curving structure covered largely in titanium, inspired the architect Philip Johnson, who toured the museum a few months before its completion, to proclaim it "the greatest building of our time." It stood as evidence of Gehry's ability to envision form that had not existed before: exhilarating, robust, and baroque in its richness and complexity. The museum could not be called anything but modern, but it was not your father's modernism. Its unusual form bore no resemblance to the stark glass boxes that most people identified with modern architecture.

Because Gehry enjoyed making models out of paper and from time to time would crumple up pieces of paper and use the resulting shape as a starting point for figuring out what he wanted to do, his designs were thought by many to be casual and random. It was the same misconception that people had had fifty years before about the paintings of Franz Kline or Jackson Pollock. Gehry's buildings were no more the result of accident than Pollock's drip paintings, and at their best they possessed a similar kind of strange, new, intense, and energetic beauty.

You could, in fact, think of Gehry's buildings as representing a kind of "action architecture," following Harold Rosenberg's famous description of Kline, Pollack, and Willem de Kooning as "action painters,"* but while Gehry's finished buildings often felt dynamic, they came into being through a very different process than that of the action painters, for whom Rosenberg's term was intended to describe their intense engagement with the canvas itself. Architecture is not painting, and not only because it needs to fulfill practical and often mundane functions as well as evoke feeling and emotion. The process by which architecture is made is entirely different: it requires that every detail be specified in advance, rather than be the product of spontaneous impulse, as well as the collaboration of engineers to assure that a design is buildable and structurally sound.

Creative imagination is necessary but not sufficient to the process of making architecture, since what is imagined must be able to be built.† In the 1950s, the great abstract expressionist painters were creating work that powerfully, even profoundly, reinvented modern painting, but modern architecture was still by and large exploring themes that it had been dealing with since the 1920s. A glass-and-steel house built in the 1950s might have seemed advanced beside a shingled Cape Cod cottage, but that new house was not as radical a reinvention as, say, the De Kooning that, if the owners were fortunate, they might have hung within it. The challenges of getting a building built meant that architectural ideas rarely bore fruit as rapidly as artistic ones: it was one thing for a painter to put a dashing brushstroke across a canvas, and quite another for an architect to make a vast, flowing, irregular, geometrically complex space real. Engineers worked nobly to keep pace, but even such striking buildings as Eero Saarinen's TWA Terminal, of 1962, at John F. Kennedy International Airport

---

* Rosenberg first used the term in 1952, in an essay entitled "The American Action Painters," in which he wrote, "A painting that is an act is inseparable from the biography of the artist."

† Here I do not mean to overlook the rich history of architectural designs that were unbuildable but nevertheless influential. From Étienne-Louis Boullée and Claude Nicolas Ledoux in the eighteenth century to Antonio Sant'Elia in the early twentieth century to Lebbeus Woods in our own time, critical architectural ideas have been developed and communicated on paper as well as through constructed work. But the history of architecture properly is primarily a history of what is built, not what is merely imagined.

in New York—perhaps as advanced an example of structural engineering as its time was capable of creating—was almost tame beside what painters of the previous decade had been doing. From time to time architects like Frederick Kiesler imagined even bolder forms still, but they were essentially unbuildable.

Gehry, deeply connected to art and profoundly influenced by it, was among the first to realize that digital technology could provide a means for architects in effect to catch up with artists. Although he did not like to use a computer himself, he prided himself on being a technological innovator as well as a maker of unusual forms, and he saw that digital technology could go beyond its most common use in architects' offices, which was to make the production of architectural drawings more efficient. It could also make it possible to engineer and construct extraordinarily complex shapes that had previously been unbuildable. He realized that almost any form that the mind could conceive, the computer could engineer. It could free the architectural imagination.

Gehry and his colleagues began to work with advanced digital software that had been invented for the aerospace industry, adapting it for architectural use. That software became the essential ingredient in making projects like the Guggenheim in Bilbao possible—the link, you could say, between Gehry's imagination and the creation of an actual building. Bilbao was not the first building made possible by the digital revolution. But it was the first to excite the public, and the first to show clearly how much the computer could revolutionize architecture and make a different kind of building— the kind of building that Saarinen had been grasping toward, with only the most primitive tools, decades earlier.

Bilbao was the first radically different new building in a long time to have an impact on the popular culture. Gehry's powerful shapes seemed to capture the imagination of everyone, not just the architectural world; the museum was one of the few buildings in modern times to be hailed as a serious and important new work by architecture critics and historians, yet at the same time be embraced by a public whose taste in architecture often did not go beyond classical courthouses and redbrick Georgian houses and generally disdained anything that could be considered avant-garde. Its popularity marked an unusual development in any field, as if a novel by David Foster Wallace were to outsell those of John Grisham, or the music of Philip Glass were to top Lady Gaga on the charts. But something like that was what seemed to be happening with the Guggenheim, as many people who generally had little use for modern architecture were going to Bilbao, and liking what they saw. Here, perhaps for the first time since Frank Lloyd Wright's spiraling structure on Fifth Avenue in New York for the same Guggenheim Museum in 1959, was a building that was at once a cutting-edge work and the subject of public fascination, even excitement.

New York, of course, had hardly needed Frank Lloyd Wright's Guggenheim to get itself on the map. Bilbao, an old industrial city in the Basque region of northern Spain, was another matter. The magnetic appeal of Gehry's Guggenheim awakened the world to Bilbao, and made the city a huge tourist destination. The museum attracted a far larger crowd than the cognoscenti of art and architecture who normally make pilgrimages to far-off museums. The stream of visitors so revitalized the city that people began to talk of unusual buildings as having "the Bilbao effect," a phrase that became shorthand for the idea that a single work of architecture could have transformational power over a place.

G ehry had been well known in architectural circles for many years, but after Bilbao's opening in 1997 he began a meteoric rise to celebrity and became the best-known American architect since Frank Lloyd Wright. Given that they had both designed pathbreaking, highly popular museums that, while forty years apart, were built by the same institution, the parallels between the two Franks were hard to avoid. In reality, however, while Wright and Gehry shared a first name, a passionate commitment to architecture, and a brilliant gift for conceiving design that was new and different from what had come before, their underlying personalities, like the buildings they designed, were in almost every way different. Wright was something of an autocrat, politically conservative and narcissistic; he was incapable of admitting fault, and he made himself the center of a circle that was cultlike in its devotion. Wright's attitude seemed to be that if you did not like his architecture, it must be because you were incapable of appreciating greatness.

Gehry was more inclined to self-doubt. He craved affection and acceptance, he wanted his architecture to please, and sometimes it seemed that he viewed those two things—approval of his work and approval of himself as a person—as almost the same thing. "It's very important for Frank to feel needed and loved, in a kind of core way, through acceptance of his architecture," Babs Thompson, an old friend of his, said. If you did not appreciate his work, "then you're not understanding him, not accepting him," she said.

Even though Gehry was ridden with angst throughout his life, his manner came off as relaxed, low-key, and amiable, and his steely determination, far from being obvious like Wright's, was hidden behind an easygoing exterior, a kind of "aw shucks" air that Gehry's old friend the artist Peter Alexander called "his gentle, humble ways." Wright was never mistaken for being modest; Gehry often was.

It would be easy to say that Gehry, born Frank Goldberg, was Jewish and that Wright came from solid Welsh stock, and to suggest that the differences in their sensibilities can be explained by their backgrounds. Gehry grew up in Toronto and in Timmins, Ontario, a small mining town, and he was conscious of anti-Semitism for much of his youth. In his mind, he was an outsider, and a financially strapped one at that. Wright grew up in the late nineteenth century in Madison and rural Spring Green, Wisconsin, on land that had long been in his mother's family, and while he was not born to money, he had a sense of entitlement that never left him. He was part of a large, tight-knit clan whose motto was "Truth Against the World," a line that Gehry would undoubtedly have found pretentious and utterly lacking in irony. Wright believed in land and all that it symbolized; he would build his famous house, Taliesin, on his family's property in Spring Green. Gehry grew up living in small apartments and city houses, and while he, like Wright, would design a house for himself that would solidify his growing reputation as an architect, it would be a remake of an ordinary house on a corner suburban lot in Santa Monica, California, as far from ancestral estates as anything could be.

Gehry and Wright did have something else in common, however. They both had fathers who were impractical men, largely unsuccessful at their careers, who never managed to support their families financially or, for that matter, emotionally. And both architects had determined mothers who offered the focus their fathers lacked, and in each case introduced them to art, music, and literature. Wright's parents divorced when he was eighteen, and William Wright disappeared from his son's life; Gehry's father remained a presence in his son's life until his death at sixty-one in 1962. Irving Goldberg was a source of both sadness and frustration to his son, who struggled, often in vain, to find reasons to be proud of his father, whom he yearned to admire. Irving had some modest design skills—he liked to make small objects out of wood, and he once won an award for the design of a window display—but he was a failure in almost every business venture he undertook, and poor health rendered him an invalid for the last decade of his life. Those years were a time of mounting frustration for the senior Goldberg, who felt that his life was a series of missed opportunities. He could be a difficult, temperamental man, and his relationship with his son was fraught with particular anguish. It was Irving's nature to direct his bitterness mainly toward those closest to him; however difficult his circumstances became, he remained resolute in his commitment to liberal political beliefs. There were always people in worse straits, Irving believed, and he never retreated from his view that they deserved help. Ultimately his legacy to his son would not be in the realm of making or designing, but in a strong belief in inclusivity, social justice, and a sense of sympathy for the underdog.

Irving's failing health paradoxically provided his son with another great gift. In 1947, after a heart attack, Irving was told that he was not likely to survive another Toronto winter, and he resettled his family in Los Angeles to escape the cold climate, bringing his son as an eighteen-year-old to the city where he would spend the rest of his life, the city with which he would forever be identified as an architect in the same way that Christopher Wren's name is linked to London or Stanford White's to New York—and the place that would shape his outlook more than any other. Many of his instincts seemed more those of an artist than an architect, and in his early years he was more comfortable spending time with the artists of Los Angeles than with his fellow architects. The city had a community of talented artists who had chosen to work outside of the epicenter of the art world, New York, and their attitude dovetailed with Gehry's instinctive sense of himself as an outsider. With the artists, he was a double outsider—outside of New York like the rest of them, and not really an artist, either.

He did not like to call himself an artist or a sculptor, in part, he told an interviewer, because "there are some artists who are offended when you use the word 'art' for a building that has toilets in it." To a query in an early interview about whether he considered himself an artist, he responded with the definitive "No, I'm an architect," four words that would become almost a mantra. But there can be no doubt that he was more interested than most architects in creating highly expressive buildings, and after the museum in Bilbao opened, his name was all but synonymous with the notion of architecture as expressive form making. And labels notwithstanding, "You can argue that Frank is the most influential artist to emerge out of Los Angeles, period. I think he is," said the Los Angeles artist Tony Berlant, one of his oldest friends. Another Los Angeles artist, Billy Al Bengston, went even further. "I think Frank is the foremost artist in the contemporary world," he said.

If the popular acclaim of Bilbao posed any challenge, it was how to avoid being merely a "brand," which Gehry undoubtedly was, and to keep going as an architect—which for him meant not just to continue designing buildings but to do it as creatively as he had done before, and to resist the many opportunities he had to turn his famous building into a formula that he could replicate everywhere. "Success is much harder to deal with than failure," Gehry said, and he meant it. He did not want to repeat himself, and he would find it frustrating when observers looked at buildings he had done after Bilbao that also had lyrically curving forms of metal, glass, or stone and thought that however striking their appearance was, they were just examples of his copying his previous work. It wasn't that at all, in his view; people who thought of his post-Bilbao work as just a continuation of the design he had created for the museum were failing to understand that what he had really done was create an altogether new architectural language, and that with each new building he was using that language to say something in a slightly different way.

Architects and critics tended to agree with this sympathetic view, and Gehry's press was generally better than that of any other architect of his generation. But fame, of course, has another side, and Gehry's reputation all but assured that the unfelicitous but pungent term "starchitect" was frequently used alongside his name. It is a word that glibly conflates the flashiness of celebrity and the more serious pursuit of design, and it is not surprising that Gehry hated it. He may have been the quintessential starchitect in the public's mind, but to him the term misrepresented his work entirely, implying that his architecture involved nothing more than eye-catching, flashy shapes. But for all his professed discomfort with the label, he had no dislike of fame itself, and some of his actions seemed designed to enhance rather than to minimize his celebrity. He allowed himself to be satirized on an episode of the television show *The Simpsons*, and he accepted an invitation from Tiffany & Co. to design jewelry and other objects for its stores and catalogs. He designed a vodka bottle, and watches, and furniture inspired by his favorite sport, ice hockey. (He had played hockey himself from his boyhood in Canada until he was into his seventies.) He allowed his friend the director Sydney Pollack—after six decades of living in Los Angeles, Gehry knew more than the average architect's share of entertainment people—and a cameraman to follow him around for months to create a reverential documentary about him that Pollack called *Sketches of Frank Gehry.*

Archetypical starchitect though he may have been, Gehry was skilled at not appearing to act the part of star. When the *Architects' Journal,* a British publication, arranged for a video interview with him in 2014 on the occasion of the unveiling of his first project in London, a residential and retail complex at Battersea Power Station, the interviewer asked why he had not designed anything there before. Gehry's reply was typically nonchalant and self-effacing. Nobody asked me, he said. His reply appeared to disappoint the interviewer, who seemed to be hoping that Gehry would use the occasion to rant about how the challenging process of getting large buildings approved in London was beneath an architect of his stature. His response, instead, was more akin to saying that he would be happy to do anything, even a small project, and that he had simply been waiting for the phone to ring with a request. He had no marketing department out there promoting him, he said. In the video, he came across as avuncular more than ambitious, as if he were the struggling head of a small studio, not the celebrated architect atop one of the best-known firms in the world.

It was a vintage Gehry performance: the architect as antistar, another reminder of how much Gehry's persona could seem to be made up of equal parts of Frank Lloyd Wright and Woody Allen. In fact, while he would often complain about not having enough work, he was busy with numerous projects of varying sizes at the time of that interview, and he often turned down work from clients whose projects he found insufficiently stimulating—or whose commitment to his architecture he found insufficient, period. He was proud of his flexibility, but he was willing to demonstrate it only to those who made it clear beforehand that they liked his work and wanted a Frank Gehry. There was no sense in coming to him if you wanted a sleek white building in the manner of Richard Meier, or a glass tower in the manner of Norman Foster, or a traditional building like those produced by Robert Stern. He counted on clients to self-select, but he could not always be sure, and he felt most comfortable with those who he knew were comfortable with him and willing to let him explore.

Early in his career, those clients had generally been as unusual as Gehry himself: many came from the art worlds of Los Angeles and New York, and almost all of them were people who enjoyed pushing the boundaries of architectural possibility. Gehry's early buildings were almost without exception designed for people with tight budgets, and he was known for his fondness for using cheap, everyday materials like raw, unpainted plywood, chain-link fencing, and corrugated aluminum, which became Gehry trademarks in the formative years of his career. While he had a few commercial clients back then, most of them were small, with one exception—the Rouse Company, a developer of shopping malls, for which he designed a headquarters building and several other structures, including his only shopping mall, Santa Monica Place. But by 1980, Gehry and Rouse had amicably parted ways, not because Gehry was unable to do the more conventional work that Rouse wanted, but because it was increasingly clear to them that his priorities lay elsewhere. "Frank, why are you wasting your time and energy fighting with commercial developers when you really have a different mission in life?" Matt DeVito, the chief executive of Rouse, said to Gehry after visiting the house the architect had just completed for himself and his family in Santa Monica. "Why don't you just do what you're good at?"

And so he did. What Gehry was "good at" was making architecture that both inspired thought and brought pleasure, making buildings that were unusual enough so that some confused them with art pieces and others found them merely bizarre. His house in Santa Monica was an old Dutch colonial that he surrounded with trapezoidal additions made of plywood and corrugated metal. It offended some of his neighbors, who wanted it taken down as an affront to their tranquil suburban street. In time, as his reputation grew, he would be asked to design museums, concert halls, libraries, and academic buildings, as well as a smattering of private houses for clients who were both rich and adventurous, like Peter Lewis, who had earned billions in the insurance business and would spend six years and more than $6 million in fees having Gehry design multiple versions of an $82 million house that Lewis would ultimately choose not to build.

With success came not only bigger budgets, but also the expectation of more lavish materials: plywood gave way to the likes of titanium. Gehry's own sensibility never really changed—at least he hoped it never did—and he viewed his big projects with a combination of pride and anxiety. He never fully shed a sense of discomfort with how far he had come since the days when he was known for turning plywood and chain-link fencing into the stuff of serious architecture. By the mid-1980s, he was mainly doing bespoke architecture, very expensive buildings for very rich clients. "I'm a do-gooder Jewish liberal to the core, and it's hard for me to think I'm solving any problems doing a rich guy's house," he told *The New York Times* in 1995.

But he did not want to be remembered solely for highly expressive buildings like the Guggenheim and Walt Disney Concert Hall, either, however much he knew that they would probably be considered his crowning achievements. He bristled at complaints that he was not building affordable housing, in part because he had never lost his youthful belief that architecture could in some way contribute to the betterment of society. Since no architect, not even Frank Gehry, could build anything unless a client asked him to, he expressed what he called his "do-gooder" instincts mainly through donating his services for small projects like a cancer center in Dundee, Scotland, that he designed in memory of his old friend Maggie Keswick, another one in Hong Kong, and later a tiny concert hall in Berlin for his friend Daniel Barenboim that he fussed over as if it were a fifty-story building. He set up an organization to support arts education among public school students in California and paid the salary of its director, whom he installed in his own office. And he became deeply involved in supporting scientific research, first through his friend and psychiatrist Milton Wexler, whose family suffered from Huntington's disease, and who established a foundation to underwrite research into genetic disease that Gehry and his wife, Berta, took on as a cause of their own. After Gehry's daughter Leslie, his eldest child, died of uterine cancer in 2007, medical research became a bigger passion still.

But charitable efforts, however sincere, were not architecture. A part of him missed the raw, low-budget projects he had begun his career with, and he continued to search for a cheaper way to make the kind of expressive buildings that he loved so that they could be accessible to people or institutions of limited means. He came to hope that digital technology would be the key. He had already shown that technology could enable the creation of extraordinary, one-of-a-kind buildings with extraordinary, one-of-a-kind shapes like Bilbao and Disney Concert Hall. Technology should also make it possible, Gehry came to feel, to design conventional buildings in such a way as to make them more engaging. If unusual forms that once had to be created by hand could now be made with the aid of software, the sort of one-of-a-kind, bespoke buildings that had been beyond the reach of commercial real estate developers would be more economical to build. He became more and more interested in proving that not only could computers make it possible to replicate something quickly and cheaply, but also that they could aid in creating unique designs. Software could allow him to do now what plywood and chain-link fencing had let him to do before: make the architecture special when the budget was ordinary.

And so Gehry had begun to work with clients like Barry Diller, the entertainment and Internet mogul, who with the real estate developers Marshall Rose, Adam Flatto, and Joseph Rose was putting up a new headquarters for his company, IAC, in the Chelsea section of Manhattan. Diller had initially been wary of Gehry, fearing that he would be both arbitrary and expensive, and that it would be too hard to control either his design instincts or his budget. Gehry had managed to convince Diller that he could both be reasonable and produce a building for reasonable cost, and Diller agreed to let him try. It was not an easy project, since building in New York is notoriously difficult and expensive to start with, and the city was an odd place for any architect to try to prove that he could adhere to a tight budget—especially an architect from Los Angeles who had originally built his reputation on what he liked to call "cheapskate architecture." But in 2006 Gehry managed to get the building, a ten-story tower of white glass whose torqued form billows out like a schooner's sails, built for something reasonably close to the price of a more conventional structure. It was a great relief, because he had been trying, and failing, to build in New York for years, including an enormous new Guggenheim Museum that Thomas Krens, the director who had erected the museum in Bilbao, had hoped to construct on the waterfront in Lower Manhattan, which could get neither funding nor planning approvals after the September 11, 2001, attacks.

Gehry had met Bruce Ratner before Barry Diller's project started, on another venture that came to naught, a design competition for a new headquarters tower for the New York Times Company in 2000. Ratner's development company was serving as the Times Company's partner, and Gehry had been invited to submit a design, which would have been his first skyscraper. He was Bruce Ratner's clear favorite. Ratner liked the way Gehry met the selection committee for the Times building. "He came and said, 'I'm Frank Gehry and I like to do buildings. Yeah, I haven't built high-rises before, but I think I can do this,'" Ratner recalled Gehry as saying. "He was so humble. He wasn't dressed particularly well. He didn't have a model. He said basically, 'I'm an architect, I do lots of things.'"

Gehry teamed with David Childs, an old friend who was a partner in the large corporate architecture firm Skidmore, Owings & Merrill, to put to rest concerns about his lack of skyscraper experience. But before the committee charged with selecting an architect announced its decision, Gehry decided he was uncomfortable with the project and withdrew. Even though he had been favored to win, his wariness of the demands of commercial building got the better of him, and he left the prize commission to one of his competitors, the Italian architect Renzo Piano. It was not the first time he had walked away from a potentially lucrative commission, fearing that he would not be happy with it. In fact, it had been a pattern throughout his professional life. As a young architect he had spurned the offer of one of his mentors to take charge of a branch office in Paris. Later he would abandon a furniture company that was being set up to market his designs and was prepared to make him famous, and possibly wealthy, as a furniture designer.

Bruce Ratner was surprised, as he was not accustomed to having an architect reject him. Usually if you were a real estate developer, it was the other way around. But Ratner, who came from a large Jewish real estate family in Cleveland, had taken an instant liking to Gehry; he liked both his low-key, easy manner and the determined ambition hidden beneath it, a combination that in some ways resembled Ratner's own nature. The two men had developed a friendly, relaxed banter, and Ratner felt disappointed more than angry at Gehry's withdrawal. He made a point of keeping up their acquaintance, and he was determined to find another chance to work with him. Not long after, Ratner asked Gehry if he wanted to take charge of the huge project he was planning for the old Long Island Railroad train yard, called Atlantic Yards—and also to design an apartment tower Ratner wanted to build in Lower Manhattan. Atlantic Yards was a long saga that ended unhappily,* but the apartment building turned out to be otherwise. At first it was envisioned as merely another large structure, and the idea of making it the tallest apartment tower in the city had not yet come to the fore. It evolved gradually, over several years and multiple iterations, in part because Gehry felt that the proportions of the lower, squatter building would be unappealing.

As with the IAC Building, Gehry had to meet the challenge of making the building economical enough for the client to build, yet at the same time visually compelling enough for him to want to put his name on it. It had to be identifiable as a Frank Gehry building, but it had to be filled with apartments that would be straightforward enough to construct easily and appealing enough to be rented to people who might not have had notable architecture at the top of their list of priorities when they went apartment hunting. It had to be Frank Gehry, but not *too* Frank Gehry.

Gehry designed a slender tower sheathed in stainless steel panels—10,500 of them—and like the glass pieces at IAC, almost all of them

---

* See chapter 16 for a more complete discussion of Atlantic Yards.

were uniquely shaped. The north, east, and west sides of the building swirl and billow in and out, like folds of fabric hundreds of feet high. Once again, it was a computer program that allowed the varied panels to be fabricated for a cost comparable to that of a more conventional stainless steel façade. The folds join to create larger patterns in the façade, swoops and curves that run up over multiple stories, but the innards of the building are fairly conventional, which both simplified construction and assured that rooms are not too oddly shaped. The tower contains nine hundred rental units, including three penthouses on the top floor.

When Bruce Ratner decided to open the building with a birthday party for his architect, the penthouses were still unfinished. In some ways that made throwing a party easy—the top floor was a huge, open loft in the sky, and it felt not unlike the raw industrial spaces in Lower Manhattan that had lately become fashionable places for product launches, fashion shows, and other events. But Ratner did not want this party to feel like a business event that people dropped into for a moment. To make the place more attractive, he had his office arrange to rent modern furniture, some of it designed by Gehry himself and some of it classic pieces by Le Corbusier and Mies van der Rohe. It was spread out through the ten-thousand-square-foot floor, creating the incongruous tableau of Mies van der Rohe's elegant leather Barcelona chairs set against unfinished walls. The caterer, Peter Callahan, set up bars and cocktail tables and filled the space with flowers. A piano was brought in as well, probably a useless gesture, since before long the room was filled with so many people that the hired pianist's cocktail music could barely be heard.

The enormous windows—the penthouse floor had exceptionally high ceilings—meant that the spectacular views competed for attention with the guest of honor, all the more so because March 19, 2011, just happened to be the night of an unusual astronomical phenomenon: there was a full moon, larger than it had been in nearly a decade. The evening turned out to coincide with what astronomers call the perigee-syzygy of the earth-moon-sun system and laymen call a supermoon, when a full moon coincides with its elliptical orbit bringing it closest to the earth, resulting in a moon that looks roughly 14 percent bigger and 30 percent brighter than a normal full moon. There had not been a supermoon since 1993, and another would not come for several years. The night was perfectly clear, which meant that everyone would see the enormous moon rise over the Brooklyn Bridge.

Bruce Ratner had been anxious about the party, but he took the unusual

Frank thanks the guests, and remembers his father, before a Gehryesque cake at his eighty-second birthday party. The architect Robert A. M. Stern is on the right.

moon as a good omen. Once his guests had had a chance to eat, drink, and look out the window, he summoned them to the north end of the building, with the midtown skyline—Gehry's favorite view—as his backdrop, and offered a toast in front of an enormous cake that was made to resemble a collage of Gehry buildings.

"One of the things about my life that I'm lucky about is that I get to meet amazing people," Ratner said. "And Frank's probably the most amazing in terms of giving me joy in meeting somebody. He's one of the few architects that's down-to-earth, a mensch. Also, he is a genius. I worship Frank Gehry. So, happy birthday, Frank."

The crowd applauded, and Gehry took the microphone. He thanked Ratner and graciously avoided discussing Atlantic Yards, although he reminded the crowd that the building they were standing at the top of had gone through multiple iterations, and at one point, after the economic downturn of 2008, it was almost cut drastically and turned into the kind of shorter, stouter building that he had hoped to avoid. He praised Ratner for going ahead with the tower despite economic uncertainty, and then he took another turn.

"This is not far from where my father was born," he said, pointing toward midtown Manhattan. "It is hard not to think of him here. I really wish . . ." His voice began to break, and then he went on: "I really wish he could be here, and see what I've built in the city where he grew up. My father never saw my buildings, and he thought I was just a dreamer. I think he would be proud of me. I wish he could have seen this building. I would like to think that he would see this building and feel that I amounted to something."

2

Canada

Frank Gehry was born Frank Owen Goldberg at Toronto General Hospital on February 28, 1929. His family, like so many first- and second-generation families of Jewish immigrants in Canada and the United States, considered survival to be a form of triumph. His mother, who had been born Sadie Thelma Caplanski in Lodz, Poland, was twenty-four when her son was born; she had arrived in Toronto as a child of eight, brought by her parents, Samuel and Leah, who were fleeing the anti-Semitism that was rampant in Eastern Europe. Samuel, who shortened the family name to Caplan when he arrived in North America, had run a successful business delivering coal in Lodz; he abandoned it amid ongoing theft from his employees that the police refused to stop. He moved his family to Holland, and from there sailed to Canada. When he settled in Toronto, he managed to open a hardware store.

Irving Goldberg, Frank's father, was twenty-eight when his son was born. Although he was never forced to flee his homeland as a child, he suffered what may have been an even greater trauma at roughly the same age as Thelma when she left Poland. Irving, who was born on Christmas Day 1900, was one of nine children of immigrant parents in the Hell's Kitchen neighborhood of New York City. His father, Frank Goldberg, for whom Irving's son would be named, was a tailor who died when Irving was nine, leaving his family destitute. Irving left school in the fourth grade, and for the next few years lived largely in the streets, a kind of New York version of a Dickensian childhood. He supported his mother, brothers, and sisters in a hand-to-mouth existence, working at grocery stores, carnivals, and anyplace else he could find that would pay a child a few cents for a few hours' labor. Irving was industrious, curious, stubborn, and restless, all qualities that he would pass along to his son, and that his son, in time, would turn to more positive benefit than his father would ever be able to do. Irving moved from career to career, and would spend much of his life searching for an occupation that might bring him some measure of satisfaction and financial reward, both of which eluded him. At various times he operated a fruit and vegetable stand, owned and operated a slot machine business, drove a truck, was a boxer, designed and built furniture, and worked in a liquor store.

Irving's restlessness took him first from New York to Cleveland, where he ran the fruit stand. Eventually he moved to Toronto, for reasons that remain obscure. His son surmised that the decision could have been motivated by the availability of a sales route for slot machines. The Toronto that Irving Goldberg settled in as a young man was a city that, outwardly at least, could not have been more distinct from rough-and-tumble New York, where immigrants set much of the city's tone. Toronto was genteel and British. In the 1930s the city had little of the cultural and ethnic diversity that would mark it several decades later, when Jane Jacobs would see in it so many of the lively qualities that had initially attracted her to New York. In the years before World War II, Toronto measured variations in its population mainly in terms of the range of Protestant denominations its citizens practiced: in the early 1930s, the city was 31.5 percent Anglican, with another 21 percent of its population affiliated with the United Church of Canada, and 15.3 percent Presbyterian. In 1923, Ernest Hemingway, who worked for the *Star Weekly*, complained in a letter that he had left Paris "for Toronto the City of Churches," where "85% of the inmates attend a Protestant church on Sunday. Official figures."

Canada in the 1920s and 1930s was generally less than welcoming to anyone whose origins were outside the British Empire. In 1923, for example, the country banned immigration from China outright. But Toronto, duller and more pompous than Montreal, had its own form of narrow-mindedness. Its size at its centennial in 1934—roughly six hundred thousand people—suggested a degree of cosmopolitanism that it was either unable or unwilling to deliver. It offered instead a combination of British reserve and midwestern American provincialism.

Jews were the first ethnic group to make any significant inroads into this bastion of middlebrow British culture. The year after Irving Goldberg was born in New York, Toronto's Jewish population stood at thirty-one hundred; by 1931, shortly after Frank's birth, the Jewish community had grown to forty-six thousand, roughly 7 percent of the total population, enough to make Jews the largest ethnic bloc in the city. If Toronto was not overly

Sam and Leah Caplan's house at 15 Beverley Street, Toronto

welcoming to Jewish immigrants, it seemed, however grudgingly, to accept the notion of a Jewish community as a permanent fixture.

But their growing numbers sometimes served only to make the Protestant majority only more disdainful, not to say suspicious, of Jews. In 1920, the city's aldermen considered a law that would prohibit advertising signs in languages other than English, a restriction clearly directed at the Yiddish signs that were beginning to appear in Jewish shops. (It foreshadowed the discomfort Toronto would have with bilingual signage generations later, when the growing power of the separatist movement in Quebec led to the adoption of a national requirement that all signage be in French as well as English.) The cultural and political climate of Toronto in the 1930s was also marked by considerable anxiety about the threat of communism, which, as in the United States, often blurred into anti-Semitism, encouraged by the presence of many Jews in the union movement, especially in the garment trades. And the Jews in staid Toronto were rarely to be found on the political right, which seemed to many Canadians only to emphasize the notion that they were outsiders. Irving Goldberg bore this out: his politics were left-leaning, and he was the opposite of genteel. If anything, he had something of the air of a tough guy from the movies, with a liberal's heart.

The core of the Jewish community was in the center of the city, north of Queen Street and east of University Avenue. Sam Caplan's cluttered hardware store was at 366 Queen Street West, and he and Leah purchased a narrow two-story brick house around the corner at 15 Beverley Street. The Kensington Market, a plethora of stalls and stands selling fish, meat, and produce, as well as religious books and artifacts, was the de facto town square of the Jewish quarter, and there were numerous small synagogues, shops, delicatessens, and community centers up and down the nearby streets. It was a dense neighborhood of small to medium-size houses, mostly brick, some of which were detached and others row houses. There were no high-rise buildings—that was for the business district farther downtown, a short streetcar ride or a long walk away—but there were numerous factories scattered through the neighborhood. The combination of residential and industrial uses assured that the neighborhood, while not a slum, would not be confused with the city's more fashionable districts, and may well have made it more welcoming to Jews. The Canada Cycle and Motor Co., a bicycle-making concern that would eventually transform into the hockey equipment company CCM, had its factory behind the original location of Caplan's Hardware a bit farther down Queen Street from No. 366, and Sam Caplan became friendly with its workers.

The Jewish quarter, like so many ethnic neighborhoods in the 1920s, felt at once connected to the rest of the city and apart from it. Its brick houses, many with front porches, looked no different from those in other Toronto neighborhoods, and from some blocks on the eastern side of the neighborhood you could see downtown and perhaps even glimpse the limestone tower of the Royal Bank of Canada, the beginning of the modern Toronto skyline. But if the architecture and the street signs resembled those of the rest of Toronto, the sidewalks were filled with residents who, unlike the houses they lived in, were not interchangeable with their counterparts on the other side of town.

The Caplans were solid members of this community. Samuel was president of his small neighborhood synagogue on D'Arcy Street, and like many laymen he attended services regularly, studied the Talmud, and refused to work on Saturdays. When Frank was older, his grandfather would send him to open the store on Saturdays while he himself observed the Sabbath. He appears to have found it acceptable for his grandson to blaspheme the Sabbath, as long as he did not do so himself. Samuel's insistence on treating Frank as if he were a *shabbas goy*, the term traditionally used to describe a non-Jew who was hired to perform tasks forbidden to Jews on the Sabbath, angered his wife, Leah. "But she went along with it," Frank remembered, because the family needed the income from the store. "What else could they do?" And it was clear that Frank loved being in the

Frank in Toronto

store and immersing himself in the vast miscellany contained within its shelves and cabinets.

When Samuel was in the store himself, Leah would cook meals for him and bring them to him twice a day. She was skilled at more than cooking, however. She was known as a neighborhood healer, and would prepare herbal remedies for ill neighbors who would come to her kitchen table or, if they were more seriously ill, allow Leah to make a house call. Years later, her grandson would remember being taken with her to the house of a sick neighbor, where grandmother and grandson sat in candlelight, as if at a vigil, and Leah used a quill pen to write Yiddish phrases on the arm of the afflicted person.

The Caplans' house on Beverley was modest by upper-middle-class standards, but it was no tenement, and the family was comfortable in comparison to many later immigrants to Toronto, who like their counterparts in American cities were crowded tightly into slums. There was a small living room facing the street, with a dining room behind it, and a large kitchen across the back of the house. The Caplans' grandson remembered the rooms as being dark, with heavy wooden furniture, lace doilies, and solid brass candlesticks. The windows were covered with thick draperies that he recalled as resembling tapestries. A telephone sat on a small stand in the dining room next to the door to the cellar, where Leah Caplan made her own red wine. In the kitchen there was an old cast-iron stove and a large table. The house had something of the air of Eastern Europe, and if it was fairly typical of the homes of Jewish immigrants of Samuel and Leah Caplan's generation, to their grandchildren it appeared at once mysterious and exotic.

The Caplans had two children: Kalman, who Anglicized his name to Kelly, and Thelma. Thelma was both intellectually and socially ambitious, and she was frustrated that her parents did not allow her to complete high school, let alone to fulfill her desire to go to college and law school. Education, they believed, was for men. They did permit her music lessons, and she had a lifelong interest in music, art, and theater, which she would in time pass along to her children. (She would also, many years later, complete high school and college on her own after raising two children, and she even managed to take some adult courses in legal studies.) Her early disappointment about her lack of educational opportunities was surely compounded by the fact that her brother, Kelly, was encouraged by their parents to go to law school, though he may not have had much interest in the law—he never practiced once he got his degree. Thelma was told to work in her father's store while she sought a man to marry.

After a brief relationship with a man that, to Thelma's disappointment, did not lead to marriage—he felt he could not afford to support her and moved away from Toronto—Thelma met Irving Goldberg. He was ambitious and goodhearted, if not as refined a suitor as Thelma might have wanted, and he was entranced with her. Years later, their daughter, Doreen, would say that "he was crazy about her, absolutely crazy about her," and while it is not entirely clear that Thelma felt quite the same level of excitement about the man her son would describe as "kind of a diamond in the rough," she agreed to marry him. They wed on Halloween, October 31, 1926.

The Goldbergs moved into the upstairs flat in a two-family house on Rusholme Road, about two miles west of the house on Beverley Street. When their son was born, they followed the Jewish tradition of naming a child for a deceased relative, giving him the first name of Irving's father, Frank. His Hebrew name, probably chosen by Sam and Leah, was Ephraim. Thelma, who had never been particularly fond of the name Goldberg, chose her son's middle name, Owen, with the thought that it might someday make a serviceable surname, should he choose to drop Goldberg altogether. The Caplans would ultimately have four grandchildren—Kelly Caplan had two daughters, Judy and Shirley, and eight years after Frank's arrival Thelma would give birth to his sister, Doreen. Frank was the only boy among Samuel and Leah's grandchildren, and his grandparents doted on him.

He returned their affection. Frank was shy but inquisitive, and if he sometimes felt awkward around other children—a birth defect, a tumor on the front of his left leg just below his knee, made him feel self-conscious and uncomfortable in anything but long pants—he could also be headstrong and determined. When he was five, his father's sister Rosie, who had married well and had more ample means than the rest of the Goldberg family, persuaded Irving and Thelma to allow her to take Frank to a surgeon to have the tumor removed. Frank, confronted with the possibility of being sedated for the procedure, bolted from the operating table before the operation could begin, and neither his rich aunt nor his parents could induce him to go through with it. The tumor would remain for the rest of his life. His stubborn refusal to submit to a situation in which he feared a loss of control, even if it offered great potential benefit, would be a pattern he would repeat throughout his life.

More than anyone else, his grandparents gave him a sense that the world was rich in possibility. He came to see them, he recalled, as a "safe haven" from his parents, whom he would describe many years later as "edgy." The Beverley Street house was an easy fifteen-minute bicycle ride from his family's house, and he spent a lot of time there. He would recall sometimes spending the night, sleeping between Samuel and Leah on the crack between their twin beds. He took joy in being in the hardware store, even before he was entrusted to open it on Saturdays; to a young boy it was a wonderland full of screws and bolts and hammers and nails and every kind of household gadget, all of it the stuff of possibility in Frank's mind. The complex, ordered clutter of the hardware store gave him a sense of both pleasure and mystery. There was always something new to discover, and he retained a vivid memory of it not only as a place that held all kinds of fascinating objects, but as a complete and whole object in itself, a collage of alluring intricacy. Later he would help his grandfather fix clocks and toasters and thread pipes and cut glass.

But the most important memories were of playing on the kitchen floor with his grandmother. Once beyond toddlerhood he would often accompany her to a woodshop on John Street, five blocks away from Beverley, where she would buy burlap bags filled with pieces of scrap wood. When they returned home, Leah would open one of the sacks and spill the irregular pieces of wood across the kitchen floor. Just as the shelves of nuts and bolts had stimulated Frank's imagination in the hardware store, the wood scraps were the raw material of fantasy. Leah would sit down on the floor with Frank and together they would build imaginary buildings, bridges, and even whole cities.

"There were round pieces that looked like bridges and freeways before [there were] freeways," Frank would recall many years later. "And I loved it. She would play with me on an equal level like an adult." He would say that when he began to think about the possibility of being an architect, he would recall making things out of oddly shaped pieces of wood on his grandmother's floor as "the most fun I ever had in my life. I realized it was a license to play." It was not just wood that Leah offered Frank. When she was baking challah she would give him pieces of dough to play with, which he turned into a kind of proto-Play-Doh.

Leah's relationship to her grandson is best known for a realm in which her influence was almost surely less significant than playing with wood scraps. Like many Jewish women in the older neighborhoods, Leah made gefilte fish, a traditional dish made of poached ground fish, as a part of the weekly Sabbath dinner on Friday evening. She would shop at Kensington Market every Thursday for a live carp, carry it home in a bag filled with water, then put it in her filled bathtub until she was ready to kill it. Frank would often accompany her

Irving, Frank, and Thelma Goldberg

to the market, and once home he would watch with fascination as the carp swam around the bathtub. "I used to go in there and watch the carp. I spent a lot of time watching the carp. And then Friday the carp wasn't there anymore and there was gefilte fish. And I didn't put two and two together for a long time," Frank recalled years later.

The powerful image of the carp remained in Frank's mind, so much so that he would talk about it often as an adult, even going so far as to suggest, not a little disingenuously, that it was responsible for the significant role that the fish shape came to play in his work. The notion that Gehry's famous fish lamps and fish sculptures, not to mention the fishlike curves of some of his buildings, owed their form to his childhood experience of watching his grandmother's carp has achieved the status of legend, encouraged by the architect who saw it, he admitted long afterward, as a way "to feign anti-intellectualism."[*]

---

[*] In fact, a number of things were behind Gehry's fondness for the fish form, including its curving shape, its scaled surface, and the idea that the fish is one of the oldest creatures in

Samuel, his grandfather, helped shape Frank in a different way, by encouraging his strong curiosity. On warm evenings he would sit with his grandson on the front porch of 15 Beverley—Samuel called the porch his "summer resort"—and talk to him "about the importance of asking questions. Why did the sun come up in the morning? Why did the trees turn color in the winter? Why was the sky blue? Everything was why, why, why. I think that has created a pattern of curiosity that has done well for me," Frank recalled.

They would also talk about the Talmud, getting "into the old arguments about 'why this' and 'why that,'" Frank remembered. It would give him a favorable impression of Judaism as a religion that asked questions constantly and seemed to take the stance that the question was at least as important as the answer. Later Frank would call this "one of the most important things we get out of being Jewish. . . . It's a kind of iterative process until you stop and say, 'Okay.' I love that. I used to love doing that with him. I studied the Talmud with my grandfather. My grandmother was very religious, my grandfather was in it for the questioning—the first word in the Talmud is 'why.' It's all about questions. I loved that shit. I don't know why I loved it. I was curious about all of that."

If his grandparents played an outsize role in his boyhood, his parents were hardly absent. Thelma, eager to impress upon her son the importance of the culture that she felt she had not had enough exposure to, took him to classical music events when he was as young as eight, and brought him often to the Art Gallery of Toronto on Bloor Street, just a few blocks away from 15 Beverley. On their first visit, Frank saw a landscape in watercolor of "hills and blue and sea," hanging in Walker Court, the museum's central atrium, that he would remember years later as the first time he had been excited by a painting and felt the potential of art not just to offer a fleeting moment of beauty, but to stop him in his tracks. It was a transformational experience, and he remembered wondering how an artist could create something that would affect him so deeply.[*]

Frank's relationship to his father was somewhat more episodic. Irving

---

nature, which Gehry intended as a somewhat facetious way of responding to the postmodern call for use of historical form. See chapter 11.

[*] He remembered the landscape as being by John Marin; it was almost certainly by another artist, since the Art Gallery of Toronto—which would eventually become the Art Gallery of Ontario, and in 2004 hire Frank Gehry to design its expansion—had no works by Marin in its collection. While the gallery's records show that watercolors by several European and Canadian artists were displayed in special exhibitions around 1937, when Thelma and Frank made the visit that he remembered so vividly, no Marin was among them.

worked hard at his business of leasing and servicing slot machines, pinball machines, and jukeboxes, but his income was erratic, and so were his moods. He could be warm and generous when things were going well, and explode with anger, often directed at his son, when they were not. Irving carved wooden toys for Frank, and he enjoyed drawing and making things with his son. His daughter recalled that he "loved to play with stuff. He loved plastic, he loved papier-mâché, and he liked wood. He just found materials interesting," a fact surely not lost on Frank.

Some business venture of Irving's—the particulars of which are lost to history—led the Goldbergs to leave Toronto for a period of several months between Frank's first and second birthdays and to live on Avenue J in Brooklyn. Whatever it was did not last, and before long they were back in Toronto. When Frank was four, things were looking up enough for the family to be able to rent a two-story brick house at 1364 Dundas Street West, not far from the flat on Rusholme. In 1937, the year Thelma gave birth to Frank's sister, Doreen, Irving's business was successful enough for them to be able to come up with the funds for a down payment to purchase the house outright. Frank recalled that it cost $6,000. "I don't know where he got the money," he said.

Even though Dundas was enough of a major artery to have a streetcar line leading west from central Toronto, it was relatively quiet and still mostly residential when the Goldbergs took up residence there. In time the street would become entirely commercial, and the neighborhood would slip from being a comfortable lower-middle-class area to a quarter for recent immigrants to the city; by 2011, the house at No. 1364 had become the headquarters of the Toronto Vietnamese Association, with a storefront evangelical church, a sports bar, and a Portuguese travel agency as its neighbors.

When the Goldbergs lived there, the house had a large, open porch with brick columns facing Dundas; it was later filled in to create more commercial space. There was enough room in front for Thelma to have a small cactus garden, and there was a small yard and a garage in the back. Inside was a bigger, more open version of his grandparents' house. The first floor had a living room with a leaded glass bay window facing out to the street, leaded glass doors between the living room and dining room, and an enclosed sun porch in the rear, beyond the large kitchen. The kitchen contained an up-to-date stove, since Irving had a particular dislike for the ancient stove at his in-laws' house. He thought that Samuel's refusal to buy a new one, which was rooted largely in his feeling that the old-fashioned stove gave food a taste that "reminded him of the old country," according to Doreen, put an unnecessary burden on Leah. Irving's strong feelings on the matter were a reminder that he could sometimes, for all his harshness, be exceptionally considerate of others.

The Goldbergs were not to spend much time in the house on Dundas after they purchased it. Later that same year, Irving was offered the chance to distribute slot machines in his own territory, which seemed like a welcome chance to make his income more stable. The problem was that the territory was in Timmins, a small mining town surrounded by dense forest, 428 miles north of Toronto. The house at 1364 Dundas was put up for rent, and eight-year-old Frank left the Alexander Muir Elementary School, four blocks away from his house on Dundas Street, where he had been since kindergarten. He, his newborn sister, Doreen, and Thelma and Irving moved abruptly to a very different life from Toronto, far from his grandparents and the Jewish quarter, far from the Art Gallery of Toronto, far from the concerts at Massey Hall, far from the Kensington Market and the carp in the bathtub. In Timmins, there were roughly thirty Jewish families, a distinct minority in a town of thirty thousand people, most of whom were of Finnish, Polish, or French Canadian descent.

Some of the Jewish families were well-to-do owners of the timber businesses and paper mills that, along with mining, were the basis of the local economy; others were shopkeepers. No one else was in "the gambling business," as Frank would describe his father's work years later. At the beginning, even though Thelma quickly joined the local chapter of the Jewish women's organization Hadassah (she would eventually become its president), the nature of Irving's work, not to mention the family's fairly modest means, meant that the acceptance of the Goldbergs into the Jewish community was hesitant at first. In time, Thelma's commitment and Irving's genial manner led their neighbors to embrace them, but Frank remembers the family's position within the Jewish community to have been "precarious" at the beginning, not a comfortable state of affairs for a family that found itself in a cold, isolated town hundreds of miles away from familiar friends and relatives, and had to cope with the pressures of a new baby as well.

Anna Gangbar, the daughter of the cantor of the small synagogue in Timmins and the sister of Tootie Linder, one of Frank's friends, said, "Growing up in Timmins wasn't easy. It was terribly, terribly freezing cold. Winters were so long you couldn't get out of your house until the snow melted." Despite the weather, Anna Gangbar said, "it was nice living there, not a big community. It was a good place to be. A lot of the Jewish community was well-to-do. But Frank's dad didn't have a profession, he was trying to make a living. It was very difficult for him in Timmins, I'm sure."

The Goldbergs settled into a wood clapboard bungalow at 8 Birch Street. There were two small bedrooms, one of which Frank and Doreen shared. The basement served as Irving's warehouse and repair shop; it was filled with slot machines and pinball machines, as well as with tools to keep them in good order. The house was smaller than the Dundas Street house in Toronto, but in Timmins the Goldbergs were able to afford the luxury of a Polish housekeeper, which allowed Thelma to join the other Jewish wives in Hadassah.

Frank remembers Timmins primarily for introducing him to two things: hockey, which became a lifelong love, and anti-Semitism, which he had been unaware of in Toronto. In Toronto, Jews either dominated the neighborhood, as around his grandparents' house, or appeared to blend into the increasingly diverse population of the city at large. In Timmins, however, there was clearly no possibility of appearing to be a majority. And the town seemed ethnically charged in a way that made it difficult for anyone's Jewish identity to go unnoticed. It was the sort of small town in which everyone knew who was Finnish, who was French Canadian, who was Polish, and who was Jewish. And religion was not the only source of tension: there was no love lost between the French Canadians and the Poles, even though both groups were largely Catholic.

Frank was the only Jewish child attending the Birch Street School, and there he had his earliest experiences with anti-Semitism. "It was mostly Poles, the Polish families that were working the mines," he recalled. When Frank was ten, he was bullied by some of the Polish children, who followed him home "and would beat me up. And finally I got up enough nerve to fight back, and I beat them up," he said. He recalled one incident in which a Polish boy chased him home from school and attacked him, "saying it was for killing Christ. I remember asking my mother why they thought I had killed Christ."

The Birch Street School had a hockey rink, which gave Frank his most important early exposure to a game he would play again as an adult and love throughout his life. The rink was shared with a French Canadian Catholic parochial school, whose students, Frank remembered, had no more fondness for the Polish ruffians than Frank did. "They saw me being beat up and so they formed a kind of gang with me," he recalled. "That's why I have this big soft spot for French Canadians."

The Goldbergs returned to Toronto during many school holidays, usually by train. "I loved taking the train, because we would leave at night from Timmins and arrive in the morning, and Union Station in Toronto is very impressive," Frank remembered. It was not just Union Station itself, a grandiose Beaux-Arts building with a colonnade of Corinthian columns and a great central hall, that excited him—it was the reminder that he and his family had, for at least a few days, escaped the harshness of Timmins.

Samuel and Leah Caplan never visited Timmins, but they took advantage of the train in another way. Every Thursday, Leah would pack a box containing her chicken soup with matzo balls, gefilte fish, and other traditional food for Friday night Sabbath dinner, take it to Union Station, and put it on the northbound train for Timmins. Thelma would meet the train at Timmins on Friday morning and carry the dinner home to Birch Street.

Frank began to mature into adolescence in Timmins, and his relationship with his father, which was never entirely free of tension, took on the added stress common to adolescent boys and their parents. Irving was particularly troubled that Frank had begun to put on weight, and told him frequently that he was becoming fat. There were times when he seemed almost to delight in bullying his son. Frank remembered one incident when he was eleven and he and his father were washing the family car together. Suddenly Irving turned the hose on his son and drenched him in water.

Yet it was also during the Timmins years that Frank had his most cherished childhood memory of Irving, who in 1940 took him on a trip by car to Chicago, where he was meeting with Mills Novelty, the company on Fullerton Avenue that provided the machines that he distributed in Canada. This time, Irving was neither distracted by work nor frustrated or anxious about it, as he often was. "My father drove his car to Chicago with me—we went from Timmins down through Windsor, Detroit, Ann Arbor, Gary, Indiana, then to Chicago," Gehry recalled. "We stayed at the YMCA because we didn't have money—we stayed in a room with cots. I remember lunch in a deli under the El. It was a bonding with my father that I hadn't had. He didn't lose his temper on me like he did all the time—I always remember that. I could almost draw the section of Chicago we were in." More than seventy years later, Frank would remember many of the specifics of the trip, including a stop in Ann Arbor to see a special exhibition baseball team play. The happy experience of the Chicago trip would never be repeated.

More typical of Frank's interactions with his father in those years was the experience he had trying to sell newspapers in Timmins. He would go to the office of the *Timmins Daily Press* on Third Avenue, the town's main street, and buy five copies of the paper for three cents each. He then would walk down the street toward home yelling, *"Timmins Daily Press!"* and usually sold three or four of the papers. He never sold all five, and frequently on his return home Irving would see the leftover papers and say to him that he was sure that Doreen, who by then was four or five, could have sold them all. To prove his point he would scoop up Doreen and the leftover papers and walk to a nearby bar where one of his machines was located. "He'd walk in with this little girl with the *Timmins Press,* and she sold it," Frank remembered.

It was hardly a fair test—few people would not want to please a cute little girl—but Irving used the story to justify his frequent taunts to his son, whom he called "stupid" and "a dreamer." His son's stubbornness, a quality that Irving himself possessed and appears to have taken pride in, seemed to him only further proof that Frank had no practical abilities to function in the world. Irving often acted as if he were convinced that Frank would amount to very little.

It is difficult not to feel that he was projecting onto Frank his anxieties about himself, since by his mid-thirties Irving could not have failed to have felt some degree of worry about whether he possessed enough practical sense to succeed in business, and indeed, whether he would amount to enough in the world. Thelma, too, in her own way projected herself and her disappointments onto Frank, but in this case the effect was more benign. She saw herself as being somewhat better than her station—she took pride in acting with dignity, and "talked about her refined English background, maybe as a joke, but she always said it," Frank remembered. She did correspond with cousins in London and "she got in her head that they were some highfalutin' something or other," he said. To Doreen, there was a presumption that the "Goldberg family was crazy and [Thelma's] family, the Caplan family, was the sane family. It's like my mother came from landed gentry and then there were these garbage people we happened to be related to but we'll try to stay as far away as we can."

Thelma's views, however fanciful they may have been, led her to encourage Frank to better himself. She believed profoundly in education, and she took him to a museum or cultural event as often as she could. There were limited opportunities in Timmins, of course, but in Toronto, Thelma and Frank would go not only to the Art Gallery of Toronto near her parents' house, they would make visits to the Royal Ontario Museum on Bloor

Street, where Frank remembered visiting mummies, and to Massey Hall, where Frank was introduced to symphony concerts. She wanted Frank to take piano lessons, but the family could not afford it. He did learn to play a few things by ear, but he never took formal lessons. "I always felt cheated that I never learned to play an instrument," he recalled. "I always wanted to play the cello. I felt drawn to the cello a lot. And I loved the piano."

Thelma's cultural ambitions for Frank got a particular boost from an unlikely source in 1941, when he was twelve and beginning to prepare for his bar mitzvah. He had continued to draw from time to time with Irving, and at one point he drew a portrait of Theodor Herzl, the Zionist leader, for an art show at the small Timmins synagogue. It was selected as the best piece in the show. Even better was the comment the synagogue cantor, who was tutoring Frank in his bar mitzvah studies, made after seeing the drawing. Frank, the cantor said to Thelma, had "gold in the hand."

Early in 1942, as Frank approached his thirteenth birthday, the family left Timmins nearly as abruptly as they had arrived there five years earlier. New regulations limiting slot machines made Irving's business suddenly no longer viable, and there was nothing else to keep the family in Timmins. They returned to Toronto in time for Frank to follow up his initial bar mitzvah in Timmins with a fuller commemoration of the occasion at his grandfather's synagogue, Etz Haim, a small congregation that worshipped in a converted house on D'Arcy Street. Because the Goldbergs' own house was still occupied by tenants, Frank and Doreen were sent to live with their grandparents on Beverley Street, and Frank returned not to his old school but to Ogden Elementary School nearby. Thelma's brother Kelly and his family were also living in the Beverley Street house, and there was no room in the overcrowded house for Irving and Thelma, who boarded elsewhere.

As Frank approached his bar mitzvah, his enthusiasm for Judaism mounted, encouraged by his living once again under his grandparents' roof. His closest friend when he returned to Toronto was a boy named Solly Botnick, who came from a highly religious family. Solly and Frank described each other as "super Jews." Years later, Frank would say that "Solly and I were bonkers about religion and Judaism. We were into proving that there was a God."

His infatuation with Judaism came to an abrupt end immediately after his bar mitzvah. At the service, he chanted his Torah portion, as is customary. On the way out of the synagogue, as he prepared to head to the local community house around the corner where a reception would be held and he would be expected to give a short speech, he encountered two old men who were members of the congregation. Excited that they had been at the service, Frank tried to engage them in a discussion of the meaning of the section of the Torah that he had just read. They brushed him off, and he got the impression that they had come solely to be able to enjoy the free drinks and food that the family of the bar mitzvah traditionally provided for the congregation. The seriousness with which he took Judaism seemed, in an instant, untenable to him. It was, in a sense, the opposite of a revelation. He felt that there had been no point to his

Frank as a young teenager

effort, and he remembered going home at the end of the day and saying to someone, perhaps his grandfather, that he now realized "there ain't no God. This is all bullshit."

He did not remember what, if any, response he got. The suddenness of his conversion from religious Jew to atheist is hard to explain, however, as the result of a single aborted conversation with two men he hardly knew. More likely, he harbored the same growing doubts about religion that are common to adolescents, and that they were held in check by his strong desire to be a good and respectful son and grandson, as well as by a boost of interest in Judaism brought on by his friendship with Solly Botnick and his renewed daily encounters with the grandparents he adored. Once his bar mitzvah was over, he may have felt, so was his obligation to accept the tenets of the faith. But given the extent to which his conversations with his grandfather revolved around the idea that Judaism respects the asking of questions at least as much if not more than the acceptance of dogma, he seemed to be rejecting not only Jewish tradition but also the premise that the questions were worth asking in the first place.

Not long after Frank's bar mitzvah and his Paul-to-Saul conversion, the Goldbergs' tenants moved out and the family returned to 1364 Dundas Street. The neighborhood had not changed significantly in the five years since they left for Timmins—there was still an empty lot on one side of their house, and a nearly matching brick house, now occupied by a dentist and his family, on the other. The Goldbergs knew many of their neighbors—some Caplan cousins lived a few blocks away, in fact—and the surroundings seemed safe enough and familiar enough that Thelma allowed Doreen as a small girl to cross the street and purchase food for the family at the Jewish grocery store, where the Goldbergs had a charge account, or to buy candy at the confectionery a few doors down the street.

While the immediate neighborhood around 1364 Dundas was primarily residential, within a few blocks there was much more to experience. The Cadbury/Neilson chocolate factory on Gladstone Avenue, which Frank remembered as "a big industrial building, with modernist windows"—one of the first times he thought specifically about modern architecture, or took note of it amid his daily surroundings—was close by, as was the Dufferin Park Racetrack. Years later, the racetrack would become a low-priced mall with Wal-Mart and Toys "R" Us stores, but when the Goldbergs lived nearby it was an active horse-racing venue, and Frank would often stop to watch the horses and trainers. When he started high school at Bloor Collegiate, an art deco brick building on Bloor Avenue, Dufferin was on his regular route to school each day. Across the street was Dufferin Grove Park, where Frank and Doreen and their friends would ice-skate. The section of Toronto extending outward from 1364 Dundas was an urban neighborhood largely suburban in scale, with all the amenities of the city a short streetcar ride away.

As Frank moved toward high school age, he began to gravitate toward a different group of friends, few of whom were Jewish. Years later he would recall only one close Jewish friend from those years, a boy named Marvin Hauser, and their relationship was driven by a mutual love of jazz, far different from his friendship with Solly Botnick. In the fall of 1942 at Bloor Collegiate he met Ross Honsberger and found, for the first time, a friend he considered a kindred soul. Honsberger, who became a distinguished mathematician and remained close to Frank into their eighties, was, like Frank, a combination of enthusiasm and skepticism. He was bright, talkative, curious about a wide range of scientific and cultural subjects, and cynical about religion, just as Frank had become. On top of that, he could play the piano.

"He was like me; he questioned everything. Like me, nothing was sacred. We read the Bible together and found 138 inconsistencies," Frank recalled.

Later, the two would collaborate on a treatise they called "Atheism and Theism," which they hoped would make an irrefutable case for the non-existence of God. At one point early in their friendship they dug a hole together because Ross "wanted to get closer to the core of the earth," in Frank's words. And they also set out to invent a perpetual motion machine, designing and trying to build a device that consisted of a pair of planks set on rollers. Doreen, eight years younger than her brother, has a childhood memory of hearing Frank and Ross argue for what she remembered as several hours about another theoretical idea that fascinated them—whether a fly was capable of stopping a train. And Ross's love of classical music and facility on the piano reinforced the interest in serious music that Thelma had begun to instill in her son. More than sixty years later, Frank would recall Ross's abilities with awe: "He used to talk about Chopin and he learned to play *Fantaisie-Impromptu*, which is amazing."

Ross did not provide Frank with his only intellectual stimulation in those years. Decades later he would remember numerous teachers at Bloor Collegiate, and say how well they introduced him to subjects that would remain meaningful to him throughout his life. Joe Noble, a physics teacher with "a big nose, ruddy complexion, a big smile . . . very husky, Irish guy" liked both Ross and Frank, and encouraged their inventive streak as well as their atheism, though he warned them that the latter would not win them popularity among their classmates. Frank fell in love with Shakespeare, Tennyson, and Conrad in his English literature class, with history in his history class, and with shop, where he liked to make objects out of wood.

Everything was not smooth at Bloor Collegiate, however. Frank was uncomfortable with writing, and he did poorly in his literature class despite his liking for the subject matter and the teacher. He was shy and hesitant to speak out in class discussions, and that, combined with his lack of writing skills, led the teacher to think of him as no more than a mediocre student. He felt even more uncomfortable when his parents would come to school for open houses. Irving, always uneasy about his lack of formal education, often did not know what to say to Frank's teachers, and made comments that embarrassed Frank. Nothing Thelma could say or do was enough to make Frank not "want to crawl under the table." He recalls feeling particularly awkward when Irving met his English literature teacher, afraid that Irving's lack of sophistication would make the erudite teacher he admired think even less of him than she already did.

For the first couple of years of high school, Frank's social life consisted in part of regular dances at the YMCA, where he somehow felt stigmatized again for being Jewish. "I would go and somehow the girls danced with me even though I had the black mark of their knowing I was Jewish," he recalled. "I had the name Goldberg. I was complicated. I was in both camps at once—I was with the goyim and with the Jews." He also played handball and Ping-Pong with Ross, and socialized with another group of friends whose common bond, it seemed, was that they were from working- and middle-class families and wanted to avoid the cliques of students from more well-to-do families. They formed a fraternity they called Delta Psi Delta, but the ties were not strong enough to keep Frank interested for the long term, and he began to drift away, seeking more intellectual stimula- tion. By then, Ross had begun to spend a lot of time with a classmate whom he would eventually marry, while Frank felt too shy and insecure to date actively.

Instead, he withdrew into reading and science, and became more com- fortable spending time on his own. What he wanted, he was beginning to realize, was stimulation, not mere company. He discovered a Friday night lecture series at the University of Toronto, and he began spending those evenings alone in the balcony of Convocation Hall, listening to lectures on subjects like electronics, transportation, and the future of electromag- netic propulsion. When he wasn't at Convocation Hall, he would be in the library, reading *Popular Science* and *Popular Mechanics*. He continued to spend time with Ross, but he was soon using much of the rest of his time outside of his classes for what had become a kind of self-education program in science.

On a Friday evening in November 1946, Frank walked into Convoca- tion Hall to hear a lecture by a visitor from Finland whose name he had not known before: Alvar Aalto, an architect from Helsinki. Aalto, gray- haired with a thick accent, showed slides of his recent buildings like the Paimio Sanatorium in Finland, and a project he was at work on in the United States, the Baker House dormitory at the Massachusetts Institute of Technology. He also brought a bent plywood chair of his own design onto the stage and demonstrated its strength.

Frank was entranced. He found Aalto charismatic, he loved the images of the buildings the architect presented, and he was excited by the bent plywood chair, which looked like nothing he had ever seen. The lecture resonated in his head long after Aalto left Toronto. Frank was sufficiently intrigued to go to the library at Bloor Collegiate and examine the voca- tional guidance shelves to see what they contained about studying archi- tecture. He found a book that outlined the program at the University of

Toronto, and nothing about the course of study resembled the beautiful and unusual modern buildings Aalto had shown. "It was designing these little cottages with stone and it was like something out of the English countryside. It didn't grab me at all. So I just put the book back," he remembered. And that was the end of Frank and architecture, he was certain.

Much later, he would wonder whether his instinctive response to Aalto had something to do with his time in Timmins. "Timmins is very northern and the aesthetic of Timmins was wood, snow, lots of trees, but there was an aesthetic connection with the Finns," he said. "There was an aesthetic that went with the Finns, and in Timmins it was raw wood, lots of pine, I fell in love with all of that."

But he soon forgot all about the lecture. Even years later, when he began to study architecture and felt powerfully drawn to Aalto's work, he did not at first remember that as a naïve and earnest seventeen-year-old he had heard the architect talk in person. It was only the sight of an Aalto chair that jogged his memory, reminding him of that night in Toronto when he first saw the same chair on a stage in Toronto, that the architect himself had been talking about it, and that this had been his first serious introduction to architecture.

As a teenager, Frank was consistently curious, but he had no clear sense of what he wanted to do with his life. He liked to draw and he liked to make things; he was fascinated by flying and was drawn to airplanes. He liked chemistry, despite having narrowly escaped serious injury as a fifteen-year-old, when he tried to combine oxygen and hydrogen to make water and caused an explosion in his bedroom, sending shards of glass into his back. An older Caplan cousin whom Frank had always liked, Arthur Rosenberg, was a chemical engineer, and Frank considered him something of a role model; for a brief time he thought he wanted to become a chemical engineer himself. On a vocational day at Bloor Collegiate, he signed up for chemical engineering and met a representative from a General Motors paint laboratory who had been invited to explain his field. Frank was polite, but his boredom was surely evident, since at the end of the day the visiting chemical engineer turned to him and said, "Frank, this ain't for you. I saw your eyes glaze over. You'll find your place, but this won't be it."

There were more immediate challenges than a career decision. Irving had never successfully restarted his career after returning from Timmins, and money was sufficiently tight so that the family consolidated their living quarters to the first floor of their house, renting out the upstairs bedrooms. Irving had started a small furniture company not long after coming back to Toronto, called Crown Products, which specialized in ashtray stands, which were sold through department stores, and it also made wooden lazy Susans. The company did moderately well for a short period, but it was in difficulty by 1945. Irving's health was in decline—he was diagnosed with diabetes that year—and he also learned that his shop foreman, whom he considered a friend, had been stealing products, selling them himself, and pocketing the proceeds. Then the Canadian government imposed a new excise tax on cigarette paraphernalia, which included ashtrays, making the retail price prohibitive. Irving tried remarketing the ashtray as a candy dish, but there was little demand for candy dishes on stands. The business collapsed entirely in 1946.

Irving was "coming apart" emotionally, Frank recalled. He had never been comfortable with authority and for most of his life he had worked on his own, but nothing he had done had been a major success, and his most recent attempt to build a successful career had ended in failure. His frustration mounted, and his relationship to Frank deteriorated badly. He repeated his old accusation that Frank was an impractical dreamer more and more often, and was physically abusive to his son more than once. His sister recalls one night when Frank awoke in the middle of the night, tripped in the dark, and broke something. Irving "beat the shit out of him," she said. He was gentler toward Doreen, who noted his erratic behavior but saw it mostly directed toward Frank. "My relationship with my father, I either have blocked out a lot or fantasized a lot of it. Because I was a little girl, he thought I was adorable," she said.

Both children remained loyal to their father. They saw his generosity, and there was always some evidence that, as Doreen later said, "Underneath all this craziness was a really sweet guy." Irving would bring poor acquaintances home for dinner, when his own business was going well he would help family members who were in difficulty, and he insisted, like Thelma, that his children treat everyone as equal. However different their temperaments and worldviews may have been, neither Thelma nor Irving was snobbish, nor were they openly resentful of people who had more than they did.

Doreen said much later that she thought that Irving may have been bipolar. He "couldn't contain himself," Frank said. "But there was something in my dynamic with him that kept me loving him as a father, so I didn't lose that. I never lost that. And I think that I understood somehow that these outbursts had nothing to do with me. He was angry and felt trapped in a lot of ways."

Irving's problems, and Frank's relationship with him, came to a head late in 1946, when Frank was seventeen and Irving had been particularly hard on him over some matter his son considered trivial. "He was having business setbacks, and after one of his tirades against me, I hit him. For the first time, I hit him," Frank said. His rashness frightened him, and he ran out the front door of the house and hid behind a nearby build-ing, assuming his father would follow and try to catch him. Irving did not appear. "Nothing. Silence. So I saunter back, look in the window, and he is lying on the floor." Irving had suffered a heart attack after his altercation with his son. Frank, deeply shaken, felt he was responsible, and for a long time would bear "a heavy burden" of believing that he had brought on his father's heart attack.

Thelma was at home when Irving collapsed, and when Frank came back indoors she was tending to her husband on the floor, having already summoned help. Irving was taken to the hospital and recovered, but it was clear that he was in a significantly weakened condition. He had diabetes and a weak heart, and his business had fallen apart. "My dad was forty-seven years old, and he was finished. He was wiped out and demoralized," Frank told the writer Barbara Isenberg years later.[*] Still, Irving did not want Thelma to work—he saw it as a matter of pride that his wife should not have to work. But he did allow her to organize what was left of Crown Products and arrange for it to be sold at auction.

Irving was told that he could not survive another Toronto winter, and that his only hope was to move to a more benign climate. His older brother Harry, who had been living in Detroit, had recently moved to Los Angeles with his wife and son, and there were other Goldberg relatives there as well. Irving decided that California was where he, Thelma, Frank, and Doreen would start their lives all over again. Harry's work still took him to Detroit from time to time, and in March 1947 Irving met his brother there and drove with him to Los Angeles. He sent his family postcards from along the way, as Thelma and Frank packed up 1364 Dundas, prepared it for sale, and disposed of what was left of Irving's business.

Thelma and Doreen remained in Toronto until Irving sent word that he had arrived and found them an apartment. He had also gotten himself

---

[*] Irving was actually forty-six, not forty-seven, when he had his heart attack.

a job driving a delivery truck for the Yankee Doodle Root Beer Company. In May, Thelma and Doreen arrived, leaving Frank with his grandparents in Toronto so that he could finish out the year at Bloor Collegiate. In June, as soon as school was out, he went back to Union Station, the site of his arrivals from Timmins, and boarded a train for Los Angeles. As he left 15 Beverley Street, Leah, who had made imaginary cities with him on the kitchen floor a dozen years before, waved good-bye from the front porch. He would not see his grandmother again.

3

To Life in the Sun

Frank stepped off the train in Los Angeles into a terminal that had the same name as the depot in Toronto but was in every other way different. In Toronto, he had boarded the train by walking through an august colonnade of limestone classical columns. When he got off at the other Union Station he found himself in a fanciful space of rounded arches, grand chandeliers, and warm colors, a fantasy of Spanish mission architecture, raised to monumental proportions. Both Union Stations were vestibules to their cities that told you instantly what the city was like, or what it wanted you to think it was like, and it was clear that Los Angeles wanted visitors to think that they had arrived in a place unencumbered by the weight of the past, a place where the architecture of Europe could inspire pleasure, not duty. In four days on the train Frank had journeyed from east to west, from north to south, and from Canada to the United States, but the trip had also taken him from cold to warm, from old to new, and from dark to light. It was a morning in June, and half a century later he still remembered the feeling he had as he walked out of Union Station into the California sun. "It was sunny and warm. The light was brighter than I was used to. Bright, bright, bright, like coming out of a movie theater." He had been in Kansas, and this was Oz.

If Los Angeles in 1947 felt exotic to an eighteen-year-old from Toronto, it was in some ways more conventional than many other American cities in warm climates. It was not a pleasing backwater, attractive to visitors mainly as an escape from the cold, like Miami or San Diego. The years of World War II had made Los Angeles central to the American economy, and it had become one of the nation's industrial powerhouses. The city may have been known to the rest of the country mainly for its film studios in Hollywood and the San Fernando Valley, but the entertainment industry, however large its influence on the culture may have been, was only the tip of a huge and very different economic iceberg. Los Angeles may not have looked like Detroit, but it was just as much built around manufacturing. Movie stars weren't the typical Angelenos; machine workers in aircraft assembly lines were.

The core of the Los Angeles economy was in defense contracting. The city's benign climate and its large harbor to the south in San Pedro, not to mention its presence on the Pacific Rim, had made Los Angeles home to much of the U.S. aircraft industry, with Lockheed, Douglas, Northrop, North American, Vega, and Vultee its pillars. Federal dollars poured in during the war years: between 1942 and 1945, 479 new defense plants were built in the area, and hundreds more were expanded. The Defense Plant Corporation, a federal agency charged with overseeing the use of government funds to build facilities for private contractors, invested more than $450 million in building or expanding industrial facilities in the Los Angeles area during the war years, the equivalent of more than $6 billion today. Employment in the region stood at 15,930 in 1938, before the war began; by 1941, spurred by manufacturing orders from overseas, it had already grown to 120,000. It would expand to employ more than 228,000 people just a few years later, at the peak of the war effort. The shipbuilding industry, almost inconsequential before the war, grew to become the region's second-largest economic force. Local shipyards had not constructed a major vessel for two decades preceding World War II; by the end of 1941, the California Shipbuilding Corporation, known as Calship, had become the nation's most productive shipyard, delivering 111 ships for the Defense Department in 1942. Calship employed 55,000 workers, and the rest of the shipbuilding industry in the region another 35,000.

The explosive industrial growth of the city in the war years right before Frank and his family arrived in Los Angeles came on top of a solid economic base, since Los Angeles had been one of the nation's leading manufacturing centers for years. It was the second-largest garment manufacturer in the country, after New York; it was a center for oil refining, steelmaking, and food processing. Even though easterners tended to think of San Francisco as California's premier city, Los Angeles had surpassed its older northern neighbor in population by 1920. Its large tracts of cheap open land and the convenience of a large harbor for shipment of goods to and from Asia and Latin America made it an ideal center for both manufacturing and warehousing, and large East Coast–based industrial companies like

RCA, Firestone, and Bethlehem Steel had based their western operations in the area for years. After the war, the influx continued, as the civilian aircraft industry grew and other wartime plants were converted to new uses as peacetime factories. The government's decision to make Los Angeles the locale for the Rand Corporation, the new "think tank" charged with studying technology and military strategies in the postwar era, further deepened the connection between Los Angeles and the developing aerospace industry. And it made manifest the idea that the city represented the future.

San Francisco was still the West Coast's banking and financial center, but it seemed increasingly to represent old money and old ways of doing things. It was becoming clear that Los Angeles was where California's economic energy was going to be focused: where new things would happen, where new fortunes would be made, even where a new kind of place would be created. San Francisco, for all its compelling beauty, was an old city, densely settled around a core downtown. It may have looked different from an eastern city, but the environment defined by its downtown office buildings and Victorian mansions was not, in the end, as different from New York or Boston or Philadelphia as the city liked to think it was. San Francisco was a city of the nineteenth century, Los Angeles a city of the twentieth. That turned out to make all the difference.

Toronto, of course, had much in common with San Francisco. Even if the shoreline of Lake Ontario lacked the drama of San Francisco Bay and the city's fairly flat topography called to mind midwestern American cities far more than California, Toronto possessed a relatively tight urban fabric, much of it shaped long before any of the Goldbergs or Caplans had settled there. Los Angeles was a different kind of urban place. Set in a dry basin surrounded by mountains on the east and north, and with the ocean to the south and west, in its early years it was no more than a small city amid a rural expanse, as if it were the lonely capital of an agricultural province. The complex system of diverting water from the mountains and valleys to its east, assembled gradually over decades, made the city's twentieth-century expansion possible; trains and trucks enhanced its growth into a large manufacturing center. And another form of twentieth-century transportation would define Los Angeles more than anything else: the automobile.

The car would affect every city, but it would shape Los Angeles more completely than any other major city in the world. Even though the city had a substantial and effective streetcar system in the first decades of the twentieth century, it otherwise provided an ideal set of conditions for a place that would build its identity around the automobile: it was spreading rapidly across the landscape at a time when cities everywhere were beginning to decentralize; it possessed an alluring natural environment that made motoring attractive, at least in theory; and, most important, it was a place that was growing at a rapid rate and whose very essence seemed to symbolize a new way of living.

For all its soaring economic strength, the city Frank and his family saw when they arrived in 1947 bore only the slightest hints of its sprawling future. The most characteristic element of Los Angeles, the freeway system, barely existed, and the old Los Angeles streetcar lines were still largely in place, centered on a relatively small, tight downtown that resembled that of an older city more than the expansive urban agglomeration that Los Angeles would soon become. The streetcar lines extended unusually far from downtown, connecting numerous communities in every direction, including many subdivisions built by Henry Huntington, who owned the major streetcar system, and their expansive reach predicted the spread-out pattern that the freeways would more firmly establish. In 1947, the year the Goldbergs came from Toronto, Los Angeles was not yet the city of cloverleaf interchanges and shopping malls, but it was already a region more than a conventional city.

Many of Los Angeles's residents had come from the American Midwest, and while their politics were often conservative, many of them had chosen to settle in Southern California at least in part out of a desire for personal freedom. The sprawling nature of the city suited them, and they found the notion of a private car far more appealing than even the most efficient transit system. By the late 1940s traffic was increasingly clogging all of the major boulevards, but the popularity of early freeways like the Arroyo Seco between downtown and Pasadena and the Cahuenga Pass freeway connecting Hollywood and the San Fernando Valley gave the freeway great allure. When Frank arrived in 1947, the Los Angeles region was just completing its first comprehensive plan for freeway construction, a ringing affirmation of its belief that the solution to automobile congestion was in building more roads, not in strengthening alternative ways to move around the city. It would take much of the next two decades to build the major parts of the freeway system, which would never be entirely completed. But by 1947 it was already clear that Los Angeles was not going to be as downtown-focused as most American cities, and that it would grow by spreading across the landscape, up hills and across plains, building an urban environment at suburban density.*

That was the city that Frank found as he arrived in the late 1940s: a city that seemed to be building itself outward with tremendous energy, filling mile after mile of land with small houses and low commercial buildings, a city that seemed unencumbered by the weight of the past. Things happened quickly, and there was little sense of a need for permanence. This was not a place for classical courthouses and grandiose museums. Los Angeles did not build with a sense of the pressures of history, and perhaps even more important, it did not have to think about building for the demands of a difficult climate. This was, more than anything else, the city of the casual.

When Irving arrived in Los Angeles, he found a small one-bedroom furnished apartment at 1723 West 9th Street, at the corner of Burlington Avenue, a few blocks south of MacArthur Park and a few blocks west of the center of downtown. It was nothing like 1364 Dundas Street in Toronto. The apartment, Doreen remembered, had "two rooms. One room was Mom and Dad's bedroom, and there was only one closet, which was in there. There was a Murphy bed in their bedroom . . . [and another] Murphy bed [in the living room], and there was a sofa, and Frank and I fought over who slept on the sofa and who got the bed. There were bedbugs, and there were lice . . . [and] terrible velvet sofas and things that you would cringe to see, and cockroaches."

Thelma, whose aspirations seemed unbroken by the reduced circumstances of her new life, did all she could to bring a sense of propriety and dignity to her dingy surroundings. There was a tiny kitchen table that could barely seat the family, let alone the guests whom both Irving and Thelma encouraged, and Thelma would set a formal table every night for dinner.

---

* The city's evolution from streetcars to freeways was helped along by the purchase of its streetcar systems by National City Lines, a corporate entity that turned out to be backed by General Motors, Firestone Tire, and Standard Oil of California, which bought up light rail systems in numerous cities to encourage their replacement with buses and, its proponents hoped, private cars. What became known as the "General Motors streetcar conspiracy" contributed to the eventual curtailment of trolley systems in dozens of cities, but nowhere was its effect more sweeping than in Los Angeles, which adopted the automobile with an enthusiasm and gusto unmatched by any other city.

"She cooked as if she were cooking for royalty in that place. We might be living in squalor, but we were royalty," Doreen recalled.

Frank remembers being a bit startled by the extent to which the apartment "was a comedown" from Toronto. Everything was shabby. The apartment had "ragged carpets and the upholstery was ragged. It was kind of really shitty. I was disappointed [but] happy to be with them."

Irving's ill health made it impossible for him to hold on to his job driving the root beer truck. He was not strong enough to lift the cases of soda that needed to be moved on and off the truck all day. Frank helped him, but it was not enough to make up for Irving's physical weakness. Irving tried to find other work, and for a time leased popcorn machines and jukeboxes to bars, which was ultimately no more successful than his similar ventures with machines in Canada. He eventually found work at a liquor store a few blocks away from the family's apartment, often covering the night shift, working until one or two o'clock in the morning. This, too, was not an easy time. "It was pretty downhill," Frank recalled. "He started drinking. He never had before, but he was sitting day after day alone. He would drink, and get belligerent, [and] he would hit my mother. He didn't mean to, he loved her."

Eventually the job at Bonnie Brae Liquor, like the others, came to an end, done in not by Irving's anger but by his affability. He enjoyed talking to the neighborhood policemen who would often come by the store late at night, and his son thinks that from time to time he gave them drinks. Local liquor laws made it illegal to sell alcoholic beverages after 1 a.m., and one night one of the officers on the beat, chatting with Irving after closing time, asked to buy something. Irving, unaware that the request was a trap, sold the policeman a bottle of liquor at 1:05 a.m., and was arrested and taken to jail. The store's license to sell liquor was suspended for two weeks, and Irving was fired. Frank thought that the effort to set Irving up was motivated by anti-Semitism, and the police refused to allow him to testify on behalf of his father.

Thelma, lonely and far from her family, did what she could to hold up the family's sagging finances. She found work in the candy department at the Broadway department store on Hollywood Boulevard, and she took well to selling. Her manner, both warm and proper, was suited to a more ambitious role than candy sales, and she was soon moved to the drapery department, where she would remain until she retired.

Thelma's success as a department store saleswoman was not enough to make up for Irving's troubles, however, and money remained tight. Frank's cousin Hartley Gaylord—born Hartley Mervin Goldberg—would remember visiting the 9th Street apartment. "It couldn't have been more than seven hundred square feet, if that. It was small. They were poor people." The family could rarely afford to go to the movies, and Frank remembered going to the Sunset Strip to watch movie stars get out of their cars and go into fancy restaurants. "My father was very personable, and he would give the parking lot attendant a few bucks so we could stand in front," Frank said. One night he saw the actress Jennifer Jones get out of her limousine, "and I thought how elegant she was." Years later, he would come to know her, and would tell her that story.

Many of Irving's relatives had settled in Los Angeles. They tended to be a more colorful group than Thelma's kin. One of Irving's brothers, whom Frank called Uncle Willie, used the name Bill Goldie, and worked for the mobster Mickey Cohen and tended bar at a tavern on Western Avenue called the Black Lite. (A sister, Rosie, who did not move to California, sold black-market nylons in Detroit, and later married a man who Doreen believed was also a mobster.) Uncle Harry, Hartley Gaylord's father, who had driven Irving across the country, went back and forth between Detroit and Los Angeles on business. Harry was married to Beulah, a woman whose eagerness to elevate her family's social position led her to change the family name to Gaylord, a name she selected, Frank remembered, after passing the Hotel Gaylord on Wilshire Boulevard. Beulah, who earlier had changed her own first name from Minnie, bestowed on her son the expanded name of Hartley Mervin Gordon Gaylord III. Hartley lived up to the image of his new name. He drove a black Plymouth convertible, joined the Alpha Epsilon Pi fraternity at the University of Southern California, and projected the image of a suave, self-assured playboy. Hartley was four years older than Frank and studying optometry, and despite the differences between them the two became good friends. Frank looked to Hartley as a social if not a professional role model. Hartley, for his part, happily took Frank under his wing, referring to him as his "kid cousin," and bringing him to fraternity parties. Eventually, Frank was spending so much time on the USC campus with Hartley that he decided to start taking night and weekend classes at the extension division.

Another cousin, Frankie Beaver—son of Irving's brother Hymie Beaver, originally Hyman Goldberg—owned a small company in the San Fernando Valley called the Vineland Company, which specialized in building and installing breakfast nooks in suburban houses. A few weeks after arriving in California, Frankie hired his younger cousin to make deliveries and installations for Vineland. Frank was paid seventy-five cents an hour.

Frank was skillful at the installation work, which he credited to having taken woodshop back at Bloor Collegiate. And he was meticulous about measurements. From time to time he was called back to correct installations of units that his cousin had measured wrongly; one of them was for Roy Rogers and Dale Evans. "I really worked hard so they'd have it ready for Christmas," Frank remembered. The famous cowboy actor and his wife found Frank "sweet and cuddly," he thought, and they were grateful enough to invite him to join them for Christmas dinner, which impressed Irving and Thelma no end. One night not long afterward, the Goldbergs were making one of their evening visits to the Sunset Strip, and Rogers and Evans drove up to a restaurant. They saw Frank and waved him over to introduce him to Bob Hope, who was in the car with them. The sight of their son talking to Bob Hope left Irving and Thelma speechless, Frank remembers. And it left him feeling awkward. He knew that he was not a celebrity himself, or someone who socialized with them. But his encounter with Roy Rogers, Dale Evans, and Bob Hope was just enough to make him stop feeling comfortable with the idea of going celebrity-spotting on the Sunset Strip; after that night he no longer joined his parents on their jaunts.

A cousin of Frank's by marriage, Arthur Joel, who was married to Frankie Beaver's sister Shirley Beaver, owned a jewelry shop on 3rd Street in downtown Los Angeles, and Frank worked for him as well. It was part-time work, helping Arthur "clean jewelry and fix watches and fans, stuff I'd done with my grandfather," Frank said. "I was handy, they knew I could fix things." He would often drive the family's ten-year-old Ford downtown, sometimes stopping at Bonnie Brae Liquors to drop off Irving, and then he would park the car atop Bunker Hill on the edge of downtown and take the venerable Angel's Flight, the funicular that ran up the side of Bunker Hill, down to Arthur's shop, Continental Jewelers, which was located at its bottom. Frank remembered taking notice of the old Victorian houses that still dotted Bunker Hill, a neighborhood that had not yet been subsumed into the commercial downtown: "It was a bit of nineteenth-century urbanism that we should have kept," he said. "I loved the old Victorian houses, but I wasn't studying architecture yet. I didn't know anything yet."

Frank didn't receive money for his work at the jewelry store. Instead, he traded his time for flight lessons. Frank had been interested in flying since a stint as an Air Cadet in Canada, and he was thrilled to have a relative who could teach him. Arthur, a former pilot trainer in World War II, owned a classic Waco biplane, and took Frank flying on the weekends, even bringing him along when he tried acrobatic maneuvers. The plane was based at Van Nuys Airport in the San Fernando Valley, and when Frank had extra time, he would drive to the airport just to watch planes take off and land. Eventually that led to a third part-time job, washing planes. He remembers once cleaning a plane belonging to the actor Dick Powell.

Flying may have topped Frank's enthusiasms in his early years in Los Angeles, but he never considered it as a career. "I didn't know what I wanted to be when I grew up. I actually thought I wanted to be a radio announcer for about two weeks. I was interested in art, always. I think I was interested in music always, because of my mother," he said. He had thought about chemical engineering, and he thought about drawing and drafting, but he remained, at eighteen, propelled by curiosity about almost everything more than by certainty about anything.

Not long after his arrival in Los Angeles, Frank had begun taking night classes at Los Angeles City College. It was free, and it was not only an opportunity to fill in some gaps in his previous education, like American history, which he had not studied at all in Toronto, but also a way to test his interest in possible careers. It was there that he took his first courses in art and architecture. He did well at drafting and was told by his professor that he had an aptitude for it. Frank next took a drawing and perspective class, which he failed. His distress at getting an F led him to take it again, and the second time around he received an A. Emboldened, he took a class he later described as "professional practice for novices" offered by a local architecture firm, where he learned very basic skills such as drawing kitchen cabinets. The teacher "egged me on for architecture," he recalls, "but I still wasn't convinced."

It was USC, the university he more or less drifted into as a result of the time he was spending with his cousin Hartley, that would make the real impression on him. His first courses were general: he took an introductory course in English and a course called "Man and Civilization" in his first semester, and got a C in both. In his next English course, in writing, he earned a D. More C grades followed in courses like "Problems of Human Behavior." In the fall of 1948, he took a course in fine arts, called "Art Appreciation," and received a B, his first grade at USC higher than a C. The fine arts program, he recalled, "was the thing that had the least requirements to get in," and by the summer of 1949, surely encouraged by his good grade as much as the relatively loose admissions requirements, he had decided to concentrate on that. He started out by taking a course in ceramics, a course in freehand drawing, and a course called "General Design." That semester was far more successful than the previous one. His lowest grade was a B, and he received two As.

In 1948, an attractive woman in her forties named Bella Snyder came to look at breakfast nooks in the Vineland Company showroom, which was three miles from her house in North Hollywood. She decided to order one, and Frankie Beaver went to the Snyder house at 6623 Lemp Street to do the measurements. Mrs. Snyder introduced him to her fifteen-year-old daughter, Anita. Frankie, who was struck by both women, decided to play matchmaker, and told them that he had a nineteen-year-old cousin working for him whom he would send to deliver the breakfast nook when it was ready. The cousin was "the right age" for Anita, Frankie said to Mrs. Snyder, and maybe her daughter might be interested. Frank had not at that point in his life had a serious girlfriend, and even after he made the delivery, met Anita, and found her appealing, he was hesitant to call her for a date. "They kept pushing me, 'Are you gonna call her?'" he recalled. "And finally I called her, and I took her to a movie. She liked me."

Anita Rae Snyder was born on August 23, 1933, in Philadelphia, to Bella, a teacher, and her husband, Louis, a pharmacist. Anita and her younger brothers, Mark and Richard, grew up in Los Angeles, where Lou and Bella Snyder had resettled in 1941. They had grown tired of the eastern winters and hopeful for more economic opportunity in Los Angeles, and they had been satisfied on both counts. Louis Snyder, who had worked for Rexall in Philadelphia, bought a pharmacy in Los Angeles, and also invested in small properties in the city, and while the Snyders did not become wealthy, they had a solidly middle-class life. The family was Jewish, but even less inclined than the Goldbergs to emphasize their ethnic background. With their somewhat generic last name, they could have been almost any middle-class suburban family, something that for Frank may well have made them seem a touch exotic.

Anita was the oldest child by several years—she was nine years older than Mark, eleven years older than Richard—and she was bright and headstrong, which put her in conflict with both of her parents for much of her adolescence. Years later, Frank would suspect that Bella's support for their relationship derived at least in part from competitiveness with her daughter, and a sense that she would be content to have Anita out of the house and be left with two cute little boys. "Her mother was pushing the whole deal, like mad. And so I think I was being manipulated. . . . I liked her mother," Frank said. Louis Snyder, like Frank's grandparents, believed that women did not need higher education, and "sent her to become a typist." Frank said Anita chafed at her father's refusal to support her intellectual ambitions, just as Thelma had done years before when Samuel Caplan would not allow her to go to college, and Anita further resented her mother's tendency to side with her father on such matters.

Anita and her father had a very difficult relationship, her brother Richard Snyder recalled. Frank, on the other hand, "saw that she had greatness [or] he wouldn't have befriended her and everything. He really doesn't like to have a relationship with someone where he is the dominating figure." Anita, Frank felt, was "brilliant," and the two bonded, at least in part, over their shared feeling that Anita had been treated unfairly by her parents.

But if Frank provided Anita with a refuge from her family, or at least from what she considered her father's oppressive view of her potential since she was a woman, Anita gave Frank an equally welcome escape from the world of his own family. The Snyders lived at a level of comfort that the Goldbergs could only hope for, and whatever the tensions in that household might have been, to Frank it seemed a world of relaxed plenty compared to his own home. He could not afford many dates, and the couple spent much of their time together at Anita's house, where, as Frank recalled years later, "they had a television. They had a swimming pool. They had fancy desserts and food and stuff. And they had a washer-dryer, so we'd take our stuff. So that was what we did on the weekends. We'd go swim in the pool whenever we could, and watch TV." Frank and Anita, like many young couples, bonded in part because their relationship gave them both a world apart from their parents.

It was in the early years of his relationship with Anita, when she and Frank were often to be found at her family's house, that Frank first met a neighbor from down the street who had become her brother Richard's best friend, a boy with an exceptional talent for music. His name was Michael Tilson Thomas, and from time to time Frank and Anita would look after him when his parents were out. Richard Snyder was attracted to the entire Thomas family, which seemed a more cultivated household than his own, and Bella Snyder, who often seemed to aspire to a more artistic world than her husband, enjoyed spending time with her neighbors as well. Michael Tilson Thomas would remember thinking of the Snyders as a

divided household: on one side were Bella, Richard, and Anita, who liked
the intellectual atmosphere of the Thomas house, and on the other, Lou
and the older son, Mark, an athlete who as an adolescent shared none of
the interest in culture that his younger brother had, and who had little
to do with the Thomas family. Frank cast his lot with Anita, Bella, and
Richard. He found watching Richard Snyder and Michael Tilson Thomas
more stimulating than burdensome. Richard Snyder recalled seeing Frank
and young Michael sitting at the piano together, playing—Frank by ear,
Michael reading the music.*

The first course Frank took at USC after deciding that he would
concentrate in the field that the university called fine arts was in
ceramics. He had a professor named Glen Lukens, who was a prominent
ceramicist, jewelry maker, and glassblower. Lukens, who was known for
marrying bright colors to raw surfaces, took a quick liking to Frank, and
asked him to assist him in testing new glazes that could be used in Haiti,
where Lukens was helping to develop a ceramics industry. Frank liked
Lukens's social awareness, his taste, and his interest in finding new ways to
experiment with an ancient art. But he liked Lukens best, he recalled, for
the importance he put on individual creativity.

"Once, I remember, the pot I put in the kiln came out so well that I
said to Glen, 'God, that's beautiful. It's just wonderful what can happen
with the kiln and all those glazes,'" Frank remembered. "Glen said, 'Stop.
From now on, when things like that happen, you take credit for it, because
you did it. You made the pot. You put the glaze on. You put it in the kiln.
You're allowed to claim credit for it, and I want you to do that.' He was
trying to make me feel part of it. That was a very important lesson that
resonates for me even now."

Lukens had recently built a house in the West Adams district of Los
Angeles with the architect Raphael Soriano, one of several prominent
modernist architects active in the city in the years after World War II.
Soriano, who had been born in Greece, was known for using aluminum
and prefabricated steel in residential designs. Lukens took Frank to see
his house, as well as to see a new house Soriano was building, where he

---

* Michael Tilson Thomas would become an internationally known conductor. In 2003 he
commissioned Frank to design a hall in Miami for the New World Symphony, which he
had founded. The hall was finished in 2011. Richard Snyder would also remain a lifelong
friend of Thomas's. See chapter 19.

Frank's early efforts at ceramics led him to try architecture instead.

met the architect.* "There was Soriano in a black beret, black shirt, black jacket," Frank recalled. "He was kind of a prima donna. He was talking about his architecture, and [Lukens] saw my eyes light up in a way he hadn't seen. And he said, 'I think you should try architecture.' He was looking out for me, kind of." Frank believed that Lukens sensed that he was not going to be a great ceramicist, but that he had significant creative potential that needed a different kind of outlet.† Frank also had a positive memory of watching Soriano "pushing steel around" and "telling people what to do."

While Frank was taking Lukens's ceramics course he met a young architect from Montreal named Arnold Schrier, who worked for Lloyd Wright, Frank Lloyd Wright's Los Angeles–based son, and was doing graduate work at USC. As easily as Frank had fallen into partygoing with his cousin Hartley, he and Schrier quickly became an architecture-touring duo. They went around Los Angeles looking at houses by Wright, Rudolph Schindler, Soriano, Richard Neutra, and others. By then Frank knew his way around the city, and knew where many of the most interesting modern houses were. And he knew that he enjoyed few things more than exploring Los Angeles, looking at the latest buildings. "I knew every building, every

---

* Frank recalled going with Lukens to see Lukens's house under construction, but he was probably confusing the timing with a visit to another house by Soriano, in all likelihood the house the architect designed for the architectural photographer Julius Shulman, since that was under construction in 1949 and 1950. Lukens's own house had been finished in 1940. Since Frank definitely visited both houses, he probably conflated the visits in memory and erroneously remembered seeing the Lukens house under construction.

† Frank's ceramics were colorful and cartoonlike, if an example in the collection of his former brother-in-law Richard Snyder can be considered typical of his work.

street, every client. We got kicked out of more places for looking at stuff," he recalled.

Arnold repaid the favor by introducing Frank to his friend the architectural photographer Julius Shulman. Shulman was at the center of the Los Angeles architecture community, or at least the community of modernist architects in the city: he documented all their work, lived in a house in the Hollywood hills designed by Soriano, and frequently entertained his architect friends. Schrier brought Frank to dinner at Shulman's, where he met the architects Craig Ellwood and Lloyd Wright, among others. Soon Frank and Shulman became friends, and Frank and Anita began going to the Shulman dinners together. A word from Julius Shulman would open the door of almost any modern house in Southern California, and he arranged for Frank and Arnold to see all of Frank Lloyd Wright's and Lloyd Wright's work, as well as the brand-new Case Study houses, the series of inexpensive modern houses commissioned by the magazine *Arts & Architecture* and built by the likes of Charles and Ray Eames, Ellwood, Soriano, Neutra, William Wurster, and Pierre Koenig.*

Julius Shulman also introduced Frank to the two giants of modernist architecture in Los Angeles, Rudolph Schindler and Richard Neutra. His reactions to the two men were markedly different. "Schindler was interesting and accessible," Frank remembered. "I'd meet him on job sites. He was a Bohemian who wore sackcloth shirts and sandals. He had a beard and mustache and flowing hair, and he was a ladies' man. . . . I liked the way he'd draw details on wood planks at the site for the guys. I was taken by the immediacy of it, and I thought the buildings were exciting. They were also accessible. As somebody who didn't have a lot of money, I could relate to them. They weren't precious or overly fussed on. They were just matter-of-fact, something that appeals to me still." Frank would say of Schindler that "I think they thought about him the way they thought about me later."†

Neutra, on the other hand, was "very full of himself. Neutra had a big ego and he was the reigning force in L.A. architecture. At the time, he had a large office, maybe thirty or forty people." Frank remembered watching

---

* The Case Study program began in 1945 as a way of demonstrating the potential of new technologies and building materials. It extended until 1966, although most of the important Case Study houses were completed by the mid-1950s. Thirty-six houses were commissioned, of which roughly two dozen were built, mostly in and around Los Angeles.

† Frank's identification with Schindler may have involved more than his belief that their personalities were similar. In his 1930s, after he grew a mustache, Frank would come to bear a considerable physical resemblance to Schindler, if photographs of the older architect in midcareer are any indication.

Neutra order Julius Shulman around and insist on setting up each shot—
normally the photographer's prerogative—himself.

Encouraged by Glen Lukens, who Frank believes may have paid some
of his tuition,* he had already begun to take architecture courses, and in
the fall of 1949 he became a full-time student in the bachelor of fine arts
program. He had entered the University of Southern California almost by
accident, starting with night extension courses that seemed interesting and
convenient as he spent time on campus with his cousin Hartley, and had
morphed in stages toward becoming a regular student while continuing to
work for the Vineland Company. In the 1949–50 academic year, his first
with a regular courseload, he took basic courses in architectural design,
architectural history, and drawing. His grades were all Bs, with a C in freehand drawing. He continued to take ceramics for one semester and started
a second semester of work with Glen Lukens. It is the only course on his
transcript that is marked "Withdrawn." By early 1950, he had made up his
mind. There was no reason to study ceramics any longer, because he was
going to be an architect.

---

* Neither Frank nor Doreen is certain how the Goldberg family found the money to pay
Frank's tuition at USC. The courses he took at Los Angeles City College were free, but
each course at USC cost several hundred dollars, an enormous amount for a family that was
merely scraping by. Presumably Frank was able to use much of the money he earned for
tuition, since there is no record of his having received a scholarship from USC, although
it is possible. Frank told Barbara Isenberg in *Conversations with Frank Gehry* that he sus-
pected that Glen Lukens might have secretly paid the tuition for his first architecture class.

4

Becoming an Architect

In the spring of 1950, Frank's grandmother Leah was found lying on the floor of her house on Beverley Street in Toronto, next to the telephone stand. She had suffered a stroke, and died a few days later. Frank was devastated. He thought of Leah not only as a wise elder, but as the person in his family who understood him the most and got inside his restless, still unformed mind. "I adored that woman. She was my whole life. She somehow got me. Looking back, she was the only one who said, 'Something's going on.'" Leah, he felt, saw his creative side even more than his mother did.

Despite Frank's closeness to his grandmother, he did not return to Canada for her funeral. Irving was behaving more and more erratically—Doreen has a recollection of his becoming angry with her and throwing a radio at her, and she remembers Thelma's constant refrain in those years being the words, "Irving, stop it!" He was clearly not up to the trip. Thelma herself, of course, had no choice but to return to Canada. It fell to Frank to stay home and keep an eye on his father. Thelma took twelve-year-old Doreen out of school, and together they went back to Toronto for Leah Caplan's funeral.

Their trip turned out to last quite a bit longer than the traditional seven-day Jewish "shivah," or mourning period. For several weeks, Thelma was detained in Canada, unable to reenter the United States, because she lacked an American passport. Since the identification she did have showed that her birthplace was Poland, American border officials were giving her an extremely difficult time. Frank and Irving, fearing that Thelma might never be able to return, contacted their local congresswoman, Helen Gahagan Douglas, for assistance. "We just innocently called her and went for help," Frank recalled. "We had no connections whatsoever, and I remember visiting her office and she was a very beautiful woman . . . she was very heartfelt and she [said] she was going to help us and she did. She got my mother back."* On June 20, 1950, roughly six weeks after Leah's death, Irving received a letter from the Immigration and Naturalization Service confirming Thelma's visa to reenter the United States.

Once Thelma and Doreen returned, things began to look up for the Goldberg family. Thelma had been doing well as a saleswoman in the Broadway's drapery department, which she eventually came to head. She was liked by both her customers and her colleagues, who called her "Goldie," or, if they wanted to be more proper, "Mrs. Goldie." Later, Thelma would be promoted again to the design department, and given charge of the store's interior design services. Frank remembers her being especially excited when she got the assignment to handle interior decoration at the house of the entertainer Sammy Davis Jr. Thelma was not a snob, but she carried herself with an air of propriety, even dignity, and she believed in appearances. Hartley Gaylord remembered her taking him to musical evenings at the home of a friend of hers in Beverly Hills. "We'd go there and we'd sit around, must have been about twenty-five, thirty people there, and someone would come up and sing at the piano. . . . It was rather elegant. Thelma always wanted us to go there, and we did so. She was just a wonderful person. She was great."

Later in 1950, Thelma's success at the Broadway allowed the Goldbergs to move out of the apartment at 9th and Burlington that for the last three years had symbolized the challenges rather than the promise of their move to California. Like most Angelenos whose circumstances improved, they moved westward. Their new home was an apartment in a four-unit building at 6333½ Orange Street, in the Miracle Mile district south of the Farmers Market at Fairfax Avenue. The walk-up second-floor flat was no mansion in Beverly Hills, but it was an improvement over 9th Street, both in its surroundings and in its space. The new apartment had two bedrooms, a separate dining room, and a back porch.

Doreen got the least immediate benefit out of the move to Orange Street: as the youngest in the family she continued to sleep on the living

---

* It not clear how Frank and Irving were able to get access to Douglas, although it was surely easier in 1950 for unknown constituents to meet their representatives than it is today. And it is not surprising that people of Frank and Irving's political leanings would have hoped that the liberal Douglas could be helpful to them. Douglas, who was married to the actor Melvyn Douglas, later lost her seat to Richard M. Nixon, in a famous campaign in which Nixon falsely accused her of being too forgiving of communism. She became a hero with the status of a near martyr to many liberals after her defeat.

room couch. Thelma and Irving got one bedroom, and the second was given over entirely to Frank, whose architecture studies by then required the workspace of a small studio. He was drafting and sketching so much that it was a challenge for Thelma to keep his room clean. "My mother used to say that he was shoveling coal in that back room, because he was using his pencil and she hated cleaning there because everything [was covered with] pencil lead, pencil dust, all over the place."

Irving's poor health and dramatic mood swings were a constant reminder, however, that things were only marginally better even after the move. Irving was working sporadically as a door-to-door salesman for Standard Coffee Company, from which he earned $2,036.80 in 1952. Like Thelma, he would try to keep up appearances as much as possible, but he was having an increasingly hard time of it. He could be jovial in front of friends and his favorite relatives—Hartley Gaylord remembers Irving visiting his family constantly, conversing warmly, and never letting on that he had severe health problems. But back at Orange Street, he could barely climb the stairs to the apartment, and by the time of the move even part-time work was becoming a challenge for him. Doreen remembers days when she would see him walk up the stairs with great difficulty, and then sit in the apartment for hours, doing almost nothing. For his young daughter, "it was really depressing. I hated coming home."

Irving's heart grew weaker, and his diabetes, diagnosed five years earlier, was poorly managed, which weakened him further and contributed to his frequent mood swings. Doreen recalls that her father "was taking three shots of insulin a day and he was drinking a dozen Cokes. And I have memories of Frank and I just begging him, crying and begging him to please stop doing it. He couldn't help it." Frank was so frustrated by his father's mental state that he took him to see a psychiatrist, but after one session the doctor told him that Irving was not treatable. "It was unconscionable for him to say that, but I didn't know better," Frank remembered.

Irving's children had to take him to the Los Angeles County Hospital several times, their anxiety made worse by the fact that they were bringing their father not to the source of the best medical care in Los Angeles, but to a place that cared for the indigent, since the family could not afford to pay the bills of a private hospital. "He was cared for by the county. It was like welfare," Doreen said. She recalled waiting with her father in a hallway of the hospital after he had another heart attack, because there were no available beds. Thelma asked Irving's sister Rosie, who lived back east, if she would help with the costs of her brother's medical care. Rosie refused. The family had no other place to turn for help with Irving's medical bills, so when the next crisis came, and the one after that and the one after that, he went back each time to wait his turn among the needy at County Hospital.

F rank had spent the 1949–50 school year officially enrolled in the bachelor of fine arts program at USC, but most of his curriculum consisted of courses related to architecture. In the spring of 1950, with the further encouragement of Glen Lukens, he was formally admitted into the School of Architecture. It was more than a routine acceptance, however. He and three other students who were also already at USC had taken enough relevant basic courses and done well enough in them that the school allowed them to skip the first-year program and begin as second-year architecture students. It was "the first time somebody said nice things about me," Frank would say about the recommendation that he enter the program as a second-year student. The four would join eleven others to make up a second-year class of fifteen who would stay together for the rest of the five-year program that would culminate in a bachelor of architecture degree.

The University of Southern California was then the only major university in Los Angeles to offer a full-fledged, degree-granting architecture program. It would be another fourteen years before the university that saw itself as USC's major local competition, the University of California at Los Angeles, would establish its own architecture and planning school, and twenty-three years before the independent school SCI-Arc, the Southern California Institute of Architecture, would open its doors. USC was the only game in town in 1950, and many of the city's most important architects taught there. The ones who didn't teach invariably appeared at the school from time to time since it was at the center of what limited academic architectural culture existed in Los Angeles in the postwar years. Its faculty of active professionals made it a place that emphasized modern architecture: USC was not, as the architecture program at the University of Toronto had seemed to Frank years before when he looked at its materials in the library at Bloor Collegiate, the kind of school that taught its students how to make pretty English cottages. At USC, you learned to design buildings that looked more like the rigorous modern structures of Raphael Soriano—he had graduated from the school in 1934—or the flamboyant modern shapes of William Pereira, whose firm was a major force in Los Angeles in the postwar years; or John Lautner, whose striking, futuristic houses made him a particularly influential figure for younger architects.

The design style that would later be known as "midcentury modern" and be closely associated with Los Angeles had a kind of spiritual home at USC, where much of the faculty consisted of the architects who were actively designing the houses and commercial and institutional buildings that were shaping the postwar city.

Frank was coming to know many of these architects through Arnold Schrier and Julius Shulman, who had already helped him build a network of professional acquaintances that grew to include other Los Angeles modernists such as Harwell Hamilton Harris and Cal Straub, who both taught at USC. He liked and admired many of them, but he was still feeling like something of an outsider. Frank was not by temperament the kind of person who wanted to join a club, and, excited as he was by the work of many of the Los Angeles modernists, and eager as he was to learn what he could from them, he wanted to imagine a future for himself that was more than just being admitted to their club. He wanted to be liked and he wanted to be admired, but he had not yet figured out on what terms. He was still learning, and he had a lot more study ahead of him before he would be ready to know what kind of architecture he would want to make. But he was beginning to sense that it had to be something of his own, something that would not look exactly like the work of his new mentors.

Not everything went smoothly in the first year of architecture school. Frank took a design studio in his second semester with an architect named Bill Schoenfeld, a recent graduate of USC who later went to work for William Pereira and would eventually direct much of the planning and design work at Los Angeles International Airport. In the spring of 1951, however, Schoenfeld was a young instructor teaching beginning architecture students, and he was not happy with the work Frank did. "They gave us little buildings to do, just basic, not very complicated," Frank remembered. But Schoenfeld called him and told him he did not think he was suited to be an architect. Schoenfeld said to "get out of architecture," Frank said. The issue may have been personal: Frank may have already shown a discomfort with the corporate style of producing architecture that Schoenfeld, given his later career, seemed to prefer. The architects Frank admired at that point, like Schindler and Soriano, were far less corporate in both their personal style and the nature of their work.

Frank wondered later if Schoenfeld's strange suggestion had its origins in something else entirely. "It could be anti-Semitism, because I ran into that. That did rear its head." Los Angeles may have been a city committed to the new, but the architecture profession was still by and large a gentlemen's profession dominated by WASPs, as it was elsewhere in the United States. There were relatively few Jews and almost no women, and many of the men prominent in the field were politically and socially conservative, more comfortable with the business side of architecture than the artistic side. And even some of the modernists seemed to limit their interest in the progressive to aesthetic matters. They had no difficulty imagining houses as sleek glass boxes in which women still did all the cooking and cleaning and men made all the decisions. In fact, for many of the architects of the era when Frank was at USC, this was the ideal. They didn't want to change the way the world worked, only the way it looked.

Frank had a somewhat different view. He had grown up around strong women, beginning with his grandmother, and since his family's arrival in Los Angeles he had seen his mother provide most of his family's support. In Anita he saw another strong woman with high ambitions, and the certainty with which he shared her conviction that her father should be more supportive of her educational goals was clearly a factor that strengthened their relationship. And both Irving and Thelma had always been liberal politically, a stance that the hard times they went through seemed only to reinforce. Everyone deserved a chance, they felt, and the frustrations they experienced themselves did not diminish this belief, or their determination to pass it along to both of their children.

Whatever the issue between Frank and Bill Schoenfeld, Frank emerged from Schoenfeld's studio with a grade of B, higher than the C he had received in the previous semester's design studio from an instructor who had not indicated the doubts Schoenfeld did about his suitability for architecture. His exchange with Schoenfeld was troubling on a personal level, but it appears to have had little effect on his long-term feelings about architecture or about himself. It is noteworthy that Frank recalled it primarily as a possible incidence of anti-Semitism, not as a source of genuine doubt about his potential.

The modernist bias of the USC architecture school led to a relative lack of interest in architectural history, particularly European. There was a limited, relatively lackluster class in architectural history that Frank remembered as "crappy slides of Chartres and cathedrals, that stuff," which the students were sometimes expected to draw, but almost never to analyze and discuss. It would be many years before Frank would begin to experience European architecture of past centuries or, for that matter, his own century, and acknowledge its importance. The influence of European modernists was central to the modernist architecture developing in Los Angeles: both Schindler and Neutra, after all, were European-born, and despite their ties to Frank Lloyd Wright, their work—Neutra's in particular—was highly influenced by the Bauhaus. But connections to Europe were rarely emphasized at USC; there was far more eagerness to view Los Angeles modernism as a thing unto itself, emerging out of the openness of the American West. Even American work by Mies van der Rohe, like his Farnsworth House in Plano, Illinois, finished while Frank was in architecture school, seemed like it came from another world from that of USC. "I hated the Farnsworth House then," Frank recalls. "I didn't hate Mies. I just couldn't imagine living in it. It seemed almost militaristic that you couldn't throw your clothes on a chair."

The one exception to the general reluctance at USC to acknowledge the importance of the architecture of other places and other times was Japanese architecture, which was appreciated by many American modernists, from Frank Lloyd Wright onward, for its simple lines, purity of space, and elegant mix of warmth and spareness. "The only humanistic thing then was the Japanese influence," Frank said, and he theorized that it developed, at least in part, as a result of the exposure many architects who fought in World War II had to Japan. It was logical, too, that California would be more open to influences from the other side of the Pacific than the other side of the Atlantic. The bias toward Japanese architecture very much affected Frank, who attributed it to his inability to feel a sense of connection to the work of Erich Mendelsohn, like Mies a celebrated German modernist who had relocated to the United States, despite his admiring Mendelsohn in a distant way.[*] When Mendelsohn lectured at USC, Frank said, "I couldn't relate to it because I was still in a Japanophile period. The Japanophile period is very strong. It still exists. It's a DNA you can't get rid of, I think. The Europeans [like Mendelsohn], I knew he was important, but I was not going to go there. [Walter] Gropius, the same. [Marcel] Breuer, the same. Corbu [Le Corbusier], the same."

Frank had no trouble maintaining a level of interest in almost all the modern architecture going up in Los Angeles, however, whatever its origins and influences. He still loved moving around the city looking at things, whether with Julius Shulman, Arnold Schrier, or his new classmates in the architecture school. His most frequent tour companion was a tall, lanky, somewhat shy student who had grown up nearby, in Pasadena,

---

[*] Many years later, Frank would visit Mendelsohn's Einstein Tower in Potsdam, Germany, of 1929, and would consider it one of the buildings he most admired.

and had started his studies at Pasadena City College and later transferred to USC. Like Frank, Gregory Walsh was something of an outsider. He also came from a family of modest means, although the Walshes were conservative Catholics, not liberal Jews. Frank remembers sensing that his friend's parents were less than pleased that their son had made friends with a Jew, and of once almost ending the friendship when Walsh told him not to be concerned about his parents' anti-Semitic attitudes because they had decided he "was one of the good ones."

Walsh, like Frank, loved music, art, and literature, and considered himself more sophisticated than his peers. And like Frank, his interest in architecture had developed not through engineering or construction or real estate, but through art. He gave up thoughts of being an artist early, largely because, in his recollection, his father thought he wouldn't make a living as an artist. The elder Walsh didn't think there was much money in architecture, either, and so his son first tried architectural engineering. But after a single semester, he realized he wasn't cut out to be an engineer, and he gave up pretending he wanted to be anything other than an architectural designer. After his two years at Pasadena City College, he felt secure enough to transfer to the program at USC, which declined to give him credit for all of his prior courses and placed him in the second-year program rather than the third. The frustration turned out to be an exceptionally lucky break for Walsh, since it meant that he became a classmate of another student with a somewhat unusual background, Frank Goldberg.

Greg and Frank met early in their USC career, but it was not until the fall of 1951, when they entered the third-year program, that they became close friends. Frank, Greg recalled, "was actually the only person that I seemed to be interested in talking to. . . . Most of those other people were clueless." But Frank "was always smart . . . he had a way of getting it, of understanding things."

"Greg and I bonded right away. It was like Ross, it became a very intense relationship," Frank remembered. "Greg is a classical musician. . . . He was an expert on Japan, so as a result of that, I started to read Japanese literature, I started looking at all of the work that connected to Frank Lloyd Wright's collection, and I memorized every temple. I could draw them." Greg would take Frank, and sometimes Frank and Anita, to concerts of classical music. Frank recalled going with Greg to hear Rosalyn Tureck play the *Goldberg Variations*.

If both Frank and Greg had cultural interests that extended far beyond architecture, they also shared a determination to take their architectural education outside the bounds of the classrooms and studios at USC. Like Frank, Greg Walsh loved to go looking at buildings, and they often went touring together. "I was always going out looking at houses by Neutra, Wright, Schindler. Nobody else in my class did that except Greg," Frank said. "And so every Sunday or something, we'd go exploring everything. Schrier and I think Anita used to come along, too. There was always something to see." They would, Frank said, unhesitatingly walk up to the front door of houses that interested them and ask to see the inside.*

"Greg glommed on to me, kind of," Frank recalled. "It was that he was a pianist. He knew classical music, which I was in awe of. He was literate. There were very few people in my class that were like that. Nobody like that. Anita was very literate. It was an easy kind of social thing." The triad of Frank, Anita, and Greg moved far beyond the bounds of USC, and Greg became in many ways an adjunct of Frank's family, so much so that Doreen would recall that "Greg was like my other brother."

Frank and Greg's view of themselves as slightly apart from the rest of their class at USC was confirmed by the way they both approached a major project in their third-year coursework, the assignment to analyze a contemporary house by an architect they admired. "Frank chose Schindler, definitely a maverick, his Kallis House in Studio City. My choice, John Lautner, was also a non-conformist; I looked at one of several houses with a hexagonal roof, supported on only three columns," Greg recalled. The choices were striking in many ways. Both Schindler and Lautner began their careers working with Frank Lloyd Wright, and both broke away from Wright to do highly original work on their own. Schindler, born in Vienna in 1887, was near the end of his career when Frank met him—he would die in 1953—but he remained a creative fount, and the Kallis house, which was just three years old when Frank studied it for his USC class, seems to prefigure many of the architectural ideas Frank would develop so fully on his own. An exploded box with slanted walls and angled roofs and trapezoidal windows, it has a raw, unfinished quality that, along with its sharp angles, could almost be said to suggest a primitive version of the house Frank would build for himself in Santa Monica thirty years later.[†]

---

* In the conversation with the author in which he made this comment, Frank concluded, "And I did what I hate when people do now, they knock on my door."

† Another of Frank's important buildings, his Danziger Studio of 1968, which he has described as showing the influence of Louis Kahn, also bears a surprising resemblance to another Schindler building, his little-known Bethlehem Baptist Church in South Los Angeles, at least in terms of its unusual massing. See chapter 7.

Lautner was no more inclined than Schindler toward the straight, simple boxes of much of the latest modern architecture; for all his originality, his work remained more clearly Wrightian, notable both for its reliance on basic geometric forms like circles and hexagons and then, in later years, for its commitment to swooping, curving, futuristic shapes that could often be even more dramatic than the ones Wright favored in his late years. Lautner was a generation younger than Schindler, his work was smoother than the older architect's, and he often aspired to a degree of spectacular effect, something the haughty Schindler would have disdained as theatrical, even cheap. Lautner was in midcareer when Greg Walsh chose to study his work, and he would continue to produce important works through the 1970s, his career overlapping with Frank's. Whatever their differences in style and temperament, both Schindler and Lautner were iconoclasts, celebrated primarily for their private houses; neither man could work comfortably with large corporate clients or commercial real estate developers, and as a consequence neither developed a large or diverse architectural practice. But they both served as exactly the kind of role models that Frank and Greg sought for inspiration in 1951.

Frank and Greg did not always have to go outside of USC to find architects who motivated them, however. They both thought Calvin Straub an exceptional teacher—"seminal," in Greg's words—in large part because he taught them to think in terms of neighborhoods and cities and not just single buildings. "Cal Straub was my third-year professor, and he liked me from the beginning . . . the first one that sort of embraced me, because remember, I'd just come out of a class with a guy [Bill Schoenfield] who said this profession's not for you," Frank recalled. "So then I go into third year, I'm resolved, I'm not going to quit, I'm not going to pay any attention to that asshole, so I have a little bit of self-confidence by then. And so Straub was talking about the neighborhood." It was, Frank recalled, "an idealistic kind of thing. The first part of the year, we did diagrams of those kinds of cities, and they're idealistic, and my politics was pretty left, so it was my kind of thing. It was just wonderful. So he liked me, and gave me good grades the first semester." Greg remembered Straub's class as "an ideal, kind of Garden City type thing" with highly prescriptive criteria for how to diagram a city. Frank might have been expected to have bristled at Straub's precise formulas for urban design, but he welcomed the chance it gave him to design communities that would include lots of social housing, which minimized any irritation he might have felt at Straub's tendency toward diagrammatic layouts. And Frank, like any student, responded well to any instructor who liked him. "He called me in one day and told me I was way ahead of everybody. I'd just been told [by Schoenfeld] that I should get out!" Frank recalled.

"I think all of us students initially were bewildered by that first semester with Straub," Greg has written in a recollection of his student years with Frank. "His 'good life' was an attempt to craft an ideal but achievable 5,000-person neighborhood unit that placed dwellings, schools, shopping and the workplace in close, pedestrian proximity; cars and people safely separated. Most of this, the legacy of Ebenezer Howard, Clarence Stein and 'Greenbelt' new towns was totally unfamiliar. Analysis of these often conflicting requirements was mostly about diagramming, not 'real architecture,' as many of our classmates complained. Frank and I did not; in trying to make sense of all this, we became friends."

For all that Frank and Greg appreciated the way in which Straub had awakened them to thinking in broader, urbanistic terms, neither particularly agreed with Straub's tendency to reduce design to formulas, which he applied to single buildings as much as to neighborhoods and cities. Straub favored a single mode of building houses, with post and beam structure, flat roof, and layouts and façades based on even geometric modules. "I recall the two of us talking about a possible negative outcome; overreliance on modular planning decisions as a substitute for visual evaluation," Greg wrote. "This conversation became an important ingredient of our attitude toward design later." Frank and Greg emerged from Straub's class, then, with a tendency to make judgments based on how things looked and how they worked, not on how well they fit into formulas—a critical lesson that, ironically, their favorite teacher had taught them by negative example.

Frank and Greg learned a great deal from another instructor, Harry Burge, who had none of Straub's social idealism but who had a pragmatic sensibility that for both of them proved a critical counterpoint to their aesthetic impulses. Burge, who Greg remembered always wore a tan smock, taught courses in professional practice, and required each student to take a house he had already designed for a practical course and "reshape it into something that 'could' be built, using construction drawings, done by the student, to scale, accurately. Transforming one's personal architectural creation was traumatic . . . practicality was purging our pristine concepts," Greg wrote. "Frank told me later that the direct no-nonsense approach to problem solving he took away from Burge's class helped him more than any other single aspect of our training to establish the way he wanted to practice architecture."

Frank's recollection of Burge was as the instructor who "wasn't in on the poetry. He wasn't in on the art. He was just Mr. Practical. . . . He said he thought I had a future and he said, 'There's one thing I want you to remember.' He said, 'No matter what you do, how little, how big, it's got to be the best thing you ever did at that point. Just remember this, because you're going to be judged by that.'"

The most prominent of Frank's influential teachers at USC was Garrett Eckbo, a California-born landscape architect who had studied at the Graduate School of Design at Harvard and who, along with Dan Kiley, helped to define contemporary American landscape design. Eckbo's stance was more oriented toward social issues than Kiley's, however; he was less interested in a minimalist arrangement of plants for aesthetic effect than in the connections between landscape and larger issues of urban planning. Eckbo's book *Landscape for Living*, published in 1950, made a case for closer connections between modern architecture and landscape design, and for most of his life he argued for the possibilities of landscape design as an agent of social change, a commitment that particularly impressed Frank, who later in his USC career became Eckbo's teaching assistant.

Eckbo, Frank recalled, "became my closest friend and family. Politically we agreed on everything . . . he was lefty."

Eckbo's politics were sufficiently left-wing to provoke what Frank would recall his "being harassed" by the House Un-American Activities Committee, whose inquiries followed a class during which Eckbo discussed his outrage about the Ethel and Julius Rosenberg case. Frank remembers that Eckbo, responding to a student's question, lectured for most of a class session about the injustice he believed was being done to the Rosenbergs.* It later turned out that the student who asked the question had been planted by the FBI as part of an investigation into left-wing activities at USC, and had deliberately goaded Eckbo into making political remarks.

This only made Eckbo more of a hero to Frank, who joined with several other liberal-leaning students to form a group called the Architecture Panel, an informal club focused on enhancing the connection between

---

* The Rosenbergs were accused of selling secret information about the American atomic bomb program to the Russians, and were convicted and executed in 1953. The case became a cause célèbre for the American left, which believed that the couple had been unfairly accused.

architecture and social responsibility. The panel had some ties to an organization called the National Council of Arts, Sciences and Professions,
which had socialist leanings, and this connection, if not the very existence
of the group, troubled the dean of the architecture school, Arthur Galleon.
He called Frank and Greg, who was also a member, into his office, and
said, "Frank, you know the road has a crest in it. If you're on the crest, you
can see both sides. So don't fall on one side or the other."

Frank did not take the hint. He remained one of the Architecture Panel's
most active members, helping to organize a series of Friday evening talks
on issues related to the social responsibility of architecture and encouraging the group to take an active position on public issues. The panel became
particularly involved in a bitter controversy over public housing planned
for the site of Chavez Ravine near downtown Los Angeles, a neighborhood occupied primarily by low-income Mexican families. The city had
purchased the land under eminent domain with the intention of building
an enormous public housing project to be called Elysian Park Heights and
designed by Richard Neutra and Robert E. Alexander. The project, which
was to have contained 24 thirteen-story towers as well as 163 town-house
units providing nearly 3,600 new low-cost apartments, would have been
the largest public housing project in Los Angeles. It was exactly the kind of
project that Frank, in his idealism, believed could demonstrate the ability
of architects to provide an answer to social problems. Not everyone agreed
with him. The project was unpopular in the city at large, and the political climate of Southern California in the early 1950s was such that most
of the opposition to Elysian Park Heights came not from people trying to
protect the poor residents of the neighborhood from being displaced, as
might have happened a generation later, but from the view, encouraged
in part by the *Los Angeles Times*, that government-built housing at such
a scale was socialist and therefore had no place in the city. It was another
reminder that Los Angeles, for all that its freeways and suburban sprawl
suggested a new kind of world, was at bottom a conservative city, many of
whose residents had emigrated from the Midwest and the South in search
of better jobs and better weather, not a more progressive society. By arguing
that it represented an incursion of socialism into the city, critics of Elysian
Park Heights managed to delay and ultimately defeat the project. However
implausible the claim of socialism was, it was taken seriously enough for
Frank Wilkinson, the assistant director of the Los Angeles Housing Authority, to receive a subpoena from the House Un-American Activities Com-

mittee.* In the end, the 254-acre site, which had been cleared of most of its original residents before the housing project was canceled, was sold to the Dodgers and became the site of Dodger Stadium.

Frank's political feelings went beyond a general sympathy for the downtrodden. He saw himself as an outsider who might never be accepted by the establishment, a view that became even stronger when he failed to receive an invitation to join the architecture fraternity at USC. He was hardly a fraternity type like his cousin Hartley, even though he did at one point join Hartley's fraternity, Alpha Epsilon Pi, but that was more because he enjoyed Hartley's company and tended to follow him than because he actively sought to belong. Eventually Frank was asked to leave Alpha Epsilon Pi, which was an all-Jewish fraternity, when he tried to pledge a classmate who was black. Snubbing Alpha Epsilon Pi, which had welcomed him, was one thing; being snubbed by Alpha Rho Chi, the architecture fraternity, was quite another. Frank, like Groucho Marx, didn't particularly value being a member of a club that wanted him. He was happy to reject the fraternity that he had already joined, and to do it by means of what was somewhere between a prank and a gesture of social protest. But he was deeply unhappy if he could not be the one doing the rejecting. He resented being excluded from Alpha Rho Chi, which Greg Walsh and several of his other friends belonged to, and he thought, once again, that the cause might be anti-Semitism. "I knew what they were doing," he said. He recalled that the experience only made his political views more entrenched. "It just fueled the liberal thing. It just made it more intense."

Meanwhile, Frank's relationship with Anita continued to strengthen. It was the first intimate relationship that either of them had had, and it was driven to some extent by their shared desire to get out of their parents' houses. But they provided each other with far more than just a sense of escape. They felt that they shared the same worldview, and the same politics. Anita believed in Frank's work, and Frank believed in Anita's determination to have a career of her own. They enjoyed each other's company. And there was no doubt about the physical attraction they felt.

---

* Wilkinson was asked about the project and his political persuasion. He refused to respond, believing that his politics were irrelevant to the project and that the committee had no justification in inquiring into his personal political views. He was then held in contempt of Congress and forced to resign.

The Goldbergs and the Snyders became friendly, and the presumption of both families was that it would merely be a matter of time before their children would marry. Richard Snyder recalls Irving and Thelma visiting his family's house in North Hollywood, and the Snyders making return visits to the apartment on Orange Street. "Thelma was bouncy and energetic and opinionated. Irving was very, very ill, but he always wore suits"—a sign that both Irving and Thelma viewed their relationship with the Snyders as something to be taken seriously. This was not a casual acquaintance, because their families were going to be joined together.

In the winter of 1952 the inevitable, or what seemed inevitable at the time, occurred. Frank married Anita at the Valley Jewish Community Center on February 2, three and a half weeks before his twenty-third birthday. His bride was eighteen. Thelma and Irving stretched their budget to buy Frank a new suit. Bella Snyder made a dress for Anita. The event was fairly small, with most of the guests from Frank's side his Goldberg relatives. Greg Walsh, who had already become quite friendly with Anita and was probably at that point Frank's closest friend, was not there. After Frank stepped on a wineglass, breaking it in the traditional end to the Jewish wedding ceremony, the party adjourned to a reception hosted by the Snyders at the Sportsman's Lodge, a quirky old Hollywood hotel on Ventura Boulevard known for its pseudo-rustic décor and ponds stocked with trout.

Before the wedding, Frank and Anita had rented an apartment on Crenshaw Boulevard near the USC campus. They had spent time fixing it up with paper lamps, beanbag chairs, and paintings by their artist friends. Richard Snyder remembers seeing a Japanese paper lamp in the shape of a fish—"He always loved fish"—and that the apartment had a youthful, casual spareness and a sense that its elements had been improvised. Its upbeat informality was a world away from the apartments and houses Frank had grown up in. At first, he and Anita seem to have treated the apartment as a project more than as a place to live, since they did not spend a night there until after their wedding. Frank was nervous as he and Anita left the Sportsman's Lodge to go home together for the first time. His cousin Hartley had slipped some condoms into his pocket during the wedding reception, but this gift did not fully allay his feeling that, happy as he was to be married to Anita, he did not fully know what it would be like to sleep with her. Both he and his bride were virgins.

The night in their apartment was a one-night stopover en route to their honeymoon in Desert Hot Springs. They stayed at the Desert Hot Springs

Motel, which had been designed by John Lautner, a destination Frank chose at least in part for its architectural pedigree.[*] It was an easy trip, not far from Los Angeles. Frank could not afford either the time or the money to do anything more, and soon he and Anita were back on Crenshaw Boulevard. Frank resumed his studies and Anita started at the first of several jobs she would take to support him while he worked toward his degree. Now that Frank and Anita constituted a household of their own, someone had to put bread on the table.

Frank would encounter several other influential teachers at USC, including the architect Gregory Ain, another member of the left-leaning faculty group. Ain, who like several other architects Frank met had recently been investigated in the wave of anticommunist sentiment, was, in Greg Walsh's words, "cynical and disillusioned" as a result of his experience, and Greg found him difficult. Frank was excited by Ain's way of teaching, however, and despite Ain's cool manner—"I could never tell whether he liked me or not, or liked my work," Frank said—he liked being in Ain's class since he was the most intellectually disposed of any of the architecture professors. "He would talk about *Murder in the Cathedral* and T. S. Eliot and he would read poetry and he would talk about architecture in a different way," Frank recalled. Frank found the notion of talking about architecture as a part of culture to be compelling, and he thought of Ain as someone who opened him up to new ways of thinking. Greg, though normally at least as inclined toward the intellectual, nontechnical side of architecture as Frank, was more put off by Ain's manner. And both of them were disappointed to find that Ain's openness to thought did not seem to translate into an acceptance of a broad range of approaches to architectural design. "His rigorous, logical approach to design seemed limiting," was how Greg put it.

Frank also studied with Edgardo Contini, a partner at Gruen Associates, a large Los Angeles–based architecture and planning firm best known as the designer of early shopping malls. Dean Gallion had found him a summer job at Gruen in 1952, and Frank would continue to work there in subsequent summers. It was a somewhat unusual match since the firm was not particularly known for public housing, which Frank considered his

---

[*] Years later, the place would be offered for sale and Frank briefly considered buying it. Eventually it would be bought by a new owner who, eager to capitalize on the fashion for midcentury modern architecture, renamed it the Hotel Lautner.

primary interest. But it was active in urban planning and Victor Gruen, the Austrian-born founding partner, was a prominent thinker on the sub-ject of evolving urban form in the postwar era, so the Gruen office was not without a connection to social issues. In any event, Frank liked the job and felt comfortable at the firm. In the summer of 1953 he helped to construct the models for what would become one of Gruen's most famous projects, Southdale, the nation's first enclosed mall, which would be completed outside Minneapolis in 1956. (As a junior summer worker, Frank had no role in the actual design.) By the time Frank became Edgardo Contini's student at USC, then, he knew him well. For Contini's USC studio Frank designed a house made of concrete panels that he felt looked somewhat like one of Rudolph Schindler's recent houses. Contini was very taken with it, gave Frank an A in his studio, and urged him to consider working at the Gruen office on a permanent basis.

Frank's interest in public housing led a classmate from Mexico, Rene Pesqueira, to ask if he would join forces with him to work on an urban planning project in Baja California, where his family knew the governor, Braulio Maldonado Sández, and Pesqueira had been given the chance to design a master plan to stimulate development in the area. It was an extraordinary opportunity for someone who had not yet even graduated from architecture school, and Frank was quick to agree. He and Rene were invited to Baja California to study the area, and given enough funds to rent a small office on La Brea Avenue back in Los Angeles, where they hired some USC colleagues and set up business as the Collaborative Pro-fessional Planning Group.

A key part of Frank and Rene's plan was a bridge across the Gulf of California to connect Baja with the mainland of Mexico, a tie that they hoped would stimulate economic development. "I remember we were all excited. We had convinced the Baja guy [Governor Sández] to fight for it. We were just kids, so anything could go," Frank remembered. Putting a bridge across the gulf, which is thirty miles wide at its narrowest point, may or may not have been possible structurally, but it turned out to be far too ambitious financially. Neither it nor any other part of the plan was ever built, and the project, as well as the Collaborative Professional Planning Group, ultimately faded away.

The experience did give Frank an idea for his senior thesis, however. Together with Rene Pesqueira, he chose a location in Baja that was part of their project site and designed a public housing complex for it. At that point the Baja master planning project remained active, and so the housing complex, too, seemed as if it might actually be built. Frank thought for a while that he had pulled off the impossible: he had found a way to design a thesis that reflected his interest in socially responsible architecture, and he had even managed to get paid for it. He remembered that the architect William Pereira, who taught a fifth-year studio, was particularly impressed at his and Rene's entrepreneurial instincts.

Greg and Frank remained as close as ever, even though Frank had partnered with Rene to produce his thesis. Greg had chosen a more conventional subject for his project, the design of a civic center for the city of Fontana, near San Bernardino, but he ended up working alongside the others in Frank and Anita's apartment, which the three appropriated as a drafting room since space was too tight at USC to produce all the drawings and models they needed. They put Masonite doors on sawhorses in the middle of the living room to serve as drafting tables, and worked for a solid month to produce drawings for both projects in Pelican brand black ink.

Anita was fond of Greg, and saw him, as Frank did, as almost a member of the family. Frank and Greg worked together to decorate the Crenshaw Avenue apartment as a Japanese house, with tatami mats, paper walls, and a lowered ceiling, for a surprise party for Frank's sister Doreen's sixteenth birthday. "He and Greg must have spent nights, weeks, doing this thing," Doreen remembered—though she also recalled her friends from Fairfax High School finding the idea of a sweet-sixteen party in an apartment turned into a make-believe Japanese house to be strange.

By the time the apartment made its next transformation, into a temporary architecture studio, Anita had become pregnant, which made the imposition of Frank's classmates and the loss of the living room even more stressful than it would have been otherwise. The prospect of having a child brought to the fore a far bigger concern for Anita, however, which was that she did not like being called Anita Goldberg. She wasn't entirely happy at being married to an architect named Frank Goldberg, either. And most of all, she did not want to bring a child into the world with that name. After growing up with the more or less ethnically neutral name Snyder, she was uneasy at the notion of one that so clearly identified her as Jewish. The political climate of the early 1950s was conducive to anti-Semitism, and who was to say how many potential clients might be lost because they did not want to hire an architect named Goldberg? Frank's instinct was not to hide his identity, and his feeling was that he wouldn't want anyone as a client who would reject an architect because his name sounded Jewish. But he was acutely aware from his own experience that being easily identified as Jewish made many parts of life more difficult, and his time at USC had made him highly conscious of the pervasiveness of anti-Semitism in Los Angeles. The last straw for Anita was the radio and television show *The Goldbergs*, which starred Gertrude Berg as a stereotypical Jewish mother. Anita did not like being burdened with a name that many people identified primarily with a caricature, and she was determined not to pass it along to her child.

Anita had an ally in Thelma. She lacked the brazen upward mobility of her sister-in-law and brother-in-law, who had gone from Goldberg to Gaylord and named their son Hartley Mervin Gaylord III (it did not trouble the Gaylords that there had never been a Hartley Mervin Gaylord I or II), but nevertheless Thelma had always felt that Goldberg was not a name that reflected her own social aspirations. She tolerated it, but welcomed the opportunity to shed it. Irving was not as sympathetic. There was nothing wrong with Goldberg, he said, and declared that he wanted it on his tombstone.[*] Frank, despite the discrimination he felt he had suffered as a Jew at the architecture school honor society and elsewhere, felt that changing his name would be a cop-out, a way of giving in to the pressure of anti-Semitism rather than resisting it. "I didn't want to do it. You have to understand, I was super lefty, I was involved with liberal causes," he has said. Garrett Eckbo told Frank he saw no reason to do it, and that, along with Irving's opposition, left Frank feeling seriously uncomfortable with the idea. He tried repeatedly to persuade Anita to forget about it.

She would not. "She was adamant," Frank said. And she wanted it done before their child was born. Anita was working as an assistant for Philip Stein, a lawyer, and he was willing to handle the legal procedure without charge for his employee, thus removing another possible objection Frank might have raised, which was cost. Frank ultimately gave in, eager to keep peace with his wife. "If you knew Anita, you knew that I had to do it. I had no way out. I was in a corner," Frank said, referring to Anita as "one tough operator." At another point he referred to his agreement to change the family name as part of a behavior pattern in which he was "placating her endlessly. I was in a mode to try to make her happy and so I bit the

---

[*] His wish was not granted, however. After Irving died on June 23, 1962, he was buried at Eden Memorial Park, his tombstone inscribed with the name Irving Gehry. Doreen has observed that he probably would have made a peace with it, however, had he lived long enough to see Frank's success and enjoy his identification with the name.

bullet and I hated it. I let her do it. I was very embarrassed."* It was perhaps a har- binger of things to come that Frank could feel that Anita was becoming difficult to please. "It was like there was an insatiable problem, always. If I brought a paycheck home, it wasn't enough. If I visited with a friend, it was no good." But Frank was committed to making his marriage work, and changing his name, he decided, was not too high a price to pay.

Once the decision to give up Goldberg had been made in principle, the question remained about what to replace it with. Frank said he did not want to change his initials, and Anita, having won the war, had no interest in fighting a small battle, so it was going to be a name beginning with G. Anita and her mother proposed

Sketch by Frank showing the profile of "Goldberg" and "Gehry"

Geary, or some variant of it, and Frank then came up with the idea of spelling it G-E-H-R-Y. His rationale for this invented spelling was some- thing only an architect or a graphic designer could have come up with. He wanted a name whose letters had a similar profile to Goldberg, which has high letters in the middle and, if spelled in lowercase letters, both begins and ends with a letter that descends below the line. In Gehry, the *h* serves the purpose of the *l*, *d*, and *b* by raising the profile of the name in the middle, and the final *y* brings the profile down at the end, like the final *g* in Goldberg. By making the name change into an exercise in design, Frank made the whole business at least somewhat more palatable.

It didn't make him feel much better about it. The change became final on May 6, 1954, but for several years thereafter, when he introduced him- self as "Frank Gehry," he would often blurt out, "But it was Goldberg," right afterward, as if to undercut the effect of the name change that he continued to find embarrassing. He jokingly referred to Johann Sebastian Bach's "Gehry Variations" in conversation with Greg Walsh, who was par-

---

* In *Sketches of Frank Gehry*, the film Sydney Pollack made about Frank and released in 2006, Frank used much stronger language to describe his capitulation to Anita's insistence on changing his name. "I was pussy-whipped," he said in the film. See chapter 17.

ticularly fond of the *Goldberg Variations*, but the sardonic humor did little to offset his basic discomfort about the decision. And Irving was particularly annoyed—"furious with me," Frank remembers—although he was too ill to do more than grudgingly accept the formality of the new name. So he, too, along with Frank, Anita, Thelma, and Doreen, became legally a Gehry, though he considered himself Irving Goldberg for the rest of his life.

The change came shortly before Frank's graduation from USC, and it was confusing to many of his classmates who had known him as Frank Goldberg, a student who more or less disappeared from the class register. Years later, Frank realized that some of his fellow students at USC whom he had fallen out of touch with had probably missed the news about his new name and had no idea what had become of him. "So there were a whole group of people who disappeared from my life and I didn't even realize it," he said. Because he knew that he would be Frank Gehry from that point onward, he had his diploma issued in his new name. But at his graduation from USC in June 1954, when he received his bachelor of architecture degree and was called up to receive his diploma as the class roll was read, he made one final gesture toward the past, asking that his name be announced as "Frank Goldberg."

For the rest of 1954, the Collaborative Professional Planning Group continued to work on the Baja California project, although the project's likelihood of being realized continued to diminish. At one point in the spring, Al Boeke, a young architect Frank had come to know through the Architecture Panel, and who had worked on the Elysian Park Heights housing project at Richard Neutra's office, encouraged him to apply to Neutra's firm for a job. Frank admired Neutra's commitment to public housing somewhat more than he liked his spare, International Style aesthetic, but he went to see the celebrated architect for an interview at his office in Silver Lake, bringing along the drawings for his housing project in Mexico. Neutra, impressed, said he could have a job and start the following Monday. "And he got up to leave and I said, 'Well, who do I talk to about how I get paid?'" Frank recalled. "And he said, 'Oh, no, when you come Monday, you'll meet with so-and-so and he'll tell you how much you will pay us for working here.'" It had not occurred to Frank that an architect as eminent and socially responsible as Neutra would run his practice like an apprenticeship academy, with young architects paying for the privilege of working beside the master. He knew he could not afford to pay Neutra, but even if he could, he had no interest in doing such a thing. He was so insulted by the idea of the arrangement that he left the office immediately after the conversation with Neutra and never returned. He did not even call to say he was no longer interested in working there.

Instead, he would return to Gruen, where he had worked happily over the previous two summers. It would not be a long stay, however, for reasons having nothing to do with the Gruen office or with architecture. Frank's start at Gruen was interrupted after a few months when, to his surprise and unhappiness, he was drafted.

At USC, Frank had been a member of the Air Force Reserve Officer Training Corps, which he joined after he became a U.S. citizen when he turned twenty-one in 1950. (Because Irving was an American citizen, Frank had the option of choosing either American or Canadian citizenship. Thelma had chosen to become an American citizen as well, and was sworn in after she successfully completed a citizenship course in January 1952.) Joining the air force, Frank thought, would be a way of continuing the interest in flying that he had begun with his cousin Arthur's flying lessons, by allowing him to enter air force flight training after graduation, a far more appealing option for military service than submitting to the draft. It was a common choice in the early 1950s, when there was mandatory military service for all physically fit males. Greg had joined the Naval ROTC, and was sent to Japan shortly after getting his USC degree.

Frank was not as fortunate. Despite having attended all of the Air Force ROTC classes and training exercises for four years, he was abruptly discharged before graduation when the commanding officer at USC discovered that his bad left knee would make it impossible for him to pass the physical exam for flight training. " 'We've made a terrible mistake,' " Frank remembers the officer telling him. " 'Because of your knee, you can't graduate.' And I said, 'Well, I've had this knee from the beginning, and you've known that.' He said, 'We made a mistake. It was overlooked and I'm sorry.' So the whole thing was a waste. I could have sued them, probably." Later, Frank thought that his cavalier dismissal from the ROTC program may have been motivated by the anti-Semitism he had already experienced elsewhere at USC.

The one comfort, he thought, was that even without his student deferment, he would be safe from military service, since if his knee was bad enough to preclude his going to flight school, it would surely disqualify him for military service as an enlisted man. But his bad luck continued. Once eligible for the draft, he was called in for a physical and examined by an army doctor who was crippled. "He looked at my leg and said, 'Man, that's nothing compared to what I've got. They found something for me to do, they'll find something for you to do.'" He refused to designate Frank as 4-F. And so Frank's architecture career had barely started when it was abruptly put on hiatus. He wasn't going to design any buildings, at least not yet. In January 1955, six months after he got his architecture degree, he was inducted into the army.

5
Dealing with Authority

I t was the worst possible time for Frank to leave home, since by then he was not just leaving Anita. Leslie, Frank and Anita's eldest daughter, had just been born, and she was three months old when Frank went to Fort Ord in Northern California for his basic training. Anita, who had stopped working in October when Leslie was born, was not happy at the thought of being alone with an infant. She had worked instead of going to school to support Frank as he went through architecture school, and when she gave up work to have a child she had expected at least to enjoy the benefits of being the wife of a rising young architect, and to feel that she and Frank were raising Leslie together. Instead, she was the wife of an army private, and Frank was hundreds of miles away. Anita did not hide her irritation when Frank came home on leave. It was, he thought, as if she felt that his army service was something that had been "done to her," robbing her of the life she had expected to be living by then. "Anita was difficult with me through all that time," Frank said—and she sometimes seemed to act as if she believed that her lot was harder than Frank's going through basic training, he felt.

She decided to move back in with her parents in North Hollywood, and she and Frank gave up their apartment on Crenshaw Avenue. It seemed like a reasonable decision, since Anita needed help with Leslie, and there seemed little point in trying to stretch Frank's army income to cover the rent for a place where Anita would feel stranded and lonely. But it was hardly a respite from family stress for Anita—Louis Snyder's health was not good in 1955, and he did not hide the fact that he was unenthusiastic about his daughter's decision to return home. "My mother tried to make everything as easy as possible, and my father tried to make the whole thing as difficult as possible," Richard Snyder, Anita's brother, who was eleven at the time, recalled.

Frank was often able to get weekend leaves, during which he and several fellow soldiers who lived in Los Angeles would share the six-hour drive south, and then drive the six hours back on Sunday evening to be at Fort Ord in time for their midnight curfew. The weekends were difficult, since the long drive to the Snyder house at 12336 Addison Street did not bring Frank to anything resembling a tranquil oasis. The tensions were palpable, and Frank remembers sensing that his mother-in-law was fully aware of how frustrated and angry Anita had become. He was sympathetic, but there was little he could do. What was all too clear was that the decision to move out of the pleasantly spare, upbeat apartment that had been their first home together, however understandable the reasons, seemed also to close the door on a casual, easy period in Frank and Anita's marriage, ending its first chapter far sooner than either of them had expected.

Whatever Anita may have thought, Frank was not having an easy time of it at Fort Ord. Basic training was physically demanding, and while he was in good shape and enjoyed physical exercise, his bad leg often put him in pain, especially during the long marches that were part of the recruits' routine. And changing his name from Goldberg to Gehry did not, he discovered, put an end to finding himself a target of anti-Semitic sentiment. Frank recalled, somewhat ruefully, "So there I was, washed out of the air force for a bum leg, doing push-ups and sit-ups for tough master sergeants like you see in the movies. I would march along with my platoon on cold misty mornings, and my leg would be hurting, so I started to falter a little bit. And when I did, this big, Neanderthal-looking guy, with his sergeant's stripes and his authority, would bellow out, 'Kikey, get back in line!' He called me that during drills, too, and I felt trapped in a prison of idiots who had no sense of me as a human being."

Frank complained to his commanding officer, who told him that the sergeant, a man named Rabachati, meant nothing by his remarks, and urged him to lighten up. Trivializing the incident infuriated Frank, who saw it less as a matter of personal offense to him than as a case of basic justice—the army was not supposed to tolerate discrimination, period. He had become friendly with several other enlisted men who, like him, were professionals who had been deferred from military service while they went to college. They were a few years older than the younger recruits and somewhat more sophisticated in the ways of the world. Most important, a couple of Frank's new acquaintances turned out to be army lawyers who had been put in charge of overseeing processing orders out of Fort Ord. "Don't worry about it, give me his name," one of the men said to Frank. The next thing Frank learned, he remembered, was that "they're processing orders for everybody, so they just processed Sergeant Rabachati. I went in one day and he was gone." He had been transferred to Alaska. "When he told me he was going to Alaska, I said, 'Isn't that terrible.' Oh, and I added, 'I'm sure you'll find lots of kikes up there.'"

Getting rid of Sergeant Rabachati hardly meant that Frank breezed through the rest of basic training. His leg continued to give him trouble, and often after extended marches it would swell, squeezing the edge of his high boots. Eventually he was sent to an army orthopedist who recognized his problem as a birth defect and ordered that he be released from the obligation of wearing standard-issue high boots, which the doctor felt were adding pressure to his defective leg. Frank was ordered to wear regular shoes instead. Since boots were required for marching, for kitchen duty, and for guard duty, the doctor's order left his commanding officers in a quandary. What were they to do with him if he couldn't march with his company or be put on guard duty or given a kitchen assignment? "Okay, what the fuck else can you do?" the captain of Frank's unit, who Frank believed was also anti-Semitic, asked him. "So I said, 'Well, I'm an architect.' He said, 'Well, redesign our dayroom.' So I did." But one small design assignment did not an army architect make, and Frank could not escape the rest of basic training. He was next sent to clerk-typist school and trained for a desk job, and then received his orders for his first assignment after Fort Ord. It was to an army engineering unit based at Fort Benning, Georgia.

The unit, Frank recalled, was assigned to "go out and measure bridges and roads, usually in advance of the troops, and it was very dangerous work. At this point, the Third Infantry Division was preparing to go on maneuvers in the swamps of Louisiana. It was called Operation Sagebrush, and they were developing a new attack mode for the kind of warfare they thought they were going to have. My job was clerk-secretary to the captain, but I wasn't very good at it." The captain seemed to agree with Frank's assessment of his clerical skills; he did not last long as a clerk. The captain asked him what else he could do, and Frank said he was an architect. "If you want to build stuff, I could get excited about it," Frank told him. "But that wasn't what he had in mind. 'Can you make signs?' he asked me. 'Can you letter?' I said I could." Frank became the company's sign maker. His

MODEL STUDIED—A Scale model of one of the new dayrooms to be built all over Third Army is studied by the three
enlisted men, all designers and decorators in civilian life, who
designed the models. Left to right are Sp3 Dominick Loscalzo,
Pfc. Orman Kimbrough, and Sp3 Frank Gehry.

A picture from *Army Times* of Frank (*right*) and his army design colleagues

first assignment was to letter a set of signs saying "Don't put paper in the urinal." He was given two weeks to make them. It was much more time than he needed, so he began to embellish the signs with elaborate script. The captain liked the results. "I had the most beautiful graphics. I had fun with it. I knew it was stupid [but] he loved them," Frank recalled.

Frank's apparent success at graphic design impressed not only his captain but the general in command of the unit as well, who was head of Operation Sagebrush. He asked Frank to prepare charts and lettering for the operation, and told him that the maneuver was still top secret. Did he have security clearance? Frank said he did not. "Well, you're a good patriotic kid, aren't you?" Frank recalled the general asking. "All the liberal organizations flashed in my head," Frank recalled. "And I said, 'I'm completely loyal to my country. Clean as a whistle.' So he swore me in. I mean, there was nothing to connect me to [left-wing organizations]. I was just a kid." Frank was given a secret, windowless room to work in while he prepared signs and charts to be used in the battlefield maneuvers.

Next, the general asked if Frank could design some field furniture, including a latrine to be used on the battlefield. He came up with a design for a two-seat latrine, in which two occupants sat back-to-back, separated by a piece of canvas. "I was into Frank Lloyd Wright at the time," Frank said—an allusion to Wright's famous desert outpost, Taliesin West, where the architect combined elements of wood and canvas. The Operation Sagebrush maneuver was roughly six weeks away, and rumors filled the

Frank's army lounge,
showing his interest
in Frank Lloyd Wright

camp. All of the soldiers, including Frank, were apprehensive. Frank's leg had continued to trouble him with throbbing, arthritic pain, and he made multiple visits to the infirmary, where he met a young army doctor who asked him to design a clinic for him that he hoped to open when he returned home to Alabama after his discharge. Frank liked the doctor, and sketched ideas each time he visited the infirmary. "And it turns out that the general was also going to the infirmary for something, and the doctor told him, 'You know that guy who works for you has a real problem with his leg, you shouldn't take him on maneuvers,'" Frank recalled. "That wasn't something I contrived or even asked him to do, but he did it." The general, impressed that Frank had not himself complained about his medical condition and asked to be exempted from maneuvers, told him that the Third Army, based at Fort McPherson in Atlanta, needed an interior designer for a project and offered to recommend him. Frank went to Atlanta and was told that Lieutenant General Thomas F. Hickey, the commanding officer, wanted to remodel all of the recreation rooms, lounges, and service clubs under his jurisdiction. It was a substantial job with a $3 million budget that involved creating a prototype that could be altered to fit two hundred different army facilities, but the general insisted that he needed an interior decorator, not an architect. Frank said he was sure he could do it, and asked to be able to prove it. "I went back and designed the whole thing, working until three or four in the morning every night," he remembered. "I built a model with furniture."

The general liked what Frank showed him, and Frank's career as an army architect had begun. He was assigned to work along with two other enlisted men, Dominick Loscalzo, a Pratt Institute graduate who had been a freelance industrial designer in New York, and Orman Kimbrough, a graduate of the Chicago Academy of Fine Arts who had done department store design. The first four of the remodeled recreation rooms (which the army called dayrooms) were scheduled to be constructed at Fort Bragg, North Carolina, and each man was told to prepare a design on his own. The officers in charge would pick their favorite, which would become the prototype. "Mine looked a lot like Frank Lloyd Wright, with too much design, and they didn't choose it," Frank said. "Like everybody who starts out, I threw everything in and overdid it." But in the end the three decided to work together and combined elements from all three designs into what Frank said "wound up being a pretty good collaboration." Frank handled the larger architectural decisions, including partitions and lighting, Dominick Loscalzo took care of furnishings, and Orman Kimbrough chose fabrics and colors.

The project was broad in its scope, but limited in its depth. Frank was permitted to make only minor architectural changes to the buildings that contained the dayrooms—he could not change their overall rectangular shape, although he could create new entrances and partitions inside. The rooms were at bottom fairly conventional, presumably because the army expected them to feel familiar and comfortable to the soldiers who would use them, and was not inclined to support cutting-edge design. As a result, Frank did not push for anything unusual or innovative. "Frank may have had better ideas than in that rectangular room, but I guess he knew we're not going any farther than this," Dominick Loscalzo said. "But he did a good job. I remember it had that feeling like the general wanted. Like your living room at home."

It was a period of great innovation in American furniture design, which was making use of new technologies to create new kinds of furniture that both Frank and Dominick were aware of. But they steered clear of it. "George Nelson had a chair, Eames had the bent plywood and then the plastic chair, [but] no, we didn't look at any of that. I don't know why I didn't, but maybe I didn't want to shock them at the time," Loscalzo said. It was one of the last times Frank would willingly design something that looked like what people had seen before. But he was realistic enough to know that there was little upside to challenging the army's sense of design. After all, it had a lot more power over his fate than a typical client.

But his assignment allowed Frank, Anita, and Leslie to live again as a conventional family. Anita and Leslie had come to Georgia when Frank was transferred to Fort McPherson, and the three resided in off-base housing. Frank was able to moonlight on the weekends with local architects, earning some extra cash. Despite his shyness he was a natural networker, and he took pleasure in getting to know a number of Atlanta architects. Among the local architects he did some part-time work for was John Portman, who was five years older than Frank and had just begun his own practice. Frank did renderings for one of Portman's first projects, the Atlanta Merchandise Mart.

In 1956, Anita gave birth to a second daughter, whom her parents named Brina. Richard Snyder remembered that his sister still seemed to be living under stressful conditions. He and his brother, Mark, along with their mother, paid a visit to Frank and Anita in Atlanta during an extended train trip planned by Bella, who believed that long-distance rail travel would not survive into the next generation and wanted her sons to have the experience of traveling across the country by train. Richard recalled Anita as not feeling particularly well, despite her pleasure at seeing her family, and he was struck by the fact that it was exceptionally hot and muggy in Atlanta when they visited, and "air-conditioning was at a premium."

Frank had remained in touch with Garrett Eckbo and Simon Eisner from USC, two of his favorite professors who both shared his political leanings. "They also knew I wasn't interested in doing rich guys' houses and that I would be more emotionally inclined toward low-cost housing and planning," Frank recalled. They encouraged him to return to school and study for an advanced degree in urban planning. Eckbo, who had gone to Harvard, suggested that Frank go to the Graduate School of Design and enroll in the city planning program so that he would have the opportunity to learn about how large-scale projects are realized. With recommendations from both Eckbo and Eisner, Frank was accepted into the program for the fall of 1956. He was granted an early release from the army so as to be able to be in Cambridge for the start of the semester. With much of his tuition paid by the GI Bill, going to Harvard felt like a fresh start—indeed, Frank felt that he would finally have the exciting beginning to his career that he had hoped for two years before.

Anita was not thrilled at the idea of moving to Massachusetts—after her stay in Georgia, she was ready to return home to Los Angeles and be an architect's wife, a prospect she considered far more appealing than being a graduate student's wife in Cambridge. But it was clear that Frank had no interest in returning so quickly to the life they had started to lead before he was drafted. And Anita had one incentive to remain on the East Coast, at least for a while. For years she had been maintaining an epistolary friendship with a Frenchwoman named Nicole, who was planning a visit to the United States. Nicole was due to arrive on the *Queen Mary* in New York in September, around the time that Frank and Anita would be heading to Massachusetts. They quickly made plans to meet Nicole and visit New York together.

Frank, Anita, and the two girls drove from Atlanta to New York in their white Volkswagen, a strenuous journey in 1956, the year before Interstate 95 would be completed. Other than the period he spent in Brooklyn as an infant, it was Frank's first visit to New York. When they met Anita's pen pal at the pier, she introduced them to a friend she had made during the voyage, a French architect named Mark Biass who was on his way to Harvard to study on a Fulbright scholarship.

It was a lucky coincidence. Biass and Frank were about the same age, although Biass had been working as an architect during the years that Frank spent in the army, so he was more experienced. He had been part of a team that won a major architectural competition in the south of France, and when the project was postponed, he decided to seek a graduate degree in the United States. Earlier that year Biass had met Josep Lluís Sert, the Catalonian architect who headed the architecture program at Harvard, at a conference of modern architects in Europe, and he decided that Harvard was where he wanted to study.

"I was going to Harvard on the *Queen Mary* with a bunch of French students and I met a girl on the boat who was the pen pal of Anita," Biass said many years later. "And this girl told me, 'I have a friend who is married to an architect, and he is picking me up at the landing platform. I think he is going to Harvard, too.'" Frank and Anita were waiting on the pier when the *Queen Mary* docked. Frank, Biass would recall, "was still in uniform. He was driving a Volkswagen with two baby girls and his wife." Frank proposed that they explore the city's architecture together. "So we did the usual tour, Rockefeller Center, the United Nations building, Lever House, and the Seagram Building, which was under construction," Biass said. It was a fast look—the architects had to get to Cambridge—and there wasn't room in the Volkswagen for Nicole, so Frank and his new friend rushed from building to building, perhaps relieved that in 1956 New York had only a handful of structures that young modern architects would deem worth visiting. They had neither the time nor the inclination to see anything more than the latest modern landmarks, and the Volkswagen was quickly back on the road before Frank had seen Grand Central Terminal, Pennsylvania Station, the Empire State Building, the Chrysler Building, Central Park, or the Brooklyn Bridge.

When Frank and Anita arrived in Cambridge, they may have wondered why they had been in such a hurry. In time Harvard would prove to be worth the trouble, but the start of their time there was something of a nightmare. The process of settling in was exceptionally difficult for Frank and his family. At first the only housing they could find was in a motel some distance from Cambridge. After several days of looking for an apartment near the campus that he could afford, Frank despaired. "It wasn't easy; we couldn't afford very much," he remembered. "The Sunday night before classes started, it was chilly and rainy. My daughter Brina was still in a crib, and my daughter Leslie was only a few years old. I was desperate. I stopped in a drugstore to call Reg Isaacs [Reginald Isaacs, the architect and planner who headed the department of city planning at Harvard]. I said, 'Professor Isaacs, this is Frank Gehry.' 'Oh yes,' he says, 'happy to have you coming.' I said, 'Look, I've got a little problem. I don't have enough money to stay in a motel very much longer, and there's nobody I can turn to.' At that point my parents were pretty tapped out, and I couldn't ask them for anything. Anita's parents probably would have helped, but I was Mr. Independent, so I wouldn't do that. So I asked him if there was anything the school could do to help me because if I couldn't find a place soon, I'd have to forfeit everything."

Isaacs said the school would do nothing to help Frank with his housing dilemma, and he provided no encouragement other than to tell Frank he should not worry about it—he could simply withdraw for now, and would be welcome to reapply to the program for the following year. "I was devastated," Frank remembered. "I hung up that phone call—I didn't know what I was going to tell Anita. Somebody in the drugstore heard me talking and said, 'I know of an apartment down the street, in a house. I know the people and I'll call them and you can go over there right now.' So I did and we got it that night."

The apartment, on the second floor of a two-family house in nearby Lexington, worked out well, but it was not the end of Frank's troubles at Harvard. In fact, his difficulties were only beginning. From the start, he sensed that his own sensibilities—shaped by Los Angeles's sprawling sense of possibility, at once modernist and populist—were at odds with the formalist rigor of Harvard. The Graduate School of Design was even more of a citadel of modernism than the architecture school at the University of Southern California, and its attitudes more dogmatic. Harvard's architectural philosophy in the 1950s had been shaped to a significant degree by Walter Gropius, the architect and cofounder of the Bauhaus in Germany, who had immigrated to the United States in 1937 to take charge of the university's architecture program. Sigfried Giedion, the Swiss architectural historian whose Charles Eliot Norton Lectures at Harvard in 1938 became the basis for his classic history of modernist architecture, *Space, Time and Architecture*, cast nearly as large a shadow as Gropius.

Gropius's Teutonic manner, not to mention his strong bias toward the European modernism that he had helped to shape, joined with Harvard's austere New England traditions to create an institution with a tone that could not have been more different from that of USC. It was not just that the two schools reflected the traditional differences in East Coast and West Coast sensibilities; USC, and Frank himself, were also shaped by an awareness of traditional Japanese architecture and a desire to use it as a source of inspiration for twentieth-century modernism, a view that was all but nonexistent at Harvard.

Frank, though he tended to be somewhat shy and self-effacing in many of his dealings with colleagues, had felt like an outsider for much of his time in Los Angeles; to some extent he even expected to find himself in that position wherever he went, and he knew how to hold his own. Especially after his long conversations with Garrett Eckbo and other Harvard alumni in Los Angeles, he had no expectation that he would find Cambridge full of architects who saw the world exactly as he did. He was not prepared, however, for the fact that he had misunderstood the nature of the city planning program at Harvard completely. He had decided to seek his degree in city planning because he thought that it would be a natural fit with his left-leaning politics; Eckbo, he recalled, had said to him "You don't want to do rich guys' houses," so city planning seemed a logical place in which to learn about more socially responsible architecture. But the Harvard program turned out to focus mainly on the political, economic, and sociological issues of cities; matters of architectural design played a relatively minor role. While there had been some discussion about finding ways to bring the Graduate School of Design's architecture and city planning departments closer together, it had resulted, at least so far, in a conference on the developing field of urban design that had been held in the spring of 1956, when Frank was still in the army. Another conference was planned for 1957, but the day-to-day academic programs remained quite distinct.

It did not take long for Frank to discover that he had enrolled in the wrong department. Charles Eliot, a city planner whose grandfather had been a revered president of Harvard in the late nineteenth century, oversaw the planning program, and he had no sympathy for Frank's view that architectural design should play a major role in city planning. At Victor Gruen's office in Los Angeles, Frank had worked on several ambitious projects to reshape both urban and suburban regions, and while he did not believe that good design could substitute for the right public policy, he was certain that the architect and planner's role was to give physical form to enlightened policy. He was far more interested in getting things built than in the sociology and demographics of neighborhoods or the problems of urban governance, all of which he considered abstract notions separate from the realities of actual designs.

The final project for Frank's first term in the planning studio was to create a master plan for the city of Worcester, Massachusetts, west of Cambridge. At Harvard, as at most design and architecture schools, final projects are presented before a jury of faculty and outside guests. Josep Lluís Sert, Charles Eliot's counterpart who headed the architecture department at the Graduate School of Design, was among those present the day that the planning students presented their term's work, which pleased Frank—he admired Sert, who had been deeply involved in Harvard's attempt to develop the field of urban design. Frank assumed that he could count on Sert to be a sympathetic critic of his project for Worcester, a counterweight to the philosophical differences he knew he had with Eliot. Frank, who was still an uneasy speaker at that point in his life, was especially nervous as he began this presentation. "I approached it like an urban design project, figuring out the ring roads and the parking and making an urban center, like I studied at Gruen," he remembered. "It was very idealistic, putting pedestrians back in the center and rebuilding the core, which was dying. I could see that as the future."

Bringing pedestrian life back into the center of older cities was indeed the future, and Frank was prescient to have proposed it at Harvard in 1956. It was not, however, what Professor Eliot had in mind. It was so far from what Eliot wanted, in fact, that he cut Frank off just a few minutes into his presentation. "Mr. Gehry, you have completely ignored the problem I've given you," Frank remembered Eliot as saying. "This is not an architecture course, this is a city planning course." And Eliot turned away from Frank and gave the floor to the next student, who presumably understood that he was expected to analyze the governance and neighborhood makeup of Worcester, not redesign its core.

Frank was shaken. Eliot's response to his project amounted to a dismissal from the course, and he was enraged. As soon as the class was over he went to Eliot's office, which was at the top of a narrow stairway that resembled a ship's ladder. Eliot, a large man, opened the door, looking, Frank thought, like Charles Laughton in *Mutiny on the Bounty*. Frank could not contain himself. "I looked at him and I said, 'You should never do what you did to me, I won't tolerate it, it's disgusting and unnecessary. And go fuck yourself.'" And he turned away and slammed the door behind him.

He then went to Sert's office, expecting that the head of the architecture program would share his furor at seeing architecture so peremptorily tossed aside. "Professor Sert, you saw what happened," Frank remembered telling Sert. "You must realize that I worked as hard as every other student there. I had a different point of view, which I think you would understand and realize that I was in the wrong pew. I would like to transfer into urban design." But Sert's loyalty to Harvard's bureaucratic ways turned out to be greater, at least in this instance, than his desire to rescue a student who had enrolled in the wrong program. Like Reginald Isaacs when Frank sought help in his housing crisis, Sert said there was nothing Frank could do except go home and apply all over again for another time. "He said, 'That's the only way. You can't just transfer like this.' He was very rigid. And I held it against him forever. I couldn't get my tuition back, and I couldn't transfer into anything I wanted," Frank said.

The one concession Harvard would make was to allow Frank to have the status of a special student so that he could audit courses for the rest of the year. He would get no degree, but he could attend any class he wanted to. To support his family he managed to get a job with Hideo Sasaki, a landscape architect, and when he was laid off—he was never sure why—he moved on to a local architecture firm, Perry, Shaw, Hepburn & Dean. What turned out to be far more important than his work, however, was that he began to delve far deeper into Harvard than he had during his semester in city planning, attending lectures and auditing courses far beyond the scope of architecture, often with Anita joining him. At that point his disastrous luck with Harvard changed entirely. Frank had never felt comfortable with rigid institutions, and Harvard in the 1950s was as rigid a place as there was. But he was intellectually curious in a way that cut across disciplinary lines, and he seemed to become only more eager to learn as time went on. Once he had the run of Harvard and no class commitments to fulfill, he began, to his astonishment, to have the happiest time he would ever experience in an educational institution.

"Margaret Mead was there in anthropology, and so was Ruth Benedict. J. Robert Oppenheimer came and gave six lectures, and I attended all of those. I saw Norman Thomas debate Howard Fast," he recalled. "Anita was interested in that and I was very interested in it as well. I was like a kid in a candy store."

Frank went to classes given by Joseph Hudnut and Otto Eckstein and Charles Haar and John Gaus, among others. And he managed to find time to hang around the architecture school even though he was not officially enrolled in its program. He became very friendly with Sigfried Giedion, the architecture historian, and Paul Rudolph, who would soon depart to head the architecture program at Yale. And he retained his friendship with Mark Biass, his French friend, for whom he served as best man when Biass married his fiancée, Jacqui, that year in Cambridge. And Biass, understanding Frank's frustration at not being an active student in the architecture program, suggested they join forces to create a joint entry for an architectural competition. The project was to design a memorial to Enrico Fermi. "A very difficult program in a very difficult site, very rigid and strict," Biass remembered. "We made a proposal and we didn't win, but we started to work together and exchange ideas." The Biass-Gehry design included a roof suspended from cables, which was intended to be a metaphor for an atomic particle, Biass recalled.

He and Mark Biass would never again collaborate professionally, though a few years later Biass would make a brief and futile attempt to persuade Frank to work with him on a project in France. But they remained close friends for the next six decades. It was a friendship based on a common love of architecture and a mutual respect unfettered by any sense of competitiveness—Biass, a more ordered and precise thinker, admired Frank's energetic, sometimes chaotically creative mind, whereas Frank admired Biass's clarity of thought and great technical skills. Mark, Frank remembered, could draw lyrical rooflines perfectly in the manner of Le Corbusier or Sert. "Sert just adored him, so he was the ace in the architecture school," Frank said.

Sert had been heavily influenced by the work of Le Corbusier, whose spirit hovered over the modernists in the Graduate School of Design as much, if not more, than that of Walter Gropius.* "Corb was very present in the culture," Frank remembered. "Corb was [Mark Biass's] hero, so all the talk was about Corb." Le Corbusier's extraordinary Chapel of Notre Dame du Haut at Ronchamp, France, had just been completed, and its startlingly expressionistic shape made it among the most talked-about buildings in the world—a 1950s version of what Frank's Guggenheim Museum in Bilbao, Spain, would become more than forty years later. "Before Harvard, I was so Japan- and Asia-centric, because of that emphasis at USC," Frank said later. "Going to Harvard, I got put in that other world, which made it imperative for me to go to Europe." Le Corbusier was also a painter, and there was an exhibition of his work at Robinson Hall, where the Graduate School of Design was housed. It excited Frank as much as any art exhibit he had ever seen. He did not know another architect who painted, and who considered painting an essential part of his work. "I knew these weren't paintings that would be sold in New York galleries," he said. "But I was intrigued with the way you could see in the paintings that he was working out a formal language, in two dimensions. I knew there was something in painting to learn from, and then I saw it actually working. It was hands-on. This guy was doing it. It didn't excite me to paint, because by then I had a reverence for painting and I knew that wasn't what I was going to do. But seeing these shapes in Corb's paintings and again in his building, I saw he was developing his own language. I realized he was painting his ideas, and that was his way of getting at it. I never forgot that. And the way I translated it in the end, for myself, is to do it with my drawings."

Harvard's second urban design conference was called for April 1957, close to the end of Frank's term of casual and wide-ranging academic immersion. He knew he would be returning to Los Angeles—Anita let it be known that, however stimulating she had found some of the lectures she attended, she had had enough of following Frank around on what she considered somewhat self-indulgent ventures like going to Harvard—and he needed to find a job. He had first thought he would return to Victor Gruen's office, where he had been content before the army snatched him away. But some conversations with Beda Zwicker, the head of planning at

---

* Soon after Frank's term at Harvard, the university commissioned Le Corbusier to design his only American building, the Carpenter Center for Visual Arts, which would be completed in 1962. Sert, who helped his mentor obtain the commission, would be deeply involved in the project, which remains after half a century Harvard's most iconic modern structure.

Gruen, made him unsure that it was such a good idea; Zwicker told him that it might not be the right place for him now, a comment Frank at first took at face value but later came to feel had emerged out of Zwicker's own insecurities. Zwicker, highly competitive, may have feared that Frank would eclipse him.

The urban design conference offered Frank another Los Angeles alternative. William Pereira, who had been Frank's thesis adviser at USC and admired his work, did not attend the conference himself but sent Jack Bevash, one of his senior colleagues. Bevash came to Harvard partly to represent his firm, Pereira & Luckman, but Pereira had given him another mission as well: to recruit Frank Gehry. Troubled by the sense that he might not receive a warm welcome at his former employer Victor Gruen's office, Frank said yes to Bevash. He had always liked Pereira, and Pereira's support for Frank's thesis work had given him early confidence in his design abilities. And Pereira & Luckman was an increasingly powerful presence on the Los Angeles architectural scene, more successful than almost any other firm in the city at raising modern architecture from the small scale of the private house to the large scale of civic and corporate projects. The firm had recently been commissioned to design the new Los Angeles International Airport on the city's west side, and its prospects appeared unlimited. It seemed to Frank an easy decision to make. Shortly after the urban design conference ended, Frank, with no exams to take, no term papers to write, or design projects to present, packed Anita, Leslie, and Brina into the Volkswagen and headed west. Anita was seven months pregnant.

6

Discovering Europe

The trip back west was long but uneventful. There was no time for detours, and the only important bit of architectural touring Frank tried to do was to visit Taliesin West, Frank Lloyd Wright's compound in Scottsdale, Arizona. When they arrived at Taliesin, Frank remembered, there was a flag flying over the property, the indication that the imperious Wright, who that spring turned ninety, was in residence. Visitors were still welcome, however, under the usual protocol: Wright's enterprise charged one dollar per person for every tour of his studio and residence complex. When Frank discovered that the ticket sellers at Taliesin expected him to pay the full charge for his two small children as well as for him and Anita, he refused and walked away. "I found that offensive," he said. "Here's me with two little daughters, and they wanted four dollars. I said, 'Go fuck yourself,' and left. I didn't like Wright's politics anyway."[*]

Back in Los Angeles, Frank, Anita, and their daughters moved into a small rental apartment in the Hollywood Hills, behind the Hollywood Bowl, and Frank began his work at Pereira & Luckman. Although finding a place to live was not as difficult as it had been in Cambridge, the family's return to Los Angeles was traumatic in a different, and ultimately more painful, way. Soon after Frank and Anita returned to California, Anita went into labor, and she and Frank went to the hospital so that she could

---

[*] Wright was not overtly engaged in politics, and his uniqueness as an architect, not to mention his strength of personality, tended to overshadow his political leanings. But he had been sympathetic to the "America First" movement opposing the nation's involvement in World War II, a movement often associated not just with isolationism but also with other conservative positions, including the anti-Semitism to which Frank was so sensitive. Wright's political views led to a twelve-year break in his close friendship with the critic Lewis Mumford, who wrote that "the America First streak in Wright is a coarse, dark vein in the fine granite of his mind."

Frank, Anita, Leslie, and Brina Gehry

give birth to their third child. The baby was stillborn, the victim, Frank was told, of a kidney problem. They gave her the name Summer. They returned to Leslie and Brina, distraught. Frank, as he had done before, escaped from his sorrows into work. Anita, at home with two other small children, had no similar option. She had no choice but to care for Leslie and Brina as she mourned her lost child.

Frank quickly discovered that his fondness for William Pereira, an architect of flamboyant and often imaginative modern buildings, did not mean that he would be happy working for him. It was not that Pereira treated Frank differently than he had expected; the problem was more that Pereira presided over a firm that was far more corporate and far less imaginative than Pereira's personality and design instincts would suggest. Much of that had to do with Pereira's partner, Charles Luckman, an architect who had started his career as a businessman. As the young president of Lever Brothers, Luckman had commissioned Skidmore, Owings & Merrill to design the celebrated Lever House tower in New York. Not long after, he returned to the career for which he had been trained. But Luckman had neither Pereira's creative imagination nor his tolerance for the quirky; if he had been daring as a client in building Lever House, he was unabashedly cautious as an architect, and produced little work of distinction.[*]

---

[*] Luckman is most famous, or notorious, for the Madison Square Garden arena in New York, completed in 1968 on the site of McKim, Mead & White's great Pennsylvania Station,

Pereira, perhaps fearing that he needed a partner like Luckman to get large-scale work, allowed him to set the tone for the firm. Pereira's name came first on the letterhead, but Luckman organized the firm's operations in such a way as to limit the creative range of the architects on the staff. Clients, Frank remembered, were made to feel important by being seated in front of a curtain, which was then drawn open to reveal the architectural scheme being presented. But it was never a single scheme: the firm's practice was to have different teams in the office do multiple schemes for a major project, and to present them in sequence to the client. "They made it very theatrical. The client would come in and they'd show him scheme one, then scheme two, and say, 'Which one do you like?' That offended the shit out of me. I couldn't take it," Frank said. He felt less as if he had been entrusted with solving a client's problem than engaged in a kind of architectural bake-off in which the results hardly mattered to Pereira and Luckman.

"I didn't like it. And I had lunch with Rudi Baumfeld [from Victor Gruen's office] one day," Frank remembered. "And he said, 'Why aren't you here, Frank?' And I said, 'Well, Beda told me it was better for me not to be.' And he looked at me and said, 'Stop it—you come back here immediately. You're part of our family.' That's when I got it that [Beda] was keeping me out."

At Pereira & Luckman, Frank had been working on designs for what became known as the Theme Building for the airport. His role in it was minor—the overall concept of the structure, which looks something like a flying saucer that has landed on huge, curving legs, was by James Langenheim of Pereira & Luckman—but he enjoyed being a part of it. He was aware, however, that the Theme Building was a kind of consolation prize given to Pereira & Luckman because the firm's original plan for the airport, which called for a huge glass dome giving access to all of the satellite aircraft gates, had been abandoned in favor of something much more conventional. The Theme Building was little more than an architectural folly at civic scale, a modernist whimsy intended to evoke the glass dome that was never built.

Frank had only been with Pereira & Luckman for a few months when he decided to return to Victor Gruen, whose office, if also large and somewhat corporate in nature, still had at least a tinge of the idealism

---

and for the Prudential Tower in Boston, finished in 1963. Both buildings were designed after his partnership with Pereira ended.

he valued. Gruen, unlike Pereira & Luckman, designed some housing, and the firm eagerly took on community planning projects, shopping centers, and downtown renewal projects. Victor Gruen seemed refreshing to Frank beside Pereira & Luckman, which he felt was hypocritical, not to say almost cynical, in its practice of claiming it was putting clients' needs first. What the Pereira & Luckman firm was really doing with its showy presentations of different options, Frank felt, was not standing behind any of its own ideas.

Leaving Pereira was a pivotal decision for Frank, not the least because he remained fond of his former teacher, who he felt had made unacceptable compromises with a partner who was so focused on the business side of architecture that he had little interest in design. Eventually Pereira himself would come to feel similarly, and the Pereira & Luckman partnership, which had begun in 1950, would be dissolved at the end of the decade. Pereira would spend the 1960s on projects that allowed him again to express his more flamboyant design instincts, such as the pyramidal tower he designed as a headquarters for the Transamerica Corporation in San Francisco and the library at the University of California at San Diego, a powerfully sculpted concrete-and-glass building shaped like a diamond in profile. Luckman's architecture, for its part, would become ever more banal once he no longer had Pereira at his side.

But the issues Frank struggled with as he made the decision to leave Pereira & Luckman only months after he had arrived were less about design style than about how the practice of architecture should work in the first place, and about how he, or any architect, could use his professional expertise to the benefit of clients and society at large. Frank knew from the beginning that Luckman, who seemed to feel that his obligation to clients was to let them pick and choose from a smorgasbord of ideas and that he had no need to demonstrate real conviction about any of them, was not a model he wanted to follow. Yet in his short time at Pereira & Luckman he grew less and less certain that Pereira was an ideal model, either, and not only because for a decade he had sacrificed his own design imagination on the business altar of his demanding partner. Left to his own devices, Frank realized, Pereira was driven more by a desire to make memorable shapes than by a clear understanding of his clients' needs. If Luckman seemed to Frank to be inclined simply to take orders from clients, Frank began to think of Pereira, unrestrained by Luckman, as an architect who mainly invented shapes out of his imagination and then tried to persuade his clients to accept them.

The problem, Frank soon realized, was not just that Pereira and Luckman were architecture's odd couple, partners without enough in common to sustain a meaningful collaboration. It was also that neither partner's view of the world was convincing to Frank on its own. Frank agreed with Luckman that architecture was, at least in part, a matter of serving clients, and he agreed with Pereira that creative form making was central to what an architect did. So why did these two things have to conflict? There had to be some middle ground, Frank thought, that embraced the polar opposites Pereira and Luckman represented. Couldn't an architect listen carefully to a client's needs, and then respond with an inventive, imaginative form that fulfilled those needs and at the same time brought joy and surprise? In other words, why couldn't the creative shapes emerge out of discourse with clients, rather than be presented as if they had sprung full-blown from the architect's head?

Frank's time at Pereira & Luckman was brief, but it turned out to be critical to his development. His few months there put his ideas about architectural practice into clearer focus than ever before. He knew even before he started to work there that he did not want to be like Charles Luckman; in coming to realize that he did not want to be like William Pereira, either, he began to develop his own vision of what he wanted his stance as a professional to be. He came to see that his way of practicing architecture was going to have to be something different from what either man represented.

Pereira would in some ways haunt Frank for years to come, because Frank's independence of mind and penchant for inventive form making, which would only grow as the years went on, could be thought in many ways to resemble the same qualities in Pereira, and he would often be mistaken for being a younger version of his mentor. Frank didn't want to be the next William Pereira, an architect remembered for the occasional bold shapes he had managed somehow to persuade clients to build. He wanted to do something much harder, which was to be as service-oriented as Luckman and as form-oriented as Pereira at the same time. He wanted to eliminate altogether the conflict that Pereira and Luckman symbolized. Like the child who seeks to smooth the differences between divorced parents, Frank wanted to find a way of practicing architecture that would resolve the dichotomy they represented.

For the near term, the office of Victor Gruen was the closest thing he would have to a resolution. Gruen, not surprisingly, was not the promised land—Frank already knew that the office had its share of politics—but he liked the nature of many of the projects Gruen took on, and he told

himself that the opportunity to work on downtown plans was serving a
kind of social good that stood for something more than Charles Luckman's corporate servility or William Pereira's arbitrary shape-making.
Frank liked his colleagues at the Gruen office, most of whom welcomed
him back warmly. And he respected Gruen, a Viennese Jew, born Vik-
tor David Grünbaum, who shared many of Frank's beliefs about social
responsibility and was increasingly becoming an international authority
on urban renewal. Gruen had envisioned his early shopping malls, like
Southland, as becoming the cores of new downtowns, and he expected
that they would provoke greater suburban density, not suburban sprawl.
He was also a passionate believer in pedestrian environments; to him, not
the least of the benefits of his new malls was that they encouraged walking
in the same way that traditional village streets did.

Gruen would later come to reject that view and realize that whatever
walking people happened to do in enclosed malls was inconsequential
compared to the damage that huge shopping malls would inflict upon
the landscape, weakening Main Streets in towns throughout the country
and replacing them with suburban sprawl. He thought his original intention for the Southdale Center, which was to come as close as possible to
replicating the experience of a traditional city street in a clean and climate-
controlled environment, had been corrupted by shopping center developers who saw malls only as vast machines for consumerism.*

But that possibility was nowhere in Gruen's mind in the 1950s, when
there seemed every reason to believe that his invention of the enclosed
mall would have a positive effect on the landscape. Frank did not envision
any more than Gruen did that malls would become synonymous with the
notion of urban decline; indeed, when he came back to work for Victor
Gruen in 1957, he felt that his work was giving him a direct connection
to the postwar reshaping of American cities. He felt privileged, in fact, to
have been assigned to work on the project that Gruen himself considered
his most important, Midtown Plaza in Rochester, New York, a seven-acre
urban retail, office, and hotel complex that was intended to revive the
city's sagging downtown. Midtown, which was finished in 1962, brought
the notion of indoor shopping into the urban core, and high-rise buildings
were a critical part of its design. Gruen had a free hand to design the inte-

---

* "I refuse to pay alimony for those bastard developments," Gruen said in a speech given
in London in 1978. He had given up on the United States a decade earlier, returning to
his native Vienna, where he worked on the conversion of portions of the urban core to a
pedestrian zone. He died in 1980.

‾rior as the town square under a roof that he had wanted his suburban malls to be, and he filled it with places to sit, decorative fountains, sidewalk cafés, and works of art. Gere Kavanagh, a young designer in the Gruen office, was commissioned to do an enormous standing clock, called the Clock of the Nations, that consisted of a central clock tower surrounded by twelve cylinders containing animated puppets from different countries. Midtown Plaza, which included two department stores as well as fifty smaller shops and six restaurants, was by any standard a sophisticated piece of modern design for a medium-size city in upstate New York. And at a time when a common response to urban decay was to use federal money to bulldoze entire neighborhoods, the idea of a privately funded downtown retail and office complex seemed a promising solution to the problem of declining downtown shopping districts: fresh, new, clean, and full of underground parking. What more could a city ask for? The opening of Midtown Plaza attracted national attention. It was covered by *Time* magazine and *The Huntley-Brinkley Report*, NBC's nightly news program.[*]

Frank gradually took on more authority at Gruen, designing portions of other shopping centers, the interior planning for an apartment tower in the Westwood section of Los Angeles, and elements of several federally subsidized housing complexes, which were his favorite projects, if only because they allowed him to feel that he was performing some kind of social benefit. With public housing he believed he was using modern architecture for the social good, just what Richard Neutra and Robert E. Alexander had been prevented from doing when the Elysian Park Heights project was stopped in Los Angeles a decade earlier.

Frank also had a major management role in Charles River Park, a complex of residential towers and a shopping mall in Boston that was another showcase project for Gruen. Frank did not design the project, but oversaw much of its execution. Charles River was completed in 1962, the same year as Midtown Plaza, and it emerged out of the identical belief, which was

---

[*] Midtown Plaza in the end would turn out to be no more truly urban than any other mall, and while its stores were successful for many years, it had little effect on the rest of downtown Rochester. In the same way that Gruen's suburban malls turned out to be a negative example, inspiring myriad projects that would have a deleterious effect on the environment, Midtown Plaza was a misguided model for urban redevelopment, entirely inward-facing, self-contained, and, by design, cut off from the city streets. It ignored the existing urban fabric, even to the point of eliminating a downtown street that was in the way of its large site. Yet it could be said to have been the prototype for many larger attempts at mixed-use urban redevelopment, including John Portman's Renaissance Center in Detroit. Midtown Plaza ultimately could not compete with the suburban malls it was designed to imitate, and it closed in 2008. It was demolished in 2010.

that if the messy disarray of old urban neighborhoods could be replaced by something clean, orderly, and new, with automobiles safely out of sight, then urban life would improve. Charles River was built on a portion of one of Boston's oldest multiethnic neighborhoods, the West End, and it was intended to replace the West End's diversity and dense urban fabric with a set of modern boxes standing in open space. Its inspiration lay in Le Corbusier's visionary schemes from the 1920s for Paris, in which the architect envisioned eliminating the city's dense old quartiers in favor of new districts of identical cruciform towers arranged evenly along wide boulevards. Gruen's use of the Corbusian model, *Boston Globe* critic Robert Campbell later wrote, was "an urban planning disaster of legendary proportions." Gruen, Campbell said, had chosen to replace the authentic city with "a managed, sanitized museum of itself."

Frank was uncomfortable with the vast scale of Charles River—later he would refer to it as "that huge monster, which I hated." But he enjoyed the responsibility he was getting in helping to manage the early stages of the project. He knew that he was not an administrator at heart, but he discovered that he had an ability to coordinate the complex process of producing a design for a major urban project, and his superiors at Gruen seemed to appreciate that. He was put in charge of project budgets, and he also became known as the office's main housing expert. "I loved doing housing. I was really good at it, and if they had a rush job, I could churn out work faster than anybody else," Frank recalled. He came to direct a team at Gruen and had twenty people reporting to him. He was under pressure to produce drawings for one project after another on what seemed like an ever-tighter timetable. But if he found the intensity occasionally frustrating, he more often found it exhilarating. He enjoyed many of his colleagues—Greg Walsh had come to work at Gruen, and so had Fred Usher, Marion Sampler, Gere Kavanagh, Kip Stewart, and John Gilchrest, architects and designers Frank knew and respected. Some had come to Gruen after working for Charles and Ray Eames, and the Gruen firm had some of the same fresh energy as the Eames office. In Frank's initial months at Gruen, he found it the kind of workplace where a person with a serious interest in art, architecture, and design could feel at home, and could believe that the work he was doing was of some social benefit.

He was working, he recalled, day and night, and many weekends. Anita was grateful that he was bringing home a regular salary, but she was increasingly upset at the demands Frank's career was making on their family life. There was little time available for Leslie and Brina, and not much for Anita, either. The life she led with Frank at Gruen was not as different from the life she had led with him in the army as she had assumed it would be. Frank had clearly decided to focus on his career. He was not unaware of the consequences: "I knew it was fucking up my marriage," he recalled, "because Anita was just furious, even though she wanted financial security."

Bella Snyder saw how unhappy her daughter was, and she shared Anita's view that the problem stemmed from Frank's side of the marriage. She suggested that her son-in-law see a psychotherapist. She went so far as to find one, Dr. James Weishaus, and Frank agreed to see him and join a therapy group that Dr. Weishaus ran. It was his first experience with any kind of group therapy, and it did nothing to help his marital situation. In fact, it underscored the seriousness of the problem. Frank quickly formed a bond with another member of the group, the wife of a lawyer, and the two shared their disillusionment over their marriages, first within the group therapy session, and later over drinks after one of the sessions. Their private encounters soon grew more intimate. They both felt an obligation to disclose their relationship to the rest of the group, but when they did, they were told that their liaison violated a principle of group therapy, and they were ordered to withdraw.

At the same time, Frank felt that his honeymoon at Gruen was ending. He was becoming less and less comfortable with the culture of a large firm at the same time that the firm was losing what had made it attractive to him as it grew more corporate in tone. "It became obvious that it was more business-oriented and things the designer types like me were doing were shoved aside," Frank recalled. "And I think from their side I was becoming a bit of a renegade, maybe a little unpredictable."

Despite his hard work, Frank was not promoted to the level of associate, as many of his peers had been. He surmised that this was because of his discomfort with making the presentations to clients that associates and partners were expected to do. He was shy, he lacked the smoothness that was expected of a corporate architect, and he knew he had a tendency to ruffle feathers. "I had a mind of my own. I was always trying to push things, and they weren't about that. Maybe I was immature," he said. Years later, speaking to the journalist John Pastier about his time at Gruen, Frank offered yet another theory for his failure to rise further within the firm: "In hindsight I think they felt that I was angry. I went through a period where I was always angry, and they didn't know what to do with that. They wanted me to be happy and I couldn't be. I couldn't fit in. I wasn't comfortable, even though I often got to work with Victor very closely, and with Rudi Baumfeld and Edgardo Contini, people who I adored and respected."

The only bright spot for Frank professionally was the opportunity he had to try his hand at some independent architectural projects in partnership with his old friend from USC and Gruen colleague Greg Walsh. Designing a small project, such as a house or apartment, on the side while still maintaining a position, and a salary, from a large architectural office is how many architects dip their toes into the difficult waters of private architectural practice, waiting until they can attract enough work to live off their own architectural fees. Large firms view such "moonlighting" with varying degrees of acceptance, and many forbid it. (Frank Lloyd Wright was famously fired from the office of Louis Sullivan in 1893 when Sullivan discovered that Wright had been designing houses for private clients on the side. The experience led Wright to open his own office rather than go to work for anyone else.)

Gruen apparently had a more liberal policy about such matters. The first opportunity Frank and Greg had was to design a small mountain cabin in Idyllwild, California, west of Palm Springs, for Melvin David, a neighbor of Anita's family. It was a simple, low-budget building, made of wood frame, concrete block, and redwood siding. It is notable less as a work of architecture than as a sad chapter in Frank's troubled relationship with his father. It is the only house Frank designed that Irving saw, and his recollection is that Irving was not impressed.

A much more serious opportunity followed: a residence in Brentwood with a $60,000 budget, a figure that, while not extravagant, could allow for a substantial house in 1958. The clients were an accountant, Edgar Steeves, and his wife, Mary Lou, whose daughter, Barbara, was dating Dick Martin, an architect who had been a classmate of Frank's and Greg's at USC. Martin, seemingly indifferent to the nepotism that has given many architects their start, felt it was inappropriate to design a house for his potential in-laws, and recommended Frank and Greg. Frank's shyness and tendency toward bluntness either were held in check or did not trouble the Steeveses, because they hired the pair after a single interview. Frank came up with the basic concept for the design, and Greg helped to work out problems and produced most of the construction drawings.

What resulted was a one-story, three-bedroom house, built of wood frame and stucco, heavily reminiscent of the work of Frank Lloyd Wright, mildly reminiscent of Richard Neutra, and showing more than a hint of Japanese influence as well. It is cruciform in plan, and sections of the

The Steeves house, which Frank designed with Greg Walsh, shows the ongoing influence of Frank Lloyd Wright in his early work.

roof extend out beyond the house to create a frame over a reflecting pool, as well as to create the image of a larger building with greater horizontal expanse. The house has a tight, formal elegance to it—characteristic of many of the modern houses built in Los Angeles in the 1950s by architects such as Harwell Hamilton Harris and Raphael Soriano, both early influences on Frank—as well as a sense of expansive, flowing space. The precision and straight lines of its plan suggest that Frank had not yet moved beyond the architects who were his first inspirations, which in many ways he had not. Yet the house has a certain esprit to it that derives from none of its precedents, and that is surely Frank's own. The horizontal lines of the overhanging roof, always a characteristic of Wright, are exaggerated here and pulled out beyond the mass of the structure at one end to become a kind of sculptural essay.

But perhaps the most important sign of Frank's presence—and the one that would turn out to mean the most to him in the rest of his work—was a certain roughness to the construction, as if neither the architect nor the contractor could be bothered with making every detail perfect, which is so often the goal in classically modern houses. The initial construction bids had come in over budget, and to get the house built without significantly changing the design, Frank and Greg hired what Greg would refer to later as a "cowboy contractor," a small builder who lacked the finesse of larger, more experienced builders. "There were some mistakes, but you know, bottom line, the house looked okay," Greg Walsh remembered.

Frank had begun to spend time with artists in Los Angeles, whose community would become more and more important to him in the following decade, and he saw how, as abstract expressionism began to give way to later movements, artists had become interested in using found objects and in breaking away from an academic concern with precision and refinement. He looked beyond Los Angeles as well, and took note of Robert Rauschenberg's "combines," collages that were part painting and part sculpture and often included elements of junk, and of Jasper Johns's interest in common objects. And his growing interest in the ordinary was not restricted to art. As he drove around Los Angeles and Orange County and saw new developments of tract houses sprawling across the region, he realized that when houses were at an early stage of construction, when they were just open frames of wood two-by-fours, he actually found them attractive. The framework, suggesting a finished shape but obviously just in mid-process, was a lot better-looking than the houses would be when they were finished. Frank loved the ambiguity of the framework, with the profile of a solid house but at the same time merely a void. As he worked on the Steeves house, he began to think that his feeling about unfinished tract houses might be more than just an amusing and quirky observation. It might have some meaning for his work.

"There was a beauty to [the houses] before they were covered up with a filigree of wood," Frank said later. "And the workmanship didn't matter. And I remember twist-turning, thinking that the artists were telling us that kind of perfection was not necessarily the right way to look at things. It was kind of contrived, not natural. And so the whole idea of letting it all hang out became another way to deal with how to build because I wasn't going to get to perfection. So if you can't beat 'em, join 'em, and see where you take it. And I think that pervades what I do still."

The roughness, Frank said, "was interesting to me, in terms of workmanship, in terms of the spontaneity of the aesthetic. It had a humanity to it, it had an accessibility to it, had warmth to it and friendliness to it. It was a lot of things that Mies was not getting. And I guess I like the prairie houses by Frank Lloyd Wright which were similar—they weren't so finicky." Designing and building the Steeves house helped Frank realize that he did not want to produce buildings of utter refinement—that he was not interested in "finicky perfection," but in something else that he could barely define, much less understand, at that point.* It might have had something to do, he said later, with his left-leaning political views. "I liked the matter-of-factness of cheap materials, not too design-y. It fit with my politics."

Frank's share of the architectural fees for the Steeves house came to $1,500. The money was not going to be used to pay debts, or to buy a house, or to build a savings account. Frank had another idea. His friend from Harvard, Mark Biass, who had lived in Los Angeles for the first two years after Harvard, had returned to Paris because a design for a hospital that he had created several years before in an architectural competition now seemed likely to be built. Frank and Mark stayed in close contact. Frank remembers that his friend "was begging me to come to Paris," although Mark recalled things somewhat differently. "Frank wrote me [to say that] I'm a little tired of life here. I'd like to come to France and look and find me a place to live, and a job."

Whatever the origins of the idea, the notion of going to Paris took hold. Anita was part of the reason. She had a pen pal there of long standing, and she had often talked of wanting to live in Paris, without seriously expecting that she would. Frank decided to use his fee to buy passage on the Holland America Line from New York to Le Havre for himself, Anita, and the two girls. "It seemed like it would be a way to repay her for all the things I got to do," Frank said. "It was her turn. . . . And Mark said he thought he could get me a job."

However impulsive the decision may have been to use his money from the Steeves house to take his family to France, Frank had no interest in leaving immediately. The tickets he bought were for a crossing nearly a year away. He felt he owed Gruen a long notice, since he was working on a number of major projects that could not easily be taken over by colleagues, and he wanted Anita to have a long time to plan for the move. At Gruen, Frank remembered, "I walked in to Rudi [Baumfeld] and I showed him the tickets and I said, 'Look, I just bought these, and they're for a year from now. So, I'm leaving. But it's good that I'm telling you a year in advance

---

* More than twenty years later, in 1981, subsequent owners would come to Frank and ask him to design an addition to the house. He produced something very different from the original work, a set of discrete elements that intersected with the original at a diagonal, deliberately breaking with the more formal axis of the 1959 house. It was one of the first times that Frank had designed a project in the form of a series of rooms as separate structures, making up a symbolic village, an idea he would return to repeatedly. While the new owners, the Smiths, were happy with the design, the local design review board was not. "They said it did not look like a house," Greg Walsh recalled, and the project was never built.

so you don't load me up with stuff, so you don't plan that I'm staying here. I'm going to leave, and I need to leave and you know I have to leave, and this is the way I want to do it. I want to do it in a way that doesn't hurt anybody.'"

Baumfeld, likely in an attempt to change Frank's mind, began assigning him more and more work on desirable projects, Frank recalled: "Three months before the due date to leave they were giving me the best projects, and I went to his office and said, 'Look, I made up my mind about the fucking tickets. Somewhere over the rainbow we can talk after I've done this about whether there's a future for me here, but honestly I don't think so.' And the year came and I walked out. And they looked at me like they didn't believe I was going to walk out."

Baumfeld, in what was probably a last-ditch effort, told Frank that the firm intended to promote him to associate. "Well, you never did, and it's too late now," Frank remembers telling him. "I don't want to be an associate." So he left and took his family back across the country and to Europe, where he and Anita, both separately and together, hoped for a fresh start.

Mark Biass and his wife, Jacqui, were living in a close-in suburb southwest of Paris, not far from Versailles, called Meudon, that had grown up around a royal woods and the grounds of a royal château. The château had been partially destroyed in the Franco-Prussian War and its remains converted into France's main astronomical observatory, but the forest and much of the landscape, originally designed by the great seventeenth-century landscape architect André Le Nôtre, remained, making the village a curious mix of aristocratic relic and small middle-class town. There were remnants of its past glory, like the orangery and formal terrace high on a hill with spectacular views of Paris. And there were small houses and apartment buildings that could have been anywhere in France.

The Biasses lived in a large crescent-shaped garden apartment building at 60 Route des Gardes. The site, which sloped sharply downward from the road, was unusual for more than its topography: it occupied a portion of what had once been the site of the "Hameau des Mesdames," a fantasy village constructed in 1779 to amuse the daughters of Louis XV, of which remained one building, a tiny stone chapel, an ancient folly tucked beside the Route des Gardes. By luck Mark and Jacqui were able to find the Gehrys a unit in the building just below their own. It wasn't the Paris of garrets and boulevards that Anita had dreamed of, but it was close enough, and the presence of close friends meant that she would not be alone when Frank was at work. For what it was worth, the five-story, curving building was of at least minor architectural note; if it was not the Paris of Haus-mann's boulevards, its graceful semicircular shape and façade of horizon-tal stripes of red brick and concrete were a far more gracious expression of modernist sentiment than the harsh concrete high-rise slabs that housed so much of the population of the city's outlying districts. The building's design took advantage of the slope. There were several entrances, all of which were across pedestrian bridges over a ravine. In the rear, parking was tucked under the structure into the side of the hill. Best of all, the curving back of the building embraced an attractive park and a playground that was ideal for two small children. The Biasses had even filled the apartment with cast-off furniture so that Frank, Anita, and the girls could feel at home in their new setting as soon as they arrived.

The apartment was a five-minute walk from the Meudon Bellevue train station, from which it was a twenty-minute ride to the Gare Montparnasse. Mark Biass had tried to line up a job for Frank in advance, but he had not been as successful on the employment front as he had in the area of accommodation, and as soon as the Gehrys were settled, Frank began to go into Paris to look for a job, doing as best he could with his modest high school French. His first choice was to work for Candilis-Josic-Woods, a Paris-based firm that was known internationally for its advanced, highly theoretical modernist urban planning. George Candilis and Alexis Josic agreed to see him, and they offered him a job. But as Frank remembered it, the pay would have been only two francs an hour. "I had two kids and couldn't live on that," he said.* So he turned the offer down, much as he had refused to work for Richard Neutra for no salary at all many years before.

When no other offers, even at two francs an hour, materialized, Frank contacted Helen Michaelis, the chief financial officer at Victor Gruen's office in Los Angeles, to ask for help. She was European, and she and Frank had always gotten along well. She offered to put Frank in touch with André Remondet, a French architect who had worked for Wallace K. Har-rison in New York in the 1930s, and had served as a French liaison officer with the Fifth Infantry Division of the United States Army during World War II. Remondet was "enamored with America," Frank recalled, and

---

* Two francs was worth less than half an American dollar in 1961. While it was still possible to live inexpensively in Paris in the early 1960s, it was unlikely that a family could be sup-ported on an income this modest. It added up to less than the amount cited in Arthur From-mer's famous guidebook *Europe on Five Dollars a Day*, which had been published in 1957.

had employed other Americans in Paris. Mark Biass had also suggested that Frank approach Remondet, but Helen Michaelis's recommendation apparently counted for more, since after he heard from her, Remondet offered Frank an interview, and then a job at four francs an hour. "At four francs an hour I could kind of make it," Frank said. The hourly pay was especially important because Frank only wanted to work four days a week to allow him time to explore as much important architecture as he could find within driving distance. He knew that having never been to Europe, he had a lot of architectural history to catch up on.

Remondet's office was on the Champs-Élysées, a long Metro ride from the terminus of the train from Meudon at the Gare Montparnasse. While it was a glamorous address—Frank watched from the office balcony as President Kennedy and Charles de Gaulle proceeded down the Champs-Élysées in a motorcade during Kennedy's heralded 1961 trip to Paris—it took roughly an hour each way to commute from Meudon. And public transportation was not going to work for the architecture touring that Frank had in mind to do with Mark. So the Gehrys borrowed some money from Anita's parents and purchased a white Volkswagen Beetle, identical to the one they had used to drive back home to Los Angeles after Frank left Harvard. He was soon driving to work and parking near the office on the elegant Avenue Foch. Years later, his most vivid memory of his commute would be of the morning he parked the car and emerged from it to find himself face-to-face with the actor Gene Kelly, who lived there. "Bonjour, monsieur!" Frank remembers Kelly saying to him. Nonplussed, Frank could only respond, "Bonjour."

Remondet's office produced a number of official buildings—he held the title of chief architect of civil and national palaces—and by coincidence he worked on a renovation of the observatory at Meudon, not far from the Gehrys' apartment. It would not be until 1975 that Remondet would win his most important commission, the French embassy in Washington, D.C., and Frank did not find most of the projects Remondet was working on in 1961 particularly engaging. His position in the office was more junior than it had been at Gruen, and nothing he was doing could equal the thrill of designing a project himself from scratch, as he had done for the Steeveses. To him, working for André Remondet was a job, a way of keeping his family fed. His real goal was simply to be in Paris, and to try to educate himself about something he had barely been exposed to in school: European architecture.

M ark Biass took it upon himself to be Frank's tutor. He started
the moment the Gehrys arrived in Paris. He picked them up at
the Gare Saint-Lazare and took them to the cathedral of Notre Dame,
where Frank remembered walking in to the sound of Gregorian chants,
haunting sounds reverberating within the Gothic vaults, a combination
of music and architecture in which both were entirely new to him. He
was overwhelmed. The next weekend they went to Chartres, and as they
approached the city on the highway, Frank was struck by the vista of the
cathedral rising above the fields of the Beauce, a Gothic vision floating in
the landscape. Biass also planned trips to see modern buildings in Paris,
to visit Romanesque churches around France, to see Roman ruins in the
south of France, and to go on to Switzerland and Germany. "We tried to
visit Paris and the surroundings together," Mark Biass remembered. "We
had a Deux Chevaux [the small Citroën 2CV], and he was following me
with his Volkswagen." Anita and the two girls almost always came along, as
did Mark's wife and family.

The trips were eye-opening to Frank. "I came from the West Coast
aesthetic, which was Japanese, Asian-centric, woodcut drawings, wood-
framed temples," Frank said. "And all of a sudden I'm exposed to things
my history of architecture teacher at USC never told me anything about,
like the great cathedrals. He showed black-and-white pictures—'This is
Chartres, this is Bonn'—but those pictures don't convey the power. When
I walked into Chartres I was furious. I said, 'Why why didn't they tell us?'"

Frank was especially taken with the solid, heavy forms of the Romanesque cathedrals. Autun, in Burgundy, brought him to a kind of epiphany—
not a religious one but an architectural one, making him feel for the first
time that ornament did not have to be prissy decoration as he had thought,
but could be an integral part of a strong work of architecture. Architecture,
painting, and sculpture could unite in a single, vast work of building. To
Frank, that notion was a revelation. "I was enough of a modernist so that
the idea of decoration was [unacceptable] until I got to Autun," he said.
"For the first time I understood how decoration could be part of a building
and could be tough and not cutesy-pie, not trivial."

The tours included modern buildings as well. Frank and Mark visited Le
Corbusier's early buildings in Paris, the Maison La Roche and the Maison
Jeanneret and the Pavillon Suisse, as well as the Villa Savoye in suburban
Poissy, deepening his understanding of the architect whose work he had
first gotten to know well during his time at Harvard. The Villa Savoye was

barely more than thirty years old when Frank first saw it, but Frank would find the architect's newer work, like the heavy concrete-and-brick Maisons Jaoul in Neuilly just outside Paris, even more compelling. The high points of his encounters with Le Corbusier's architecture came not in Paris but in a rural valley near Lyon. After a visit to the early Romanesque church at Tournus, in Burgundy, Frank and Mark and their wives drove to see Le Corbusier's latest project, the Dominican monastery at La Tourette. To Frank, the huge concrete structure perched on a hillside, at once harshly elegant and utterly serene, was a revelation. "I became more Eurocentric," he said. "So Japan, bye-bye." Mark recalled that his wife, Jacqui, and Anita were not permitted to go beyond the chapel, the only part of the complex open to all visitors, whereas he and Frank as men were allowed to walk through the cloister, mixing with the monks. They were content to leave their wives waiting while they explored every inch of the building.

The more expressionist shape of Le Corbusier's chapel at Ronchamp, in eastern France, another recent work that Frank visited on a separate architectural pilgrimage, shifted his perspective at least as much as the powerful sculptural form of La Tourette, and would have a more direct influence on his work. So would the rough, rounded shapes of the Romanesque churches, which probably affected him more than anything else he saw in France. He found less appeal in delicacy after seeing these churches and Le Corbusier's recent buildings; for all their differences, both made him realize that buildings could possess both great solidity and unusual, fluid shape, and that the best of them could demonstrate both of these qualities at the same time. Schindler, Neutra, and the architects of the Case Study houses of Los Angeles, long his primary influences, were moving to the sidelines, along with Japan. No longer did lightness and precision seem like such certain virtues. He already sensed that he would have designed the Steeves house differently had the commission come in 1961 instead of 1958.

There were other trips, including to Spain to see Gaudí's work in Barcelona, which would become another important influence on Frank, reinforcing his growing sense that straight lines were not as essential as USC had taught him to believe. He also went to Holland and to Italy. They were joined on some of their excursions by Greg Walsh, who had left Victor Gruen's office a few months after Frank did. Greg, too, had decided to take some time off to travel. He had been deeply affected by his time in Japan, but he knew little of Europe. He attached himself to Frank and Anita much as he had done in Los Angeles, and he was just as eager as

Frank to be spending as much time as possible looking at both old and new architecture. If there was any tension during the time that Greg joined the Gehrys, it was over the fact that he and Margaret Knudsen, a designer who was his traveling companion, had a very different budget. Greg was single, and unlike Frank, he had some savings. He and Margaret drove in a rented convertible, while Frank, Anita, and their children squeezed into their tiny Volkswagen. "We'd meet them on the road and they'd want to go to fancy restaurants and we couldn't afford it," Frank recalled. "So they went to the fancy restaurants and we went to the crappy restaurants. It was funny traveling with them. We went all the way down to Rome."

After the Gehrys had been living in Paris for the better part of a year, Anita's happiness began to fade. Mark Biass recalls that she had begun to complain, as she had years before, that she had put aside her own studies to support Frank and then to raise their children, and she wanted her life to be different. "So Frank told me, 'We'll have to go back to the United States,'" Mark said. He had just begun to work on a design competition for a new city in Normandy, and he and Frank had discussed working together on it. "But he told me, 'No, I can't—I have to go back,'" Mark said. "And so that was the end of our French collaboration."

Frank and Anita decided to remain in France until the summer of 1961. Frank was unhappy about going home, but he took comfort in his decision to open his own office once he was back in Los Angeles. Architects' careers tend to develop slowly—many do not win significant commissions before they are approaching middle age—but patience had never been Frank's primary virtue, and neither had being subordinate to a boss. In any event he knew that if he was going to have a shot at important work when he was in his forties, he needed to begin the process of establishing his identity as an independent architect long before that. He had turned thirty-two in February, and he felt more than ready to go out on his own.

Then, a month before the Gehrys were scheduled to leave, Frank received a surprising message. Victor Gruen had come to Paris, was staying at the Ritz, and wanted to see him. Frank went to meet his former employer at the hotel, and assumed that they would sit down over lunch. Instead, as Frank recalled, "He said, 'Show me Paris.' So I said, 'Sure, how long you got?' He said three hours. I said, 'Okay, I'm going to show you my favorite place.' And so we went to a grocery store and picked up stuff to make sandwiches, just me and him and Leesette, his wife." Frank took the Gruens to a little-known site outside the city, the location once occupied by the Machine de Marly, the vast water-pumping station near

Versailles that had been created in 1684 to serve the fountains of Versailles, which consumed nearly as much water as the city of Paris. Marly, one of the great engineering efforts in French history, originally consisted of fourteen waterwheels, each thirty-eight feet in diameter, and more than two hundred pumps. It had been replaced long before by newer systems, but in 1962 some remnants of an old pumping building remained, and the adjacent riverbank had become a park, an early version of a landscape created around an industrial relic. It was relatively little-known, and it had become Frank's favorite picnic spot.

Frank and the Gruens spread out a blanket and had a picnic lunch, and Frank remembers Victor Gruen telling him how much he liked discovering a part of Paris that he had never seen. Then, as they were driving back to the hotel, he told Frank why he had wanted to see him.

"He said, 'I'm opening an office in Europe, and leaving the L.A. firm to the other partners,'" Frank recalled. "'I'm coming back to be in Paris and I'm opening a small office and I want you to run it.' Now, at this point I was so poor, and he offered me ten times what I was making, and a way to stay there, which I really wanted to do, because I loved it. And I looked at him as I was getting out of the car, and I said, 'Victor, that's the kindest, most wonderful offer anybody could ever make, but I can't do it because I've committed myself to going home and starting my own thing and I'm pretty much set. I know it's going to be tough, but that's what I've got to do.' He got furious with me. He slammed the door and drove off."

It would not be the last time that Frank would walk away from something that held great promise of benefiting him both professionally and financially, but it still left him feeling uneasy. He told himself he was saying no to Gruen for Anita's sake, that as he had come to Paris for her benefit, he would return to Los Angeles in the hope of making her, and their marriage, happier. But there was another reason that he turned Victor Gruen down. He did not want to be working for anyone else any longer. If he was going to be an architect for the rest of his life, he wanted at least to be able to control what he did. He knew he wouldn't always have the luxury of picking and choosing among projects and doing only the ones he felt would be most meaningful. But if he had to take on projects to pay the rent, at least he would be making those decisions himself. He was tired of having other people determine his fate.

7
Restart in Los Angeles

When Frank and Anita and their children returned to live again in Los Angeles—via Toronto, driving cross-country in their Volkswagen shipped from France—they came back to California for good. Neither Frank nor Anita would ever live anywhere but Los Angeles again. Frank was excited about the possibilities of setting out on his own as an architect, and after his long months as a draftsman in André Remondet's office, he was more than ready to return to designing. He could still be shy and awkward among people he didn't know well, and he was uncomfortable promoting himself in the hope of getting work. Still, the experience he had gotten at Victor Gruen, Frank felt, "gave me the confidence to go out on my own."

And he felt better prepared than he had been before the trip. If his architectural instincts had begun to develop as he learned about California modernism at USC, and his horizons had expanded further as he began to think about European modernism at Harvard, his sojourn in France, by giving him his first direct experience with great buildings of the distant past, increased his awareness and knowledge of architecture exponentially. The most rewarding part of the trip by far was the time spent looking at European architecture with Mark Biass and, later, with Greg Walsh, and he felt energized by much of what he had seen. He was eager to start conceiving things that would give his new knowledge, gestating over many months, a chance to reveal itself. He knew that he would not begin to discover how his excitement about Romanesque churches and the twentieth-century work of Le Corbusier and Gaudí would affect his architecture until he had actually begun to design.

Feeling ready to design buildings on your own, however, is not the same as doing it. Architects need clients, and clients are not easy to come

by when you are a young architect who has been living abroad for fifteen months. Frank needed some income, and to avoid taking a job with
another firm, he did freelance work, mainly for Carlos Diniz, a former
colleague from Gruen, where he had been an artist charged with making
architectural renderings. It was a critical skill in an age before computers,
when renderings were the only way other than models to show clients what
their architect envisioned. Diniz, whom Frank's sister, Doreen, remembered as being so talented that "he could sell a building even if it was a
piece of crap," had left Gruen and established his own business doing
renderings and presentations for other architects, and he hired Frank to
help. "I could draw trees and buildings but I couldn't draw people," Frank
recalled. In this sphere of drawing, though, that was hardly a liability.

Money remained tight, however, and Frank and Anita and their daughters rented a house at 6623 Lemp Avenue in North Hollywood that the
Snyders had once occupied and that Louis Snyder, Anita's father, still
owned. "I think my father kept everything he had ever owned—he had lots
of properties," Richard Snyder, Frank's brother-in-law, recalled. Bella Snyder thought her husband should have simply given the house to the Gehrys. But "he was not that sort of person," Richard said, and he remembered
that "there was some discord between my parents" over Louis's refusal to
make the house a gift and his decision to charge his daughter and son-
in-law rent. Frank and Anita eventually bought the house for $14,000, an
amount that presumably was sufficient to assuage Louis over the loss of
rental income.

Frank remembers having "a pretty steady stream of projects" once he
and Greg, who seemed destined to play Sancho Panza to Frank's Don
Quixote, opened up their architectural practice together. But whatever
the quantity of work there may have been in the very early days—no complete records remain—none of the early projects were very large, or paid
much in the way of fees. More troubling than financial pressures, however,
was the fact that for all that Frank's responsibilities at Gruen may have
bolstered his confidence, his independent practice offered little opportunity to use any of the skills he had developed there. He "could take on a
multistory building. I wasn't afraid of it, because I had already done it. It
wasn't a mystery to me," he remembered. "I understood shopping centers
backwards and forwards. I knew department store people, and I knew construction. I could write contracts and letters. I could handle budgeting."
What he lacked were clients who needed those skills.

Although Frank remembered it as a time when "we kind of cobbled together a living," there was clearly enough money coming in to allow him to rent a small house at the corner of 5th Street and Broadway in Santa Monica to use as an office. It was a tiny house—barely bigger than a garage, Frank recalled, and it was across the street from the Santa Monica bus station. A portion of the house was sublet to Gere Kavanagh, Frank's friend and former colleague from Gruen, who would remain an office-mate, though never actually a design partner, for a number of years, not only in the 5th Street house but also at the larger office that succeeded it. The house had one room that could serve as a private office. Frank took possession of it, although his recollection is that he rarely used it and spent most of his time in the main room, where Greg and Gere had their desks.

That Frank would presume to take the sole private office suggests that he had a sense of a clear hierarchy: he, not Greg, would be in charge. In fact, his relationship with Greg was considerably more complicated. Frank was only beginning to develop a sense of conviction of his creative abilities as a designer, and his sense of himself, even after his experiences in the army, at Victor Gruen's office, at Harvard, and in Paris, was still marked more by insecurity than self-assurance. If Greg's quiet manner made it quickly apparent that Frank was the dominant personality of the two, Frank never-theless needed Greg as much, if not more, than Greg needed him. Greg drew elegantly, and had the patience for small details, unlike Frank. Tall and well-spoken, Greg was far more at ease with clients than Frank was, and more sophisticated culturally. He had been to Japan, and knew not only its architecture but also its art and music. Greg was a talented pianist, whereas Frank, who loved music, knew relatively little about it and had no musical talent. Frank could be enthusiastic, but rarely in those days could he be described as charming; Greg was both enthusiastic and charming. He had the air of a sophisticated, self-assured WASP, which Frank, ridden by anxiety and aware of his own rough edges, envied. (That Greg was in fact Catholic and not Protestant hardly mattered.)

Frank valued Greg as a friend and as a critic of his work; since their days together at USC he had always trusted Greg's insights, and never felt that he was motivated by the competitiveness he often felt from other classmates. "I was shy, I was insecure intellectually, and I couldn't talk to clients," Frank said. "Greg was the front. He could talk the talk, he could make the presentations, and I just sat in the back." Frank and Greg would exchange thoughts, and critiques of each other's drawings, so constantly that it sometimes seemed as if they represented a single design sensibility.

They shared a passion not just for making architecture, but also for experiencing it, learning from it, and talking about how it connected to the rest of culture. They were so accustomed to firing up each other's enthusiasms that Frank recalls not being conscious that many of the key design ideas that they were developing had originated with him: "I didn't know who was doing what. I didn't, I never thought about it that way. I always thought we were working on everything together," he said later.

Doreen felt that her brother had lacked an awareness of his own gifts since his student days. "I don't think Frank knew how talented he was. And he tended to think everybody was better than he was. He'd gotten an inferiority complex," she said. "And so Greg Walsh comes along. He didn't seem to have any guilt. So it must have been appealing. And he was sweet. He's still sweet. And he adored Frank. He was like a brother. He was like Ross Honsberger in a way—Ross Honsberger in architecture."

Frank, a determined loner in some ways, was needful in others. He had always relied on close friends both to share his enthusiasms and to balance elements of his personality. If there is anything that Ross Honsberger, Mark Biass, and Greg Walsh shared, it was that they were each more knowledgeable than Frank about something he wanted to know more about. They were also somewhat more methodical and more attentive to detail than he was, and they seemed able to project a sense of being suave and self-assured, something Frank could not do at all. Most important, while all three of them seemed to display little or none of the angst that Frank so often felt, their steadiness seemed to come at no cost to their ability to feel passionate about what interested them. Frank was attracted to friends who seemed determined to experience life with the same intensity that he did, yet who looked like they were having an easier time staying on an even keel.

Like many architects, Frank relied heavily on family and friends to send projects his way—or even to invent them—to help get his architectural practice off the ground. Doreen encouraged the parents of a man she was dating to hire Frank to design a small house for them on Prospect Street in Hollywood, which he did. It was not as ambitious an effort as the Steeves house, but it was another work he could claim to have built from the ground up.* More significant, at least in terms of the amount of work

---

* The original owners of the house lived there for the rest of their lives, according to Doreen. By chance, Frank and Berta Gehry's son Sam would purchase a house across the street many years later.

it yielded, was a relationship that came from Anita's side. Wesley Bilson, whose brother was married to one of Anita's close friends from high school, had married the daughter of the owner of Kay Jewelers, and he had money to invest. He was interested in going into real estate development, and had begun to talk with Frank about working together before the Gehrys went to Paris. When they returned, the conversations got more serious. Bilson had a property on Highland Avenue in Santa Monica that was suitable for a small, six-unit apartment house. It was an old residential neighborhood not far from the ocean, poised between the more prosperous parts of Santa Monica to the north and the shabby precincts of Venice to the south.

Bilson and Frank formed a development company along with another architect, Fereydoon Ghaffari, who had been in Frank's class at USC and had also worked at Gruen for a time, and two engineers, Moshe Rubenstein and Joseph Kurily. Frank, along with Greg, was to provide the design in exchange for a share in the ownership of the project. Wesley Bilson was the primary investor, but Anita's father agreed to invest some money, as did Thelma Gehry, whose long years of working as a saleswoman at the Broadway department store had given her some modest savings.

The building at Highland Avenue, which was called Hillcrest Apartments, was Frank's largest project up to that point, and his most revealing. It seems at first glance to be a conventional six-unit building of wood and stucco, and its design bears some resemblance to the traditional California bungalow style, once prevalent in that part of Santa Monica but already beginning to disappear, as well as to the neighborhood's newer form of vernacular architecture, the small apartment buildings, two or three stories high, that are essentially stucco boxes set atop open parking garages. Frank liked the ordinary, unpretentious feel of the neighborhood, and he wanted the building to fit comfortably into its context, an unusual, even startling idea in 1962, when most modern buildings designed by architects were conceived more as abstract objects, pure shapes set down on their sites with little regard to what was around them. The notion that an architect designing a building in an established neighborhood might have an obligation to make the building feel connected to its surroundings, or at least to take the nature of the surroundings into account, had been something of a truism for much of architectural history, and it is commonly accepted today. But it had been largely set aside in the 1960s, when it so often seemed, at least to architects, that the best way to improve an old neighborhood was to tear it down and start over.

Hillcrest Apartments on Highland Avenue in Santa Monica

Frank's desire to make his building seem like a natural part of its old Santa Monica neighborhood, then, was almost radical. Yet Frank had no more interest at that time than he would later in truly mimicking the buildings of the past. Hillcrest is most notable, in the end, not for the things about it that resemble more common buildings, but for the things that do not. The little apartment house is full of elements that reveal Frank's instinctive desire to break away, to design details that were different and very much his own, as if he could not help himself from continuing to invent. Even where his overall intention was to fit in, his instincts led him to stand out and to do things in a unique way.

From the street, Hillcrest looks fairly unexceptional: a two-story structure of white stucco, with a shingled, gabled roof, projecting decks with wooden balustrades, and a parking area at grade level. The composition of the façade, however, reveals the design to be somewhat more complex. Each level has three sliding doors opening to a wooden balcony. The two doors on the left are on the plane of the façade; the one on the right is recessed on both floors, creating a void that balances the mass of the chimney, which is farther to the right. The result is a subtle asymmetrical arrangement of solids and voids.

The entry to all six units in the building faces the right side, which similarly balances solids and voids, in this case projecting bays that read as floating masses of white stucco playing off against wooden stairs and balustrades. The entry area feels almost like a tiny piazza, and it is reached either by walking from the street or by taking a half flight of stairs up from the parking area, an arrangement intended to assure that tenants and visitors alike have the same experience of entry. Perhaps most notable of all is the care Gehry took in detailing elements constructed of wood, such as balustrades, stairways, and the benches that flank the entry area, all of which were clearly an attempt to give the building the air of something more urbane. The balustrades were designed with vertical pieces that, instead of ending at the level of the deck, are set slightly in front of it and extend below it, creating a strong pattern of vertical lines. The underside of the stair is a composition of open horizontals, leading to a floating landing supported by a metal lally column. These are minor details, but they are major early signals of Frank's developing instincts. Confronted with a tight budget and eager to design something special at the same time, he figured out a way to craft elements that would give the building some distinction at little or no extra cost.

Viewing the building from the side also reveals the steep gable to be little more than an ornamental front. Instead of covering the entire structure, as it appears to be doing from the street, it rises to a peak just behind the façade and then goes right back down again, so from the side it appears just to be a steep, hollow triangle, as if a folded piece of paper was set atop the house. The gable's front side provides shade for the upper-level decks, but in every other way it seems, at first glance, to be an indulgence, a false front at odds with the rest of the building, perhaps even a very early foray into the realm of architectural playfulness that would come to be known as postmodernism.

Hillcrest was completed in the same year that Robert Venturi finished the house for his mother in Chestnut Hill, Pennsylvania, an iconic work of postmodernism that contains numerous traditional architectural elements reinterpreted, made thinner and more obviously pictorial, and used with ironic intent. Frank was not a postmodernist and never would be, but he had some of the same misgivings about modern architecture that Venturi did in the early 1960s, and he shared an interest in what Venturi would later call "ugly and ordinary" architecture. Four years after Frank designed Hillcrest, Venturi would publish a seminal book, *Complexity and Contradiction in Architecture*, in which he wrote, "I like elements which are hybrid rather than 'pure,' compromising rather than 'clean,' distorted rather than 'straightforward.' . . . I am for messy vitality over obvious unity . . . for richness of meaning rather than clarity of meaning," words that could describe Frank's motivations as well as his own. Frank, like Venturi, was increasingly uncomfortable with the banal, corporate direction modern architecture had taken, and he was beginning to strive for a way to create something that would make for richer experience. His work would follow a very different trajectory than Venturi's, but like Venturi, he felt that the plain modern box was a dead end, and he liked neither the rejection of ordinary buildings and neighborhoods that it presumed nor the notion that austerity was the route to architectural pleasure.

Frank knew that Hillcrest was no more than a primitive, awkward beginning, and he had no idea where it would take him. He felt afterward that he might have gone too far in his desire to make the building fit into its old neighborhood, especially when Esther McCoy, the most eminent writer on California architecture, who lived nearby, let it be known that she didn't think much of it. "She thought it was derivative, historic [and] she was a modernist," Frank said. Looking back at Hillcrest, he described what he was trying out as "doing my fitting into the neighborhood without copying the neighborhood." The problem, he came to realize, was that "I was trying to talk to the neighborhood and I didn't have a vocabulary to take it somewhere."

The development venture that Frank and Wesley Bilson formed purchased two other sites in Santa Monica, and Frank began work on designs for the apartment projects that he expected would follow Hillcrest. Neither appears, at least from renderings, to have been as unresolved, or as fertile, a design as Hillcrest: one rendering suggests a building strongly derivative of the work of Frank Lloyd Wright and the Prairie School, while the other seems like a conventional modern multiunit apartment building. Then again, Hillcrest can seem fairly conventional at first glance, too, and it is impossible to know how Frank would have put his stamp on either of these buildings, neither of which was ever developed beyond a rough concept.

Instead, the development venture was terminated, for reasons that are not entirely clear. Frank felt a growing conflict between his role as the architect and his role as a part owner, and he worried that the two could not be reconciled. His partners wanted to take money out of the venture, and he wanted it to stay in so as to build better buildings. There may also have been tension between Frank and Wesley Bilson, whom he alternatively described as "overbearing" and "a great guy." But Frank was gradually coming to conclude that he was not comfortable trying to be a real estate developer and an architect at the same time, whatever potential financial gains there might be. He had already shown a willingness to walk away from situations that he did not think would ultimately be to his professional benefit, and his decision that this venture fell into that category was surely part of the reason the development company came to a quick end.[*]

Bilson, however, remained a valuable source of work, at least indirectly, since Frank's next substantial project was a regional headquarters and warehouse for Kay Jewelers in Los Angeles, along with Kay stores in Redondo Beach and Buena Park. The office building on Fairfax Avenue, like Hillcrest Apartments, bears little resemblance to the architecture Frank would design a few years later, and like Hillcrest it can seem at first glance to be more conventional than it is. And yet like Hillcrest it appears less conventional the more you look at it, and it becomes easy to see how Frank was struggling in the early 1960s to find a way to make architecture that would feel new, cost little, and have the expressive, even the emotive, quality of older buildings. For Kay Jewelers he produced a two-story structure of concrete, wood, glass, and red roof tile, with a vaguely Japanese air. The head of Kay had told Frank that he admired Japanese architecture, and Frank was happy to oblige with a building that makes almost no literal use of Japanese elements but manages to convey the sense of serene order, quiet formality, and rich texture that Japanese temples possess. The façade is marked by a formal colonnade, loosely evoking the columns that are often hidden but are a critical part of the structure of a Japanese temple, here remade as cylinders of concrete topped by boxy capitals. It is as if Frank stripped the Japanese temple of its most characteristic element, its pagoda-style roof, and then reshaped it in accord with the classical architecture of the West to end up with a façade that is an abstracted synthesis of a Japanese and a Greek temple. The expansive windows, framed in wood, are set back from the columns, as if to emphasize the temple-like quality. The side walls of the building, meanwhile, project forward, becoming floating planes that from the front appear to enclose the façade in a vast frame, a Los Angeles storefront with grandiose airs. The Kay building

---

[*] Despite his misgivings about playing the role of developer and architect at the same time, Frank would repeat at several other points in his life the pattern of investing in real estate in the expectation that he would be able to be the project's architect. Few of these projects went ahead in the early years, although he would later be successful investing in real estate along with his partner Larry Field. See chapter 17.

originally had a small Japanese garden in front, a compromised version of Frank's original idea, which was to have a garden surrounded by a high wall that was to be interrupted by a tiled pergola that would serve as the entrance. The building was conceived, then, as being at least slightly more Japanese than it now appears to be. But the warm formality with which it addresses the street remains.

The pace of work began to accelerate after the Kay project, which was completed in 1963, and the two Kay stores in 1964. Frank's early clients the Steeveses commissioned him to design a five-story office building for Santa Monica, which was to have been a structure of glass and concrete in two different textures. It was abandoned when costs turned out to be too high, and Frank had to hire a lawyer when the clients sued to demand the return of his $15,000 architectural fee because they had decided not to go forward. He was able to hold on to the fee, but the painful episode was a further reminder of the economic precariousness of an architect's life. His next project, a small industrial building for the Faith Plating Company, a metal plating concern in Hollywood, thankfully had no such problems, and while it was smaller than the Steeves office building would have been, it was substantial enough to stand as the marker of a new direction, away from the historical references of Hillcrest and Kay.

Frank had been interested for some time in the commercial architectural vernacular of Los Angeles, the ordinary buildings that he, and almost everyone else, tended to refer to as "dumb boxes," and he would spend much of his free time photographing warehouses, derricks, and factories around the city.[*] He was not the only person to be intrigued by the city's ordinary industrial buildings. The British architectural historian Reyner Banham, who a decade later would write a critical book on Los Angeles, saw the simple box as the basic building block of the city's identity.[†] But Frank's interest was less academic and more pragmatic. Was there a way to make something more out of this, he wondered—a way to make the dumb box speak? At Faith Plating, he put a plain stucco box atop a brick base, and broke the solid façade only with two large rectangular window-

---

[*] Gehry's photographs of the industrial landscape of Los Angeles would be included by the curator Frédéric Migayrou in a retrospective exhibition of his architecture at the Centre Pompidou in 2014. See chapter 21.

[†] Banham's *Los Angeles: The Architecture of Four Ecologies,* published in 1971, was one of the first works by a prominent architectural historian to paint Los Angeles in an almost entirely positive light. It was published a year before Robert Venturi, Denise Scott Brown, and Steven Izenour's *Learning from Las Vegas,* which also called for serious examination of what might be thought of as the modernist vernacular for the age of the freeway.

The Danziger Studio on Melrose Avenue, Los Angeles

like openings in the upper level and a wide, deep, framelike enclosure of stucco around the front door. What resulted resembles a conventional building, but it is almost too conventional, turned into something plainer and simpler than a child's drawing. Or so it first appears. But here, too, Frank was exploring ambitious formal ideas—solids and voids, receding and projecting planes, heaviness and lightness, openness and enclosure—within the context of a design that was not only an essay in formalism, but also an attempt to comment on the architectural potential Frank saw in the banal, ordinary commercial architecture of Los Angeles that almost everyone else disdained.

Faith Plating, which was finished in 1964, turned out to be a trial run for a project that would follow later that same year, the Danziger Studio and Residence, also in Hollywood. The client was Lou Danziger, a prominent Los Angeles graphic designer who was on the board of Faith Plating and may have been influential in helping Frank get that job as well. He had met Frank through his close friend Frederick Usher, a designer

who had been an early collaborator of Charles Eames. Frank believed that
Danziger had at first wanted Usher himself to design the building, but that
Usher declined and recommended him.[*]

Whatever the circumstances that brought it about, the Danziger project
was a major turning point. The design, a composition of boxes covered in
a form of stucco that was called "tunnel mix," a material generally used
only for freeway underpasses and tunnels, was blunter than Faith Plating,
but considerably larger, more complex, and more powerful. Frank was so
determined to find a material that would have a rough texture similar to
the one he remembered seeing on the exterior of Le Corbusier's chapel
at Ronchamp that he rented special equipment to test the material on a
garage in Venice to prove to the contractor that it could be used on a conventional frame building. It was an early example of his stubborn determination to have things his way.

Frank's decision to use an industrial material on a domestically scaled
building was only one sign of his intention to elevate the "dumb box"
into something that could no longer be mistaken for an ordinary building. Even though the Danziger Studio revealed little to the street, there
could be no doubt that an architect's hand was behind it. The two tall,
oblong boxes, set parallel but one offset from the other, were positioned
as carefully as pieces of minimalist sculpture; from the front, facing busy
Melrose Avenue, a matching garden wall functioned as a third box, giving
the composition greater depth as well as a horizontal element. Smaller
boxes pushed out from the roof with high clerestory windows to bring in
natural light, while at the base of the building Frank stopped the stucco
a foot or so above the sidewalk, creating an oversize reveal that made the
masses appear almost to float.

The building was an essay in balancing masses and planes, a three-
dimensional modernist composition. While it responded to the immediate context of a busy commercial street by turning inward toward the very
Southern California element of a garden, its massing seemed also to evoke
the American Southwest, as well as the work of a very unsouthwestern

---

[*] The sequence is not entirely clear, and it is not certain how either project came to Frank.
Since Frank is certain that Usher played a role in his obtaining the Danziger commission,
it is possible that Usher had mentioned Frank's name to Danziger before the Faith Plating job, and Danziger, as a board member of Faith Plating, suggested that the company
hire Frank, and then later asked him to do his own studio and residence after Usher had
declined that commission. It is also possible that Frank and Faith Plating came together
through other means, and that Usher recommended independently of the Faith Plating job
that Frank design the Danziger project.

architect, Louis Kahn, whose somber, brooding, solid buildings sought a new expression of modernist monumentality and were then beginning to attract wide notice. Frank may also have seen a Baptist church designed by Rudolf Schindler in 1944 in South Los Angeles, a series of windowless stucco masses with horizontal lines, to which Danziger bears at least a passing resemblance.*

Reyner Banham, who would write admiringly of the "deft authority" of Frank's design, saw other influences: he would observe that the Danziger Studio resembled "the design of studio houses in Europe in the twenties," and he suggested comparisons to the Dutch modernist Theo van Doesburg. "What is important and striking," Banham wrote, "is the way in which this elegantly simple envelope not only reaffirms the continuing validity of the stucco box as Angeleno architecture, but does so in a manner that can stand up to international scrutiny. The cycle initiated by Schindler comes round again with deft authority."

Banham's invocation of Schindler underscores the extent to which the Danziger Studio seemed somehow entirely of Los Angeles, to belong on funky Melrose Avenue and not in Amsterdam or Santa Fe. Danziger did not mark the beginning of Frank's career by any means, but it did mark the beginning of his reputation as an architect on his own. It was clear that he did not fit into established categories. His ability to bring into harmony such diverse influences as California modernism, Louis Kahn, and the pueblo architecture of the Southwest, not to mention European modernism from the 1920s, was a sign that his maturity as a designer was evolving rapidly: few architects had combined modernist lightness and solid, monumental weight without having these two things feel contradictory. Frank was beginning to reveal himself not only as a gifted maker of three-dimensional compositions, but also as an architect with an unusual ability to unite opposites, to pull together different influences, as if his greatest goal were to transcend conflict and through his architecture bring different forces into accord.

---

* The Bethlehem Baptist Church, Schindler's only church, was abandoned for years and nearly lost, then rediscovered and painted in 2014. It awaits restoration. It was designed for an African-American congregation that had parted ways with its original architect, an African American named James Garrott. Steve Wallet, a San Diego architect who has researched the history of the building, has proposed that Gregory Ain, who was part of the circle of Los Angeles modernists that Frank had come to know at USC and who knew both Garrott and Schindler, introduced the congregation to Schindler.

A s Frank's practice began to grow and the family's finances became, if not comfortable, at least less anxiety-provoking, Anita decided it was time to go back to school and get the education she had craved as a young woman. With both their daughters in school—Leslie was ten and Brina eight—there was no reason Anita had to be home all day. The family had moved to a new house Anita had found on Kennard Avenue in Westwood, close to the campus of the University of California at Los Angeles. Anita started at junior college, then switched to UCLA, where she studied Russian literature. She liked higher education, and once she had earned her bachelor's degree, she continued on to get a master's in social work, the field she had decided would be her career.

Frank's feelings about Anita's return to school were mixed. He knew it was what she wanted, and he had no desire to be married to a woman whose ambitions went no further than being a housewife. If there was an issue for him in Anita's decision, it was not her desire for higher education and a career of her own, which he had always supported. It was his awareness that Anita's academic life would pull her into her own world, further away from his. He missed the days when he could feel that his career was something they shared. At the beginning, it had seemed to symbolize a joint future. But that was a long time ago. Now the connection Anita felt to Frank's career seemed to be expressed mainly in terms of her resentment over the sacrifices she had made for it. Frank had hoped that there would be a way for her to feel engaged with what he did in a more positive way, but there was no sign that Anita had any inclination to make that happen. Still, if Anita felt more fulfilled in her own life, perhaps she would not complain so much, and life would at least be calmer. So Frank never questioned her decision, though as Richard Snyder observed, it was not entirely clear whether he was supporting her new academic career because he took joy in helping her realize her dream, or because he felt he had no choice but to repay a debt to her. "Is this reparations or is this generosity?" Anita's brother asked, knowing, surely, that it was both.

If Anita was happy at last to be doing what she had wanted, it did not translate into happiness in her marriage. Frank continued to leave most household and parental duties to her, and as his practice grew, he felt justified in spending more and more time at the office. He had recently gained an important new client, the Rouse Company, the development company behind the new town of Columbia, Maryland, for which he was designing several buildings. Now a major portion of his work was not even in California, and required him to make frequent trips across the country.* For Anita, things had not changed as much as she had expected from a dozen years before when she worked as an assistant in a law office so that Frank could go to architecture school. She was still fitting her life around his.

Whatever benefits the year in Paris had brought faded, and as Frank became more engaged in his work, their marriage seemed to become only tenser and more distant. Their worlds by day had become almost entirely separate, and Frank was increasingly absent from the house in the evenings and on weekends. He loved his daughters and enjoyed playing with them, but he managed to set aside large amounts of time for them so infrequently that the pleasure he felt at fatherhood sometimes seemed more of an abstract concept than a reality—at least to Anita, Leslie, and Brina.

Work was not the only reason Frank was often absent from home. He had no major romantic entanglements, at least not yet, but he had found something else at least as enticing. In the mid-1960s, as his architectural practice began to grow, he began to spend much of his time in Venice, Ocean Park, and the other parts of Los Angeles where artists tended to live and work. Art had interested him since his early days at USC, when he explored becoming a ceramicist, and as he became more accustomed to making his own designs and running his own office, he found himself increasingly interested in many of the issues that artists dealt with: exploring perspective, shape, color, materials, and light, and finding new ways to express what they saw. Frank had no desire to give up architecture, but he wanted to use architecture to do many of the same things he saw artists doing. He found the work of Los Angeles artists like Billy Al Bengston, Ed Moses, Ed Ruscha, Ken Price, Robert Irwin, Ron Davis, Tony Berlant, Larry Bell, Peter Alexander, and John Altoon far more compelling than the work of most of his architectural contemporaries. The artists, Frank realized, made it their business to interpret the world, not to take it as it was. He took no small amount of satisfaction in the fact that some of them were equally intrigued by what he did. He remembered first meeting Ed Moses on Melrose Avenue in front of the Danziger Studio, which Moses had gone to see. Frank said, "When I went to the project site one day, Ed Moses was standing there. I knew who he was when he introduced himself, and I was so excited that he was interested. He was very

---

* For a complete discussion of his work with Rouse, see chapter 8.

complimentary and brought around some of his guys, like Ken Price and Billy Al Bengston. They would hang out at the site during construction."

Moses recalled the encounter somewhat differently—he had known Lou Danziger for some time, and as he remembered it, he had met Frank at the suggestion of a friend who thought he might be able to help Moses with the design of a new studio, after which Frank invited him to see Lou's building under construction. "When Frank first came to my studio in Beverly Glen he wore a blue suit with cordovan shoes," Moses said. It was so early in Frank's career that he was still dressing more as he had when he worked for Victor Gruen. However it happened that Ed Moses first saw the Danziger Studio, he liked it. "I loved the place, it was a terrific design with the rough-blown stucco on the outside . . . more like a Southwest kind of structure," Moses said. And he liked its architect. Moses's encounter with the Danziger project would mark the beginning of what would become one of Frank's closest friendships. And it led Moses to suggest to some of his artist friends that they see Frank's work, after which Frank began to spend more time with Moses and the other artists. "I said, 'This is Frank Gehry—he's a friend of mine, an architect who is very interested in painting,'" Moses said. "It was very unusual for an architect—most of them never got out of their own territory." Soon, more or less by default, Frank had become part of their circle.

It was a circle defined, at least symbolically, by the Ferus Gallery, which had been started in 1957 by Walter Hopps, a gifted and impassioned if somewhat eccentric twenty-four-year-old curator, and Ed Kienholz, a thirty-year-old artist who used found objects to make tableaux of social commentary. Hopps and Kienholz envisioned Ferus as a place where other young local artists could show their work and, if they were fortunate, sell a piece or two. Kienholz, like Ed Moses, Robert Irwin, Ed Ruscha, James Turrell, and the other artists Frank would come to know, had all made a deliberate decision to settle in Los Angeles instead of amid the artistic and commercial hothouse of New York, in large part because they wanted no part of its pressures. In the 1950s, Los Angeles was the un–New York. It had no "art scene" to speak of. There were no major art museums in the city and no modern galleries of consequence. There were many serious Los Angeles collectors, but for the most part they filled their walls with paintings they had gone to New York to buy, and they had few interactions with local artists. If being away from the center of the art world felt like career suicide for some artists, distance was exactly what the ones who gravitated to Los Angeles were seeking. They found it liberating. They could do what they pleased, away from both New York's critical eye and its commercial intensity.

But they needed someplace that would bring them together and try to sell their work, and they wanted to do it in an environment that would be different from the staid precincts of New York galleries. At that they certainly succeeded: the opening show, which featured assemblages by the artist Wallace Berman, was raided by the Los Angeles police for obscenity. "Kienholz and Hopps had no finite criteria for selecting Ferus artists apart from attitude. Friends recommended friends. Berman suggested showing Ed Moses," Hunter Drohojowska-Philp wrote in *Rebels in Paradise: The Los Angeles Art Scene and the 1960s.* After a year, Kienholz decided he was more suited to be an artist than a gallerist, and he sold his share back to Hopps, who in turn sold it to Irving Blum, a debonair New Yorker who had recently relocated to Los Angeles.* Blum kept Ferus focused primarily on the emerging artists of Los Angeles, but he expanded the gallery's quarters on La Cienega Boulevard and sprinkled its schedule with a few exhibitions of cutting-edge New York artists, including Andy Warhol. It was a skillful way of raising the gallery's profile while not diluting its identity.

By the time Frank began to spend time with the Ferus artists in the mid-1960s, the energetic Blum, an ambitious businessman, had taken over day-to-day management from Hopps. The gallery remained the artists' clubhouse, but it became slightly more a gallery and slightly less a clubhouse. And it was no longer unique: a handful of other galleries had sprung up to sell the work of Los Angeles artists, including one run by Rolf Nelson, who married Doreen Gehry in 1966. But family ties were not enough to keep Frank away from the gravitational pull of Ferus, which remained the gallery most closely identified with the increasingly visible Los Angeles art world.

The community of Los Angeles artists was unusually close. "I don't think we had the pressure that the artists in New York had—we were free spirits, experimenting. Everything got passed around—the drugs, the girls, the ideas," Chuck Arnoldi, a younger member of the group who became another of Frank's closest friends, said. "The art scene here was very small, everybody knew everybody. . . . Frank had the reputation of sometimes buying some art, which made him very attractive to artists, because nobody sold anything. But that wasn't why people liked Frank. I think Frank just

---

* Blum may have purchased Kienholz's share directly from him. Their accounts, recounted in *Rebels in Paradise,* differ.

felt like one of the guys. And we just, you know, ate, drank, talked, and hung out. And he was interested in what we were doing. Anybody that was interested in what you were doing was just immediately, you know, taken into the scene, because there was no, there wasn't a big audience."

Frank had a unique role in the artists' group. While he fairly quickly became one of what Tony Berlant would call "the band of brothers," he was always a bit different, and not only because he was an architect and the others were artists. There was nothing about Frank that was blasé. If anything separated him from the artists, it was his eagerness to learn. At the beginning, it was enough to make one of the de facto leaders of the group, the artist Billy Al Bengston, ask Moses, "Who is this little putz you keep bringing around?" "He was like, 'Gee whiz,'" said Ed Ruscha, who described Frank as "the least bombastic person I've ever known." To the artists, he seemed to be always around, listening with a careful ear, looking at everything everyone else was doing, and learning what he could from it. "Frank had an insatiable appetite—I'd never met an architect like that," Ed Moses said. Frank knew exactly what he was doing. "I felt in an art-centric place, whether I put plumbing in it or not," he said, and he felt comfortable with the artists in a way that he didn't with most architects. "There was a powerful, powerful energy I was getting from this scene that I wasn't getting from the architecture world. What attracted me to them is that they worked intuitively. They would do what they wanted and take the consequences"—something that most architects, in Frank's experience, were less and less willing to do.

For the artists, Frank felt, the craft and the art were one. "It wasn't two separate acts, and that intrigued me. I was hoping an architect could do that.

"Their work was more direct and in such contrast to what I was doing in architecture, which was so rigid. You have to deal with safety issues— fireproofing, sprinklers, handrails for stairways, things like that. You go through training that teaches you to do things in a very careful way, following codes and budgets. But those constraints didn't speak to aesthetics. When I got close to these guys, I'd hang out at their studios and watch them work and observe how they dealt with things, and it was very different. I was terribly enamored with the directness of it and the Mount Everest–ness of it, how they had to confront a white canvas. That whole process seemed so much more likely to produce beautiful work than the architectural process did. I knew pragmatic things had to be taken care of, and I could do that, but it wasn't enough."

Most of the artists had studios in the then-funky precincts of Venice, south of Santa Monica, a part of the city with a messy mix of the grandiose and the mundane that Frank found especially appealing: Venice was shabby more than plain, and it represented the opposite of the pristine perfection he had been taught to aspire to as an architect. He was particularly taken by the tendency of several of the artists to redesign their studios at regular intervals, and often to leave sections raw or unfinished. Billy Al Bengston built his own furniture, put up partitions, and then knocked them down when he had a fresh idea. The notion of celebrating incompleteness and change was a far cry from the perfect, pure, and permanent objects Frank had been taught to aspire to in architecture school and in his work at Gruen. Larry Bell opened up a section of wall in his studio to expose the studs, then covered it with glass. "So you were looking at the studs as if they were a picture, and I loved that," Frank said.

He willingly took on small design projects for many of the artists, largely out of friendship although it was also a way of reminding them that he too was a creative person, not just a hanger-on. While Bengston could give Frank a hard time—he criticized him for being a "name-fucker" and would later call him "the best thief of all time" for the way he integrated the artists' ideas into his work—he was deeply admiring of Frank, so much so that he insisted that Frank design the installation for the retrospective he was to have in 1968 at the then-new Los Angeles County Museum of Art, a somewhat vapid series of classically inspired pavilions designed by Frank's former mentor William Pereira.[*]

It was not Frank's first project at the museum. Three years earlier, thanks in part to Greg Walsh's deep familiarity with Japan, he and Greg had been asked to design an exhibition called *Art Treasures of Japan*. The exhibition design made use of wood and had colored fabrics hanging from the ceiling, and it had a quiet, handsome order to it. But it did not suggest what Frank would do the next time he was called to produce a design for an exhibition in the museum's ostentatious precincts.

Bengston, who was often photographed with his motorcycle and whose

---

[*] Pereira received the commission as a compromise between museum trustees who wanted to hire Mies van der Rohe and a trustee who insisted on Edward Durell Stone. At LACMA Pereira restricted his fondness for unusual shapes to the act of breaking the museum into separate pieces, and his banal design demonstrated none of the qualities that had attracted Frank to him. Pereira's little-admired building did, however, inspire one of Ed Ruscha's most famous paintings, *The Los Angeles County Museum on Fire*, in the collection of the Joseph H. Hirshhorn Museum in Washington, D.C.

work frequently used spray lacquer similar to that in custom car finishes, was the first of the Los Angeles artists to have a solo exhibition at the museum. He wanted the exhibition to capture some of the spirit of the group, and he made it clear to Frank that he wanted him to do more than tell the curators where in the gallery to put the walls. Bengston left the look of the exhibition up to Frank, and to make the project even more of a collaboration, he asked Ed Ruscha to produce the catalog and gave him similar license.

Frank recalled that the museum's curators were somewhat nervous about his involvement, though they may have been more anxious about the very idea of a Bengston show in the first place. They reminded him that there was a minimal budget for the installation, hoping that would keep things fairly standard. It had the opposite effect. "I asked them to take me down to their storeroom, where they had piles of plywood with paint on them," Frank said. "I asked what they were doing with the plywood and they didn't know, so I took it and made [the] exhibition. It was so cheap they couldn't deny it." The sheets of plywood were either unpainted or painted in various colors, and Frank insisted that they be installed as they were, with no further painting. "I guess maybe I told them we'd paint it, but then when it got up it looked so great that we kept it up," he said.

Frank, still excited by the way the artists treated their studios as architectural works in progress, decided that some of the exhibition should resemble Bengston's studio and living quarters, with the art placed as if it were on living room walls, while other walls would be made of the randomly colored plywood or corrugated metal. It also included a wax figure of Bengston on a motorcycle. At first things did not go well between Bengston and Frank, who thought the artist would send over his own furniture. When he failed to do so, Frank called a furniture rental business and asked for four sets of living room furniture. He saw what had arrived and thought it had nothing to do with either his idea or Bengston's aesthetic, and he tried to get it out of the gallery before the artist could see it. But Bengston got there first and was livid. "He started yelling at me and calling me all kinds of things. It freaked me out because, as you can imagine, I loved Billy. I wanted to make this the best thing ever for him. If I bombed, they wouldn't let me in anymore. There was a lot riding on it for me," Frank said. Bengston ended up getting furniture more to his liking, the rift quickly healed, and the exhibition went on to be a success. It raised Frank's profile, and most important of all for him, it cemented his connection to the community of artists.

If Frank had begun to consider his artist friends to be a kind of surrogate family, it was with good reason. His relationship with his own family was increasingly distant. Two years before the upbeat event of the Bengston show, his deteriorating relationship with Anita had reached a crisis point. He was miserable when he was at home, and he felt racked with guilt for spending so much time away from his family. Work and the artists were a partial distraction, but he knew that the situation was not sustainable.

Ed Moses suggested that Frank seek the counsel of his psychotherapist, Milton Wexler, an analyst who had trained as both a lawyer and a psychologist, and had treated a number of artists, actors, and other creative people, often without charge. Among Wexler's patients was John Altoon, a charismatic and much-loved artist in the Ferus group who had a history of hospitalizations for mental illness. Wexler's methods were unorthodox. He tended to become involved in the lives of many of his patients, and he sometimes socialized with them. He would later have a professional relationship with one of his patients, the director Blake Edwards, with whom he coauthored the scripts for two films, *The Man Who Loved Women* and *That's Life*. Wexler met Altoon when Altoon was hospitalized in nearby Camarillo and another of his patients, Laura Sterns, a painter and friend of Altoon's, told him that Altoon was a gifted artist who she felt could flourish on his own with the right treatment, and urged Wexler to help her get Altoon released. The two went to Camarillo and arranged to bring Altoon back to Los Angeles, where he became one of Wexler's patients.

Wexler liked to treat patients in groups, and Altoon was in a therapy group made up primarily of artists. It was also unusual in that Wexler treated all of the artists at no charge. Altoon suggested to Ed Moses that he join the group, and Wexler met him and agreed to make a place for him. Moses, in turn, encouraged a woman named Donna O'Neill to join the group, and then he suggested that Frank meet Wexler and see if he felt comfortable enough with him to become a patient.

Frank was reluctant at first. Later he would write that Moses needed to "push" him into therapy "because, like a lot of people who rely on their creativity, I had a mystical sense of what it is to be an artist. You recognize that the source of your talent is your identity, so you don't want to tamper with yourself." For a long time, Frank expressed his ambivalence about therapy by sitting in silence, listening to everyone else in the group but saying almost nothing himself. He said he felt shy and intimidated by how easily the other people in the group seemed to talk. He did not feel capable of being articulate about anything, let alone the private matters that are usually the stuff of therapy. "Then one night, the entire group turned on me," Frank wrote. "They attacked me, saying who did I think I was, sitting there, judging them, withholding." Afterward, Wexler said that the others were right, and that in his view Frank's silence communicated arrogance, not humility. "You asshole, don't you see what they see?" Wexler said to Frank.

Frank would recall that conversation as an epiphany. "Nothing was the same after that," he wrote. "It wasn't even that I talked that much more, though I did. The change went deeper. I was able to dismantle the wall I had built around myself. I began to listen. I don't think I had ever listened before. But I heard what people were saying, heard it clearly. The more I listened, the more interested I became in them."

It may not have been as instantaneous a transformation as Frank remembers it, but there can be no doubt that Milton Wexler would become one of the most important people in his life. When Frank entered treatment, in Wexler's words, "he lacked a lot of confidence. He was talking often about being bankrupt, and he meant more than just monetary bankruptcy, he meant bankrupt in his relationships, bankrupt in his ability to get his clients to accept what he was doing. He was using all kinds of subjective techniques and trying to trick them into accepting his special vision, and he was very uneasy about it because none of it seemed to work." Wexler believed that Frank learned how to behave with his clients because of the need to explain his work to his therapist, who admitted to knowing almost nothing about architecture. "I think it helped him to take on the role of the adult in the relationship," Wexler told Sydney Pollack. "And also instead of trying to seduce his clients, I think he took on more adult roles in relation to his clients. He began to teach them as he was trying to teach me, to tell them what they needed to see, how they needed to see it. I think in that sense my naïveté was probably a very valuable asset in the therapy in some strange way."

Not only would Frank become one of Wexler's most devoted and committed long-term patients, but he would also grow close to Wexler's family, particularly his daughter Nancy, and would become deeply involved in the medical research foundation that the Wexlers founded, the Hereditary Disease Foundation, to fight Huntington's disease.* Most important, Milton Wexler would become Frank's mentor, counselor, and adviser, an older person whose judgment he trusted and whom he would turn to first to help him through any difficult period. It could not have been hard to see that Frank viewed Wexler as the father Irving had been incapable of being: an ideal father he respected and sought out, not a father he tolerated with a mix of love, anger, and frustration.

When Frank wrote about his first experience with Wexler's therapy group, he recounted the story primarily in terms of its effect on his professional life, and how he learned he could attract more clients and satisfy them more fully if he could manage to see their projects as they saw them, not merely through his own eyes. In a sense, he was also acknowledging that for all the solidarity and sense of common purpose he felt with artists, he knew that his obligations as an architect were different. He was a creator, but a creator who had to listen to his clients.

It was hardly the case that Frank was unable to hear his clients' requests before he entered therapy and that Milton Wexler transformed him in one triumphant moment into a caring and responsive listener. But he did come over time to believe that he could not be successful without an engaged and sympathetic client, that he had as much responsibility as the client in building a relationship, and that his projects could improve as a result of changes suggested by clients. He did not mind having a design go through multiple iterations in response to clients' comments, and he believed that good feedback improved his work. In fact, as his career went on, the criticisms that would bother him most were not complaints from people who found his buildings startling or even ugly, but protests that he was inflexible and arbitrary. When he was viewed as an artist who could only go his own way rather than as an architect who could respond to clients, he felt as if he were not just being criticized, but misunderstood in a fundamental way. If Frank was disappointed when people did not like his architecture, he would be deeply hurt, even angered, by accusations that he shaped his buildings entirely out of his own head and did not engage in discourse with his clients. Nothing bothered him more than the suggestion that he was not able to listen.

---

* Milton Wexler's wife had Huntington's disease. Although the Wexlers were divorced, Wexler devoted much of his life to the cause of the genetic disease that would affect others in his family.

The help Milton Wexler gave Frank in understanding his own creative process extended over many years, but Wexler moved more quickly to help him through other, more personal issues in his life. Like any therapist, Wexler delved into his patients' past, and Frank talked about his grandparents, his parents, and in particular the unresolved issues he had with his father. "Milton gave Frank a second childhood—he re-raised him," said Nan Peletz, a painter and architect who met Frank though Philip Johnson.

And Wexler led him to a resolution of his most immediate personal problem, which was what to do about his marriage. Frank had agonized over his unhappiness for so long that the state of indecision itself had become a part of his self-identity, and he knew he had trouble giving it up. The decision was only made harder by Wexler helping him to understand that he had contributed to the troubled state of his marriage not only by his physical absences, but also by being emotionally absent and withdrawn much of the time when he was physically present. "I held away from her because she pushed me away, and I let myself be pushed away because it was nasty," he said.

In August 1966, Frank and Anita had a particularly painful conversation about their marriage, during which Anita not only berated him again for spending too little time with her and the girls, but confessed she was having an affair. Frank was actually relieved as much as he was angry. Her infidelity made his decision at least somewhat easier, and it relieved his guilt about his own indiscretions. He did not confess to her that he had been having an affair with Donna O'Neill, whom he had met through Milton Wexler, and who had become a client. It was simpler to take the moral high ground in regard to Anita, even though he was fully aware that he did not deserve it. He knew leaving would mean stepping away from his children, breaking up his nuclear family. He went to see Wexler the next day, and the therapist told him that time had run out: he needed to make a decision. "Milton said, 'Look, I can't keep on treating you, it is too nebulous,'" Frank recalled. "'So here is the game. If you want to continue, you go home and leave, you move out on your own, or you commit for three months to stay there and make it work.' I looked at him and said, 'I will take the former.' And I went."

Frank went back home and told Anita he was moving out. Then he went straight to the home of actor Ben Gazzara and his wife, the actress Janice Rule, whose casual Sunday afternoon parties he had been attending for some time, often with John Altoon and his wife, Babs. He felt comfortable with the Gazzaras and told them of his decision. In Frank's recollection, the Gazzaras said he would feel better if he were in a comfortable place where his household needs were taken care of and "not in some sad-sack bachelor apartment." They called the Beverly Wilshire Hotel and reserved a room for him, and he checked in that night.

Anita and the girls remained at the house in Westwood. Things did not get easier once Frank had made his decision, and the divorce was not a cordial one. Anita remained angry, and did all she could to limit Frank's access to his children; she also told Richard Snyder, her brother, that she did not want him to remain in contact with Frank. She told Frank's mother and sister, both of whom adored Leslie and Brina, that they were no longer welcome, and that they should no longer consider the children a part of their lives. If either Thelma or Doreen tried to speak to the girls by telephone, Anita would hang up the phone, and when Thelma tried to visit the house, she slammed the door in the face of the woman who was her children's grandmother.

The marriage had lasted fourteen years, and Anita apparently concluded that if it was truly finished, she wanted as few reminders of Frank in her life as possible. The one exception was the house on Kennard Avenue, where Anita would live for the rest of her life, including through her subsequent marriage to George Brenner, whose last name, to Frank's distress, Leslie would decide to take as her own, becoming Leslie Brenner, as powerful a sign as there could be that the family he had made with Anita no longer existed.

8
Independence

Frank arrived at the Beverly Wilshire Hotel with no plan as to how long he would remain there, or where he would go afterward. He could not easily afford the $60 per night cost, but he realized that Ben and Janice Gazzara had been right: he needed an alternative to rattling around a dreary, empty bachelor apartment, where his loneliness would be unbearable. A posh hotel in the middle of Beverly Hills was, if nothing else, an upbeat distraction. A more prominent Los Angeles bachelor, Warren Beatty, also lived at the Beverly Wilshire, and Frank would see him from time to time.

"He had to go someplace to lick his wounds, and he went to the fanciest place he could find," his sister, Doreen, said. "He didn't have a penny. It was a really incredible thing to do." Frank, Doreen thought, was trying to make a conscious break with his past, and went to the Beverly Wilshire in part as a way of trying out a new identity. "He became a playboy. And that's what I felt. But he didn't have it in him. I mean, he was a fake playboy. Because he's not that kind of guy," his sister said.

Whether or not the identity of a playboy living in a fancy hotel suited him, Frank could hardly afford it, and after three months, he moved out. A colleague from Victor Gruen's office let him know of a studio apartment that was available in a high-rise building on Doheny Drive at the edge of West Hollywood, and Frank moved into it, even though it offered no place for his children to stay if they visited, and had the anonymous quality of a newly divorced man's apartment that he had been hoping to avoid. But for the moment, it would do.

M ilton Wexler did not set up his therapy groups primarily as a way of helping his patients to meet one another, but it almost seemed that way for Frank. His connections to people in the movie business stemmed largely from people he first met in Wexler's group: Blake Edwards, Carol Burnett, Jennifer Jones, and Dudley Moore all became friends, and some of them became clients as well. So did Donna O'Neill, the friend whom Moses had sent to Wexler before he urged Frank to consult the therapist. Donna O'Neill's husband, Richard, had inherited a large ranch in San Juan Capistrano, south of Los Angeles, and the O'Neills, who lived most of the time in Los Angeles, wanted to build a series of structures on the ranch, culminating in a new house. Richard O'Neill wanted the buildings to be inexpensive, and they turned to Frank.

The O'Neills would end up building only a simple hay barn, which Frank remembers as costing $2,500. But it would become one of his most important early structures, and the first building whose form would clearly show the influence of his discussions with his artist friends. The O'Neill hay barn is like a piece of minimalist sculpture, as the Danziger Studio had been, but this time the simple shape of the box has been replaced by a trapezoid, and the brooding, solid quiet of Danziger replaced by an active sense of movement, even intensity. It goes without saying that there is more architecture here than the simple task of protecting hay and farm implements from the weather could possibly have required: Frank, finding a client who he felt understood him and was sympathetic to his experimentation, was not going to let the opportunity pass.

Still, the structure hardly feels overdone. It consists of a set of columns (actually telephone poles), arranged to form a large rectangle. Sitting atop them is a trapezoidal roof, tilted so that it is lowest on one corner and highest on the diagonally opposite corner, which creates a powerful perspective illusion; the building looks from one corner as if it were about to fly away, and from another as if it were far larger than it is. The walls, which do not reach the ground, are made of corrugated metal. If the shape is something of a conceit given the simplicity of the program, the structure as a whole still conveys a sense of spareness, not of excess. Frank used simple, basic materials, and arranged them in such a way as to create a structure of unexpected power, not to say beauty. To make something both unexpected and beautiful out of ordinary materials would become a goal of much of Frank's work, and the O'Neill hay barn, minor work though it is, stands as a remarkably resolved beginning to that quest.

The O'Neill hay barn, which was intended as the beginning of a series of structures on the O'Neill ranch

Frank wanted to do something special for Donna O'Neill. He had known the O'Neills for some time, but soon after he received the commission, which was before his marriage to Anita had ended, he and Donna became lovers. He was "madly in love," he recalled. Donna was flamboyant, arty, and in every way "a free spirit—she did what she wanted," Frank said. It was hard to imagine a woman who, outwardly at least, could be more different from Anita. Their relationship began one evening following a cocktail party with many of Frank's artist friends at the apartment the O'Neills maintained in Hollywood. Anita was not present. There was no food, only drink, and toward the end of the party the group, thoroughly drunk, decided to adjourn to a nearby restaurant. Frank was a bit puzzled when Donna—"dressed in black, like Carmen from the opera"—asked him if she could ride along with him rather than with her husband, but he wanted to be courteous, so he agreed. Shortly after the group had arrived at the restaurant, Donna announced that she was not feeling well, and asked Frank if he could drive her home. "I was innocent. I looked around and thought her husband should drive her home," Frank said. "She said, no, she wanted me to drive her. So I got the car and drove her. She said, 'I don't feel good, you better carry me in.' I took her in, she pulled me into the bedroom, flopped on the bed, grabbed me by the neck, and pulled me down. What do you do? He's going to be coming home in about thirty minutes and here I am wrestling with his wife. It was one of those life-changing experiences. I got out of there before he got home."

The next morning, Frank was scheduled to meet the O'Neills at the ranch to talk about their building project. He called Ed Moses first thing in the morning, terrified that Richard O'Neill would have discovered what had happened and would order his wife to cancel the appointment. Moses laughed and told him that he was not the first man that Donna had seduced, and that Richard knew of her affairs. So Frank drove to San Juan Capistrano. "I went to the ranch to meet them and if you don't think I felt awkward looking at her, looking at him, trying to figure out what they wanted me to do," he said. "Finally, Dick left and she grabbed me again. We became really close, friends. She came along at a time when I needed that desperately. We hung out for about six months."

The relationship was not always smooth. One day Donna asked Frank to meet her for a drink at the Beverly Hills Hotel, and he expected that the two of them would remain together for the evening. Instead, Donna said she wanted to meet at the hotel because she had plans to see a friend from out of town who was staying there, and that she was heading to his room. Frank was shaken: it was a cruel way to end a relationship. Weeks later, Donna called and told Frank she still wanted to see him, and asked him to come down to the ranch in San Juan Capistrano. Frank, still infatuated with her, agreed. They continued to see each other on and off, but the relationship gradually transformed into a warm friendship that continued until Donna's death, several years later, from cancer. In 1973, long after their romantic relationship had ended, Donna hosted an extravagant benefit at the ranch for Milton Wexler's foundation fighting Huntington's disease. The event confirmed the ongoing tightness of the Wexler Hollywood circle: Ben Gazzara, Gena Rowlands, Peter Falk, Elaine May, Walter Matthau, and John Cassavetes were all there, along with Frank, Ed Moses, Billy Al Bengston, and Tony Berlant.

The hay barn, which Frank would call "a labor of love," would turn out to be the only thing he ever managed to build on the property. He designed a house as well, but it was never constructed. Richard O'Neill may not have been as tolerant of his wife's extramarital activities as Ed Moses had thought. O'Neill never paid Frank's fee, perhaps assuming that it had been paid in the form of his friendship with Donna.

In 1967, at around the same time the O'Neill barn was under construction, two other women would take on roles in Frank's life. One was a beautiful, shy, but self-assured Panamanian named Berta Aguilera; the other was a lively, outgoing woman named Babs Altoon, the wife of the artist John Altoon. By then Frank had moved his office to a building on San Vicente Boulevard in Brentwood, just east of Santa Monica, and the practice was large enough to need an office manager. Berta had recently arrived in Los Angeles from Panama and was working for an insurance company, living with a cousin, and looking for a more interesting job. Through a roundabout series of connections that involved a bartender at the Daisy, a bar Frank and several of the artists frequented, and the bartender's wife who worked with Berta's cousin at a hairdressing salon, she heard about the opening in Frank's office and went for an interview. Frank took an instant liking to her, and he told her that the most important part of the job was answering the phone and protecting him from interruptions when he was designing.

Berta

Berta's English was far from perfect, but she understood enough to realize that she would have a hard time handling a job that involved so much use of the telephone. She was deeply disappointed, because she found everything else about Frank's office much more appealing than the insurance company. But she was certain it wouldn't work, and she thought Frank was as aware of the problem as she was. Frank, however, thought he had actually offered Berta the job, and that she would come back a couple of weeks later to start work. When she never showed up, he called her and asked her to dinner. She accepted, thinking he intended only to press her further to come and work for him. Berta did not at first realize that the invitation—which was to Casa d'Oro, a casual Italian restaurant on Santa Monica Boulevard, near his old house in Westwood—was her first date with the man she would eventually marry. Not long afterward Frank would introduce her to several of his friends at a barbecue on the roof of Billy Al Bengston's studio in Venice, and they began to be seen as a couple.

When Berta did not become Frank's office manager, he offered the job to Babs, who had once considered becoming an architect and was looking for work. She said yes, and stayed for two years, during which time she and John, who had always been good friends of Frank, became still closer to him. After working with Greg for as long as he had, Frank had no hesitation about employing a friend, and he liked that he was extending a helping hand. The help was reciprocal: for most of the time until John Altoon's sudden death in 1969, Frank would have dinner at the Altoons' every Thursday night. He considered John Altoon one of the most gifted artists he knew, and like the others in the artists' group, he felt that Altoon had a particular magnetism. In Billy Al Bengston's words, "We were all scratching for the kind of style and grace that he embodied. He was a totally brilliant craftsman and an intuitive observer, much more so than any of us. You could take him into a place where you are the best friend of everybody and after five minutes nobody would talk to you. They couldn't stay away from him. He was a total magnet. One day I went over to visit his studio and Lenny Bruce was in there taking notes. [Altoon had] a sense of humor, balance, style, grace."

He was also seriously bipolar, and was on heavy medication. One night early in 1969, the Altoons were at a party along with Bengston, and John complained of not feeling well. Bengston offered to drive him home or, if necessary, to the hospital, and shortly after they got into his car he realized that they were near the home of Leonard Asher, a doctor and art collector whom they all knew. So they drove instead to Asher's house, where Asher gave him some medication. Altoon began to have convulsions, and a few minutes later he was dead, presumably of a heart attack.

It was a huge loss for the group, not only because Altoon's promising artistic career was cut short at age forty-three, but also because Altoon's large, generous personality had been so central to the dynamic of the artists' circle. "I think it was all held together by John Altoon. He was like the pope of the scene, and we all revered him," Frank said. "He was a little more out there than everybody else, and everybody was just in awe of that. When he died, the joint split apart. It wasn't the same afterwards."[*]

---

[*] Altoon's reputation did not take off after his death, as is sometimes the case with an artist, and he has never been as well known as Ed Ruscha, Billy Al Bengston, Ken Price, Larry Bell, or many of the other Los Angeles artists. That Altoon had destroyed much of his work, probably as a result of his illness, did not help, since not a large body of his art remains. But

Babs Altoon was devastated, and too shaken to continue in her job. She went off on a short vacation in Hawaii with Ed Janss, a prominent collector who was friendly with many of the artists, including Frank, and Janss's wife and child.* When Babs returned, Frank decided that she needed a longer time away from Los Angeles. He had an obligation in Columbia, Maryland, in conjunction with the projects he was doing for the Rouse Company there, and he suggested that she accompany him there. She could see some of the work that she had known in her role as office manager. After that, he told her, they could go on to New York.

They would end up going much farther. In New York, they attended a dinner party given by the artist Roy Lichtenstein and his wife, Dorothy, and saw other friends, mostly from the art world. At the Lichtensteins' Frank saw that Babs was still having a difficult time. "I said, 'Babs, you've got to get away. Why don't you go to London?' She said, 'Would you want to go?' I said, 'I'll take you.' So we went. In those days, you could just buy a ticket. Within hours, we were flying to London. We had no idea where we were going, where we were going to stay," Frank said.

In London, Frank and Babs found a hotel and took adjacent rooms. They considered each other friends, not romantic partners, and by then Frank had been dating Berta fairly regularly. He and Babs talked easily with each other about their intimate feelings, a relationship that may have been made easier by the fact that neither had romantic expectations. They made a joking pact that when they turned sixty-five, they would marry, which Berta found amusing. ("When sixty-five came and went, we said, 'Let's make it seventy-five,'" Babs remembered. "Seventy-five came and went, and we've never discussed it again.") Babs became for Frank almost like another sister. He felt protective of her in a way that he would of few people who were not members of his family. In London, he remembered, he heard the sound of her crying through the wall between their rooms, and he tried to cheer her up by taking her shopping for clothes on Carnaby Street. They shopped first for things for Babs, and then Frank asked her for advice on choosing a few things he could bring back as gifts for Berta.

---

his paintings and drawings, both abstract and figurative, are among the finest works to have come out of Los Angeles in the 1950s and 1960s. In 2014 the Los Angeles County Museum of Art mounted a major retrospective of Altoon's work, organized by the curator Carol Eiler, and two books of his work were published at the same time. Thus forty-five years after his death an Altoon revival can be said to have begun.

* Frank would design a house in Los Angeles for Ed Janss a few years later, which Janss would build with several adjustments to Frank's plans, making it an early but significantly compromised Gehry residence.

During the course of their stay in London they saw a number of friends, some of whom mistook them for a couple and did not seem to believe Frank's demurrals. One night Frank brought Babs to dinner with the architectural historian Reyner Banham, who was back home in London writing his book about Los Angeles. But Babs's spirits barely lifted in London, so Frank decided to try crossing the Channel to Paris. He took her to the Champs-Élysées to see André Remondet's architecture office, where he had worked, and then to other places where he had spent time when he and Anita lived in Paris. It was Frank's "memory lane" trip, Babs realized, but she didn't particularly mind, and she enjoyed seeing places that had been important in his life. Later in the trip, high on some marijuana they had brought along, they went to the Eiffel Tower, took the elevator to the top, and ran all the way down the stairs. Finally, Babs began to relax. "We were screaming and hollering, and having so much fun. We went, did the whole goddamn thing, all the way to the bottom," Frank said.

Later, Babs would leave Los Angeles and return to New York, where she would become especially close to the artist Jasper Johns, whom she had met years before, when Johns had been in Los Angeles working on a series of his early prints. John Altoon did not get along with Johns, but Babs liked him, and their friendship grew after Altoon's death. She had introduced Frank to Johns when Altoon was still alive, and over time Frank and Johns became close as well. It would be a significant friendship, since by then Frank was becoming as interested in New York artists as he was in their counterparts in Los Angeles. His close connection to the Los Angeles art scene would never diminish, but his interest in Johns, Roy Lichtenstein, and others was a sign of more than the enthusiasm he felt for the art they were producing. It was a clear way of giving himself a broader reach beyond Los Angeles. Ed Moses and Billy Al Bengston might be known as Los Angeles artists, but Frank Gehry was not going to be known forever as a Los Angeles architect.

Frank would give Johns some help with renovations to his studio on Houston Street in Lower Manhattan. He soon became friendly with James Rosenquist, Claes Oldenburg, and Robert Rauschenberg, among others. Rauschenberg, already one of Frank's most important artistic influences, would become another close friend. The artist's "combines," painting-sculpture hybrids that integrated found objects into painted canvases, were among the first works of postwar high art to include ordinary, everyday, cheap objects, and Frank found them exciting, not to say liberating. If an artist as serious as Rauschenberg could use found objects, Frank felt, this legitimized his instincts about using cheap ordinary materials in serious architecture. Without Rauschenberg, Frank felt, he might not have had the nerve to bring chain-link fencing or unfinished plywood into his buildings.

Jasper Johns would establish an even more important connection when he introduced Frank to one of his closest friends in New York, a freelance curator named David Whitney. Whitney, who was close to most of the New York artists, especially Andy Warhol, would become a good friend of Frank's. He was also the partner of the well-known architect Philip Johnson, whose work at the time, a somewhat decorative and highly personal variation on classicism, could not have been further from Frank's own. In fact, it was exactly the kind of architecture that Frank found insipid. But Johnson, who was also an architectural historian and the first head of the architecture and design department of the Museum of Modern Art, was a powerful intellectual presence in the field, whatever his own work may have been like. By the late 1960s he had already assumed the role he would play for the rest of his life as simultaneously the dean, patron, éminence grise, and Svengali of the architecture world. Frank was eager to meet him, and he assumed that once he had come to know both Jasper Johns and David Whitney, an invitation to meet the master would follow quickly.

But it did not. "It's too soon," Jasper Johns told him. "You're not ready yet."

Frank's relationship with the Rouse Company began almost by accident. David O'Malley, a former colleague from Victor Gruen's office in Los Angeles, handled Gruen's work for Rouse, a large shopping center developer, and had recently moved to Maryland, where Rouse was based, to be closer to his client. The company considered itself one of the more enlightened builders of shopping malls in the country, and its founder, James Rouse, was by any measure an unusual real estate developer: despite having made much of his fortune in suburban shopping malls, he was sincerely interested in urban planning, affordable housing, and equal opportunity, and cared deeply about the future of cities. In time he would become known for building "festival marketplaces," large urban retail complexes like Fanueil Hall in Boston and the Inner Harbor in Baltimore, a genre he all but invented. In the mid-1960s, however, his focus was on building an entirely new town outside Baltimore that he envisioned as an ideal community, and to which he gave the name Columbia.

O'Malley was eager to play a role in Columbia, and he saw it as a way of leaving Gruen and going out on his own. But he did not feel he could do it by himself, and thought of Frank as an ideal partner. He persuaded Frank to come to a party at his house in Maryland when Frank came east on other business, and introduced him to Mort Hoppenfeld, an architect who had joined Rouse's staff to oversee the planning and design of the new town. "I didn't know I was being interviewed, but I was being interviewed," Frank said. "He said he wanted me to come back and meet with Jim Rouse." Frank told Hoppenfeld that he was tired of traveling on his own and didn't want to leave his wife and children to return east again so soon, and Hoppenfeld invited him to bring Anita and the girls along. All four Gehrys returned to Maryland the following weekend, and Rouse and Frank met. They hit it off quickly. Though Rouse's aesthetic taste was far more conventional than Frank's—indeed, it was almost conservative— Frank found everything else about him appealing. The developer, he said, was "a do-gooder like me. . . . He was liberal, he was interested in a lot of the same things I was—people and human scale." Rouse clearly took just as quickly to Frank. Before the Gehrys left on Sunday, Mort Hoppenfeld called to offer Frank the position of chief architect for Columbia.

He turned it down. "I said, 'Look, I just spent my life starting, getting ready to start a practice. I have an office in Santa Monica. It doesn't have a lot of work. But I'm independent and I don't want to go back. Thank you very much. I'd love to work with you, but thank you very much.' Anita and I got on a plane." It seemed as if Frank had once again passed up an opportunity for financial security because he feared it would compromise his independence. It was becoming a common pattern in his life.

Yet when the Gehrys got home to Los Angeles late Sunday night, they got a phone call. "It's Mort Hoppenfeld, [who said,] 'Oh, okay. We know you won't come work for us, but we want you to do the first building, so come back tomorrow,'" Frank remembered Hoppenfeld telling him. "So Monday, I was on the plane, and that's what I did." It was the beginning of an eleven-year relationship that would ultimately bring Frank ten different commissions, including his first large buildings, his first venue for music performance, and his first opportunity to actually build one of his designs for an office building. This time, holding firm for his independence hadn't cost him the work. He could have his freedom and get the big jobs—or so it seemed.

Frank had no desire to relocate to the East Coast, so it made sense to join forces with Dave O'Malley, just as O'Malley had hoped. O'Malley resigned from Gruen, and along with Greg Walsh became a part of almost all of Frank's enterprises. The three formed a new firm: Gehry, Walsh & O'Malley, with offices in California and Maryland. The new operation was legally separate from the original office in California, but all three men had a partial ownership interest in both firms.

The new firm's first venture was a small exhibition building for Columbia, where the developer could showcase plans for the new town. It was followed by a firehouse, and then by the first of Frank's buildings to receive major public attention, the Merriweather Post Pavilion, an outdoor concert hall seating three thousand that Rouse had commissioned to accommodate summer concerts by the Washington Philharmonic at Columbia. Both the schedule and the budget were exceptionally tight. Gehry, Walsh & O'Malley had seventy working days, or roughly three months, and less than half a million dollars to work with. More confining still, Frank was required to use a steel joist roofing system that had already been ordered by Rouse. Rouse and the engineers had for all intents begun to design the project. Frank was brought in to try to give it architectural resonance while remaining within the parameters already set.

He did so in a way that confirmed his ability to use simple, straightforward materials and work within tight constraints and come up with an unusual and notable piece of architecture. The pavilion is the O'Neill hay barn writ large. The dominant feature of the design is a huge, trapezoidal roof, set on an angle and supported by six columns. The roof is fan-shaped, widening as it moves away from the stage. The steel joists supporting it are exposed, and the sides are covered in unstained Douglas fir.

The pavilion opened on an unforgettable night in 1967. A heavy storm came up just after the concert began, and because there had not yet been time to finish the walkways around the pavilion, concertgoers had to exit by walking through mud under torrents of rain, only to find their parked cars mired in deeper mud. The party Rouse had planned to celebrate the opening was washed out entirely. In spite of the conditions, the concert itself came off without a hitch, and both Frank's design and the work of Christopher Jaffe, the acoustician, were well received, all the more because the horrendous weather seemed to have minimal effect on the quality of the sound in the hall. It received a positive review from Harold Schonberg, the music critic of *The New York Times*, who called it "an unqualified architectural and acoustic success . . . probably the best-sounding outdoor hall in the United States. It may be hard to believe, but the Merriweather Post Pavilion of Music is better than most regulation concert halls. . . .

Never does one have to strain to listen. The hall is large, but it has the intimacy of a much smaller enclosure."

Frank had returned to Los Angeles by the time Schonberg's review appeared in the following Sunday's edition of the *Times*. He was spending his usual Sunday afternoon at the home of Ben and Janice Gazzara. He remembered, "Esther Williams and Fernando Lamas were there, as were other dignitaries of the silver screen. Ben was saving the review because he was so proud of me, and he read it out loud. When he finished reading it, I swam in the pool with Esther and Fernando. I had arrived."

Rouse was happy working with Gehry, Walsh & O'Malley, but after the first few projects were completed, Frank had serious second thoughts about the partnership. David O'Malley had proven to be almost too enthusiastic a partner. He was so determined to build the firm into a sizable practice that he had lined up far more work on the East Coast than Frank could keep up with, including plenty of projects that had nothing to do with Rouse. O'Malley was happy to design the smaller projects himself and not bother Frank with them, but in Frank's view that only made things worse. It was one thing to have O'Malley as a partner executing projects Frank had designed, but quite another to have him designing things himself that would have Frank's name attached to them. Frank wanted the office to be successful, but not to the point of churning out designs that weren't his and that he didn't like. He told O'Malley that he wanted to dissolve their partnership. He offered to turn over to O'Malley his share of their joint firm in exchange for O'Malley's giving up his share of ownership of the operation in Los Angeles.

Once again, Frank had decided to walk away from a lucrative situation because he felt his independence, and in this case his reputation, was threatened. He assumed this would mean the end of the work with Rouse and that his former partner would continue on his own as the company's architect. When the partnership was dissolved, Frank went to see Mort Hoppenfeld, who had been his original backer at Rouse, and explained his decision. "Thank God," Frank remembers Hoppenfeld saying when he heard that the partners were splitting. "We want you to do our new headquarters, and we don't want him."

Frank had been prepared to walk away—in fact, he had walked away—but this time he had been given the chance to return on his own terms. Jim

Rouse agreed with Hoppenfeld's suggestion that Frank design the company's new headquarters, which would be on a suburban site in Columbia, and Gehry & Walsh, minus O'Malley, was given the job. The project in many ways would be the opposite of the music pavilion. It would have a long timetable, and a more generous budget. Frank was awarded the commission in 1969, and the building would not open until 1974.*

The Rouse headquarters is a long building of white stucco, three stories high, with horizontal windows of dark glass, and its massing stepped back in certain sections to allow for open terraces. From a distance it appears more like a conventional suburban office building than it is. Wooden pergolas surround the building at its base and cover some of the terraces, their softer different texture, warmer material, and smaller scale playing off against the crisp form of the white stucco and glass. Inside, Frank was more innovative. The building is an early experiment in open office design, and one of the first to have a raised floor with wires running underneath, allowing for complete flexibility of workstations and office partitions. The lighting was indirect, shooting upward from fixtures Frank designed to reflect off the smooth ceiling, which was unencumbered by ducts, since all heating and air-conditioning vents were in columns. The interior was anchored by a central "street," a skylit atrium that gently hinted at the design of a shopping mall.

Some of the lighting innovations at Rouse emerged out of designs Frank had been developing for another commercial client, Joseph Magnin, the California department store. Rudi Baumfeld and Edgardo Contini from Victor Gruen's office had suggested to Magnin that Frank would be a good choice to design the interiors of two new stores, one in Costa Mesa and the other in Almaden, near San Jose. Magnin was a client that had more in common with the Rouse Company than with the O'Neills, but Frank never considered himself above commercial work, and he willingly took it on. A department store was a fascinating problem—a machine for selling—and he was intrigued by the challenge of figuring out how his

---

* Rouse remained in the building for forty years. In 2004, the Rouse Company was sold to General Growth Properties, which continued to use the bulding as a regional office. In 2014, the Howard Hughes Corporation, the successor to General Growth, converted the building into a Whole Foods supermarket. Hughes was respectful of the building's pedigree. A press release from the county executive praised the conversion as "preserving and highlighting this Frank Gehry original." Later, Hughes would establish a much more substantial relationship with Frank's firm and invite Gehry Partners to prepare a design for a condominium tower in Honolulu.

architectural instincts could yield a new department store that would both function better and be more aesthetically appealing than the familiar older ones.

He took on two collaborators: Gere Kavanagh, his longtime friend and officemate, and a newer officemate, Deborah Sussman, a Los Angeles graphic designer who had formerly been with Charles and Ray Eames and had opened her own practice, which she first based at a spare desk in the San Vicente office of Gehry & Walsh. Their contributions turned out to be essential: both women, each of whom took charge of one of the Magnin stores, brought a vital degree of color and energy to the designs, rescuing them from what might have been, for Frank, an uncharacteristic degree of austerity.*

Frank's notion was that department stores had become a cluttered mess, with poor design overshadowing the merchandise itself, and he wanted to simplify the look in the hope that the things on sale would take on more prominence. And he thought that the rapid changes in fashion should allow a department store interior to be far more flexible than it had been. "The usual store is a static type of thing. But fashion isn't static. It's fickle and changeable," he told *Furnishings Daily,* which published pictures of the first Magnin store under the headline "Things to Come . . . Now."

The design was clean, if hardly minimalist: Frank designed a hidden lighting system at Costa Mesa capable of changing the color of the light on the selling floor, and for Almaden tall display modules he called "trees" that were freestanding square columns that held merchandise on all sides, topped by large panels facing in all four directions that could be changed to accommodate any kind of graphic design or signage. The trees were at once signs and racks, they could be seen from across the floor, and they could be added or subtracted easily. It allowed the store manager to "experiment, change and refine the display systems, the departmental relationships, and the décor," Frank told *Stores* magazine. "He doesn't just have to make the best of a given inflexible environment, which doesn't permit him to change his mind."

Frank's most striking, or at least his most purely architectural, innovation was the glass display boxes he placed in front of the façade of the Costa Mesa store. They were as tall as a traditional department store window, and

---

* Sussman, often with her longtime partner Paul Preszja, would go on to become one of Los Angeles's most celebrated graphic designers. The firm of Sussman & Preszja was in charge of the graphic identity for the 1984 Los Angeles Olympics and did numerous projects for the Walt Disney Company, among other prominent clients. Sussman died in 2014.

at least as big. With one gesture he had transformed the window from a two-dimensional element to a three dimensional one, and transcended the flat, blank façade of the typical suburban department store.

F rank had not been happy in the small apartment on Doheny Drive that he had taken after leaving the Beverly Wilshire. It was too small to allow him to host his daughters, and it was a long drive from West Hollywood to Santa Monica and Brentwood, where his office, most of his friends, and most of his day-to-day life were. It was also far from the water—from Marina del Rey in particular, where Frank kept a small boat and liked to sail. Years before, some friends at USC had introduced him to sailing, and while he had neither the time nor the money to pursue it avidly, it had become over the years something more than a casual pastime. For a long time he would rent sailboats with Sam Rose, a Rouse executive who was also a sailor, and eventually the two bought a small sailboat together. Frank felt relaxed on the water. It was an escape from the stresses that seemed always to surround him, and there was something he particularly liked about the purity of a sailboat. "The sails," he would say later, "make an architectural space."

There was a much more convenient housing option on the west side of Los Angeles that fit Frank's needs perfectly, an apartment that he still had in the Hillcrest building in Santa Monica. But Frank had turned it over some time ago to Doreen and her husband, Rolf Nelson. Milton Wexler encouraged Frank to tell Doreen that he was sorry, but that he needed to take the apartment back and that she and Rolf would have to leave. Frank was reluctant. It seemed cruel to do that to his sister. But the more he thought about it the more he began to feel that only a sense of martyrdom could allow him to remain in cramped and inconvenient quarters at Doheny solely so Doreen could go on living at Hillcrest, in real estate that belonged to him.

Wexler was not one to encourage his patients to feel like martyrs, and the therapist "egged me on so I could move into my own apartment and I would have more self-respect," Frank said. "So I evicted Doreen. Essentially I said, 'I have a very bad need and you guys should figure out something else.'" Doreen left—she had no choice—but she was furious. She did not speak to her brother for months, and their relationship, which had always interwoven both deep affection and sibling rivalry, would be shaky for a long time afterward.

Having a more respectable place to live would also help Frank's deepening relationship with Berta. There was not yet talk of marriage, but they were spending more and more time together, and Frank was increasingly coming to appreciate Berta's fierce intelligence, her warm spirit, and her deep loyalty to him. She seemed as grounded and as comfortable in her own skin as Anita had been insecure, and the contrast to his former wife was instantly apparent. Berta was beautiful, soft-spoken, and gracious. Most important of all, she was fascinated by Frank's work but seemed indifferent to the fame and celebrity that were beginning to attach to it. Frank was far from immune to the lure of friendships with famous and powerful people—his artist friends had been teasing him about name-dropping for years—and he knew how rare it was to come across someone who admired him for his creative gifts, could support him emotionally, and yet keep him grounded at the same time. Berta's great strength, Billy Al Bengston said, was that she could be both Frank's "support mechanism [and] shit detector," capable of protecting Frank not only from everyday pressures but also from the riskier side of his own ambition.

T he artist Ron Davis was something of a latecomer to the Los Angeles group. He was born in the city, but grew up and went to school in Wyoming, and did not come back to his hometown until the mid-1960s, after he had begun to establish his career as a painter. It was long after the early days of the Ferus Gallery, but Davis, who was roughly the same age as many of the artists in the Ferus group, came to know many of them well. It was no surprise that he and Frank became friends also.

He would become Frank's most important early residential client. In many ways it was a natural alliance: Davis's large, intensely colored abstractions explored geometric shapes and the illusions of perspective, which were among the issues that preoccupied Frank. Davis was interested in how the things he was trying to do in two dimensions would play out in three-dimensional space. He wanted an architect who would understand and respond to his work, and who would enjoy working in collaboration with him. And he had been successful enough as a painter that he had the wherewithal to build a stand-alone structure to serve as a house and studio.

Davis purchased a three-and-a-quarter-acre former horse farm in the Malibu hills, and in 1969 he asked Frank to work with him to design a building that would give him space to produce large paintings, to store his work, and to provide flexible living space. Those requirements were fairly easy to quantify. Davis's desire for the house to relate in some way to the ideas within his art was understandably more difficult. The first step, Esther McCoy would report in *Progressive Architecture*, was when Davis stretched string across the site to determine vanishing points. Davis and Frank would work on the design for the better part of three years, meeting weekly unless Frank's schedule took him out of town. It was, Davis said later, "a labor of love for him; he certainly didn't make any money on the project. I gave him a couple of paintings, and he gave me endless time and endless wisdom." Davis referred to the project as his "fantasy," and described Frank as "a marvelous architect who can relate to an artist's fantasies."

What Frank—or Frank and Ron Davis—came up with was a huge box of corrugated metal, trapezoidal in plan, with its roof slanted on an incline that reflected the slope of the mountains. The structure was nine feet high at its lowest corner and rose to twenty-nine feet at the highest. Setting a slanted roof atop walls that were not at right angles meant that all four walls were of constantly varying height. The walls were broken with large picture window openings, some of which were rectangular and some of which were trapezoids, and the front door was a huge square of glass set within a pivoting frame. Sections of the roof were cut out to create a twenty-foot-long opening for skylights.

The house owed a significant debt to the O'Neill hay barn, only here the ideas Frank had begun to explore in the hay barn expanded to the scale and complexity of a full-fledged building. The building was as plain as the hay barn in one sense. It cost only $16 a square foot, a minuscule amount even then. In the most literal sense the design was just an assemblage of straight lines making up four walls and a roof. The result, though, was anything but a simple box. The angles gave it a dramatic sense of perspective; the unusually shaped windows and skylights sent abstract shadow lines across the white walls and wood plank floors, and the whole achieved a sumptuousness that was all the more striking for the blunt, industrial quality of its shape and materials.

The fifty-eight-hundred-square-foot interior was largely open, a rural version of an artist's loft. Davis had specified that flexibility was important to him, and Frank at one point considered putting all the partitions on wheels, and even designed movable stairs to allow Davis to shift access to the platforms that gave some of the space an upper story. Both client and architect realized that the notion of partitions and stairs on wheels would in the end be a conceit, more clever than practical, and so Frank divided

Frank at work on the Ron Davis
house, 1970

the interior into a major living space, roughly seventeen feet high; a den and office area atop a balcony; a double-height dining area; a kitchen; and a master bedroom area, in addition to Davis's studio workspace. In the center, a long double partition contained two bathrooms within it as well as painting storage.

Davis moved into the house in 1972, and a few years later he and Frank would expand its living area by inserting additional balconies and partitions into the space, making the sections slightly more separate, if hardly conventional. "He decided he wanted rooms," Frank told *The New York Times* in 1977. "It's now completely different. But I think it's really okay." It was an early example of Frank's disinclination to play prima donna. Early on, he had referred to the house as "a big barn we could play with," and he was true to his word. If Ron Davis wanted things to be flexible, Frank was not going to argue, even if it meant that the original concept of the house was somewhat compromised.

By one interpretation, however, the Davis house was never quite as unconventional as it may have appeared to be. It was designed at a time when the austere boxes of glass, metal, wood, and concrete that had been modernism's ideal—the California houses of Neutra, Schindler, Soriano, Buff & Hensman, and many of Frank's other mentors—were in eclipse, and many architects were looking back toward the traditional, shedlike house shapes that the modernists had disdained in favor of their flat-roofed boxes and wondering if there was not something to be learned from them. Robert Venturi's house for his mother in Chestnut Hill, outside Philadelphia,* may have been the most mannered attempt to evoke the traditional image of the house, but in California, Charles Moore, Donlyn Lyndon, William Turnbull, and Richard Whitaker of MLTW had produced a more popu-

---

* See the discussion of Venturi in chapter 7.

lar, if not more academic, work of new architecture that alluded to old forms in their design for Sea Ranch, a vacation community on the coast north of San Francisco. Sea Ranch, completed in 1965, was an assemblage of wooden sheds with slanted roofs, carefully organized into a sculptural composition that stood out powerfully against the Pacific. Sea Ranch did not look like a traditional house, but it did not look like a modern box, either, and it had a gentle, amiable quality that was widely admired.

Was the Ron Davis house Frank's attempt to add his own somewhat different voice to that of the shedmakers as they broke away from modernist boxes? Or was it his attempt to be more modern still, to use cheap, industrial materials to create an object that would be tough, not easy, and that would make the last generation of California modernists seem, if not timid, then at least excessively genteel?

Not the least of the reasons the Ron Davis house remains such a powerful and important work is that Frank managed to do both of these things at once. The house underscores his tenuous but important connection to the postmodern movement in architecture that was coming into its own as he himself was establishing his own voice: he was motivated by many of the same issues that concerned the postmodernists, especially their feeling that modernist architecture was ascetic, limited in its emotional range. And he was comfortable, as the postmodernists were, looking at the architecture of the past and trying to learn from it.

But for Frank the architecture of the past could never be more than a kind of conceptual inspiration. It could certainly not be an object of even loose replication. He wanted things to be new, and he wanted to explore aspects of abstract form that the previous generation had not probed deeply enough. Ultimately he was dissatisfied with the simple modernist box not because it didn't do enough to call to mind elements of a traditional house—as Venturi, Moore, and other postmodernists would try to do in their work—but because it didn't push the invention of form far enough. The midcentury modern houses of California seemed prim to Frank. And if his voice as an architect had not yet been fully defined by the time he designed Ron Davis's house, it was certainly clear that it could not be called prim.[*]

---

[*] Davis and his wife lived in the house for many years, making internal adjustments from time to time, often in collaboration with Gehry. They eventually sold it and moved to Taos,

The Ron Davis house brought Gehry the widest recognition of his career to that point. Not only would Esther McCoy write about the house in *Progressive Architecture,* but it would be the subject of a story in *The New York Times Magazine,* then a prominent venue for the presentation of contemporary residential architecture, titled "Studied Slapdash." The *Times* piece, the first extended presentation of Frank's architecture in a national general-interest publication, said that "while Gehry has designed a space that offers a significant amount of freedom . . . he has subtly kept himself in control at the same time. The unusual space is never neutral: it forces one to think of the nature of space, the nature of walls, the nature of enclosures. Doing this is a primary mission of serious architecture, and for all its play at being casual this is serious architecture indeed."[*]

New Mexico. Subsequent owners, including the actor Patrick Dempsey, have protected the overall structure but have added elaborate landscaping outdoors and made the house more conventional within. *Architectural Digest* published a story on the house in 2014, referring to it as the "warm, artfully decorated home" of the actor and his family. The Dempseys' art collection includes a light sculpture by Robert Irwin and pieces by Ed Ruscha, however, so there is some distant connection to the house's origins. The house was sold in 2015 for $15 million.

[*] I was the author of the piece; it was the first time I wrote a story on Frank Gehry.

9
Easing the Edges

Frank was hardly timid, but his outward manner sometimes suggested a degree of hesitation, even reticence; he often hovered in the background, and he was neither a keeper of journals nor an active letter writer. But he was neither meek nor tentative in his views, and as he passed his fortieth birthday in the winter of 1969, it was clear that he was increasingly comfortable asserting himself. He did so very much in his own way, and he remained soft-spoken, with nothing in his personality, at least on the surface, that echoed the increasingly strong, even flamboyant character of his architecture. Milton Wexler had helped him understand that it was into his work that he needed to pour his turmoil and creative energy, and that his architecture was ultimately the most satisfying outlet he would have for his angst. His growing self-confidence as an architect and as a thinker did not play out in the creation of a self-conscious artist's persona; his manner remained easygoing and understated, even as his ego strengthened. The curious, enthusiastic, eager, and somewhat insecure person he had been in his twenties and thirties did not disappear as success and achievement were layered on top of it. Frank was ever more determined to have his way, and he was at least as ambitious as any of his architect or artist peers, but he did not remake himself to get what he wanted. Instead, he was figuring out, in part through Wexler, how to make the most of the personality he already had. He did not try to make his insecurity disappear by cloaking himself in arrogance. Instead, he became quite skilled at appearing to be far more relaxed and low-key than he actually was.

Not long after he turned forty, the magazine *Designers West* devoted a page to a commentary by Frank that summed up his views about architecture, creativity, and the future of his profession. It is a remarkable document, in part because while Frank was always comfortable talking to the press and giving interviews—and paid far more attention to what the press had to say about him than he would pretend—he actually wrote very little himself, and so it stands as a rare position paper by an architect who, however freely and frequently he spoke about his work, has produced almost no writing about it.

The piece took the form of a short essay that opened with a powerful, almost subversive declaration. "Architects mostly practice in fear of their clients, and thereby compromise the quality of their service," Frank said. He went on:

> Our architectural vocabulary is better than our client's; our visual intellect is more highly evolved; we are the experts and that is why we are hired. I want to provide services at my highest possible level and to do so I have to deal with the real issues, the clearest statement of the problem uncluttered by "How it was done before" or "Give them what they want" hang-ups. I have to question every facet of the client's problem to be solved and finally assume responsibility for my solutions.

From anyone else, this might be a justification of the kind of self-importance and indifference to clients of which architects have often been accused. But Frank had not fallen prey to the allure of *The Fountainhead*, and he had no desire to remake himself in the image of Ayn Rand's smug Howard Roark. He did not deny that architecture was a service business as much as it was a creative pursuit. He did, after all, refer twice to the idea of serving clients, both times presenting the notion of service as a goal of his profession, not a roadblock to it.

So how does this jibe with Frank's interest in hearing what his clients wanted, and the comfort he had always felt in revising his designs in response to clients' comments? He had never wanted his clients to be completely passive, to be merely the patrons who would foot the bill for his fantasies. But he was even more frustrated by passive architects who treated the act of design as if they were merely order takers for their clients. He believed that an architect needed to bring to a project something that the client could not have imagined himself. If the architect could not inspire his or her client to accept fresh thinking, he felt, what was the point? As he had discovered a few years before, when he worked briefly for Pereira & Luckman, he wanted to be neither like William Pereira, who invented extravagant forms that often seemed disconnected from their uses, nor Charles Luckman, who brought almost no design ideas of his own to the table.

The *Designers West* essay went on to include Frank's thinking about the future of transportation and housing as well as his views about the values that should be inherent in architectural practice. He was remarkably prescient about a number of things, including the role of technology, and he understood that the pace of change was accelerating rapidly. "Buildings are less permanent—land values and rapidly changing needs make change the rule," he wrote. "We need a system which responds to what is really going on."

Frank's comments about transportation reject the notion of conventional public transit systems such as subways and monorails as inconsistent with the American preference for the automobile. How, then, to improve transportation and not violate the progressive political agenda to which he remained loyal? His idea here was to find a new way of making automobiles practical:

We thrash around with predigested solutions to a complicated problem we can't even define. The monorail, the subway and an improved ground system, even if they could be financed and built within a reasonable time don't begin to provide the flexibility and freedom of choice and prestige of the private automobile. We are hooked by our value system. A monorail might get the people out of the ghetto to get jobs but with their first paycheck they'll buy a car. Maybe if an analysis were made of all the costs involved in owning a car, including wasted time in traffic, parking at home and elsewhere, insurance, maintenance, etc. we might find out that for the same amount of money per capita per year you could have rental cars delivered as needed and taxicabs to fill in the gaps. Less cars would remain parked. It's an oversimplification but a thought.

Frank had, in effect, envisioned in 1969 a business that would appear four decades later: Zipcar.

The *Designers West* article also proposes that the technology of the space program, then at its height—it appeared just before American astronauts landed on the moon for the first time—be used as a way of providing power to residential buildings. "Suppose we separate a unit of dwelling into two parts: (1) The mechanical, electrical and waste disposal system, and call that the power pack; (2) the shelter," Frank wrote. He went on:

"Might it be possible to give part one as a problem to be solved by scientists and engineers. . . . I could imagine solutions using printed circuitry, solid state electronic packages, transistors, a system for capillary waste absorption, etc. etc. and with a lot of refinement something to be sold at Sears or White Front like any other appliance." His idea was that technology could function as a kind of "plug-in" system, suitable for any kind of house. "The shelter part becomes a problem to be solved to suit any taste level and any budget, but the power pack could be used for multi-family shelters, and for single-family shelters, from high-rise to tents," he wrote.

Most revealing of all were Frank's general observations on the practice of architecture, which he presented in a section called "On Goals":

> The value system we inherited and the combination not only of what we say we believe in but what we actually believe in when tested, is the force that moulds our environment. If we consider that force to be a train speeding along a track, we can be dragged along by it, we can hang on to it or we can be pushed by it. Somewhere up the track is a switch point where we can divert the train, just as somewhere there must be a point where the force of our value system can be modified. I'm trying to find that point in my work. Where do I have to be to effect a change? Where is the realistic point of attack? . . .
>
> To redesign the environment we really have to redesign our whole value system—question the sacred cows—and ask ourselves what we really want, what has priority.
>
> For each project in my office we define our goals and set up a priority system. As we work with the client and begin to absorb the pressures to compromise we have a yardstick to measure our changing course. This makes it possible to intelligently evaluate the pressure in terms of our goals and decide whether or not to accept the change and if not, having completely identified the pressure we can at least attempt to reason with it.
>
> In practice we find that this system forces a greater depth of involvement between architect and client in the programming and the whole design process ultimately leading to the solving of more aspects of a project than is usually possible.

Frank wanted to envision himself as a force for change in the profession, and he was characteristically pragmatic about his ambitions and how they might be executed. He was asking, rhetorically but sincerely, what would be the most effective way to bring about an unusual, not to say radical, vision. And he was explaining that he tried to operate his office with the same value system, with the goal of bringing rational analysis to what most people would almost surely consider unusual, even irrational, goals.

It was clear that by the spring of 1969, Frank had begun to see himself as an architect who would produce unusual forms that were not pure flights of fancy, but would be anchored in reason. That notion of highly imaginative form that, however unusual it might seem, would be a rational response both to human needs and to a client's specific program—that would not, in other words, be the arbitrary creation of an architect—would underlie the rest of his career.

Frank concluded the *Designers West* piece with a statement that at first might appear to contradict his commitment to rational thinking: "I suggest that we are really involved with illusion and maybe it's possible to develop an architecture of illusion. A system which satisfies mass taste levels but which is easily changeable and becomes a valuable tool to elevate the taste level—a new visual vocabulary—spaces changeable by the turn of a dial."

But once again, his words are not quite what they might seem, and they provide considerable insight into his aspirations. Illusion, to Frank, was not the soft make-believe of, say, Disneyland. What he had in mind was more the exquisite, often profound pleasure of abstraction. The architecture of illusion, to Frank, was architecture of high aesthetic ambition, architecture capable of evoking a feeling of transcendence. At the same time, however, he yearned for his work to be popular, and he felt profoundly the need for architecture to be comfortable, not unsettling. That, in the end, was what meant the most to him: to be ambitious, even radical, and to be popular at the same time. His reference to "mass taste" underscores how important public acceptance was to him. And yet he was determined not to pander to existing levels of popular taste. "Illusion," to Frank, was not falsity. It was a word that he meant to evoke the highest aesthetic intentions.

Frank was nothing if not earnest. His hope was to create architecture that would be at once avant-garde and popular, assertively modernist and yet embraced by the public. It may have been naïve, but it was surely not cynical. His attitude was very much his own, and it had little in common with the culture he had known in the 1950s and 1960s, as he was coming of age as an architect, when modernism often sought to establish itself as a thing apart from the mainstream. Indeed, this had been the case for much of the history of twentieth-century modernism, which, while it sometimes aspired to popular acceptance, rarely achieved anything close to it. And for every movement that, like the Bauhaus, sought to win over the public, there were other strains of modernism that were disdainful, even suspicious, of popularity. Challenging the status quo was the priority for many modernist artists and architects, and they did not often view artistic aspiration as having much to do with public acceptance. They yearned for success, but at the same time they were suspicious of what too much public approval might represent. For many artists and architects, avant-garde credentials and popularity were for all intents and purposes mutually exclusive.

It was an implicitly elitist view. Frank wanted it to be otherwise, at least so far as his own work was concerned. He wanted his work to make people comfortable, however unusual it was, and he wanted it to have room for a range of different things. "When I was doing houses, I would never commandeer the interiors with my own furniture and my own designs like Mies van der Rohe or Frank Lloyd Wright," Frank told Barbara Isenberg. "I was the opposite. I wanted people to bring in their stuff to make it their own and interact with what I had done." Clutter, Frank admitted, was something he found comforting.

His sensibility, crafted as much by his and his family's liberal political views as by his aesthetic tastes, sought to synthesize the conflict between the creativity of the avant-garde and broad popular taste, much as he had tried to resolve the conflict between William Pereira's inventive shapes and Charles Luckman's accommodation to his clients. Frank wanted to see himself as a creative power. But it was every bit as important to him to be seen as an architect who could resolve the conflicting forces around him—and who would be welcomed by all.

That was surely why he embarked on an unusual project in 1968 with his sister, Doreen, to teach fifth graders in a Los Angeles public school about how cities come into being. Under the aegis of the Artists-in-Schools program of the National Endowment for the Arts, Frank and Doreen used the Westminster Avenue School in Venice for a pilot program that would restructure the curriculum around an imaginary city that the students would design and build themselves. It was Frank's idea that mathematics, history, science, and civics could all be taught through an exercise in city planning. He and Doreen invented a scenario in which a new element they named Purium that could make garbage biodegradable had been discovered on a rural piece of land, and a city needed to be built quickly to house the workers and their families who would mine the material and get it out to the rest of the world. Frank and Doreen worked with the fifth graders to design the city and build it with blocks, showing them the difficult choices that had to be made, such as the decision to remove trees to make way for highways and housing. They designated some students as politicians, others as builders, and others as protesting citizens so as to demonstrate the realities of city building.

Frank and Doreen treated the project almost like an exercise in improvisational theater. It did not sit well with the classroom teacher, who, after agreeing to work with them, eventually ordered them out of her class, finding their approach to teaching too freewheeling for her taste. The optimistic start of the project and its disappointing end were documented by the filmmaker Jon Boorstin in a short film entitled *Kid City* that centers on the escalating tension between the outsiders—Frank, with shaggy hair and a mustache, and Doreen, with long, straight dark hair in the manner of Joan Baez—and the prim teacher. To Frank, the problem was that the teacher did not want her students exposed to the rough-and-tumble of real life. "All we're talking about is trying things and taking chances," he said on camera, using a line that he would repeat for the rest of his life. The teacher, Frank said, was "taking all the conflict out of the project because it was too hard to deal with. [But] the conflict is the real involvement in the

Frank and Doreen collaborate on a project to teach grade school children about city planning, 1971.

city planning process that we were looking for. Making a beautiful object wasn't at all what we were trying to do."[*]

Frank's closeness to Los Angeles artists had long before expanded to include many of their more famous New York counterparts like Jasper Johns, James Rosenquist, and Robert Rauschenberg, and through Johns he had become friendly with the curator David Whitney. Frank was particularly eager to meet Whitney's partner, the architect Philip Johnson, but that had so far failed to happen. Johnson was celebrated less for his own work than for the unusual role he had created for himself within the architecture world. He had begun his career as the first curator of architecture and design at the Museum of Modern Art, and later on he made himself in effect the entire profession's curator, selecting those younger architects whose work he admired, getting to know them, and then giving their careers a boost by referring new jobs to them. His patronage was motivated by self-interest at least as much as by generosity; he craved the stimulation of new ideas that younger architects brought him, and he knew that any help he gave them would be repaid in loyalty. Johnson, like Frank, believed deeply that architecture involved the making of art as well as the solving of functional problems, and while his own architectural output was at best uneven, his buildings never failed to suggest the presence of a sharp mind trying to express an idea.

By the time the article about the Ron Davis house was published, Frank was in his mid-forties and on the verge of national recognition. He was becoming exactly the kind of pathbreaking architect Johnson liked getting to know; as someone who was also a friend of David Whitney and Jasper Johns, Frank thought it was about time that he had an introduction to the master himself. Finally the word came through Tim Vreeland, a Los Angeles architect who taught at the University of California at Los Angeles and was friendly with Johnson's circle. Johnson had asked Vreeland to set up a tour of important new work for him to see in Los Angeles, and had asked that the Ron Davis house be included.

"Ron Davis thought Philip was coming to see his paintings, because he

---

[*] Neither Frank nor Doreen gave up an interest in arts education, or in using city building as an educational tool. Doreen would devote much of her career to developing a program she called "Design Based Learning," and Frank many years later would embark on a major philanthropic effort to bring arts education to California schools, hiring his friend Malissa Shriver, the wife of Bobby Shriver, to administer it.

couldn't imagine that he would want to see my work. And I knew he was coming to see the building," Frank remembered. He went to Malibu several hours before Johnson was due to arrive, and he and Davis got stoned. They were somewhat giddy by the time Johnson arrived, accompanied by Vreeland. Johnson characteristically said little when he visited a new building; he walked around it quickly, and immediately saw that the form of the house was in part a play on the illusion of perspective. "It looks like there are vanishing points, but where are they?" Johnson said to Frank. "How did you do it?" He walked through the entire house but showed no interest in Davis's paintings. The roughness of Frank's architecture was not Philip Johnson's way of making buildings, to say the least: Johnson, weaned on Mies van der Rohe and fond of expensive buildings throughout his life, was not instantly comfortable with Frank's rough-hewn, "cheapskate" architecture. In those days he was more preoccupied with figuring out how to line elevator cabs with marble.

But Johnson had a better nose for what was new and important than almost anyone else practicing architecture, and he presumably found something compelling in the Davis house, even if he was not moved, as he sometimes was with work he admired, to begin imitating it. Whether because he saw that Frank and Davis were stoned or because he was rushing on to his next stop, he said almost nothing to Frank as he left, but urged him to call if he came to New York.

Frank needed no more than that hint, and soon he and Johnson were in frequent contact. He would visit Johnson regularly at his office in the Seagram Building on Park Avenue, show him his new work, and share architectural gossip. From time to time Frank would be a guest at Johnson's corner table at the Four Seasons restaurant, which Johnson had designed in 1958 and where he maintained what amounted to an architectural salon for several decades, lunching every day with architects, scholars, journalists, and critics whose conversation he found stimulating.

Frank Gehry and Philip Johnson seemed like an odd pair: Johnson the elegant, self-styled *architecte du roi*, Gehry the celebrator of the messy, the incomplete, the cheap, and the raw. But both men valued intelligent discourse, and they found it in each other. And Johnson's endorsement gave Frank a degree of credibility, not to mention exposure, among his counterparts on the East Coast, who considered Johnson the arbiter of serious intention in architecture. While Frank had no desire to give up his identity as a Los Angeles outlier, he knew that he needed some connection to New York if he were truly to have a national reputation. To be welcomed into

Philip Johnson's circle meant that he was no longer just a California architect. He had, in at least a symbolic sense, arrived.

The *Designers West* article never directly addressed the question of the
relationship of architecture to art, but the subjects Frank chose to
focus on in the piece underscored, at least implicitly, the extent to which
he considered himself an architect and not an artist. However much he
obsessed about form, however much projects like the O'Neill hay barn and
the Davis house could seem to have been driven by purely aesthetic issues,
he did not see form as an end in itself. It was always connected to human
activity, to functional use, and to place. He wanted to push the boundaries
of architectural form so that they would embrace more of the concerns of
art, but that was not the same as rejecting the concerns of architecture in
favor of those of art. Few things bothered Frank more than being thought
of as an artist and not an architect, when all he felt that he wanted to do
was to build real buildings for real purposes in the real world.

His worry that he might not be viewed primarily as an architect would
have significant implications for one of his most ambitious early ventures, an outgrowth of his interest in plain, everyday industrial materials:
his designs for furniture made of cardboard. He had been thinking about
cardboard since the Joseph Magnin department store project, when he
was experimenting with means of making flexible displays, and he continued to play around with the material in his office, where it was used
mainly to make architectural models. But he was convinced there were
other possibilities.

In 1969, as the Magnin stores were being completed, Frank was asked
to reshape the artist Robert Irwin's studio for a special symposium, a discussion with artists and scientists from NASA on art and technology. The
budget for the one-day makeover was, as usual, tight, and Frank made
some simple seating out of stacks of cardboard, which seemed like a way
to transform the space that would be both cheap enough to fit within the
budget and unconventional enough to allow it to seem, if a bit funky, at
least vaguely futuristic at the same time. The result excited him, and he
continued to work with cardboard. He had been using corrugated cardboard, which bends easily, to represent the ups and downs of terrain in the
site models he made in the office, and at one point he remembered sitting
at his desk, looking at the exposed end of the corrugated sheet with its open
ridges. "I thought, That's beautiful," he remembered. "Why don't I just

use that? So I started to make shapes with it, which were very fuzzy, with a nice texture. I loved it, because it was like corduroy. You get a texture that's pleasant, and I could make a tabletop that wasn't very heavy, which seemed promising. It trumps folding the cardboard, and very efficiently you get a structure that's very strong and aesthetically looks great." Frank had made a key discovery: when single sheets of corrugated cardboard were bonded together into layers with the corrugation set in alternate directions, they became exceptionally solid, yielding a material as strong as wood, and far more flexible.

Before long, with Robert Irwin's help, Frank had put together a desk and a file cabinet made of cardboard. The desk became the reception desk in his office, where it would be an immediate signal to visitors that this was not the kind of architectural office outfitted with the sleek Knoll and Herman Miller furniture that you saw everywhere else. It was softer than common modern furniture, and if it was a bit funky, it was also warm and surprising, a combination Frank loved. The reception desk was only the beginning. The challenge of making new things out of cardboard captivated several of the artists besides Irwin, including Larry Bell, as well as Greg Walsh and others in Frank's office. Soon there were more kinds of furniture: partitions, shelves, chairs, side tables. Frank devised a round side table with a highly finished, lacquerlike cardboard top that was strong enough to stand on. He later gave it to his friend Donna O'Neill. Irwin helped to design an armchair, which led Frank to come up with what would become one of the best-known pieces, a side chair made out of a long, narrow slab of corrugated cardboard that was upright at the top to form the back of a chair, bent into a seat, and then below the seat bent back and forth in the shape of an S to provide support in place of legs. It was dubbed the Wiggle Chair for its squiggly shape, which yielded other pieces as well. There was also a rocking chair, a chaise lounge, and tables and dining chairs.

It seemed inevitable that at some point the idea would arise that these things could be more than quirky experiments for Frank's office. Robert Irwin, who often dropped by Frank's studio, was particularly enthusiastic, and he told Frank he thought there should be some commercial possibilities in the idea. Frank was dubious about trying to make and sell cardboard furniture, and resisted the idea of going into business, despite Irwin's continued prodding, until he was asked by his friend Rudy Gernreich, a prominent fashion designer, to share the platform with him at a program he was scheduled to present at the Hotel Bel-Air on fashion and design.

Frank spoke about his experiments with cardboard furniture, and a businessman from New York named Richard Salomon was in the audience. Salomon, who owned Lanvin-Charles of the Ritz, prided himself on his ability to serve as a business partner to highly creative people and build major brands around their names. He had persuaded the fashion designer Yves Saint Laurent to go into partnership with him to expand the range of his fashion production from haute couture to ready-to-wear by creating Yves Saint Laurent Rive Gauche, and he had built Vidal Sassoon into a high-fashion chain of hairdressing salons. Salomon was excited by the idea of cardboard furniture, which he thought could give him the potential to revolutionize the home-furnishings market the same way that he had been revolutionizing high-end fashion and hairdressing. And he was taken with Frank personally. This bright, soft-spoken young architect from Los Angeles, Salomon thought, could be the third star in the constellation of brand-name designers he was building. Consumers hadn't known the names Yves Saint Laurent or Vidal Sassoon before he invested in them and built their businesses, and it didn't matter to him that Frank Gehry wasn't already a household name. In fact, he liked it better that way: he could guide the process of turning Frank into a famous designer.

They agreed on Easy Edges as a simple, easy-to-remember brand name, and on May 15, 1972, Frank applied for and received U.S. Patent No. 4,067,615 as the inventor of a process for "furniture or other similar load-bearing structural article [that] comprises a laminate of flat, corrugated cardboard pieces conforming generally to the cross-sectional shape of the article . . . [in which] individual pieces are secured together adhesively." Frank then formed a company, along with Robert Irwin and Jack Brogan, a fabricator who had made many of Irwin's art pieces and whom Irwin had brought in to help with fabrication of many of the cardboard furniture pieces. Brogan helped refine the designs, and recalled having figured out how to make the pieces lighter, which would significantly improve their salability. He set up a facility in Venice, where industrial real estate remained cheap, to do the manufacturing.

Richard Salomon made an initial investment to get the venture started in exchange for 40 percent of the company. He was close to Marvin Traub, the head of Bloomingdale's, who shared Salomon's excitement about what Frank was doing. Not much had happened in contemporary furniture design since the Danish modern trend of the 1950s, at least in terms of ideas that might be affordable and would appeal to the mass market, and Salomon and Traub thought that Easy Edges had the potential to have a major impact on the home-furnishings business. Traub had positioned Bloomingdale's as a shaper of trends and as a store with a younger sensibility than its competitors, and he assigned Barbara D'Arcy, who designed Bloomingdale's famous model rooms, to do a room of Easy Edges furniture. The debut of the furniture line was treated as if it were an art opening. Traub put the store's marketing weight behind the venture, and Frank was interviewed in newspapers and magazines. Photographs of a Volkswagen Beetle lifted up on three pieces of Easy Edges furniture were used in advertising as a way of showing the material's strength. Easy Edges seemed about to become the hottest thing in interior design.

And it was, briefly. *House & Garden* published a spread with pictures of the model rooms Barbara D'Arcy had designed at Bloomingdale's, and the *Los Angeles Times*, in a story headlined "Why Didn't Somebody Think of This Before?," called Easy Edges "the most astonishing furniture of our generation. It is cheap—$80 for the Sleigh chairs—and amazingly sturdy. Practically nothing can go wrong with it in normal usage. And it's completely and honestly different." *The New York Times Magazine*, for its part, weighed in with a piece called "Paper Furniture for Penny Pinchers" that referred to the Easy Edges pieces as "strong, graphic shapes with a strength and solidity that compares favorably with modern design in plastic and metal." The *Times* also observed that cardboard furniture has sound-absorption properties, and suggested that it could reduce noise by 50 percent, "certainly an advantage for a family dining table." The article praised the low prices of Easy Edges and suggested that it would first become the furniture of choice for young and trendy Bloomingdale's customers, after which, the author predicted in a curious aside, it would "find its way into low-income housing."

Whatever it might cost to buy Easy Edges pieces, however, it soon became clear that far more money than Salomon or Frank had envisioned was going to be needed if the business was to grow big enough to service the orders that seemed likely after the rush of favorable publicity. Salomon agreed to put significantly more cash into the venture. His additional investment would have diluted Frank's ownership stake and put Salomon in effective control of what could turn out to be a substantial business. The lawyer Frank had hired to represent him with Easy Edges, Arthur Aloff, was not convinced that going ahead with the deal was in Frank's best interest, and discouraged him from agreeing to it, in part because he felt that the initial royalty terms were too low.

But Frank had another problem. The acclaim Easy Edges was receiving frightened him. He had begun making things out of cardboard as a side-line to his architectural work, and he started to worry that if Easy Edges was too successful, it would take up so much of his time that it would be hard for him to go on designing buildings. More troubling still, what if he became known as a furniture designer and not as an architect? He became anxious that he would be just another designer working for a large corporation, and no matter how much money he made from it, no matter how much his name was connected to it, he would no longer feel independent. The notion that the success of Easy Edges might provide him with an income stream that could subsidize his architectural work, and thus might support his career as an architect rather than undermine it, did not occur to him. He could not see beyond his fear that he would be losing control over his own work.

He asked Vidal Sassoon if he could meet with him, and the two had a drink at the Beverly Hills Hotel. Sassoon had become rich and famous with Richard Salomon's backing, and Frank knew that he was being groomed to follow in the same path. "Tell me about these guys," Frank said to Sassoon. "Do you want to be this?" Sassoon asked him, referring to the celebrity that he himself had become. "You're going to become the Yves Saint Laurent of furniture. They're going to market you. You're going to be in every book, every magazine. Your life won't be your own."

That was exactly what Frank was afraid of. Even if his lawyer could force Richard Salomon's hand and negotiate a better royalty deal, Frank feared that he would still end up like Vidal Sassoon: a brand, not a creative figure. If a celebrity hairdresser could acknowledge that there was a cost to this kind of business arrangement, Frank thought, what would it mean for an architect to commit to such a deal? He went back to New York and made an appointment to see Richard Salomon at his office at 730 Fifth Avenue. Frank was fond of Salomon, an avuncular man seventeen years his senior who took pride in his ability to nurture young talent. Salomon had three sons of his own, and in many ways he had begun to see Frank as a de facto fourth son. And from Frank's standpoint, Salomon seemed to be a benign father figure. Certainly the older man's eagerness to support him and invest in his future stood in clear contrast to the angst-ridden relationship he had had with Irving.

Frank walked into Salomon's office and immediately asked for a drink to calm his nerves. Salomon gave him one, and Frank poured out his feelings. It was a painful conversation. Frank told Salomon that he had decided not just to reject a restructuring of their business arrangement, but to pull out of Easy Edges altogether. And he had no desire to give up the rights and let Salomon or anyone else keep the company going without him. It was his design, and his patent. He had come to the conclusion that he did not want to continue with Easy Edges, and that he did not want anyone else to, either. There was no choice but to shut down the venture that had started with such excitement and promise. Unlike most new businesses that close, Easy Edges would be ceasing operations not because the world did not have enough interest in its product, but because the world had perhaps too much interest in it—at least for Frank.

Salomon was shocked, angry, and deeply disappointed. He felt that Frank was not only passing up an opportunity to get rich, he was showing indifference to the warm and meaningful relationship that he believed the two of them had. He was hurt at what he considered Frank's rejection of his support. However, Salomon's reaction was nothing compared with the fury that Frank's decision unleashed in Marvin Traub, who telephoned him in a rage. "He called me and he started yelling at me," Frank remembered. "He said, 'You son of a bitch, you can't promote this kind of thing and [then abandon it]. I have $150,000 worth of orders.' And he said, 'You gotta fuckin' make those orders or I'm gonna to sue your ass.' So I had to make the orders." But that would not be so easy, because Jack Brogan, who had been fabricating the Easy Edges furniture, was also so angry at Frank's decision to close down the venture that he refused to make any more pieces. Brogan had gone into debt to purchase equipment to make the Easy Edges pieces, and now he would have little use for it, and no income to cover its cost. Robert Irwin, too, was furious at Frank, and it would be years before either Irwin or Brogan would speak to him again.[*] Frank found a small factory in Orange County to make the pieces, and fulfilled his obligation to Bloomingdale's. His recollection was that he lost more than $100,000 on them.

The impulse that led Frank to say no to Victor Gruen when Gruen offered him the chance to run his office in Paris had reared its head again.

---

[*] According to Brogan, he was forced to sell his studio to cover the debt he had taken on to build his fabrication facility for Easy Edges. He considered suing Frank, having believed that the venture was on its way to bringing significant profits to everyone who was involved with it, including him, and that Frank closed it down solely because he wanted complete control over the operation, denying him the income he believed he was due. Brogan said that he did not pursue the suit because he and Frank were "both in the art community" of Los Angeles, and he did not want to engage in what would become a public battle. Frank acknowledges that Brogan lost money, but recalls offering him some funds later in partial restitution. Brogan still has a number of the original Easy Edges pieces in storage.

Once more Frank was turning away from an opportunity that held considerable promise of financial security out of fear that he would be compromising his independence as a designer. His old political instincts that led him to be suspicious of corporations didn't help matters in this case, and neither did the fact that Richard Salomon, like Victor Gruen before him, was an elder mentor. Frank's fondness for both men was genuine, but something in him resisted allowing himself to be under the wing of either one of them, and caused him to interpret their support as a way of trying to control him. Only Milton Wexler, it seemed, who had no direct involvement in any of Frank's work, could mentor him without experiencing rejection.

When Frank had turned down Victor Gruen's offer in Paris, the only person the decision affected other than Frank was Gruen himself, who had to deal with his disappointment and then find someone else. Easy Edges, however, was another matter entirely. It was more than an idea; it was up and running, and many people, like Richard Salomon and Jack Brogan, had invested substantial time and money in it. So, of course, had Bloomingdale's, and other retail distributors. There had been advertisements placed, articles written, and orders submitted. When Frank "pulled the plug," as he put it, he was abandoning both the people and the companies that had joined with him and supported his design ideas. It may have felt to Frank like a bold decision to retreat from Easy Edges to focus fully on his architectural practice, but it was also a selfish, even narcissistic, one. In the belief that he was protecting his artistic integrity, he abandoned friends and other people who had believed in him. Unlike his rejection of Victor Gruen, his decision to forsake Easy Edges left plenty of collateral damage.

Furniture was not, however, the only use Frank would make of cardboard. At the same time he was beginning his experiments with cardboard furniture, in 1970, he tried an even bolder use of the material at the Hollywood Bowl. Originally opened in 1922 in a natural amphitheater called Daisy Dell, the outdoor concert venue had recently become the summer home of the Los Angeles Philharmonic. The Bowl's concert shell, in use since 1929, had a series of concentric arches not unlike the proscenium of Radio City Music Hall.* Its acoustics had always been somewhat prob-

---

* The concert shell went through multiple incarnations in the Bowl's first few years, including a version designed by Lloyd Wright, the architect son of Frank Lloyd Wright, for the 1927 season. It was pyramidal in shape and was said to have had good acoustics, but many concertgoers found Lloyd Wright's aesthetic as jarring as his father's, and it was demol-

lematic, and they became more so with the presence of noise from the nearby 101 freeway, which had not existed in the Bowl's early years. Seating expansions had changed the shape of the natural bowl and further compromised the sound quality, and musicians in the orchestra complained that they could not hear one another or solo performers. If the Bowl was to work for the Philharmonic, something needed to be done, and quickly. Ernest Fleischmann, who had recently become the executive director of the Los Angeles Philharmonic and brought the orchestra to the Bowl for a summer season, called on Frank, whose recent Merriweather Post Pavilion in Columbia, Maryland, had been the most successful outdoor concert venue of the previous decade.

It was another crash program, but also another opportunity to enter the world of music, and it was Frank's first professional dealing with Fleischmann, a brilliant, demanding, and temperamental music executive who would eventually play a critical role in a far more important job both in Frank's career and in the cultural life of Los Angeles: Walt Disney Concert Hall. In 1970, the stakes were more modest. Between the 1970 and 1971 summer concert seasons Frank worked with the acoustician Christopher Jaffe to create what was in effect a stage within the stage, a structure made up of sixty cardboard sono-tubes, three feet in diameter, some standing vertically like classical columns, others placed across the top like round beams. It was another example of what Frank liked to call "cheapskate architecture": simple solutions using common, inexpensive materials that by being used in a new context were perceived differently. The Hollywood Bowl design elevated cardboard far beyond the scale of furniture and made it the stuff of monumental architecture, although flanking the stage with rows of tubes mimicking columns without capitals certainly had more of the air of pop art playfulness than serious classicism. But it was visually attractive, and it worked.[*]

Frank asked Deborah Sussman, the graphic designer who had worked with him on the Joseph Magnin department store project, to join his team for the Hollywood Bowl, and Sussman produced bright graphics that were

---

ished at the end of the season. Wright was given another chance the next year if he agreed to build a shell in an arched shape, which he did, but that one was destroyed by rough weather. A firm called Allied Architects built the permanent shell that Gehry altered in 1970–71, picking up on Wright's second design.

[*] Frank's use of cardboard tubes as an architectural element predated by more than a generation the work of Shigeru Ban, the Japanese architect who won the Pritzker Prize in 2014, in part for his unusual use of cardboard in projects such as his temporary cathedral in Christchurch, New Zealand, constructed in 2013 out of cardboard tubes.

in keeping with Frank's casual architecture. The cardboard tubes turned out to be so inexpensive that they were replaced annually for the rest of the decade, until funds were available for a more permanent solution. When Fleischmann decided the time had come to move beyond the cardboard tubes, Frank came up with a new scheme that consisted of fiberglass spheres of varying sizes suspended from the roof of the old arched shell, whose curving lines again became fully visible to the audience.*

Frank's success at the Hollywood Bowl was followed by another collaboration with Christopher Jaffe, the Concord Pavilion, set on an open rural site in Northern California, roughly thirty miles east of Berkeley. Another outdoor venue for concerts, the pavilion is at once one of his boldest early buildings and one of his most deceptively simple. Atop a semicircular bowl Frank placed a square roof, two hundred feet on a side, covering the seating area as well as the stage. The roof is supported by an enormous steel truss set on a concrete wall behind the stage and on two huge concrete columns in the front. The truss, painted black and twelve feet deep, is far and away the dominant element, and from a distance it appears to float: a gigantic, dark, mysterious, hovering machine.

The pavilion is more austere than much of Frank's work, and larger in scale. Yet it is not just a kind of proto–high tech, an expression of machinery made sleek and powerful. There is surely a hint of that, but more telling is the way in which the truss tapers to a thin edge on both sides, making the huge, heavy metal structure seem unexpectedly light, and giving the pavilion, at least in profile, a distant kinship to the trapezoidal shapes of smaller, earlier projects like the O'Neill hay barn and the Ron Davis house.

It also owes a debt to the Merriweather Post Pavilion in Maryland, whose wood structure appears to hover over the seating area in a similar way. Unlike a conventional outdoor performance space such as the Hollywood Bowl, where the architecture is limited to the shell over the stage, in both the Post and Concord pavilions Frank brought the architecture out to cover the audience. It was a way not just of protecting them from the rain, but also of making the implicit point that his architecture belonged to everyone and not just to the performers onstage: it was not something to look at while you listened, but something to experience fully from the audience. The structure and its expansive roof also served to frame views of the surrounding landscape, done in collaboration with the landscape

---

* Frank later made other changes and additions to the Hollywood Bowl, including an open-air dining pavilion in 1982.

Frank Gehry stands in front of his newly completed house in Santa Monica, 1978.

An early example of a Gehry fish lamp, made of ColorCore Formica, from 1983 on

A selection of Gehry Easy Edges furniture on display, along with the later Cross Check and other bentwood chairs

FRANK O. GEHRYS MÖBEL
FRANK O. GEHRY'S FURNITURE DESIGNS

Ron Davis house, Malibu, 1972

Loyola Law School campus, with Gehry's allusion to a classical façade facing a central square, built from 1979 to 1994

Rear façade of the Guggenheim Bilbao, facing the Nervión River, 1997

The main façade of the Guggenheim Bilbao is framed by the older buildings of the city, with Jeff Koons's sculpture *Puppy* in the foreground.

Museum of Biodiversity in Panama, 2014

Walt Disney Concert Hall on Grand Avenue in downtown Los Angeles, 2003

Interior of the Walt Disney Concert Hall

Fondation Louis Vuitton at the Jardin d'Acclimitation in the Bois
de Boulogne, Paris, 2014

Detail of the glass sails that surround the building

From its narrow end, the Fondation Louis Vuitton resembles a ship
sailing forward across the reflecting pool.

Gehry designed the exhibition at the Los Angeles County Museum of Art with attention to the scale and color of the sculptures of his friend Ken Price, 2012.

Aboard *Foggy*, January 2015

architect Peter Walker. If the Post Pavilion was a "cheapskate" version of an idea for outdoor musical performance, the Concord Pavilion was its grander, more fully realized sibling, ambitious as engineering and landscape design as well as architecture.

Concord is surrounded by an artificial berm influenced by the earthworks of the artist Robert Smithson. Frank had asked Smithson to consider working with him on the project, and the two made plans to meet, but Smithson died in a plane crash before the meeting could take place, so Frank decided to create his own Smithsonesque design, with Peter Walker's cooperation, in homage to the artist. The berm's interior is a grassy lawn that serves as an overflow area for concerts; on its exterior is a long, curving chain-link fence marking the border of the property. When you approach the pavilion, only the berm and the fence are visible. From afar, the fence, which has been likened to a metal necklace, has a stark, blunt clarity that is more like the enclosure around an industrial site than a cultural facility. That was no accident: Frank was increasingly coming to think of chain-link fencing as he had thought of plywood and two-by-four construction studs, as a material unjustly rejected by his fellow architects because they found it plain, boring, or ugly. To Frank it was none of those things, and he began to wonder whether the interlocking mesh of chain link could be used for something more than enclosing a piece of land.

He was encouraged in his thinking by Pete Walker. Frank's daughter Leslie was attending the California Institute of the Arts in Valencia, where one of Walker's children was also a student. Both men had noticed a large power station with massive chain-link fencing along the freeway en route to Valencia. "I kept looking at it and thinking about it. I liked it," Frank said. "I had thought about playing with chain link before, because every building I do has a chain-link fence around it, like Concord, so it seemed like I should try to deal with it in some way."

Pete Walker's firm, Sasaki, Walker & Associates, was working on a waterfront park for Long Beach, California, and Frank was given the assignment of designing a pavilion and conservatory for the park. Walker came to Frank's office to discuss the project after he had made one of his trips to Valencia, and he asked Frank if he had ever considered using chain link as something more than a fence.

"Funny you asked," Frank said. He had been thinking the same thing, and he produced a trapezoidal pavilion with all its walls and roof made entirely of chain-link fencing, set on a steel framework. The structure was L-shaped in plan, and the roof sharply slanted, so from any angle it would appear to be an unusual abstract shape. Inside was an entire landscape with trees that from a distance would appear almost like shadows behind the metal mesh. The structure would change dramatically in appearance as the sun moved around it, yet it would always be light, with little visual weight, an almost ghostly presence.

The conservatory pavilion was never built, but it nevertheless became one of Frank's seminal projects. Not long after it was designed, he was called back to Concord to add a freestanding box office separate from the seating bowl, and he came up with another raked-roof design to be constructed entirely of chain link, which he called a "shadow structure." This one was built. From a distance it looks almost like a translucent version of the Ron Davis house, sitting alone in the landscape. Within a few years, Frank would use chain link in so many projects, both residential and commercial, that the material would become, at least for a while, the equivalent of his signature.[*]

A mid the turmoil over Easy Edges, Frank's personal life was becoming at least slightly more stable. He continued to grow closer to Berta, and he took her with him on a trip to Finland in 1972, the same year as Easy Edges. It was before the line had made its debut, and Frank had the idea of visiting the studio of Alvar Aalto, the great Finnish architect whose lecture he had attended in Toronto in 1946, when he had never heard of Aalto, or of any other architect. Over the years Frank had come to deeply admire Aalto, whose work was modern but characterized by a warm humanism and formal imagination that separated it from the rigid modernism of the Bauhaus. Aalto was also celebrated as a furniture designer, and many of his chairs, stools, and tables in light-colored wood were becoming staples of modern design. If they were not as cheap as Easy Edges, they emerged out of a similar desire to create simple, unpretentious, and affordable furniture

---

[*] Philip Johnson, known for absorbing and recasting the work of many architects he admired, would erect a small structure of chain-link fencing on his estate in New Canaan, Connecticut, in 1984, which he dubbed the "Gehry Ghost House." It was only partially an homage to Frank, who by then Johnson had come to know well: the house was symmetrical, with a traditional design and a split gable in the center, so its shape was not at all like something Frank would have done. It calls to mind more the work of Robert Venturi, whose own house of 1962 had a famous split gable on its façade. In a way, the Gehry Ghost House was Johnson's skillful synthesis of Frank and Venturi, who shared many ideas but produced utterly different work.

of modern design. Frank had the thought of showing the master some of his ideas for Easy Edges, and he called the architect's studio.

Aalto, who was seventy-four, was away, but Frank was told that he and Berta were welcome to visit the studio. He was in awe. Aalto's staff "realized I was a total nut about him," he said. "They put us in his office and they said, 'You're welcome to sit here as long as you like. He's not coming back, just don't touch anything.' So I sat in his chair, at his desk for a couple of hours with Berta there and we just looked around on our own, drank it all in." Before he left, he met the architect's wife, Elissa, and showed her pictures of his Easy Edges furniture. She reacted with indifference, which disappointed Frank, who had hoped that she would see a connection between Aalto's furniture designs and his own.* If Elissa Aalto failed to perceive one kind of connection between her husband and Frank Gehry, Frank himself failed to see another: Alvar Aalto was a model of the architect who had designed modern furniture that had become highly successful at no cost to his reputation as an architect. He was known first and foremost for his buildings, and his stools, tables, and chairs helped support his architectural practice. Aalto's career demonstrated that Frank's fear that success at furniture design would come at a cost to his architectural practice was not a necessary outcome. Even though his visit to Aalto's studio in the months before the release of Easy Edges was presumably still fresh in his mind, it did not occur to Frank that Aalto's success at blending architecture and furniture design could be a model for his own career.

Berta was a good companion in Finland, the first major trip she took with Frank. She was an equally good companion in Los Angeles: she liked most of his friends, and they appeared to like her. She had studied cultural anthropology and she was an avid reader. Frank enjoyed her company far more than any of the women he had seen since his divorce. The possibility of marriage was obvious to both of them. Berta asked less of him than Anita had, and his reaction to her warm and quiet manner was to want to do more for her. It was always his inclination to be generous when he did not feel pressured into it. If he felt cornered, he would run the other way.

But Berta, fourteen years younger than Frank, was eager to have children, and Frank, pained by his divorce and his strained relationship with Leslie and Brina, had no interest in becoming a father again. He was in

---

* Many years later, Elissa Aalto, by then a widow—Alvar Aalto died in 1976—would call on Frank in his office in Los Angeles, and he would tell her, "He is my hero."

his early forties, and his career was beginning to take off. Even if parenting would be less stressful with Berta than it had been with Anita, it was insufficient reason to repeat a phase of his life that in many ways he was relieved had passed.

The fact that Berta was Catholic and Panamanian was less of a concern, at least from Frank's standpoint. He was not an observant Jew, and he thought of himself as worldly and cosmopolitan, the sort of man fully comfortable with the notion that his family would embrace different cultures and backgrounds. Thelma Gehry, if a bit uncertain at first about Berta's background, quickly saw that she was making her son happy, and she set out to become Berta's friend. Berta's own family was less certain about Frank. Not only was he not Catholic, but he was divorced, and the idea of Berta marrying a divorced man with two children who was fourteen years her senior did not please them.

Frank and Berta broke up and reconciled several times, mainly over the issue of whether or not to have children. Berta's quiet, easygoing manner masked a strong will, and it was not an issue she was prepared to compromise on. She loved Frank, but she would give him up if he would not allow her the opportunity to become a mother. If he would agree to have children, she was prepared to stand by him, and to convince her family that her future was with Frank, whatever they thought.

Berta got her wish. She became pregnant, and Frank realized that his desire to be with her far outweighed his reluctance to have more children. They were married at the home of her cousin on September 11, 1975. It was a far more modest event than Frank's first wedding, but it would have a much happier and longer-lasting outcome.

Shortly after their marriage, Frank and Berta planned a trip to visit her family in Panama, after which they would go on to Peru to see the Inca ruins at Machu Picchu. That had to be postponed when one of his most temperamental clients, the industrialist Norton Simon, for whom he was designing a small gallery and guesthouse in Malibu, became enraged when he heard that Frank planned to be away from Los Angeles for an extended trip. Simon told Frank that he would be in violation of his contract if he were not available for regular meetings and site inspections. Frank had met Simon through his wife, the actress Jennifer Jones, who was a fellow member of Milton Wexler's therapy group, and so he felt he had no choice but to agree to put off the trip, even though the postponement was "an indignity we had to suffer because of Norton." The job had already caused

Frank an unusual degree of frustration, in part because Simon liked to make changes during construction. At one point he decided to substitute a new roof tile he had found for the original one Frank had specified, and insisted that Frank install it without reengineering the roof to take into account the different size and weight of the new tiles, a decision that would have troubling consequences.

Frank told Berta that the trip—in effect, their honeymoon—would have to be pushed back to accommodate to Simon's demand. The trade-off was that they would go instead over the Christmas holidays, and Berta would be able to spend Christmas in Panama with her family. It would be Frank's first meeting with Berta's father.

Both the meeting with Berta's family and the visit to Machu Picchu appear to have gone well—or at least there were no problems that Frank would remember that overshadowed the ongoing issues with Norton Simon, who was not placated by the postponement of the trip. Simon tracked Frank down on one of the three telephone lines going into Cuzco, the ancient Inca capital near Machu Picchu, and told him he was firing him as his architect. "It was devastating, in the middle of my so-called honeymoon," Frank said later. Making the situation worse was that he and Berta were both experiencing some altitude sickness in Cuzco, which is eleven thousand feet above sea level. Simon's actions, Frank felt, were "sadistic."

When Frank and Berta returned in January, Simon called him again, this time to say that the architect he had hired to finish the job was having difficulty understanding what to do. "You'd better fucking get in here and finish it," Frank remembers Simon saying to him. He went back and oversaw the completion of the house, more out of duty than loyalty to Simon. The job had begun with warm feelings, both because of Jennifer Jones and the Milton Wexler connection, and also because Simon, a prominent art collector, was gracious in allowing Frank to spend time with his collection and talking about it with him. But working with Simon turned out to be an altogether different experience from chatting with him about his art collecting. When the house was finished, Simon would complain about leaks, which Frank said came about because of Simon's substitution of new roof tile, since the roof structure had been designed to accommodate tiles the size of the ones Frank had chosen, and the new ones did not fit as precisely. Frank remembered getting a phone call from Simon's assistant, who said to him, "Mr. Simon wants you to know that he's sitting at his desk and the water is pouring in. It's raining and the roof is leaking on his desk. He doesn't want you to come here. He just wants to tell you that's what's happening."

"And I said, 'I'm just gonna quote from another episode like this where [Frank Lloyd] Wright had the same phone call,'" Frank said. "And he said, 'Madam, move your chair.' And I hung up."

Frank's pleasure at being married to Berta did not change all of his habits. He still worked constantly. "I'm intense about my work and I spend every waking hour on it," he told Peter Arnell a few years later, in an interview for the monograph Arnell was preparing on Frank's work. "I love my kids, my wife, but I'm so intensely involved with my work that I forget birthdays, anniversaries—I never remember anything personal."

Far more problematic than absentmindedness was Frank's agreement to go ahead with a trip to Israel, Greece, and Egypt with his old friend the artist Ed Moses. The idea of visiting the countries that could be considered the origins of Western culture had originated when Frank and Moses were smoking marijuana with their friend the sculptor Ken Price. "If you really want to understand it all, you go there. If you want to find Nirvana [as an artist] that's what you gotta do," Frank remembers Price saying. Price did not, however, go on the trip. Moses, who had recently separated from his wife, was eager to go but had no desire to travel alone. Frank offered to come with him. He assumed that he could count on Berta to be more reasonable about such things than Anita had been, and he liked the idea of traveling with a friend to places that could mean a lot to both of them. There might not be another chance to do this, he told himself, since he would soon have a small child again. That he was leaving behind a pregnant wife to take the trip was a fact that he conveniently chose to put aside in his mind.

The trip began well in Israel, where Frank was able to meet Teddy Kollek, the longtime mayor of Jerusalem, who was particularly interested in the physical development of the city and five years before had established an international committee to advise on it. Having the chance to share his views with a celebrated mayor who cared about architecture pleased Frank no end. Moses, too, was able to get some professional benefit out of the trip. Through the Pace Gallery he was given an introduction to the head of the Israel Museum. The two men "were wined and dined all around," Moses recalled. "I said, 'Frank, are you proud to be a Jew now, seeing this whole situation, [the] magnificence of it?'" Frank and Moses

Frank joined Ed Moses
on a trip to Greece right
after his marriage to
Berta.

also spent time with the violinist Itzhak Perlman, who was on tour in Israel at the time, and they attended one of his concerts. Later they traveled to Masada to see the ancient fortress site beside the Dead Sea.

They went next to Greece, which was considerably less successful.[*] The problem was not in the architecture and ancient artifacts they had come to see, but in Frank's feeling that Moses, newly single, was as interested in meeting women in Greece as in seeing historic sites. Frank had no interest in other women and was racked with guilt for leaving Berta at home not long after their marriage. He knew he had taken advantage of her because she had not exploded in fury over the idea of such a trip, as Anita might have done. Throughout the trip Frank and Moses were on a tight budget, and by the time they got to Greece they had begun to quarrel over money. The two shared a room, which made for complications when Moses had romantic interludes. After about a week and a half, they parted ways. Moses went on to Egypt by himself, and Frank returned to Los Angeles to resume his married life. The trip was not without consequences. Frank's relationship with Moses was badly damaged and would not recover for years. And Frank discovered that Berta, however calm she may have appeared on the surface, was hardly happy about his absence. She would remind him about it for years to come.

---

[*] In 1975 it was not possible to travel directly from Israel to Egypt, which would have made more sense in geographical terms.

I ssues with old friends like Moses or with clients like Norton Simon seemed to recede in Frank's mind as Berta's pregnancy advanced. She was due to give birth in April 1976, and wanted to have a natural childbirth. Doreen volunteered to be her labor coach and accompany her to Lamaze classes, a role that Frank, aware of his own strengths and weaknesses, had declined. Doreen had always gotten along well with the women in her brother's life, and Frank's marriage to Berta had eased some of the strain in his relationship with her, despite her deep unhappiness over his decision to evict her from the Hillcrest apartment.

That apartment would become Frank and Berta's first home as a married couple, and it was where they were when Frank placed a panicked call to his sister very early in the morning of April 13 to say that Berta appeared to be going into labor. Her mother, who had come from Panama, was making breakfast, Doreen remembered, while Frank "was hysterical, absolutely hysterical beyond himself."

"Is she okay? Is she okay?" Frank would ask Doreen over and over again, while Berta's mother held her rosary. The calmest people, it seemed, were Doreen and Berta herself. But Frank managed to get them all to the hospital, where he spent most of his time in the waiting room, too anxious to be in the birthing room with his wife.

A few hours later, with Doreen's help, Berta gave birth to her first child and Frank's first son. They named him Alejandro, Alejo for short. Frank's second family had begun.

10

A House in Santa Monica

rank's relationship with the Rouse Company was to some extent an unlikely one, and not only because he was separated by a continent from his Maryland-based client. Rouse was a commercial real estate developer whose founder, James Rouse, was impassioned about cities, economic opportunity, and affordable housing, despite having made most of his money building suburban shopping malls, and he understood the notion of civic and public space far better than most of his competitors. He had established his company's relationship with Frank mainly on the basis of shared social ideals, not a common architectural interest. Even though Frank had designed the Rouse headquarters and other buildings for Rouse's new town, Columbia, in Maryland, it was not surprising that he had never been asked to design one of the company's shopping centers.

That changed with the start of Santa Monica Place, a Rouse project in Frank's hometown that he asked Rouse if he could design. How could he not, when it was just blocks away from where he lived? The project emerged out of Santa Monica's long and unsuccessful attempts to revitalize its aging downtown shopping district, which, like the cores of so many older cities, had lost business to new, large suburban malls. In 1960 the city commissioned Victor Gruen, Frank's old boss, to study the problem, and Gruen suggested that 3rd Street, the main shopping street, be converted into a pedestrian promenade, and that the city build large parking garages and try to attract a major department store. After a dozen years, the first two recommendations had been implemented to modest success, but the city had been frustrated in its attempt to interest a department store in coming downtown, so the planners decided in 1972 to up the ante and make three downtown blocks available for a large, multiuse retail complex. Frank realized that the site could allow for a development with apartments, hotels, and offices, a more expansive version of Midtown Plaza, the Victor Gruen project he had worked on years before in Rochester, New York. He still believed in the potential of urban renewal projects like this to turn around troubled downtowns, and he persuaded Rouse to let him produce a design, which the Rouse Company would have to present to the city in competition with proposals from other developers.

As it turned out, Rouse, which had never done a project in California, was one of only two final competitors. The other was Ernest Hahn, whose company was California's largest mall developer, and whose projects back then could only be described as conventional at best. In May 1974, Hahn and Rouse were both scheduled to present their proposals to the Santa Monica city council. Hahn's presentation consisted of detailed cost estimates more than design, and he showed written commitments from a department store and a hotel operator. Rouse, exhausted from a European business trip that had concluded just before he went to California, collapsed just before starting his presentation. It was rescheduled for the following week, and Rouse, on the advice of his doctors, decided not to return to Santa Monica and asked Frank to make the presentation himself.

It turned out to be a wise strategy. Rouse couldn't beat Hahn at the numbers—its project simply wasn't far enough along to allow them to show the same commitments—but the developer knew that with Frank's design he had something more exciting to show than Hahn's banal concrete boxes, and he decided to take a chance on Frank's ability to impress the city council with what looked like a lively, socially active urban space. The council agreed, and voted unanimously to award the land to Rouse.

Frank's basic design concept was to try to tie the project into the surrounding urban fabric, placing low-rise buildings around the perimeter that would connect to the scale of the existing buildings on neighboring streets. In that sense, it was the opposite of most malls, either urban or suburban, which tend to face inward, indifferent either to surrounding streets or, in the case of suburban malls, parking lots. Frank's plan was to place the taller hotel and office slabs largely in the interior of the site.

Opposition from citizens' groups delayed the project for years. The objections ranged from unhappiness with the idea of the city condemning land and offering financial incentives to a private developer to questions about the wisdom of placing an enclosed shopping mall in the benign climate of Southern California two blocks from the Pacific Ocean, no matter who paid for it. The citizens' groups sued the city, and after they lost in trial court, Santa Monica, a famously liberal city whose leaders were not eager to engage in an extended court battle, settled by agreeing to numerous concessions in exchange for allowing Santa Monica Place to go ahead. The city agreed to use some of the new taxes that the project was expected to bring in to rehabilitate low-income housing, and to build new vest-pocket parks, and Rouse agreed to contribute to local funds for child care and battered women.

An unintended consequence of the delays and negotiations was that the project itself was reduced in scope, and what was finally built was much closer to a standard shopping mall than what either Frank or Rouse had envisioned. There were two department stores—one of them a branch of the Broadway, the store where Thelma Gehry had worked for many years—and two parking garages, as well as an arcade of smaller stores. The parcel of land that was available for the reduced-size version of Santa Monica Place was roughly square, and Frank put the department stores in two corners diagonally opposite each other, and the parking structures in the remaining two corners. A diagonal arcade—the actual "mall"—sliced through the site at a slight angle. The department stores were permitted to design their own buildings, and the only elements left for Frank on the outside were the exteriors of the parking structures and the sections of the façade where the central shopping arcade faced the street. He managed to bring a certain choppy energy to his design of the mall entrance, which looked more or less as if the sleek white stucco façade of the Rouse Company headquarters had been cut into pieces and the pieces mixed up and reassembled into a jagged, asymmetrical composition. To some extent it suggested a theme he would explore in many of his later projects, which, like Santa Monica Place, seemed random and disordered at first glance, but were in fact carefully and precisely planned.

The most notable aspect of the architecture of Santa Monica Place, however, was the exterior of the concrete parking garage at the southern end of the project. Frank covered one entire side of the garage in blue chain-link fencing, four stories of it, and atop that he placed a huge sign made of white chain-link fencing, spelling out SANTA MONICA PLACE in letters two stories high. He could not have been unaware that the deliberately hazy quality of the words fabricated out of chain link evoked the work of Ed Ruscha, one of his favorite Los Angeles artists, at a vast scale. Using words at all was a rare venture into graphics for Frank, who generally disdained placing any kind of large lettering on his buildings and preferred to have his architecture serve as its own sign. But at Santa Monica Place there had been less opportunity to create recognizable architecture than he had expected, which he found frustrating; he knew also that he had to find a way to make the project easily identifiable from an adjacent free-way, Interstate 10. His friend Robert Irwin was working on art pieces that involved scrims, and he realized that he could use chain link as a gargantuan form of scrim, a translucent metal curtain pulled across the exterior of the parking garage. Its enormous size made the chain-link wall and sign of Santa Monica Place Frank's most conspicuous exercise in the material, but in some ways it was among his least adventuresome. It was just a huge, two-dimensional wall covering, and Frank had already begun to come up with far more unusual uses for it. If the chain-link sign was nothing like what you would see in any other shopping center, it was tame by comparison to much of the other work Frank was doing. His friend Craig Hodgetts, talking to him about the sign, said, "You didn't accomplish anything with that," and Frank did not disagree.

Still, Frank saw his use of chain-link fencing as a benign, even earnest attempt to break away from the common associations of the material and look at it on its own terms. Chain link may have been invented as nothing more than a fence material, but Frank was convinced that it could be used for things other than keeping people out of places, and that it did not have to have the negative connotations that had led the set designer Oliver Smith to use it to signify a dangerous locale in his sets for the Broadway musical *West Side Story* twenty years before. Frank had already shown at the Concord Pavilion box office that chain link could create a kind of "shadow architecture," a structure that seemed at once solid and void, and he expanded on that idea not long afterward at the Cabrillo Marine Museum in San Pedro, south of Los Angeles, with an entire series of trapezoidal structures in chain link, effectively a mini-skyline. The museum was near the port of Los Angeles, and its industrial site was as far from the rural environment of the Concord Pavilion as could be imagined. Frank described the site in a comment at once sincere and ironic: "The site was a parking lot . . . it has chain-link fences, industrial type buildings, and big water tanks. In front are lots of large ships. I'm a very traditional architect in the sense that I am interested in context."

Concerned about context though he may have been, Frank's contrarian instincts were hardly absent so far as chain link was concerned. He knew, he said later, that "everybody hates it. So that's when I started doing some stuff [with it]." His goal was not to provoke irritation but recognition that chain link is a ubiquitous material, and that most people don't think about it or even notice it until the context in which it is seen has changed. Frank remembered visiting the home of the lawyer Mickey Rudin, whom he had met through Milton Wexler, and noticing how the chain-link fencing around Rudin's tennis court was a prominent part of the view from the living room, the dining room, the kitchen, and Rudin's bedroom. "I see I've converted you to chain link," Frank told Rudin. "No, that's just my tennis court," Rudin replied. "I said bingo, that's the denial thing," Frank said. That material was everywhere, and why pretend it wasn't? Instead of denying its ubiquity, why not use it more creatively?

Frank found a factory in downtown Los Angeles that made chain-link fencing, and went to visit. He had thought that it would be an easy matter to produce chain link in a variety of colors, and discovered that while it was not challenging from a technical standpoint, the factory's management had no interest in turning the material into a custom item. We don't need to bother, Frank remembered the chain link manufacturer telling him. They produced unpainted chain-link so quickly and easily and sold it in such large quantities that it wasn't worth the trouble and extra expense to produce smaller amounts in different colors. The only color other than unpainted silver that they produced willingly was dark green, because it was popular for tennis courts.

As his projects like the Concord Pavilion box office and the Cabrillo Marine Museum show, Frank was quick to exploit the design possibilities in chain-link fencing. To him it was a scrim, a gauze, a transparent mesh that could be put together into almost any kind of shape. His fantasy was that it could yield a kind of "instantaneous" architecture. "You could call the chain-link guys and you could give them coordinates and they could build a structure," Frank said. But even more than the forms he could make it into was the very ordinariness of the material, its plainness and lack of pretension, that gave him pleasure. "I love the way it looked," he said. "It had a humanity to it and it had an accessibility to it. It wasn't precious. It allows people to be who they are at the time. So, it's the antithesis of the Farnsworth House, in which every detail is perfect. You got to go there and if you don't make the bed as soon as you get out, it destroys the world."

Chain-link fence, then, was the anti-Mies material—something that expressed casualness, funkiness, ambiguity, the appearance of incompleteness, all things Frank responded to and wanted somehow to have his architecture contain. Milton Wexler, however, did not see chain link that way at all. Frank's psychiatrist thought of chain-link fencing more in terms of prison yards than tennis courts, and he was troubled by Frank's fondness for it. "He thought I was expressing anger with the chain link and that I needed to do these angry things with this corrugated metal and things, to piss people off, to get attention," Frank said. "And he was very critical about that to me. He said it was a waste of time."

Frank usually accepted Wexler's suggestions, rarely challenging him. This time, however, was different: Milton Wexler wasn't telling him how to conduct a relationship but how to make architecture, and Frank decided to take him on. "I confronted him. I said, 'How dare you tell me that. You can't do that,'" Frank said. "I said, 'Architecture's intuitive, it's a magic trick. I don't know where it comes from. Stop it.'"

It was an important conversation, in part because it was one of the rare times that Frank pushed back against his therapist. Generally, he did not argue with Wexler. He instantly abandoned his longtime practice of smoking cigars, for example, when Wexler asked him if he realized how many people around him, including Wexler himself, disliked cigars and found smoking to be a messy, selfish, and unattractive habit. When it came to architecture, though, Frank realized that however insightful, even brilliant, he might find Milton Wexler to be, Wexler was seeing architecture not as he himself did, but in a more conventional way. The man whom Frank had relied upon to see all things with a fresh eye could not in fact see Frank's own subject with much freshness at all. To Frank, chain-link fencing could be pure, geometric form, a kind of big metal mesh, but he realized that Wexler had difficulty getting beyond its common associations, which resonated with issues of restriction and enclosure and authority. Usually Frank, like most patients, needed his therapist to help him to see patterns that he was unable to perceive himself, but this time it was he who saw beyond the surface, and Wexler who could not.

Wexler had a tendency to be stubborn. So, of course, did Frank, but he rarely displayed that side of himself to his therapist, who more often saw him either in the grip of indecision or, as with his decision to give up smoking, willing to accede quickly to Wexler's suggestions. But the two had never confronted an issue that could be considered more about architecture than about Frank's psyche, and when the matter of chain link arose, Frank showed neither ambivalence nor any inclination to accept what Wexler was saying at face value. He was so annoyed at Wexler that he even considered quitting therapy.

Frank did not deny that he was capable of anger, and eventually he came to see that Wexler was motivated by a desire to search for the basis of that anger and was not trying to tell him how to make architecture.

But Frank's feeling about chain link, as about so many design choices he made, was intuitive. He had said that to Wexler, but he felt some frustration at his inability to elucidate it convincingly. He could not, at least back then, explain adequately why he was so certain that his fondness for the material was motivated not by seeing chain link in the conventional way but by the exact opposite of that. It was because he did not see the material as others did that he could envision its potential to be something else altogether. It was, he felt, a matter of imagination—and if Milton Wexler had great imagination so far as the human psyche was concerned, he had far less, Frank believed, when it came to matters of physical form.

The notion of a new house began modestly enough. In 1977, with Alejo approaching the toddler stage, Frank and Berta were beginning to feel squeezed in the apartment at Hillcrest. Designing a house for himself and his family from scratch had occurred to him, as it crosses the mind of almost every architect, but he felt no sense of urgency about it. He felt no urgency about moving at all, since any new house, even an existing one, would be a statement to the world about his architectural taste and judgment, if not his design skill, and he was not sure that he wanted to take that on. It was not the first time this had happened. Berta recalled Frank's mother, Thelma, telling her, " 'You know, when you-know-who'—that was how she would refer to Anita—'when you-know-who wanted a new house, I told her she would have to find it herself.' " And Anita had found the house on Kennard Avenue in Westwood, to which Frank dutifully moved.

Doreen remembered hearing Thelma giving Berta the same advice. "My mother said, 'Honey, he'll never buy a house . . . go and get one,' " Doreen said. "And my mother was right. She knew this guy. He couldn't, you know? And I think she understood that if it was he who made the move to buy the house, then he had to do something with it, but if his wife chose the house he could just say, 'My wife chose the house,' and then do battle, architectural battle with it, which is what I think happened."

Berta had recently begun to work at the office as a bookkeeper. She had been called in by Frank to help when he discovered that his bookkeeper had not bothered to balance the office checkbook. Berta's efficiency at untangling the mess seemed to deepen their partnership, giving Frank even more of a feeling that she understood how he worked and how he thought, and it made the notion of designing a house seem more palatable. Still, he did not feel ready, either emotionally or financially, to design a house for his family from scratch, and it made sense to buy an existing one, at least as a starting point, and renovate it. Berta began to look at houses in Santa Monica, where she and Frank wanted to remain. What intrigued her most was a slightly run-down Dutch colonial house painted a dull salmon pink at the corner of 22nd Street and Washington Avenue. "The first moment I went through it I thought, 'Frank can do things to this house,'" Berta said.

The house was in a pleasant, quiet neighborhood that was not Santa Monica's fanciest but hardly undesirable. The streets were lined with trees, and the immediate neighbors were mostly one- and two-story single-family houses. The house had a backyard for Alejo to play in, and it was reasonably convenient to Frank's office, which by then had moved to an industrial building on Cloverfield Boulevard. Perhaps best of all, it was not one of those Spanish-style houses that are ubiquitous in Los Angeles, which might have made Frank feel as if he were living in a cliché. If anything, it could more easily be taken for an ordinary suburban house on the East Coast. But at bottom it had no strong architectural presence to speak of, which Frank counted as a plus.

The Gehrys bought the property for $160,000, putting down $40,000 that Frank was able to borrow from Fred Weisman, the Los Angeles art collector and businessman for whom he had completed an office building in Columbia, Maryland, and some small projects in Los Angeles. He mortgaged the rest. As he began to think about what to do with the house, he made a list of what he considered the place's positive attributes. He liked the giant euphorbia cactus in the backyard, the row of tall cedar trees along the north property line, and the fact that it was on a corner and two stories high. He also listed "pink asbestos shingles, white clapboard siding, a green asphalt shingle roof, and original windows with small and large glass panes" as things he liked about the structure itself, along with the narrow oak flooring and paneled wood doors inside.

The house appeared to be between fifty and sixty years old, and even though it was ordinary as Dutch colonials went, such houses were unusual enough in Los Angeles that the profile of its gambrel roof stood out. More important, it gave Gehry an architectural foil. He was not sure what he wanted to do to the house, but he was certain that he did not want to bury it within his own architecture. He knew that it would be easy to alter the old house beyond recognition, or to expand it on all sides so that the original structure disappeared behind new, Gehry-designed façades. It would be much more difficult to figure out how to engage this old house in some form of architectural discourse—to weave his own very different kind of architecture in and around it and make the conversation work. It had to be, in part, a purely formal discourse, a play of shapes, of solids and voids, of transparency and opacity, but it had to be just as much a dialogue between old and new, and between the ordinary and the extraordinary.

"I wasn't trying to make a big or precious statement about architecture or trying to do an important work," Frank said shortly after the house was finished. "I was trying to build a lot of ideas." At the same time as he was trying to use the house as a way of working out his ideas in their most advanced form, he also had to fulfill the needs of his family. Berta had become a quiet, determined, and unwavering advocate of his work, but she was also in effect his client, and from her standpoint the renovated and expanded house had to have a large kitchen—"Frank and I have in common the fact that at our grandmothers' houses everybody spent most of their time in the kitchens," she said—as well as ample play space both inside and out, and a staircase that would be safe for Alejandro.

The house had a gestation period of several months as Frank developed different ideas. The design owed a debt to a few projects he was working on at around the same time, including a renovation and expansion of Gemini G.E.L., the fine art lithography studio owned by his friends Elyse and Stanley Grinstein and Sid Felsen, to which he added first a new stucco façade, wrapping the front of the existing building, and later a new wing with a stairway skewed off the structure's grid, placed under an angled skylight with exposed wood framing. Gemini's owners, who thought of themselves as providing a place in which artists could explore new ideas, were more than happy to let Frank do the same with their building, and several details that became common in his work can be traced to the studio. But it was far from the only project that connected with his house. A small renovation of a suburban house from the 1950s in West Hollywood, the St. Ives house, in which Frank wrapped an addition with an expanded kitchen, stairs, and entrance around three sides of the old house, was a particular, if cautious, model for his initial scheme, in which he surrounded the original house with new rooms on the first floor.

He used that simple version in the plans he submitted to the city of Santa Monica for a building permit, but he hardly considered it final. As he was working on his own house in 1978 he was also designing three other houses, none of which would be built, but all of which gave him the chance to experiment with ideas that would influence the design of his own house, in turn influencing the other three. All three projects—the

Gunther house, the Wagner house, and the Familian house—made use of chain link as an architectural element, and all three were more complex, less geometrically pure compositions than the Ron Davis house. And all three were designed to give the suggestion that their construction was not yet fully complete.

The Familian house, which would also have been in Santa Monica, is the largest and most ambitious, based on a forty-by-forty-foot cube, built in wood framing covered in white stucco, containing main living areas, and a hundred-foot-long rectangular structure, also of stucco over a wood frame, with bedrooms. It marks an important early point in a theme Frank would explore much more seriously later on, which was the notion of dividing a program up into multiple smaller structures and putting them together to suggest a village. But the most striking thing about the Familian house is not the fact of its separate sections but the fact that both portions look as if they have exploded, with numerous projecting spaces, bridges, and stair-wells, most of which are designed to look like the unfinished wood-frame tract houses that Frank so liked until their structure was covered up. You are struck with a sense of irregular lines, of energy moving in all kinds of directions.

Frank later described these houses as "sketching with wood" and said, "I guess I was interested in the unfinished—or the quality you find in paintings by Jackson Pollock, for instance, or de Kooning, or Cézanne, that look like the paint was just applied. The very finished, polished, every-detail-perfect kind of architecture seemed to me not to have that quality. I wanted to try that out in a building."

If the clients of these three houses were ultimately unable to see them built, that would not be the issue with Frank's own house. Any problem here would be more due to Frank's distraction with other projects and reluctance to make final decisions about what he wanted to do with the house. He was prone in many of his projects to a tendency to continue designing and redesigning, driven not by a search for perfectionism— the quality that is behind so many architects' obsessive reworking of their designs—but by his own distinctive combination of anxiety and ongoing curiosity. Frank's inclination to keep on sketching was usually tempered by his clients' timetables. But this time there was no external force to push him along other than his recognition that however much more patient than most of his clients Berta might appear to be, it would not be in his interest to keep her waiting forever. He was as aware as she that their Hill-crest quarters were feeling more cramped as Alejo grew bigger.

At the beginning, Frank did most of the work on the house himself, hesitant to take his colleagues away from paying clients to focus on a project that he hadn't figured out fully for himself yet. Then, early in the design process, he found an unexpected lieutenant, a young architect named Paul Lubowicki. Frank had met him only a few months earlier at Cooper Union in New York, where John Hejduk, the longtime dean of the architecture school at Cooper, who had admired the Ron Davis house, had invited him to talk about his work. Frank spent some time with the architecture students in their studio, and particularly liked what Lubowicki, a student in his final year, was doing. He suggested that Lubowicki call him. When Lubowicki followed up, Frank proposed that he come out west for six months, which would allow both of them to see if working in the Gehry office was a good fit. (It was something Frank would do a number of times with students whose work had impressed him, but to whom he was not ready to offer a permanent job.) When Lubowicki arrived to start work and Frank showed him around, he noticed the preliminary sketches for the house, which at that stage looked something like a version of the Ron Davis house placed in front of the old Dutch colonial.

"I said, 'I really like that,'" Lubowicki said. "I latched on to his house. . . . A few days later he said, 'I want you to work on the house.'" Lubowicki was exactly what Frank wanted: young, eager, and without any predetermined views of what the house should be. Lubowicki made a model from Frank's early sketch, and when it was done, Frank, with Lubowicki at his side, began to play with the model. "Let's cut away at it," Frank said. He was determined to push the house beyond the Ron Davis house, and he took a knife and cut the front section apart in the center, breaking the new façade into two parts, with an opening in the middle to serve as the entryway.

The cut was not just a technique of model-making; it was, in a sense, a metaphor for the way Frank was seeing the whole design—as a composition made of slices and slashes and clashes, of colliding forms and textures, solids and voids, all seeming random but considered as meticulously as any Miesian detail. If Frank's work had some of the quality of action painting, the house was like the sketches Franz Kline did on pages torn from the telephone directory, where Kline's new and bold lines of force played off against the more genteel, ordered background of the old printed page. Here Frank's architecture was Kline's brushstrokes, and the old house was the printed page of the telephone book.

Designing the house was also, Lubowicki thought, "a way for Frank to escape. It was during the time he was working on the shopping center,

A side view of the
Gehry house from
Washington Avenue

Santa Monica Place, and not really enjoying it." Lubowicki would become
Frank's assistant, sounding board, and general factotum on the house, and
the recipient of sketch after sketch. "Every day he'd come up with five
sketches, but I didn't know anything. I had never designed a building,"
Lubowicki said. But Lubowicki seemed well suited to Frank's ad hoc process, and with the help of Greg Walsh, who as always remained at his desk
to unravel problems or to act as an interpreter of Frank's wishes, the design
was completed. Through some of his artist friends Frank found a young
contractor, John Fernandez, who took on the job of building the house.
It was finished in time for the Gehrys to move into it by September 1978.
Frank rented a U-Haul truck to bring their belongings from their old apartment. He remembered driving to 22nd Street with Alejo on his lap, even
though he knew it was unsafe.

   The house as built both summed up Frank's work to that point and
propelled it forward. The old two-story structure was surrounded by a new
structure of corrugated metal, sharply angled but only one story high, with
the old house visible from all sides, poking up through the midst of the

The Gehry kitchen in Santa Monica, with the wall of the old house on the left

new. The corrugated metal façade was broken at the corner, and again along the side, by large expanses of exposed wood framing covered in glass. In the front of the house, the roof of the new extension became a deck, enclosed by large sections of chain-link fencing, one of which seemed to slash through the air like a flying wedge. On the side, one of the sections made of exposed wood frame and glass was in the shape of a cube, appearing to burst through the corrugated metal wall. With its slanting lines, protruding corners, and crooked windows, the house "employed an original vocabulary of crude industrial materials . . . arranged into a composition of lopsided cubes, exposed-stud walls, and other unruly shapes," the critic Herbert Muschamp wrote.

If Frank appeared to be attacking the old house by surrounding it with alien forms and materials, he also seemed to be no more sympathetic to the original structure on the interior. Many of the walls and ceilings were removed or stripped back to their framework, and the tiny original rooms were opened up to make a larger, flowing living space on the ground floor that had one solid white wall, one wall of unpainted plywood, and another of exposed studs. Wooden joists were left exposed in the ceiling, sections of which were removed to create open lofts in what had been the attic.

A new kitchen and dining area were added on the side, under the glass of the exposed wood-frame sections, which bring natural light and the play of shape and shadow directly into the space. The kitchen was given a floor of asphalt, poured directly over the ground, like a driveway. The exterior wall of the old house divided the kitchen from the living room, so that it was ambiguously poised between feeling like an indoor room and an outdoor one.

The kitchen was punctuated by a huge old Roper range that Berta Gehry found and purchased secondhand; sitting on the asphalt floor, it seemed almost like an enormous old Packard about to rumble down the length of the room. The stove is a kind of found object, slightly funky but enlivened by being shifted into a new context, which of course is something you could say about the entire original Dutch colonial house. The stove has an easy, obvious playfulness that helps soften Frank's interventions to the house. At first glance the old house appears casual, relaxed, and forgiving, while Frank's additions seem crisp, hard-edged, and visually jarring. The stove is the clearest indication that the situation is a bit more complicated than that. Its relaxed presence lightens the house and signals that Frank's intentions were gentler than they might appear.

Frank's architectural voice was developing rapidly, and however startling, even bizarre, many of his forms seemed, they were not pompous or smug. Frank was not dogmatic, and his architecture was not the self-righteous expression of a theory, but much more of an intuitive, methodical formal exploration. If it stood for anything, it was his belief that architecture had no business being reduced to the simple and pure geometric forms of minimalism. "In this world, you cannot make things clean and simple and hermetic. . . . Architecture can't clean up the mess singlehandedly, and what I see in the architecture that pretends to clean up the mess is contrivance. I don't think you can do it, that you can clean it all up so easily, sweep all the mess under the carpet, I think architecture should deal with the mess."

Perhaps the most remarkable thing about Frank's architecture that was beginning to become clear was his gift for making unusual shapes that seemed, if not natural, then at least relatively unself-conscious. The house, both inside and out, had a quality that was strange and different, but once you got over the shock of seeing it for the first time, it could seem amiable, even benign. If the house had any implication for the rest of Frank's work, it was that the unusual qualities of his architecture were quirkily cheerful rather than ominous.

The architect Charles Moore, a perceptive critic, understood this when he wrote, "It seems to me that delight is especially strong in this house, which is, for all its astonishing differences with what's around it, a cheerful and pleasant addition to a cheerful and pleasant neighborhood. The neighbors aren't so sure, but it has the same kind of 'Maybe it seems naïve but you know it isn't' apparent ingenuousness that makes houses built out of bottle glass or broken plates or other unusual materials become monuments that people travel halfway around the world to see."

Moore was correct in observing that many of Frank and Berta's new neighbors saw it otherwise. "It looks like a Tijuana sausage factory," a man told Paul Lubowicki before the house was finished. John Dreyfuss of the *Los Angeles Times* wrote a piece with the headline "Gehry's Artful House Offends, Baffles, Angers His Neighbors" that attempted to be sympathetic to the house, describing Frank as a nationally respected architect who "has put his money and talent where his heart is, in a structure that reflects many of his highly unusual and controversial design theories." But the article made clear that Dreyfuss's favorable view of the house was not shared by most of Frank's neighbors, some of whom, the *Times* writer said, referred to the house as "the prison." A woman who lived down the street, who had attempted legal action to stop its construction, wrote to the *Los Angeles Times* claiming that the house had been abandoned when the Gehrys took a short vacation after moving in, the implication being that the city should take advantage of the opportunity to swoop in and demolish it.

Even less-hostile neighbors thought the house was unfinished. It did look something like a construction site. To many of the neighbors, it was a direct attack on their taste, their values, and their judgment. Frank claimed that he was merely reflecting the reality of the world around him and presenting it as he saw it. "There's a smugness about many middle-class neighborhoods that bothers me," he said. "Everybody has his camper truck out front. There's a lot of activity related to hardware and junk and cars and boats. But the neighbors have come around and told me, 'I don't like your house.' And I say, 'What about your boat in the front yard? What about your camper truck? It's the same aesthetic.' They say, 'Oh, no, that's normal.'"

It was not unlike the argument he had given to Mickey Rudin about his chain-link fencing. You have this stuff all around you, Frank said, so why are you denying it? His neighbors, he believed, were hiding behind a veil of gentility that existed more in their imagination than in reality. The messy, industrial stuff was all around them—what was so terrible about trying to make something out of it?

"My attitude is that, despite everything, I'm attracted to those kinds of neighborhoods," Frank said. "Throughout my life, for better or worse, I have always been associated with the middle class. It's what I am. I'm kind of chameleon-like, I guess. Fit into the neighborhood. Fit into the environment. I like that. I sort of nestle in."

To the neighbors, Frank was hardly nestling in, or if he were doing so, it was more in the manner of a subversive, an architect who had come not to participate in the world that they knew and trusted, but to undermine it. They did not want to be told that the houses they felt comfortable in and the neighborhood they liked were an illusion, and that Frank was offering a design that represented a kind of truth. To his neighbors in Santa Monica, he may well have seemed something like the kind of neighbor that people in Ipswich, Massachusetts, found the writer John Updike to be when he participated in the local suburban culture and then took it apart in the eloquent, biting satire of his novels. But people in Ipswich did not have to read Updike's novels, while everyone who drove down 22nd Street or Washington Avenue in Santa Monica had no choice but to see Frank Gehry's house.

Berta, once again, proved a godsend. She loved her new house and was happy to say so, and her cool, unflappable manner provided a calming influence around the neighbors. If the house seemed provocative, Berta was the opposite. She would express her frustration with angry neighbors in private to Frank, but in public she came off as straightforward and matter-of-fact in expressing the pride she felt in the house, and in explaining why she found it to be exactly the comfortable environment in which she wanted to raise her child.

The neighbors calmed down, although before long they had to cope with a problem that proved as troublesome to Frank and Berta as it did to any of them—the constant flow of traffic past the house. The building had started off as a neighborhood curiosity, but John Dreyfuss's article made it famous all over Los Angeles, and by mid-1979, when the house was described by *The New York Times* as "a major work of architecture—perhaps the most significant new house in southern California in some years"—it had become a magnet for architects, students, and architecture buffs from all over the world. Some of them just drove by, slowing down as they passed the house; others parked and walked around, and a few bold ones went up and rang the doorbell. Frank felt mildly flattered by the attention but had no desire to give up his and his family's privacy to turn the house into a tourist attraction, and Berta had far less patience for the public spotlight than he did. The Gehrys soon added a small front gate.

Their two sons—Samuel Gehry, whom his parents called Sami, was born in 1979—would grow up thinking it was a fairly natural thing to live in a house that everyone wanted to see. "I never had a bad play date in that house," Alejo Gehry remembered. "It was a great place to play hide-and-seek, to run around and have a good time."

"I remember going to friends' houses and wondering why their walls were straight and their windows square," Sam Gehry said. "I'd go to friends' houses and their couches matched. We didn't even have a couch." Still, Frank's sons were not immune to the desire, common to most children, to live in a conventional way and to have what their friends had. As he grew older, Sam remembered, "I thought it would be nice to live in a finished house." He recalled looking with envy at an ordinary white stucco house nearby with a glider on the front porch. "I wanted to live there."

F rank took pleasure in showing the house to friends and colleagues, and he did not expect them all to like it. He hoped architects would at least understand what he was trying to do, and he was disappointed when Arthur Drexler, the influential curator of architecture at the Museum of Modern Art, visited the house and once back in New York began to make deprecating remarks about it that made their way back to Frank. "He didn't like it, and he didn't like my work. He thought it was a joke," Frank told Barbara Isenberg.

If snide comments passed through the architectural grapevine—most likely conveyed by Philip Johnson, who was close to both Drexler and Frank, and liked nothing more than to stir the pot—was how Frank learned what Drexler thought of his house, the writer Lillian Hellman informed him of her views in a different manner. Frank had met Hellman at a benefit party for Milton Wexler's Hereditary Disease Foundation, and they quickly hit it off when Hellman invited him to consider doing a project for her on Cape Cod.* He invited her to a large dinner party he and Berta

---

* Frank visited Hellman in Massachusetts, but the project never went ahead. He remembered that, when they first met, she told him that she had studied architecture at MIT, which turned out to be another instance of Hellman's well-known habit of embellishing her past.

were giving at the house. Hellman arrived and asked where the powder room was. She disappeared, emerged just before dinner was served, and sat down at the table. After five minutes she got up, said she was not feeling well, and departed.

Not long afterward Frank and Hellman encountered each other at another party. Hellman, Frank remembered, leaned over to him and said, "You're mad at me—you haven't called me."

"No," Frank said. "The last time I saw you was the night you weren't feeling well and you left my house."

She was actually feeling fine that night, Hellman told him. "I hated it," she said. "That's why I left—because I hated your house."

Frank's house, however, was just one of the things that was building his national reputation. His contacts in the art world were beginning to bear fruit on the East Coast, where Christophe de Menil, whose Texas-based family was known for its patronage of important, often younger artists and architects, asked him to remodel her town house in Manhattan, a former carriage house on the Upper East Side. Christophe had grown up in an early Philip Johnson house in Houston commissioned by her parents, Dominique and John de Menil, surrounded by her family's sweeping collection of twentieth-century art.[*] Her brother François would soon ask the architect Charles Gwathmey to build him a large beachfront villa in East Hampton, and this house would be Christophe's opportunity to show that she, too, could be a patron of cutting-edge architecture in the family tradition.[†]

The stakes were high for Frank as well. Philip Johnson, who relished his role as architectural kingmaker, knew the de Menils well, but then again, so did almost everyone in New York's art world. If the project would be relatively invisible in a literal sense, since its lower levels would be entirely hidden behind the original façade, it would be symbolically one of the most visible pieces of architecture in New York, since it would be carefully watched by people who were coming to matter to Frank a great deal.

---

[*] The de Menils asked the couturier Charles James to design the interiors, to which he gave a voluptuousness and rich sense of color that Johnson felt contradicted the Miesian restraint of his architecture. As a result, Johnson never allowed the house to be included in surveys of his work.

[†] The de Menils also commissioned Philip Johnson to build the University of St. Thomas in Houston, and they built the Rothko Chapel and the Byzantine Frescoes Chapel in Houston as well. Dominique de Menil asked Louis Kahn to build a permanent home for her art collection, a project that Kahn had not begun at the time of his death in 1974; in 1981 she hired Renzo Piano to design the Menil Collection, which opened in 1987.

Frank proposed gutting the entire interior of the carriage house. He wanted to ask Gordon Matta-Clark, the artist who was known for his "building cuts," sculptural pieces in which he removed sections of abandoned buildings, to craft the demolition as a site-specific art piece. Frank planned a swimming pool, kitchen, entertaining spaces, and guest quarters on the lower levels, and then, with these as a base, proposed building what were in effect two towerlike structures, one with a private living room, bedroom, and bath for Christophe, and one with the same series of rooms for her daughter. The plan was in some ways an inversion of what he was in the process of doing with his own house: instead of enclosing an old façade with new construction, he was placing something new as an object inside it. The two towers, which were linked by a bridge, were freestanding sculptural objects, and they marked another step in Frank's ongoing attempt to break down the elements of a building program into separate parts, making a house into a metaphorical village.

It was not to be. After multiple revisions and refinements, Christophe de Menil finally decided that the project was too expensive, too complex, and too time-consuming, and she asked Frank to simplify it into a more routine renovation. He reluctantly agreed. She had been a difficult client, making frequent demands, changing her mind, and asking for a disproportionate amount of his time, and if there was not to be an important design at the end of all this trouble, why bother? But the instinct that had so often led him to walk away from situations in which he felt he did not have enough control lay dormant this time. He began to oversee a simple renovation of the carriage house. After the work had started, de Menil ended a meeting by letting him know that she did not require his services any longer. He left her house, got into a yellow cab, and felt himself beginning to cry. He was not sure whether he was feeling a delayed reaction to the loss of the more ambitious project he had dreamed of building for Christophe de Menil, or relief that he would not have to deal with her wants any longer. [*]

S o much for Frank's triumphant entry into New York architecture. He would pursue several other projects there, including one in which

---

[*] The carriage house was later purchased by the art dealer Larry Gagosian, who seemed to have developed a specialty in taking over de Menil residences, since he also bought François de Menil's Gwathmey-designed beach house in East Hampton. As if to close the circle further, Gagosian became Frank's dealer, specializing in selling the fish lamps he would build from the mid-1980s onward.

he was an investor, a pair of industrial buildings on Lafayette Street on the northern fringe of Little Italy that he planned to convert into a small village of artists' lofts. That, too, did not come to fruition. New York was a hard nut to crack, and it would be years before he managed to complete a project there.

At the same time, the period just after he completed his house was a productive one back home. Several important residential jobs in Los Angeles were completed, making up for the failure of the Familian, Wagner, and Gunther houses to go forward. The most significant was for Jane Spiller, a designer who had worked for Charles Eames and later gone to film school, where a film project about Los Angeles artists brought her into contact with Frank. She remembered visiting his office and seeing the plans for the Ron Davis house, and Frank's enthusiasm for the corrugated metal exterior he was planning. A few years later, Spiller purchased a small, narrow lot in Venice. She called Frank and asked him if he would consult with her on a house for the property, which she wanted to design herself to save money. Frank told her he could not work that way, but that he was eager to design a building in Venice, a neighborhood whose messy disarray appealed to him. In exchange for the freedom to use his own design concepts, he said he would promise a house with a low construction cost as well as modest design fees. Spiller agreed, and a four-year design process began that, like all of Frank's best work, was an experience of constant give-and-take between architect and client. "I would bring ideas, Frank would bring ideas, and he would do sketches," Jane Spiller said. "I often think that Frank is like a conductor or a composer, and there are many other people involved, but without Frank, you wouldn't have the symphony."

Spiller wanted to fit a single-family house for herself as well as a small rental unit onto the property. Frank was able to make use of ideas he had been developing in his own house and in the project for Christophe de Menil to create a house in the form of a vertical loft, with a generosity of space inside that comes as a surprising contrast to the tight exterior. The Spiller house is sheathed in corrugated galvanized steel, and it has multiple projections of wood, some of which contain exposed framework behind glass. Spiller's portion of the house is built in the form of a three-story, fifty-foot tower: ostensibly a way of allowing a view of the ocean a few blocks away, it is also an echo of what Frank had been trying to do with the de Menil project in New York. The small rental unit squats in front of it, close to the street, with a garden courtyard between the two.

A few blocks away, on Indiana Avenue in the Oakwood section of Venice, Frank made another go at being a part-time real estate developer. He had already joined forces with his artist friend Chuck Arnoldi to buy a building in Venice, and Arnoldi, convinced that real estate values would rise and the artists would be forced out of the area, wanted to do something before gentrification made the area—which in the 1970s was considered too dangerous to walk in after dark—no longer affordable. He came up with a plan to buy land and build artists' lofts. Laddie Dill, another artist friend of Frank's, joined Arnoldi in purchasing a long, narrow lot that could accommodate three units, and Frank agreed to contribute his services as an architect in exchange for a one-third share in the partnership.

Arnoldi and Dill were willing to let Frank do anything he pleased— "Frank was the architect, and we just let him run with it," Arnoldi said— and Frank came up with the notion of placing three freestanding structures in a row, one at the street, one in the back of the lot, and the other in between. He thought of them as boxes whose shape he would vary by carving away a different portion of the box, and each would be sheathed in a different material. One building would be covered in green asbestos shingles, one in plywood, and the other in pale blue stucco. Each had an exaggerated architectural element: a stairway in one case, a bay window in another, a chimney in the third. All three structures would have modest living accommodations on the ground floor and high, open studio spaces above.

The buildings had an unusual history. The construction process was casual enough that no one realized until the project was nearly done that the contractor had somehow managed to reverse the plans, flipping the buildings so that the studio that Frank wanted to be closest to the street was at the far end of the lot. Worse, the inversion meant that the houses faced the wrong way, and had a solid wall where there should have been windows admitting natural light.

Frank agreed to carve new windows on the opposite side, which solved that problem and brought more natural light into the studios, actually improving them. But they did not sell quickly. Venice was a lot further from major gentrification than Chuck Arnoldi had thought, and the combination of a sluggish economy and ongoing concerns about the neighborhood's safety meant that the partners were left holding the Indiana Avenue houses for much longer than they had expected. After months, one was sold; later, the actor Dennis Hopper purchased another.

Hopper eventually bought a second one, and then the third, and gradually turned the grouping into a private compound, something altogether different from what Arnoldi, Dill, and Frank had in mind. He also expanded the complex and hired another architect to do an additional structure next door on Indiana Avenue that was intended to be compatible with Frank's initial trio of small buildings. If someone as well known as Hopper, a prominent actor, filmmaker, photographer, and artist, wanted to be on Indiana Avenue, it demonstrated, if nothing else, that within a few years the neighborhood had gentrified beyond even what Chuck Arnoldi had envisioned—and also that Frank's work was beginning to become well enough known that other architects were starting to imitate it. But whatever the Indiana Avenue project did for Frank's growing reputation, he never made any money from it at all.

Not long after the completion of Santa Monica Place, Frank and Berta had Matt DeVito, the chief executive of the Rouse Company, to dinner at their house, which was still fairly new. DeVito was not entirely sure what to make of it, but one thing was absolutely clear to him: what Frank had designed for himself was very different from what he had been doing for the Rouse Company, and he sensed immediately Frank's heart lay in the house and works like it, not in designing commercial buildings for large developers.

"Frank, you don't like Santa Monica Place, do you?" DeVito asked him.

Frank did not want to offend DeVito, whom he genuinely liked, but he did not want to lie to him, either. "No," he said.

"Why are you wasting your time and energy fighting with commercial developers when you really have a different mission in life?" DeVito asked. "Why don't you just do what you're good at?"

Frank knew instantly that DeVito was right. He did not want to design buildings just to pay the rent, and he had never intended to build his practice around that kind of work. Even though Rouse was not a typical developer, the experience of designing Santa Monica Place had made it clear to him that the company was not exactly interested in blazing new trails in design, either. He may have shared Jim Rouse's passion for reshaping urban centers, but that hardly meant Rouse and his colleagues shared Frank's passion for reshaping architecture.

It was also becoming clear, even before Matt DeVito had his conversation with Frank, that the Rouse Company's interests and Frank's were diverging. Rouse had begun to develop what it called "festival marketplaces," downtown retail complexes that were intended to serve as public urban spaces, the first of which, Faneuil Hall, opened in Boston in 1976. It was designed by Benjamin Thompson, an architect more sophisticated than a typical shopping center architect but with none of Frank's desire to push the boundaries of architecture. Thompson was a more natural match for Jim Rouse and Matt DeVito, who had formed a tight working relationship with him during the planning of Faneuil Hall, and they were working together on similar projects in Philadelphia, Baltimore, and New York. It was not clear whether there was going to be room for Frank at Rouse, even if he wanted to keep working for the company. There were no more corporate headquarters or summer music pavilions to be built, and Frank was certainly not going to take on the conventional suburban malls that were the company's bread and butter.

Frank could not get the conversation with DeVito out of his mind. Usually he was the one who walked away from potentially profitable ventures that he felt would require him to make unacceptable compromises; this time, Matt DeVito asked him essentially why he hadn't already left Rouse. DeVito could have been trying to encourage Frank to step aside so that he did not have to tell him there was no more work in the pipeline for him, but even if Frank had seen that and understood that Ben Thompson had taken over as Rouse's favored outside architect, it would only have intensified Frank's recognition that the time had come to put an end to the relationship.

Characteristically, once he made the decision, he turned it into something bolder and more sweeping than it might have been. He decided not only to step aside from Rouse, but also to stop seeking other commercial work similar to what he had been doing for the company. He resolved to focus himself totally on making the architecture he cared about, and to accept the consequences of that decision.

The first consequence was unavoidable: his office, which had ballooned to several dozen people, largely as a result of the steady flow of fees from Rouse, had to shrink. Matt DeVito had come to dinner on a Friday night, and Frank spent the weekend trying to decide what to do. On the Monday morning after his conversation with DeVito, he let more than thirty of his employees go. He wanted a small office, with little enough overhead that he could afford to focus on work he cared about. Greg Walsh stayed on, and so, of course, did Berta, on whom Frank increasingly relied for advice as well as bookkeeping acumen. He was ready to start over again.

II

Fish and Other Shapes

Frank's decision to downsize his office and focus his practice solely on architecture that would give him the chance to express himself was a case of his characteristic tendency to walk away, writ large. Now he wasn't turning down specific opportunities that he didn't feel good about after they had been offered. He was rejecting them in advance and saying that if someone had a job that would not allow him to do something interesting, they should not bother to knock on his door.

It could seem like an arrogant way to do business, and in some ways it was, though in Frank's case it was driven not by arrogance or overconfidence so much as his recognition that he would be miserable if he had to spend his life designing shopping centers and office parks. He had no certainty that his smaller office would be as successful as his larger one was on its way to becoming. But he felt he had to reset, or rebalance, his practice lest it turn into the kind of large architectural offices he worked at early in his career, none of which he ever envisioned as a model for what he wanted to run himself. He feared a conventional kind of success far more than he feared artistic failure. He saw his decision as merely reorganizing things so that he could do what he thought he did best, which was to solve architectural problems in a way that made an artistic statement at, he hoped, no cost to functional utility.

His reset brought him closer to a group of local architects, all somewhat younger than he was, who believed as he did that architecture had an artistic component to it, and were determined to evolve new forms of expression. Frank's success as well as his seniority had made him a kind of de facto leader of the group, which included Thom Mayne and Michael Rotundi, who then practiced together as the firm Morphosis; Craig Hodgetts and Robert Mangurian, who called their firm Studio Works; and

Roland Coate, Eugene Kupper, Frederick Fisher, Peter de Bretteville, Coy Howard, Frank Dimster, and Eric Owen Moss. Some of them had worked for Frank at one time or another, and several were connected to the Southern California Institute of Architecture (SCI-Arc), an alternative architecture school in Santa Monica that had been founded in 1972.

In the late 1970s, the group loosely constituted a kind of "Los Angeles School" of architecture whose most notable characteristic, other than a basic seriousness about both form and theory, was probably a rejection of gentility. Although they went about it in very different ways, all of the architects of the Los Angeles School were eager to make buildings that had a bold, sometimes raw intensity that would have been unwelcome on the East Coast.

In this sense they shared a lot with Frank, who was clearly the group's central figure. Thom Mayne recalled returning to Los Angeles after getting his master of architecture degree at Harvard and being "immediately struck by something palpable that was going on in the architecture community. . . . The mood was strikingly different, more optimistic, more open, more creative than what I had seen in Cambridge or New York during my tenure at Harvard." Mayne remembered that his partner, Michael Rotundi, picked him up at the Los Angeles International Airport and was so eager to show him Frank's new house, which was then under construction, that he insisted they go to Santa Monica before Mayne even dropped off his luggage at home. "It was a powerful blast of something contemporary and new, something that could never have been done anywhere but L.A.," Mayne later wrote of his first visit to the house.

At around the same time, a gifted New York architect named Frank Israel, who was close to both Philip Johnson and Robert A. M. Stern, accepted an invitation to teach at UCLA and decided to move to Los Angeles. Johnson introduced the two Franks, who quickly hit it off. In Frank Israel, Gehry had found a colleague who was as comfortable talking about Culver City as Rome, who was as fascinated by the sprawl of Los Angeles as by the grandeur of Romanesque cathedrals, and who, like him, wanted to make architecture that looked different from the architecture of the past but was as grounded in a humanistic sensibility. "Frank and I have a lot of common ground. Both of us absorb our surroundings, recast what we see, and examine how those realities impact on the human psyche," Frank would write in an introduction to a monograph on Israel's work. "There is a human quality to his work that could only derive from a deep understanding of, and a deep concern for, the people around him. Where others have pulled abstractions out of the sky to justify their designs, Frank has grounded his work in the realities of human necessity and desire." It was perhaps the most generous homage to a younger architect he ever wrote. In Frank Israel, more than in any of the young architects who worked for him, Frank Gehry saw much of himself, and his own sensibility.*

Israel, perhaps because he was a recent transplant, was never considered a part of the Los Angeles School. It fell to Thom Mayne, who was teaching at SCI-Arc, to organize an exhibition and lecture series in 1979 that would galvanize the notion of the school. The exhibitions were somewhat ad hoc—Mayne had rented a large loft in Venice that had an empty gallery space attached to it, and he took it upon himself to produce a series of informal weekly shows accompanied by lectures. Each architect was given a week, during which he (the architects were all men) would have his work on display and would give a talk. John Dreyfuss, who was then the architecture critic of the *Los Angeles Times*, gave the casual event historic gravitas by deciding to write a separate review of each architect's exhibition. The *Times*'s decision to mark the events with an entire series of articles probably did as much as anything to establish the notion of a Los Angeles School of young architects who were doing important and creative things that the East Coast establishment would never consider. "Many of them have not built much," Dreyfuss wrote, "at least partly because they are unwilling to compromise their artistic principles."

Frank was the architect in the group with the highest profile by far, the one who had not only built several buildings but had begun to achieve a national reputation. At that point none of the others were known outside of Los Angeles, whereas Frank was already hobnobbing with Philip Johnson and the circle of architects Johnson called, with intended irony, "the kids," a group that included Robert A. M. Stern, Charles Gwathmey, Michael Graves, Richard Meier, Robert Venturi, Stanley Tigerman, and Peter Eisenman. A year before Mayne organized the exhibition and lecture series in Los Angeles, Frank's membership in Johnson's circle had been confirmed when Johnson asked him to come to Dallas to participate in a design symposium marking the occasion of Johnson's receiving the American Institute of Architects' Gold Medal, its highest honor.

---

* The monograph was published in 1992. Frank Israel would design a number of notable houses in Los Angeles and elsewhere and become one of the most respected figures in the generation following Frank Gehry. His career was cut short in 1996, when he died of AIDS at age fifty.

Philip Johnson's AIA Gold Medal in 1978 was marked by a gathering of the architects he called his "kids." *Left to right:* Frank, Michael Graves, Charles Moore, César Pelli, Philip Johnson, Charles Gwathmey, Stanley Tigerman, Peter Eisenman, and Robert A. M. Stern

"The kids" came en masse to Dallas to make a collective stand for the notion that aesthetics mattered at least as much as plumbing. The year after Mayne's lecture series, Johnson came to Los Angeles for the opening of the Crystal Cathedral, the extravagant glass church he had designed in Orange County for the television evangelist Robert Schuller. Frank and Berta drove down to Garden Grove to join Johnson and David Whitney at the opening service on a warm Sunday morning. Then, back in Santa Monica, the Gehrys hosted Johnson, Whitney, and a number of other visitors at a celebration dinner at Michael's, at that time one of the city's newest and most fashionable eateries.

It was like Frank to want to try, at once, to tie himself to a well-known elder on the national scene like Philip Johnson and also to be such an elder himself at home in Los Angeles. He yearned for acceptance both by the architects elsewhere whom he was coming increasingly to consider his peers and by the younger architects in Los Angeles whom he saw as being influenced by him. He wanted, like Johnson, to be simultaneously the elder statesman and the enfant terrible, both an eminence and a fresh creative force.

For all that Frank's architecture could not have been more different from Philip Johnson's decorative postmodernism, his actions were more like Johnson's than he realized, since he, like Johnson, welcomed the stimulation of younger figures around him. He had never worked in isolation: from Greg Walsh to the artists to younger architects in his office like Paul Lubowicki, he had always shaped his work, in part, by the exchange of ideas he craved. Now, at fifty, Frank watched the work of architects in their thirties like Eric Owen Moss and Thom Mayne carefully. He had designed the most talked-about house in Los Angeles, if not in the entire country, and he had become, by default if not by design, the central figure around whom the growing community of cutting-edge architects in Los Angeles revolved. But how was he going to stay fresh, and stay ahead of the next generation?

That was part of the reason he made the change in his office, which was soon followed by a physical move from the industrial space he had been occupying for the last decade on Cloverfield Boulevard in Santa Monica. Chuck Arnoldi had rented a studio in a building on Brooks Avenue in Venice, near the beach, and when a large space behind his studio became available, Frank decided to move his office into it. Venice had become even more of a creative center than it had been in the 1960s, when Frank first joined the community of artists who were beginning to move into the area. In the early 1980s, the gentrification that would drive all but the most successful artists out of Venice was only beginning to percolate. Craig Hodgetts saw Frank's relocation to the heart of Venice as being a recognition that he needed to renew his connections to younger creative people, and also as a validation of the importance of the Los Angeles School architects' group.

"When Frank Gehry, then conducting a largely commercial practice from a spacious industrial loft, decided to join the club and relocate into a cramped, messy storefront a few yards from the beach, it was clear that what had begun as a coagulation of misfits was emerging from the shadows," Hodgetts wrote later.[*]

Frank's delicate dance as both leader and follower is visible in a famous photograph taken of several members of the group on the beach in Venice in 1980. Frank is closest to the camera, but he looks away and stands slightly apart, while most of the other architects are arrayed in a casual

---

[*] Hodgetts's comment, written with his former partner Robert Mangurian, appeared in an essay written for *A Confederacy of Heretics*, a book published by SCI-Arc and the Getty Center as part of a 2013 symposium at SCI-Arc organized to look back at the Los Angeles School and evaluate its impact thirty-four years after Mayne's series of lectures and exhibitions. Frank was the only one of the original architects who did not contribute a current statement to the book, citing, according to a note on a blank page of the catalog, "insufficiently detailed memories to offer anything substantive." He was much discussed during the symposium, but he did not attend.

Frank joins, but stands slightly apart from, his younger colleagues on the beach in Venice, California, 1980. *Left to right:* Frederick Fisher, Robert Mangurian, Eric Owen Moss, Coy Howard, Craig Hodgetts, Thom Mayne, Frank

semicircle and are looking directly into the camera. Frank looms larger than the others, but he is not quite with them.[*]

Not long before the photograph was taken, Frank had been in the other Venice, participating in the Venice Biennale, the biennial international architecture exhibition that has often served as a marker of the preoccupations of the moment. For 1980, the theme was "The Presence of the Past," and the curators, led by Paolo Portoghesi, invited numerous architects, including Hans Hollein, Michael Graves, Robert Venturi and Denise Scott Brown, Robert A. M. Stern, Ricardo Bofill, and Charles Moore to design full-scale façades, which were set up side by side to form a street of false fronts, called the Strada Novissima, within Venice's historic Arsenale. Between the Strada and the wall of the Arsenale was a small exhibition of each architect's work, which could be entered by walking through that architect's façade. The Biennale was intended to be an inves-

---

[*] The photograph was taken for *Interiors* magazine to accompany an article by Joseph Giovannini entitled "California Design: New West Side Story."

tigation of postmodernism and the role that history could or should play in the making of new architecture.

Frank was invited to participate, and characteristically he came up with a solution that managed both to undermine the theme and to trump it. His "façade" was an open framework of wooden two-by-fours, which made not only his exhibition but also the wall of the Arsenale visible from the Strada. He composed the framework around the view from the Strada toward the window, with diagonal pieces to suggest the illusion of perspective. By making a visual connection to an element of the historic building the basis of his design, Frank managed, in his view, to be more closely tied to the Biennale's true historic context than the other architects, all of whose façades were self-contained architectural objects that could have been anywhere. His façade served as an allusion to his other work—an aspect he shared with the other participants—and also as a reminder that historical monumentality can be evoked in a variety of ways beyond the more direct replication of historical elements favored by many of the postmodernists. The critic Germano Celant, who would write frequently about Frank's work, said of the Biennale project, "In the end the most radical intervention is decidedly that of Frank Gehry, the California architect who has refuted monumentalizations and imitations by proposing a woodframe skeleton through which to view the sixteenth-century architecture of the arsenal 'in perspective' thus turning this postmodernist rebirth into what might be called a 'renaissance of the Renaissance.'"

Frank's desire to "answer" postmodernism, and to show that there was some way he could acknowledge the influence of history without appropriating its architectural forms, had been brewing for a long time before the Venice Biennale. Postmodern architecture "was decorative, soft and pandering and all the things I didn't care about, and I didn't know how to deal with," he recalled to Barbara Isenberg. "The rest of the world seemed to be excited about it, but I was left behind. The train left the station with a new conductor, and I didn't know how to get on it."

Frank had long sympathized with the feeling that modern architecture had worked itself into something of a dead end, and he understood, at least intellectually, the appeal of looking with renewed sympathy at the historical architecture that a previous generation had all but dismissed as irrelevant. But for all that he understood the limits of modernism at the time, it was never in his nature to look backward, and he could not even conceive of mimicking the forms of the past.

His combination of sympathy for the aims of the postmodern movement and disdain at its methods was very much behind what would become one of his most famous shapes, that of the fish, which he would use both as a complete form in a series of lamps and sculptures, and as the inspiration for the complex curves of many of his buildings. No small part of the pleasure he took in his appropriation of the fish shape was that it felt for him like a way of mocking the notion of copying the forms of the past. You want history? I'll give you history, Frank was saying. At a lecture at UCLA he went right to the point, saying that he could not understand why architects were going back only as far as the Greeks when they could go back millions of years—to prehistoric times, to one of the most primal forms of all, the fish.

Frank may have been making jokes when he said that the fish represented the return to history that the postmodernists advocated, but he was altogether serious about seeing it as an inspiration for architecture that would be both more sensual and more geometrically complex than the conventional modernist box. The double curves of the fish form fascinated him. So did its delicate skeleton, light and graceful in itself, and the way its form suggested movement. Even the scales, which suggest that the fish is not quite so pure an object as it first appears, appealed to him as a reminder that such a sensuous shape can be made up of many little parts that come together, rather like his architecture. The fish, he said, offered "a complete vocabulary that I can draw from." It gave Frank, an architect who generally shied away from conventional forms, the opportunity to use one of the most familiar shapes there is and make it his own. And if the fish allowed him to thumb his nose at historicism, it allowed him to do the same to critics who found his work too abstract, too unusual, or too distant from forms they recognized. No one could fail to recognize a fish.

Frank first experimented with using the fish as an architectural form in the design of an entry colonnade for the Smith residence, his 1981 proposal for an expansion of the Steeves house, in which "jumping fish" set a rhythm for the series of columns. As he had done at the Venice Biennale, he at once acknowledged traditional architectural form and subverted it. That same year he tried to blow a fish up to the size of an entire building in his design for a hotel in Kalamazoo, Michigan, part of a larger downtown renewal project that was ultimately designed by another architect. Kalamazoo would have been only half a fish anyway: he cut off the head, and stood the lower half of the body vertically, so that it could be taken, at least from a distance, as a sinuous tower. Later he proposed a sculpture of an entire fish, balanced on its tail, as the centerpiece in the courtyard of the complex of studio lofts he was working on in Lower Manhattan, another project that was never realized.

At around the same time, Frank was invited to participate in a project initiated by the Architectural League of New York that paired architects with contemporary artists and asked them to create something that neither would be able to do on his own. Frank's partner was the sculptor Richard Serra, with whom he would have a close but eventually rather tortured relationship. Frank and Serra concocted a gargantuan bridge to connect the Chrysler Building with the World Trade Center, both of which could be seen from the windows of Serra's downtown Manhattan loft. Serra designed the supporting pylon at the Chrysler Building end, which would have been a huge tilted pylon set in the East River. Frank designed the pylon at the other end, which he envisioned as a skyscraper-size fish, rising out of the Hudson River and holding the bridge's cables in its teeth. Here the fish made thematic sense in a way that it did not in Kalamazoo. It was leaping out of the water and catching the cable, a witty reversal of the normal relationship of a fish to a casting rod. (It is hard not to think that Frank was highly influenced here by his friends Claes Oldenburg and Coosje van Bruggen—sculptors very different from Serra—since the bridge fish, like Oldenburg and Van Bruggen's work, is a familiar object blown up beyond monumental scale to yield something at once amusing and disquieting.)

Frank continued to look for ways to use the fish as a design element and not merely as a metaphor for his architectural aspirations. In 1983, he proposed a glass fish, this time set horizontally, as a pavilion for an exhibition of architectural follies organized at the Leo Castelli Gallery by Barbara Jakobson—the first time he proposed creating a fish at the scale of a small building, with the interior a single room. The Castelli fish was to be accompanied by a coiled snake, which Frank envisioned as a private prison, its inmate supervised by the occupant of the pavilion—a rare instance of his creating a semblance of a narrative for one of his projects, rather than letting its forms speak for themselves.

He flirted from time to time with other creatures as well. He envisioned an abstracted eagle as the crown of the skyscraper he proposed as his entry into a mock architectural competition in 1980 that was intended as a contemporary homage to one of the most famous architectural contests of all time, the 1920s competition to select a design for the Tribune Tower in

Chicago. Another eagle topped the pediment of a porch he designed for the house of the architectural historian Charles Jencks, which Jencks did not build.

But not all of Frank's early attempts to insert biomorphic form into architecture were unrealized. His design for the restaurant Rebecca's, not far from his new studio on Brooks Avenue in Venice, was completed in 1985, its most striking feature a pair of large Gehry crocodiles hanging from the ceiling. There was also a chandelier in the form of a glowing octopus, and two large standing lamps that, like the Kalamazoo project, took the form of the body of a fish, without its head. Rebecca's turned out to be an occasion for Frank to commission several of his artist friends to create other elements of the restaurant. Ed Moses made a window with images of tarantulas, Peter Alexander made a mural in black velvet, and Tony Berlant designed the front doors.[*]

In 1983, after Frank had been playing casually with the form of the fish for a couple of years, he was approached by the Formica Corporation, which had recently introduced a new plastic laminate called ColorCore.[†] To draw attention to the design potential of its new product, Formica was commissioning noted designers to create new objects with it, and asked Frank to be part of the group. He agreed, as much because he was intrigued by the fact that the material was translucent—at least in lighter colors—as with its color consistency. At first he did not think of the project as having any connection to his interest in the fish form, and he started to use the translucency of ColorCore as the basis for glowing lamps that had nothing to do with fish. One of his first lamp designs was essentially a box, which Frank, frustrated, felt was little more than a version of Isamu Noguchi's famous paper lamps rendered in Formica. It was only when one of the prototype lamps was accidentally broken that he noticed that it had shattered into shards, with rough edges that reminded him of the scales of a fish. Suddenly he realized that his ColorCore project could be a lamp in the form of a fish.

And thus the first set of fish lamps was created in 1983, almost by accident, not as a deliberate design project so much as part of a corporate effort to promote a new material. Frank had little expectation that the lamps

---

[*] Rebecca's had a brief run as a fashionable gathering place for Venice's artists, architects, and their followers. It closed in 1988 and was demolished.

[†] Unlike traditional plastic laminates, which have color only on the surface, ColorCore features color that extends all the way through the material, giving it edges that are the same color as the surface.

would have commercial potential. He sketched a series of variations and asked Tomas Osinski, an artist and craftsman who had helped him with other projects over the years, to help him fabricate a variety of lamps out of ColorCore Formica that would highlight the translucency of the material. Frank kept the first fish lamp for himself and Berta and turned the second one over to Formica, and then one of the lamps was seen by an art dealer, who offered him $100 for it. Word of the lamps began to spread through the art world, and the collector Agnes Gund asked Frank to create one as an engagement gift for her brother, the architect Graham Gund, which Frank sold to her for $1,000. Requests from Philip Johnson, Jasper Johns, and Victoria Newhouse soon followed, and in 1984, Larry Gagosian, quickly sensing that the lamps had become a fashionable item to collect, put twenty of them on exhibit in his gallery in Beverly Hills. A new Gehry art world commodity was born.[*]

It was only a matter of time before someone would try to get Frank to design an actual building in the form of a fish. In 1986 a developer competing for a waterfront site in Kobe, Japan, asked him to create a large restaurant for the site, and brought him to Kobe. Over dinner with the developer and his colleagues, they asked him if he liked to make sketches on napkins. "So each guy had to have a sketch on a napkin," Frank said. "One of the sketches I made was a fish floating on the sea. They said, 'Gehry-san, please, fish.' So I made the thing." Frank forgot about the doodles and returned to Los Angeles. He produced a design for the restaurant and sent it to his clients, who called him in dismay. Where was the fish? They had expected a building that looked like a fish. "They said they didn't like the design. They wanted a fish, and they wanted it like the drawing," Frank said. "And I said, 'I can redesign this thing for you, but it will take two or three weeks.' They said, 'No, no, no, it has to be done by Monday morning.' It was a competition, but they didn't tell me. I said, 'No, I can't get it done, I'm very sorry.' And I hung up. It was 10 p.m., L.A. time. Midnight, they called again, said, 'Gehry-san, is okay, we take your drawing and make building, you don't have to do anything.'"

The thought of the Japanese developer trying to build from Frank's napkin sketch was horrifying enough to send Frank into the office on a Saturday morning. He asked Greg Walsh, who spoke Japanese, to work with

---

[*] It would be the beginning of one of Gagosian's most durable art objects, since Frank would continue to make fish lamps for years. Gagosian was still marketing them in 2013 and 2014, when he put on a series of exhibitions in his galleries around the world to show the recent examples.

Fishdance Restaurant in Kobe, Japan

him, and they assembled a collage-like design by combining elements of his earlier work: an angled structure covered in white metal that resembled a slice of the Ron Davis house, a copper-clad building that was an abstract rendition of a coiled snake, and a seventy-foot high sculpture of a fish leaping upward, based on one of the fish lamps. It was to be covered in chain link, at once a piece of monumental sculpture and the restaurant's iconic identity. "We made a still life of those three pieces, and then put Greg on a plane to Japan," Frank said. "He stayed there for a month, and they built it." It took ten months to complete the project, which was named Fishdance Restaurant and quickly became a landmark of Kobe.

Frank's attachment to the shape of the fish, and his determination to use it as an inspiration for everything from large-scale sculpture to lamps, was hardly intended as a serious statement about postmodernism, let alone as a way of connecting him to the postmodern architects who reveled in their use of traditional architectural forms. Frank's fondness for Philip Johnson and his respect for Johnson's intellect were deeply felt, but his feelings about Johnson never led him toward any sympathy with Johnson's increasingly decorative, and often rather simplistic, historic borrowings, or to consider putting aside the intense and visceral discomfort he had always felt about the idea that new architecture should mimic old.* His dislike of anything that could be viewed as copying would always be fundamental to his outlook.

But Frank was every bit as suspicious of the view that new architecture, whatever it looked like, could emerge full-blown from its designer's mind, with no connection to what had come before. He had no reluctance to admit the profound influence that great architecture of the past had on him; he just did not understand why it was necessary to express his admiration for historic architecture by copying it. There were more sincere forms of flattery for Frank than imitation. He also understood another of postmodernism's underlying presumptions, that certain kinds of architectural forms evoked certain associations, but here, too, he felt he could accept the premise without allowing it to lead him in the same direction as most of the postmodern architects. He believed that architects had accepted a false polarity: it was as if modernists wanted to design new things that had almost no resemblance to what had come before, while postmodernists sought to design new buildings that bore far too much similarity to the architecture of the past.

Frank's complex relationship to the postmodern movement in architecture had been evident for years, particularly in early projects such as the Hillcrest Apartments in Santa Monica. But in general what common cause he felt with postmodernism manifested itself mainly in the way he shared the postmodernists' unhappiness with austere, institutional modern architecture, not in the forms he designed as an alternative to corporate modernism. At heart he was a confirmed modernist with a postmodernist's sensibility, whose instincts were leading him more and more toward an architecture that did not fit into either category—and indeed seemed not to fit any label at all.

In 1978, he began work on a project that would represent, in one sense, his closest brush with postmodernism, and at the same time would demonstrate how tenuous his connection to that movement was: Loyola Law School, a law school affiliated with Loyola Marymount University, which occupied a tiny campus of its own in the Westlake section of Los Angeles,

---

* It is unlikely that Johnson, for his part, would have expected Frank to share his postmodern stance, or would even have wanted him to. Johnson could be cynical and careerist, but he was smart enough to prefer a circle of intellectual equals to a crowd of blind acolytes. And he surely knew that Frank's respect for him was based more on his intellect than on his architecture.

just west of downtown. It was an awkward location, an urban outpost separated by several miles from Loyola's main campus in West Los Angeles, too far from the center of downtown to capture what energy the old core of Los Angeles might offer, and at the same time too close to downtown to have much of a neighborhood identity of its own. Frank knew that part of town all too well: the dreary little apartment Irving had rented at 9th and Burlington that had been the Goldberg family's first home in Los Angeles was just four blocks to the west.

Loyola's location may have been low-key and banal, but the school's tone seemed more in line with Frank's ambitious nature, not to mention his political leanings. A Jesuit institution, it had a long history of encouraging students to enter public interest law, and it was the first accredited law school in Los Angeles to require its students to devote time to pro bono work. The school's administration recognized that its buildings, dull commercial structures more suited to an office than to a campus, offered students little in the way of places in which to meet, to socialize, and to feel a sense of connection with the school, and Loyola asked several prominent local architects to discuss how they might upgrade the small campus to give the school a greater sense of identity.

Frank was not the front-runner. He recalls that the school was leaning toward Charles Moore, whose easygoing, upbeat, and colorful postmodern work could well have been seen as a surefire route to an inviting campus. Moore, who had established a practice in Los Angeles a few years earlier after stepping down as dean of the school of architecture at Yale, was the bigger name of the two. Frank's work was edgier by any measure, and the Loyola administration had shown no sign of wanting to equate its tradition of social responsibility with architectural innovation.

But Frank had two things in his favor. He could speak with conviction about the issue of neighborhood identity, not only because he had spent a few years of his life a few blocks away, but also because he was unsparing in his criticism of the existing state of the small Loyola campus, which had been designed in 1963 by a large Los Angeles commercial firm. And perhaps more important, when the school was interviewing architects, one of the faculty members involved in the selection process was a professor named Bob Benson, who was an ardent Gehry loyalist and would later commission Frank to design a house for himself and his family in nearby Calabasas. Benson, Frank remembered years later, "was gutsy. And he convinced them."

The Benson house, a low-budget, playful composition of two small boxes joined by second-story bridges, would turn out to be one of Frank's many early explorations of the notion of breaking up the program of a building into several smaller, freestanding units, an idea that the Loyola campus would bring into full flower. Shortly after he got the job, Frank, searching for a design that would enhance day-to-day interaction between students and faculty as well as help make the school more recognizable, took a trip to Rome. He walked through the Roman Forum, and it occurred to him that there might be a way he could conceive of Loyola similarly, as a collection of disparate objects that came together to create a civic identity—in effect, as a village of little buildings.

The associations between classical architecture and the law were obvious—almost too obvious, since they presented Frank with the challenge of evoking the Forum without being too literal about it and indulging in the mimicking of historical form that he had never been comfortable with. He was determined to try to figure out a way to allude to classical architecture without actually copying it. "I decided I could have those symbolic columns without going postmodern," he said.

He did. The master plan Frank devised for Loyola, which would be completed in phases that would continue to 1994, was his most cogent response to the challenge of postmodernism. It was also his most advanced attempt at urban design, and in many ways the wittiest project he had produced. The centerpiece was a trio of small buildings—a classroom building, a lecture hall to serve as a moot court, and a chapel—set in front of a long four-story building containing a student center, meeting rooms, seminar rooms, and offices. The space between the buildings was more like the piazza of an Italian town than an academic quadrangle. The large building had a yellow stucco façade, exaggerated in size to enhance its role as a backdrop to the smaller buildings.* Frank punched plain, conventional-looking windows into the façade, then broke the box apart by adding lively open stairways at each end and splitting the façade in the middle, opening it up to contain a large, angled central stairway leading to a gabled

---

* It was not the only time Frank indulged in the postmodern gesture of an exaggerated façade. His branch building for the World Savings and Loan Association in North Hollywood, completed in 1980, addresses the parking lot and entry door with a three-story-high stucco wall set atop a one-story structure: a "false front" designed to enhance a sense of monumentality and give the auto-oriented bank building some feeling of urbanity. It is austere in its details, but otherwise could almost have been designed by Robert Venturi. Frank's shop in Santa Monica Place for Bubar's Jewelers, also completed in 1980, is a similar essay in postmodern exaggerated urbanism.

section of glass. The overall composition managed to demonstrate at the same time the idea of a calm, ordered façade and of intense, disordered activity within, as if one of Frank's more characteristically active designs had crashed into a façade by Aldo Rossi. To the architect Henry N. Cobb, who was an early admirer of Frank's despite the very different work he himself did as a partner of I. M. Pei, the stairways "twist and turn with such irrepressible abandon as to seem utterly and blissfully liberated from any constraints of economy, engineering or function." The stairways, Cobb wrote, "when seen together with the rigorously ordered openings in the wall from which they spring, offer an eloquent metaphorical speculation on the complex and ever-problematic relationship between freedom of action and the rule of law in human society."

Frank's design for Loyola both accepted postmodernism's belief in the idea that public buildings should have formal, dignified faces and sub-verted it by breaking it in two to yield something far more visually engag-ing and revealing than the plain façade would have been. He played the game of acceptance and subversion even more overtly in the little lecture hall building, whose brick façade is punctuated by four large freestanding concrete columns. The columns have neither bases nor capitals, and they stand on their own with neither frieze nor pediment atop them, a classical façade that has been boiled down to its essence and turned into a minimal-ist sculpture.

It is a remarkable little building, because it manages through abstrac-tion to evoke the idea of a common classical courthouse more powerfully than most literal copies of traditional buildings are able to do. So, too, with the chapel, a wood-frame building sheathed in glass and Finnish ply-wood* that has a frontal gable, a rounded, apselike shape at the rear, and a campanile made of wood framing enclosed in glass. Frank referred to the chapel as "a Monopoly house with an apse," and together with the campa-nile, it calls to mind a set of references as diverse as an Italian cathedral, a Quaker meetinghouse, and a New England barn, woven together into a new and altogether coherent form. The glass façade set over wood framing deepens the architecture further, bringing both modernity and transpar-ency to architectural forms that have normally been associated with the ancient and the opaque.

The chapel almost didn't happen. Some of the Loyola administration

---

* The plywood was later replaced with copper sheet metal, a more durable material.

wanted something that would more directly demonstrate the school's Catholic affiliation, and Frank recalled that he was accused of being blasphemous in his playful but frankly nondenominational design. He remembered telling his clients that his wife was Catholic and that he would be happy to design a separate Catholic chapel if they wanted one, but that the building he had come up with fit the spirit of the law school and its diverse student body. The chapel—perhaps because of Bob Benson's intervention—went ahead as Frank designed it.[*]

The final building in the trio, a small classroom structure, extends the theme of turning classical elements into abstractions, in this case a gray stucco box with a freestanding colonnade in front and a second, smaller colonnade on top in front of a large light monitor, a kind of rooftop sign shouting out the idea of classicism. This building bears a striking resemblance to a series of pieces created a few years before by Tony Berlant, one of Frank's Los Angeles artist friends, entitled *The Marriage of New York and Athens*, architectural sculptures that Frank made no secret of admiring.[†] One of the pieces in Berlant's series resembles a classical temple that has a sharp, jagged cut in its side wall, a juxtaposition of classical order and modernist intervention that calls to mind Frank's design for the larger building at Loyola that had so impressed Henry Cobb.

All of the Loyola buildings, and especially the lecture hall/courthouse and the chapel, stand as clear signals of where Frank was going in his work. Nothing here was a neutral box—it is worth comparing Frank's chapel, say, with Mies van der Rohe's chapel at the Illinois Institute of Technology in Chicago, a plain box of brick, steel, and glass that was intended to demonstrate the universality of Mies's architectural language. Frank had no more interest in a universal modernist architectural language than the postmodernists did, and he shared their pleasure in making reference to symbols and time-honored associations. Unlike Mies, he did not mind the historical connections between, say, bell tower and nave and the idea of worship, or between a Greek temple and the idea of justice. He would play the same game as the postmodernists—but he would play it his way, and

---

[*] Frank was less successful in persuading Loyola to go ahead with another aspect of the design, which was to have Ed Ruscha do a painting for three blank panels in the lecture hall/moot court building. Ruscha proposed a mural with the words WHAT IS THE LAW? The dean of the school did not believe it was serious, and rejected it. Several years later Loyola indicated that it had changed its mind, but Ruscha refused to go ahead with the work.

[†] Many years later, Frank would display several of Berlant's sculptures from this series in the entry arcade in front of his studio.

in doing so he would manage to transcend the whole debate and redefine it on his own terms.

As Frank's reputation continued to grow, his office began again to expand. If there was any downside to this, it was that the problems of day-to-day administration that had long plagued him became harder to avoid. Even with Berta handling much of the financial administration, there was more to do as the firm grew, and Frank wondered if he should take on a business partner so that he could spend more of his time designing and less of it managing. "I was always looking for a savior, for someone to do the business part, because I wanted to design," he said.

Frank's friend Peter Walker, the landscape architect, suggested an architect named Paul Kruger, who had recently left a firm in Boston and was looking for a new position. Frank and Kruger met, and despite Kruger's reluctance to relocate to Los Angeles, Frank agreed to establish a second firm, called Gehry & Kruger, that Kruger would manage from the East Coast and that would work in tandem with Frank O. Gehry & Associates in Venice.

It was no more successful than Gehry, Walsh & O'Malley. Frank had trouble getting along with Kruger's staff, and soon regretted his decision to allow Kruger to operate an affiliated firm in Boston rather than be based alongside him in Los Angeles. He decided that the arrangement was adding to his administrative woes, not reducing them, and after less than a year he severed the relationship, essentially paying Paul Kruger for a divorce.

In the early 1980s, Frank's reputation seemed to be expanding faster around the country and the world than in Los Angeles. Being seen as the Los Angeles member of an international coterie of notable architects did not necessarily translate into jobs at home. Nevertheless, his local stature still grew, if more gradually than elsewhere, and his telephone continued to ring with inquiries about local jobs. Several of them were for more prestigious clients than he had been accustomed to. In 1981 he produced a design for a speculative office building in Studio City that the developer Keith Kennedy was planning in association with the Screen Actors Guild, a project that, while never built, turned out to be one of the most inventive of his variations on postmodern themes: a 140,000-square-foot structure whose façade consisted of alternating flat, windowed sections and recessed sections containing high columns and what appeared to be landscapes of small, generic buildings clustered as if in Italian hill towns. The larger sections were office blocks, and the scenographic groupings of little build-ings were to contain retail shops. It was as if Frank had taken some of the ideas he was using at Loyola and inserted them as pictorial niches within a much larger, modernist framework, once again both celebrating tradi-tional buildings and subverting them by placing them within an altogether different context—a context that, on its own terms, would have been an unusual and compelling architectural composition.

But some of Frank's larger Los Angeles projects began to be realized. In 1982, the producer Samuel Goldwyn asked him to renovate an undistin-guished midcentury office building on the edge of Beverly Hills as a head-quarters, a project that offered only minor design opportunities but led to Frank's selection as architect for a large new regional branch library in Hollywood that was to be named for Goldwyn's mother, Frances Howard Goldwyn. The library was a highly visible project with a $3 million budget, and Frank produced a set of three glass-and-stucco boxes that were gener-ously, even grandly, scaled, conferring a kind of modernist monumentality on the notion of reading. If the building had any significant shortcoming, it was that its three boxes, which were really small towers, had an aloofness uncharacteristic of Frank's work, and that, combined with the city's insis-tence on fences and a high stucco wall for security, gave the project the air of a military installation more than a community library. Perhaps it was not surprising, then, that the library, while well used, was not resoundingly popular. A few years after its completion the cultural critic Mike Davis took the building to task in his book *City of Quartz,* calling it "undoubtedly the most menacing library ever built, a bizarre hybrid (on the outside) of dry-docked dreadnought and Gunga Din fort." It was obvious hyperbole, but a reminder that what Frank could consider a benign exploration of abstract form might have a very different meaning for other people. Davis's sharp critique, which also criticized Loyola Law School for the inward focus of Frank's Italian piazza design, suggested that Frank allowed aesthetics to justify projects that were more like fortresses than inviting public places, and that he was motivated more by a willingness to satisfy powerful clients than by the left-wing politics he claimed to espouse.

Frank, whose fierce ambition had never gotten the better of his desire to be liked, was shaken by Davis's attack, which served, if nothing else, to remind him that however much he continued to see himself as an outsider in the power structures of both Los Angeles and the world of architecture, to most people he was looking more and more like an insider. At the same time that he was working on the Goldwyn Library, however, two other projects made it clear to him how unresolved his status in Los Angeles continued to be.

The first was the California Aerospace Museum, a commission from the state of California that was to be completed in time for the 1984 Olympics in Los Angeles. It was an exciting project for Frank to take on, not only because it would be larger and more visible than the Goldwyn Library, but also because of his long-felt fondness for aviation. A new museum for old airplanes was in some ways a dream job.

The museum had been given an old armory building in Exposition Park, adjacent to the USC campus, and the original expectation was that it would be renovated. Frank argued that the $5 million budget was inadequate to permit a meaningful renovation of a building as large as the armory, and that for the same cost he could produce a smaller, simpler new building that would give the young museum a distinct identity that would be difficult to achieve within the old armory at any cost. The argument that architecture could define an institution's identity was one that Frank would make often in his career, and this time it worked. The state architect's office agreed to let Frank construct a new building in front of the armory instead of renovating the old building.

Frank produced a building of sheet metal, stucco, steel frame, and concrete that seemed, from the outside, to consist of two large masses, one angled and the other more boxy, with a viewing tower in between. Inside, the building is more of a continuous exhibition hall, eighty feet high, punctuated by ramps, bridges, stairs, and skylights, with airplanes, satellites, and space probes hanging within the space.

John Clagett, an architect who worked in Frank's office on the project, recalled how Frank started the design process by putting the museum's program into a large, simple, boxlike building. Then, Clagett said, "he would take to subtracting parts of the box, with swaths selectively sliced away, often in a literal way, X-Acto knife carving away a foam core model. Many variations later, a three-dimensional diagram would emerge. A composition of solids and voids would take the place of the original super-box. A process of reasoning would give slices a rationale, as glazed openings, entryways. Cut-away portions of the initial box would sometimes return in quick fashion, sometimes at a reduced scale, sometimes in a different location, as skylight boxes, etc. His design approach at CAM was a curious mix; at times it resembled that of a Renaissance sculptor, carving away at the block until a form emerges. But what emerged was not in any strict sense premeditated, but laced with accident and fortuitous circumstance."

Clagett's description of Frank's design process for the California Aerospace Museum could apply to many of his projects, of course; it underscores the extent to which Frank tried to balance his purely sculptural impulses with the fulfillment of an architectural program. He would never be interested in sculpture for sculpture's sake, but he would always try to find a sculptural solution to an architectural problem. In other words, fulfilling the architectural program was always his goal, not making a piece of sculpture. Yet sculptural techniques were a key part of how he would choose to solve architectural problems.

The California Aerospace Museum would be best known, however, not for the shape Frank would give it, but for his decision to attach a plane to the building's exterior, as literal a sign as there could be for what the museum was about. His original idea was to place a Messerschmitt Bf109, a German fighter aircraft, on the exterior, aiming down toward the building. "It's my Jewish guilt, that they should be aware that this could happen again, that was my intent," he said.

The museum board was, understandably, not taken with the notion of displaying a German fighter plane, particularly in such a way as to appear to be about to fly into the building. Neither were they entranced with Frank's idea that the elevator shaft be designed to resemble a missile silo. But another notion of Frank's, that the façade contain a forty-foot-tall hangar door, remained, perhaps less for the reason he wanted it, which was to evoke the industrial architecture of an airplane hangar, as because it was useful as a way of moving display aircraft in and out of the building.

And once they got over the notion of a Messerschmitt, the museum's board decided it liked Frank's idea of attaching a plane to the front of the building, just so long as it was something other than a German warplane — and that it be positioned to appear to be taking off from the building, not flying downward toward it. A Lockheed F-104 Starfighter from the 1950s was selected, partly in homage to Lockheed's founding in Hollywood in 1926.

The presence of the airplane shooting upward from the façade made the building — and, by extension, its architect — much talked about in Los Angeles. It was Frank's largest public building in the city thus far, and it was well received by the local critics. Leon Whiteson, writing in the *Los Angeles Herald-Examiner*, called the aerospace museum "a forceful reassembly of shattered shapes in one coherent yet lighthearted sculpture that captures the energy of space travel."*

The aerospace museum project had barely begun when Frank received a painful reminder that, however much his stock was rising outside Los Angeles, he was a long way from being established as the city's favorite architectural son. A group of prominent collectors and artists, frustrated by what they felt was the Los Angeles County Museum of Art's slowness at recognizing the growing stature of the local contemporary art scene, had been talking for some time about the idea of a new museum that would focus on contemporary art. At the center of the group were Marcia and Fred Weisman, well-known collectors who were good friends of Frank's—Fred Weisman had helped him finance his house, had given him the commission to design an office building for the East Coast Toyota distributorship he owned, and had approached him from time to time about other projects. No other architect in the city had closer relationships with local artists, or, for that matter, with important artists, collectors, and gallery owners in New York, whose support for the project, while perhaps not essential, would certainly be helpful. As the project was getting started, Marcia Weisman asked Frank to study the feasibility of putting the museum in the old Pan-Pacific Auditorium, a landmark Art Moderne exposition structure on West Beverly Boulevard that had been vacant for a decade. He looked at the old auditorium and made some casual sketches, gratis, to show how it might be converted into a museum. As the plans got more serious, the city offered the possibility of locating the museum within a large skyscraper complex called California Plaza that was going up downtown. Tom Bradley, the mayor, and Joel Wachs, a city councilman with a strong interest in the arts, eventually brokered a deal mandating the developer set aside 1.5 percent of the project's budget to build the museum on Grand Avenue. Frank was invited to another meeting at Marcia Weisman's house in Beverly Hills to talk about the new site, and he did not think he

---

* The museum later became part of the California Science Center, and was renamed the center's Air and Space Gallery, perhaps to avoid confusion with the Aerospace Museum of California in Sacramento. It was closed in 2011 as part of a reconstruction of the Science Center's facilities to accommodate the permanent display of the space shuttle *Endeavour*, and its future has been uncertain. The building was named to the California Register, an official listing of historically significant buildings, in 2012.

was making a particularly bold assumption in thinking that wherever the new museum ended up, he was more than just a front-runner for the job of designing it—he had all but gotten the commission. If he did not deserve it by right, he had earned it by his position in the city's art world.

The museum's founders, it turned out, had other ideas. After the meeting at Marcia Weisman's, Frank heard that the artists were planning to get together again to discuss the project, and he expected to be invited. Then he learned that the meeting had taken place without him, in part, he was told, because the artists, some of whom were his old friends, had decided that they wanted to control the project themselves, and believed that any architect, even Frank, would have priorities contrary to their own. The artists failed to consider that the developers behind California Plaza who were paying much of the cost of the building, the city administration that was hoping to use the new museum to spur further downtown renewal, and the collectors who would be giving paintings and additional funds to the museum would all also have priorities that ran counter to theirs, and that Frank, paradoxically, might be a stronger advocate for keeping the artists' interests in the forefront of the project than another architect might have been. For some of the artists, of course, Frank was still the young architect who had run around the fringes of their group, eager for access to them. It was difficult for them to conceive that someone whose relationship to them had been more than a little sycophantic might have the stature to design a major art museum.

Either way, whether Frank was viewed as insufficiently respectful of the artists or as too bedazzled by them, it amounted to a rejection, and he was deeply hurt. It hardly helped that the painter Sam Francis, whom Frank had never been particularly close to but who was involved in the artists' committee for the museum, had become a friend of the Japanese architect Arata Isozaki and wanted him to design the museum, or that Arthur Erickson, the Canadian architect who was designing the towers at California Plaza, hoped to do the museum as well, making the process more complicated still. Finally the decision was made to interview six architects. Max Palevsky, a collector who was also part of the founding group of the museum and headed the architects' search committee, called Frank to say that it was necessary for political reasons to include a local architect on the list, and asked him to agree to be interviewed even though, Palevsky said with more candor than tact, he was not going to get the job.

Being brought in as the token Los Angeles architect only compounded the sense of insult. Still, Frank, whose instinct always led him to be easygoing until he saw absolutely no hope in a situation, agreed to meet with the committee. He knew the group was leaning toward Isozaki, and decided he had nothing to lose in being as blunt with them as Palevsky had been with him. It would be difficult to work with an architect who lived halfway across the world and spoke a different language, Frank said to the committee. And he added that he thought the situation would be tougher still for Isozaki, because the museum had to be built in coordination with a major commercial real estate project whose developers had little interest in the museum themselves, and no experience in working with people like Isozaki.

Frank did not get the job. But he was not punished for his candor. Once design work had begun, it was clear that the new Museum of Contemporary Art was going to take much longer to build and cost much more than the group had first thought; since there was no chance it would be ready in time for the 1984 Olympics, as originally hoped, something needed to be done to show that the museum was in business. Pontus Hulten, the founding director of the modern art museum at the Centre Pompidou in Paris, who had been recruited to Los Angeles to become the first director of the new museum, and his deputy, Richard Koshalek, invited Frank to dinner at a Japanese restaurant near his house in Santa Monica. They told him that the city was making a pair of old warehouses in the Little Tokyo section of downtown available to them as a temporary facility so that they could be open in time for the games. They were going to call it the Temporary Contemporary, and they wanted Frank to design it.

"I looked at them, and I said, 'You mean a consolation prize? You don't need to do that,'" Frank said. "But they said they really wanted me to do it. They said it was going to be historic—and they were right in the end about that—and I was the only one who could do it." Frank liked the idea, but he felt sufficiently bruised by the treatment of the selection committee that he did not want to give Hulten and Koshalek the satisfaction of having him agree on the spot. "Don't torture me anymore," he remembers telling them. "I've done my duty already." Hulten and Koshalek asked him to think about it overnight, and they agreed to talk again the following day.

Frank was still unsure what to do when his home phone rang at eight o'clock the next morning. It was Coy Howard, a young architect who was close to many of the artists in town and had been present at many of the meetings about the new museum. Howard knew all about the Temporary Contemporary, and asked Frank if he had been offered the job of designing it. It was clear to Frank that Howard thought he deserved the job himself, and was hoping that Frank would decline. Howard's phone call was just enough to stimulate Frank's competitive juices, and he overcame his reluctance and spoke to Richard Koshalek, who told him that the museum was not interested in any other architect for the job and that both he and Pontus Hulten felt strongly that Frank was the only architect who would know how to convert the old warehouse into a viable museum.

Frank was always happier being pursued than being the pursuer, and it did not take too many more entreaties on the part of Hulten and Koshalek to seduce him. He just needed to be romanced sufficiently to soothe the lingering hurt over his rejection for the museum's main building. Once he had accepted the job, the Temporary Contemporary turned out to be one of his simplest projects—there was a budget of only $1.2 million, much of which had to go into seismic upgrading and mechanical systems, so there wasn't much opportunity for architectural expression. Frank didn't mind, since he pretty much liked the old warehouses as they were, and believed that their combination of plainness, expansive size, and lack of pretension made them as good a place for the display of contemporary art as there could be. He cleaned and sandblasted the steel trusses and wood joists, painted the walls white, added ramps and stairs to bring the space up to the requirements of the building code, and then, to create some sense of exterior presence and give the museum a kind of Gehryesque outdoor foyer space, ran a canopy of steel framing and chain-link fencing down the length of the building's entry side.

The project was an enormous success, not least because of Frank's intuitive sense of how much to change the old warehouses and how much to leave them alone. His interventions were modest but surefooted, and while it was clear to anyone entering the Temporary Contemporary that it was an industrial building, not a purpose-built museum, no one could see it and not know that Frank had redone it. In 1982, as the project was getting started, the notion of converting old industrial space into a venue for the display of contemporary art was largely untried. The Bankside Power Station, in London, which would become the Tate Modern, was still operating as a power station in 1981, and the idea of turning it into a museum would not be proposed for another decade. The factory buildings in North Adams, Massachusetts, that would become Mass MOCA in 1999 were abandoned and derelict when the Temporary Contemporary was built; the factory that would become Dia:Beacon on the Hudson River in New York in 2003 was still making paper boxes. When the Temporary Contemporary opened its doors in 1983, Frank could feel that he had all but established a new genre of museum design. The Temporary Contemporary was at the beginning of what would become an international tidal wave of factories, warehouses, and industrial spaces converted into arts institutions, and Frank was the architect at the vanguard of this movement. Moreover, he had gotten his project open three years before Isozaki's main building for the Museum of Contemporary Art on Grand Avenue was ready. If that wasn't going to help him feel that his position as the preeminent architect in Los Angeles's art world had been vindicated, nothing would.

12

Onto the World Stage

E ven before the Temporary Contemporary was ready for its first exhibition, Richard Koshalek, who had taken over as director of the Museum of Contemporary Art from Pontus Hulten, was eager to show off the rich potential of the space. Mixed-media collaborations were in vogue, and Koshalek invited Frank to join forces with the dancer-choreographer Lucinda Childs and the composer John Adams to produce a dance piece as the first event in the new building. Adams offered a musical piece he had written previously and did not participate actively in the collaboration, but Frank and Childs worked closely together to shape the space to best show off her choreography in the form of a dance, called *Available Light,* that she choreographed specifically for the space. It was the kind of collaboration Frank liked best—not each artist working separately, but trying to create together so that each influenced the other. Frank reshaped the interior to respond to Childs's choreography, while she choreographed her dance to respond to his architecture. "We wanted to make something that none of us would have done alone," Frank said. "That is the essence of collaboration. When you agree to collaborate, you agree to jump off a cliff holding hands with everyone, hoping the resourcefulness of each will insure that you all land on your feet."

Frank loved the idea of using the building for performance, and he created a forty-foot-wide split-level stage, behind which he hung a scrim made up of layers of chain link. The chain link, he said, was not only for aesthetic reasons: he could use the same pieces that were scheduled to become part of the exterior canopy as soon as the contractor was ready to install them in the days following the performance. He hung theatrical lighting from the ceiling and covered a clerestory window behind the stage with layers of red gel, creating, he hoped, the image of a distant

sunrise or sunset. Childs's choreography called for the dancers to enter
and leave the stage on three separate stairways, effectively expanding the
performance area across much of the Temporary Contemporary, which
Frank encouraged. "I was interested in inaugurating the building so that
the patrons of the museum would have a sense of how big it is," he said.
Not long afterward, he had the opportunity for another collaboration, this
one with his old friend the Los Angeles artist Peter Alexander and an even
older friend—the young man whom he and Anita had occasionally looked
after in the early years of their relationship, the Snyders' neighbor Michael
Tilson Thomas. Thomas's musical gifts, apparent even in childhood when
Frank was taking care of him and his friend, Anita's brother Richard, had
blossomed into a major conducting career, and in 1981 he returned to
Los Angeles as the principal guest conductor of the Los Angeles Philharmonic. To celebrate the opening of the 1984 Olympics, the Philharmonic
asked Frank to collaborate with Thomas and Ron Hays, a designer of laser
and video animations, for a special performance of Aaron Copland's Third
Symphony at the Hollywood Bowl. Thomas would conduct, and Frank
would create a special visual presentation to accompany the music.

Frank wanted to replicate the effect of the skies in J. M. W. Turner
paintings, and he remembered that Peter Alexander, whose studio was
near his office in Venice, had been painting a series of skyscapes. Alexander and Frank selected portions of his paintings to project at enormous
scale around the proscenium of the Hollywood Bowl, in effect turning the
bowl into the venue of a huge *son et lumière*. "Gehry rushes in where most
architects fear to tread: into places like museums and theaters to create
things that are generally temporary (anathema to most architects) and that
must be produced in a relatively short span of time on modest budgets,"
wrote the curator and historian Mildred Friedman. "Yet for Gehry, such
activities are enriching, stimulating, and on occasion inspiring."

All was not performance, of course. Frank continued to do plenty
of buildings, and despite his promise to himself that he would do
only aesthetically meaningful work post-Rouse, he was happy to take on
commercial projects if he felt they offered him real design opportunities,
or if he liked the client. He produced an exceptionally urbane small retail
cluster, Edgemar, that managed to combine a courtyard, a hint of the
shopping mall, and the streetscape of a village, all within his own distinctive, angled vocabulary, and also included space for the Santa Monica

Museum of Art; a showroom in Houston for the furniture manufacturer Sunar-Hauserman; and a much bigger project for one of that company's best-known competitors, Herman Miller, for which Frank designed a factory and office building on a 156-acre site near Sacramento. The Herman Miller project consisted of separate warehouse, processing, and assembly buildings, placed precisely to create an angled open space between them in which Frank created a three-story copper-clad pergola. (The project also contained a meeting room designed by Frank's old friend the Chicago architect Stanley Tigerman.)

The most ambitious commercial project Frank would work on in the 1980s, however, was never built: a mixed-use development for Turtle Creek in Dallas that would have contained an office building, a condominium tower, a hotel, and town houses. He envisioned the office tower as a round structure of glass that would have appeared to be slightly twisted at its base, while the high-rise condominiums were to consist of gridded sections with frequent setbacks, as if boxes had been piled irregularly one atop the other. Designed for a Dallas-based developer, Vince Carrozza, for whom Frank had previously designed a smaller project in Oklahoma City that was also not built, the Turtle Creek project was a chance for Frank to think about the challenge of a multitower urban complex on his own terms. He began to develop ideas that would bear fruit in other projects, some of them almost two decades in the future.

As he was working on Turtle Creek, Frank received a call from another real estate developer who would become far more important in his life, Richard Cohen. Cohen, who then lived in Boston, had become interested in an old loft building at 360 Newbury Street in Boston, in a somewhat run-down section of Back Bay. The building needed renovation and expansion, and Cohen asked his friend David Ross, who ran the Institute for Contemporary Art in Boston, if he could suggest an architect who might bring some flair to the project. Ross had noticed that Frank was getting increasing national attention even though most of his completed work was in California, and he suggested that Cohen contact him.

Frank and Cohen, who was younger by eighteen years, hit it off quickly, and Frank produced a design that at once restored the original building and altered it dramatically. He added a new eighth floor topped with projecting struts, copper-and-glass canopies, and new façades faced in lead-coated copper in the rear, turning 360 Newbury into what at its completion in 1988 was a striking, not to say highly unusual, juxtaposition of old and new: an early-twentieth-century industrial building with a late-twentieth-century overlay. Cohen was happy with the process of working with Frank, pleased with the result, and impressed by Frank's ability to win over the Back Bay Architectural Commission and the Boston Redevelopment Authority, which had to approve the design—and did, with only minor revisions. (Among them was the elimination of a Claes Oldenburg and Coosje van Bruggen sculpture of a huge tea bag that was to go on the roof.) The project was an economic success, Cohen believed, "primarily because of the architecture," which turned it from an anonymous old building into a minor landmark. Cohen followed 360 Newbury Street with a commission to design a new sixteen-story office tower in downtown Boston. That second project never went forward, but it hardly seemed to matter, since the two began a friendship that would continue for decades, even though they would not complete another project together for more than twenty years.

E ven as Frank had his sights set on large projects, he continued to design houses for clients he found stimulating and sympathetic. There was a certain self-selection process to becoming a Gehry client: he rarely had to turn people down, because by the early 1980s his work had become well enough known that most of the people who approached him had already decided that they wanted a Frank Gehry house. You did not come to 11 Brooks Avenue in Venice to ask for a house that was already fully formed in your own head. You came in the hope that Frank would surprise you. And you had to be the sort of person who was willing to live in a surprise.

Frank had several clients who fit that description in the 1980s, and his work with at least three of them yielded houses that were significant milestones in his career: the Sirmai-Peterson house, in Thousand Oaks, California, completed in 1986; the Winton guesthouse, finished in Wayzata, Minnesota, in 1987; and the Schnabel house, in the Brentwood section of Los Angeles, finished in 1989. All three of the houses were little villages of one kind or another, places where Frank continued to play with his notion of breaking up a single building into a composition of several separate structures. He liked to quote Philip Johnson's remark that the greatest buildings often consist of a single room, and to think of this as the spur to conceiving of a work of architecture as a collection of building-rooms.

The Winton House was the first to begin. It was unusual in a number of ways: it was Frank's only residential project built outside California (he designed numerous houses elsewhere, but never managed to get any of

Winton House, Wayzata, Minnesota

them built); it did not have a particularly rigid program, although the brief called for space that could house the owners' visiting grandchildren and that they would find appealing; and it was built beside the owners' original house, designed by none other than Philip Johnson in 1952 for the director of the Minneapolis Institute of Arts. The owners, Mike and Penny Winton, had purchased the house in the 1970s, and they approached Johnson first in the hope that he would be willing to expand his original house to include guest space for their expanded family. Johnson never replied, and the Wintons, eager to find an architect of stature, began to look elsewhere. They knew Martin and Mildred Friedman, who had just begun the long process of organizing the first retrospective exhibition of Frank's work for the Walker Art Center in Minneapolis, and after talking with the Friedmans, reading about Frank, and traveling to Los Angeles to meet him, they decided they had found their architect.

Frank was understandably pleased at the Philip Johnson connection, but he worried about whether Johnson would feel that he was trying to upstage him by creating an adjacent building in response to his early work. "I didn't want to mess around with Uncle Philip's baby," he said. He put the guesthouse on the other side of a hedge, so as to emphasize its separateness,* and conceived it as a sculptural composition of six different shapes, arranged in a pinwheel, and each covered with a different material: lead-coated copper, stone, painted metal, Finnish plywood, and brick similar to the brick Johnson had used. One shape had a tapering, thirty-five-foot-high light tower; another had a curving top; and another had a tall chimney. Unlike Frank's other "villages," which were built for mild climates, the elements of the Winton house butted up against one another and were connected inside to protect against the Minnesota winters. Having the shapes touch gave the composition an added degree of energy; it became less like a set of little buildings making up a mock townscape than like a still life. Frank liked to compare it to Giorgio Morandi's still life paintings of jars and bottles, which the understated power of the Winton House composition does in fact resemble. But to the extent that the comparison with Morandi makes sense, it reduces the Johnson house to the status of backdrop behind the still life, making Frank's work the real subject.[†]

For Mark Peterson and Barbara Sirmai, whose three-acre building site had a small lake and overlooked a ravine, Frank produced an arrangement of boxy forms, less a Morandi still life than an active, zigzagging

---

* Frank was uncharacteristically, and unnecessarily, timid here. When the house was completed in 1986, the Wintons, observing that the hedge compromised the strong architectural dialogue between the two houses that they had hoped for, had it removed, to the benefit of both buildings.

[†] The Wintons were exceptionally satisfied clients. They remained in the house until 2002, when they sold the property to a real estate developer, who divided it into three lots. The Johnson house and the vacant parcel sold quickly, but the unusual form of the Gehry house discouraged buyers. After two years of trying to sell it, the developer, Kirt Woodhouse, donated it to the University of St. Thomas. It was taken apart, moved 110 miles to a conference center the university owned in Owatonna, and reconstructed there in 2011. It no longer has the Philip Johnson house as an architectural foil and it is not sited as subtly as it was on the Winton property, but under the guidance of Victoria Young, a professor of architectural history at St. Thomas, the house was well cared for and became the only Gehry house that could be visited by the public. But the university decided in 2014 to sell the land, and it sold the house at auction in 2015 to a private owner, who is now re-erecting it on a site in New York, with completion expected in 2018.

version of some of his earlier houses. He arranged the main living spaces in an extended, cross-shaped structure clad in metal and gray stucco that deliberately echoed the cruciform shape of a church; a tall light tower marked the crossing, the living room formed the nave, and a fireplace nook was the apse. He finished the design when he was on a vacation trip with Berta to visit her family in Panama, and the presence of so many Catholics around him, he said, put churches front and center in his consciousness— reminding him of the Romanesque churches that had so excited him in France. The bedrooms were in adjacent square structures of stucco and concrete block and set at different levels to reflect the topography of the site. One bedroom was connected to the main house by bridge and the other by tunnel. A courtyard was between the three main structures.

The Schnabel house was designed for Rockwell Schnabel, a career diplomat, and his wife, Marna, an architect who had worked briefly for Frank after she graduated from the University of Southern California. During the years that the house was being designed, Rockwell Schnabel served as the U.S. ambassador to Finland, a posting that gave Frank the welcome opportunity to return with Berta to Finland to visit the Schnabels and work on the design. The house that resulted was the most ambitious, if not also the most elaborate, residence Frank had done up to that point, where ideas he had developed in the Winton and Sirmai-Peterson houses were most clearly realized.

The Schnabel house was a modern villa, if a five-thousand-square foot residence broken up into multiple smaller structures can be called a villa. As in the Sirmai-Peterson house, Frank used a metal-clad cruciform structure with a high light monitor as the centerpiece, but this time it was less like a church than a great village hall surrounded by a whole series of outbuildings: a skylit office for Rockwell Schnabel topped by a dome in the shape of a copper globe; a two-story stucco wing containing the kitchen, a two-story family room, and two bedrooms; a stucco garage with a staff apartment in a box above it, rotated off the axis of the garage; another bedroom in its own structure, topped by a sawtooth skylight; and a columned master bedroom pavilion one level below the rest of the house, set on a shallow artificial lake. The entire site was conceived as a two-level walled garden. It was Frank's most sophisticated house, embracing at one point or another almost all of the design ideas he had been exploring through the 1980s. The Schnabel house contains elements that allude to the Indiana Avenue houses and the Spiller house, among others, as well as to his more recent houses. It is an intense hive of architectural activity that neverthe-less manages to appear serene, even sumptuous, while still remaining true to Frank's architectural voice. Neither the tranquil still life of the Winton House nor the tiny village of Sirmai-Peterson, the Schnabel house was both a set of notable parts and a majestic whole.

One major residential commission in the mid-1980s did not turn out as well as Schnabel, and it was to have major repercussions to Frank's life and practice. In 1984, the billionaire collector and philanthropist Eli Broad, who had been among the founders of the Museum of Contemporary Art, asked Frank to design a house for him and his wife, Edythe, in Brentwood. Frank was uneasy: Broad had a reputation for being a difficult client, and he had been part of the group that chose Arata Isozaki over Frank to design the museum. If this was another consolation prize, like the Temporary Contemporary, but this time with a client known for interfering, Frank did not want it. Broad persisted, and in time Frank gave in, persuading Broad to sign a contract that gave Frank however much time he needed to design the project, and no limit on the budget. He thought that would keep him free from Broad's meddling.

It did, up to a point, but it did not keep him free from Broad's impatience. Broad did not object to Frank's design. Quite the contrary: he was ready to accept it long before Frank was. Two years into the project, Frank was still refining and reshaping the plans, and Broad was desperate to begin con-struction, so much so that when Frank insisted that the design was not yet finished, Broad took the plans and gave them to Langdon Wilson, a large corporate architectural firm in Los Angeles with a reputation for getting commercial projects built efficiently. The house was finished under the supervision of Randy Jefferson, an architect at Langdon Wilson. It adhered more or less to Frank's intentions, or at least his intentions as they were at the time Broad ran out of patience and fired him.[*] Yet Frank was so angry with Broad that he refused to acknowledge the house as his work,[†] and in the agreement that dissolved their contract, he insisted that Broad not refer to the project as a Gehry house. The Broads invited Frank multiple times to see the finished house, and he refused all of their invitations.

---

[*] The Broads hired an interior designer to furnish the rooms, so the inside of the house bears less resemblance to Frank's original scheme than does the exterior.

[†] While the house is absent from all books and published documentations of Frank Gehry's work, it is included in a private list of projects maintained for internal use in his office, where it is described as "unbuilt."

M ildred Friedman, who encouraged Mike and Penny Winton to hire Frank, was the first museum curator to take a serious interest in his work. Along with her husband, Martin, the longtime director of the Walker Art Center in Minneapolis, she organized the first major national exhibition of Frank's architecture, which opened at the Walker in September 1986, by which time Frank had designed both the Winton and Sirmai-Peterson houses and was at work on Schnabel and the ill-fated Broad house.* It was surprising that an institution in the Midwest would be the first to acknowledge Frank with a major retrospective exhibition, but the Walker under the Friedmans had a reputation for cutting-edge exhibitions and for supporting the careers of numerous artists before larger institutions did. By setting her sights on Frank, Mildred Friedman was simply extending the museum's modus operandi to architecture. She did not even know Frank when she decided to do the show. "I had looked at a lot of his work that had been published, and it looked interesting and unusual and unique," Friedman said. "So I just called him on the phone, probably in '84, I guess, and said hello. I asked, 'Have you ever been to the Walker Art Center?'" Frank knew of the Walker and its reputation, and he and Friedman—who was younger than Frank by six months—quickly found themselves talking about artists they knew in common. By the end of the call, they had become so friendly that Frank invited Friedman to come to Los Angeles to continue the conversation in person. When she arrived at Frank's studio in Venice, Friedman said, "It was like meeting your brother." She would spend the next two years commuting between Los Angeles and Minneapolis, gathering material and working with Frank to decide how the exhibition would be presented.

The Architecture of Frank Gehry was a major coup for the Walker, not least because Frank, ever anxious about how the public would perceive his work, decided to pour his full energies into designing the exhibit as well as providing material for it. It occurred to him that he could make it an opportunity for visitors to experience his work, not just to look at it, and he came up with four room-size structures that he placed, like little freestanding buildings, in the galleries of the museum, a 1971 structure designed by Edward Larrabee Barnes. The Walker, at once understated and lively, was

---

* After its run at the Walker, the exhibition traveled to the Harborfront Museum in Frank's hometown of Toronto, the Museum of Contemporary Art in Los Angeles, the High Museum in Atlanta, and the Museum of Contemporary Art in Houston, concluding its run at the Whitney Museum in New York.

one of the most admired small museum buildings in the United States, its success underscored by the way its relatively stark, modernist architecture provided both a sharp contrast and a benign backdrop for Frank's work.

The structures, all of which could be entered, ranged from ten to twenty feet long, and from eight to ten feet high. One, not surprisingly, was a fish, built of lead scales fastened to a wooden frame; another was a curving object sheathed in copper, a section of which rose up like a chimney; another was a ziggurat covered in the same reddish plywood from Finland that Frank had used on the chapel at Loyola Law School; and another was a roofless room of corrugated cardboard, in effect an architectural riff on Frank's Easy Edges furniture. None was a miniature of an actual Gehry building—Frank was too smart for a gesture as cute as that—but collectively they gave a sense of what Gehry buildings were like.

The exhibition had plenty of conventional documentation as well. Arranged all around the structures and on the gallery walls were drawings and photographs of Frank's work, as well as models, including particularly handsome ones of Frank and Berta's house in Santa Monica and of the campus of Loyola Law School. The exhibit also included pieces of Easy Edges furniture, as well as a few fish lamps suspended within the fish structure, where their surroundings gave them an unexpected resonance. The exhibition generated a book-length catalog with essays by the architectural historian Thomas Hines, Rosemarie Haag Bletter, Joseph Giovannini, Pilar Viladas, the art historian and artist Coosje van Bruggen, and Friedman herself. It was actually the second book on Frank's work to appear—his good friend Peter Arnell and Arnell's partner Ted Bickford had put together a substantial monograph that Rizzoli brought out the year before the Walker show—and the collective impact of the two seemed to confirm how much Frank's reputation had grown since the completion of his house a few years before. Hines, in his largely biographical essay, wrote of Frank that "frequently depressed by perceived past 'failures' and, by his own admission, 'paranoid' about the future, Gehry could not deny that for the last ten years, his stock and his star had been steadily rising. . . . Gehry had indeed achieved fame, notoriety, and international prominence as one of the era's most provocative and creative architects." Hines wrote of the "increasingly euphoric critical acclaim" Frank was receiving for his architecture, which, Hines said, "in its powerful, brutal, ugly-beautiful way, continued to reflect the pain, anger, tensions and ambivalences of its times."

Coosje van Bruggen, who was married to the artist Claes Oldenburg and worked in partnership with him, wrote an essay that was both a paean to Frank for his understanding and sympathy for artists and a memoir of her and Oldenburg's various attempts over the years to collaborate with Frank. She and Oldenburg had met him in 1982 when they were invited to visit the Gehrys in Santa Monica and taken on a tour of the house by Alejo, who was six, and Sam, who was barely three, "Alejo assuring us that it was all right to step on a chain-link floor, while Sami pointed out the black and white Ellsworth Kelly print that hung above his bed," Van Bruggen recalled.

Van Bruggen went on to quote Frank as telling her that he tended to be influenced by living artists more than dead ones, because "they are working on the same issues I am," and he said to her that "three artists I especially looked at, and still look at and learn from, are Richard Serra, Don Judd and Claes Oldenburg." The friendship developed quickly. A year and a half after they first met Frank, Van Bruggen and Oldenburg spent two weeks at the Gehry office in Venice, looking at current work, sailing with Frank and Berta in the small boat that they kept at Marina del Rey, and trying to figure out a project that they might collaborate on. Van Bruggen and Oldenburg came up with a piece called *Toppling Ladder with Spilling Paint* to be installed on the Loyola campus, but that, like the tea bag they proposed for Richard Cohen's building in Boston, was more of a response to Frank's architecture than the genuine collaboration that all three of them envisioned.

In March 1984 an opportunity arose. Germano Celant, a critic and art historian who had written an essay for the book on Frank's work that Peter Arnell and Ted Bickford produced, invited Frank, Oldenburg, and Van Bruggen to take on a one-week project with his students from the Politecnico di Milano. They proposed a new neighborhood to be added to Venice. Frank suggested that it include, among other things, a fire station in the form of a coiled snake, and Oldenburg and Van Bruggen proposed an office building in the form of a grand piano as well as a theater library in the form of a vast pair of binoculars standing upright, like two small towers.

The Venice project was never intended to be real, but it provided the basis for a performance piece that Frank, Oldenburg, and Van Bruggen did for the Venice Biennale in 1985, entitled *Il Corso del Cortello* (*The Course of the Knife*). Using a gigantic version of a Swiss Army knife as a ship and a stage in front of the Arsenale, the three each played a character with artistic ambitions: Oldenburg a souvenir vendor who sought to be a painter, Van Bruggen a travel agent who wanted to be a writer, and

Frank as "Frankie P. Toronto," a barber who wanted to be an architect. Anita and Frank's daughter Brina also played roles in the costumed drama. Frank, wearing a suit made of fragments of classical architecture, proceeded to create his own drawings over projected images of old Venetian buildings, a symbolic act of new art supplanting old, not unlike Robert Rauschenberg's famous erasure of a De Kooning drawing in 1953. But Rauschenberg created his piece in the privacy of his studio; Frank, for the first and only time in his life, was engaging in performance art.

Frank as "Frankie P. Toronto" in Venice, 1985

Just before leaving for Italy, Frank received another commission: Camp Good Times, a place for children with cancer that was to be built in the Santa Monica Mountains near Los Angeles. When Frank returned from Venice he told the client he would take on the job if Oldenburg and Van Bruggen, as well as the landscape architect Peter Walker, could work with him. Frank, Oldenburg, and Van Bruggen all felt strongly that they did not want to each tackle a different part of the project, but to have all of it be designed by the entire team. The group spent months trying to figure out how to create a set of buildings that did not evoke common objects directly, as Oldenburg and Van Bruggen's sculptural pieces did, but would somehow be more like them than Frank's work otherwise would have been—to find a meeting point between Frank's architecture and the artists' sculptures. They used mostly maritime imagery, and produced an infirmary with flying sails for shade, a dormitory in the form of a bridge over a gully, a large dining hall building that had wavelike shapes, an entry porch that called to mind both an inverted ship's hull and Frank's early projects with open wood framing, and a kitchen in the shape of an old-fashioned milk can.

But this supposedly real project never got any further than the imaginary plans for Venice. After working closely with Frank and the others for more than a year, the camp's organizers concluded that the design, in Frank's words, "was too 'arty' and that the kids really would like something more rustic—a normal camp. [They] suggested Huckleberry Finn as a metaphor." It turned out that they had wanted all along the kind of sentimental, picturesque, not to say Disneyland-like design Frank had hoped to avoid. Unable, or at least unwilling, to produce that, the team decided it had no choice but to give up the project. It was a painful loss. The Gehrys and the Oldenburgs had become close, and Frank, Van Bruggen, and Oldenburg had labored long and hard over the camp. They produced something that was neither self-conscious nor precious, and not at all condescending, as they felt, not surprisingly, that a "Huckleberry Finn" design would be. Frank believed that "there's a kind of sentimentality in looking back to Twain that relates more to my generation than to the kids who are going to be using this camp."

The Gehry-Oldenburg combine would get one more chance, closer to home on Main Street in Venice, California. Fred Weisman had asked Frank to help him find an old industrial building that he could convert into a home for his art collection, and Frank found one that had been used by the local gas company. Weisman liked the location, which associated his museum with the Venice art scene. The building had just been sold to a Los Angeles real estate investor named Larry Field, who specialized in seeking out undervalued properties, and Frank went to see him on Fred Weisman's behalf.

Field, who had not yet closed on the property, realized he had a chance to flip it for a huge profit, but he took a liking to Frank and proposed that they go into partnership, with Weisman providing money and Frank contributing his architectural services in exchange for an equity stake. Frank agreed, and it turned out to be the beginning of another of his unlikely friendships. Field was a straight-talking, no-nonsense businessman from the Bronx who had little interest in aesthetics and was a conservative Republican. But he liked Frank's unpretentious manner, and was impressed by his determination and focus. Frank, in turn, liked Field's directness and thought he was always fair, unlike many of the people he had dealt with in business. Both men were nonnatives who had become deeply engaged in Los Angeles, and they had come to the city for a similar family reason, the search for a mild climate for a close relative who was ill: in Frank's case his father, and in Field's his wife. Later, when the building on Brooks Avenue housing his office went up for sale, Frank would turn to Field for advice on how to buy it. Frank eventually bought the building in partnership with Chuck Arnoldi and another friend, Jack Quinn, a lawyer and art collector.

On the Main Street site Frank had found for Fred Weisman, he and Weisman envisioned the old building as the anchor of a much larger development that would include retail and office space and artists' studios as well as space to display Weisman's art collection, but the project soon ran into community opposition. Weisman was impatient with the delays and lost interest in the site. He offered Frank an unusual deal: if Frank would give him some of the art he owned, Weisman would turn over his share of the property to him. Weisman took a painting by Ed Moses, among other things, and Frank found himself the majority owner, along with Greg Walsh, to whom he had given some of his stake in the building.

Walsh, doggedly loyal to Frank but also far more interested in a quiet, contemplative life, was beginning to seem slightly out of his element as the office grew bigger and Frank jetted around the world. He was content to remain in Frank's shadow, but Frank worried from time to time about Walsh's welfare. He was unmarried and had neither partner nor children, and Frank wanted him to have some resources.

Walsh ended up with a roughly one-third ownership in the project, but with Fred Weisman gone, there was no clear plan for the building that made economic sense. Venice was still a gritty, raffish environment with only glimmers of gentrification, and for a time Frank and Greg rented the building to the artist Niki de Saint-Phalle, who used it as a studio to produce her oversize sculpted figures.

The solution came through one of Frank's clients, an artist named Miriam Wosk, who had commissioned Frank to build an unusual penthouse and studio atop a small apartment building in Beverly Hills. (It took the form of a small village, a residential version of Loyola on a rooftop.) Wosk was close to Jay Chiat, the advertising executive who founded the firm of Chiat/Day and who not long after would become famous for his Apple advertisements. Wosk introduced Chiat to Frank at a dinner she gave before a concert at the Hollywood Bowl. It was another client acquaintance that quickly turned into a close friendship, as well as a useful business relationship, a pattern that was becoming increasingly common in Frank's life. Many architects manage to turn their friends into clients; Frank seemed to specialize in turning his clients into friends, and the friendships often lasted longer than the client relationship. Fred Weisman, Richard Cohen, and Ernest Fleischmann, the executive director of the Los Angeles Philharmonic, were at the beginning of what would become in time a much longer list.

Chiat was an unconventional thinker who felt comfortable with Frank, and would ultimately hire him to design offices for Chiat/Day in Los Angeles, Toronto, and New York. A decade later, his firm would include Frank among the famous faces of creative iconoclasts in Apple's "Think Different" campaign. Chiat would also commission Frank to design a house he wanted to build in Telluride and another in Sagaponack, Long Island.*

When Jay Chiat first met Frank, he was looking for new office space for his expanding agency, and he had no interest in conventional Los Angeles locations like Beverly Hills or Century City. He preferred the creative energy, not to mention the edginess, of Venice, and he asked if Frank would be interested in being the architect. Frank said yes, but it didn't occur to him at first to propose his own property as the location—the idea of a major advertising agency in such a marginal location seemed unthinkable even to him. Later Miriam Wosk told Chiat that Frank controlled some property there, and he asked to see it. Chiat promptly offered to buy it for slightly over a million dollars. "We didn't have a million, so it was a good offer," Frank said, and he accepted it.

To replace the old gas structure, Frank produced a design for a long, low office building with one section with a curving façade and another section that resembled an abstract version of tree branches. Something was needed to tie the two disparate sections together, and one day when the two were meeting at Frank's office, Chiat, who liked the design so far as it went, grew impatient at Frank's uncertainty about how he would complete the composition. "He said, 'Come on, Gehry, you can do better than that,'" Frank remembered. "He said, 'What are you going to do there?' And I said, 'I don't know.' We drank wine and he said, 'You must have some idea.'"

At that moment, Frank didn't. He looked up and saw a small model of the building-size binoculars Oldenburg, Van Bruggen, and he had proposed as a library for the other Venice, grabbed it, and plopped it down in front of the model for the Chiat/Day office. "That's great," Jay Chiat said. Frank was less certain. He hadn't really meant to suggest that the binoculars should go on Main Street. "Claes will never let us do that," he said, and he reminded Chiat that Oldenburg's projects were all site-specific, and that the binoculars had been conceived as a pair of towers

---

* Neither house was ever built. They would have been the only Gehry houses in either Colorado or the Hamptons.

The Chiat/Day
building on
Main Street in
Venice, California,
with Oldenburg
binoculars

for a very different site in a very different Venice. Chiat didn't care. He
insisted that Frank call Oldenburg and Van Bruggen and tell them that he
wanted them to redesign the binoculars to become a part of his building.
"So I called him, and I said, 'I know this is a long shot: would you do the
binoculars for this guy who wants them for his entry?'" Frank recalled. "I
said to Claes, 'In order for you to do these binoculars, you have to become
an architect.' He said, 'What does that mean?' I said, 'You have to put
windows in it.'" Oldenburg, it turned out, loved the idea, because it would
give him and Van Bruggen the chance they had been craving, which was
to blur the distinction between sculpture and architecture. So long as the
binoculars were a functioning part of the building and not just a work of art
placed in front of it they were willing to redo the work for Chiat/Day. The
upright binoculars, which reached the full three-story height of the building, were constructed in black to contrast with the copper sheet metal of
one wing and the off-white stucco of the other. The space between the
two lenses, which looks like a grand portal, became the entrance to the
building's parking garage—a perhaps implicit acknowledgment that in Los
Angeles, street entrances are secondary to automobile entrances. The inte-

rior of the lenses—the "towers"—served as a library and conference area for Chiat/Day.*

F rank, Claes Oldenburg, and Coosje van Bruggen would work together one more time, for a client who soon became as much a part of Frank's life as Jay Chiat: Rolf Fehlbaum, the chairman of Vitra, a maker of modern furniture based just outside Basel, Switzerland. Fehlbaum had run the company, which his parents founded as a maker of shop fittings, since 1977. They had branched into furniture in 1957 by licensing from Herman Miller the European rights to manufacture the furniture designs of Charles and Ray Eames and George Nelson, and a few years later Vitra began to commission furniture of its own. Fehlbaum, a passionate student of design who had written a doctoral dissertation on the French philosopher and social theorist Saint-Simon, took to heart his subject's desire for a more utopian industrial environment uplifted by the arts. Spurred on by a fire in 1981 that destroyed Vitra's manufacturing facility in Weil am Rhein, Germany, just across the Swiss border, he proceeded to rebuild it into a showcase of modern architecture. Fehlbaum's first commission was to the British architect Nicholas Grimshaw, who designed a factory constructed of prefabricated corrugated metal that could be erected quickly to get the company back in operation after the fire. Grimshaw designed a master plan for future expansion that Fehlbaum expected to follow. And then he met Frank Gehry.

Fehlbaum had been trying to meet Frank for years, ever since he saw the first Easy Edges furniture. He was fascinated by Los Angeles—he would end up buying the entire collection of furniture prototypes created by Charles and Ray Eames—and he had visited many Gehry buildings. He wrote to Frank, asking if he would consider designing something for Vitra, and Frank, wary of getting back into furniture, never bothered to reply. After the Grimshaw factory was finished in 1982, Fehlbaum decided to honor his father's seventieth birthday by commissioning a sculpture by Claes Oldenburg and Coosje van Bruggen as a gateway to the campus. He was visiting the Oldenburgs at their studio in New York to talk about the

---

* The discovery of contaminated waste on the site delayed the project, and it was not ready for occupancy until 1991. Not surprisingly it quickly became known as the Binoculars Building. Chiat/Day remained for less than a decade: needing more space, it moved to other quarters in 1998. The building is now the Los Angeles base for Google.

work, and as he recalls, Frank turned out to be there. Fehlbaum immediately invited them all to visit the campus together.[*]

Once at Vitra, accompanied by Berta, Alejo, and Sam, Frank provided another set of eyes and helped Oldenburg and Van Bruggen site the sculpture, which was called *Balancing Tools* and consisted of an enormous hammer, pliers, and screwdriver—three tools of the upholsterer—arranged to make a kind of triumphal arch. Rolf Fehlbaum tried, this time in person, to interest Frank in designing furniture for Vitra. The two had gotten along exceptionally well—"I came from a very simple background. We were modest people. But we bonded. I had my insecurities, Frank had his," Fehlbaum said.

Even though Frank found Fehlbaum a welcome mix of intellectual and gemütlich—the combination he liked best in a person—and Fehlbaum's admiration for his work was beyond doubt, Frank remained nervous about returning to furniture design and continued to maintain that he was more interested in designing buildings than chairs. So Fehlbaum decided he would come up with an architectural commission: a "little shed" that would house his ever-expanding collections of modern design, and would also serve to honor his mother as the Oldenburg sculpture had honored his father. It could be placed in front of a second factory building that he was planning to build beside Grimshaw's.

Frank was dubious, even though it would be his first job in Europe. The job was too small to justify his fee and the time he would need to spend in Weil am Rhein and traveling back and forth to Los Angeles, he told Fehlbaum. He didn't want to saddle his friend with the burden of paying an excessive architect's fee so he could make a profit, and neither did he want to risk their friendship by accepting the standard fee for a small job and resenting it. "Frank is not greedy, but he is always worried about money, that something terrible would happen," Fehlbaum said later. "But he is a fantastic, wonderful, and warm man."

And then Fehlbaum had an idea. Why couldn't Frank do the new factory as well as the small building in front of it? Then the project would be big enough to justify a larger fee, and more trips from Los Angeles. Nicholas Grimshaw was not pleased—he had expected to be in charge of any

---

[*] Frank's recollection is slightly different. He believes that the European trip came first, and that Fehlbaum, knowing that he was acquainted with the Oldenburgs, took advantage of the fact that they were traveling together and urged them all to come to Weil am Rhein to see the proposed location for the sculpture.

The Vitra Design Museum

ongoing expansion—but Fehlbaum had already begun to conceive of the campus in a new way, not as an ever-growing complex by Grimshaw but as a collection of significant buildings by different architects. Vitra manufactured chairs by all kinds of different major designers; why couldn't it build buildings by all kinds of different major architects?

Frank quickly agreed to the expanded commission and designed a relatively simple factory building that he felt complemented the Grimshaw building beside it. "For me, it was a defining experience to see the two structures by Grimshaw and Gehry side by side: the same volume, the same costs, the same function. And I found the co-existence of two different approaches much more interesting than two Gehrys or two Grimshaws," Fehlbaum said.[*]

Meanwhile, Fehlbaum, who had said he considered the notion of building his own museum "pretentious," acknowledged to himself that his growing design collections required something more than what he had

---

[*] The Vitra campus would eventually grow to include Zaha Hadid's first completed building as well as work by Herzog and de Meuron, Tadao Ando, Álvaro Siza, and SANAA. Fehlbaum gave it the address of 2 Charles-Eames Strasse.

been calling a mere shed. He encouraged Frank to design a highly expressive building that could be used for all kinds of art and design exhibitions. Inspired by the freedom Fehlbaum had given him, Frank turned the job he had been reluctant to take into one of his key works, the Vitra Design Museum. Finished in 1989, it is a mix of shapes that seem to have crashed together: a composition made of swooping curves and angled boxes, its forms seem to swirl about with an intensity that is altogether unlike the serene order of the Winton guesthouse, which, by comparison to Vitra, seems almost genteel. The even white color of the plaster exterior belies the tremendous energy within the form, which has an intensity that Frank had not demonstrated since his own house a decade before. Inside, there are skylights, level changes, and a sense of moving, dynamic space throughout. But there are also plenty of plain, vertical white walls for paintings and, more important for showing Fehlbaum's collections, platforms and podiums for showing furniture and other objects. For Frank, Vitra was a new chance to prove his belief that dramatic and different architectural form did not have to come at the price of function. He had always done his best work for clients he felt comfortable with, and Vitra was, among other things, an affirmation of how comfortable he was with Rolf Fehlbaum, and how comfortable he would continue to be with the design of places for the display of art.

It had not been easy to characterize Frank's work for a long time, and Vitra's powerful, expressionist form made it no simpler. In 1988, Philip Johnson, by then tired of postmodernism's historical ruffles and flourishes, had decided that it was time for a change, not just in his own work, but in his view of what was the style du jour. The next trend in architecture, Johnson decided, was a return to modernism in the form of sharp, angled forms, their slashing quality in some ways as much of a rebellion against the pure and perfect geometries envisioned by the early modernist architects as postmodernism had been. Several critics called this movement "deconstructivism," an allusion to the Russian constructivist movement of the 1920s and 1930s; others, including the critic and architect Aaron Betsky, called it "violated perfection." Johnson, who had been the first curator of architecture and design at the Museum of Modern Art, temporarily reclaimed his old post to organize an exhibition at the museum that he hoped would confirm the rise of deconstructivist architecture, or at least get it into the newspapers. Johnson and his co-curator, Mark Wigley, who was then a professor at Princeton, selected seven architects to represent what Wigley would call a "sense of dislocation" and an architecture of "disquiet." He wrote, "What is being disturbed is a set of deeply entrenched cultural assumptions which underlie a certain view of architecture, assumptions about order, harmony, stability and unity."

Frank was selected as one of the seven, along with Daniel Libeskind, Zaha Hadid, Rem Koolhaas, Bernard Tschumi, Peter Eisenman, and the firm of Coop Himmelb(l)au, and models and drawings of his own house in Santa Monica were featured. He was hardly going to argue with Philip Johnson, who he knew felt strongly about including him, or to complain about having his work shown at the Museum of Modern Art. Still, he found the experience troubling. He was unsure how much he really had in common with the other six architects, or whether he really wanted to be grouped with them at all. He admired several of them, but that was beside the point. He did not believe that his work challenged assumptions about order and harmony—in fact, quite the contrary. Wigley's observations about deconstructivist architecture suggested the opposite of what Frank believed he was doing, which was seeking another kind of order, and showing that harmony could be found through something other than the classical tradition. The text of the exhibition catalog referred to the unusual forms he had added to his house as if they represented a kind of unconscious, simmering beneath the surface of the original house and bursting out to challenge it. Frank had never felt that he was attacking the old house. To him, what he had added to his house was more like an exuberant layer of celebratory form, dancing on the surface of the old house, breaking through its walls, and in the end establishing a content, if unorthodox cohabitation with it.

Frank's house had been finished for nearly a decade by the time the *Deconstructivist Architecture* show opened, and in recent years his creative impulses had yielded work that was very different from it: even if Frank's house could be called deconstructivist, projects like Loyola Law School, the Winton House, and the Vitra Design Museum demonstrated how inadequate that label was as a way of describing almost everything he had been trying to do in the years since. While the Museum of Modern Art was presenting Frank as a deconstructivist, he was overseeing the completion of Vitra, a project that was altogether different. And it was Vitra that would point to the direction he would take in the years to follow.

The decade would end with a welcome recognition that Frank was more than one of seven architects practicing in what Philip Johnson had decreed the mode of the moment. It came not from a museum but from the jury that awarded the Pritzker Architecture Prize, which since its founding in 1979 by the Pritzker family of Chicago had been given annually to an architect whose work "has produced consistent and significant contributions to humanity and the built environment through the art of architecture." In its first decade the Pritzker, which came with a stipend of $100,000, had been given to I. M. Pei, Philip Johnson, Kevin Roche, James Stirling, and Oscar Niemeyer, among others, and it was widely considered the most prestigious prize an architect could win, an acknowledgment that he had earned his way into an architectural pantheon.

Frank was in Amsterdam with his client Ernest Fleischmann, the executive director of the Los Angeles Philharmonic, when the phone rang at his hotel. "Frank, you've won the Pritzker Prize," Bill Lacy, who managed the prize for the Pritzker family, said to him. "Don't be silly," Frank said. "Venturi hasn't won it yet." And he hung up. Lacy called back. "He said, 'Hey, buddy, this is real—you just can't tell anyone,'" Frank remembered. "So I called Berta and then I couldn't go to sleep."

The Pritzker Prize is presented each spring in a different location of architectural distinction, and in 1989 the ceremony was to be at the Todai-ji temple, an ancient Buddhist temple in Nara, Japan. The location pleased Frank. "Since I was a Japanophile already, I knew the temple," he said.

The Pritzkers sent Frank and Berta first-class tickets for a flight from Los Angeles to Japan, and they found themselves on the same plane as Lacy and J. Carter Brown, the director of the National Gallery of Art, who chaired the jury. Not everything went smoothly. Lacy and Brown, Frank remembered, teased him for much of the flight about the acceptance speech he would be expected to make, and asked him whether he had written it yet. It was the most important speech he would ever give, they told him, and it needed to be thought through fully in advance.

It was Frank's habit to speak off the cuff—he did not like written texts—and he assumed that Lacy and Brown, knowing that, were just trying to give him a hard time. He would be fine, he thought, with a couple of gracious and casual thank-yous. Then he arrived and looked at the program, and he realized that the Japanese fondness for protocol meant that he actually did have to try to say something meaningful, and that he would be expected to talk for several minutes. He got up at five o'clock on the morning of the prize presentation and sat in his hotel room as Berta slept, trying to figure out what to say and writing it down.

The ceremony was in the morning, and after Jay Pritzker welcomed the guests, Kenzo Tange, the Japanese architect who had received the prize two years earlier, was asked to speak. Tange spoke in Japanese about the Todai-ji temple and the importance of the prize and then, to the astonishment of both Frank and the Pritzker family, went on to say that so far as he could tell, Frank's work had nothing to do with the great architectural heritage of the temple or, for that matter, with that of the Pritzker Prize. It was a surprising insult, and if nothing else, it underscored the extent to which Frank's work was still viewed as disturbing, even threatening, by many of his profession's established practitioners. Frank's comfort with speaking extemporaneously defused the tension. He rose, and before he turned to his text, he looked toward Tange and said, "I realize I will have to work harder."

He expressed his happiness and gratitude, and then he went on to deliver one of his few extended reflections on his values and motivations:

> I am obsessed with architecture. It is true, I am restless, trying to find myself as an architect, and how best to contribute to this world filled with contradiction, disparity and inequality, even passion and opportunity. It is a world in which our values and priorities are constantly being challenged. It is simplistic to expect a single right answer. Architecture is a small piece of this human equation, but for those of us who practice it, we believe in its potential to make a difference, to enlighten and to enrich the human experience, to penetrate the barriers of misunderstanding and provide a beautiful context for life's drama.
>
> I was trained early in my career by a Viennese master to make perfection, but in my first projects, I was not able to find the craft to achieve that perfection. My artist friends, people like Jasper Johns, Bob Rauschenberg, Ed Kienholz, Claes Oldenburg, were working with very inexpensive materials—broken wood and paper, and they were making beauty. These were not superficial details, they were direct; it raised the question of what was beautiful. I chose to use the craft available, and to work with the craftsmen and make a virtue out of their limitations.
>
> Painting had an immediacy that I craved for architecture. I explored the processes of raw construction materials to try giving feeling and spirit to form. In trying to find the essence of my own expression, I fantasized the artist standing before the white canvas deciding what was the first move. I called it the moment of truth.

Architecture must solve complex problems. We must understand and use technology, and we must create buildings that are safe and dry, respectful of context and neighbors, and face all the myriad of issues of social responsibility, and even please the client.

But then what? The moment of truth, the composition of elements, the selection of form, scale, materials, color, finally, all the same issues facing the painter and the sculptor. Architecture is surely an art, and those who practice the art of architecture are surely architects.

Our problems as architects increase in complexity as time goes on. We have difficulty with the art of city building. We are finding ways of working together, artists and architects, architects and architects, clients and architects. The dream is that each brick, each window, each wall, each road and each tree will be placed lovingly by craftsmen, client, architect and people to create beautiful cities. Adding the extra time and money at the beginning is essential. This very temple, Todai-ji, is a symbol of a great collaborative effort in its time, bringing together many thousands of people and talents to create incredible and lasting beauty.

Frank then thanked his mentors, and the Pritzkers, before concluding his talk in the same tone with which he began. "Since the announcement of this award, I have been asked many times by reporters what I intend to do with the money," he said. "I have said, of course, that I am going to finish my house and tear down the construction fence."

13

Walt Disney Concert Hall: First Movement

For one group of people in Los Angeles, the news that Frank had won the Pritzker Prize was an occasion for relief as much as celebration. The five members of the architectural selection committee of the Los Angeles Music Center had made an audacious decision just a few months before when they chose Frank to design the new concert hall that was to be added to the center. The Music Center had conducted an international search for an architect, and in the summer of 1988 narrowed the list to four names: Gottfried Bohm, of Germany; James Stirling, the British architect; Hans Hollein, of Vienna; and Frank Gehry. If Frank had been the token local architect six years earlier when the Museum of Contemporary Art was choosing its architect, this time he was a serious contender.

But he was still something of a long shot when the interview process began. To some members of the Music Center board he was still the city's bad-boy architect, connected more to the Venice art scene than to downtown halls of power and culture. Choosing Frank in their view was hardly the way to show that Los Angeles was a sophisticated global city. They saw the committee's selection of the local architect over three international superstars, all of whom had won the Pritzker Prize, not as an act of caution, but as the riskiest decision they could have made. Yet if those voices were not entirely silenced when Frank himself won the Pritzker, they were surely muted, and to the committee, the news of Frank's prize came as a sweet vindication of the wisdom of their choice. It could still be called daring, but at least it could no longer be thought provincial.

The project was the Walt Disney Concert Hall, and it had its origins in May 1987, when Lillian Disney, Walt Disney's eighty-seven-year-old widow, offered a gift of $50 million for the city to build a new hall for the Los Angeles Philharmonic. The orchestra had suffered for years with the bad acoustics and banal architecture of the Dorothy Chandler Pavilion, the main hall of the Music Center, and Lillian Disney thought a new concert hall would be an excellent memorial to her husband. She wanted the hall to be "one of the finest in the world," she wrote, and put no conditions on her gift except to require that the hall be built on the vacant block to the immediate south of the Chandler Pavilion, that construction be started within five years—and that she have the final say as to the choice of an architect.

Since the hall was technically to be a part of the Music Center, the center's board took charge of the planning once Lillian Disney's gift had been accepted. Frederick M. Nicholas, a real estate developer and attorney who was active on the boards of both the Music Center and the Museum of Contemporary Art—where he had overseen the six-year design and construction process of the building by Arata Isozaki just down the street—seemed the logical person to take charge of the project. Nicholas, who viewed himself as a supporter of great architecture, wanted Lillian Disney's assurance that she was committed to having a major architect design the hall before he agreed to take on the job. Mrs. Disney agreed, and told Nicholas that good acoustics and the presence of a garden as part of the project were also of great importance to her. Nicholas took on the task, putting together a committee to work with him. To isolate the process of architect selection from any political pressures, he organized a subcommittee consisting of the deans of the two major architecture schools in Los Angeles and the directors of the city's three major museums to serve as a panel to settle on an architect. While Lillian Disney had the right to veto the selection, she indicated that she was unlikely to do so.

Nicholas asked his friend Richard Koshalek, the director of MOCA, to take charge of the subcommittee. Koshalek, Nicholas, and several members of the Philharmonic management and of the orchestra quickly embarked on a series of trips to great concert halls around the world, and began to put together a list of potential architects. They started with eighty, then reduced the group to twenty-five, who were invited to submit their qualifications for further consideration. Lillian Disney invited the subcommittee to her house in Holmby Hills, where they looked at slides of the architects' work and reduced the field to six: Bohm, Stirling, Hollein, Harry Cobb, Renzo Piano, and Frank. After interviewing all six, the committee and subcommittee decided to eliminate Cobb and Piano, and on March 17, 1988, they announced the names of the four finalists and gave each $75,000 to prepare a preliminary design.

A backlash arose almost immediately to Frank's inclusion among the finalists. "You can't pick Frank Gehry; we're going to be the laughingstock of the whole universe," Fred Nicholas remembers a prominent Angeleno saying to him. "It can't be Frank Gehry," Koshalek was told by Ron Gother, a lawyer who worked for the Disneys. "The Disney family can't have a plywood or a chain-link concert hall." Gother went so far as to call Frank and tell him that there was no point to his remaining in the architectural competition. "Walt Disney would not have wanted his name on a Gehry building," Frank remembers Gother saying. That Frank no longer made much use of plywood and chain link, and that his growing stature was confirmed by the national tour of the Walker's exhibition of his work—which right then happened to be on view at the Museum of Contemporary Art in Los Angeles, adding an ironic twist—seemed to matter little to the city's old establishment, which made it clear to the Koshalek committee that any architect would be more acceptable to it than Frank. Koshalek was able to quiet the criticism by threatening to go to the press with the story that members of the city's power structure were trying to interfere with what was supposed to be an impartial process. But it was clear that Frank had an uphill battle. Just after they had chosen the four architects who would be invited to compete, the selection committee took a private, informal poll, and it turned out that a majority of the committee favored Stirling, remembered Richard Weinstein, who as dean of the architecture school at UCLA sat on the committee.

"They were scared to death of Frank," Richard Koshalek said of the city's leaders. Some did not want a prominent architect at all—Koshalek was told by one member of the Music Center board that everyone could save a lot of trouble by just updating the plans for the Dorothy Chandler Pavilion and duplicating it next door—but the possibility that Frank might end up with the commission created such anxiety on the part of the board that Koshalek's committee was asked to provide only comments about the four architects instead of ranking them in order of preference, and to agree not to make any public comments about its deliberations or any differences it might have with the board.

Working on early models for Walt Disney Concert Hall with Michael Maltzan

"They asked us to waive the right of going to the press if there was a disagreement between us and the Music Center board. And we instantly returned a response to the lawyer that we would publicly resign," Richard Weinstein remembered. The board backed down, and the committee retained its right to make a public announcement of its recommended architect. If the Music Center or Lillian Disney disagreed, they would be in the embarrassing position of having to explain why they were rejecting the recommendation of their own impartial panel of experts.

While all this was going on, the four architects had begun to work on their designs, and the committee invited them to present their preliminary concepts and hear comments and suggestions. It was seen as an opportunity to see how responsive the architects would be to criticism, but Frank, Richard Weinstein recalled, was the only one of the four who later made substantial changes in response to the interim comments. He was also the only one who responded to every element in the Music Center's program for the new building, and the only one who continually asked questions. "There was criticism of each of the schemes, and the only one who changed their scheme was Gehry. And the only one who met every single question embedded in the brief was Gehry," Weinstein said.

In November, the competitors came to Los Angeles to present their final schemes to the concert hall committee and the architecture subcommittee. Each architect was given a conference room in which to set up his materials and make his presentation, and the committees moved from room to room. Bohm was scheduled to go first, and Frank remembered that he emerged with a smile, convinced that his presentation had gone so well that he all but had the job. "Come to lunch and have champagne with me," Bohm told Frank. Frank declined. He was to present that afternoon, and he didn't want to have anything to drink. Moreover, he wasn't entirely sure that Bohm was correct.

In fact, all three overseas architects made tactical as well as architectural errors. Bohm produced an almost laughably grandiose scheme that looked to John Walsh, the director of the Getty Museum and another member of the Koshalek committee, as if it had been designed for "zillions of tiny people." Stirling, told during the interim review that the balcony of his hall looked as if it would have unworkable sight lines, returned with his scheme unchanged, an act that the committee found arrogant, while Hollein came up with a design for a hexagonal hall filled with literal allusions to Walt Disney characters, a gesture that the committee viewed as patronizing.

Beside these three, Frank seemed the epitome of reason and even modesty. He tried his best to distance himself from his reputation as wild, and the committee was impressed with the extent to which he had listened to their earlier comments. Frank's understated, "aw, shucks" manner, even to those who knew that it was at least in part a façade masking his driving ambition, struck the right tone with a committee that, after Gottfried Bohm, was inclined to be skittish about architects who made grandiose pronouncements. His design, which called for a stage surrounded by the audience, was heavily influenced by Hans Scharoun's Berlin Philharmonie, the building from 1963 that at the time was considered the most distinguished concert hall of the late twentieth century—and a favorite of the committee members who toured halls at the beginning of the process. Frank also included a glass-roofed conservatory that he called "a living room for the city," and which gave the building a public component that seemed populist in a far more convincing way than Hans Hollein's Disney statues. Frank also included a musicians' garden, which was seen as a generous acknowledgment both of the needs of the orchestra members and of Lillian Disney's love of flowers and gardens.

Frank knew that his presentation was well received by the architecture subcommittee, but he was also certain that several members of the Music Center remained highly skeptical of the notion that he should be trusted to design the most important civic building in Los Angeles. Yet by the time the four presentations were over, it was clear that the other architects had damaged their chances so much that Frank was the only one left standing. The Music Center's concert hall committee met in a borrowed conference room at the Crocker Bank downtown to hear the architecture committee's report. Each of the Koshalek committee members spoke and offered his comments on all four designs. John Walsh concluded by calling Frank's design "the only one I'd really want to see built for the Philharmonic" and arguing that Frank, far from being a risky choice, was the safest option, given what the committee felt was his understanding of both Los Angeles as a city and the Philharmonic as an orchestra, as well as his ability to be "a reliable, down-to-earth, businesslike builder of buildings that work." Walsh described Frank exactly as he wanted to be described, but it took a few days, and several more meetings, before the leadership of the Music Center agreed.

"Mrs. Disney said she'd like it to be Frank Gehry because of the beautiful garden he's created," Koshalek remembered. The members of Fred Nicholas's concert hall committee may have had other reasons, but in the end they saw no reason to disagree with her.

Frank had to leave soon after his presentation for Switzerland and Germany, where he was scheduled to work on his project for Vitra. He had just arrived in Zurich when the phone in his hotel room rang. It was Fred Nicholas. "I need you back here on Sunday at three p.m.," Nicholas said. "I think it's probable that you won it." Frank rushed back to Los Angeles and met one final time with the committee, which appeared to be holding Hans Hollein, who was also there, in reserve in case this last discussion with Frank left them with any misgivings. At the end of the meeting, he was told only to come back to the Founders Room at the Dorothy Chandler Pavilion at nine the following morning. He brought Berta along with him, still not absolutely certain of the morning's agenda. He arrived to find the boards of the Music Center and the Los Angeles Philharmonic, along with the committee members and the press, gathered to hear an announcement: the architect for the new Walt Disney Concert Hall had been chosen, and it was Frank Gehry.

At that point Frank had fewer than forty employees; while his office had grown, it was still smaller than it had been when his work for Rouse came to an end and he made the decision to downsize. He had several young designers of exceptional talent working for him, such as Edwin

Chan, a gifted young architect who had joined Frank a couple of years earlier upon graduating from Harvard and who would come to play a critical role in the office for the next several decades; Michael Maltzan, who would leave in a few years to establish his own practice but who been one of the key designers of the scheme that won the Walt Disney Hall competition; and Robert Hale, who had played a major role in Loyola Law School and the Temporary Contemporary.

Many of the other architects on his staff, however, were recent graduates who liked the idea of having a stint at Frank Gehry's office on their résumés, and remained for only a couple of years. Even the more senior people in the office had no experience with projects as large and complicated as Walt Disney Concert Hall would be. Frank knew that the office had to change. The competition scheme, however challenging it had been to create, was still not much more than a preliminary design. The process of turning it into something buildable and practical would take years, and would reshape Frank's practice. To start the process of getting Disney Hall done, he hired two architects who would work closely by his side for the next several years, and would play a major role in giving his office its identity: Craig Webb, a talented designer who had been working for Barton Myers, and Jim Glymph, who had overseen the completion of the Los Angeles Convention Center for Gruen, Frank's former firm. Webb knew a lot about theaters and concert halls, and Glymph had experience in managing large and complicated projects. Along with Michael Maltzan, they would be Frank's core team.

Neither Webb nor Glymph was interested in spending his career in a huge corporate firm, but they wondered at first if they were going to fit into Frank's office, which at times seemed more like an artist's atelier than an architectural office capable of producing large and complex building projects. To Glymph, Frank seemed like a creative artist surrounded by people who were more interested in protecting him than in showing him how things could be done. He said as much to Frank in his first interview, which took place in Fromin's delicatessen in Santa Monica. "I can't work with you in your practice as it now is," Glymph told him. Frank seemed to agree that they were a poor match, and the meeting ended uncomfortably.

A week later, Frank called Glymph. "Let's try again," he said. This time they went to Madame Wu's, a Chinese restaurant, and they talked for four hours. "I know I have to change the way I run my practice," Frank said. And Glymph agreed to come. "I immediately wondered what I had gotten into," he said. "I spent the first months fixing leaks in Frank's buildings.

Greg Walsh was overloaded, trying to direct all of the young kids," many of whom, Glymph believed, had made aesthetic decisions without understanding their practical impact, believing that they were serving Frank's larger goals. One of Glymph's first jobs as the office's "Mr. Fixit," as he called himself, was to figure out why one of the rooms in Miriam Wosk's penthouse was getting wet. He discovered that the flashing, the metal strips installed for waterproofing at the edge of the roof, had been installed upside down over the contractor's objections. The young architect working on the project overruled him because he thought that the upside-down flashing better reflected Frank's aesthetic. Glymph, who quickly saw that Frank had a practical side with no more patience than he himself harbored for that kind of reasoning, told him that the mistake was his responsibility and that if he valued his relationship with Miriam Wosk, he had no choice but to pay the costs of repair and replacement. Frank did.

Glymph, a stocky, bearded man who seemed part techie, part hippie, came to see himself as the bridge between Frank's creative and pragmatic instincts. He liked the fact that, as he put it, Frank understood that "his buildings had to work better because they looked so weird. If the program didn't fit, he knew that the building wouldn't work."

It was one thing to fix the Wosk penthouse, quite another to build a concert hall. The trouble began fairly quickly. After an exciting start that included trips abroad with Ernest Fleischmann to visit great concert halls—Frank was on one of those trips when Bill Lacy called him in Amsterdam to tell him he had won the Pritzker—Frank soon found himself caught between the Los Angeles Music Center, which would own the building; the Los Angeles Philharmonic, which would occupy it; Los Angeles County, which owned the land and had agreed to build the parking garage underneath the hall; the city of Los Angeles; the Disney family; and the various contractors and consultants who had a role in the project. It was sometimes hard to know who was the client. The interests of the different parties did not always match, and Frank could not afford to alienate any of them. The fact that the client was a kind of multiheaded hydra was one of the reasons that Disney Hall would end up taking sixteen years to complete, and would be one of the longest and most painful roads Frank would travel.

And there was another, even bigger obstacle placed in Frank's path. He was told that his office could not design the hall by itself. Another firm would have to join with him to execute the working drawings, the documents from which the building is actually built. This was more than just having another firm relieve him of some of his workload. If, as the architect Gregg Pasquarelli has said, "architects don't build buildings, we build instruction kits for other people to build buildings," someone else was going to have the right to build Frank's instruction kit. Frank found that humiliating, which it was; although assigning the preparation of working drawings to a larger firm, called the executive architect, is a relatively common practice when a smaller firm does the design, he knew that he was giving up a significant degree of control, which was always painful to him. But he was trapped: he could hardly refuse the job, since he had already accepted it with much fanfare, and to resign over this would seem petty. And it would be challenging enough to handle the design of such a complicated building adequately. His office had never produced working drawings for a project remotely as complicated as this one, and it was understandable that the Music Center felt that he needed an executive architect working beside him. But the arrangement meant that Frank was limited to deciding what the building would look like. The executive architect would figure out how to translate his ideas into built form. And if the executive architect found some of the forms so unusual that he didn't know how to get them built, what was to happen then?

That was Frank's fear. Seeing no way out of the situation, he decided to work with a firm run by an architect he knew, Daniel Dworsky, an architect two years his senior who had played football at the University of Michigan before deciding to establish his career in Los Angeles. Dworsky was a modernist who had worked for Raphael Soriano, William Pereira, and Charles Luckman, architects who had been influential in Frank's life, and while the sports facilities, airports, and commercial buildings that Dworsky Associates was known for bore no resemblance to the architecture that Frank produced, the two had always had a friendly relationship.

The collaboration, such as it was, turned out to be a disaster. The Music Center wanted to move quickly, and Dworsky was ordered to begin working drawings before Frank had completely finished his design, which was becoming ever more complex as he reworked it repeatedly. Frank was increasingly interested in curving, fluid forms, the kind of shapes he had begun to explore at Vitra, and the emerging design for Walt Disney Concert Hall grew progressively more distant from the preliminary scheme that had won the competition.

The design was expected to be different, so that was not in itself a problem. But it was becoming different in ways that looked increasingly challenging to build, and were nearly incomprehensible to the architects who worked at Dworsky Associates. Jim Glymph, realizing that the only way the increasingly complex shapes that Frank was conceiving in his mind were going to get built was with the aid of computers, rapidly brought the office to the forefront of technology. He persuaded Frank, who had never used a computer himself, to allow the office to work with computer software developed for the French aerospace industry. Called CATIA (Computer Aided Three-dimensional Interactive Application), it had been invented to create construction documents for airplanes, whose shapes had complex curves not unlike the ones Frank was designing. CATIA could also calculate stresses, aiding the work of engineers, and made it economical to create unique pieces instead of using identical elements over and over again.

It was a huge leap, since Frank's office did not even make much use of the simple CAD (computer-aided drafting) systems that were becoming popular in architects' offices in the 1980s. But while CAD could speed up the task of preparing two-dimensional drawings, early CAD systems could not handle complex three-dimensional forms, as CATIA could, and create what amounted to a virtual 3-D model of a building on a computer screen. Frank's office first used CATIA to assist in producing the drawings for an enormous fish sculpture for the Barcelona waterfront, a project that was commissioned in 1989 and had to be ready before the 1992 games, a tight schedule that could not have been met without digital technology. When it became clear that CATIA was what had made it possible to finish the project on time and on budget, Jim Glymph said, "that got Frank's attention—he had not wanted computers before."

Suddenly, Frank was a believer. He still had no interest in using computers himself, but he realized that they could translate his ideas into something buildable in a more efficient way than he had ever thought possible—and that the more complex the forms he imagined in his head became, the more digital technology would be necessary not just to get things built efficiently, but to get them built at all. He trusted Glymph to use the computer as a way of supporting, not changing, his architecture. "The ground rule for bringing computers into the office was that it shouldn't interfere with Frank's design process," Glymph said. "Frank always thinks in three dimensions, and one of the challenges was that two-dimensional drawings make these non-Euclidian buildings difficult to build." Frank was also aware that the built versions of two important projects that followed Vitra, Team Disney in Anaheim, an administration building for Disneyland, and the American Center in Paris, both of which combine curvilinear forms with boxy ones, were less ambitious than he had first imagined they would be. As he conceived shapes in his head that were more and more complex geometrically, translating them into buildable structures was becoming increasingly challenging, both physically and economically. With CATIA he saw that he could get his buildings built with fewer compromises. The computer, Frank realized, could be the tool that freed him from limits.

For the first year or so, the process of designing Walt Disney Concert Hall moved ahead in fits and starts. "I think we did fifty or sixty different models of different hall configurations," Michael Maltzan, who was the project designer, said. Then, in 1991, with the advent of CATIA, it began to accelerate. The final scheme called for a rectangular hall, set at an angle to the street, surrounded by a more sculptural form that Frank began to think of as a kind of wrapping that peeled away to reveal the hall within. As Frank became more comfortable with CATIA, his forms became even more fluid and began to resemble huge sails, billowing in the wind. He wanted to have the curving planes clad in stone, which he felt would enhance the building's civic dignity and remove any lingering doubt that he was still wedded to the cheap materials he had been known for earlier in his career. CATIA, at least theoretically, would be able to direct the cutting tools that would make it economically feasible to cut pieces of stone in multiple complex patterns to fit on the huge, curving structural framework that he envisioned.

Unfortunately, Dworsky Associates was not experienced in CATIA, and the more complicated the design got, the harder it seemed to be for them to make sense of it. Frank's fear that Dworsky would not understand his work well enough to determine how to build it was turning out to be true. Even though Craig Webb was assigned to a desk in Dworsky's office to facilitate coordination, the drawings were becoming a source of frustration rather than clarity. Contractors, confused by drawings they did not understand, put in high bids to protect themselves, and the project looked like it was going to be far over its budget before construction even started. Michael Maltzan remembered that there was an office poll to guess the final cost of the project, which in 1992 was estimated to cost $210 million, more than four times Lillian Disney's gift. And that number seemed destined only to escalate further.

Relations between the Gehry office and the Dworsky office grew tense. In addition to preparing construction drawings, Dworsky was also in charge of determining how the hall would meet the requirements of building codes, which meant that Dworsky, not Frank, was the architect whom public officials generally dealt with on the project. Adding to the pressure, Los Angeles County had to start building the parking garage that was to go beneath the hall before the design for the building above it was complete so as to meet Lillian Disney's deadline of a construction start within five years of her gift. When the ceremonial groundbreaking took place in December 1992, it was actually only the garage that was started, not the hall above it.

At the beginning of 1994, construction on the hall itself had still not started. The Northridge earthquake in January led to a decision to redesign the underlying structure to a steel-brace frame, adding more delays and still more costs. That August, the concert hall committee announced that it needed another $50 million on top of the $210 million, and fundraising had stalled. It began to seem possible that the building might never be built at all, and no one wanted to donate money to a project that was doomed. County officials were becoming especially dubious, and they began to talk about declaring the hall in default of its lease on the site and renovating the parking garage so it could be a stand-alone structure. Richard S. Volpert, an attorney for the county, said the county administration was prepared to abandon the project as beyond the ability of Los Angeles to realize. "If you throw enough money at it, you can build an atom bomb, fly to the moon, build the Disney Concert Hall," was how Volpert put it.

By the end of 1994, it was clear that the project was not moving forward. Frank was devastated. It was not just that his most important building was stalled, perhaps indefinitely, but that he was viewed by many people in Los Angeles as an irresponsible designer of unbuildable fantasies. It was the most painful criticism imaginable, because he considered himself more practical than he was generally given credit for, and he had expected that Disney Hall would demonstrate not only his creative potential but also his ability to handle large and complex projects effectively. Instead, it was being viewed as an expensive folly. Dworsky's drawings turned out to be "virtually useless," according to Richard Koshalek. Frank felt that his reputation in Los Angeles was beginning to unravel not because he had tried to control too much, but because he was able to control too little. Dworsky's failure to produce suitable working drawings, Frank believed, had brought the project down.

Frank's friendship with Daniel Dworsky came to an end, but that was the least of it. It was clear that the combination of Disney Hall's complicated political structure, with so many different public and private entities believing themselves to be in charge, along with an executive architect who did not understand how the building Frank was designing could be built, was not the right formula for creating a work of architecture that would be challenging to build even in ideal circumstances. Frank had felt from the beginning that having a separate executive architect was a mistake, but there was no sense in being vindicated if the cost of being right was seeing Disney Hall come to a halt.

Frank had always viewed himself as an outsider, albeit one who was happy to be invited inside so long as it was on his terms. He thought that Walt Disney Hall would be his opportunity to become a part of the city's establishment; instead, he felt that the Los Angeles establishment had conspired to defeat him. A couple of years earlier he had enjoyed being recognized around town as the architect of the city's new concert hall, but by 1994 he began to fear showing up in restaurants and at dinner parties, where Disney Hall was often the subject of mocking remarks like Richard Volpert's, and even people he didn't know would give him a hard time about its problems. The younger architects in the office felt that Frank seemed less fully engaged in his work than he had been when Disney Hall was still an active project. "It was harder to get him excited. It was a different Frank for a couple of years," Michael Maltzan, who had been the leader of Frank's Disney Hall team, said.

Frank was angry, and he could not take refuge solely in his work, as he was accustomed to doing, because the largest and most ambitious project he had ever attempted was precisely the source of his black mood. So he turned away from Los Angeles, which was making him so uncomfortable that he took advantage of every opportunity he had to travel out of town. For the first time since he had gotten off the train at Union Station in 1947, he thought seriously about living somewhere else. He considered moving his office to New York, or even Paris; at one point he even thought about relocating to Newport, Rhode Island, where his old friend the architect Richard Saul Wurman had settled happily a few years earlier. Frank and Wurman, an idiosyncratic architect who, like Frank, could be counted on to enjoy talking about almost anything, found his greatest success when he invented a celebrated conference program called Technology, Entertainment and Design, or TED. Frank participated in several of the early TED conferences, along with another old friend of both his and Wurman's, the architect Moshe Safdie.

Wurman, who had settled in an old Newport mansion, was especially excited at the thought that Frank might do something similar. He reminded Frank, who loved to sail, of the temptations of Newport's coastal location, and the opportunities it offered for sailing up and down the East Coast. Wurman went so far as to look at an empty power plant that he thought might be converted into an office. But Berta was completely opposed to the idea of moving to the East Coast, which she considered a place to visit, not to live, and she reminded Frank that he had not thought through the daunting challenges of moving an established architectural practice all the way across the country. In the end, the temptation that other cities held for him was illusory: it was not so much what they were that interested him as the fact that they were far away from Los Angeles. When Disney Hall stopped, Frank told the *Los Angeles Times*, he felt like a pariah in his own city. Given his history of walking away from uncomfortable situations, it was not surprising that his first impulse was to leave town.

The solution turned out to be not a permanent move, but a lot of time spent on airplanes. Some of it was purely in the realm of escape. Frank and Berta took an extended driving trip through Europe in the spring of 1994 with their friends Irving and Marilyn Lavin, Renaissance art historians who lived in Princeton, that was in some ways a latter-day version of Frank's travels with Mark Biass and his wife. The Lavins and the Gehrys traveled together through Spain and France, looking at Romanesque churches—Irving Lavin remembered being surprised by how interested Frank was in Romanesque architecture—and making a stop in Dijon that would turn out to be particularly meaningful for Frank. The Lavins showed him the work of the fourteenth-century Netherlandish sculptor Claus Sluter, who was celebrated for his ability to evoke a sense of flowing fabric in stone, and Sluter's work would be revelatory for Frank, his most striking new experience with old art since his early travels in Europe. Sluter's sculptures, which Lavin described as "huge and voluminous figures with huge and voluminous crinkling drapery," would start Frank thinking about the notion of evoking the draping of fabric in solid form. The cowls that draped many of Sluter's figures would directly influence many of the shapes that Frank would develop as pieces of architecture.

For all of Disney Hall's problems, Frank's practice was flourishing elsewhere. He may have felt that the Gehry name had come to connote failure in his home city, but he was a prophet with plenty of honor outside his own land, and he was happy to fly to wherever the commissions were to be

"Fred and Ginger," a
symbol of Prague's revival

had. His reputation in Europe, where he had been admired for years, had received another boost in 1991, when Philip Johnson, who was in charge of the American entry to the Venice Biennale that year, decided that the exhibit should consist solely of work by Frank and Johnson's other favorite, Peter Eisenman. "Gehry and Eisenman are unmatched," Johnson wrote. Of Frank, he said, "his risks revolve around the architectural possibilities of unexplored shapes and untried materials, and his muse is Art." (Eisenman's muse, Johnson said, was "Philosophy.") Frank Gehry and Peter Eisenman did represent opposite poles of Johnson's aesthetic interests: Frank saw architecture as experiential, whereas for Eisenman it was an intellectual quest.

Germany and Switzerland were particularly eager for Gehry buildings. In 1994, the year Disney Hall stopped, Frank was asked to design a trio of high-rise office buildings in Düsseldorf, Der Neue Zollhof, and there were new projects in Berlin, Frankfurt, Hannover, Rehme, Bad Oeynhausen, and Bielefeld, Germany. A corporate headquarters building for Vitra, which Rolf Fehlbaum had set him to work on even before the Vitra Design Museum was done, was nearing completion outside Basel; a major project for Prague, the swooping office building known as "Fred and Ginger" or the "Dancing House" that would become a symbol of the city's revival, had been commissioned in 1992 and was under construction when Disney Hall came to a halt. Its easy, flowing form was integrated closely with the old streetscape, and it would manage the difficult trick of both representing Prague's new freedom and standing as a reminder that Frank was far more interested in relating to the existing urban context than he was usually given credit for.

And there was much more. The American Center in Paris, Frank's first project in France, was nearly complete in 1994, its curving limestone surfaces offering a hint at smaller scale of what Walt Disney Concert Hall could look like if Frank's design were built. Samsung invited Frank to design a large museum for Seoul, and closer to home, Paul Allen asked him to do a museum in Seattle honoring Jimi Hendrix. Meanwhile, Frank's art museum in Minneapolis for the University of Minnesota, named for his old friend Fred Weisman, had recently opened, as had a center for the visual arts in Toledo. At the same time, he was adding to his workload by entering design competitions for buildings around the world, as if he felt he could ward off his post-Disney melancholy by getting on ever more airplanes to ever more places.

He also had a lot of mouths to feed. When Disney Hall was active, Frank had expanded his office still more. In 1992 he hired Randy Jefferson, the architect from Langdon Wilson who had completed Eli Broad's house a few years earlier. While Frank still had not been to the Broad house himself—Eli and Edythe Broad, after inviting him several times and being rebuffed, eventually stopped trying—he concluded that if Jefferson, who like Jim Glymph was known as a skilled manager of complex situations, could get the Broad house built, then he clearly understood the firm's work, and he might be trusted to relieve Frank of some of his managerial duties. Frank decided to give Jim Glymph and Randy Jefferson each a 20 percent ownership stake in the firm, and he changed the name to

Gehry Partners.* Glymph and Jefferson bonded further with Frank over their shared ownership of something else, a sailboat. Both men enjoyed sailing, and after several successful excursions, Frank suggested that the three of them buy a boat together. Not the least of the pleasures of their sails, Frank recalled years later, was that it gave him and Glymph, who smoked a great deal of marijuana, a pleasant place to get stoned. David Whitney, Philip Johnson's partner, regularly provided Frank with marijuana, which he invariably brought to share on the water.

Giving Glymph and Jefferson a stake in the firm was a further step toward professionalizing his office at just the time that, ironically, the problems at Walt Disney Concert Hall were giving him a reputation as a maker of costly follies. Frank did not offer a share in the firm to the one person he might have been most expected to, Greg Walsh. Walsh remained deeply loyal to Frank, and Frank continued to feel a personal loyalty to him, but Walsh was increasingly on the margins of big projects, uncomfortable with the growing reliance on CATIA and other forms of digital technology. He was an old-fashioned architect who was comfortable drawing, not using a computer. By 1991, it had become clear that his seniority in the firm no longer translated into a key position, and he was less and less at Frank's side in major projects. His role evolved into that of mentor to young architects in the office and as the possessor of the firm's institutional memory, the one person who was likely to remember as much, if not more, than Frank did. That was useful, but it was not enough. Frank decided that the time had come to let Greg go, and he tried to drop hints in the hope that Greg would recognize that the best way to preserve their forty-year friendship would be for him to leave.

Greg, who knew no professional life except at Frank's side, was aware that he did not have an essential role in the firm as it was evolving, but for several months he stayed on, obviously uncomfortable but unable to bring himself to move. Frank, unwilling to fire his friend outright, became increasingly critical of his work, thinking that this might lead Greg to leave in frustration. It was passive-aggressive behavior in the extreme, and its cruelty accomplished little except to make Frank feel guilty and to increase the tension between them. Greg spoke to David Denton and Robert Hale,

---

* For years, the firm had been known as Frank O. Gehry & Associates, even though Frank rarely used his middle initial any longer. Correspondence to him was often mistakenly addressed to "Frank O'Gehry," which at first he found amusing. The error was repeated so often, however, that it became an irritant, and so he dropped the middle initial from his signature.

two senior architects who worked closely with Frank, and then, early in 1991, he sent Frank a handwritten letter that amounted to a plea for more meaningful things to do and offering to work on a half-time basis.

Still unable to bring himself to have a direct conversation about the future with Greg, Frank asked Jim Glymph to intervene. Glymph took Greg to the outside deck of the office on Cloverfield Boulevard, where the two had a long and emotional conversation. There was no meaning-ful position for Greg in the firm as it evolved, Glymph told him, and the only way his long friendship with Frank was going to survive was if he saw himself only as a friend, no longer as a colleague.

A few days later, Greg went into Frank's office and told his friend that he had decided that his usefulness to Gehry Partners was at an end. He began a new career, teaching at SCI-Arc, the Los Angeles architecture school, and working occasionally on smaller projects with a couple of other local firms. He began to spend more time with music, another interest that had bound him to Frank early on. From time to time he returned to the office to help with archives and other matters connected to the firm's history, and Frank, relieved to have a problem out of his way, welcomed him. If the arrival of Jim Glymph and Randy Jefferson symbolized the evolution of Frank's practice on the organizational side, the departure of Greg Walsh was its emotional symbol, the last remnant of the days when the office was small, scrappy, artsy, and irreverent.

Those days brought another transition in Frank's life. A few years ear-lier, when he won the Pritzker Prize, he hadn't used the money to finish his house, as he had jokingly promised, but he did put the $100,000 prize money toward another house, a small cottage in Brentwood for his mother, Thelma, who had always dreamed of a place of her own. It had a small back garden, and Frank designed a trellis and a porch so that Thelma could sit outside. By the early 1990s, her memory was fading, and one day she told Frank that she thought it was time to plan the garden party.

"What garden party?" Frank asked.

"You know, the one we have every year," Thelma told him.

Frank played along and asked his mother whom she wanted to invite.

"The usual people," Thelma said.

There had never been a garden party, but Frank, seeing how much the idea meant to her, flew her brother, his uncle Kelly, and his wife to Los Angeles from Toronto, invited Thelma's surviving cousins, added a few of his and Berta's friends, and hired the New York Bagel Company, whose shop he had designed years before, to cater.

There was a crisis when Thelma, whose vision of the party seemed to grow grander every day, told the gardener to cut down all of the trees in her garden, her neighbor's garden, and along the street to allow more room for her guests. When the gardener hesitated at removing trees that Thelma did not own, she called Frank and insisted that he help. He rushed over to his mother's house and explained to her that he was sorry, but that the party would have to be a bit smaller than she had hoped it would be. He promised her that it would still be a success.

And it was. Sam Gehry, who was studying the violin, played; Thelma delighted in seeing her brother and the rest of her family; and she took pleasure in hearing toasts and speeches in her honor. She was, for that one afternoon, the grand hostess she had always imagined herself to be. The memory of that happy day carried her until she died, not long afterward, in the house her son had bought for her. It happened in 1994, while Frank was in Japan giving a lecture. He received a phone call saying that his mother's condition had worsened, and he canceled his plans and rushed back to Los Angeles. It was too late; Thelma was already gone.

Thelma Gehry was buried at Eden Memorial Park, but it was not beside Irving: when Irving died, the family could not afford to buy two adjacent plots, and the spaces beside him were taken. Thelma was buried higher up on the hill, and Frank purchased extra burial plots on either side of hers, just to be sure, he said, that she would not feel squeezed by strangers. After Thelma's casket was lowered into the ground, the family walked down the hill to Irving's grave. It was the first time Frank had been there since Irving's death, thirty-two years before, and the first time his sons had been there at all.

It was also one of the few times that all four of Frank's children were together. Sam, who was fifteen, had brought with him a tiny sculpture of a fish, which he laid atop his grandfather's headstone, sharing this family totem as a way of symbolically connecting Irving not just to Frank's success but also to all that his family had become in the years since his death. It was a poignant gesture that brought Irving, who had always thought of himself as Goldberg, into the full scope of being a Gehry, and conferred on him in death the role of patriarch that he had not ever fully assumed in life.

It was a moment, Frank would recall, of family closeness, and of his awe at his son's sensitivity. By then, Frank's daughters were in their thirties and Alejo and Sami were both teenagers, and all four children had suffered somewhat from a lack of attention on Frank's part. He loved all of his children, but had never been good at bringing himself to take as much time away from his work, or from the social connections with artists and architects and friends who stimulated his work, to spend with them as he felt he should have. Both boys grew up assuming that he would be in his office every weekend, and when they were younger, he would bring them along and let them run around while he worked. They hardly grew up with a sense of entitlement, however: Sam remembered thinking, as a small child, that Greg Walsh was the owner of the firm, since he seemed to have the more serious demeanor, and that Frank worked for him.

Alejo, Sam, Berta, and Frank

Occasionally, if Berta was busy, Frank would leave the boys alone at home on a Saturday. Once, he left for work and saw them in front of the television, watching cartoons. "Don't do that all day—if you're that lazy you'll have grass growing out of your ears," he told them. In the afternoon, after playing outside, they returned to the television, and when Alejo heard Frank's car pulling up to the house, he ran outside and scooped up some handfuls of grass. He gave some of it to Sam, and the two of them tucked it into their ears. Frank came upstairs to find them on his bed. He was furious to find his sons still watching television. "Didn't I tell you," he started to say, and then he saw the grass and broke into hysterical laughter. He really wanted nothing more than an easy, relaxed time with his sons, which was why, when Alejo was five and asked him what he looked like without the mustache he had worn since the 1960s, Frank immediately went into the bathroom and shaved it off. (He was less accommodating when Alejo, looking at his father clean-shaven, asked him to please put it back. He never grew his mustache again.)

Neither boy had a particularly easy time in school. Alejo, who was dyslexic, had an up-and-down academic career that included five years at a school for learning-disabled students. He had an exceptionally strong visual sense—as a child, he could identify almost all the artists whose works hung in Frank and Berta's house—and he dreamed of being a doctor, he recalled, until the day he took a biology class and lost interest entirely. A gifted art teacher at Santa Monica High School encouraged Alejo to pursue his interest in art, and he ended up graduating from the Rhode Island School of Design.

Sam was more intrigued with architecture, but at first thought that he would be an industrial designer, and after graduating from the Los Angeles County High School of the Arts in 1998, he enrolled at Maryland College of Art in Baltimore. After three years, unsure of himself and of what he wanted to do, he took a year off. Frank encouraged him to come back to Los Angeles and help around the office on furniture and other products he was working on. "He swindled me," Sam said. "I was soon working on buildings." Later, Sam would come to function as a kind of apprentice in the office, and after several years of uncertainty about whether he could follow his father into his profession, he worked briefly for another architect in Los Angeles, then spent a year in Vienna studying architecture. He came home for the summer to work at Frank's office, and he never left. In 2006, after he had begun his career as an architect, Sam sent his father an e-mail. "Everything I did in your office inspired me to do the best I can at whatever I do and I'm really grateful," he wrote. "Thank you. You have helped me understand what I like to do. Thanks, Pop. Love, Sam." Frank was so pleased that he kept a printout of the e-mail on his desk. It was more than parental pride. Sam's e-mail reminded Frank that however challenging he had sometimes found his children, they could bring him a kind of satisfaction he felt from nothing else.

Frank also introduced his sons to hockey, almost by accident. On a family trip to Sun Valley, where he wanted them to learn to ski, he wondered how it would feel to wear ice skates again, something he had not done since his teenage years in Canada. While Alejo and Sam were at ski school, Frank rented skates, went into the ice rink, and promptly fell over backward. That only reinforced his desire to skate again, and back in Los Angeles he started taking lessons at a rink in the San Fernando Valley. He remembered how much he had liked hockey growing up, and he brought the boys to the rink. Soon the three were skating together. The boys were eager to join a youth hockey team, and Frank, pleased at their interest,

Devoted to hockey, Frank named his bent plywood chair for Knoll the Cross Check.

promised Berta that he would handle the responsibility of taking them to and from practices and games. Not surprisingly, he did little of that, since he was beginning to make frequent trips abroad and was not in Los Angeles regularly enough to be a reliable team parent. "So I got to know every ice rink from Torrance to Panorama City," Berta said. "I became a hockey mom."

It was not long before Frank's talent for crossing paths with famous people began to assert itself in hockey, too. He met the producer Jerry Bruckheimer, who was taking lessons at the same rink. Bruckheimer was starting a Hollywood hockey team, which he invited Frank to join. Maureen Chartraw, a consultant for Knoll, the furniture company for which Frank was designing several chairs,* was married to a professional hockey player, Rick Chartraw, who was then playing for the Los Angeles Kings, and the Chartraws invited Frank and the boys to come to a Kings game. Frank was as much of a fan as his sons, and at least as thrilled to meet the players. He decided to start an office team, which was called the FOG,

---

* Lest there be any doubt of the role hockey played in Frank's life, or in the development of the Knoll furniture, Frank named the chairs, which were made out of bent slats of maple, the Cross Check and the Hat Trick.

after his initials. He was the center, and Sam and Alejo joined as well, along with Michael Maltzan and Paul Liebowicki, among others. Frank played with the team until he was past seventy, when his persistent back pain made it too difficult to keep skating.

Things were never as easy for Leslie and Brina as they were for Alejo and Sam. Despite their school problems, Frank's sons were raised by loving, cohabiting parents, an experience his daughters had not had since they were small children. Frank tried to maintain contact with them when they were growing up, but visits were sporadic after Anita's remarriage, and there were periods when he and his daughters had almost no contact at all. Once Berta had become an active presence in Frank's life, she encouraged Frank to make greater efforts to spend time with them, and after the wedding—which neither daughter attended—Berta tried her best to be an engaged stepmother, urging Frank to include Leslie and Brina in family events. But in those days she had her hands full with two young boys, and Leslie in particular was moody and withdrawn much of the time. She and Brina would write notes to Frank as children, telling him how much they missed seeing him. Leslie, who would graduate from the California Institute of the Arts in Valencia, was a talented artist. She once drew a series of cartoons that showed a child's face and a man with a mustache in each panel, alternately smiling and frowning at each other. In the final panel, the figure of the child—obviously Leslie herself—is kissing the man with the mustache, her father, and he is smiling.

For Alejo and Sam, Berta's natural ability to balance loving warmth, firmness, and clarity kept the household on the kind of even keel that Leslie and Brina rarely experienced. Although Berta had worked at Frank's office since before Sam was born, mainly overseeing bookkeeping matters, she took it as a matter of course that her lot was to juggle office and parental responsibilities. She got into the habit of bringing work home and doing it while her sons were being tutored, or as she sat on the cold bleachers at hockey practice. And she could handle Frank in a way that Anita never could. "My mom ran the house," Alejo said. "If my dad came home in a bad mood, pissed about some developer or something, my mom would say, 'Frank, remember, we don't work for you. We're your family.'"

The transition from the funky atelier by the beach in Venice to the tech-driven world of Gehry Partners in a sprawling industrial building on Cloverfield Boulevard in Santa Monica was also connected to the long saga of one of Frank's most idiosyncratic and impassioned clients, one whose relationship with him could only be called unique: Peter Lewis, the billionaire chairman of Progressive Insurance Company. Lewis met Frank in 1984, shortly after he had purchased a large plot of land to build a new house for himself in the suburbs of Cleveland, his company's headquarters city. A friend told him that Frank Gehry was lecturing at the city's museum of contemporary art; he knew little about him except, Lewis wrote later, that he was "a rising star." Lewis recalled his first impression: "I expected to see someone glamorous, but Gehry was short, stout and professorial. He wore an ill-fitting suit and looked out at his audience through rimless glasses. I was spellbound by his modest descriptions of how clients' objectives evolved into the lyrical, light-hearted structures flashing on the screen behind him. I experienced Gehry as an artist as much as an architect. He was impressively insightful, profound and imaginative, but seemed like a down to earth guy. . . . I imagined my enthusiasm and resources could supercharge Gehry's enormous talent and let him accomplish something wonderful." The crowd surrounding Frank after the lecture was so heavy that Lewis never had the chance to introduce himself. Two years would pass before he called Frank in Los Angeles, told him he had heard him speak in Cleveland, and asked him if he would design a house for the twelve-acre property he had in the rural outskirts of the city.

Lewis soon flew to Los Angeles, and the two spent an afternoon together, touring several Gehry houses, including Frank's own, which Lewis found exciting. They bonded quickly: both men, as Lewis said later, were "iconoclasts, analysands and political progressives," similar, it seemed, in everything except the size of their bank accounts. Lewis imagined that he was giving Frank the same kind of opportunity that Edgar Kaufmann had given Frank Lloyd Wright when he commissioned Fallingwater, and he dreamed of being the same kind of patron, who would make possible a magnificent one-of-a-kind house that would become a landmark in the history of architecture, that he would live in it with pleasure for the rest of his life and then leave it to the public.

He told Frank he was prepared to spend $5 million on the house of his dreams, gave him a $5,000 advance payment toward a fee, and promised to pay him for however much time he wanted to put into thinking creatively about the project. Because he found Frank's own house so intriguing, Lewis wondered aloud whether there was any sense in retaining the existing house on the property and trying to do something similar with it. After nine months, Frank called to say he was finding the problem frustrating, and asked if Lewis would mind tearing the house down. Lewis had always intended to demolish the old house, and hadn't expected that Frank would take his inquiry about keeping it so literally.

The design process started again, and Lewis asked Frank if he could promise to deliver a design to him in person in Cleveland in six weeks. Frank agreed, and showed up with an enormous model of a compound of small buildings, arranged in the shape of a U around an open courtyard. One building, to contain a game room, was set in the middle of the courtyard and resembled a coiled snake; there was a glass garden pavilion in the shape of a fish; and other sections with stainless steel roofs and black glass floors, all in different geometric shapes. It was around the same time that Frank was working on the Schnabel and Winton houses, and there was a clear connection to both.

But the Lewis house was the most cutting-edge of them all, and Peter Lewis was thrilled with it. He was ready to move ahead on Brookwood, as he called the house, as fast as Frank could in converting the design into a set of construction documents, which Frank promised to have by March 1986. That deadline came and went, but Lewis, excited that at least part of the reason was Frank's increasing visibility around the world—he was building Vitra, his first European project—thought he could be patient for a little while longer. He tried to sweeten the pot by asking Frank to design a new headquarters for Progressive in downtown Cleveland, a project that Frank initially declined and referred to Philip Johnson, who suggested Peter Eisenman; eventually Lewis went back to Frank and persuaded him to produce a design for the building, which Frank envisioned as a fifty-four-story tower with a Claes Oldenburg sculpture at the top.

A Gehry skyscraper topped by an Oldenburg, not surprisingly, was not greeted with unanimous praise in Cleveland, and it was never built—the board of Progressive, initially enthusiastic, grew increasingly unhappy at finding itself the center of an architectural debate, and thought Frank was better suited to being Peter Lewis's personal architect than its corporate one. The headquarters project distracted Frank and further delayed Lewis's house, which made only minimal progress in 1988 and 1989, by which point Walt Disney Concert Hall, the events surrounding the Pritzker Prize, and Frank's increasing preoccupation with newer projects made for further delays. "Like some fervent groupie, I continuously pleaded with Gehry to work on Brookwood," Lewis recalled.

In the meantime, Lewis financed some of Frank's fish sculptures and fish lamps, and waited for him to turn again to Brookwood. When he did, it coincided with the development of the CATIA system, and the house became a de facto laboratory for Frank's experiments with the digital software, the place where he tested how well the software could help design and engineer the extreme shapes he was conceiving. Lewis continued to encourage Frank's most adventuresome thoughts, and the house, further stimulated by Lewis's decision to add separate outbuildings as guest quarters for his grown children, became ever more elaborate. Lewis's business was going well, and he continued to be excited by the project—"Frank was getting more and more famous and I was getting more and more rich," he said, and he was clearly having a wonderful time.

Frank had discussed with Lewis his longtime interest in collaboration, and Lewis, perhaps on the theory that there was always room for one more at the party, agreed with his suggestion that Philip Johnson, a native of Cleveland, would enjoy being a part of the project; Johnson ended up designing the guesthouse structure. Lewis also commissioned Claes Oldenburg to do a monumental sculpture of a golf bag, Richard Serra to design a car-size tunnel for the entry drive, and Frank Stella to design a gatehouse.

It was becoming quite a large party indeed, and an expensive one. After more than three years of ongoing studies and evolving designs, Lewis, knowing that the project had long before passed far beyond his original $5 million budget but having no idea by how much, asked Frank over dinner what he guessed the cost had risen to.

"Probably about fifty million dollars," Frank told him.

"How much is Bill Gates's house costing?" Lewis asked.

"I don't know, but I read in the paper that it's fifty-five million," Frank said.

"Then we're okay," Lewis said to Frank.

But they were not. Lewis continued to encourage Frank to design new iterations of the project, and then, in the spring of 1995, he read an article in a special issue of *The New York Times Magazine* called "Houses as Art," in which the design for his house was published along with houses by architects like César Pelli, Charles Gwathmey, and Robert Venturi, and the value of building a house as a custom work of architecture was discussed at length. Unfortunately, the Lewis house was portrayed as the ultimate rich man's extravagance—a case of excess on the part of the client, not the architect—and Lewis was shaken. Frank did not help matters when he was quoted in the article as saying, "I'm a do-gooder, liberal to the core, and it's hard for me to think I'm solving any problems doing a rich guy's house. I said to [Lewis], 'Why don't you just build a little $5 million house and give the rest to charity?'"*

It was disingenuous, to say the least; Frank had hardly tried to curb Lewis's enthusiasm. In his mind, Lewis said later, he had figured that he might be willing to go as high as $40 million for everything, including the art pieces, the architects' fees, and other costs. When he came to meet with Frank and his staff a few weeks after the article appeared and put the question to Jim Glymph, there was an awkward silence. "For Christ's sake, give me the numbers," Lewis said. Glymph then told him that he thought the total cost of the project by then had climbed to the neighborhood of $82.5 million.

"That's crazy," Lewis said. "We're done." And he headed to the airport, determined to walk away from the project. On the flight back to Cleveland, however, he began to have regrets. He had spent ten years on the project and paid $6 million in fees to Gehry Partners; the thought of writing all of that off troubled him. When he landed, he called Frank and asked if the project could be scaled back to cost $40 million. Lewis recalled that Frank at first refused, saying the project was what it was and couldn't be compromised. Frank recalled otherwise, and said he told Lewis that he believed that a revised and simplified version could have been built for $24 million. But the spell, such as it was, had been broken, and the house never moved forward.

Peter Lewis's relationship with Frank, however, continued, or at least it resumed after several months during which the two barely spoke. Frank felt that Lewis had goaded him on, claiming to be indifferent to cost, and had failed to realize that he had pushed the house into the realm of an institutional project more than a domestic one. The high cost, Frank believed, was the inevitable result of the enormous size and unusual forms his client

---

* I was the author of the *Times* article. I had interviewed Gehry on the subject of the Lewis project many months before the article appeared, and he was in one of his periodic waves of self-doubt, questioning the validity of many of his projects, not only this one. I was interested in exploring the broader question of "high art" houses and the role of architect-client relationships, and the article referred to the problems that can ensue when a client gives an architect unlimited freedom. "The client who loves architecture so much he leaves his architect alone may not be serving architecture at all, for the truth of architecture is that its essence comes out of turning mundane, real-world needs into art," I wrote. "Almost invariably, an architect's best work comes out of a strong, sometimes even painful, dialogue between client and architect. If the client who can only say no is impossible to contend with, the client who can only say yes is not really any better." I did not become aware until many years later that Peter Lewis took those words as being directed at him, and that the article played a role in his decision to cancel the project.

had wanted, not to mention the fact that, in his wish that Brookwood be an ongoing institution after his death, it had many of the characteristics of a museum. Lewis, for his part, felt as if he had been made to look foolish, especially in the pages of *The New York Times*.

The collapse of Brookwood was not a conventional clash of two large egos, though both men had them, and both were badly bruised. But Frank and Peter Lewis ultimately wanted the same thing—an extraordinary work of residential architecture that would cause the world to take notice—and neither of them really understood the cost of it, not only in dollars, but emotionally. Peter Lewis saw the house as the representation of a kind of idealized version of himself, and he wanted it to confirm his greatness as a patron; he did not understand that such a house would transform him more than it would represent him. Frank, for his part, failed to realize that even the client who says there are no limits does not entirely mean it.

Still, the affection between the two men was genuine, and neither wanted to give up the friendship. Frank came to see Lewis in Cleveland a few months after the project was canceled, and told him how much the years of work on the house had meant to him. It was, Frank said, like a MacArthur "genius" grant, a sum of money he got to develop his most advanced ideas, with no strings attached. Lewis gracefully accepted the compliment. "Gehry schooled himself in the complex tools of a radically new architecture, emerging as a seminal artist of the twenty-first century," he said. "I paid the tuition and savored the glow of being his client."

Although Peter Lewis never built his house, he would a few years later make two other Frank Gehry buildings possible through his philanthropy: the Peter B. Lewis Building at the Case Western Reserve University's Weatherhead School of Management, finished in 2002, and the Peter Lewis Science Library at Lewis's alma mater, Princeton, which opened in 2008, both of which made use of ideas and technology that Frank had begun to develop while working on the house. And Lewis would remain in close contact with Frank for another reason as well, connected to an event that had occurred back in 1993, two years before the house project came to an end, when Frank introduced him to Thomas Krens, the director of the Guggenheim Museum. Krens and Lewis would become friendly, and Lewis would join the Guggenheim's board, eventually becoming its chairman. Over the next decade the three of them—Krens, Lewis, and Frank—became a close-knit trio, working together, traveling together, and planning the future of the Guggenheim, as Krens became the most important client of Frank's life.

14

The Guggenheim and Bilbao

W hen Thomas Krens first asked Frank to design a museum,
it came to very little. It was 1987, and Krens, the director
of the Williams College Museum of Art in northwestern
Massachusetts, had been struck by the contrast between the genteel college community of Williamstown, where he lived, and the gritty, economically depressed old industrial city of North Adams just to the east. At the
center of North Adams was the enormous, sprawling factory complex that
once belonged to the Sprague Electric Corporation, which had abandoned it years before. Why, Krens thought, couldn't the factory buildings
be converted into places for the display of contemporary art? Much new
art required bigger spaces than most museums could provide, and it would
be a way of revitalizing the troubled city.

Krens's idea, which eventually became Mass MOCA—the Massachusetts Museum of Contemporary Art—owed something to the Temporary
Contemporary in downtown Los Angeles, the old warehouse that Frank
had converted into exhibition space in 1983. So it was not surprising that
Krens contacted Frank in Los Angeles and asked him to come to North
Adams along with two other architects he also admired: David Childs of
Skidmore, Owings & Merrill, and Robert Venturi. He wanted Childs to
design a master plan for the factory complex and for Frank and Venturi
to somehow collaborate on a design to convert the factories into galleries.
Frank's rough-hewn, raw aesthetic, Krens thought, would marry as well
with old brick factories in the Northeast as it had with the warehouse in
Los Angeles, and he felt that Venturi, who was known for a certain, vaguely
pop sensibility, would be an intriguing partner.

Krens, a tall, tightly wound man who rides motorcycles and has a tendency to talk in somewhat elliptical, cryptic phrases, had already gotten a

reputation as a museum director who thought boldly and took daring risks; it was entirely in character for him to convince three prominent architects to collaborate on a huge project that he had no funds to complete. The three produced a design that, not surprisingly, was too expensive to build, and Krens turned to a Massachusetts firm that had an expertise in restoring older buildings. But while Frank's design died quickly, his relationship with Krens flourished—as with so many people Frank encountered who explored the notion of doing a Gehry building, a personal attachment arose that outlived the project.

In the case of Tom Krens, it did not take long for the attachment to bear fruit. As the Mass MOCA saga was unfolding, Krens was negotiating with the Guggenheim Museum to become its next director, and by early 1988 he had left Williamstown and settled in New York. Krens was hired in large part as a result of his desire to expand the Guggenheim into an institution with multiple international outposts through which its collection and temporary exhibitions would circulate. He envisioned it as an international museum "brand" that would take advantage of the growing demand for modern art museums around the world, and he quickly entered into negotiations to establish a Guggenheim in Salzburg, Austria, which would have been designed by the Viennese architect Hans Hollein. The Salzburg museum had not yet gone forward—it would ultimately not be built—when Krens was approached at the opening of an exhibition of the Guggenheim's collection in Madrid by representatives of the government of the Basque region of Spain, which planned to convert a huge old wine warehouse in the city of Bilbao into a cultural facility. The project was part of a larger program that sought to increase tourism as a means of economic development after Bilbao's old industrial economy declined.

Krens initially doubted whether Bilbao, a city far from established tourist routes, had the kind of potential he was looking for. He decided to reconsider when, on his first visit to the city in April 1991, he was taken to meet with the president of the Basque region, who made it clear that the government was prepared to pay the full cost of the museum as well as to pay the Guggenheim to build and run it. Krens then saw the Alhóndiga, the ornate cast concrete structure that the Basques wanted to convert into a museum. He was troubled by the limitations of its low ceilings and closely placed structural columns, and he was skeptical as to whether either that building or an adjacent parking garage was good enough to work. But with Salzburg stalled, Krens decided it was worth devoting a bit more time to exploring the possibilities in Bilbao. In May, just a month after his first visit, he asked Frank if he would to travel to Spain and offer an opinion as to the suitability of the Alhóndiga.

Frank, who had never before been to Bilbao, admired the ornate exterior of the old building and urged that it be retained, but he agreed with Krens that unlike the buildings in Los Angeles and North Adams, it could not easily be converted into a good museum. At dinner with their Basque hosts, he recommended that they find another site and build an entirely new building. He knew just where it should go: exploring the city, he had come upon a largely vacant industrial site at the edge of downtown at a bend along the Nervión River that was being used to store old automobiles.* He loved that it was visible from multiple parts of the city, that it was beside a major bridge, and that it seemed connected to Bilbao's industrial heritage. Tom Krens agreed that the riverfront site was preferable, and he went so far as to tell the Basques that the Guggenheim would not agree to be a partner in a museum in the old Alhóndiga. But there were problems with obtaining title to the riverfront site, which was divided among multiple owners, and for a short while it appeared as if the whole project was dead, caught between Frank and Krens's unwillingness to use the old building and the unavailability of the new site.

It was not. The Basque government was convinced by the arguments in favor of a new museum along the riverfront, and managed to acquire the land. Krens was asked to find an architect. From there, the project proceeded with unusual speed. Krens decided to hold a simple, invited competition limited to three architects. He would let the Basques make the final decision, but he would select the competitors himself. Krens chose one architect from Asia, Arata Isozaki; one from Europe, Wolf Prix of the Vienna firm Coop Himmelb(l)au; and one American, Frank Gehry. He asked a close friend of his, Heinrich Klotz, the former director of the Deutsches Architekturmuseum in Frankfurt, to serve as the professional adviser to the competition. The terms for the architects were challenging. They were each paid $10,000, a small sum for such an effort even in 1991, and not given any specific requirements as to what kind of materials to use to explain their concept for the museum to the jury. The architects were invited to visit the site in late June or early July, and their designs were due on July 20, leaving less than a month to develop a concept.

---

* Frank and Krens each believed that he had come up with the idea for the site first. Krens saw it while taking a morning run, which he believes was before Frank visited. While their recollections of the discovery of the site differ, they agree that they both thought immediately that it was ideally suited for the museum.

Frank and Berta did not go to Bilbao until July 5, and Frank began to sketch as soon as he returned to their hotel. His line drawings, which can appear as casual as doodles, almost always contain the essential idea of a project, and in Bilbao on stationery from the Hotel Lopez de Haro he sketched a plan that showed the museum and the adjacent bridge, along with marginal notes about views to and from the building, and a pair of drawings of the north elevation from across the river. Along with a map of Bilbao to which Frank had added strong red arrows indicating vistas toward the site from various vantage points in the city, the drawings made it clear from the beginning that he was envisioning the museum not as an isolated sculptural object but as an active form that would engage with its surroundings. "How do you make a big monolithic building that's humane? I try to fit into the city. In Bilbao I took on the bridge, the river, the road, and then I tried to make a building that was scaled to the nineteenth-century city," he said.

Frank almost never started a design with a predetermined shape. He liked to begin by "playing"—a word he used far more often than "working" when he talked about how he went about designing things—with wooden blocks of different sizes, each representing a portion of a building's functional program. He would then stack or array the blocks in what he felt was both a practical and an aesthetically pleasing composition. It was part a massing model, part a way to test how well a building's program could fit into the designated area. Only after that was done would he begin to embellish the design with his more characteristic shapes.

Frank asked Edwin Chan to be his lead designer on the project, a sign of how much confidence he had come to have in Chan, who by then had been in the office for almost six years and was better at interpreting Frank's ideas than anyone else, Michelle Kaufmann, another architect in the office, would observe later. "Frank would just do a sketch and Edwin would know exactly what to do with it," she said. "Edwin was always right next to Frank" at presentations to clients, she recalled. "It gave Frank support and confidence as if he had worked out every detail himself." Chan was not quite Frank's alter ego, but Frank trusted him to know instinctively where he wanted a project to go. He asked Chan to prepare a preliminary block model for Bilbao while he was still in Spain, walking the site and thinking about its relationship to the city. Since Frank was not returning directly to Los Angeles—he was going to New York for Philip Johnson's eighty-fifth birthday party, and then to Boston for a meeting on another job—Chan brought the model to New York so that he and Frank could work on it together for a day. They borrowed office space from the architect Peter Eisenman, and Frank began to tweak the model by adding sail-like forms made of scraps of white paper.

Over the next week, with Frank back in Los Angeles, the building began to assume its shape, with a nearly continuous outpouring of simple cardboard or wood models. As in most projects, Frank would use models as design tools. Although the firm was rapidly assuming expertise in CATIA software, Frank did not go near the computers himself; he thought of CATIA entirely as a tool of execution, not creation. His practice would be to review a model with the team of architects assigned to a project, study it intently, and suggest a few tweaks, after which the model shop would produce a new model that incorporated his changes and the process would begin again.

It was essentially the process Frank used with all of his projects, although for the competition scheme for Bilbao, the timeline was compressed to the point that there were often multiple models in a single day, as Frank would test and reject various ideas in quick succession. And at the early stages of Bilbao, as with so many projects, he continued to sketch whenever he had a spare moment on an airplane, or in a hotel room, producing rough drawings that could seem like scribbles but were always explorations of a new thought in a design process that he was never very eager to bring to an end.

His desire to keep going was in large part a reflection of his ongoing insecurities, his constant worry on every job that he had not yet gotten it quite right and needed to keep trying. For all that he loved the messiness and inconsistency of the world and wanted his architecture to celebrate it, Frank was at bottom a driven perfectionist. And he liked the design process itself and the sense of endless possibilities that existed when a design was still in formation. Once any design was finalized, all possibilities but one went away, and Frank did not like giving up the feeling that a project had multiple solutions and could go in multiple directions. Every building needs a final design in order to be built, of course, but Frank was unusual among architects in that he always felt mixed emotions at the conclusion of the design process. For him, that moment was less a time to celebrate the arrival of an ideal solution than the time when the quest to do it better must cease and he had to forgo other options.

For Bilbao, there was never a thought of enjoying the luxury of an extended period of design and redesign, at least not during the competition phase. Frank's entry was due in Frankfurt, where the jury, hosted by Heinrich Klotz, would be meeting just two weeks after he and Berta returned from Bilbao. His pragmatic instincts, so often subsumed beneath his desire to ruminate over problems, would have to prevail.

And they did, but this time at no cost to his aesthetic ambitions. Under pressure, Frank and Edwin Chan produced a design that included a large, metal-clad section containing an atrium, with galleries of various shapes, many clad in limestone, projecting off of it. The model that was sent to Frankfurt showed a building that contained one enormous gallery that stretched, like the hull of a boat, underneath the bridge that crossed the river onto the site, culminating in a tower that rose just beyond the bridge. It was, like most of Frank's other work since Vitra, a highly complex, active sculptural form, with elements that splayed out in unexpected directions and curving planes that seemed almost to float in space. No single geometric shape summed it up, although to some people the main part of the museum, the assemblage of huge, curving metal surfaces arranged in a sculptural composition around the atrium, resembled the leaves of an artichoke, or the petals of a flower. There was some resemblance to portions of Walt Disney Concert Hall, whose design was still evolving, and to the just-completed Weisman Museum in Minneapolis and the American Center in Paris, which was in design and would be finished in 1994. The Weisman and the American Center would be Frank's last significant buildings to be designed before CATIA software became his office standard, and both buildings show in primitive form many of the ideas he would develop later, much more fully, with CATIA.

Frank's victory in the Bilbao competition was not a foregone conclusion. He did not receive a majority of the seven votes at first, but neither did either of the others. Isozaki, who a decade earlier had won the Museum of Contemporary Art competition in Los Angeles to Frank's chagrin, produced a fairly bland, monolithic building that was eliminated early on, but Wolf Prix's design, like Frank's made up of multiple sections of varying shapes extending under the bridge, was another matter, and the jury was impressed by it. The Basques were also concerned that Frank would be too preoccupied by Walt Disney Concert Hall, which at that point had not yet sputtered to a halt, to devote enough time to Bilbao. "Our challenge is going to be to get enough of Frank's time for this building ten thousand miles away when he has this huge project in his hometown," said Juan Ignacio Vidarte, an official of the Basque regional government who later became head of the local authority that built the museum. But the Basques were unwavering in their desire to have a building that could become a recognizable symbol, like the Sydney Opera House by Jørn Utzon, and while it was clear that either Wolf Prix's or Frank Gehry's design could provide that, Frank's design seemed to hold out the most hope for iconic status. After two days of deliberations, the jury decided to offer the Guggenheim to him.

Then, of course, the real work began. As with Disney Hall, it would take years to create a final design, and Frank would get the time he craved to play with multiple possibilities. Krens, not surprisingly, turned out to be a highly engaged client. He believed that museums could come in many forms, from the most architecturally expressive to the least, and he had no doubts as to where on that continuum he envisioned Bilbao. In contrast to some of the other Guggenheim branches Krens was planning around the world, a few of which were no more than interior display spaces within other buildings, he wanted Frank's structure to be "the apotheosis of the stand-alone building," a place with a powerful identity of its own, something he wanted at least as much as the Basques did.

Krens wrote a long letter to Frank just two weeks after he had been given the commission, outlining his and the Guggenheim architectural review committee's thoughts. He praised the connection to the riverfront site, in terms of both materials and design, and noted the potential for large exhibition spaces. There was less enthusiasm about the tower Frank had planned for the section of the site that went just beyond the bridge. And they knew that the exact form of the atrium and the galleries, not to mention the placement of the building's front door, still remained to be worked out. Krens worked closely with Frank and his colleagues, and flew from New York to Los Angeles for monthly meetings in Frank's office, a practice that went on for several years as Frank, assisted by Edwin Chan, continued to play with different arrangements of shapes. "The relationship I had with Frank was like that of an editor to a writer," Krens said.

Once the final agreement with the Basque government had been worked out, Vidarte, in his new role as head of the new Basque entity called the Bilbao Project Consortium, would sometimes come to Los Angeles, but it was clear from the start that Krens, not the Basque government, would be the hands-on client. It was Krens, for example, who wanted the gargantuan, 400-foot-long gallery on the main floor, which contains a 340-foot-long work by Richard Serra, called *Snake*, which the Guggenheim had purchased for $22 million. Frank had wanted the gallery divided into three parts, but that would have made the installation of the

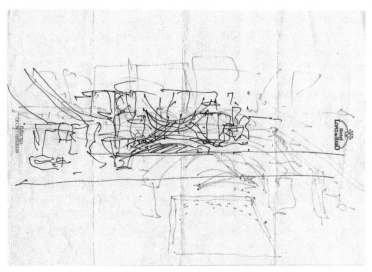

The first sketches for the Guggenheim were done on the stationery at the Hotel Lopez de Haro in Bilbao.

Serra impossible.[*] It was also Krens who insisted that the building have six galleries that were conventional and not sculptural in shape, a request that would ultimately help Frank defend the design against charges that it was insufficiently accommodating to the needs of art.

Not the least of the things that made the project unusual was the freedom Krens was given by both the Guggenheim's board and the Basques to direct the project himself. The Basques, he said, "had only one criterion: don't go over the budget. It was an ultimate dream for both the architect and the client: it was a two-person project. Frank and I got to play together once a month for five years."

The $100 million budget was not extravagant, but it was at least assured, unhindered by the financial worry that already hung over Walt Disney Concert Hall. Bilbao was not dependent on whether enough money could be raised: the funds were in hand, and that alone was sufficient to allow Frank's imagination to flow freely. He and Edwin Chan spent most of 1992 and 1993 refining the design, no element of which Frank, characteristically, wanted to consider final. The flowerlike sculptural pattern that would become the primary image of the building covered more or less of the structure at various times, and at one point it was abandoned altogether in favor of a square atrium, which Frank quickly deemed to be a

---

[*] Frank and Richard Serra had been close friends for many years, and shared ideas and admiration of each other's work. The installation of Serra's huge work in Bilbao caused some degree of strain between them. Later the tensions would expand and would lead to an estrangement. See chapter 17.

The shape of the museum in Bilbao begins to emerge.

mistake. In subsequent versions the original form returned, ending up only around the atrium, its curving surfaces repeated in the shape of the long gallery wing, which became more boatlike as it evolved. Boxy sections, one sheathed in limestone and the other bright blue, were set in counterpoint to the curves.

Frank's final design managed both to allude to Frank Lloyd Wright's rotunda in the original Guggenheim in New York and to turn it into something else, a room so soaring, so swooping, so contorted, and so full of natural light that it made Wright's space seem almost staid. Wright's ghost hovered over the project, since Frank was creating a similar kind of building for the same institution, and he knew that he had to both pay homage to the master and go beyond him. If Wright showed in 1959 that architectural space did not have to be enclosed in a box, Frank nearly half a century later demonstrated that architectural space did not have to be defined by a single system of geometry or, for that matter, by any conventional order. His building, more visually energetic than Wright's Guggenheim, seemed to taunt chaos: it appeared, when first looked at, to be not just arbitrary but wild.

In reality, it was neither arbitrary nor wild. Frank may have enjoyed invoking disorder, but his way of doing it was to push to the edge, never to go over it. At bottom he was more interested in finding a new order, and in making new ways to instill a sense of comfort, than in creating anything truly chaotic. The architecture of Bilbao would articulate his larger goals more clearly than ever before: he wanted less to shock than to find a fresh and different way of using architecture to produce the sensations of satisfaction, comfort, and pleasure that more traditional buildings did. The shapes of Bilbao were visually exciting, but never bizarre; they could even be said to have had a certain naturalness to them, and there was nothing about Frank's design that challenged basic instincts about space and proportion. It was exciting, not disorienting. And the building would end up functioning far better than Wright's Guggenheim as a container for various kinds of art. The galleries inside Bilbao, the architectural historian Victoria Newhouse would write, "offer an architectural context for contemporary art equivalent to what many artists have demanded for centuries. Here, Gehry's architecture of movement has produced flowing forms that appear as film stills, motion caught and made definitive at a particular moment." And unlike most contemporary museums, Newhouse observed, the Bilbao Guggenheim had a range of gallery shapes and sizes, making it suitable for all kinds of art.

The pressure to stay within the budget was real, and Frank had to make some compromises. The most significant was with the tower he had planned for the eastern end of the site, beyond the bridge, which was never the strongest point of the original design—it was too large in proportion to the rest of the structure, and its galleries would have felt isolated. It was eventually modified into a purely symbolic tower, with exposed steel framework to suggest a link to the site's industrial past, and curving planes sheathed in limestone to echo the forms of the museum. It remained, however, in some ways an appendage, with an ambiguous relationship to the remainder, and it does not appear in most of the better-known photographs of the building. It was something of a tail, irrelevant to the iconic image.

Designing the building was one thing; building it would be quite another, as the struggle over the working drawings for Walt Disney Concert Hall showed. Frank was particularly concerned about how the exterior, once he had shaped it to his liking, would appear in the light; he had first envisioned the building as clad primarily in lead-coated copper, which is neither glaringly reflective nor solid and dark, but has a warm, changing glow. Environmental risks with lead put an end to that idea, and he needed to find a new material that could both be fabricated into the curving shapes he had designed and reflect light in just the way he wanted.

It was not easy. Stainless steel was a possibility, and Juan Ignacio Vidarte remembers seeing Frank sitting in a chair in the middle of the empty museum site, staring at panels of stainless steel in a variety of finishes, hoping to find one that he thought looked good under the exact light conditions of that part of Bilbao. He didn't like any of them, but reluctantly agreed to the one he found the least industrial and cold. Then he came up with what seemed at first to be an outlandish idea, which was to use titanium, a more exotic metal. It had the characteristics he was looking for, but it was expensive and rarely used on buildings, so there was little data about how well it would perform, especially when panels of it were bent into the shapes Frank had designed. Frank hardly minded the risk of using a new material, and everyone agreed with him that it looked best. "But we all thought it was not going to be possible because we could not afford it," said Vidarte, who recalled the debate about titanium to be one of the few moments of real tension in the project, since Frank seemed to be digging in his heels.

Then, by unusual luck, there was a drop in titanium prices when the contractors were preparing bids, and the metal, usually more expensive than steel, became affordable. It brought with it, however, a new set of challenges: titanium is exceptionally strong and could be milled in panels only a third of a millimeter thick, far thinner than steel—so thin that the panels would have a tendency to billow and flutter in the wind, meaning that the surfaces of the building might not always appear completely smooth. Close up, the museum would seem textured. Frank decided that this would only enhance the richness of the exterior, and that the slight billowing of the titanium should not be considered a failure to make a perfectly smooth surface; along with the soft reflections of the light, it would further enhance the building's appearance.

The curving steel framework on which the titanium panels were hung "like wallpaper," in Randy Jefferson's words, could not have been constructed without the CATIA software that Jim Glymph was developing for the office, which determined the shape, size, and placement of every single piece of steel necessary to underpin the complex shape that Frank had imagined. Bilbao was the first building for which CATIA played a role in almost every aspect of the design and construction process. The software was more than just an aesthetic enabler; it was even more necessary as an engineering tool, helping the architects design the structural framework, calculating the structural stresses at each point of the building, and determining the most economical way to construct the curving forms

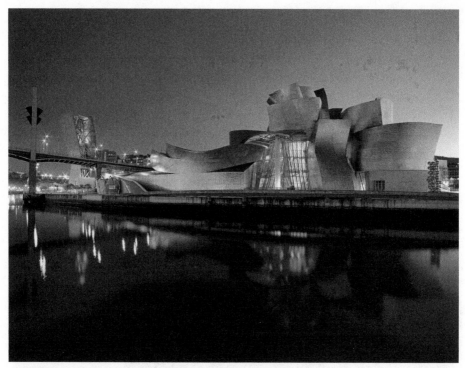

The Guggenheim at night—the view from the Nervión River

primarily out of straight pieces of steel, which were set at slight angles to one another to create the outline of a curve, and then specifying the exact dimensions of each piece. It "helped the contractors understand how these shapes could be achieved," Juan Ignacio Vidarte said, and its precision "lowered the degree of mistake possibilities." And if Frank wanted to vary a shape or a curve, CATIA could instantly calculate the structural implications, and make clear whether or not the change was practical. Frank, who still preferred not to use the computer himself, quickly realized that without digital software his design for Bilbao would never have gotten beyond his imagination, since it would have been impossible to build.

The good fortune of the project continued after construction began in October 1993. It took four years, and it came in, as the Basques had insisted, on budget. In fact, it was $3 million *under* budget, according to the accounting in Frank's office, which put the final cost at $97 million. The technical and management expertise that Jim Glymph and Randy

Atrium of the
Guggenheim Bilbao

Jefferson had brought to Frank's office, along with the CATIA system, all helped control costs. And this time there was never any thought of having the working drawings done by another architect, as with Walt Disney Concert Hall. Frank had to answer to Tom Krens and the Basque government, but not to another architect.*

By mid-1996, a year before completion, it was already becoming clear that something special was happening in Bilbao. The Pritzker family, which had helped to establish the stature of the Pritzker Prize by holding its presentation celebration each year in a different, architecturally significant site around the world, set Frank's building as the site of the 1997 prize

---

* There was a Bilbao architectural firm, called IDOM, that served as local contact and as a kind of coordinating partner, a common arrangement when a building is designed by an architect who is based a great distance away. However, IDOM was not empowered to challenge Frank's authority, as Daniel Dworsky had been in Los Angeles.

ceremony at the end of May. It turned out to be not quite finished—the opening had been postponed to October—but that hardly mattered to the architectural notables who journeyed to Bilbao to hear Sverre Fehn, the Norwegian architect who won the prize that year, praise Frank for managing to erect a building that so faithfully preserved "the genius idea" of his original sketches. "This museum by Frank Gehry expresses the instant of freedom," Fehn said.

An even more significant visitor, however, had come to see Bilbao a number of months before. Philip Johnson, traveling through Europe, arranged to tour the almost-finished building. Frank was not there, and Juan Ignacio Vidarte showed him around. Later, Johnson told both Charlie Rose and Sydney Pollack that he had been so overwhelmed by the museum that he was moved to tears as he stood in the atrium. He pronounced the Bilbao Guggenheim "the greatest building of our time."[*]

From that point on, it was almost a question of who could get there first and come up with the highest praise. Herbert Muschamp went over the summer of 1997, before any art was installed, and reviewed the museum not in the regular architecture column of *The New York Times* but in the form of a cover story in *The New York Times Magazine* titled "A Masterpiece for Now." Muschamp wrote, "The word is out that miracles still occur, and that a major one is happening here. Frank Gehry's new Guggenheim Museum won't open until next month, but people have been flocking to Bilbao, Spain, to watch the building take shape. 'Have you been to Bilbao?' In architectural circles, the question has acquired the status of a shibboleth. Have you seen the light? Have you seen the future? Does it work? Does it play?"

And then, in a phrase that would become one of the most remembered lines he ever wrote, Muschamp called the museum "the reincarnation of Marilyn Monroe." He went on, "What twins the actress and the building in my memory is that both of them stand for an American style of freedom. That style is voluptuous, emotional, intuitive and exhibitionist. It is mobile, fluid, material, mercurial, fearless, radiant and as fragile as a newborn child. It can't resist doing a dance with all of the voices that say 'No.' It wants to take up a lot of space. And when the impulse strikes, it likes to let its dress fly up in the air." Muschamp's piece, not surprisingly,

---

[*] Johnson returned to Bilbao in 1998 with Charlie Rose to film an interview about the building, and said, "Architecture is not about words, it is about tears. I get the same feeling as I get in Chartres Cathedral." He then began to cry once again, for Rose's camera.

became the most famous among the hundreds of things written about the building: it was by turns brilliant and self-indulgent, a tour de force more than a work of journalism.

Muschamp examined the building solely as an outpost of American culture. "If you want to look into the heart of American art today, you are going to need a passport," he wrote. It was left to other critics, many of whom considered Bilbao no less extraordinary than Muschamp did, to probe the other aspects of the building: its workings as a museum, of course, and also its connections to Basque culture and politics. Not the least of the many remarkable aspects of the project was the willingness of the Basques to express their nationalistic impulses by commissioning a work of cutting-edge architecture by an architect with no connection to their region or even to their country: an event that could seem as anomalous as if the Irish Republican Army had brought the Sydney Opera House into being. Nationalism, so often a restrictive force, in Bilbao was bringing forth a culturally enlightened internationalism. The Basques were telling the world that they wanted to be known for their willingness to support the most advanced architectural ideas, whatever they were and wherever they might come from.

It happened, of course, because the Basques were not the Irish Republican Army, or Hamas, or Al Qaeda. While the region had a radical separatist arm, ETA, which was capable of extreme violence, the deeper currents in Basque politics and culture were more bourgeois, and more traditional. Bilbao, the historical industrial and banking center of northern Spain, was in many ways the generic European provincial city, filled with plazas and statues and fountains. If the proper folk of Bilbao deplored the political killings committed on behalf of the separatist movement, they were hardly opposed to the Basque-centric instincts behind them; despite the extreme differences between the Bilbao mainstream and ETA, they were united by a powerful sense of identity as Basques first and Spaniards second. The Basques were a curious cross between canny developers and political rebels, and most of Bilbao was content to use boosterism as a way of expressing nationalist impulses. For them, building an art museum that would dazzle the world would help the city achieve its fondest wish: not merely to see its economy revive, but to give Bilbao and the Basque region an identity apart from that of Spain.

When the building was formally dedicated in late October 1997, the presence of King Juan Carlos and Queen Sofia—who symbolized Spain, not the Basque country—gave ETA the occasion for one last attempt at cataclysmic, violent protest. Members of the separatist group, posing as a team of gardeners, hid multiple explosives in the foliage of *Puppy*, a forty-three-foot-high topiary sculpture by Jeff Koons that Krens had placed in front of the building in amiable counterpoint to Frank's architecture. Their intention was not to destroy the sculpture but to assassinate the king, and it almost came off. The police managed to prevent the explosion, but not without a shootout with ETA that left one officer dead.

The Koons, the king, and the museum emerged unscathed, and the opening went on. There was a black-tie dinner attended by numerous artists, art collectors, and members of the Guggenheim board, including Peter Lewis, as well as Frank, Berta, Frank's children, and Frank's former brother-in-law Richard Snyder, who had remained in close contact with Frank and Berta but had never met his younger children. Alejo Gehry remembers his father grabbing him at one point before the dinner and bringing him over to an unfamiliar middle-aged man. "This is Uncle Rick," Frank said, introducing him to Anita's brother. Snyder and his partner, the designer Paul Vincent Wiseman, had always been close to Leslie and Brina and had often stepped in to make peace when tensions arose between Frank and his daughters, and they quickly brought Alejo and Sam into their circle. The ongoing relationship with Frank was primarily familial, but from time to time Snyder had also advised him on legal and business matters. In particular, he had urged him to retain the rights to the images of his buildings so that he could profit from their replication in souvenirs and other objects. Snyder saw, sooner than most of Frank's friends and family, that there was a Gehry "brand" developing, and he encouraged Frank to make the most of it.

If the attempted terrorism discouraged visitors, there was no sign of it, since the public began to pour into the Guggenheim the morning after the private opening events at more than twice the rate that had been predicted. Projections had been for five hundred thousand visitors a year, but almost four million came within the first three years, contributing roughly $455 million to the regional economy and $110 million in regional taxes. The additional taxes were more than enough to reimburse the Basque regional treasury for the cost of the building. Suddenly, Bilbao seemed neither a declining industrial city nor a place inhibited by fears of terrorist violence, but a powerful tourist magnet. According to *Forbes*, 82 percent of the visitors to the city had come specifically to see the Guggenheim, or were extended their stay because of it. And the benefits of the acclaimed museum were not just economic; as Juan Ignacio Vidarte told the *Financial Times*, it meant that "we recovered our self-esteem."

The Guggenheim was not just a fad, a trendy attraction destined to fade quickly. The allure remained undiminished. In 2012, fifteen years after the opening, the museum was still attracting a million visitors a year. No wonder, then, that the phrase "Bilbao effect" entered the language, and came quickly to signify the role a spectacular work of architecture could play as a catalyst for economic development. While few, if any, such efforts elsewhere would have quite the success of Bilbao, where very specific architectural, political, managerial, and economic factors all contributed to the positive result, the Bilbao Guggenheim and Frank's name both soon became synonymous with the more general idea that architecture could provide a certain magic, a "wow" factor that would be a force of powerful cultural allure.

By this token, Herbert Muschamp's desire to see the building as the embodiment of a particularly American attitude made some sense, even if it ignored the motivations of the Basques. Frank's work represented emotion as much as intellect and emerged out of intuition far more than theory; like all of his architecture, Bilbao was at once pragmatic and idealistic. If, as Vincent Scully has written, a historical theme of American architecture has been a tendency to loosen up European architecture, to make things a bit more picturesque, more emotionally appealing, and sometimes less intellectually rigorous,* at Bilbao Frank was doing something along similar lines. It was a work of architecture that showed Europe the same intense, potent energy that the American abstract expressionists had done decades earlier, and it extended into architecture the notion that there was an American instinct that was different from the European and was something very much its own. Also, it brought American architecture into the realm of the twentieth-century avant-garde. Before Bilbao, the international architectural avant-garde tended to be far more theory-driven, not to say academic; Bilbao represented a new paradigm, a cutting-edge building that reflected an American impulse.

The Guggenheim Bilbao, then, was not just the most important building of 1997, or of the 1990s; it was, as Philip Johnson had predicted, the

---

* It is a point Scully made frequently, most memorably in his *American Architecture and Urbanism*, where he interpreted American Beaux-Arts and eclectic architecture as a softer, more visually inviting, looser version of European prototypes—something Scully generally meant as a compliment.

building of the era. Less than a decade after the completion of his first European building for Vitra, Frank had designed another in Europe, and this one was being hailed as the most important new building in the world. There could be no doubt now of his stature: not just an international figure, he was looking more and more like the most important architect anywhere.

He was, characteristically, thrilled at the reception Bilbao received and full of doubt about it. Was he really as good as people were saying? Or was the whole thing simply a mad idea that he had somehow persuaded the world to believe in? Frank had never felt that his finished buildings were quite as good as he had wanted them to be; it was not just that he was always seeing little details he thought he could have done better, but that he was never able to escape flashes of doubt that his basic concept was right. And Bilbao was his most ambitious building yet, which meant that even all the praise it had gotten could not render him free of worry.

"When I saw Bilbao for the first time," he recalled, "I said, 'Oh my god, what have I done to these people?'"

His anxieties notwithstanding, the extraordinary success of the Guggenheim in Bilbao changed Frank's life. It presented an unusual challenge because, despite his great ambition, he had always been more flustered by success than failure. "Before Bilbao, he could always feel that he was the underdog, misunderstood and struggling," said Michelle Kaufmann. It was a position that Frank felt naturally comfortable in. "It was tough for him not to have all those forces to push up against," Kaufmann said.

The acclaim of Bilbao also removed the office even further, if that could be imagined, from its beginnings as an informal atelier. Before Bilbao, Michelle Kaufmann remembered, Frank would wander from desk to desk around the office and make casual sketches to show architects how he wanted something done. After Bilbao, she observed, if he made a sketch, an assistant would sometimes spirit it away for the archives and hand over a photocopy to be used as a reference tool.

After Bilbao, Frank was a celebrity in worlds outside art and architecture that had until then paid him relatively little notice. Everyone wanted a piece of his time, and he received constant requests to duplicate the image of Bilbao in other kinds of buildings. Most of them he ignored or, if the client was prestigious enough, tried to turn down gracefully. He was thrilled with the acclaim of Bilbao, but he did not want to copy it, and he was uncomfortable with the notion that clients would come to him because they wanted him to produce something that resembled the Guggenheim. He was much happier with the idea that clients would hire him because they wanted to be surprised. It was important to Frank that he not turn the success of Bilbao into a formula.

At one point not long after the building was finished, he was approached by Steve Wynn, the casino owner, who was interested in having a Gehry-designed casino in Atlantic City. It was an unusual interview: Wynn flew Frank in his private plane to New Jersey to see the site, and then persuaded him to continue eastward and show him Bilbao, which Wynn had not yet visited. They brought along Philip Johnson, who was happy to take advantage of an opportunity to see the building again (as well as to meet Wynn and see if he could get a commission out of the casino magnate himself).

As the men flew across the Atlantic, Frank recalled, he and Johnson played with sketches and models while Wynn sat in his private cabin making phone calls. Frank overheard him telling friends what a coup it was to have Frank Gehry and Philip Johnson on his plane. But when Wynn emerged from the cabin, he showed little interest in the actual designs they were sketching, and Frank began to wonder if Wynn's interest in him was driven more by his new level of fame than by a desire to engage with his work. When they got to Bilbao, Johnson enthused about the building as usual, and Wynn seemed pleased.

"I think I've found my architect," he told Frank.

Frank paused for a moment before responding.

"Well, I don't think I've found my client," he said. Even though Wynn said only positive things about Bilbao, Frank could not shed his misgivings. Once again, his instinct led him to walk away from a lucrative situation because he felt uncomfortable and sensed that he would not have the kind of working relationship with a client that he liked and, at this stage of his career, felt increasingly entitled to ask for.

"The way I think about it," he said later, "is that if it looks like we're not going to get along, it's going to be difficult for everybody. So we'd better not do it."

Tom Krens understood as well as anyone that the circumstances of Bilbao were unique, but he felt little hesitation about trying it again. In fact, he was so emboldened by the success of the Bilbao Guggenheim that less than a year after its opening he decided that the time had come for a new Guggenheim Museum in New York, not to replace Frank Lloyd Wright's building—Krens knew how iconic it was, and how critical it was to his institution's image—but to supplement it, and to give New Yorkers a taste of the new architecture that the Guggenheim had come to symbolize around the world.

This time, Krens saw no need for an architectural competition. He went right to Frank and asked him to design a new, expanded Guggenheim Museum, and he knew just where it should go: in Lower Manhattan, where it could connect to the growing cultural activity both in downtown Manhattan and in Brooklyn. Krens had already tried once to expand the Guggenheim downtown, with a branch designed by Arata Isozaki on the ground floor of an old industrial building on Broadway in SoHo, but that modest project had had minimal impact.[*] Krens, characteristically, decided that the solution was to double down and replace the small downtown Guggenheim with a building far larger than the main Guggenheim uptown, or the new one in Bilbao. This museum would be so big, in fact, that it could not fit on a conventional site. Krens wanted to obtain the right to build on city-owned piers at the waterfront, first on the Hudson River and later, in a more fully developed version, along the East River at the foot of Wall Street, where the new building could sprawl across the equivalent of several blocks along the open waterfront. Frank responded to Krens's wishes and designed a project that made Bilbao seem almost restrained. David Dunlap of *The New York Times* would later describe it as a "titanium cloud," as apt a phrase as any for a building whose swirling metallic forms were lifted high atop stone-covered piers. The museum would have contained more than four times the gallery space of the original uptown Guggenheim, reached up to four hundred feet, or nearly the height of a forty-story building, and sat on almost six acres of open space and gardens.

New York, however, was not Bilbao, where Krens had both a government checkbook at his disposal and the promise of autonomy in the planning process. He decided that the best way to build support for the building was to commission Frank to make an elaborate model, which he installed in an anonymous space the Guggenheim rented in an old office building

---

[*] It would close in 2001 and be replaced by a large Prada store designed by Rem Koolhaas, another of Krens's favorite architects. Koolhaas designed a pair of Guggenheim branches in the Venetian Hotel in Las Vegas that opened in 2001; neither attracted the expected level of visitors, and one section closed after only two years. The other closed in 2008.

on Varick Street. Krens invited members of the press, collectors, artists, supporters of the museum, and politicians to see the model and have private, off-the-record briefings about his plan to construct the gargantuan museum, expecting that he would line up enough opinion-makers, artists, and donors in advance in support of the project that its construction would be a foregone conclusion. Unfortunately, he failed to explain his strategy either to Ronald Perelman, the financier who was then the president of the Guggenheim board and his nominal boss, or to many of the public officials whose approval would be necessary for the project to go ahead. According to *Vanity Fair*, news of the new museum leaked out in the press before either the governor of New York, George Pataki, or the mayor of New York City, Rudolph Giuliani, knew about it, and Perelman, who was close to both men, was furious. He considered the venture to be no more than exploratory, and thought that he, the governor, and the mayor had all been blindsided by Krens's tactic of showing off Frank's model before the board had made an official decision to announce the new museum.

Peter Lewis would turn out to be Krens's savior. Lewis had become increasingly active on the Guggenheim board, and he had taken quickly to Krens's expansion plans. By 1998, Krens, Lewis, and Frank had become, for all intents and purposes, a tightly functioning trio: with the potent combination of Lewis's money, Krens's drive, and Frank's architecture, the three friends felt they could accomplish anything. Lewis pledged $250 million toward the estimated $950 million cost of the Gehry New York Guggenheim, and the three of them saw little reason why Ronald Perelman or anyone else should prevent the project from moving full speed ahead. By the middle of 1999, Perelman had decided to leave the board, and Peter Lawson-Johnston, a Guggenheim relative who had been serving as chairman, became the honorary chairman. Peter Lewis took over as chairman of the Guggenheim.

But things did not turn out as the Krens-Lewis-Gehry troika had hoped. First, while the Giuliani administration had come around to approving the plan for the new museum and promised $67.5 million in city funds, there were few signs of other money. Peter Lewis's contribution and the city's totaled roughly a third of the project budget, but the museum was making little progress in finding the other two-thirds. In fact, it was having increasing trouble covering its general operating budget, since none of Krens's other expansion efforts had worked out nearly as well as Bilbao, and Lewis and other board members were writing more and more checks to cover deficits. Then came the terrorist attacks of September 11, 2001, and New York went into a tailspin. It would have been challenging enough to build anything in New York in the difficult time following 9/11, but there was no chance at all that an expensive and largely unfunded new museum could move forward then in Lower Manhattan, just a few blocks from the site where the twin towers of the World Trade Center had stood. The project was for all intents and purposes dead.

The faint hope that the new Guggenheim might play a role in post–September 11 reconstruction efforts kept it from being formally abandoned until the end of 2002, by which time it was clear that the planners in charge of Lower Manhattan did not see a vast Frank Gehry museum as part of their road map to recovery. By then, the Guggenheim's financial problems had become more severe, and while Krens had not given up on his quest for continued expansion, Peter Lewis, who had rapidly become the museum's largest donor—he would ultimately give $77 million to the Guggenheim—was beginning to become disenchanted with his friend. Their relationship would spiral downward over the next several years as Lewis, whose personal flamboyance hid a focused and sober business sense, increasingly took issue with what he considered to be Krens's loose financial management and determination to expand at all costs. At the beginning of 2005, the friction between Frank's two close friends culminated in a boardroom showdown. Lewis decided that the time had come for Krens to leave, and he asked the rest of the board to support his decision. When the board did not agree, Lewis resigned.

Frank had tried to broker a peace between his two friends, and at one point went so far as to invite Krens to join him and Lewis on Lewis's yacht as they traveled in Norway. But the conflicts ran too deep, and there was no peace to be made. Frank was stuck awkwardly in the middle, all the more so because Krens had replaced the abandoned New York project with an even bigger commission for Frank: a Guggenheim on Saadiyat Island in Abu Dhabi, announced in 2006, the year after Peter Lewis left the board. Frank produced a design with eleven enormous conelike structures, curving sections of blue glass and boxlike gallery sections clad in stone, all arrayed around a four-story atrium and connected by glass bridges. It was an extravaganza on a grandiose—perhaps too grandiose—scale.

For a while, the Abu Dhabi project would keep the collaboration between Krens and Frank going strong, even after 2008, when the members of the Guggenheim board, three years after rejecting Lewis's attempt to squeeze Krens out, changed their minds and relieved him of day-to-day operating responsibilities. Krens was named "senior advisor for international affairs" and charged with overseeing the Abu Dhabi project, which at that point was the only one of his many expansion efforts that seemed to be moving forward. But it did not take long for Abu Dhabi, too, to fall prey to uncertainty and delay, and in 2011, with construction still not started, Krens would be eased out altogether. Frank remained on the project, waiting for construction to begin[*] and struggling with charges that the Guggenheim was complicit in the discrimination against immigrant workers that was common in large projects in the United Arab Emirates. Troubled by suggestions that he had been untrue to his liberal roots by participating in a project that violated human rights, he hired a human rights lawyer, Scott Horton, to represent him and to gain assurances that the Guggenheim was abiding by international standards governing the welfare of workers.[†] With Horton's assistance, Frank became a strong public advocate of improved conditions for construction workers. His public stance may or may not have had a significant impact on the treatment of workers, but it did exempt him from the brunt of the criticism that was directed toward the Guggenheim and other institutions building in Abu Dhabi, and toward other architects who have been working actively in the region.[‡]

But however things played out in Abu Dhabi, the partnership between Frank Gehry and Tom Krens was over. It had brought forth the most famous

---

[*] The Abu Dhabi project was part of a complex of museums in the new Saadiyat Island cultural area, with other projects by Jean Nouvel, Norman Foster, and Zaha Hadid. Originally the Abu Dhabi government had planned to build them all at once. It soon acknowledged that not even the vast financial resources at its disposal would overcome the challenges of constructing four enormous and complex museums at the same time, and a decision was made to build them in sequence instead. Frank's project had still not begun in early 2015, although the office had been asked to update the design in preparation for possible construction, so seeing it built still seemed possible, if far from certain.

[†] In 2010, at the urging of Scott Horton and Frank, the Guggenheim and the Tourism Development and Investment Company of Abu Dhabi, the organization that was building the museums, issued a joint statement asserting that they were both "deeply committed to safeguarding the rights and welfare of employees at the Guggenheim Abu Dhabi Museum site."

[‡] The problem did not go away, and attracted more public attention in 2014 after Zaha Hadid was widely criticized for suggesting that labor conditions were the concern of governments and not architects. Late in 2014, Richard Armstrong, Krens's successor as director and Frank's new client at Abu Dhabi, felt compelled to remind advocates of workers' rights that the Guggenheim was not technically the organization in charge of constructing the building. But he acknowledged that the museum was hardly a neutral observer, and he repeated his statement that the Guggenheim was "deeply committed" to fair labor practices.

building in the world, transformed tourism, reimagined the museum, and changed the role of architecture as a force for urban redevelopment. Frank and Krens had produced what was arguably the most important building of the late twentieth century, and neither of them could have done it alone. But it would not happen again. There would be only one Bilbao.

15

Walt Disney Concert Hall:
Second Movement

ecause the success of the Bilbao Guggenheim was almost a foregone conclusion before it opened—even before the 1997 Pritzker Prize ceremony was held there, the world of architecture was
abuzz with talk about Frank's building long before it was finished—back
home in Los Angeles it became harder to think of the stalled Walt Disney Concert Hall as anything but an embarrassment. A small provincial
city in northern Spain could build the most advanced Gehry building yet
designed, and Los Angeles, his home city, couldn't get one off the ground?
It was clear that the world was looking at Bilbao as Frank's most important
work, and that the Spanish city was already rising in stature as a result of
Frank's contribution to it. If Bilbao, a city less than a tenth the size of Los
Angeles, could make this happen, then why couldn't Los Angeles? How
could it consider itself a world city when it had all but abandoned its most
ambitious piece of cultural architecture before construction had barely
begun?

To Richard Riordan, the mayor of Los Angeles, these were not rhe-
torical questions. Riordan, a businessman who was mayor for eight years
beginning in 1993, was particularly troubled by the view that his city was
not a world-class cultural center, and he understood that opinions would
never change unless Disney Hall was built. He also realized that there was
only one private citizen who combined the philanthropic clout, political
connections, and cultural credentials needed to help restart the dormant
project, and that was Eli Broad. Broad had invested huge amounts of his
energy as well as his money into building the city's reputation as a cultural
center, and the acclaim Bilbao was getting was to him an implicit source
of shame for Los Angeles. Frank Gehry was increasingly being hailed as

Sketch of the final design of the façade of Walt Disney Concert Hall

an architect of international stature, and he felt that Los Angeles could not afford to look to the world as if it were rejecting the architectural efforts of its most famous son. Yes, the building was complicated and expensive, and yes, he knew as well as anyone how difficult Frank could be, but there were ways to deal with all of that, Broad told the mayor. The important thing was that the project had to get built, somehow.

Broad and the mayor shared a belief that strengthening downtown Los Angeles was key to the ongoing health of the city, and the task of downtown revival was difficult enough without the embarrassment of the aborted concert hall in the middle of it. Some of the early schemes for Disney Hall had included a hotel and other commercial space on the site to support the city's wish that the hall be tied directly to the renewal of downtown, and while those studies were eventually abandoned in favor of giving the full block to the hall, there was still a plan to develop the block just across Grand Avenue as commercial space in tandem with the concert hall.* Broad, despite having made his first fortune as a builder of suburban tract

---

* The plan want through multiple iterations and eventually morphed into a pair of towers designed by Frank that were to be built by the Related Group, a New York developer. By the middle of 2015, however, construction had still not begun.

housing, clung to a vision of Los Angeles as a more traditionally organized city than it was, and he particularly felt that it needed a strong downtown core to be taken seriously as a world city. He may have first gotten rich from sprawl, but he believed in density. That the cultural and economic vitality of Los Angeles by 1996 could be said to have proven the opposite — that it had managed to become one of the great cities of the world even with many of its strongest elements not clustered in a traditional, dense center but scattered along its boulevards and freeways, and so its success might be a model for a different kind of urban form — was a notion that Broad either could not grasp or chose not to see.

But whether the primary motivation was a belief that a strong downtown was the linchpin of a strong Los Angeles or a desire to overcome the embarrassment the city faced in the light of the triumph of Bilbao, it was clear that something had to be done to get Walt Disney Concert Hall moving again. And so Broad and Riordan launched a campaign to revive the project. They called it "The Heart of the City," playing to the notion that they would have more success raising funds to complete the hall if they portrayed it as the key to giving Los Angeles a healthy center than if they sought money solely to build an important piece of architecture. "People didn't believe it could be built; they thought it was a black hole for money," Broad said. He and Riordan promised to sequester the funds in a construction account and return the money to donors if construction did not go ahead. Broad then gave the fund $15 million, and Riordan made a $5 million personal donation, after which they lined up support from a number of the city's largest businesses. The oil and gas company ARCO, Wells Fargo, Bank of America, and Times Mirror, then the parent of the *Los Angeles Times*, all made seven- and eight-figure gifts. The effort was helped along by the easy relationship that Riordan, an amateur hockey player, had with Frank. Shortly after the campaign began, Riordan recalled, he and Frank were both playing in a men's league at local rink. "As our hockey game intensified, I checked Frank into the boards. We faced each other and I couldn't help myself from shouting, 'You're going to build Disney Hall or I'm going to murder you!'"

The Walt Disney Company, which had had an uneasy relationship with the Disney family since Michael Eisner became its chief executive more than a decade before, had contributed nothing toward the construction of the hall. But Disney reversed course when the campaign started and came up with $25 million. Since Frank was one of many celebrated architects whom Eisner had brought into the Disney fold—in addition to the administration building at Disneyland, he had designed projects at Euro Disney and an ice rink in Anaheim—the company's change of heart was as much a gesture of public support for Frank as for the Disney family.[*]

The campaign to restart Disney Hall did not ignore the building's architectural significance. On March 4, 1997, as the campaign was launching, a full-page advertisement ran in the *Los Angeles Times*, signed by architects from around the world. It had been organized by Thom Mayne as a reminder to the city's business and political community that the architecture world was watching what happened in Los Angeles. Around an image of Frank's final, revised design for the hall, a headline proclaimed, "Build It and They Will Come." The rest of the ad consisted of five columns of small type listing the names of more than two hundred architects, architecture historians, and critics from around the world who "wish to offer their support for this visionary design by Frank Gehry." The signers included celebrated architects like Philip Johnson, Rem Koolhaas, Arata Isozaki, Richard Rogers, Robert A. M. Stern, Peter Eisenman, Robert Venturi, Denise Scott Brown, Tadao Ando, Harry Cobb, and Richard Meier, as well as many local practitioners. Many of the signers were architects whose work was quite different from Frank's. But what was perhaps the most telling sign that the tide was turning was that one of the signers was Frank's nemesis, Daniel Dworsky.

Dworsky's own role in the project was at an end; probably the most significant impact Bilbao had on the progress of Disney Hall was not to allay concerns about its design but to resolve issues about how it should be built. Frank's office had handled every part of the Guggenheim project, including the working drawings, and the museum had been completed on time and on budget, which appeared to justify Frank's contention that the problems at Disney stemmed less from his design than from his not being allowed to control every part of the architectural process.

Still, he was hardly out of the woods, and it would be some time before he would be in a position similar to the one he had had at Bilbao. Eli Broad, who had been to Bilbao and admired it, seemed to view its success

---

[*] Ron Miller, Walt Disney's son-in-law and Diane Disney Miller's husband, had been the company's chief executive before Eisner, and was pushed aside by the Disney board of directors when they decided to hire Eisner in 1984. The company's success under Eisner led to frequent references to him as the heir to Walt Disney's legacy, which did not further endear him to the Disney family.

only as proof that a complicated and unusual Gehry building was build-able, not that Frank should be in charge of building it. While he did not accept Dworsky's contention that the problem with the working drawings stemmed from the fact that Frank's design was so complex as to be virtually impossible to construct—Bilbao had proven Dworsky's charge hollow—Broad had not given up on his belief that Frank could be difficult and slow, as he had found him to be with his house, and he still viewed him as an artist capable of making imaginative shapes, not as one capable of execut-ing demanding projects.

Broad was convinced that the problem the first time around was poor management, and he laid much of the blame for that at the feet of Fred Nicholas, who had chaired the concert hall committee and overseen the project on behalf of the Music Center and Los Angeles Philharmonic boards. Broad squeezed Nicholas out of the project, but it was not to make more room for Frank. Giving Frank greater control over it was not the solution, "because of past history," Broad told Calvin Tomkins of *The New Yorker*. Broad's solution was to more or less take charge of the entire enter-prise himself and turn it into a "design-build" project under the control of a contractor, who would commit to building it for a fixed price and select an architect to oversee it.

Frank was furious, and not only because he saw the history of Broad's house repeating itself on a larger and more public scale. Finding the money to get the building finished did not entitle Broad to treat the project as if it were his own house, Frank believed, and he resented being margin-alized a second time on his own building. He reacted as he often had in difficult situations—by walking away. First he stalked out of a conference room in his own office when he saw that Broad had come to a Disney Hall planning meeting, saying that he did not want him in his studio. Then he decided to walk off the entire project and submitted his resignation, saying in effect that he could not work under the conditions that Eli Broad was demanding, and that he would take his name off the building, just as he had at Broad's house.

"Some people have said that 75 percent of my building is better than none," Frank wrote in a letter to Broad that was published in the *Los Ange-les Times*. "That's the way you did your house, and you are satisfied. Maybe you can do it again. My obligation to myself and to the Disney family makes it impossible for me to agree to such a process." And then he let loose his frustration to *The New York Times*. "They don't want to listen to me because I'm the creative type," he said. "They dismiss me because I'm the 'great genius,' and every time they say this, I cringe. I've been geniused to death."

It was the Disney family that came to the rescue. Diane Disney Miller, one of Walt and Lillian Disney's two daughters, lived a relatively private life in the wine country of Napa, far from the pressures of Los Angeles in which she had grown up. But she had taken over her mother's role as the family's most active participant in the project—Lillian Disney was in her late nineties, and would die at the end of 1997—and she had grown fond of Frank, in whom she saw some of the creative instincts of her father. She invited Frank and Berta to visit her at her ranch in Napa, and confessed to them how troubled she was by the pressures on the project. She recalled that her father had told her that whenever there was a dispute between creative people and business managers, he almost always found it was in his best long-term interest to side with the creative people.

Diane Disney Miller wanted to do the same thing. She decided that her family would cover the costs of having Frank's office do the working drawings. Miller told the concert hall committee that she was not releasing the remaining funds in her mother's trust until Frank gave her the okay. "We promised Los Angeles a Frank Gehry building, and that's what we intend to deliver," Miller announced. She did not want her father's name on a building that Frank himself did not want to stand behind, so she let it be known that if the finished building were not satisfactory to him, it would not be just his name that would be removed from it—she would take her father's name off it, too.

Diane Disney Miller played the one card that could trump Eli Broad. The committee overseeing the concert hall, which had been deferring to Broad, could not overrule the wishes of the family whose name was on the building, especially not if it was offering additional funds. Broad gave in, and the project proceeded with Gehry Partners as the sole architect. Construction started, or restarted, in November 1999, more than ten years after Frank was selected as the architect.

The design had continued to evolve, although the basic thrust of it remained what it had been when the project went on hold in 1994: a roughly rectangular hall seating approximately twenty-two hundred, its interior of Douglas fir, placed at an angle to the street, surrounded by large, curving planes that enclosed lobbies, other public spaces, and support space. The building as a whole could be said to have a vague resem-

The final model of the main entry of Walt Disney Concert Hall

blance to an artichoke with a box as its heart, or to a Spanish galleon with huge sails billowing in all directions.

Originally the exterior was to be covered in pieces of stone, but the ongoing pressure on costs, as well as the success of Bilbao's titanium exterior, led Frank to switch to stainless steel. He had rejected the option of a metal exterior once before, in 1994, and he continued to believe that stone would be both softer and warmer. But when it turned out that steel would cost $10 million less than limestone, he conceded, and adjusted the shapes of the curving sails slightly to make them somewhat simpler and stronger to compensate for the fact that metal was visually lighter than stone.

It turned out to be a wise decision, and the even, brushed finish of the fifty-one hundred plates of stainless steel that make up the sails give the building a luminous glow,* not to mention a crispness and visual sharp-

---

* Residents of a condominium apartment building to the southwest found the building not luminous but glaring in the afternoon sun, the result of a decision to use polished rather than brushed steel to distinguish a section on that side containing the Founders Room, which Frank wanted to stand out slightly from the rest of the structure. The problem was resolved when the steel on the section causing the reflection was sanded to a finish similar to that of the rest of the exterior.

ness that it would not have had if it had been sheathed in stone. While Frank had been intrigued by the implications of combining the advanced structure and shape of the building with a material as dense and traditional as stone—to him, the inherent contradiction between the solidity of stone and a sense of movement represented a challenge to his talent for expressing the difficult and ambiguous—he soon saw the potential of steel to create a brighter and more visually powerful exterior. It turned out to be the right thing to do for architectural as well as financial reasons. The billowing waves of steel became in short order a civic symbol of Los Angeles.

They also represented something relatively new for Frank, which was the extension of cladding material beyond what was being cladded. The billowing steel, in other words, did more than cover similar, billowing shapes underneath it. In many of his earlier buildings, such as the towers at Düsseldorf or the American Center in Paris and the Weisman Museum in Minneapolis, Frank produced unusual shapes and figured out how to construct and cover them; at Walt Disney Concert Hall he began to create exterior sheathing that extended out beyond what it was covering and suggested a shape of its own. Some of the steel sails, in other words, seemed to exist more for exterior effect than to cover anything, as if they had been created solely to make the exterior an elaborate and dynamic sculptural composition. The steel sails seem to fly, and they made the enormous building feel light and full of movement.

It was, of course, an architectural tour de force. But more important, it revealed yet again the extent to which Frank, for all his passion for what was new, his determination to do something that had never been done before, and his commitment to the most advanced technology, was also trying to break free of one of modernism's most cherished practices and create his own form of ornament. The great sails were a symbol of the new, but they were also a way of creating decoration, of giving the building an element that existed solely for visual pleasure. Frank was consciously going against the puritanical strain that had always run through modernist architecture, the belief that a building needed to be "honest," "pure," and "rational"—that ornamentation was not just a self-indulgent frill and a useless return to historical copying, but an ethical transgression, a violation of modernist principles.

At Walt Disney Concert Hall, perhaps, Frank definitively proved the fallacy of this argument by producing a design that was utterly modern and new and yet, in a way that was very much his own, unapologetically rich and textured. At Disney Hall he revealed, even more powerfully than

before, that he wanted to find a way to preserve what might be called traditional architectural values—not by using traditional architectural forms,
but by demonstrating with new kinds of forms that architecture exists not
only to serve functional needs but also to create visual and emotional pleasure. Walt Disney Concert Hall, in Frank's mind, was an ode to the joy of
architecture.

It was also an ode to the joy of music. Classical music had played a
role in Frank's life since his mother had taken him to his first concerts in
Toronto in the 1930s. His long friendship with Greg Walsh had deepened
his connection to music, which continued to grow throughout his life. By
the time he began work on Walt Disney Concert Hall he was a sophisticated and knowledgeable listener. He was no musical professional, but he
could be described in a way at least as meaningful for the designer of a
concert hall: as an ideal audience member.

Frank's interest in music made him a willing partner to the hall's acoustician, Yasuhisa Toyota of Nagata Acoustics in Tokyo. He knew, as Michael
Maltzan said, "that no matter how spectacular the building was, if the
hall didn't work acoustically, it would be judged a failure." It helped that

The wood interior of the hall was studied with a large and precise model.

Toyota shared Frank's admiration for the Berlin Philharmonie by Hans Scharoun, as well as Frank's inclination toward a complex rather than a simple form, but most important was that Frank did not present Toyota with a completed auditorium design and ask him to make it work acoustically, but rather expected to develop the form of the auditorium together with the acoustician.

The final form of the hall emerged out of a genuine synthesis of their ideas. Frank agreed to make the room symmetrical, which is uncharacteristic of his work, but everything else about the space is Gehryesque in its complexity, with sixteen different seating sections arranged in terraces, balconies, and mezzanines on all sides of the orchestra, which is positioned neither in the middle nor at the end, but roughly a quarter of the way into the space. There is an unusual sense of intimacy for a hall seating more than two thousand. The room is lined in wood veneer over plaster, and the ceiling, also of wood, consists of convex sections that, like the stainless steel on the exterior, curve and billow in a way that resembles fabric more than a hard material. A brightly colored, Gehry-designed floral pattern is used for the upholstered seats and carpets, Frank's acknowledgment of Lillian Disney's love of gardens. (The building also has an exterior garden for which Frank designed a fountain by recycling pieces of Delft pottery, which Lillian Disney collected.)

The gestation period of Walt Disney Concert Hall was so long that Ernest Fleischmann, the ambitious and demanding executive director of the Los Angeles Philharmonic for nearly three decades—and a consistent champion of Frank's work—retired in 1998 at seventy-five, as the hall was about to resume construction. Fleischmann had worked closely with Frank on every detail of the project, from seating arrangements in the hall to backstage accommodations, and his retirement could have been yet another setback both to the project and to Frank personally.

Fortunately for Frank, Fleischmann was replaced with Deborah Borda, the energetic, exuberant, and determined director of the New York Philharmonic, who decided to take the job in Los Angeles in large part, she said, because she found the prospect of the new hall so exciting. Borda recalled seeing a picture of the hall in *The New York Times* a few years before. "I thought it was the most amazing thing I'd ever seen, and I'm not a visual person," she said. "I would not have come to Los Angeles except for the hall." Before Borda agreed to take the job, she asked to meet not only with the board and with Esa-Pekka Salonen, the music director, but also with Frank. "I immediately fell in love with him," she said. "I felt a different kind of connection." Borda and Frank became good friends, far closer than he and Fleischmann had been, and she became an impassioned and perceptive advocate of the project. Her enthusiasm was critical, and once she arrived she became for all intents and purposes the primary client, even though the larger entity of the Los Angeles Music Center remained technically in charge.

Borda, a woman whose geniality masks an unshakable will, asked Frank for one thing before she agreed to take the job in Los Angeles. She was distressed that during one phase of cost cutting, office space for the orchestra administration had been removed. She had no intention, she said, of moving all the way across the country to preside over the construction of a new home for her orchestra and then spending the rest of her working days off in some rented office space. The least she could ask for, she told Frank, was that she and her staff be able to work in the new building. "I said to Frank that before I accept the job I need a promise from you that you will design an office wing," she said. "I'll raise the extra money." He did, and she did. Frank added a stone-clad box to the south side of the site as an administrative wing. While it added $10 million to the cost, it allowed the building to function not just as a performance space but as a true home for the entire Los Angeles Philharmonic organization.

The final cost of the building was $207 million, considerably more than the original budget in 1988, but on target with the estimates made a decade later when the final version was completed and construction restarted.* The cost of Walt Disney Concert Hall would be a touchy subject for both Frank and the Philharmonic for years, since it was often compared with the much lower budget of the first iteration of the building and the difference taken as evidence that Frank's buildings invariably exceeded their budgets. More than a decade after the hall was finished, Frank was still responding to writers who described the project as fraught with cost overruns, defending his ability to stay within the budget.

Still, it was a challenge to stay within the $207 million budget. There was pressure toward the end to reduce expenditures, and Frank was asked

---

* This $207 million figure refers to what are known as "hard costs," or the actual cost of physical construction alone. The total project cost, including fees for architects and engineers, legal fees, borrowing costs, and the funds expended in the failed set of working drawings done by Dworsky Associates, was $270 million.

to forgo a portion of his firm's fee. It was ultimately reduced by $7 million, which Frank agreed to so long as the funds could be considered a contribution to the Los Angeles Philharmonic. The orchestra went along with his request, and Frank and Berta Gehry are listed as major benefactors on the donors' wall in the lobby.

The hall was largely complete at the beginning of 2003, but Deborah Borda wanted to wait until that fall to open it. She and Salonen thought the orchestra needed time to adjust to playing in the new space. "If you have been playing on a lousy violin and then you have a Stradivarius, you need to learn how to play on it," she said. The hall opened with three concerts in late October. It was not easy to decide what music should be played first, and Frank, joining his enthusiasm for music to his possessiveness about the design, worked hand in hand with Borda and Salonen as they made their decisions about what should open the hall. The three became a de facto programming committee, and met for weekly dinners at Vincenti's restaurant in Brentwood to discuss program options. They ended up with Charles Ives's "The Unanswered Question," a Bach prelude for solo violin, Mozart's Symphony no. 32, and Stravinsky's *Rite of Spring* for the special program on the first night; the orchestra's regular season would start the following week, with a single work: Mahler's vast Second Symphony, *Resurrection*, probably the best test of all of the hall's acoustic potential.

The opening evening, which followed a week of free previews for schoolchildren and other invited groups, was the biggest event downtown Los Angeles had seen in a generation. Spotlights flooded Frank's stainless steel sails with light, there were fireworks, and Grand Avenue was closed to traffic to make room for a huge tent to shelter a celebratory postconcert dinner. Even Frank, who for the last several years had usually dressed in nothing more formal than a black T-shirt, came in black tie.

The most unexpected event, however, was not the opening concert but a private dinner that was held on the stage a few nights before. Frank hosted it, and the guest of honor was Eli Broad. Berta, with her combination of sharp political instincts and general goodwill, had convinced Frank that it made no sense to continue their feud, especially since Frank had won most of the important battles. There was more than enough good feeling surrounding the hall now, Berta said, so why not appear magnanimous in victory and share some of it with Broad?

As usual, Berta's intuition was right. "You've all heard that Eli and I have been at each other, but look at what we've built," Frank said at the dinner, toasting Broad. "The result is beautiful, and we're both proud of it." Broad then stood up and raised his glass. "What can I say?" he responded. "Frank's right and this is a priceless building."

Critical response to the building was immediate, and almost entirely positive. Frank, for so long the whipping boy, was the new hero of downtown. Herbert Muschamp, whose admiration for Frank was certainly no surprise, was as excited as he had been at Bilbao: "Disney Hall is the most gallant building you are ever likely to see," he wrote in *The New York Times*. The hall, Muschamp wrote, brought him to "aesthetic ecstasy," and he went on to say, "Audience, music, architecture were infused by a sensation of unity so profound that time stopped."

If other critics did not soar to Muschamp's heights of hyperbole— Anthony Tommasini, the music critic of *The New York Times*, had some minor quibbles about the acoustics—they came close. Alex Ross of *The New Yorker* said of Disney Hall that "in richness of sound, it has few rivals on the international scene, and in terms of visual drama it may have no rival at all. . . . The music seizes you from all sides. The painting-on-a-wall illusion shatters; the orchestra throngs the air."

Ross noted that the hall was not only an architectural phenomenon but a social one in that it had ignited interest all across the city, including from people who had not heretofore displayed any interest in classical music. He understood, as Muschamp had, that Frank had produced something unusual, even for him, and that Walt Disney Concert Hall was much more than an exhilarating essay in form and space. It was a work of architecture that served music in a way that had a particular significance in the twenty-first century, when electronic reproduction of sound has made traditional concert halls nearly obsolete. In an age when anyone who can afford an iPod has the ability to carry high-quality sound in his or her pocket and can hear music on demand, anywhere and anytime, what is the incentive to attend live concerts of classical music? Disney Hall provided exactly the inducement that was needed to encourage people to put down their earphones and buy concert tickets. Frank's new building was a place in which the emotional power of the architecture could equal the emotional power of the music, a place in which the pleasures of being in great public space could once again be united with the excitement of live performance: a surrounding that held forth the promise of bringing musical experience to new and triumphant heights.

The same year that Walt Disney Hall opened, Frank also celebrated the completion of a much smaller hall, the Richard B. Fisher Center for the Performing Arts at Bard College in upstate New York. It was a project he took on largely out of respect for Leon Botstein, Bard's president, who had a second career as a respected musicologist and conductor. Botstein, who had long dreamed of having a serious hall for performance on Bard's rural campus, approached Frank in 1997, when Disney Hall was not yet back on a firm footing. Despite Bard's small budget and out-of-the-way location ninety miles north of New York City, the chance to do another concert hall appealed to Frank, especially when the client was a musician.

The building that resulted, with its wood-paneled auditorium and voluptuous, curving panels of stainless steel on the façade, might seem like a simple, casual sketch for the vastly larger Disney Hall. In the open landscape at Bard, however, the stainless steel reflects the sky and the trees, and it can give the building a soft, ephemeral quality, altogether different from the monumentality of Disney Hall. But the most important aspect of this building might be that its softly curving steel does not cover the build-

The Fisher Center at Bard College

ing's boxy, ordinary, highly functional rear, making the steel in effect a kind of ornamental façade. Here, as in many of his earlier buildings, Frank revealed again how distant his own architectural sensibility was from the classic modernist rhetoric about "honesty," geometric purity, and so forth. The Fisher Center can be seen as a plain building with an ornate façade, more like a nineteenth-century theater or opera house than an abstract modern concert hall, but with Frank's flowing forms as the decoration.

Not all of Frank's post-Bilbao projects were as simple. In 1995, he was approached by Paul Allen, the Seattle billionaire and cofounder of Microsoft, who was a passionate admirer of the rock guitarist Jimi Hendrix, a Seattle native. Allen wanted to build a museum in tribute to his musical hero, and while he did not have a clear sense of what he wanted it to look like—his own architectural taste at the time, he admitted, was somewhat conservative—he knew that he wanted it to be an unusual building that would in some way reflect the creative spirit of Hendrix's music. "His music is very organic, psychedelic, sounds that go up and down, are both delicate and powerful," Allen said. "I came up with the term 'swoopy.' I wanted the feeling of colorful, psychedelic art."

Allen's sister, Jody Allen, who would play a major role in the Experience Music Project, as the museum would come to be named, suggested that Frank would be a logical architect for the unusual building her brother had in mind. Paul Allen had not yet been to Bilbao and was only casually familiar with Frank, but once he had looked at a few other architects' work, he decided his sister was right: if anyone could possibly figure out how to express the idea of Hendrix's music in architecture, it would be Frank. A visit to the Gehry office in Santa Monica was arranged, at Frank's insistence—Allen, who is famously shy, had indicated that he preferred to communicate by e-mail, but Frank said he would not work without at least some face-to-face meetings, and he also wanted Allen to soak up the atmosphere in the office and look at some of his other work. When the two men met, Allen at first said little and just looked around, waiting for Frank to draw him out. Frank showed him through the office, and remembered that Allen stopped to admire the model of a conference room that was roughly in the shape of a horse's head, part of Frank's design for the atrium of the DZ Bank in Berlin. Allen told Frank that he appreciated its "swoopy" form. For his part, Allen recalled being excited by the models for Walt Disney Concert Hall, which was then in its period of hiatus.

Frank's low-key manner, which could frustrate some clients, turned out to be just right for Allen, who was as happy looking at models as directly engaging in conversation. But Allen soon grew comfortable with Frank and began to talk about his love for Hendrix's music and what he wanted the building to be. Frank had never been an ardent fan of Jimi Hendrix—"I was always the liberal Jewish lefty, more into Pete Seeger and Woody Guthrie," he said—but he tried to get a better feel for Hendrix by listening to recordings and talking to Craig Webb and Jim Glymph, both of whom were rock guitarists. Then he went to a guitar maker in Santa Monica and got a bunch of broken pieces of old guitars, wondering if he could put them together into an architectural composition.

At first the building seemed to Frank too diagrammatic and literal. "It was guitar strings flying in the air," he recalled. "I had to make the forms more rooflike." There were many iterations, and at some point along the way Allen, preoccupied with other ventures, delegated much of the work of coordinating the project, at which point Frank lost the easy and frequent give-and-take with a sympathetic client that he depended on to refine his ideas. The final version was something of a compromise, a series of different shapes in different-colored metals that, taken together, make a vague

The Experience Music Project in Seattle

attempt to allude to a shattered Fender Stratocaster guitar. But the sharpness and boldness of that idea is lost in what comes off looking more amorphous, a flowing rather than shattering shape. Yet there is also some of the unbuilt Peter Lewis house in it, a reminder that Frank's "MacArthur grant" was continuing to pay dividends.

The Experience Music Project opened in 2001, an event that had more of the air of a rock concert than an art museum opening. Jim Glymph remembered that he and several of his colleagues from the office gathered before the opening to smoke marijuana in Frank's hotel suite, a get-together that ended abruptly when Frank, worried that word would get out that he was hosting a pot party, shooed them all out. However high the spirits may have been at the opening, the Experience Music Project was not received with the general sense of acclaim Frank had become accustomed to since Bilbao. Herbert Muschamp, who usually could be counted on for enthusiasm about anything Frank did, referred to it as looking like "something that crawled out of the sea, rolled over, and died." But the unusual, almost liquid form of the building certainly pleased Allen, whose view was that since Hendrix's music was not to everyone's taste, any building that accurately reflected him would inevitably be controversial. What mattered to him, he said later, was that Frank had figured out how to "capture the exuberance of Jimi Hendrix's music in a building. I don't think anyone else could have pulled it off, and I think it's a masterpiece."

If the Experience Music Project was not Bilbao, another building, the Ray and Maria Stata Center for Computer, Information and Intelligence Services at the Massachusetts Institute of Technology, brought Frank more serious concerns than carping from critics. MIT hired Frank in 1998 to design a huge new center for computers and artificial intelligence on the site of one of the most historic structures on the campus, the casual, rambling Building 20, where radar was developed during World War II. The old building's very informality—it looked like an army barracks—suited the scientists who worked there, and they were not pleased at the prospect of its removal, which meant that Frank started the design process with at least some of his constituency opposed to having anything new built at all. "They were suspicious by nature of architecture," he said. An even bigger problem was that the building had to house seven different departments whose views did not always agree, and the university was not speaking to its architect with a single voice. "I had a seven-hundred-person client," Frank said. "I had the president of the university, two hundred some faculty, and four hundred students."

To engage its sprawling, amorphous client, Gehry Partners set up a special Web site devoted to the planning process, which was updated weekly with the firm's latest sketches, ideas, and notes. MIT students and faculty were invited to post comments, and at the beginning of the process, Frank said, "I got a lot of hate mail." Gradually the comments became more constructive, but Frank was still frustrated by the conflicting demands of the scientists who would be using the building. "They said they wanted to be alone, and they also wanted to be together," he recalled. "And so we showed them how they could have their own little rooms, and how they could just push the walls away and be together. They hated it." He showed them other models of ways in which spaces could be arranged, and finally settled on one that would have a mix of private and communal spaces, set around a large common space that would serve as both an atrium and a street, wending its way through the long building. Frank tried to give the design some of the casual, easy feeling of Building 20.

To a certain extent he did: the result, a sprawling, highly expressionist building of curving, slanted, twisted, torqued, and rounded towers of multiple colors and materials, whose distinct sections make it look almost like a miniature city, is jaunty, even exhilarating. And a central public space envisioned as a kind of indoor street was generally a success. Robert Campbell of *The Boston Globe* described the building as "a metaphor for the freedom, daring, and creativity of the research that's supposed to occur inside it." But creating a metaphor for scientific creativity is not the same as serving the needs of creativity, and to some of the scientists working in the building, Frank's version of casual seemed, in its way, as rigid as Mies van der Rohe. They saw the Stata Center not as the expression of flexibility that they had hoped for, but as an all too inflexible statement by a strong-willed architect. Frank and his colleagues had spent months working closely with the MIT scientists in the hope of producing something that responded to their needs. The problem, in the end, was that what many of the researchers really wanted was to have something as neutral as Building 20 had been—not so much a piece of architecture that tried to respond to their needs as a leftover building that had no architectural aspirations at all.

Hardly everyone felt that way about the Stata Center, however; plenty of the scientists liked it, and found it spirited and energizing. Irving and Marilyn Lavin, art historians who were close friends of Frank and Berta's and made a point of visiting almost every Gehry building, recalled walking through Stata and seeing a student working with her computer in a nook off the "student street," the main public space. How did she like it? the Lavins asked her. Did she find it confusing to get around? "She said, 'I just love it, it's my favorite place on earth, because I never know what I'm going to run into,'" Irving Lavin said. "She said every move you make is unexpected. I found that very moving, the way that the building worked for this kid, who is presumably learning to be a computer programmer, making connections between unconnectable things"—for which Frank's building in effect served as both metaphor and inspiration.

However mixed its reception, a couple of years after its opening in 2004 the building certainly seemed to be one of the high points in MIT's drive to become a more inventive architectural patron, an effort that also included new buildings by Steven Holl, Charles Correa, and Kevin Roche. Then, in 2007, the administration of MIT turned against Frank, claiming that a section of the building that served as an outdoor amphitheater was causing leaks and structural deficiencies in the building, and filed suit against Gehry Partners and the contractors, Skanska and NER Construction Management. The building did in fact leak in several places, which Frank attributed to last-minute changes made to save money, most of which he said were ordered by MIT against his wishes, although he did not dispute that one of the changes did originate in his office and acknowledged that he had responsibility for it.

The problems were corrected and the suit was settled—"amicably," according to all parties—in 2010. The whole matter might have faded away—after all, the Stata was far from the first building to have leaks that were repaired, with the costs covered by insurance companies—but for a campaign begun by John Silber, the former president of Boston University across the Charles River, who saw the Stata Center as the symbol of all that he thought was wrong with contemporary architecture. Silber put a picture of the building on the cover of a book that he titled *Architecture of the Absurd: How "Genius" Disfigured a Practical Art.* There was little doubt who Silber believed was the "genius" who was destroying architecture: it was Frank Gehry, and Silber did more than make the Stata Center the poster building for indefensible and irrational architecture. The book attacked a number of architects, including Daniel Libeskind and I. M. Pei, but Silber saved his worst vitriol for Frank and attacked almost everything he had ever done, with erroneous charges that not just Stata but all of his buildings were badly engineered and badly designed, that they all cost more than they were supposed to and, Silber clearly believed, far more than they were worth. Silber's conclusion was that Frank's buildings were made up of elements that served "no obvious purpose unless to prostrate all visitors before the gigantic ego of the architect," he wrote, in a reference to the stainless steel roof elements of the Fisher Center at Bard.

The book was a polemic, a rant for which Frank's architecture proved an easy target because it could seem so willful and arbitrary. To Silber it was unthinkable that the odd shapes of Gehry buildings could have emerged from a rational planning process, or from any degree of cooperation with a client. None of his specific charges about the Stata Center turned out to be true, save for the error that Frank admitted and corrected. Errors by the contractor and not Gehry Partners turned out to be responsible for most of the problems, including the most serious one, which required rebuilding the amphitheater. In the end, Frank's responsibility turned out to be relatively minor. But he was the building's designer, and he was more of a public figure than the contractor, the president of MIT, or anyone else connected to the building, and so he was the natural target of complaints. The combination of Silber's polemic, the lawsuit, and the bewilderment of those MIT scientists who had trouble dealing with any unorthodox work of architecture left Strata, in many ways one of Frank's most thoughtful buildings, with a mixed legacy.

Things went far better with Frank's next ventures in Europe, the three curvy, leaning towers he designed for Düsseldorf, known as Der Neue Zollhof, that were completed in 1998, and the project for Berlin, DZ Bank, that had intrigued Paul Allen when he saw its model in Frank's office. Berlin was different from almost anything Frank had ever been asked to do. It was, first, a bank headquarters, with a lavish budget. And it was on a prominent site in Pariser Platz—opposite the Brandenburg Gate, beside the Hotel Adlon, and adjacent to the memorial to the Jews slaughtered in the Holocaust that Peter Eisenman was designing. Frank's previous projects in Germany did not seem to have aroused feelings one way or another so far as his Jewish identity was concerned, but designing something on this emotionally charged site in the heart of Berlin was another matter.

The location presented him with another challenge. The authorities in charge of urban planning in the reunified Berlin in the 1990s were committed to a traditional view of urbanism: buildings were not permitted to be too high or too unusually shaped, and they had to be built out to the street line and aligned with their neighbors. It was a prescription that, as in many cities, pushed architecture toward a degree of homogeneity, and it had the virtue of preventing certain kinds of design disasters. But it also limited creative responses, and it was not the kind of regulation that encouraged Frank's approach to architecture.

Frank's solution was unusual, and made the building remarkable in his oeuvre. He designed a sleek five-story façade of buff-colored limestone, its material matching the surrounding buildings, although he did not replicate any of their details, and instead figured out a way to follow the dictates of the planners while expressing his own ideas. The windows are deeply recessed, and the balcony balustrades are floating planes of glass; the geometry feels almost too heavy and solid, as if it were designed to protect something within, which is exactly what it does. The main part of the

Atrium of DZ Bank in Berlin, with its "horse's head" conference room

building consists of offices around a wood-paneled atrium with a glass roof, and in the center of the atrium is a four-story-high structure of stainless steel, its curvy form resembling an enormous, abstract horse's head. Like all of Frank's unusual shapes, the horse's head required the digital capabilities of the CATIA system, all the more so because the bank insisted on a level of refinement that went beyond Bilbao and other projects. In Berlin, the stainless steel panels were set in perfect seams so that the form would appear as if made of a single piece, like an airplane, rather than overlapping slightly, like shingles.

The structure contains an elaborate conference center, but its real purpose is to be the pearl in the oyster, the moment of architectural intensity that is the reason for the heavy protective shell. What Frank did in Berlin to solve the problem the planners' demands set before him was to turn his architecture inside out. Instead of making his architecture a sculptural form that he played off against the rest of the city, he made it into something that he could play off against himself. The building as a whole became a kind of Cartesian grid, a rational backdrop against which the irrational form of the horse's head engages in lyrical counterpoint. Unlike most of Frank's other buildings, where emotion was as visible as it might be on a psychoanalyst's couch, in Berlin he was offering sensation hidden within a discreet, controlled interior. It was what he had planned to do in the town-house interior he had designed long before for Christophe de Menil, which was never built; now, decades later, he was once again experimenting with the creation of powerful architectural space that would be hidden entirely behind a conventional façade. It was, in a sense, a metaphor for public propriety and private, internal passions. But in Berlin the formal, somber façade took on another meaning as well: an implicit acknowledgment of the complex feelings a Jewish architect would inevitably have designing a building on a prominent site in the center of a city where Jews once felt it essential to keep private thoughts bottled up within themselves. Most of all, Frank was showing here, in a way that he had not explicitly done in a built work until now, that he could represent passion and dignity together.

The restraint demonstrated in Berlin would provide a template for one of the few large museums Frank would work on after Bilbao, the Philadelphia Museum of Art, where he was asked to reorganize and expand the galleries without altering the iconic façade of the museum's classical 1928 building, which contains the famous "Rocky steps." When Anne d'Harnoncourt, the museum's longtime director, who greatly admired Bilbao, asked him in 2002 if he could figure out how to improve and expand the Philadelphia museum in a way that would be just as appealing as Bilbao while staying within the confines of the original structure, designed by Horace Trumbauer and Julian Abele, Frank was excited by the challenge. He saw it as a chance to demonstrate that he was not interested solely in creating unusual sculptural objects and that he could defer to other architects when deference was called for. D'Harnoncourt's sudden death in 2008 delayed the project, but it continued under the guidance of Gail Harrity, one of Thomas Krens's lieutenants in the Bilbao project who had become the Philadelphia museum's chief operating officer, and Timothy Rub, D'Harnoncourt's successor. They worked with Frank to develop a new gallery space underneath the front steps and to reorganize almost all of the museum's interior workings and display spaces. Philadelphia, Frank thought, was the un-Bilbao, the natural complement to the Guggenheim, with none of his architecture on the outside and all of the thrills hidden on the inside.

Back home, or partway home, in Chicago, the post-Bilbao years also gave Frank his chance to have the Pritzker family, his good friends since he had won the Pritzker Prize in 1989, become his clients, at least symbolically. The Pritzkers did not tend to socialize with the winners of the prize that bore their name, but Frank once again had managed to carve out a special category for himself. Jay Pritzker and his wife, Cindy, had a winter home in Rancho Santa Fe, outside San Diego, and a casual invitation to Frank, Berta, and their sons to drive down from Los Angeles for a visit had led to an ongoing friendship between the two families, as well as to an invitation to Frank to join the Pritzker Prize jury and help determine future winners. The friendship was based on far more than a common love of art and architecture. Cindy and Jay Pritzker had a relaxed irreverence that appealed to both Frank and Berta. They were not above sharing their worries and anxieties; like Frank and Berta, they were sophisticated people of the world whose ambitions did not hide an unpretentious, low-key manner. Cindy Pritzker, in particular like so many people, found Frank an easy person in whom to confide.

When Richard M. Daley, the mayor of Chicago, in 1997 promoted the idea of creating a public-private partnership to construct a new park over railroad yards adjacent to the Art Institute on Michigan Avenue, it was almost inevitable that the Pritzkers, as the city's preeminent philanthropic and business leaders, would become involved. Jay Pritzker had suffered a stroke earlier that year, but Cindy played an active role on the art committee for the park, which was to be completed in 2000 and called Millennium Park. The master plan was by Skidmore, Owings & Merrill, who, in deference to the mayor's professed fondness for flower and planter beds, had designed the park in a traditional style. Cindy Pritzker was not impressed. To her, a park with gaslights and ornamental ironworks was not the way to commemorate the arrival of the twenty-first century.

"I didn't understand what millennium they were talking about," she said. "I thought it was terrible. It wasn't the sort of park we should build. I said if you build with someone like Frank Gehry, you wouldn't need anything else." In that case, she was asked, would her family be willing to support bringing Gehry in? She polled her children, who shared her eagerness to underwrite what would be Frank's first piece of architecture in Chicago. It made perfect sense in Pritzker's mind: Chicago was known as America's first city of architecture; with Bilbao, Frank was considered America's preeminent architect, and the Pritzker family, as donors of the Pritzker Prize, were closely associated with supporting important new architecture. Having Frank design something for Millennium Park would bring all of these things together.

A lifetime of Chicago politics had taught Cindy Pritzker to know when to stay in the background, and she thought the project had a better chance of succeeding if she let the invitation to Frank come from the mayor and the rest of the planning committee. She and her children would provide the lead gift, but she wanted the city to be invested in the project. A delegation went from Chicago to Los Angeles to ask Frank if he would consider designing a band shell to serve as a focal point of Millennium Park. At first he declined, telling them that there was no way he could get such a project completed in time for the millennium, two years away. "So one of them said, 'That's too bad, because we know someone who will be very disappointed in you,'" Pritzker remembered. "He said, 'Who's that?' They said 'Cindy.' He said, 'I'll do it.'"

Frank designed what became in effect an outdoor music pavilion, a new, and far more elaborate, version of the Hollywood Bowl or the Merriweather Post Pavilion from the early days of his practice. The final design for the band shell, named for Jay Pritzker, who died in 1999, has Frank's characteristic ribbons of stainless steel, exuberantly billowing around the stage. A metalwork trellis arches over the seating area, which contains four thousand fixed seats and room for another seven thousand people on the lawn, containing sound amplification equipment that gives the pavilion acoustics more like those of an interior concert hall than an outdoor music venue.

As with all of his projects, Frank went through multiple versions of the design, and initially favored one that was simpler and heavier than the final scheme, with a more visible structure. "It was a very simple model that I think he was relating to Chicago—it was a big shoulder thing and it was sort of maybe Louis Sullivan or Frank Lloyd Wright," Cindy Pritzker recalled. "He said to me, 'You know, this is very Chicago.' And I said, 'I know, but I want it to be very Frank.'"

And so it became. Cindy Pritzker knew Frank well enough to know that however much he loved Chicago and was excited to be adding something to its architectural legacy, he was never going to do his best work if he was trying too hard to fit into a historic architectural tradition. She knew when he was being too self-conscious in his design, and she made it a point to remind him that he needed to relax and be himself. It had been her idea to have him design the pavilion in the first place, which she did because she felt that Chicago could benefit from having a Frank Gehry, not because she felt Frank could benefit by trying to "Chicagoize" his architecture. Persuading him to put that idea aside was a contribution Cindy Pritzker made to the project that was as important, in some ways, as any other.

All of Millennium Park, which also included a monumental sculpture by Anish Kapoor and a fountain and electronic sculpture by Jaume Plensa, ran behind schedule and did not open until 2004. The Pritzkers honored Frank twice around the time the pavilion opened. They scheduled the presentation of the Pritzker Prize for 2005 at the Jay Pritzker Pavilion, the second time a Frank Gehry project was used as the locale for the event in its yearly rotation to a different architecturally significant location around the world. And Tom Pritzker, who had taken over from his father as head of the family enterprises, invited Frank and Berta to join him, his wife, Margot, and his mother on a trip to China that coincided with Frank's seventy-fifth birthday.

The Pritzkers and the Gehrys would make several other trips together to distant locations, including to India, and as Frank became closer to the Pritzkers over the years, he began to tease Tom and his family about when he would receive another Pritzker Prize. "We all said, 'Yes, you should, but you're not going to,'" Cindy Pritzker said. On the trip to China, however, Tom Pritzker decided it was time to play a friendly joke on Frank. The Pritzkers told Frank they wanted him to accompany them to a Buddhist temple that was being reconstructed, where there would be a luncheon to mark Frank's birthday. Frank was seated next to a man in robes who was described as the priest in charge of the temple. "I know your work and I understand that you have won an important prize, but you've done so much important work since, you deserve another one," he said, speaking through a translator.

"You see?" Frank said to the Pritzkers. Then, Cindy Pritzker remembered, "Tom got up and spoke. And he said, 'This is one of our prizewinners and special laureates. His name is Frank Gehry. And, as a matter of fact, he has done so much for our prize that we've decided to award him another medal.'" Frank was called to the front of the room and handed a box. Within it was a fake Pritzker Prize medal. The Buddhist priest and the staff at the temple, it turned out, were all employees of the Pritzkers' hotel in Shanghai, who had been cast in an elaborate ruse to pretend to give Frank a second Pritzker Prize. When Frank looked at the medal, he saw that the name on it, instead of Frank Gehry, was Frank Goldberg.

16

New York: Trials and Triumphs

E ver since the painful moment early in his career when his designs
for Christophe de Menil's town house were abandoned, New York
City had been, for Frank, the unattainable, the mountain that he
would try repeatedly to climb, only to find himself sliding back down. In
1987, his friend David Childs, a prominent design partner at Skidmore,
Owings & Merrill, invited him to collaborate on an entry into an invited
competition to replace Madison Square Garden with a trio of office towers
and an improved version of Pennsylvania Station below; nothing came of
it except a general sense that the two had gotten along, despite their very
different sensibilities, and they both agreed that someday they should try
again. Frank, Childs would remember, "was so eager to know how everything worked in a tall office building—he was like a sponge. All the technical stuff interested him, not just the aesthetics." In 1996 Warner Bros.
invited Frank to make a proposal to redesign the exterior of One Times
Square, and a few years later the developer Ian Schrager asked him to
design a hotel for a site on Astor Place. Neither of these projects went
ahead, either.

Frank's first completed work in New York would turn out to be not a
skyscraper but a suite of rooms inside a skyscraper: a cafeteria and private dining rooms for Condé Nast, the magazine publishing company that
owned *The New Yorker*, *Vogue*, and *Vanity Fair*. Frank had been friendly
for years with S. I. Newhouse, the publisher who owned Condé Nast,
and his wife, Victoria, an architecture historian. The Newhouses were
prominent art collectors, avid followers of architecture, and close friends
with Philip Johnson and David Whitney; they had been introduced to
Frank and Berta at a dinner party given by Jill Spalding, a mutual friend,
in Brentwood in the early 1990s. It had been another of Frank's instant

friendships: they talked not only about art and architecture, but also about music, an interest they shared. Before long the Newhouses were visiting Frank's house and several of his other works in Los Angeles. A few years later, Frank and the Newhouses would travel together to Japan, and then they would bond even further over music when Frank took the Newhouses to a concert at Lincoln Center and introduced them to György Sándor Ligeti, a twentieth-century Hungarian composer whose work he particularly admired. Victoria and Si Newhouse would become avid fans of contemporary music, and later Frank would encourage Victoria Newhouse, who had written a book on the architecture of contemporary museums that was highly admiring of Bilbao, to take new concert halls and opera houses as her next subject.[*]

It was not long after meeting Frank, when he was showing them around the Schnabel house in Brentwood, that the Newhouses began to think about becoming Frank's clients as well as his friends. In 1995 they invited him to build a weekend house for them in Bellport, on eastern Long Island, where they had purchased a waterfront site. Frank joined Si Newhouse on a helicopter ride out from Manhattan to see the site, and began to work on a design for the publisher and his wife. He produced a scheme that was to have consisted of several boxy and round sections arranged around a courtyard, which was to be covered by a large sculptural form facing toward the water. The house had echoes of the Schnabel house and the Winton guesthouse, woven together with the cowl-like shapes that called to mind some of the more public work he was doing at the time, such as the "horse's head" conference room in Berlin. The Newhouses were eager participants in Frank's working process, and shared his feeling that the house they envisioned was emerging, step by step, out of a continuous dialogue among the three of them. As it moved toward a final version, however, external circumstances intervened. The attractive waterfront site was also close to a main road, and the more the Newhouses thought about it, the more uncomfortable they became with building their dream house where they could never be fully free of traffic noise. When a neighbor threatened to object to seeing anything new built on the property, they decided to abandon the project altogether.

"That made us all the more eager to work with Frank," Victoria Newhouse said. As the house design was proceeding, Condé Nast was making

---

[*] Newhouse's book *Sight and Sound* (New York: Monacelli Press, 2012) referred to Disney Hall as "a landmark of the twenty-first century."

plans to move to a new skyscraper at Times Square, and Si Newhouse asked Frank if he had any interest in designing the offices. He declined: he knew that designing hundreds of identical editors' cubicles was not the job for him, no matter who the client was; he also knew that Newhouse, however genuine his admiration for cutting-edge art and architecture, viewed those pursuits as a personal passion, not as a business matter, and he feared that he would find Newhouse a less supportive client at the office than he had been at home. James Truman, then the company's editorial director, proposed that instead of asking Frank to design the entire office, perhaps some special portion of it might be found. Why not a cafeteria for the staff? Truman suggested. The project, which expanded to include a series of private dining rooms, would fill only half a floor, but Frank considered it a much more interesting opportunity than designing the office would have been. "We had the greatest time working on that," Victoria Newhouse said. "We would fly out every month and 'play' with Frank."

Although the cafeteria project was far smaller than the kind of jobs Frank was now doing, he knew that the Newhouses wanted it to be special, and that designing a gathering place for the editors of some of the world's most influential magazines would bring this room more attention than many freestanding buildings. And it would mean he had done something in New York at last. Frank's hopes were realized. The Newhouses, partly in sorrow over the curtailment of their house project, gave him free rein, and he began to experiment with curving glass partitions, trying to duplicate in glass the same kind of curving, swooping forms he had been making in metal. The room, which cost $12 million, had more than seventy enormous pieces of glass, each bent and curved in a slightly different position, set under a titanium ceiling. It was laid out mainly as a series of rounded booths, in effect giving almost all of the occupants a seating niche not unlike the ones Philip Johnson had designed at the Four Seasons restaurant, long a favored haunt of Condé Nast editors.

But unlike at the Four Seasons, where every material spoke of luxury, Frank wanted to coax special effects out of common materials: along with the voluptuously curving glass, there was bright yellow Formica on all the tabletops. The ordinariness of the Formica was in deliberate contrast to the extravagance of the curving glass partitions, and Victoria Newhouse remembered being impressed with Frank's determination to fine-tune the mix of materials. "On one of our visits we sat down and looked at what he had done, and he said, 'Oh, this is awful, it looks like a nightclub.' We

Edwin Chan (*left*) oversees David Nam and Anand Devarajan completing a model of the proposed New York Times Building.

admired the fact that he himself felt it wasn't right, and we had implicit faith that he would make it right."

In 2000, not long after the Condé Nast cafeteria was finished, another opportunity arose for Frank and David Childs to collaborate on a skyscraper. This one was for an unusual client, the New York Times Company, which had joined forces with the real estate developer Forest City Ratner to build a new headquarters building on Eighth Avenue, not far from its longtime home off Times Square. The *Times*, despite passionately advocating the value of architecture in its pages, had a long history of ignoring its critics' advice when it came to its own facilities; most of its offices, including its main newsroom, were mediocre places at best, neither efficient nor well designed. In the late 1990s, a younger publisher, Arthur Ochs Sulzberger Jr., saw no reason that the paper needed to remain in a building constructed around the demands of a printing plant when all of its printing was being done elsewhere, and he envisioned a fresher, more progressive face for the company in the digital age. Sulzberger organized a committee that included Herbert Muschamp, the architecture critic, and charged it with coming up with a list of distinguished architects. The company decided to ask a small group of architects to produce conceptual schemes for a new building.

It was no surprise that Frank was high on Muschamp's list. But others on the committee were equally convinced that Frank should join the competition. Aware that his lack of skyscraper experience could be considered a liability, he asked David Childs once again to join forces with him, and they set about producing a scheme to compete with proposals by Norman Foster, César Pelli, and Renzo Piano. Excited by the prospect of designing a building that would somehow express the spirit and the energy of *The New York Times*, Frank and Childs studied the paper carefully, met with editors and writers, and tried to understand the process of producing a daily newspaper. They came up with a design that attempted to marry Frank's interest in wavy, curvy forms with the glass towers that Childs's firm, Skidmore, Owings & Merrill, specialized in, with a large, glass-enclosed newsroom at the base, and undulating planes of glass twisting slightly as they rose forty stories into the sky and splayed out at the top. A huge version of the *Times*'s Gothic logo was at the top, turned into an abstraction by being imprinted on Frank's curving glass. Both the executives of the newspaper and of Forest City Ratner, somewhat to Frank's surprise, reacted positively, and he and Childs were given to believe that they had the inside track.

Then everything began to fall apart. Childs began to wonder if the project was really as much of a collaboration as he had intended it to be; while he liked the final result, he had no doubt that there was a lot more of Frank in it than of Skidmore, Owings & Merrill, and he was not comfortable being perceived as merely in a supporting role. He dropped hints that he might prefer to step aside, which would have made executing the project especially difficult for Frank. Then the executives of Forest City and the Times Company who were working on the project let it be known that once the project got under way, they wanted to have weekly meetings in New York, and that all of the principals, including Frank, had to commit to being there.

Frank was happy to come often to New York, but he was not going to promise to be there every week, which to him felt tantamount to moving there. No other client had ever put him on so rigorous a schedule, and he began to wonder if the *Times*, for all its good intentions, was beginning to act less like an idealistic newspaper trying to become a patron of architecture than like any other big corporation or real estate developer. He called

David Childs and proposed that they withdraw. Childs, already anxious about being perceived as playing the pragmatist to Frank's artist, did not argue. He composed a simple letter of resignation from the competition, which he convinced Frank was more in both of their interests to send than a version Frank had drafted, an emotional paean to the aspirations of architecture. They sent Childs's letter and returned the $50,000 that each competitor had been given toward the expenses of preparing their design.

And so Frank once again had walked away from a situation that could have been a landmark moment in his career. While he and Childs had not been formally chosen, every signal was that they were about to be, and both the newspaper and Bruce Ratner of Forest City were stunned by their decision to withdraw. The last thing they had expected was to be fired by an architect before they had even hired him. Frank had come to like most of the people he had met at the *Times*, but he had also become keenly aware that Arthur Sulzberger was not Si Newhouse, and that even the chairman of the New York Times Company had to deal with a board of directors, stockholders, and a bevy of managers and editors. The question of whom his client would really be nagged him; the problems with MIT and Walt Disney Hall as multiheaded clients were still all too raw. The prospect of dealing with a large public corporation gave him the same anxiety and foreboding he had had long ago when he walked away from the opportunity that Victor Gruen had offered him in Paris: it was not worth doing if he was going to give up the feeling that he was in control.

Frank was back in New York City on September 11, 2001, his twenty-sixth wedding anniversary, working on another New York project that would not come to fruition, the renovation of Lincoln Center. Marshall Rose, a real estate developer whom Frank had met during the Madison Square Garden project and who was married to the actress Candice Bergen, was active on the board of Lincoln Center, and suggested that Frank would be the right architect to inject a shot of adrenaline into the campus of the staid cultural complex, whose major buildings were nearly half a century old. At one point Frank was asked to look into the notion of putting a glass roof over Lincoln Center's central plaza, and he agreed to study its feasibility. The dramatic scheme would become public in 2002, before his studies were complete; Frank was not even certain that he was committed to the idea, but published images of Lincoln Center's famous plaza covered by a vaulted roof of glass caused such a public outcry that the center's board ended up not only rejecting the plan but deciding that it no longer wanted to work with Frank at all. At Lincoln Center his name became in a way the opposite of what it was in Bilbao, so closely associated with an unpopular design that he was no longer viewed as a credible architect for the project, even if he were to propose something completely different.

Frank's fall from grace at Lincoln Center would not occur until the following year, however, and on the morning of September 11, all seemed well in New York. The huge, sprawling new Guggenheim Museum for downtown still seemed plausible, despite the problems in raising the money to build it. Frank was preparing for a presentation meeting scheduled with the construction committee of Lincoln Center, which was eager to hear his thoughts. Alejo, who was living in the city after graduating from the Rhode Island School of Design, was finishing a mural he had produced for a new Issey Miyake store in Lower Manhattan, which was opening later in the week. Frank had designed the interior, a small job that he had agreed to do so that he could collaborate with his son. Early that morning Berta arrived at the airport in Los Angeles, expecting to board a flight to New York, where she was looking forward both to celebrating her anniversary and to the unveiling of Alejo's mural. It was going to be a wonderful family week in the city.

Frank was still in his room at the Four Seasons Hotel on East 57th Street at the time of the terrorist attack that brought down the towers of the World Trade Center. He watched the events unfold on television and by looking out the window toward the shattered skyline. Berta's flight, of course, never took off, and the Issey Miyake store canceled its opening celebration. The city had ground to a halt, but Frank was startled to get word from Lincoln Center that his meeting was still on. Deeply shaken and sure he was not at his best, he made his way through most of the presentation, then said he felt uncomfortable, excused himself, and walked back to the hotel. He tracked down Alejo as well as Leslie and Brina, both of whom were by then also living in New York, and they all made their way to the Four Seasons, where Frank would remain for the next several days, while Berta and Sam stayed in Los Angeles. He communicated mostly by phone to his New York friends, including Herbert Muschamp, who lived just a few blocks from the Trade Center site and was too stunned to leave his apartment. Issey Miyake, equally upset, stayed in his room at the Mercer Hotel, Frank remembered. Frank heard from Peter Lewis, who was in the duplex apartment he maintained on the Upper West Side, and Renzo Piano, who had come to the city on behalf of one of his clients and, like

Frank, was stranded until air service resumed. Lewis, Piano, and Frank's children provided distraction as Frank waited for things to normalize so he could return to Berta in Los Angeles.

Like almost every architect, Frank found it impossible not to think about what should happen on the site of the World Trade Center. He felt strongly that something had to be built—leaving the land empty would be a kind of nonresponse, he felt, and he imagined "a space that is so magnificent it would engage the world," he told Deborah Solomon, who interviewed him in *The New York Times Magazine*. "It could be an indoor park with a lake in it." In the spring of 2002, when he was teaching the seminar he did every other year at Yale, he assigned his students the challenge of designing "a building that could be spiritual . . . a symbol of openness and tolerance" for the site. And he used the class's travel budget to take the students to Istanbul to see the Hagia Sophia in the hope that it would provide inspiration.

But a few months later, when the Lower Manhattan Development Corporation, the agency set up to oversee rebuilding, set up a competition to create a master plan for the site, Frank refused to participate, telling *The New York Times* that it was "demeaning" for the corporation to pay the architects it invited to compete a fee of only $40,000, a fraction of what it would cost to prepare a design. "I can understand why the kids did it, but why would people my age do it?" he said. "When you're only paid $40,000, you're treated as if that is your worth."

It was one of Frank's rare public relations gaffes. His lifelong anxieties about respect and money, and his tendency to equate the two, had blinded him to the fact that most of his fellow architects thought of participation in the rebuilding of the World Trade Center site as a patriotic duty, not a source of income. Both Peter Eisenman and Charles Gwathmey attacked him in public forums after his interview with Deborah Solomon was published. Frank appeared not as if he was defending the professional stature of architects, but as if he were demanding more money for performing what many of his colleagues thought was a civic obligation. And then, for good measure, he was accusing his fellow architects of selling themselves cheap.

Ever since the overwhelming public response to Bilbao a few years before, Frank's relationship to many of his peers, especially to many of the other architects who had been part of Philip Johnson's "kids" circle, had been characterized by a slight, simmering tension. He was one of them, and they admired his work. Yet his wide fame was a reminder that he had also achieved something that had eluded the rest of them, and there were undercurrents of jealousy. Frank had not achieved his renown by pandering to popular taste or by "dumbing down" his architecture, so his peers could not resent him for that. They were waiting for him to make a misstep, and his statements about building at Ground Zero gave them a reason to pounce.

The Lower Manhattan Development Corporation, however, seemed to bear no grudges. After it selected a master plan by Daniel Libeskind that called for several office buildings, a memorial, and two cultural buildings, the corporation offered Frank the commission to design one of the arts buildings, a performing arts center that was to include a new home for the Joyce, a prominent dance theater, and the Signature Theater Company, a nonprofit Off-Broadway theater. That, too, would turn out to be a long saga that would end in disappointment. Frank's design, a series of cascading boxes, was estimated to cost more than $400 million, but the Lower Manhattan Development Corporation had only a quarter of that in its budget and expected the rest of the money to be raised privately. Political turmoil, frequent changes in the nature of the program, fund-raising problems, and site complications caused by the construction of adjacent buildings led to multiple postponements, continual requests to Frank to redesign the project, and no clear starting date. The Signature eventually gave up and decamped for midtown, where it was offered the chance to have a custom-designed home of its own in the lower floors of a new high-rise apartment tower on West 42nd Street. The company's management had enjoyed working with Frank and was as frustrated as he was by the long delays downtown, so they invited him to come along and design the new theater complex. It was a small job but a happy one, and he produced one of his finest interiors, a set of three distinctive theaters that served as a reminder, like the Fisher Center at Bard, that for the right client he was capable of designing inventive and functional projects on a tight budget.

When the new Pershing Square Signature Theater opened in 2012, the performing arts center on the World Trade Center site had still not begun construction, and the program changed yet again into a multidisciplinary arts center in which the Joyce, which had waited patiently for a decade, would play only a partial role. At the dedication of the Signature complex, Mayor Michael Bloomberg hailed Frank and said that New York "needed more Frank Gehry buildings," but the new president of the downtown center, Maggie Boepple, had already let it be known that she did not share the mayor's and the Signature Theater Company's belief in Frank. She had barely communicated with him since she took over management of the troubled arts center in 2012. He had been waiting for instructions about how he should redesign the project yet again, but heard nothing. Instead, late in the summer of 2014, almost exactly ten years to the day from when it was announced with great fanfare that Frank Gehry had been engaged to design the performing arts center, officials told *The New York Times* that they had decided to start all over again with a new architect. Frank was never notified, and it was only when a reporter from the *Times* called him for comment that he learned that he had been fired.

B y then, however, the New York curse had been broken, at least some-what, in 2007 by the completion of Frank's first freestanding building in the city, the headquarters of IAC, the holding company of Internet-related businesses headed by Barry Diller. Diller, an executive with a pow-erful instinct for the new, wanted to move his company to the Chelsea waterfront, and he acquired a site on West 18th Street, a block away from the High Line, the elevated freight train tracks that were in the process of being converted to a new public park. And he wanted a notable building

IAC Building in Manhattan

that would serve as a public symbol of his company the way the Seagram Building, Lever House, the Woolworth Building, and other New York headquarters structures of earlier generations had done.

Diller asked Marshall Rose, an old acquaintance, for advice on finding an architect, and Rose, still eager to help Frank make a mark in New York after the Lincoln Center episode, suggested he call Frank. Diller initially said no—Frank Gehry was too strong-willed, he said, and he feared that he would be expensive and difficult to control. Rose urged him to meet Frank, telling him that Frank, like Diller, loved to sail, and that they could at least talk about sailing if they didn't see eye-to-eye about architecture. The two men spent a day together in Los Angeles and spoke for hours. Diller was as impressed with Frank's low-key manner as he was with the Walt Disney Concert Hall, which they toured together. Diller decided he could collaborate with Frank, and hired him in 2003 without interviewing another architect.

The ten-story glass building that Frank designed for IAC and Marshall Rose's company, Georgetown, which became his partner in the venture, was in some ways a continuation of the ideas Frank explored in the Condé Nast cafeteria: an essay in swooping, curving glass, this time assembled into an entire building. Diller wanted the building to be white, and Frank obliged; both men liked the idea that the form bore a certain resemblance to a set of sails billowing in the wind. Glass buildings often feel brittle, but this one came off as relaxed, as if the glass had been molded like clay. The white glass and the curving shape made the building look a bit like a computer rendering.

Frank produced fifty-one different models during the year it took to design the project, which put to rest any concerns Diller might have had about Frank's willingness to be flexible. For Frank, however, the most important challenge was not aesthetics alone, but their connection to economics. Diller insisted that the building be roughly competitive with other high-end Manhattan office space, which meant that while it would be far from cheap, Frank would have to stay within a clear budget. Far from troubling him, the constraints excited him: if the IAC project was going to be his chance to prove that he could build something in the tough environment of New York, why not, he felt, show that he could do it at a reasonable cost as well? New York, Frank decided, would be where he would put to rest the complaint that had dogged him for years: that his work was extravagant and expensive. It was worth giving up the high ambition of Bilbao and Walt Disney Concert Hall if the world could see that he had pleased the demanding Barry Diller and put up a distinctive, functional, and economically viable building in the middle of Manhattan. Then maybe people would stop thinking of him as a crazy artist who had no interest in the practical side of architecture.

It was a struggle, in part because Diller turned out to be a client who really did want a bespoke building. Some of the early versions included faceted pieces of flat glass placed at slight angles to one another, which Frank thought would be a cheaper way to give the impression from a distance that the surface was curved. Why, Diller asked, were there little lines across the windows, where the faceted pieces joined? He pushed Frank to find a way to curve the glass on the exterior, and eventually Gehry Partners was able to work with a European curtain wall company, Permasteelisa, to produce 1,437 milky-white glass panels, almost all of them slightly different in shape, at a cost that Diller and Marshall Rose were willing to accept.

Frank's frequent visits to New York gave him a chance for numerous dinners with his circle of New York friends like Claes Oldenburg, Richard Cohen, Martin and Mildred Friedman, and Herbert Muschamp, with whom he also had a regular Sunday morning telephone call. He did not see a great deal of his two daughters, both of whom were living in New York. Leslie, an artist and jewelry designer who had worked for several years as a copy editor at *House & Garden* magazine, was living in an apartment Frank had purchased for her, trying to further another career as a writer. Frank's old friend Gere Kavanagh, who knew Leslie as a child and reconnected with her when she was at *House & Garden*, remembered having lunch with Leslie in the cafeteria of the Condé Nast Building, where *House & Garden* was published. They were surrounded by Frank's curving glass partitions, titanium panels, and yellow tables, but Leslie had made it clear that she did not want to talk about her father. Kavanagh, fond of Leslie and eager to resume the friendship, did not mention him, and the two had a warm and lively conversation. But the irony of their surroundings did not escape her. "I thought, wow, is this a collage of life," Kavanagh said, realizing that she was talking to her old friend's daughter in a famous space he had designed, a fact that neither of the women acknowledged. "But we had a wonderful time," she recalled.

Brina lived in Brooklyn, where she worked as a yoga instructor after several years at *The New York Review of Books*. Frank recalled that on one of

Leslie Gehry Brenner

the rare nights when he was having dinner in New York with Brina, the writers Joan Didion and John Gregory Dunne, whose work often appeared in the *Review*, were in the same restaurant and came over to their table to say hello—to Brina, not to Frank, who realized that he had by then become so accustomed to celebrity that he did not imagine that two famous people would be coming to greet his daughter and not him. He had enough perspective to view the event with amusement, but it served as a reminder that the subject of fame and the demands it made was still a sore point with both of his daughters. They felt that he had never had enough time for them when they were growing up, and in response, like many people who feel powerless and have no way of asserting themselves except to withdraw, both of them often told him they were busy when he called to say he was in New York and wanted to see them.

Frank's relationship with Brina was not helped by an incident that occurred in the mid-1990s, when Brina was working for Frank's old friend Peter Arnell, who in his publishing days had produced Frank's first monograph in his advertising and branding consultancy. Arnell told Frank that on a recruiting trip to the Rhode Island School of Design he had met Alejandro, and had been impressed by his talents as an artist and graphic designer. Would Frank mind if he extended a job offer to his son? Frank realized instantly that it could be a problem for Brina, who might, he thought, feel possessive about her status in the office of one of his old friends. He asked Arnell to make sure that Brina was comfortable with having her half brother as a colleague. She was less than thrilled with the idea, and the situation was not improved when Berta, usually the person who could be counted on to resolve family tensions, lost her temper and in no uncertain terms told Brina that she had no right to be angry. Ultimately both Brina and Alejandro did work for Arnell, but the stresses did not disappear.

Both Leslie and Brina could be described as high-strung, and there could be tensions between the two of them that were as serious as any with Frank. In 2008, the sisters had not spoken for some time to each other or to Frank when Richard Snyder, their uncle—and the only person in the family who seemed able to maintain good relations with everyone, including his former brother-in-law—called Frank to tell him that Leslie was not well and it was imperative that he call her. At that point Leslie had become somewhat reclusive and rarely left her apartment. Her uncle was one of the few people she spoke to with any frequency.

Frank called her, and Leslie brushed off any questions about her health. "It's a woman thing, and not too serious," she told her father. Frank had not spoken to his daughter in months, but he could tell from the tone of her voice that something more was going on. Leslie had already had a surgical procedure that she had not told her father about.

"I said, 'Leslie, I'm taking over, I'm going to get you help,'" Frank recalled. He called his friend Nancy Wexler, Milton Wexler's daughter, who ran the foundation to combat Huntington's and other genetic diseases that her father had started, and lived in New York as the partner of Herbert Pardes, the doctor who headed the New York–Presbyterian hospital system. Wexler and Pardes arranged for Leslie to be admitted to the system's hospital at 168th Street and to have exploratory surgery. It turned out that Leslie had Stage 3 uterine cancer that had gone undetected by her previous doctors, and that she was gravely ill.

Once Frank took charge of the situation, far from rejecting her father's help, Leslie appeared to welcome it. "I did what a father does, and I realized that I should have done that long before," Frank said. He realized that he had used Leslie's withdrawal as an excuse to distance himself from his daughter instead of pressing to become more engaged, and he was overwhelmed with regret. He called Brina, who told her father that she and her sister had not been getting along, and that she was hesitant to see Leslie. Frank was unhappy, but he decided it would be only fair to give Brina time to process the news of her sister's illness, and went on to make an even more difficult call, to Anita. He told his former wife that their daughter had cancer and was in serious condition. He told Anita to get on a plane to New York as soon as she could and said that he would pay for her ticket.

For the next several months, Frank would play a new role as paterfamilias to his original nuclear family. Brina put aside her objections and came to visit Leslie in the hospital; when she arrived, he left the two sisters alone in Leslie's room. When he looked in on them later, he saw them hugging, and he felt that he had begun, in a small way, to heal the wounds of his broken family. Some of his duties involved juggling worlds that until then he had managed to keep entirely separate. Anita met Sam and Alejo for the first time during her trip to New York for Leslie's surgery; Sam remembered feeling sufficiently ill at ease passing time in Leslie's hospital room with Anita that he and his fiancée, Joyce, offered to go downtown and clean up Leslie's apartment for her, the only thing they could think to do that could be helpful to Leslie and also take them away from the hospital. There was an awkward moment of a different sort when Anita, Frank, and Brina were in a hospital waiting room and Elaine May and Diane Sawyer walked by on their way to visit Mike Nichols, who was a patient on the same floor as Leslie. May and Sawyer were excited to see Frank, urged him to go down the hall to visit Nichols, and paid little attention to his former wife and daughter. To Brina and Anita, it seemed like the old story of their family time giving way to Frank's public identity, and they were livid.

Still, Frank, often accompanied by Berta and sometimes by Alejandro and Sam, was Leslie's most regular visitor. Alejandro and Sam became closer to both of their sisters, and Alejandro and Leslie had the happiest time they had ever had together when Leslie invited her brother to share some of the medical marijuana she had been given. "We got stoned as hell and we had a blast," Alejandro said. Nancy Wexler and Herb Pardes were regular visitors as well, and when Frank could not be in New York with Leslie, he would phone her several times a day. He arranged for meals to be sent by courier from the Lowell Hotel on East 63rd Street, where he often stayed, because she disliked the hospital food. Leslie liked that, not only for the food itself but because the gesture made it clear to her—perhaps for the first time—that her well-being was her father's priority. They had long conversations, and Frank held her hand as he sat beside her bed. He took pleasure in feeling close to his daughter at long last. They spoke candidly with each other, and they both understood that Leslie would not recover. Leslie, who had no heirs, agreed with Frank's suggestion that she bequeath her estate to the Wexlers' Hereditary Disease Foundation.[*]

Leslie died on November 16, 2008, less than six months after her diagnosis. It was one month after her fifty-fourth birthday. Anita, who had returned to New York a few days before, was with her, and so was Berta, along with Frank's sister, Doreen. Frank had left briefly. He and the rest of the family

---

[*] Leslie's estate consisted primarily of the value of her apartment. Frank matched the gift with his own funds and directed that they be used to support an annual award that the Hereditary Disease Foundation would give in Leslie's name. The Leslie Gehry Brenner Award for Innovation in Science, Frank wrote in a letter to his friends, "reflects Leslie's many talents and gifts—originality, creativity, spontaneity, precision and rigor—all critical attributes in a scientist."

gathered the next morning in his hotel room—he and Berta were at the Peninsula this time—and Doreen and Brina went together to the funeral home to collect Leslie's ashes. Frank knew that Leslie would die, but the moment still came as a shock, and he was numb. He recalled talking to Tom Krens, who called him about an urgent matter regarding the Guggenheim project in Abu Dhabi, and agreeing to talk to him because he thought it would distract him momentarily from his grief.

Leslie's ashes were brought home to California, and a few weeks later the family group came together one more time to honor her. Frank arranged for a sailboat to take them all to scatter Leslie's ashes in the ocean off the coast of Malibu. It was a slow and painful journey, three miles out to sea, the closest point at which it was legal to scatter the ashes, the quiet shattered only by the sound of the boat's motor, which the captain explained was necessary because the wind direction meant that it would have taken hours to travel that distance by sail power. Frank found the noise especially irritating, and he was relieved when they could return under sail, the motor silenced.

At the three-mile point, Frank and Anita stood together and scattered their daughter's ashes in the water. Richard Snyder, who was there, recalled noting that Berta had stood at the other end of the deck, a respectful distance away, with Alejo and Sam beside her. With her instinctive sense of propriety, she understood that this was the one time that Frank belonged back at Anita's side. When the boat returned to shore, Frank took everyone to the Pacific Dining Car, the old-fashioned steakhouse near his house in Santa Monica, where he had reserved a private room for the group, which included Anita's brother Mark, whom Frank had not seen in years, and her husband, George Brenner. It was the only time that all of the Snyders and all of the Gehrys had ever been together. Frank sat at the end of a long table, overwhelmed with emotion as he thought back to the years when Leslie was growing up. He stood, raised his glass, and offered a toast to his former wife. "I still love you," he said to Anita.

B ruce Ratner, who had grown exceptionally fond of Frank during their meetings about the Times building project, made a point of staying in touch with him after Frank and David Childs withdrew from the project. Ratner let him know that his company, Forest City Ratner, had a number of other things in the works, including an unusual site in Lower Manhattan just south of the Brooklyn Bridge that he thought would be ideal for a very tall apartment tower. And he was beginning to work on Atlantic Yards, a twenty-two-acre project over the Long Island Railroad yards in Brooklyn that was to contain eight million square feet of housing, retail, offices, and a new arena for the New Jersey Nets, the basketball team that Ratner had purchased and planned to move and rename the Brooklyn Nets.

Neither project was a midtown Manhattan skyscraper, but collectively they represented several times more square footage than the New York Times tower. Ratner ended up inviting Frank to do all of it: first to create the master plan for Atlantic Yards and to design several high-rise buildings for the site and the Nets arena, and not long afterward to design the Manhattan apartment tower. The New York work would become the mainstay of the office, which at one point grew to 240 people.

Atlantic Yards would prove to be one of the most frustrating experiences of Frank's career. It was the largest project he had undertaken, and while he welcomed the opportunity to engage in large-scale urban design, it did not necessarily play to his strengths. The glass-enclosed arena he designed as the project's centerpiece was spectacular, and it might have been one of his finest projects. He understood both the excitement of an arena and the role it could play in the cityscape. But the towers were another matter. Almost all of Frank's projects had worked best as one-of-a-kind designs, set off against the urban context. As Bilbao and other projects showed, he could be highly responsive to the context, but he was still designing for the foreground. At Atlantic Yards, however, what he was designing had to be the context. In the hope of creating a sense of background and foreground, he tried to make some of the towers—there were to have been sixteen—understated and focus primarily on the ornate, 620-foot-tall main tower, which he named Miss Brooklyn. But the juxtaposition of plain and fancy looked more like a Gehry bought for full price placed next to several bought at discount.

The project was controversial from the beginning. People objected to its scale, to its placement—it would create a wall of large buildings between the neighborhoods of Fort Greene and Prospect Heights—and to the public subsidies that were a part of it. And most painfully for Frank, the opponents suggested that Ratner had hired him not for his design skill, but in the cynical hope that his reputation would draw attention away from the issues that concerned them. If this were a Frank Gehry project, it couldn't be dismissed as just another gargantuan, developer-driven real estate project, went the logic. And Frank's prestige did in fact help the project surmount some of its political hurdles. But it was at a cost to his own reputation. The novelist Jonathan Lethem, like many Brooklynites, opposed the project, and wrote an open letter to Frank in the online magazine *Slate:* "I've been struggling to understand how someone of your sensibilities can have drifted into such an unfortunate alliance, with potentially disastrous results."

Frank did not reply. And if Bruce Ratner had thought that Frank's name would serve as an insurance policy against controversy, he could not have been more wrong. The project faced numerous lawsuits, and while Forest City Ratner ultimately prevailed, the legal maneuvering delayed the development for years. Frank may have paid a higher price, at least in terms of his reputation, than Forest City Ratner. Jonathan Lethem was not alone in questioning whether Frank had made an unacceptable compromise; many of the critics who could be counted on to write admiringly of his work felt that he had made a mistake, particularly since many of his ideas had been discarded as the project went through multiple revisions to cut costs. "It's fair to ask whether Mr. Gehry and other gifted architects have made a pact with the Devil, compromising their values for the sake of ever bigger commissions," wrote Nicolai Ouroussoff, who had succeeded Herbert Muschamp at *The New York Times.*

By late 2008, with nothing started after more than four years, Ratner had to face a serious problem. The economic crisis that autumn made it impossible to get financing for the apartment towers, and it was clear that they would have to wait. The arena, however, couldn't wait. Legislation allowing new arenas to be tax-exempt was due to expire at the end of 2009, and Ratner could not afford to build the arena without the tax exemption he had counted on. He could not go back on his commitment to bring professional basketball to Brooklyn, or delay it. At Ratner's request, Frank had designed the arena to be closely integrated into the rest of the project—the connection was one of the design's strongest points—but without the apartment towers it would have to be redesigned, quickly, as an entirely different, stand-alone building that could be started before the end of the next year.

"There was no way that Frank could do that," Ratner said. "We had to start from scratch." But Ratner did not actually plan to start from scratch. He decided that the most efficient way to meet the timetable was to find an existing arena that fit the dimensions of the Atlantic Yards site, and see if its architect could rework those plans for Brooklyn. If the aggressive schedule made it impractical for Frank to continue as the arena architect, Ratner's idea that another architect's building could be used as a template made it unthinkable.*

Losing Atlantic Yards and the arena came at a terrible time for Frank, just after Leslie's illness and death. He was well aware that the combination of political and economic problems meant that the apartment towers of Atlantic Yards could not be built for years, and he did not blame Bruce Ratner for that. But he had been counting on the arena. It was the part of the project that he was the most excited about, and given how popular the pending move of the Nets basketball team to Brooklyn was, the arena had been largely immune from the controversy that dogged the rest of Atlantic Yards. Frank was devastated by the news that the project was now going to be designed by another firm.

Ratner took pains to assure him that his other job was not in jeopardy. The Manhattan apartment tower had been a leap of faith for both of them. Frank, in his late seventies, would finally get to build a skyscraper; Ratner, for his part, was putting to the test his instinctive belief that however controversial things might be in Brooklyn, Frank's name would add value to an upscale apartment tower in Manhattan. When he had first proposed asking Frank to do the tower in 2004, he told his executives that he was sure that a building by Frank Gehry could bring higher rents. Some, he recalled, were skeptical. "I said, 'Let's go around the table and everybody write down what higher rent we'll get,'" Ratner said. "Some wrote forty cents [per square foot], fifty cents. Somebody said 10 percent more. So I said, 'Don't worry about it. You're going to get more rent, even if it costs more money.'"

Ratner, like Barry Diller, was cost-conscious, and Frank had to make the building at least roughly competitive with conventional structures. Once again, he took this requirement as an opportunity to prove that if he was not the cheapest architect around, neither was he was an architect whose buildings were by their very nature irrational, difficult, and expensive. "I'm passionate about the challenge to show that good architecture doesn't cost more than schlock," he said.

It would turn out to cost more than "schlock," but not so much as to

---

* The arena that Ratner used as a model was the home of the Indianapolis Pacers, designed by Ellerbe Becket. The banality of the building troubled him, however, and he decided to use the Indiana building only as a rough template, and hired the architecture firm SHoP to rework Ellerbe Becket's plans and give the arena, which was called Barclays Center, more character.

make the project infeasible for Ratner, since Frank willingly accepted the idea that the interior of the building—the elevator, stairs, and apartment layouts—could be relatively conventional, maximizing efficiency. Once again, he took this constraint almost as a matter of pride, because it gave him a chance to demonstrate that he could produce a highly original, one-of-a-kind building that was still practical for a developer to build. Within that, however, lay a paradox: the building had to be different enough from Frank's other work to be economical, and similar enough to his other buildings that it would be identifiable as being by Frank Gehry. In other words, it had to be at once conventional and unique. And it had to some-how prove that Nicolai Ouroussoff was wrong; he hadn't made a pact with the Devil.

Frank's first move was to convince Forest City Ratner that the sixty-six-story building that resulted from simply applying the New York City zoning laws to the site would not do: it felt too stout and bulky to him. He argued for a taller, thinner tower that, while more costly to build, would also have a greater number of expensive upper-floor apartments with spec-tacular views. He experimented with multiple shapes: undulating, swoop-ing towers that seemed like narrower versions of his design for the New York Times Building, twisting towers, curving towers with setbacks, and towers with different twisted sections placed one atop the other, like blocks. As with many of his projects, he relied on models as the centerpiece of the design process, and over the two years of the design process his office would construct several dozen of them, each different from the one before. Frank would look at each one on its own, as if it was a small sculpture, and then he would place it in a large model of the tower's Lower Manhattan neighborhood for the more important test of seeing how it would look in the skyline.

At the same time, on his trips to New York he would look at older tow-ers, trying to analyze them more carefully than he had ever done before. The Woolworth Building was near the site, and he saw the thinness and delicate grace of Cass Gilbert's gleaming terra-cotta tower, once the tallest building in the world. He looked at newer towers by César Pelli, whose tall buildings he admired, he said, because Pelli "understood how to get to an essence and not overdo it. There's clarity." He noticed that Pelli's buildings always seemed to have a clear shape, and that the corners were usually not given over to windows. "So I decided that the corners would be solid, and the only game was the bay window," he said. He realized that the underlying structure didn't have to have an undulating shape if the façade could be made to fold in and out in a dramatic way, which bay windows could do. Having a lot of large, extruded bay windows also offered another advantage: since the rooms would be fairly conventional in shape, any wall containing a bay window would have some added panache, making ordinary rooms, in a sense, feel more Gehryesque.

But a tower whose architectural distinction came only from bay windows, Frank realized, would be banal: if the windows were stacked, they would look like stripes, and the whole thing might bear a disturbing resemblance to a building Frank did not admire, the General Motors Building, a rectangular slab whose façade consists of alternating rows of bay windows and white marble columns. So he set to figuring out how to move the bay windows around, to place them not in vertical rows but in a more inventive arrangement. That was when he began to envision them as flowing in a sculptural form, with a curving façade. He thought of the conversations he had had with his friend Irving Lavin, the Renaissance art historian, about Bernini and Michelangelo, and he thought that the building in some ways evoked the flowing forms of Michelangelo's sculpture, rendered in metal, draped over a slab. But it did not feel right somehow. It felt too rounded to him, as if the curves were fighting with the sharper outline of the slab underneath.

After working on the design for much of one day, Frank went home, went to sleep, and awoke in the middle of the night. "I woke up and thought, 'Bernini,'" he said. "If you look at the edginess of Bernini's folds, they're more architectural." He made a quick sketch of the tower with crisper lines, then went back to sleep. The next morning, he went into the office and stopped at the desk of Susan Beningfield, a young designer who had been assigned to the project. "Do you know the difference between Michelangelo curves and Bernini curves?" he asked. "Yes," Beningfield said. He handed her his drawing from the night before and told her to rework the façade into sharp Bernini curves. Beningfield took the most recent design for the seventy-two-story tower and made its architectural form less fluid and more like folds of fabric hundreds of feet high, with the bay windows at the peak of the swirling folds. The Bernini folds turned the entire façade into a vast bas-relief. From some angles, the building could look as if a breeze were blowing ripples across its surface.

As with all of Frank's buildings, designing was one thing, and making was quite another. Covering the exterior required nearly ten thousand steel panels, almost all of which were different because of the irregular pattern of bay windows swirling down the façade in the manner of sculpted fabric

8 Spruce Street, with the
Woolworth Building to
the left

by Bernini. Permasteelisa, the Italian company that had worked on other
challenging buildings for Frank, was brought in to review the preliminary
design, and its estimates were far above Ratner's budget. It took two years to
refine the design to bring the cost down to the equivalent of simpler panels
of the same material and still not compromise Frank's basic idea.

There was one major change: Frank had initially planned for the glass
of the windows to align with the billowing form of the façade, but curving
glass, not surprisingly, proved too expensive, and it was replaced with flat
glass panels set back from the projecting folds. Again, the office's digital
software made the difference, since it allowed such precise calculations
about each panel's exact shape and where it would fit in the overall pattern
that contractors did not need to inflate their estimates to allow for changes
and the unforeseen problems that arise when decisions about exactly how
certain elements will fit together are not made until the construction pro-

cess has begun. Six subcontractors bid to install the stainless steel panels once the design was set, and they all bid under the budget.

Because the curves fall at different points up and down the façade, there are technically some two hundred different apartment layouts, although the variations from floor to floor are slight. Frank decided to make the south side of the exterior entirely flat, dropping the billowing curves not to save money, but because he liked the idea of having the building look different on that side, as if it had been sliced in two. It reminded him, he said, of a geode, and he felt that it was much more powerful than a building that had been decorated on all sides. To Frank, the tower was not a whole and complete sculptural shape like the Chrysler Building, but a functional slab that had been brought to life by the ornamented panels hung on its exterior. Making one side flat was the final step in the process of moving the design away from the elaborate shapes he had started with and confirming that it was instead a more conventional slab hung with decoration. Technology for Frank was not a route to standardization but a way of making a unique, ornate object that would be affordable to produce.

Bruce Ratner had originally planned that the apartments on the upper floors of the building would be sold as condominiums, while the ones on the lower floors would be rented. The financial crisis of 2008 changed his mind, and all of the apartments were constructed as rental units. Frank was more concerned when Ratner proposed a much more drastic change, which was to stop building the structure at the midpoint and erect only the lower floors to save money. Ratner was worried that it would be difficult to fully rent a building that was to contain more than nine hundred units. Frank was appalled at the thought of eliminating a portion of the building. He had not taken on this project to build a stump, he thought, and he argued that the awkward proportions of a shorter building would undercut all of his architectural ideas. Everything would have been designed differently from the beginning if the plan had been for a smaller building, he said. Ratner, trusting his instinct that the market would recover, decided to move forward.

When the building was finished, it was marketed under the name New York by Gehry, which, however flattering it may have been to Frank, seemed to anoint him as an architect who had a private vision of the city that Bruce Ratner was now making available to everyone. Still, Ratner's early hope was more than borne out: the building, which was also known by its address, 8 Spruce Street, filled quickly despite its huge size. And the recession that had almost caused Ratner to cut short the tower had receded, so much so that 8 Spruce Street was able to command higher rents than anything else in Lower Manhattan. With 8 Spruce there was no doubt that Frank had achieved a major aesthetic success in New York at last, and at the same time he had shown that he could do more than make spectacular museums and concert halls. He could also make a developer a lot of money. By 2011, there was at least some sense of victory in New York, even if the defeats outnumbered the wins.

17

Frank at Eighty

rank's determination to prove that good architecture, or at least his
architecture, did not have to be outrageously expensive was more
than just an attempt to please clients like Bruce Ratner and Barry
Diller. It was something he believed, deeply. Few things bothered him
more than being dismissed as an architect whose buildings were impractical and too expensive. Long after the Guggenheim in Bilbao was finished, when its status as one of the most important buildings of the age
was beyond dispute, Frank was still going out of his way to object to char-
acterizations of it as expensive. "One thing that nobody knows is that my
buildings come in on time and on budget," he said to Jori Finkel of *The
Art Newspaper* in 2014. "Bilbao was built for $300 a square foot, which was
the budget."

In fact, not everything was completed on time. In 1999, Frank took on
his first project in Latin America, the Biomuseo, an environmental center
and museum devoted to showcasing the natural resources of Panama. The
organizers, aware of Berta's background, correctly guessed that he would
be unlikely to turn down an invitation to design a project in her native
country, particularly not one planned for one of its most visible sites, at the
Pacific Ocean entrance to the Panama Canal. Frank designed an exuberant assemblage of shedlike structures with orange, red, yellow, blue, and
green roofs, his most colorful project ever. But problems with funding as
well as with the quality of the local workforce delayed the project for years,
and it took until 2014 to get it finished.

Frank's insistence on being viewed as an architect who was not extravagant was a way of reconciling the two very different sides of his persona—
the part of him that identified with ordinary people, with the family he
had never chosen to reject even as he moved far beyond the world of his

parents, and the part of him that craved fame, status, and the friendship of prominent people. He wanted to believe that his values had not changed from those days, despite his success. And in many ways they had not. He and Berta continued to live in the house in Santa Monica, which was famous but hardly grand; for all its notoriety, by Los Angeles standards it was modest for the residence of a famous person, with neither much land nor much privacy. The Gehrys had expanded it slightly in 1993 to allow their growing sons more space,[*] and a few years later they purchased an adjacent lot to allow room for a larger yard, a garage, and a studio. But even after Frank's friend the landscape architect Laurie Olin helped them create a new back garden, the lot still felt relatively tight and enclosed, a far cry from an estate property.

How and where an architect lives inevitably takes on disproportionate meaning, and this was particularly so in Frank's case, where the question of his choice of domicile played directly into the anxieties he had always felt about his image. Too ordinary made it look like he was denying the success he had a right to enjoy; too grand felt like he was denying the origins he continued to feel proud to identify with. The house in Santa Monica just a couple of blocks north of the messy commercial strip of Wilshire Boulevard still felt like just the right combination of distinctiveness and ordinariness.

Although Frank talked often about moving, he was motivated as much by restlessness as anything else. In 2002 he went so far as to purchase three adjoining lots on Harding Avenue in the southern portion of Venice, near Marina del Rey, where he kept his boat, for which he designed a residential compound for himself and his family. He was curious as to what he could produce if he set his mind once again to the challenge of designing a house for himself and Berta, twenty-five years after doing the house in Santa Monica. But he was more than a little ambivalent about the whole idea, since he had always felt comfortable with the mixture of radical architecture and modest surroundings that the Santa Monica house represented. Both he and Berta identified closely with it, and he would feel a certain vindication when the American Institute of Architects gave the

---

[*] The expansion did not significantly alter the appearance the house from the street, but it did make some portions of the interior more conventional, and Frank knew that he had taken just a bit of the radical edge off of it. "Taking one for the team," is how he explained it to Barbara Isenberg. Philip Johnson told the director Sydney Pollack that he thought Frank had "ruined" the house, but that it was forgivable because he had done it for his family. "He has higher things in the world, forget architecture, he has love. I say that's fine, but build another house."

house its Twenty-Five Year Award in 2012, an award given annually to a distinguished work of architecture that has withstood the test of time.

Then again, if the Santa Monica house was even on the radar for consideration as a historic building, maybe it was time for Frank to try something else, if only to show how much it still meant to him to continue to "make it new," in Ezra Pound's famous injunction. Frank worked on plans for the Venice house for several years, and it became another one of his design laboratories, this one at a tiny scale compared to Peter Lewis's house, and self-funded. Still, it grew large enough to include a music room that he planned to make available to the Los Angeles Philharmonic for visiting performers to use as practice and recital space, guest quarters, and an apartment for staff to look after his and Berta's needs as they got older. But neither Frank nor Berta ever felt fully committed to the project. Their disenchantment began when, during the extended period while they awaited planning approval, neighbors began to dump garbage on the empty lot; the Gehrys hired a gardener to landscape the property and keep it looking neat, and when that did not stem the flow of garbage, they surrounded the property with a fence and a locked gate. Vandals broke the lock repeatedly, and Berta began to have serious doubts as to whether she wanted to live in that neighborhood at all. Many of their neighbors had been friendly, but Venice was clearly not as safe as Santa Monica, and also, did it make economic sense to build something so elaborate in that part of Los Angeles? Berta was also not so sure she wanted to take care of a large house. Neither she nor Frank liked the idea of live-in servants. And they both decided that they liked Santa Monica better as a place to live. In 2007, five years after they had bought the property and Frank had begun the design process, he and Berta decided to abandon the project.*

N ot the least of the appeal of moving to Venice was that it would have brought Frank and Berta much closer to their office, which in 2002 moved to a warehouselike building on Beatrice Street in Playa Vista, south of Venice and not far from the airport. The drive from the house in Santa Monica to Beatrice Street was hardly a long commute by Los Angeles stan-

---

* Frank and Berta held on to the property and considered building a house there for investment. Eventually they turned it over to their son Alejo and his wife, Carrie, who began plans to build a house there in 2015. It would be designed by Frank, but simpler and smaller than the one he had planned for himself and Berta.

dards, but it seemed far by comparison to the old office on Cloverfield Boulevard, which is only a few blocks from the house, and it was slightly more distant than the studio on Brooks Avenue in Venice that Frank had in the 1980s.

Larry Field and Frank bought the white concrete-and-glass building at 12541 Beatrice, a midcentury modern box with an open, two-story-high interior, as an investment as well as a location for the office, making Frank both landlord and tenant. He renovated the building with such a deliberately light touch that the only indication of his work on the exterior is a small aluminum sign projecting from the building and hung vertically, reading GEHRY PARTNERS. One wing of the building was rented to the Media Arts Lab of TBWA, the company that did Apple's advertising, a unit of the former Chiat/Day that had once been in Frank's Binoculars Building on Main Street in Venice; Gehry Partners took the rest of the structure, and the two companies were separated by an open arcade filled with brightly colored outdoor furniture Frank had designed for Heller. The sculpted furniture, made of resin, is the first indication that it is not just anyone's office, but it is not until you go inside, into a reception area with plywood furniture, white walls, a Chuck Arnoldi painting, an acrylic sculpture by Craig Kaufman, and one of Frank's Formica fish—later replaced by a metallic bear—that the place begins to look like Frank Gehry works there.

Beyond the reception area is a series of glass-walled offices for administrative staff, including Berta, arranged around an open area filled with architectural models. The walls are something of a Gehry museum, and what they contain goes beyond Frank's architecture. There are several signed jerseys from National Hockey League players, posters of exhibitions of Frank's work, pictures of him with prominent people like Martha Stewart, and a still from the episode of *The Simpsons* that featured Frank, who voiced his own cartoon character. He originally placed his own office between the administrative area and the huge high-ceilinged drafting room where the firm's architects work. It was a strategic location: almost everyone had to pass by it coming or going, and with glass walls looking out in three directions, Frank could see much of what was going on in the office. Just as important, everyone else could see him. He was less interested in privacy than in being visible to everyone who worked for him and everyone who visited.

Frank gave the room a long countertop desk, installed along the length

The Gehry Partners studio at 12541 Beatrice Street

of one wall and a portion of another, two of his "Experimental Edges" cardboard easy chairs, and a conference table with a plywood top and eight of the "hockey stick" chairs Frank designed for Knoll. It is even more of a Gehry museum than the outside room, with memorabilia lining the walls and bookshelves: framed photographs of Frank with Philip Johnson; with Leonard Bernstein; with Esa-Pekka Salonen, the music director of the Los Angeles Philharmonic when Walt Disney Hall was built; with Bill Clinton, Arnold Schwarzenegger, and Shimon Peres. There is a picture of Frank's old friend Jay Chiat, and another of Berta as a child, and one of Sam and Alejo. Atop a long, low bookshelf are a small bust of Thomas Jefferson, a snow globe containing a tiny model of Walt Disney Concert Hall, a model of Frank's unbuilt Turtle Creek project for Dallas,[†] and a model of the Inland Steel Building in Chicago, the modernist tower by Skidmore, Owings & Merrill.[‡] There are also two small fish sculptures, a model of a

---

[*] Experimental Edges, a line produced for three years beginning in 1979, was an attempt to revive the idea of Frank's corrugated cardboard furniture with somewhat more striking, rough-hewn pieces than the original company, Easy Edges, had produced. This time there was no attempt to reach the mass market; the pieces in this new line of furniture, at once grander in scale than Easy Edges and shaggier, were presented unapologetically as art pieces.

[†] See chapter 12, page 238.

[‡] Frank owned a small portion of the building through a partnership organized by his friend Richard Cohen, and designed a new security desk for the lobby.

sailboat, several small massing models that show possible designs for sky-scrapers, and a small model of Frank and Berta's house in Santa Monica.

On the bookshelf are mostly art books: four separate books on Bernini, a book called *Medieval Castles of Spain*, a book on Italian frescoes, and books on Georges Seurat, Barnett Newman, Louise Bourgeois, David Smith, Chuck Arnoldi, and Richard Prince, among others. One of the few architecture books in the room is the complete works of Erich Men-delsohn, who designed the Einstein Tower in Potsdam, one of Frank's favorite buildings. It has been placed on the shelf next to a large volume called *The World's Best Sailboats*. The design of the office may be modern, but as usual with Frank, it is as far from minimalist as you could imagine. Like his house, the space is a collage, an assemblage of objects that looks cluttered at first glance but has been placed with precision. Nothing is there by accident, and every one of the objects is meaningful to him.

The main room of the office has a kind of messy grandeur to it, like the assembly-line area of a factory: a huge space 25 feet high and 275 feet long, with plywood desks for roughly a hundred people arranged in large clus-ters. The plywood furniture gives the arrangement a temporary air, even though the workstations are arranged in permanent rows. All the archi-tects, from Craig Webb down to the newest intern, work at similar open desks. There are models everywhere, some of which are small enough to fit on a desk and some of which are as big as a small room. The models are rarely perfect, pristine presentation models; they are as often as not made of cardboard or wood, and sometimes several models of the same project are together, a record of Frank's thought process.

In 2012, Frank decided it was time to move—not the whole office, just himself. He abandoned his office on the main floor and turned it into a meeting room, leaving all the memorabilia in place, giving it a quality somewhere between a working space and a shrine. To replace it, he built a large second-floor work suite overlooking the main room for him, his chief of staff Meaghan Lloyd, and a handful of assistants. He gave himself a large office with an outside window and a sundeck filled with more of his Heller outdoor furniture—the old office had no outside windows at all—as well as a library with room for a full collection of architecture as well as art books, a conference room, two bathrooms, and a kitchenette. Frank's own office is still enclosed in glass, with sliding glass doors; a large balcony, where his assistants sit, overlooks the main space. Frank can still see almost everything that is going on, and it is as easy as it had been in his old office for anyone to see whether or not he is in. But it is not as easy to drop in: there is something about ascending the stairs that makes a visit seem less casual than it was before. Frank's private office is now clearly an inner sanctum, and while it is still transparent, it presides grandly over the rest of the office. This time he put a coffee table and four of Le Corbusier's "Grand Confort" chairs in tan leather in the middle of his space, set in a circle—classic modern chairs that, however informal their arrangement, suggest a more decorous place than his old room downstairs. The new office upstairs is more comfortable than the old one, but it is hard not to feel that it is part retreat, part watchtower.

Even though Frank and Berta's Venice compound was never built, the time spent on the project was hardly for naught. It gave Frank the opportunity to observe at close range both the design skills and the management ability of the architect in his office he had assigned to the project, a young Yale graduate named Meaghan Lloyd. Lloyd had first met Frank in 1999, when he was teaching at Yale. She was a second-year graduate architecture student, and she had signed up for a studio course Frank taught every other year.* Frank had assigned the students the problem of designing a cathe-

---

* He had begun teaching part-time at Yale in the 1980s when César Pelli was dean, then stopped, finding the coast-to-coast travel too taxing to his schedule. When Robert A. M. Stern became dean of the Yale School of Architecture in 1998, Stern prevailed upon Frank to return, and agreed on a schedule in which Frank would teach one design studio course every other spring, with assistants to allow him to avoid coming to New Haven every single

dral to be built adjacent to MacArthur Park in Los Angeles, but Lloyd had
only just begun her design work when her father died, and she needed to
leave New Haven and return home to Illinois. She came back to school
late in the semester, far behind schedule, worried that she might never be
able to complete her cathedral scheme. One of Frank's teaching assistants
suggested to her that she might be better off giving up her project and
dropping the course. She was pondering that when Frank encountered her
in the design studio the night before his students were scheduled to make
a final presentation of their completed projects. "I found her sitting alone,
making her model, cutting up paper. It was so poignant," Frank said. "She
was behind the eight-ball." Lloyd remembers that Frank approached her
and did not say a word about her project. "He said, 'How are you doing,
kid? How is your mom?' I thought, wow, I don't know you but you are
the coolest person," she said. "He was humane and matter-of-fact. I said I
wanted to come and work for him."

Lloyd "figured it out at the eleventh hour and did a pretty successful
project," Frank recalled. He was impressed. When he had drinks with the
students later, several of them asked about coming to work in his office.
"They asked, 'How do we become you?'" he said. "I said, 'Well, you could
come to the office for a while, but I can't guarantee you full-time employment.' I think I offered them six months." And he warned them, Lloyd
remembered, that being known around the firm as one of his former students could be difficult. "He said, 'You won't like it, that people will hate
you if they know I know you, and they won't want to talk to you.'" It was an
odd admission by Frank that his office was not always the warmest place,
and that its culture tended to reflect his driven inner ambition more than
his casual, easygoing exterior.

Despite Frank's warning, Lloyd and another student in the class,
Anand Devarajan, took him up on his offer, and went to work in Frank's
model shop. They both rose quickly—Devarajan would become a design
partner—but Lloyd's career took several unusual turns both before and
after she worked on the design for his Venice house. Not long after she
had arrived at Gehry Partners in 2000, Frank overheard her and some of
the other young women in the office talking about the difficulty they had
meeting young men in Los Angeles. "I said, 'Come over on Sunday—

---

week of the term. For years, Frank donated his teaching fees back to Yale, to be used for
scholarships in honor of his friends Stanley Tigerman and Frank Israel, both Yale architecture graduates.

Meaghan Lloyd at work on the model for the unbuilt Gehry house in Venice

Alejo and his friends will be there and we're all going sailing.'" The afternoon had a result Frank did not envision. Lloyd did meet a young man
she liked—Alejo Gehry. The two dated for a while, and at first kept their
relationship secret. "Then Meaghan started showing up at family events,"
Frank said. Lloyd was highly poised, bright, and easygoing; she combined
strong ambition with midwestern warmth and kindness, and Berta became
exceptionally fond of her. Meaghan's romantic relationship with Alejo
ended, but by then she had been given charge of the Venice project, which
meant she continued to spend time with both Frank and Berta. She was
becoming, like Michelle Kaufmann several years before, one of the office
staff members who became a part of the Gehrys' extended family.

Around the time that Frank and Berta canceled their building plans,
Frank, approaching his eightieth birthday and still as active as ever, had
begun to think he needed to find a young staff member who could accompany him on trips, handling logistics and serving as a high-level assistant,
a kind of chief of staff. He envisioned it as a position that might be rotated
among younger architects. Berta, who enjoyed traveling with Frank on
major trips but had no desire to be his aide-de-camp, suggested that
Meaghan would be an ideal first occupant of the new position. Frank had
admired her manner ever since he saw how she had handled the difficult
situation in which she found herself after her father's death, and he took

Berta's advice and offered her the job. She accepted, thinking it would be a good learning experience for a year or two. Soon she was accompanying Frank all over the world, getting to know all of his clients, and becoming, by virtue of their travel time together as much as by the stock he put in her judgment, his primary sounding board for ideas and strategy.

Like the period a dozen years earlier during the dark days of Walt Disney Hall, when Frank's initial burst of European work took him away from Los Angeles, it was a time with a huge amount of work in far-flung places. In her first year on the job, Lloyd went along to Abu Dhabi on trips for the Guggenheim project, to Hong Kong to help him evaluate the site for the Hong Kong Swire, a new condominium tower, and on multiple trips to Europe and throughout the United States. They were traveling, she estimated, 60 percent of that first year, and would establish such a successful working relationship that Frank put aside his plan to think of the chief of staff position as one that he would appoint a young architect to for a year or two, like a Supreme Court clerkship. He let her tenure be open-ended, and she would end up remaining in the job for years, taking on more and more responsibility. It did not take long for Frank's clients to understand that when they heard the words "Frank is coming to the meeting" the meaning, almost invariably, was "Frank is coming to the meeting, along with Meaghan."

Not too long after Frank and Berta had given up their plans to build the Venice house, perhaps in part as a way of making up for its loss with something else that could mark the passage of time in a positive way, Berta began to plan a celebration for Frank's eightieth birthday. Frank had said that he had no particular desire for a party, and certainly not a big one, but Berta knew better than to take him at his word. Together with Amy Achorn, his assistant, she began to go through his contact lists, figuring out whom might be appropriate to invite.

It became a far larger event than she at first envisioned, in part because she and Achorn kept thinking of people who had been important in Frank's career and whom they occasionally saw though they were not close friends, but who Berta thought should be there if the party was truly to be a retrospective of Frank's life and the people who had been meaningful to it. And then there was the question of where to have the party, which would be bigger than anything that could fit in the Gehrys' house. Amy Achorn looked at party venues all over Los Angeles, including the Peterson

Automobile Museum, before Berta suggested that it might be worth trying to find a place that had a closer connection to Frank. "How about the TC at MOCA?" she said, referring to the Temporary Contemporary, which had been renamed the Geffen Contemporary. The museum was happy to offer the space, which was the only building of Frank's in Los Angeles other than Walt Disney Concert Hall big enough to contain what turned out to be a gathering of roughly five hundred friends, family, clients, artists, employees, and fellow architects. Berta and Amy wanted to include everyone whom they thought mattered to Frank—and to be sure to avoid anyone they thought would make him uncomfortable. Berta omitted a handful of people who she thought had treated him badly, including a few architects she felt had been unfairly critical of her husband.

"That was kindergarten stuff," Berta said, referring to letters the architects had written about him, "and this was an adult party. I had a definite 'no' list. Frank is very forgiving, but the Spanish blood in me doesn't let me do that."

The event was held on Friday, February 27, 2009, the night before Frank's actual birthday. It filled the sprawling galleries of the Geffen Contemporary, and while Berta had hired the Patina Group, which ran the restaurant in Walt Disney Hall, to cater, it was more an evening of loud music and copious consumption of alcohol than of leisurely dining. The guest list erased any doubt that Frank was now more than an internationally known architect; he was a general celebrity, and there seemed to be more famous Hollywood faces in the crowd than prominent architects. Brad Pitt, an architecture buff who had met Frank a few years before and had made a number of visits to the office to pursue his curiosity about design—he found Frank a willing tutor—was there, along with Bill Maher, Maureen Dowd, and the actors Donald Sutherland, Laurence Fishburne, and Kevin McCarthy. McCarthy, one of Frank's earliest Hollywood friends, who came with his wife, Kate Crane, had just turned ninety-five. He would die the following year, and the party would be the last time the two old friends would see each other.

The actress Sally Kellerman led the crowd in singing "Happy Birthday" when a gigantic cake, Patina's attempt to replicate in pastry the swirling, stainless steel forms of Walt Disney Hall, was rolled out. Mayor Antonio Villaraigosa toasted Frank as one of the city's leading citizens. Tom Krens, representing the art and architecture world, toasted him with a story about how Frank was never satisfied with the design of Bilbao and would continually tinker with his plans, and Arianna Huffington told the assembled

Frank and Berta welcome guests to Frank's eightieth birthday party.

Frank and Brad Pitt at Frank's eightieth

Sam and Alejo Gehry and their aunt, Doreen Nelson, watch the toasts at Frank's eightieth.

crowd, "I have written a book about Picasso, but until I met Frank Gehry I had not met a genius who is nice. Frank Gehry is the friendly genius." Fishburne, who belonged to a motorcycle group with Krens, told a story about bringing Frank along on one of his rides. "And sometimes I'd, you know, smoke a bit of marijuana and he would be riding with me and I would think, 'Oh, my God, I have the greatest living architect on my motorcycle, and what if I crash?'"

Frank, dressed in his characteristic black T-shirt and black suit jacket, talked with almost everyone; for him it was the world's largest cocktail party, and the center of the action in the huge space was wherever he was standing. He drank enough vodka that his memories of the evening were vague, but warm and happy. "I said when I was eighty I would slow down," Frank said that night. "Well, I did, but not much. I don't feel like eighty. I guess you never think you're the age you are."

M any of Frank's artist friends were present that evening. One who was missing was the sculptor Richard Serra, whose career had had some unusual parallels with Frank's. Not only did Serra share Frank's driving ambition and his intense commitment to work, but the two had been closely tied together by Bilbao, where Tom Krens had ordered Frank to design a huge gallery to accommodate Serra's enormous work entitled *Snake*. Most important, Serra and Frank had many of the same interests in shifting, twisting, torqued, and turning forms. Serra explored in his sculpture many of the same shapes that Frank did in his architecture, and for years the two men eagerly learned from each other. Frank's curving metal planes surely owed something to Serra. And Serra was so intrigued by Frank's work that he often dropped by the office to see the latest projects, even if Frank was not in, and would talk to the younger architects and offer comments.

Both men understood that pure art is a different pursuit from architecture, and while each in his way celebrated the differences, neither was ever totally certain that the other man's work did not come close to crossing into his own turf. Serra's monumental pieces in his *Torqued Ellipses* series created quite beautiful, even profound spaces, almost like roofless chapels, and entering them was in a sense a kind of architectural experience. And Frank's work, of course, was the inverse: while he never tried to hide that he was solving functional problems and not making pure, abstract form, almost all of his work managed to give the viewer some of the experience of pure art. Indeed, Frank's desire to confer the aesthetic experience of art in the course of fulfilling the functional demands of a work of architecture was at the core of his intentions.

Did this make architecture a higher calling than art or not? To Serra, the need to deal with mundane concerns made architecture itself mundane, and he came increasingly to resent the notion that an architect could be an artist. After Bilbao, when Frank's building got considerably more attention than Serra's monumental permanent installation within the vast gallery that Frank had designed, Serra became impatient at the frequent references to Frank as a great artist. When Charlie Rose raised the question with Serra on his public television program, Serra bluntly told him that he didn't like hearing Frank described as an artist, and that he, the artist, could draw better. Later, he said to Calvin Tomkins of *The New Yorker*, "Now we have architects running around saying, 'I'm an artist,' and I just don't buy it. I don't believe Frank is an artist. I don't believe Rem Koolhaas is an artist. Sure, there are comparable overlaps in the language between sculpture and architecture, between painting and architecture. There are overlaps between all kinds of human activities. But there are also differences that have gone on for centuries."

What could have been just a friendly disagreement between two men whose careers had risen in parallel, who for a long time had "talked to each other through our work," in Frank's words, and who shared a passionate intensity about art and the making of space, grew in the years after Bilbao into a more serious feud. Serra did not have Frank's eagerness to be liked and lacked the affability that runs like a contrasting vein through the marble of Frank's ambition, and he began to refer to Frank as if he as an architect had made a conscious, hostile incursion into Serra's territory as an artist. Frank, easily wounded, retreated, and the disagreement between the two friends hardened into a distant coolness.

Another old acquaintance who was absent from Frank's celebration, presumably because he was on Berta's "no" list, was Fred Nicholas, the Los Angeles lawyer who had been involved in the architect selection processes for both the Museum of Contemporary Art and Walt Disney Concert Hall. Their relationship had had a number of twists and turns over the years, given the disappointments and rejections Frank experienced with both of these cultural projects, and it had collapsed altogether in 2007 when Circa Publishing Enterprises LLC, an entity controlled by

Nicholas, sued Frank over a share of the royalties from a line of jewelry Frank had designed for Tiffany & Co.

The background of the case was not in dispute. In 2003 Frank signed a contract with Circa, which had previously marketed some other Gehry-related items, agreeing to give the company half the proceeds of jewelry that he might design. Nicholas returned the contract in 2004, which Frank took to mean that he no longer considered it binding. However, when Frank later made a separate deal directly with Tiffany and began to design a line of jewelry and vases, bowls, and cups that was launched in 2006, Nicholas insisted that he was entitled to half of Frank's income from Tiffany. Frank's lawyer, Patricia Glaser, argued that Nicholas's decision to return the earlier contract voided Frank's obligation to him. The case was pending at the time of Frank's eightieth birthday party, and went to trial before Los Angeles Superior Court judge Jane L. Johnson later in 2009. In January 2010, just before the lawyers were scheduled to present their closing arguments, the judge accepted Glaser's motion to dismiss the suit. Nicholas was not entitled to anything, Judge Johnson said, because he could not enforce an agreement that no longer existed. The lawsuit brought to a sad end a forty-year relationship that Frank had always felt slightly uncomfortable about. To Frank, Nicholas seemed always to be doing things for himself while pretending to be helping him.

The unpleasantness of the lawsuit notwithstanding, Frank's foray into jewelry design was a great success, at least for a while. It was surely a further validation of his celebrity status, and if it could appear that he was trying to exploit that status by extending it in a new realm, he took genuine pleasure in working with the Tiffany staff, whose standards impressed him. The company was happy to market him to the hilt: he was the first new designer from whom Tiffany had commissioned original pieces in a quarter century, and the Frank Gehry Collection was launched with considerable fanfare at elaborate parties in both the main store on Fifth Avenue and the Tiffany branch in Beverly Hills. "Rooted in an exquisite understanding of materials and structure, the collection explores the expressive potential of precious metals, wood and stone," the company's press materials proclaimed. "Like his buildings, Mr. Gehry's jewelry and home collection exude vitality, with Tiffany skillfully realizing the spontaneous twists and turns of the architect's inventive style."

Despite the air of hype, many of the pieces were elegant, and some of Frank's favorite shapes translated reasonably well into jewelry. The collection was divided into six "lines," Fish, Orchid, Fold, Equus, Axis, and

Torque, and included bracelets, pendants, rings, necklaces, and cuff links. What Frank called Fish were more like tiny teardrop-shaped objects than the scaled fish of his lamps, and they were particularly effective when tiny fish of sterling silver, ebony, and other woods were clustered together into a large, jangling bracelet. The Torque group included twisted forms, including a square silver ring whose shape twisted as it turned.

The positive start to Frank's collaboration with Tiffany did not continue. The excitement brought strong sales at first, but the numbers did not continue at that level. Frank felt that despite the attention that surrounded the launch, Tiffany had decided that he was not going to be the company's next Paloma Picasso and had failed to advertise the collection sufficiently to keep sales high. Frank and Tiffany did not see eye-to-eye on the what future phases of their collaboration should be, and within three years the collection was discontinued, the relationship dissolved, and the jewelry relegated to the status of a cult item on eBay.

Still, the eagerness with which Frank began his collaboration with Tiffany and jumped on the company's publicity bandwagon was in stark contrast to the way he had handled Easy Edges, his furniture line, back in the early 1970s, when he abruptly walked away from what was showing all signs of being a successful venture. He feared that the success of Easy Edges would mark him in the public eye as a furniture designer and not as an architect, and that it would be too difficult to make architecture the focus of his creative energy. By now, more than three decades later, he was sure enough of his reputation that he could afford to be a bit looser with it, and play around with other things simply because he thought they would be fun as well as lucrative. And while he was ambivalent about many things, being famous was not one of them.

That, surely, is why Frank had had no hesitation about going along with the idea of an episode of the animated series *The Simpsons* based on him and his work. The plot was simple: the residents of Springfield, aware of the acclaim of Walt Disney Hall and believing that their town needs to become more sophisticated, are motivated by Marge Simpson to request that Frank design a concert hall for their city. Marge writes a letter to Frank, who at first is so uninterested that he crumples the letter and tosses it on the ground, at which point he looks at the crumpled paper and is inspired to use it as the basis for a design. "Frank Gehry, you're a genius!" he exclaims to himself as he looks at the crumpled ball of paper. The concert hall is built, but after a disastrous opening night it becomes clear that Springfield residents have no real interest in classical music, and the build-

Frank presents his design
for Springfield's concert
hall in *The Simpsons.*

ing is turned into a prison. Frank agreed to play himself in the episode, which was aired on April 3, 2005. He enjoyed the gentle satire, but before long he had come to regret the whole venture. No other architect had ever been the focus of an episode of *The Simpsons*, and Frank was beginning to feel that his celebrity came at a price. For all its goodwill, *The Simpsons* reinforced the misconception that Frank was not a serious and thoughtful designer and that his buildings were wild, irrational creations, no more deliberate than a crumpled sheet of paper. "It has haunted me," Frank told Fareed Zakaria on CNN. "People who've seen *The Simpsons* believe it."

More accurate, not to say more reflective, was the full-length documentary film about Frank made by another of his longtime Hollywood friends, the director Sydney Pollack. The film, *Sketches of Frank Gehry*, released by Sony in May 2006, was directed by Pollack and produced by Ultan Guilfoyle, a respected cinematographer who had made a number of films about art and architecture. Pollack narrated the film himself and gave it a slightly naïve quality: he admitted at the beginning that he had never made a documentary and knew relatively little about architecture, but that he was intrigued by the way that Frank, like himself, faced the challenge of doing creative work that had to respond to more severe constraints than pure art did. The film contained interviews with artists like Chuck Arnoldi, Ed Ruscha, and Robert Rauschenberg singing Frank's praises, and there were also appearances by the likes of Michael Eisner, Michael Ovitz, Dennis Hopper, and Barry Diller. But the best parts, not surprisingly, were those in which Pollack, who knew better than to try and analyze Frank too directly, engaged him in a relaxed conversation, and as a result the film took on an amiable, casual tone that captured Frank's sweet-natured angst. "I'm always scared that I'm not going to know what to do," Frank says as the film opens.

The one exception to the laudatory tone of the film was an interview with the Princeton art historian Hal Foster, who felt that Frank was trying too hard to intrude into the realm of sculpture and produced buildings that provided spectacle more than architectural rigor. It was not a new argument—it was, in a sense, a refashioning in academic terms of the view of Frank presented on *The Simpsons*—but it was one rarely heard in academic circles any longer by the time the film appeared. The film also included footage of Frank's two most valued mentors, Milton Wexler and Philip Johnson. It was probably the last filmed interview either of them ever did—Johnson died at ninety-eight at the beginning of 2005, and Wexler, also at ninety-eight, in March 2007—and each of them described Frank with a combination of pride and awe. Very different men, they spoke in a similar tone of gentle warmth, as if they both knew it would be their last chance to go on record about him.

The self-effacing side of Frank, the side that was more Woody Allen than Frank Lloyd Wright—the "aw, shucks" part of him that was always real even if it never explained his full character—was in evidence when Sydney Pollack's film opened in Los Angeles. Frank was too nervous to stay in the auditorium to watch the audience's reaction. "Let's get out of here," he said to Pollack. Along with Michelle Kaufmann and Edwin Chan, who had accompanied him from the office, they went to the bar of the Chateau Marmont hotel in West Hollywood and finished a bottle of wine. They slipped back into the theater just before the film ended. At the first showing of the film in his hometown of Toronto, Frank was so anxious that he reached out and grabbed the hand of Lisa Rochon, the architecture critic of the *Globe and Mail*, who was sitting next to him.

18

The Legacy of Technology

For all his fierce ambition and determination to stand out, Frank did not like to think of himself as an architect of the elite. He wanted to see himself more as an architect who designed buildings for everyone and was appreciated by everyone. The difference between him and other popular architects, he felt, was that he could please the public without pandering. He aspired to be popular by elevating public taste, not by descending to it. That was not a conceit: it is what he did at Bilbao, and again at Walt Disney Concert Hall, where he made serious and innovative architecture accessible to people who would normally have no interest whatsoever in such things. He would do so again and again throughout his career, making distinctive places that bridged the gap between high architectural culture and the general public.

Yet he was also becoming increasingly interested in another aspect of architectural populism, in the making of everyday buildings where people lived, worked, studied, and played. He wanted to be able to show that the quest for the special architectural experience could be fulfilled by making better versions of commercial buildings as well as by making unique buildings, like Bilbao. After all, if Frank could elevate the ordinary, he would not be the architect who had sold out to fame and fortune; he could still be, in the critic Michael Sorkin's words, "the bleeding-heart Canadian nebbish," the unpretentious architect who stayed true to his own origins and to his own and his family's political beliefs, even as he came more and more to travel in the world of the rich and famous. He would realize the ambitions that had led him years before to spend so much of his time working with the Rouse Company, a client who still represented an unfulfilled desire, even though he had parted ways with them decades earlier. Frank had never made peace with the fact that he had not been able to satisfy fully either Rouse's demands or his own standards in the design of the Santa Monica Place shopping center. Its failure still gnawed at him.

And if he could build for developers without compromising his own aesthetic ideas, he would also show that he had not abandoned his own beginnings in the "cheapskate architecture" of plywood and chain-link fencing that he had invented. For all that his architecture had moved beyond the rough-hewn quality of his early work, he wanted to feel that the idea behind it remained with him, part of his DNA, and that he had figured out a way to bring that same mix of pragmatism and poetry to the challenge of designing big buildings in the real world. He wanted to show that practicality, high aesthetic ambition, and creative imagination could coexist in a skyscraper just as easily as they had in a small Los Angeles house.

If Frank's desire to prove that he could make practical and profitable buildings went back at least as far as his frustrated ambitions with Rouse, it took on a new and more urgent coloration in the age of digital technology. He wanted to prove that the digital software his office had worked so hard to develop would not just make the building process more efficient, but would also make it more creative, and would allow the kind of unique structures he craved to be produced in a world that was moving ever faster toward standardization. That was a critical difference between Frank's view of digital technology and those of many other architects and engineers, for whom digital architecture was mainly a means of designing and constructing buildings more quickly and cheaply, standardizing elements that in the past might have had to be designed individually.

For Frank, it was the opposite: a way to make it possible to design and build a one-of-a-kind work of architecture that would otherwise be unaffordable. Being able to build unusual designs for projects whose programs were not unusual at all, like the office building for IAC and the apartment house for Bruce Ratner, and to show that he could do them for a cost that would not be too far above the price of more conventional buildings, became more and more important to him. That some aspects of these buildings were not as distinctive as what people had come to expect when they heard the name Frank Gehry mattered less to him than that they proved a point: that he could do them in the first place. However good, even great, the architecture of buildings like Bilbao and Walt Disney Concert Hall was, he wanted more than that for his legacy. It was not in his nature, he felt, to design only bespoke architecture, even if he could do it as well as or better than anyone else.

Frank's tendency to appear casual, even indifferent, to administrative and business matters was something of an affectation. He thought about money frequently. Although he never shed his early anxieties about it, he was also genuinely interested in the nature of business. Even if he did not want to spend most of his time engaged with the deals he embarked on with Larry Field as they assembled a set of investment properties, they were not something he swept under the rug; he took pleasure in discussing them with Field. And he made it his business to understand the fine points of every contract his office negotiated with a client, even though he had not done the negotiating himself for decades. He liked thinking about his practice from a strategic standpoint. He had hired Randy Jefferson and Jim Glymph not only to make it possible for his office to produce Bilbao and Walt Disney Concert Hall, but also to organize his practice so that it could produce large and complex projects, and to help build the firm into the kind of organization that could compete with big architectural offices that did not have his creative abilities. With that level of technical expertise combined with his creative strength, Frank reasoned, his office would have an unusual advantage.

For a while, it worked exceptionally well. Randy oversaw much of the administrative work of the firm, which included not only general office administration but also what could be the more demanding task of managing the work of the teams executing major architectural projects and producing construction drawings. Jim was in charge of technology and also played a role in management. Craig Webb and Edwin Chan were the co–design heads, and each supervised a group of designers who, in turn, were divided into smaller teams to work on specific projects. Frank's decision to share ownership with Randy Jefferson and Jim Glymph and not with Craig Webb and Edwin Chan was a curious one, given how essential design was to him and to his reputation. His rationale was that however talented Webb and Chan might be, he could, in a pinch, do their design work himself. But he knew he could not do the technical work and management that he counted on Jefferson and Glymph for. Jefferson was particularly cognizant of that, and at one point before the new name was final he suggested to Frank that a better name for the firm would be Gehry, Glymph & Jefferson.

Frank tentatively agreed. Before the name change was final, Jim Glymph, the calmer of the two, spoke up. "He said, 'Are you crazy? This brand is based on Gehry, and doing this will only diminish it,'" Frank remembered. Frank decided Glymph was right, and reversed course. Gehry Partners it was, and would remain. For a dozen years, from 1992, when Randy Jefferson arrived, to 2004, when he departed, the five men ran the firm together. "We *were* Frank Gehry," Randy Jefferson said.

Few things in Frank's professional life have remained stable for long, or fully buffered from the pressures of personal life. In the case of the management team of five, the first cracks came not as a result of something in Frank's own life, but when a horrendous double tragedy struck in Randy Jefferson's family. His teenage son was killed in a motorcycle accident, which was followed not long after by the death of his wife. For several months, Frank tried to give Randy time to mourn and made few demands on him. But the situation was complicated by the fact that Randy had become involved with a female colleague in the office before his wife's death—they would eventually marry—and after a while Frank began to wonder if the deference he was giving Randy was being used less to help him recover than to allow an awkward office romance that was distracting him from any productive work.

As with Greg Walsh, Frank's dislike of confrontation made it too difficult for him to fire Randy directly. When he finally decided that the situation was untenable, he asked Jim Glymph to speak to him. Not only did Frank believe that Randy was not functioning adequately in his job, but that he and his wife-to-be, who worked on the administrative side of the office, were not working comfortably with Berta, who for some time had been the firm's chief financial officer. Challenging Berta's authority was not the route to success at Gehry Partners, and Randy's time in the office came to an end. He had seen Frank's practice through the triumphs of Bilbao and Walt Disney Hall and played a critical role in transforming it into a different kind of firm from the one that Frank had run on his own. But that job was done, and it would be up to Frank, with the help of Jim Glymph, to maintain it.

Frank rarely spoke publicly about how he ran his office, but when he was invited to participate in a symposium commemorating the opening of the building Peter Lewis had given for the Weatherhead School of Management at Case Western Reserve University in 2002 he decided to use his talk as an occasion to talk about the operations of the office, and to defend his ability to be efficient. "I want to say something about how I run my world, because it is very businesslike, and you will probably be shocked to hear that," he said. "People think that we're flaky artists, and there is no bottom line, but I have a profitable office."

Frank was exceptionally proud of the fact that, unlike many of his architect peers, he had begun his practice on a shoestring, not with inherited wealth, and he believed that gave him a certain discipline, as well as a determination not to exploit anyone who worked for him. He refused to use unpaid interns. "I also insisted that people who worked for me get a Christmas bonus, a cost-of-living increase every year, vacations, and all of these things. That was built into the culture from the beginning," he said. He took particular umbrage at the frequency with which many architects used students as free labor to produce designs for architectural competitions. "It's very easy to recruit kids who will work for nothing," he said. "A lot of my friends do that. That's like taking drugs. Once you're on it, you can't get off it."

Frank structured his fees differently from most firms, and charged a general fee for the work of Gehry Partners and a specific "design fee" for his personal involvement. It could seem like a way of exploiting his celebrity as a designer, which it certainly was. But he also saw it as a way of separating his role in a project from that of his colleagues, and of paving the way for the eventuality that someday Gehry Partners would be only partners, and not Gehry.

That, however, was a long way off. Frank had no intention of retiring, and he recognized, he said, that "there is no way that, if I leave, the office is going to be able to do what I do. It's a very personal kind of work." He felt strongly that he wanted to develop younger talent that could in time stand on its own, and he had particular praise for Edwin Chan, whom he described in his talk as among the most gifted, but also the most enigmatic, of his designers. "The first five years working with me, he sat there and didn't say a word," Frank said. "Then I would say to Edwin, 'What do you think about what we're doing?' He would look at me and say, 'I don't know, what do you think?' That went on for the next five years. Then I realized he became a monster. He started moving stuff around. . . . We were doing a project in Korea that never got built [the museum for Samsung] but every time I went on a trip and came back he had moved the auditorium. He was impeccable. He had incredible reasons for it. He's really brilliant. He doesn't sleep at night and he comes back the next morning and moves the auditorium."

Moving the auditorium, in Frank's view, was a form of what he liked to call "play," and it was largely instinctive. "A serious CEO, you would imagine, does not think of creative spirit as play. And yet it is," he said. "Creativity, the way I characterize it, is that you're searching for something. You have a goal. You're not sure where it's going. So when I meet with my people and start thinking and making models and stuff, it is like play." He recalled a time when the office was exploring different options for the design of Walt Disney Hall and he went so far as to play the theme from the old television show *Rawhide*, with the chorus "Rollin', rollin', rollin'," in the hope that it would stimulate thought. More often, however, the office was quiet, with long periods during which Frank would stare at models, pondering options and proposing tiny tweaks.

For all that Frank admired Edwin Chan and believed that Chan had developed the ability to anticipate what he himself might have wanted, he was hardly ready to turn over his practice to him or anyone else. His thoughts about how Gehry Partners might work without him were vague and constantly shifting; he enjoyed toying with different organizational schemes as an abstract exercise, and just as he often did with different design options, putting off a decision was a way of maintaining the illusion that every option was still possible. With building projects, clients eventually forced him to commit to one plan or another, but nothing was forcing his hand with the office. His health was decent, and he knew no life other than work, family, and a social life that more than ever blurred into his professional life as he became more famous.

Instead of figuring out how to phase himself out, Frank decided in 2002, when he was seventy-three, to turn the firm's expertise in digital software into a new, stand-alone company. When the firm began to use the CATIA software that had been developed for aerospace as a way of making it feasible to build his more extreme designs, he did not envision that it would have any applicability beyond Gehry Partners. After all, who else did buildings that looked like his—and if someone wanted to try, why should he make it easier for them? But it had been clear for a long time that one of the most important elements of the software his firm had developed with Dassault, the French-based owner of the CATIA system, was the way that it made it possible to monitor the steps of design, engineering, and construction more closely, and minimize confusion and miscommunication among the dozens of architects, engineers, consultants, and contractors working on a project. Those issues affected all construction projects, and Frank realized that CATIA could be used to add efficiency and discipline to almost any complex construction process.

He asked Jim Glymph to explore creating a technology company that could allow the technology Gehry Partners was developing to be used by other architecture firms. Glymph believed that there was potentially a huge financial benefit in this, since it could provide some long-term economic stability for Berta and his children, given how uncertain the future of Gehry Partners as an architectural practice was without him. Even if Frank could overcome all his ambivalence and establish a viable succession plan, the track record for multigenerational architectural practices was not encouraging. Few firms that were organized around a single creative designer succeeded in lasting much beyond the end of that designer's career, and Frank knew that for all he had tried to operate Gehry Partners as a practical business and not as a purely creative workshop, its reputation came from his creative ideas. A technology company would at least provide his family with a more solid asset, Glymph argued.

Frank was less certain than Glymph that such a company would be the route to financial stability. Yet the idea had an even more important appeal to Frank, one that could mean far more to his public legacy. It could provide a solution to what he considered one of the most troubling trends in architecture, a steady reduction in the authority of the architect as a consequence of the increasing complexity of the construction process. The problems he had experienced in the first iteration of Walt Disney Concert Hall, when he was prevented from overseeing the construction documents himself, may have been extreme, but they were not unique. Architects were losing control over the execution of more conventional designs as well. Once considered the master builders, the professionals with authority over every step of the building process from design through construction, architects were increasingly being pushed to the margins, victims of a process that was believed to be too complex for them to understand. Licensing the technology the firm was developing could only strengthen the position of architects and improve the profession's ability to hold its own amid data-driven engineers, developers, and financial institutions, Frank thought. In his words, it could "re-empower the architect."

Dennis Shelden, an architect who worked with Jim Glymph to establish Gehry Technologies, described the trend as a separation between design and execution in which construction managers, special consultants, and financial authorities, brought in to assure efficiency and economy, took on more and more authority. Frank was offended at the idea that the architect could be considered merely a shape-maker whose primary job was done once a design was accepted. He became more and more interested not only in his own reputation but also in the status of his entire profession, and he was convinced that the software his office had developed could make a difference.

By 2002, almost every architectural office operated with digital systems, but almost none were as sophisticated as the CATIA software that Gehry Partners had developed. Frank, who barely used a computer himself—he thought of it entirely as a tool that other people used to help execute the designs that he created on paper and with models—was surprised to discover that his office was more technologically advanced than larger, more corporate architectural practices like Skidmore, Owings & Merrill and Kohn Pedersen Fox. "We are way ahead of them technically, we're way ahead of them organizationally," he said. "I just can't believe it. I always thought of them as the business guys." Bilbao, Dennis Shelden said, "was not just an architectural point in time. It was a technology and method point in time as well. Now a lot of people are doing aspects of that"— but Gehry Partners had been first. Gehry Partners was ahead because the software it had developed, from its beginnings with the fish sculpture in Barcelona through buildings as different as the museum in Bilbao and the office building for IAC, was focused almost entirely on helping architects meet the challenge of getting unusual designs built. That was exactly the reason a stand-alone technology company might make sense, Frank realized. It could both sell software and train other firms in its use.

The new company, which was created in partnership with Dassault, was named Gehry Technologies. Frank at first hesitated to put his name on it out of concern that other architects would be reluctant to work with a firm named after someone who competed with them in other realms, but Jim Glymph convinced him, as he had done once before, that his name was still a strong selling point. After all, without its association with Frank, the firm could be mistaken for just another technology company.

The venture turned out to be a mixed blessing. "The success of Bilbao and Walt Disney Concert Hall was supposed to translate into success for this company, but it didn't," Glymph said. Part of the reason, he realized, was that his own strength lay more in developing the technology than in creating a company. "I was a fish out of water, but I was the company's biggest asset," he said. He felt that the new venture was pulling him away from his primary work at Gehry Partners, and he sensed that his relationship to Frank had begun to deteriorate. Glymph was also dealing with some severe personal problems. His wife had been diagnosed with schizophrenia, and Frank urged him to see Milton Wexler, which he and his wife both did. It was not enough to save either his wife or his relationship with Frank, which continued to decline. After two unhappy years during which Glymph could feel the long-standing closeness between him and Frank ebbing away, he agreed to Frank's request that he depart from both Gehry Partners and Gehry Technologies. It was a more amicable separation than Randy Jefferson had had—Glymph told Frank that he trusted him to offer fair terms and he was not going to hire a lawyer. Frank bought him out of his ownership stake, and Glymph, like Jefferson, was gone. Frank never again offered anyone else a share of the firm. And he disposed of the sailboat that he, Jefferson, and Glymph had owned together and bought another one, all his own: a forty-four-foot fiberglass-hulled Beneteau First that he named *Foggy*, a play on his initials, and berthed at the California Yacht Club in Marina del Rey, where Sydney Pollack and John Calley had proposed him for membership a few years before. By then, his most frequent architect sailing companion was Greg Lynn, an avid sailor and expert in digital architectural technology whom Frank had tried to interest in joining Gehry Technologies.

Gehry Technologies continued, with Dennis Shelden, as its chief technology officer, playing a major role in keeping the company going. It grew from twenty-five employees in 2005 to more than a hundred in 2008, and provided digital modeling for such well-known projects as Herzog & de Meuron's "Bird's Nest" Olympic stadium in Beijing; Diller, Scofidio + Renfro's renovation of Alice Tully Hall at Lincoln Center in New York—a job that Frank had lost years before; and the museum in Mexico City built to house the art collection of the billionaire Carlos Slim. Frank decided to bring in a professional manager. He hired Dayne Myers, a former management consultant with McKinsey who had founded an Internet fantasy sports game company called Imagine Sports. Myers convinced Frank that his expertise would compensate for his lack of experience in either architecture or construction, and he joined the company in 2009. Neither Frank nor Myers was ever completely certain about what they wanted Gehry Technologies to be doing, however, and the emphasis varied from developing new versions of software to advising architectural firms about different technological systems to serving the construction industry.

In the fall of 2011, Frank convened an architectural advisory board in the hope that it would help set a clear direction for the company, which Frank hoped to position as the most elite consulting firm in digital architecture. He gathered an impressive group including Moshe Safdie, David Childs, Wolf Prix of Coop Himmelb(l)au, Ben van Berkel of UN Studio, David Rockwell, Richard Saul Wurman, and Greg Lynn. Some, like Lynn, were

considerably younger than Frank and had spent their careers at the vanguard of digital technology; others, like Safdie and Wurman, were Frank's
old friends and contemporaries who, like him, understood the importance
of technology but whose architectural roots were in a predigital world.
The group gathered in New York, in a conference room at 7 World Trade
Center overlooking the site where Frank still expected his performing arts
center to be built.

T he daylong conversation turned out to be primarily a lament over
the diminished role architects felt they had in the building process.
"Why do people go to construction meetings? They go for reliable, hard
information, and they believe architects have failed them," Safdie said.

"They think we are just decorators," Frank said.

"So what are the tools that GT can give us to reestablish the integrity
of information, so that we can take back control?" Safdie asked. "A lot of
wishful thinking goes on in our profession."

"We gave away the profession a long time ago," Van Berkel said.

Frank turned the conversation in a more practical direction. "A lot of
the problem is insurance," he said, and argued that insurance companies
covering architects for malpractice had long encouraged them to reduce
rather than increase their level of responsibility in construction projects.
Gehry Technologies had the potential to reverse this process, he argued.
"If the insurance companies realized that Gehry Technologies could provide a trail of everything that happened in a project," they would welcome
it, he thought, if only because it could provide a clear, unchallengeable
record of who was responsible for every change made at every point in the
history of a project's design and construction.

The combination of Dayne Myers and Frank was never a natural match.
Frank hired Myers because he had convinced himself that Gehry Technologies needed a professional manager with experience in the world of
technology, but he never believed that Myers shared his desire to direct the
company's technological expertise toward restoring power and authority to
architects. He was a management hired gun, not an architect or even a person with any unusual degree of passion for architecture. His interest seemed
to be the construction industry. When Frank spoke to Myers about his
desire that the company focus on using its technology to address the challenges to the architectural profession that Frank was so concerned about,
Myers's tone, Frank thought, was condescending. Myers also approached

Autodesk, the largest maker of architectural software, about investing in Gehry Technologies, over Frank's objections. Gehry Technologies had a longtime partnership with Dassault, the French company that had created the CATIA software, and Dassault and Autodesk were bitter rivals. Frank thought it was highly unlikely that Myers's plan to play them off against each other would work, and it did not. The company's relationship with its original partner deteriorated precipitously. Myers's priority, Frank thought, was not to manage Gehry Technologies but to turn it into a highly visible commodity that might someday be sold outright to either Autodesk or Dassault, or to some other large tech company.

A more urgent problem was that Myers was burning through money rapidly, expanding Gehry Technologies beyond what Frank and the company's small board, which included his friend Larry Field, thought reasonable, to the point that the company's finances were spinning out of control. Frank decided that Myers had to go. Myers, unlike Jim Glymph, did not leave willingly or gracefully. He refused to accept the financial settlement Frank offered, and threatened to bring the matter to arbitration, as his contract permitted. Frank found the matter upsetting—the arbitration hearing would make it impossible for him to take his preferred position of avoiding confrontation, and he would have to listen to Myers's lawyers claim that he had mistreated the man he had hired as a chief executive officer. His anxiety about the arbitration made him unusually irritable and short-tempered for several months.

The result made at least some of the pain worthwhile. Frank turned again to his friend Patricia Glaser, the litigator who had gotten the lawsuit Fred Nicholas brought against him on his Tiffany jewelry deal dismissed. Glaser, tough and fiercely loyal to Frank, once again vanquished her opponent on Frank's behalf. The arbitrator ruled against Myers on all counts and said that Frank had just cause for dismissing him and had not acted unfairly. Glaser made such a strong case that the arbitrator ruled that Myers was entitled to no financial settlement whatsoever, and that he also would have to pay Frank's six-figure legal costs. Frank's initial reaction to winning the arbitration was not unlike the doubts he often felt when he looked at his finished buildings for the first time. He felt guilty, and he momentarily wondered if he had gotten away with something. He asked himself if his fiduciary duty to Gehry Technologies' shareholders required him to insist that Myers pay his legal bills, as the arbitrator had ordered. But like most of his initial doubts about the validity of his architecture, his moment of doubt quickly passed, and he accepted the arbitrator's ruling with a surge of relief.[*]

When Frank decided to replace Dayne Myers, Dennis Shelden, the chief technology officer, was the most experienced employee Gehry Technologies had. But however talented Shelden was, he was not the person to dig the company out of a management hole, Frank thought. He turned instead to the person he had come increasingly to rely on to solve problems, coordinate his movements, and understand everything he was thinking and doing: Meaghan Lloyd. Over the objections of Larry Field, who liked Lloyd but worried about whether she was capable of running the company, Frank named her chief executive officer of Gehry Technologies.

This time, his instincts were right. Within a year she had stabilized the company and stemmed its losses. But Lloyd could not turn Gehry Technologies into the large, stand-alone company that Frank had hoped to build. It was going to be too difficult for the company to go it alone. Selling it to either Dassault or Autodesk was conceivable, but the company would have been devoured. In the hope of keeping at least some independent identity for Gehry Technologies, Lloyd negotiated a merger with Trimble Navigation Ltd., a manufacturer of global positioning systems. Trimble had recently purchased from Google a company called SketchUp that made software for three-dimensional architectural modeling, and it was eager to move further into the realm of architecturally related software. But however much the deal with Trimble would allow Frank to continue his quest to use technology as a means of enabling architects to take more responsibility in the building process, it meant the end of his dream that Gehry Technologies would become a lasting business on its own.

R andy Jefferson, Jim Glymph, and Dayne Myers were not the only people whom Frank had become disenchanted with after giving them great authority over parts of his firm's business. Long before things ran aground with Myers, he began to lose the deep affection he had felt for Edwin Chan. Chan, a soft-spoken, elegant architect from a well-to-do Hong Kong family, had joined Frank's office almost by accident after his graduation from Harvard. At architecture school he had never been par-

---

[*] Myers, claiming that he had no funds, then initiated a second arbitration. In March 2015 the parties agreed on a revised amount.

ticularly interested in Frank's work—his hero was the more cerebral Peter Eisenman—but he was intrigued by Frank's close relationships to artists, and he liked the idea of moving to Los Angeles as an alternative to Boston, which he found "claustrophobic." So he applied for a job, thinking it wouldn't hurt to spend a couple of years with Frank Gehry, as many young architects did. "I never thought I'd stay very long," Chan said. It helped that Frank's old friend Harry Cobb, who headed the architecture department at Harvard when Chan graduated in 1985, told Frank that Chan was one of the best students he had ever had. He was offered a job.

At first, as Frank remembered in his talk at Case Western Reserve University, Chan was nearly invisible. He labored quietly, carefully observing not just the design process, but Frank himself. It was a time when the office was just beginning to do larger projects—winning the competition for Walt Disney Hall was still three years away—and "the development of the architecture at the office was at a critical juncture. We were searching for something new, something more fluid," Chan remembered. The Vitra Design Museum outside Basel, the American Center in Paris, and the Weisman Museum in Minneapolis were being designed, and they did more than extend the geographical reach of Frank's work. They made it clear that Frank was taking the first steps that would lead to Bilbao.

Edwin Chan was excited by the design direction Frank's work was taking, and he became more and more engaged with it. Frank, in turn, became more and more engaged with Chan once he began to play an active role in the office, and he became one of Frank's favorite sounding boards for ideas. Frank was impressed not only with Chan's design instincts, but also with his manner. He was cultivated and articulate, and he was the kind of sophisticated second in command whom Frank could trust to fill in for him at a client meeting. Soon Chan was working side by side with Frank on the American Center, and then on the Weisman. When the Bilbao project began, it seemed only logical that Chan should be a key member of that design team as well. Frank began to talk about how well Chan's instincts mirrored his own, and how much he enjoyed their exchanges. Chan became one of his most important design lieutenants, and Frank, always energized by "someone to play off of," began to describe Chan in the flattering terms reserved for a favored protégé. "Edwin was like family," he said.

Edwin Chan played an even more important role in two major, cutting-edge commissions after Bilbao was completed: an office and research building for Novartis, the pharmaceutical company, on its campus in

Frank and Edwin Chan (*right*) present a model for the Novartis building to Daniel Vasella, the company's chief executive officer.

Basel, and a museum for the Fondation Louis Vuitton in the Bois de Boulogne in Paris. Both buildings were in effect sculptures in glass at civic scale, reinterpreting many of the forms and ideas Frank had expressed as opaque structures of metal in projects like Bilbao and Walt Disney Concert Hall into transparent glass. Both represented another technological leap as well as a new form of visual drama. Novartis was finished first, in 2009: a kind of enormous, amiable, see-through beast, it brought a sense of lyricism and movement to an otherwise more sober campus of ambitious buildings by architects like Tadao Ando, David Chipperfield, and SANAA. Both the visibility of the underlying wooden framework playing off against the voluptuously curving glass and the overall lightness of the building gave Novartis, in some ways Frank's most advanced building so far, an unexpected connection to his earlier work. The Fondation Louis Vuitton, which opened in 2014, was larger, more elaborate, and more striking still.

Edwin Chan's part in developing both buildings was second only to Frank's own, and that of the ever more essential digital software. Yet by the time Novartis opened, and long before the Fondation Louis Vuitton was finished, he was no longer in Frank's employ. His intended few years in the firm had stretched to twenty-five, and he decided in 2010, he said, that it was time for him to go out on his own. But it was not without a push from Frank, who, as he had with so many high-ranking people in his firm, began to feel that Chan had worn out his welcome. Chan's ability to envision Frank's thinking, at first such a boon in the design process, started to make Frank a bit uncomfortable. It was one thing to be able to work closely, hand in hand, in developing a design; it was another to be dealing directly with clients, as Chan, confident that he could speak for Frank and at ease with the most sophisticated clients, seemed often to be doing. Having an associate who had established his own direct line to the management of LVMH, the French conglomerate that owned Louis Vuitton, was in many ways an asset, but it could also be worrisome. It had been decided a long time ago that there was only one name on the door. When Chan showed officials at LVMH the model of an interim design for the Fondation Louis Vuitton before Frank had signed off on it, Frank interpreted Chan's act as a challenge to his authority.

What finally brought Edwin Chan's career at Gehry Partners to an end, however, were more internal matters. As head of one of the two major design teams in the office—the other was run by Craig Webb—Chan oversaw a group clustered at the west end of the enormous workroom, and he had begun to erect small partitions to separate the architects who worked under him from the rest of the office. It was a gesture that went against the visual openness that was key to every part of the design of the office, including Frank's own quarters. On top of that, the firm's business managers pointed out to Frank that Chan's group had been spending far more time on the design process than the project budgets had provided for, which would require Gehry Partners either to bill LVMH for a significant additional amount beyond the design fee that had already been negotiated or to give up much of the profit it had expected from this high-profile project. Neither prospect was pleasant. And there would have to be an awkward negotiation with LVMH, since the firm would have no choice but to admit that it had failed to monitor its own work adequately.

The responsibility for the problem was not Chan's alone—Mark Salette, another partner, oversaw the contractual aspects of the relationship with LVMH, and as the architect most closely connected to project management, he should have prevented it. He would leave Gehry Partners not long after the discovery of the problem. But Frank, having put so much faith in Edwin Chan, felt all the more disappointed in Chan for operating in what seemed to him to be a presumptuous fashion. It was time, he decided, for his longtime protégé to move on. This time, Frank broke the news himself, but he did it gently. "I've been reluctant to do this, I don't know how I should do this," he said to Chan. "But your father is gone, and if I were him, I'd say it's time for you to take a shot—cut the ties and try and get the experience you need." Operating on his own, Frank thought, would be a way for Chan to figure out the realities of business, something Frank believed he had done neither in his own life nor at the firm.

Chan took an extended leave to think the matter over. Calling his departure a leave made it no less startling to the other people in the firm, since most of them had never known the office without him. Things were cordial enough with Frank that Chan returned briefly after a year to help out with a particularly challenging project in China, Frank's entry into the competition for the National Art Museum of China in Beijing. But it was just a cameo appearance. Chan set up a small office in Venice and began to seek work on his own. He understood that he was never coming back for good.

19

From Dwight Eisenhower to Louis Vuitton

After Walt Disney Concert Hall opened to great acclaim, Frank could have been in a position to choose what work he wanted to take on, and to a certain extent, he was. But he tended to say yes as often as he said no, in part because he worried about money and the challenges of keeping his office going, in part because of his continuing desire to show that his architecture was not only a matter of unusual and one-of-a-kind, "bespoke" buildings, and in part because he found it difficult to say no to a client he liked, or whose problem intrigued him. In 2004, for example, he did exploratory work for urban projects on Boylston Street in Boston, in the Chelsea neighborhood of New York, and on Grand Avenue opposite Walt Disney Hall in Los Angeles, as well as a master plan for Harvard's expansion across the Charles River into Allston. He also created a design for a museum in Hong Kong, a prototype gas station for Hess, a library for Deerfield Academy, and an amphitheater for New Orleans, as well as a redo of the façade of Saks Fifth Avenue in New York and, also in New York, a scheme for a fish sculpture that would have been done for the 2012 Olympics had the city won its bid to host the summer games.

Some of these projects never progressed beyond initial sketches, or even as far as having any sketches at all, although they are all listed in the chronological catalog of works that the office created for internal use. The following year Frank embarked on a plan for a huge resort in Singapore for the One and Only chain of luxury hotels, designed in collaboration with his friend Greg Lynn, as well as a cultural center for Istanbul, an urban renewal project called Park Central in Las Vegas, and the second of what would be three versions of a redevelopment plan for a large, triangular site in Barcelona. None of these would go ahead.

Still, 2005 was an unusual year, since it marked the official beginning of two of Frank's more unusual projects of the decade: the Fondation Louis Vuitton in Paris and the Cleveland Clinic Lou Ruvo Center for Brain Health in Las Vegas, a center for the study and treatment of Alzheimer's disease. They were produced for two of Frank's most distinctive, not to say different, clients, Bernard Arnault, the chairman of the French luxury conglomerate LVMH, and Larry Ruvo, a liquor distributor from Las Vegas. What the two men shared was an admiration for Frank's work, and an iron determination to get a project built against difficult odds.

Frank's relationship with Arnault began in 2002, when he was told that Arnault had recently visited the Guggenheim in Bilbao and wanted to meet him. Frank had no immediate plans to be in Paris, but Arnault traveled often to New York, and they set up a date for lunch there about a month later. Arnault, accompanied by his cultural adviser, Jean-Paul Claverie, who had first brought Arnault to see Bilbao, told Frank that he had been astonished by the museum, that he was amazed that anyone could imagine such architecture, and that he would love to work with him.

Frank was grateful for the compliment but a bit taken aback when Arnault then began to talk about a Louis Vuitton store in Tokyo. LVMH was increasingly making its mark in terms of cutting-edge design, and the idea of a Frank Gehry store in a major international city fit neatly into that strategy. But it was not the kind of commission Frank dreamed of, or increasingly felt himself entitled to. It was not until a subsequent conversation that Arnault's intentions became clear. He wanted to build a major museum to house his and the company's art collections and to underscore its role as a cultural patron. He wanted it to be in Paris, and he wanted Frank to be the architect.

It did not take Frank long to agree, although his commitment would not be finalized until after he had gone with Arnault, his wife, Hélène, and Claverie to see the unusual site, which was at the edge of the Bois de Boulogne in a section called the Jardin d'Acclimatation that contained mainly amusements for children. Arnault's company controlled a lease on the site that had been the property of Boussac, the holding company that owned Christian Dior, which had come into the possession of LVMH when it acquired Dior. A nondescript two-story building containing a bowling alley occupied the site, which was the only reason that constructing the museum inside the enormous park was even remotely possible, because LVMH could claim that it was replacing a mediocre old building with a better new one, not disturbing virgin land. Still, public objections to the project were fierce, particularly from neighbors who lived just outside the Bois de Boulogne near the site, and it would take a dozen years for the building to be designed, to win the necessary approvals, and to be built. It was an arc more than twice as long as it took to design and build Bilbao, and almost as long as that of Walt Disney Concert Hall.

Arnault would not be deterred. His longtime rival François Pinault, the owner of the luxury group Kering, LVMH's main competitor, had just abandoned plans to build a private museum on the Île Seguin in the Seine, largely because of public opposition, and took his collection to Venice instead. It was especially important to Arnault that he succeed in Paris where his rival had failed, and LVMH was prepared, not to say eager, to spend the $143 million building the museum would cost. Yet if the project did not have the financial challenges that had faced Walt Disney Concert Hall, Arnault's willingness to spend money created a new set of objections in a country in which nearly all cultural institutions were publicly owned, publicly managed, and publicly paid for. Building museums is the job of the state, not that of private corporations, some critics argued. Was Frank just letting himself be used as a vehicle to improve a rich corporation's image? Was his pleasure at being pursued by one of the richest men in Europe getting in the way of his sound judgment about putting architecture above commerce?

Then again, Arnault and Claverie were willing to put architecture above commerce themselves. They made it clear that they wanted a cutting-edge design and encouraged Frank to think without limits. They asked only that he provide ample amounts of fairly traditional gallery space. The building, in other words, could look however Frank wanted it to, as long as there were plenty of straight white walls and rectangular rooms inside it. LVMH also agreed to cede the building to the city of Paris fifty-five years after its opening, which removed at least some of the objections to the private nature of the enterprise. In time, the Fondation Louis Vuitton would become public property like most other museums, at no cost.

At first, the natural setting of the Bois de Boulogne seemed almost too much of a blank slate for Frank. It had none of the urban elements he liked to play off of, as at Bilbao, and putting a highly expressive building into a garden only heightened the risk that it would be interpreted as a piece of sculpture. But Frank came quickly to realize that the long tradition of glass buildings in nineteenth-century parks like the Bois de Boulogne could give him a compelling starting point, and he began to talk about the notion that the building should be a twenty-first-century version of the Grand Palais, just a few miles down the Champs-Élysées. And a monumental work in glass had the benefit of connecting to some of his other work at the time, experiments with curving glass like the Novartis building in Basel and the IAC headquarters in New York.

Curving glass walls are the last possible surfaces anyone would knowingly choose as a way of displaying paintings. But out of that contradiction came the essential idea of the design, which was to make the building in effect two buildings: an opaque structure containing galleries, clad in nineteen thousand white fiber-reinforced concrete panels, its boxy forms stacked unevenly one atop the other, as Frank had done in some of his early buildings; and then, wrapping around it, another structure of glass in the form of twelve enormous, floating, curving glass sails that serve as both roof and walls, and make up both the façade and the top of the building. The composition of the glass sails gives the building its drama, while the arrangement of the galleries within the white structure—which Frank and his colleagues came to call the "iceberg"—serves the basic function of displaying art. The separation, to Frank, was a response to the criticisms, generally exaggerated but nevertheless persistent, that his museums were too eccentric to show art well. This way, he concluded, "I could be myself" by creating a building that would have a striking shape as its public face, but would still possess fairly neutral display spaces.

Bernard Arnault and Claverie, who would oversee the project for LVMH, accepted the overall concept early on. Claverie called it "an iceberg wrapped in a cloud." Frank, as usual, was dissatisfied and wanted to keep designing. He and Edwin Chan played for months with different arrangements of the glass sails, even as Arnault insisted that the design not stray too far from its origins. Like Eli Broad with his house, Arnault was comfortable with Frank's initial sketches and wanted to be sure that Frank built the building that he first conceived. He wanted refinements, not changes. Unlike Broad, however, Arnault was prepared for a long and challenging period of determining how to engineer the structure, as well as an extended public process of review. Either one might put elements of the design at risk.

The engineering, worked out with the help of Gehry Technologies, was highly complex, and involved a superstructure of concrete and steel, with huge steel trusses, girders, and columns, as well as steel and timber supports that met the ground at an angle and were dubbed "the tripods." Frank being Frank, the boxlike gallery sections, while conventional

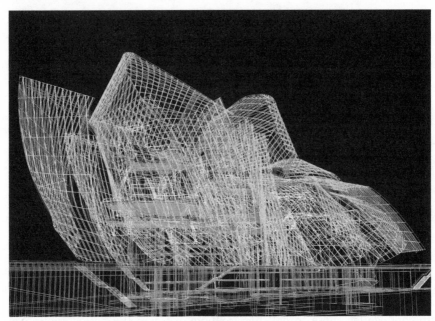

A 3-D image of the Fondation Louis Vuitton generated by the CATIA system

enough for flexibility and for easy display of art, are hardly plain boxes; they have enough curves and bends to them so that roughly 60 percent of the nineteen thousand concrete panels are uniquely shaped. The panels are attached to the structure by means of an armature of welded steel, curved and bent to reflect the shape of the walls Frank had designed.

A separate, secondary structure of steel and wood, attached to the "tripods," supports the twelve glass sails, which are made up of thirty-six hundred glass panels, every one of which is curved, and every one of which is unique. The glass is fitted into a third structure of stainless steel, attached to the secondary structure, that holds each in place, like the mullions in a gigantic window. It is Frank's boldest work of pure structure, and his most frankly spectacular. In Bilbao and Walt Disney Hall the underlying structure is mostly hidden, but at the Fondation Louis Vuitton almost all of it is visible, and the huge timbers and steel trusses and girders provide much of the building's visual drama.

Daunting as the structural problems were, the political challenges often seemed equal in magnitude. The biggest stumbling block—other than the notion that the proper outcome would be to build nothing at all, which some Parisians would have preferred—was connected to the building's height, which rose to roughly 160 feet at its highest point. When the city of

Paris granted planning permission in 2007, it specified that the new building, like the old one it replaced, had to be two stories high. As a result,
there are only two stories of galleries above the ground level. But the idea
that the building is two stories high is a technicality, not to say a conceit,
since there are outdoor terraces beside and above the gallery boxes, and
the glass sails that cover them rise far above the rooftop spaces that they
protect. Frank's "two-story" building is more than twice as tall as the two-
story building it replaced.

An organization devoted to the protection of the Bois de Boulogne
filed suit to stop the project, and in February 2011 succeeded in having the
building permit revoked and work halted. Frank was furious and, according to the architect Jean Nouvel, who had been a vocal defender of the
project, referred to the protesters as "individualistic, uncouth Philistines."
It was like Frank to be upset, but an odd choice of words from a man
who prided himself on being individualistic, and who was certainly accustomed to being called uncouth. Frank said that the phrase was Nouvel's,
not his. Grateful though he was for Nouvel's support, he also claimed not
to have made the other remark Nouvel attributed to him, which was that
he was "outraged by the selfishness, lack of civic pride, and ignorance"
behind the lawsuit.

The project was saved not by public statements but by behind-the-
scenes politicking. The mayor of Paris, upset at having his planning permission overruled by an administrative court, appealed. The National
Senate stepped in and, at the end of March, after work had been stopped
for two months, passed a bill exempting new cultural buildings of national
importance from certain planning regulations, in effect trumping the lawsuit. Bernard Arnault's resolve, not to mention his and Jean-Paul Claverie's
political clout, would redound to Frank's benefit.

It is hard to imagine a client more different from Bernard Arnault than
Larry Ruvo, whose fortune came not from internationally known
symbols of luxury but from a liquor distributorship in Las Vegas. Where
Arnault is reserved, Ruvo is effusive. Where Arnault works with a steely
focus, Ruvo gives the impression of being amiably scattered. What they
share is an admiration for Frank and a belief that his architecture could
help them achieve a personal dream. For Arnault, the dream was to confirm his and his company's position as not just rich and successful, but
as symbols of French culture to the world. For Ruvo, it was to honor the

memory of his father, who had died of Alzheimer's disease in 1994, with a treatment and research center that would demonstrate a new and more civilized approach to patient care.

Arnault did not have to work hard to persuade Frank to take on the job once he and Jean-Paul Claverie explained their vision for the Fondation Louis Vuitton. With Ruvo, it was another matter. He had been raising money for Alzheimer's research since a year after his father's death, in part through a series of benefit dinners cooked by celebrity chefs, and in 2005 he hired a Las Vegas architectural firm to design the facility he had in mind. He thought the plans looked decent enough, but they sparked no enthusiasm when he tried to raise funds for construction. Ruvo realized, he said, that "I've got to package and market this so the world knows we're serious. I know what a celebrity chef will do for a restaurant"—perhaps a celebrity architect could do the same for a center for Alzheimer's disease.

Mark Appleton, the California architect who had designed Ruvo's house, told him that the man he wanted was Frank Gehry. Ruvo managed to wangle his way onto Frank's calendar, but when Ruvo arrived at Beatrice Street and was ushered into Frank's office, Frank was less than gracious. He had little interest in seeing a liquor distributor, and didn't recall having agreed to meet with him, and he didn't want to work in Las Vegas. He had turned down much bigger jobs there. To Frank, Ruvo had come for the worst possible reason: not because he had been floored by Frank's work, as Bernard Arnault had been at Bilbao, but because he wanted a famous name.

Frank did not even rise from his chair to shake Ruvo's hand. "Listen, I'm not doing a building in Las Vegas," he said. Ruvo was livid. "You made me fly down here to tell me that you're not going to do a building in Las Vegas? You have to be the nastiest, the meanest human," he said. And he began to swear at Frank in his best Las Vegas manner.

Thus began what would become one of Frank's closest late-life friendships. "Sit down," Frank said to Ruvo after his tirade. Ruvo began to tell the story of his father, a Las Vegas restaurateur, of his illness and decline and of Ruvo's inability to find adequate care for him in his home city. Frank started to warm up, and he told Ruvo about Milton Wexler and how important it had become for him to support the research into Huntington's disease that Wexler's foundation had begun. The men talked for more than three hours, and by the end of the meeting, Frank had agreed to consider the project if Ruvo would meet Milton Wexler and expand the program to include Huntington's research. Three weeks later, Ruvo and his wife, Camille, returned to Frank's office. Frank turned to Camille Ruvo and said, "I want to make mud pies with your husband. I like him. I'm doing the building."

Given his long-standing interest in science and medical research, it was curious that Frank had never been asked to design a health care facility before. The chance to do one for a private client rather than for a hospital or university bureaucracy was too good to turn down, he decided. And he really was drawn to Larry Ruvo, who was in the end more naturally his type than Bernard Arnault—scrappy, enthusiastic, eager to learn. Still, Frank had to face the question any ambitious architect faces when trying to design a serious building amid the casinos of Las Vegas, which is how not to seem like he was a string quartet attempting to play Mozart when he was surrounded by brass bands playing John Philip Sousa. The problem was mitigated slightly by the fact that Ruvo's four-acre site was in downtown Las Vegas, not along the Strip, but the image of the Strip pervades the city. And the immediate surrounding was a relatively bleak area of urban renewal, without even the vulgar energy of the Strip.

Whatever his original motivation, Larry Ruvo turned out to be Frank's favorite kind of client, eager to talk about what he wanted but trusting entirely in Frank to give it physical form. The design for the Cleveland Clinic Lou Ruvo Center for Brain Health, as the institution was called— Ruvo had affiliated it with the huge Ohio hospital, and expanded the scope to include care for patients with multiple sclerosis and Parkinson's disease—would turn out to be a kind of miniature campus, something Frank had not done since Loyola Law School in downtown Los Angeles. Here, the architecture was far more adventurous than at Loyola, and one of the wings, a huge hall intended not only for the center's use but also as a venue that could be rented out for major events, became one of the most striking spaces Frank had ever created. Multiple curving surfaces of stainless steel are set one against the other, as if they had crashed together; the composition forms both the walls and the ceiling of the space, and all of the stainless steel sections are punctuated with windows. The effect, from a distance, is of a building in the midst of an explosion. The combination of conventional punched windows and Frank's unusual clashing shapes is compelling: it is as if normalcy had begun to disintegrate.

Inside, the distinct elements house a single, spectacular space, with the windows covering all the curving surfaces of walls and ceiling like wallpaper. The sense of a collision evaporates, and as in all of Frank's finest spaces, the things that make the room feel unusual turn out not to make it uncomfortable, and there is a sense of both grandeur and enclosure. The rest of the complex consists of a series of treatment and research wings in the form of stacked white boxes, each floor offset a bit from the next, a practical but still visually engaging backdrop for the intensely active sculptural section. It was the same juxtaposition of functional boxes and sculptural excitement that Frank had designed for the Fondation Louis Vuitton—just a lot smaller, with the sculptural form in front of the other section rather than all around and atop it. Larry Ruvo got his campus, and Frank succeeded in building a piece of serious architecture in Las Vegas with minimal compromise.

W hatever else the success of Walt Disney Concert Hall brought, it did not lead to an outpouring of requests that Frank design concert halls, just as the acclaim of Bilbao did not lead to a rush of museum commissions. The circumstances of Walt Disney Hall, like those of Bilbao, may have seemed too special to be reproduced easily in other cities; it could also be that administrators of other symphony organizations, even if they shared in the general admiration of the hall, may have feared it would be too challenging to follow a similar course with Disney Hall's architect. One musical director who was not in the least intimidated by Frank, not surprisingly, was Michael Tilson Thomas, who had known him since childhood. Thomas and Frank had renewed their acquaintance when Thomas served as assistant conductor at the Los Angeles Philharmonic in the years before Walt Disney Hall, and they had stayed in touch, joined both by their shared love of music and the friend they had in common, Frank's former brother-in-law, Richard Snyder.

Thomas was as different from Larry Ruvo as Ruvo was different from Bernard Arnault: a brilliant conductor, he was known not only for his musical direction but also for his passion for musical education, something he had inherited from one of his mentors, Leonard Bernstein. In 1987, Thomas created the New World Symphony, the only advanced academy in the United States designed to train talented musicians for roles in symphony orchestras. The original funding came from Ted Arison, the founder of Carnival Cruise Lines, who wanted it located in his hometown of Miami Beach, and for years it occupied a renovated movie theater on Lincoln Road. As the organization grew, it needed more teaching and rehearsal space as well as a proper concert hall with good acoustics, and Thomas

recalls mentioning the inadequacy of his makeshift home to Richard Snyder, who in turn said something to Frank.

"And Frank says, 'Oh, well, you want a building? I'll build you a building.' Just like that," Thomas said. The conversation took place in Aspen in
2002, where Thomas was teaching at the Aspen Music Festival and Frank
had agreed to appear at the premiere of a film that Peter Lewis had commissioned about his long and productive process of working with Frank
on the design of the house that was never built. "It was so moving, he said,
'You just need to have a space where you can really do this, and I just
see the whole thing, I really would like to build this building for you,'"
Thomas said. "That was a big honor, someone like Frank saying that to
you." Thomas went back to Miami and mentioned Frank's interest to several people on his board, who reacted, he said, "with a mixture of ecstatic
delight and horror." The organization had not yet even made a decision to
build a new building, and one of the most famous architects in the world
had all but proposed himself for the job. Frank's interest, Thomas said,
was "polarizing." It excited some people who thought that a Gehry building would immediately thrust the New World Symphony into the international spotlight, and intimidated others, who worried that the challenge of
designing, building, and paying for a building by Frank would be more than
a relatively small orchestral academy in Miami could bear. Some members
of the board may have been mindful of the experience of the American
Center in Paris in the early 1990s, which all but did itself in when it asked
Frank to build a more ambitious structure in Paris than it could manage.

Nothing of the kind happened in Miami Beach. The city, eager to cooperate with the orchestra, offered a plot in a redevelopment area near the
convention center facing a new park, and Frank went to work. His long
relationship with Michael Tilson Thomas was helpful, if only to reassure
Thomas how seriously Frank took the needs of musicians. Still, Thomas
said, he was surprised at the extent to which Frank wanted to study details
of how the organization worked. "He said, 'In terms of our relationship, the
more you tell me what you want and what you like and what you don't like,
the better the building will be that you'll get. You have to really tell me,'"
Thomas said. Thomas was also surprised when Frank asked him to drive
him around Miami Beach to look at architectural details so that he could
see how the building might relate to the rest of the city. Thomas, though,
had another request, one that had little to do with Miami but a great deal
to do with Frank's general architectural inclinations.

"I said, 'Okay, could it look like Kurt Schwitters's apartment?'" he asked Frank, referring to the famously intricate sculptural environment the artist created in the 1930s in his home in Hamburg, in which he turned whole rooms into a vast modernist collage. "And he said, 'Yes, it can.'"

Frank's first scheme for the New World Center, as the project was called, seemed less like Schwitters's apartment than like some of his other projects in which he had broken up different elements into separate buildings. He envisioned a group of structures along what Thomas called "a wandering, winding street," containing practice rooms, teaching spaces, and rehearsal halls, growing larger building by building and culminating in a concert hall at the end. The entire thing was to have been under a glass canopy. It was too ambitious, or at least too costly, for the New World Symphony, and Frank suggested putting all the functions into a single, large box. "We'll put the juice on the inside," he said. The symphony went along with his idea, resigned, in Thomas's words, to thinking of it as a sad compromise. "And then somehow in the process of doing that it became really exciting, a Frank building turned inside out," Thomas said.

The structure that was built has no shortage of drama. From a distance

The New World Symphony

it appears almost like a fairly conventional glass-and-metal box; closer in, it becomes clear that there is intense activity inside. The façade facing the park is divided in half vertically. The left side is transparent to reveal to the public key elements of the interior, including a rehearsal room, a central atrium, and a grand staircase, all with many of Frank's characteristic sculptural shapes; covering most of the other half is a gargantuan video screen that can project a live image of concerts inside to people outside, who can attend the concert virtually while they picnic in the park. The building is effectively porous: what is going on in the interior projects onto the exterior, and people on the exterior can see into the interior. The hall itself, which seats 786, roughly a third the capacity of Walt Disney Hall, has the same combination of serenity and energy as the larger hall, but rendered in simpler, less expensive materials—as at the Bard College concert hall done several years before, Frank was determined to show that he could deliver his kind of architecture to a client with a budget.

And in Miami he found a new way to produce spectacular effects for moderate cost. Suspended over the stage are several huge curving white panels that seem at first to be an inexpensive form of Gehryesque decoration but in fact that turn out to be projection screens. They can show videos or color projections to accompany a particular musical program, or can simply be a means of using technology to continually redefine the appearance of the room, giving the hall in effect an infinite number of potential redesigns. If the New World Center is not Frank's most lavish building, it is one of his most energetic, and it may be the one in which he most fully embraced technology as not just a tool to help get the building built, but as a way of shaping the experience people have of his architecture.

Frank came close to designing another building for the study of music, and its loss in 2014 troubled him greatly. The Juilliard School of Music, where one of his good friends, Ara Guzelimian, serves as provost and dean, was considering establishing a branch with a partner in China, and invited Frank to work on the plans. He traveled to China twice at his own expense, thinking of it as a contribution to Juilliard, and even though he did not have a signed contract, he began to design the project with the understanding that he had been awarded the commission. Julliard apparently thought otherwise, and after more than a year of work and multiple planning meetings in New York, Los Angeles, and China, the school's president, Joseph Polisi, informed Frank that there would be a search for another architect.

For reasons that were never specified, but that Frank thought had something to do with objections by the Chinese to his proposed fees, the deal was off. As he often did when something failed to work out, "My first thing was to worry about what I did wrong—I'm Jewish, I go there," he said. But a review of the correspondence showed nothing to suggest that Juilliard ever intended any architect but him to prepare the design for its new conservatory in China. Frank, who was sometimes accused of being too demanding in contractual matters, this time had been far too lax, and had worked for Juilliard on good faith. When he received his honorary degree from Juilliard in the spring of 2014—was it a consolation prize? he wondered—he mentioned to the chairman of the Juilliard board, Bruce Kovner, that he did not feel he had been treated fairly, and Kovner promised to look into it. However, Frank never heard from him again.

The letdown involving Juilliard followed a much greater disappointment in China the previous year. In 2012, Frank, along with Zaha Hadid, Moshe Safdie, and Jean Nouvel, had been invited to prepare a scheme for the National Art Museum of China, a major project in Beijing. It was the scheme that brought Edwin Chan back into the office briefly, and Frank was exceptionally proud of the result, which pushed his work forward in a way that went beyond even the Fondation Louis Vuitton. Frank, working with David Nam, designed a façade of undulating waves of what he called "translucent stone," a kind of super-advanced form of glass block that he developed specifically for this project. Unlike any of his previous work, the building was to be a large, symmetrical box: the undulations, and the movement of light through the glass, were the substitutes for the clashing elements that made his other buildings appear dynamic. It is the first design of Frank's that could be described with words like "stately" and "majestic," and it is the closest he has ever come to designing a building that might loosely be called classical. But what was most remarkable about it was that these qualities seemed to make it no less Gehryesque. The undulating, heavy, translucent glass block really did appear to have the liveliness and sense of movement that characterizes most of Frank's work, here joined to the dignity and formality of a more traditional stone building.

Frank was so pleased with the project that he would have been unhappy had he lost the competition under any circumstances. But he had lost under unusual, and particularly painful, ones. After the three architects presented their schemes to officials in Beijing in 2013, there was a long period of silence, and no announcement of a winner. Eventually the commission was revealed to have been given to Nouvel, but his design had evolved from its original version, which was dark, almost black, into a seemingly translucent building that appeared at first glance to bear no small resemblance to Frank's. Frank was furious. Even if Nouvel had not literally copied his design—and Nouvel's building, when it was formally unveiled in September 2014, turned out to have as many differences from Frank's as similarities—it nevertheless seemed to him to be too close for comfort. He and Nouvel had always been competitive, but Frank experienced the changes in Nouvel's museum design not as normal competition but as something different, something that, to him, went beyond the bounds of a normal contest.

Bernard Arnault, Larry Ruvo, and Michael Tilson Thomas did not constitute the full range of Frank's notable clients in the post–Disney Hall period. Jerry Perenchio, the billionaire owner of Univision, asked him to design a small office building for a site in the center of Beverly Hills, which Frank did with pleasure, still eager to have more work visible in his hometown. Perenchio told Frank he was happy with the design, and then abruptly abandoned the project before construction started. It was the kind of setback that at another point Frank would have found so painful as to be disabling, at least for a short while. Now he just moved on, busy with work for other clients like Maja Hoffmann, an art collector who was an heiress of the Hoffmann–La Roche pharmaceuticals fortune, and who had coproduced Sydney Pollack's film *Sketches of Frank Gehry.* [*] Hoffmann, who described herself as an "enabler" of art, commissioned Frank to design a structure that would serve as the centerpiece for the "Parc des Ateliers," her plan to transform Arles, in the south of France, into a contemporary art center. W magazine described the project as "a kind of think tank–cum–laboratory for contemporary art complete with a public garden, as well as exhibition spaces, archives, and housing for artists in converted old factory buildings," some of which were to be done by the New York architect Annabelle Selldorf. Frank's original scheme, which called for two towers in the center of Arles, was scaled back after objections from the National Commission for Historic Sites and Monuments that it would obscure views of historic buildings and threaten the status of Arles as a UNESCO World Heritage Site. In 2014, construction began on the revised version, which consisted of a single, twisted tower of aluminum blocks, twelve stories high, rising out of a cylindrical glass base with a glass roof. It is scheduled to be completed in 2018.

------

[*] See chapter 17.

Maja Hoffmann knew the art world and the full scope of Frank's career as well as anyone. Mark Zuckerberg, the founder of Facebook, barely knew of Frank at all before he hired him to design a new headquarters for his company in Menlo Park. Zuckerberg made no claims to be interested in architecture. His company had been talking with Gensler, a large corporate firm that specializes in corporate buildings, when Bobby Shriver, a close friend of Frank's whose sister, Maria Shriver, was then married to the California governor, Arnold Schwarzenegger, suggested to Sheryl Sandberg, Facebook's chief operating officer, that the company talk to Frank instead. Shriver knew that Frank was eager for more large commercial projects and that he would welcome the chance to do one relatively close to home.

An architect in his eighties did not seem like the most natural choice for Facebook, a company whose founder had not yet turned thirty. And Silicon Valley was not known for its interest in architecture; many companies seemed to have the same attitude toward serious architecture that their hooded sweatshirts expressed toward high fashion. When Frank and Craig Webb flew up to Menlo Park to meet with Zuckerberg for the first time, Frank remembered, Zuckerberg's first words to him were "'Why would someone of your reputation want to do this?' I said, 'You have a fantasy about what I am.' And then I asked Zuckerberg, 'What is your dream? What do you want?' He said his ideal would be one big room. And I showed him pictures of my office."

That, Frank thought, clinched the deal, although the decision to hire Gehry Partners did not become final until Frank and Zuckerberg had the chance to spend some more time together. Frank and Berta invited Zuckerberg and his wife, Priscilla Chan, to dinner at their house in Santa Monica one Saturday night. The four of them got along, and Zuckerberg signed Frank up on Facebook, which he had never used. He would not become a regular on the site—he had little interest in social media—but he got the job.

If it took Zuckerberg a short while to become fully comfortable with Frank, it took Frank and Craig Webb some time to be sure that they would feel comfortable working for Facebook. They knew little of the ways of Silicon Valley, but they were certain that the one company before Facebook to have demonstrated a serious interest in architecture, Apple, was not a client they would have wanted to have. Apple had recently hired Norman Foster to build a sleek, minimalist headquarters in the form of a vast glass doughnut, an abstract geometric object that could not have been more different from anything that Frank would have produced. Frank's casual-

Mark Zuckerberg reviews the model for the new Facebook headquarters with Frank and Craig Webb.

ness and his fondness for rough edges would not have been a good match for Steve Jobs. If an architecture of pure and perfect geometric shapes was the only thing that Silicon Valley wanted, it would have to look elsewhere. But Facebook was not Apple. Facebook had renovated its present campus, which it had taken over from Sun Microsystems, in a somewhat funky, disheveled style, much closer to Frank's work than to the stark minimalism that appealed to Jobs. The old office even had some partitions made of plywood that looked like they might have been the work of a young architect trying to imitate Frank.

When Facebook's real estate team came to Beatrice Street to visit Frank's office, they confirmed the desire to have something just like what Frank had, only bigger. It turned out that they meant bigger by a lot. Zuckerberg's desire to have everyone in a single room, however, and the company's insistence on a tight budget—another difference between Facebook and Apple—posed the risk of having the project end up looking like a Wal-Mart warehouse surrounded by a sea of cars. The only way to avoid that, Frank decided, was to hide the parking underneath and turn the entire roof of the building into a landscaped park. He designed what may be the largest workspace in the world, a single room covering ten acres that can hold more than sixteen hundred employees, who will park their cars, in effect, under their desks. Skylights bring in natural light, and there are several garden areas within the room as well as all across the roof. Frank did his best to make it feel casual, rambling, and open to the world. Yet at that scale it may be impossible for it not to feel somewhat regimented, or to have the bland vastness of a convention center. And whatever it looks like, it is a huge suburban office complex to which most workers will commute by car, reinforcing the suburban sprawl of Silicon Valley.

But Facebook was a happy client: As the building was nearing completion in early 2015, the company asked Frank to design a second building of the same size, and to make some preliminary studies for housing and other buildings that would make Facebook an even larger presence in Menlo Park. And when the first employees moved into the building in April, Zuckerberg posted a statement on Facebook saying that the project was "finished ahead of schedule and under budget. It's the only construction project I've ever heard of achieving this." For Frank, ever sensitive to charges that his buildings were too expensive, Zuckerberg's words came as sweet vindication.

The enthusiastic reactions Frank received to the Fondation Louis Vuitton, the Lou Ruvo Center, the New World Center, and Facebook, not to mention most of his other projects from the post–Disney Hall decade, left him ill prepared for what he would encounter in Washington, D.C., after he received the commission to design the national memorial to Dwight D. Eisenhower in 2009. He had never built anything in the capital—a design he did in 1998 for an expansion of the Corcoran Gallery of Art was abandoned when the museum ran into financial problems—and a memorial to be constructed by a government agency was not the sort of project he normally sought. Working for the federal government was never easy, and a project like this, which would require multiple layers of public review, meant that several public agencies would have the legal right to review his design. No one person was going to be the enlightened and engaged client that Frank always sought to "play with," as he liked to say. (At the Corcoran, he had David Levy, the director, a client whose enthusiasm, if not his financial resources, recalled that of Thomas Krens.) Instead of play, there would be government bureaucracy, as well as a public that would have plenty of opinions of its own about a memorial to a president. But in the period following the loss of the huge Atlantic Yards project in Brooklyn, the office needed work, and Frank knew that he could not afford to be as picky as he would have liked. When the Dwight D. Eisenhower

Memorial Commission, an official body charged by Congress in 1999 with creating a memorial to Eisenhower, solicited interest from architects to design a memorial to the World War II general and thirty-fourth president of the United States, Craig Webb encouraged Frank to respond. He was placed on an initial list of forty-four architects that was narrowed to a short list of finalists, and then he got the job.

His design—which, not surprisingly, bore little resemblance to the turgid classicism of so much of official Washington—provoked an aesthetic and political firestorm. The commission, which included Eisenhower's grandson, the historian David Eisenhower, unanimously selected Frank after reviewing a preliminary version of his design. But when David Eisenhower's two sisters, Anne and Susan Eisenhower, announced their strong opposition to Frank's scheme, insisting that Frank's unusual design was inconsistent with their grandfather's taste, David Eisenhower abruptly resigned from the commission and distanced himself from his previous support. The sisters, meanwhile, found common cause with a conservative-leaning private group, the National Civic Art Society, that was devoted to stopping the project on the grounds that it was not a classical design, which it believed was the only suitable style for a memorial in Washington.

Frank, who admired Eisenhower greatly—when he was in the army, he was assigned to the division that Eisenhower had once commanded— began the design process with his usual earnestness and enthusiasm. Encouraged by Craig Webb, he read books about Eisenhower and then read Eisenhower's speeches. He was especially moved by a talk Eisenhower gave when he returned from Europe to his home town of Abilene, Kansas, in 1945, just after V-E Day, when the victorious Allied commander spoke less about his own accomplishments than about the value of coming home, and of recalling his boyhood. Eisenhower's essence was a particular challenge to translate into physical terms, Frank felt, because not only was he the first president since Ulysses S. Grant to win fame initially as a victorious general, but he was also known, unlike Grant, for a quiet modesty. How do you show military triumph in World War II, depict the peacetime leadership that led to the start of the space program, the interstate highway system, and the desegregation of schools in the south, and portray modesty, all at the same time? "I fell in love with him," Frank said. "His modesty was his strength. He knew what he wanted, and he was as tough as nails."

The project was a double challenge: in addition to representing Eisenhower convincingly, a design had to deal with an exceptionally difficult four-acre site south of the National Mall near the U.S. Capitol, a concrete

Gehry Partners' design for the Eisenhower Memorial

plaza bisected by a diagonal avenue. Frank decided that the solution was not to make the monument a building, but rather a kind of park that would improve the site, which was right in front of the Department of Education, a bureaucratic modern box from Washington's least successful architectural era. He consulted Robert Wilson, the director, who urged him to use Eisenhower's boyhood dreams in Middle America as a focus for the memorial. As Frank pondered Wilson's suggestion and thought about how he could define the memorial and at the same time obscure the ungainly façade of the Department of Education while not blocking views and light for the workers inside it, he realized that he needed something that would be both large and semitransparent. He had recently seen tapestries made by the artist Chuck Close that used digital technology to weave fabric to replicate the appearance of photographs, and he wondered if it might be possible to do something similar with woven metal. His first idea was to create woven versions of scenes from Eisenhower's life, such as people celebrating V-E Day.

Unfortunately, for all their technical ingenuity, the early models looked uncomfortably like billboards. Eventually the tapestries evolved into more of a backdrop, an evocation of a rural landscape that loosely suggests the farm where Eisenhower grew up, and that Frank hoped would play off neatly against the real trees that would be part of the new park. Most important, the tapestries would prevent the concrete monolith of the Department of Education from overwhelming the design and becoming the defining element of the aesthetic.

Susan Eisenhower in particular was not fond of the tapestries, or of much else about the design, which called for eighty-foot-tall, ten-foot-wide concrete cylinders faced with limestone supporting the tapestries, and large blocks of stone in front of them, containing quotations from Eisenhower's speeches, as well as statues representing Eisenhower as both president and general. At a congressional subcommittee hearing in 2012, Susan Eisenhower cited comparisons between Frank's design and billboards, missile silos, totalitarian architecture, the fences around Nazi concentration camps, the Iron Curtain, and tapestries depicting Ho Chi Minh, Mao, Marx, and Lenin. She attributed these observations to others, but that was something of a hedge, since she surely knew that there were few ways to upset Frank more than by suggesting that something he had designed called to mind a Nazi concentration camp.

Anne Eisenhower, for her part, thought the tapestries would be impossible to maintain, and would soon become dirty and ridden with bird droppings. The sisters met with Frank and Meaghan Lloyd, along with Carl W. Reddel, a retired brigadier general who serves as the Eisenhower Memorial Commission's executive director, and his deputy, Victoria Tigwell, in Frank's suite at the Peninsula Hotel on one of his visits to New York. The session was cordial, and Anne Eisenhower said that she found Frank "a great listener." Frank, for his part, reasserted how comfortable he always was with the notion of revising his designs, so long as he felt that his basic ideas were respected and understood. He would be happy to make further changes, he said, so long as he did not have to abandon his overall concept. But that was exactly what the Eisenhower sisters wanted him to do, so the effect of the meeting was to change nothing at all.

In addition to the sisters' belief that they, and not the Eisenhower Memorial Commission, had the right to determine the design of an Eisenhower Memorial, Frank also had to cope with the chorus of architectural classicists who found his design objectionable; with the loss of the Eisenhower Memorial Commission's most committed member, Senator Daniel Inouye of Hawaii, who died at the end of 2012; and with the complex planning bureaucracy of Washington, which requires public monuments to be approved at each stage of design by both the National Capital Planning Commission and the Fine Arts Commission. And if all of those obstacles could be overcome, there was Congress, which had to be willing to appropriate money for construction of the memorial, as only planning funds had been provided thus far. In 2012 Congress eliminated construction funds for the memorial from its planned budget—largely a case of political grandstanding, a gesture to Frank's opposition, since the memorial was not ready to be constructed anyway. A final version of the design had not been determined, final approvals received, or construction drawings executed. Still, things were unpleasant enough that the secretary of the interior, Ken Salazar, stepped in to try and mediate. He was not successful. It was not clear how much the Obama administration actually supported the design, since President Obama named Bruce Cole, an outspoken opponent, to a seat on the Eisenhower Memorial Commission. In the spring of 2014, a House committee went further and called for a new design competition, a move that, if enacted, would effectively have fired Frank and started the process anew. It was easy to see how Jeffrey Frank, a former *New Yorker* editor who had written a biography of Eisenhower, could write that the design "has managed to achieve something rare in Washington: true bipartisan spirit, almost everyone hates it."

Frank considered resigning and came close to doing so at several points. He would change the arrangement and type of statues, he would vary the Eisenhower quotations, he might even reduce the number of tapestries and cylinders that he wanted to have as stand-ins for classical columns. But if he had to eliminate them altogether, he felt, what would be left would not be a revised version of his idea, but almost nothing of his idea at all.

He also felt few people in the architecture community seemed willing to defend him. He was a hero when he designed a building like Bilbao or Walt Disney Concert Hall, but when he was under attack, most of the critics and fellow architects who were so lavish with praise somehow seemed otherwise occupied. There was support from some unlikely quarters, like Witold Rybczynski, the writer and professor of architecture at the University of Pennsylvania who was a member of the Fine Arts Commission and generally sympathetic to traditional architecture. Rybczynski referred to Frank's design in *The New York Times* as "a roofless classical temple," and said he had no doubts about its appropriateness for Washington. He urged the critics of the design to let Frank do his work without subjecting him to continuous nitpicking. "Compromise and consensus are important when devising legislation, but they are a poor recipe for creating a memorial," Rybczynski wrote.

Frank, anxious as ever about his reputation, did not consider the possibility that many of his peers were simply not enamored of the memorial design, and that it was their architectural judgment, not any lack of loyalty, that was preventing them from speaking out. For all his lifelong worry about what people thought of him, it did not occur to him that the architects he respected, and who he knew respected him, might have simply viewed this one as a miss, as one of those moments when Babe Ruth strikes out. And while the scheme was clearly the most serious and ambitious attempt to articulate a new memorial language for Washington since Maya Lin's Vietnam Veterans Memorial of 1981, it was also unlike anything else that had ever been built. It was hard to visualize, and there was little to compare it to. It was not clear how well the tapestries would work at full scale, or how the cylinders—as tall as an eight-story building—would appear standing on the streetscape. Would they be ennobling, or oppressive?

In 2014, after the House committee denounced the project and urged that it be abandoned and a new design competition started, things began to look up. Some help, perhaps inadvertent, came from an unlikely source: Darrell Issa, the conservative Republican from Southern California who headed the House Committee on Oversight and Government Reform, and whose politics were generally antithetical to Frank's, rejected the notion of starting over. Issa met with Frank, and then urged a scaled-back design. He asked the Eisenhower Memorial Commission to forward two alternative schemes to the Commission of Fine Arts and the National Capital Planning Commission, one of which would eliminate Frank's tapestries and columns. Issa's notion, presumably, was to send the responsibility for the decision down the road to the next bureaucratic station, freeing Congress, the Eisenhower Commission, and Frank himself from the responsibility for the aesthetic decision.

Frank was pleased that Issa was not trying to kill the memorial outright. But he would have none of the two-version solution. He said he would resign rather than submit the stripped-down version. The Eisenhower Commission was divided. Yet a majority of the commission backed Frank and put forward only one design, a further reduced and simplified version authorized by Frank. He agreed to take away tapestries that were to have been at the east and west ends of the site, leaving the five main ones in the center, and to reduce the number of columns. The Commission on Fine Arts approved it in October, and voted final approval in June 2015. An editorial in *The New York Times* praised the outcome: "The commission persevered and Mr. Gehry adapted, creatively changing some aspects but never stalking from the field of battle in artistic umbrage."

20

An Archive and a Legacy

T he approval of the Fine Arts Commission did not mean that the battle over the Eisenhower Memorial had been won. The relentless criticism of the design continued, and it took an emotional toll on Frank, especially coming after the two setbacks involving buildings in China: the loss of the National Art Museum of China to Jean Nouvel, and the loss of the Julliard-sponsored conservatory in China that he was all but certain he was going to be able to design. Frank experienced each as a kind of betrayal. He had long been close to Nouvel, who had been one of the most ardent defenders of his Fondation Louis Vuitton design for Paris, and he had many good friends at Juilliard, which had granted him an honorary degree in the spring of 2014. And he increasingly considered any opportunity to design a space for music to be a special privilege.

Still, while he had lost plenty of commissions over the years and was certainly accustomed to having controversy surround his work, he had little experience with the kind of personal charges that were being leveled in the Eisenhower controversy. Sometimes he would make light of them, as he did one morning early in 2015 when Shimon Peres, the former president of Israel, came to visit the office in Los Angeles. Frank gave him the personal tour of the studio that he customarily offered prominent visitors, and when Peres paused to admire a model of the Eisenhower memorial, Frank looked plaintively at his guest and explained that the Eisenhower sisters did not approve of it. "I don't know what's going to happen here," he said. "I'm having problems with the *mishpocha*."

Justin Shubow, the driving force behind the National Civic Art Society, went so far as to argue that Frank was motivated by a desire to destroy, not to support, Eisenhower's legacy. In a 153-page screed that was as much a personal attack on Frank as an architectural treatise, Shubow described Frank by saying that "his avant-garde prior works—which glorify chaos, danger, and pandemonium—are antithetical to everything that Eisenhower stood for." Shubow went on to say that Frank's values were "also antithetical to the orderly, harmonious style of the Monumental Core and the nation's capital, not to mention the order and balance of the American form of government." Citing as evidence the Pritzker Prize jury's citation about Frank, which used adjectives like "iconoclastic" and "impermanent" and praised his ability to create architecture to express "contemporary society and its ambivalent values," Shubow concluded, "Needless to say, iconoclasm, impermanence and ambivalence are not the virtues of a national presidential memorial." He conveniently ignored the fact that the citation had been written twenty-three years earlier and had nothing to do with Frank's intentions for the memorial.

It was one thing to have people not like your work, and it was another to be called un-American. Frank went so far as to hire a well-connected Washington lawyer, Gregory Craig, to assist him in a public relations strategy. Frank's public presence, usually an asset, seemed almost to have become a liability in Washington, where it appeared that his every word was taken out of context or deliberately misunderstood. In a city in which insincerity is the coin of the realm, Frank's earnestness was getting him nowhere. Eventually he gave in to the instincts of conflict avoidance that had always been part of his management style but had rarely entered into his dealings with clients, and he let Meaghan Lloyd and John Bowers, the design partner in charge of the memorial, represent him at hearings and meetings in Washington.

Frank was, after all, a man in his eighties, and it was not unreasonable for him to want to free himself from at least some degree of stress. He was lucky enough to be healthy, but he worried about his energy, about his weight, and, increasingly, about his back, which seemed to be giving him more and more trouble. He had spinal stenosis, a narrowing of spaces in the spine that puts pressure on the spinal core and nerves, with the potential to cause extreme pain. He had one procedure in Los Angeles, which provided temporary relief. In 2011 Nancy Wexler and Herbert Pardes recommended that he see Dr. Robert Snow, a prominent neurological surgeon in New York. In the summer of 2011, just a few months after the celebration of his eighty-second birthday at the top of the 8 Spruce Street apartment tower, Frank was back in New York to undergo surgery at Columbia-Presbyterian

Hospital, where Leslie had died three years before. It was a painful operation, and Frank recuperated for the first few days at the Greenwich Hotel
in Tribeca, until he could fly home to Los Angeles.

He traveled by small chartered jet. For the last couple of years he had
done most of his domestic flying by private plane. He did not own a plane
and had no intention of buying one, but he had concluded that if he was
going to keep to his pattern of constantly flying around in his eighties, he
had to relieve himself from the pressure of standing in airport security
lines and squeezing into commercial aircraft. His contracts with clients
allowed him to be reimbursed for the equivalent of first-class commercial
airfare, and his office calculated that over the course of a year the difference between those reimbursements and the cost of leasing private jets
was roughly $200,000, an amount Frank decided he was willing to pay to
assure himself the relative tranquillity of a private plane. Without it, he
decided, he could not keep going at that pace.

By early September 2011 he was feeling well enough to return to the
office, and his normal, chaotic life resumed. There seemed to be ever
more work on his plate. It was not just ongoing big projects like the Fondation Louis Vuitton in Paris and the Guggenheim Abu Dhabi; he had
recently finished an expansion and renovation of the Art Gallery of
Ontario, an especially meaningful project since it was around the corner from his grandparents' house on Beverley Street, and was the first art
museum he had ever visited. Being asked to take it on was a meaningful
symbol of respect from the hometown that he had left more than half a
century earlier. So was the commission from David Mirvish, a prominent
Toronto theater producer and real estate developer, to design a high-rise
condominium complex just a few blocks away from the museum, which
would be one of the tallest buildings in the city and would give Frank a
chance to expand on the ideas he began to explore in the 8 Spruce Street
tower in New York.

There was also plenty of work much farther afield: a business school in
Australia, a condominium tower in Hong Kong, and a luxury condominium for the new neighborhood being built around the Battersea Power Station in London. In early 2015 he began work on an enormous mixed-use
development closer to home, on Sunset Boulevard in West Hollywood,
that would contain more than two hundred apartments, retail space, and
a large plaza—in effect an urban village—on a two-and-a-half acre site.
And he would take on his first project in Hawaii, planning a portion of
Ward Village, a high-rise project in Honolulu for the Howard Hughes

Frank revisited his grandparents' house at 15 Beverley Street when he was in Toronto to work on the Art Gallery of Ontario down the street.

Corporation, whose chief executive, David Weinreb—a successful investor and real estate developer who had begun his career as a singer—became the lastest in the string of unusual clients with whom Frank's professional relationship quickly morphed into an unlikely friendship.

Frank was leaving a lot of the design work on some of the major projects to trusted designers like Craig Webb, David Nam, and John Bowers, and by choice spending more of his time on several smaller things that he had agreed to do only because they were meaningful to him, like a small pavilion for Michael Eisner's house in Aspen and an intimate, elliptical concert hall he was designing for Daniel Barenboim's West-Eastern Divan Orchestra in Berlin. Frank accepted no fee for the Berlin project, which he thought of both as a personal tribute to Barenboim and as a way of showing his admiration for Barenboim's attempt to use music to bridge the political and cultural chasms of the Middle East.

He was also deeply involved in another music-related project, a school and performance complex in Barquisimeto, Venezuela, for the National Center for Social Action Through Music, a project he had been invited to design in 2012 by Gustavo Dudamel, the young Venezuelan conductor who had taken over the Los Angeles Philharmonic from Esa-Pekka Salonen in the fall of 2009. Dudamel, a product of Venezuela's ambitious program for teaching classical music to children, continued to direct a youth orchestra in his native country, and knowing of Frank's strong interest in arts education, he arranged for Frank and Deborah Borda to visit the program in Venezuela. "It knocked our socks off to see these little kids playing classical music," Frank said. "There is no place in the world where an arts education program like this exists." Designing a new home for the program in Barquisimeto, Dudamel's native city, was a project that seemed to combine all of Frank's interests, and he quickly agreed to do it.

The project would sit on the back burner for years, delayed first by the illness of Hugo Chávez, the president of Venezuela, and then by a period of uncertainty after Chávez's death. The country's troubled relations with the United States seemed only to be declining further under the policies of Chávez's successor, Nicolás Maduro, whose government was widely perceived as antidemocratic, and by the end of 2014, when Frank and Dudamel were invited to return to meet with Maduro, the political situation in Venezuela was in considerable turmoil. Dudamel, as a native of Venezuela, might have a continued interest in working with the Maduro government, but Frank's decision to offer his services to a regime that was commonly viewed as anti-American, not to say corrupt, seemed harder to understand. Frank defended himself mainly by offering a standard demurral. "I'm not involved in the politics," he said. "I'm involved with arts education. If anything I was doing contributed to their politics, I wouldn't do it." His admiration for the arts education program that had been developed in Venezuela was certainly sincere, as was his claim that it was the project that interested him, not the politics of the government that was his client. But it seemed like a weak argument compared with the strong position he had taken on workers' rights at his project for the Guggenheim in the Middle East. Frank was having trouble admitting that it was going to be difficult to continue to work for the government of Venezuela and not be tainted by its politics.

In Los Angeles, at least, Frank could focus on projects that truly were disconnected from politics. He had agreed to advise the Los Angeles Philharmonic on a series of productions of Mozart operas to be designed by architects, and he set to work on the first one himself: a *Don Giovanni* that Dudamel would conduct at Walt Disney Hall in the spring of 2012. Reviewing the opera, Zachary Woolfe of *The New York Times* wrote that

Frank "filled the stage with huge icebergs of crumpled paper. . . . It was an eerie, elegant study in white, with the strangeness that should permeate *Don Giovanni*." Frank's opera was followed the next year by *The Marriage of Figaro*, designed by Jean Nouvel, and by a production of *Così Fan Tutte* in 2014 designed by Zaha Hadid.

Frank also took on the installation of two major exhibitions at the Los Angeles County Museum of Art. One was a show of the work of Alexander Calder, which opened in late 2013, for which Frank designed a series of white platforms and curved backdrops that responded to the color and movement of Calder's sculptures with what could only be called energetic understatement. It was preceded by a retrospective of the work of one of Frank's most cherished friends from the Los Angeles art scene in the 1960s, the sculptor and ceramicist Ken Price, which was scheduled for late 2012. Frank and Berta had collected Price's work since the early years, and the exhibition would have several of their pieces.

Price had lived in New Mexico since 1971, and he had been ill with cancer. It was not clear whether he would survive to see the exhibition, and Frank worked closely with him to learn how he wanted his pieces to be shown, treating Price in effect as his client, along with Stephanie Barron, the museum's curator. Price died at the end of February, several months before the September opening and shortly after Frank had visited him in Taos to present the final version of his design, which he thought of as a personal tribute to his friend.

The show was in the exhibition gallery in the Resnick Pavilion, a large, bland box by Renzo Piano that, left alone, would have swallowed up Price's work, much of which was as small as a ceramic teacup. Frank designed what was in effect a series of rooms inside the space, bringing down the scale to accommodate Price's small sculptures and creating a clear processional movement. Some of his characteristic angles were present, but they were muted, as if to suggest that Frank wanted to show that he was there, but at the level of a whisper. The installation was painted entirely in white; everything about the design was intended to allow Price's colorful work to be front and center. Price created some large sculptures toward the end of his life, and Frank placed most of those at the end of the gallery, in the only part of the space that had a window and natural light. Frank left this last section largely undefined, as if he had decided to step aside and let his final gesture to his friend be natural light and open space.

Frank, who rarely liked to write anything, agreed to write a short essay about Price for the museum's catalog. It was one of his gentlest and most eloquent pieces of writing. "I have a personal affinity for ceramics," he began. "Before I studied architecture, that was my first art class. I made stuff that was ridiculously funny, so I became an architect instead." He recalled buying Price's work early on, including a cup held up by snails, for $200. "From the beginning I thought about the forms of his cups and sculptures," Frank went on. "They were like buildings. There is one cup that has a little twisted piece on the top. When I look at the California Aerospace Museum that I designed in the early 1980s, with the airplane coming out of the building, and then look at the cup, I think the similarity of form was totally unconscious." In a comment that says as much about how he hoped he would be perceived as it does about Price, Frank went on to explain how much he admired Price for continuing late in life to make new kinds of work. "It may not be completely successful, but he had the courage to try. That's what I loved about him, and why I've been inspired by him all these years. . . . His work has a sense of clarity and an unselfconscious sense of humor. It speaks volumes; it speaks of pleasure and love, and speaks of beauty without bravado."

The pain of Ken Price's loss would be duplicated many times, and it sometimes seemed to Frank as if the people closest to him were disappearing, one by one. Ben Gazzara had died in New York of pancreatic cancer just a couple of weeks before Price, making February 2012 a particularly difficult month. At the beginning of 2013, Ada Louise Huxtable, the writer and critic who had become a good friend during the years she and Frank served together on the Pritzker Prize jury, also died of cancer. Frank traveled to New York to speak at her memorial service, as he had done a few years before when Herbert Muschamp went after a long bout with lung cancer and Frank found himself speaking before an audience in the auditorium at Renzo Piano's New York Times Building, the building that he had almost gotten to design. Toward the end of 2014 he again flew across the country to fulfill a similar duty for Mildred Friedman, the curator who had been so critical to his career in the mid-1980s, when she mounted the first major retrospective of his work at the Walker Art Center in Minneapolis, and who, with her husband, Martin, had remained a close friend of his ever since.

The hardest loss of all, surely, was also the most sudden: Peter Lewis, who died suddenly of a heart attack at the age of eighty on November 23, 2013. Frank flew to Cleveland for Lewis's funeral at the imposing, gold-domed Temple Tifereth Israel at University Circle, where he was asked to speak along with Anthony Romero, head of the American Civil Liberties Union, and Shirley Tilghman, who had just stepped down as president of Princeton, Lewis's alma mater, to which he had given the Peter Lewis Science Library, designed by Frank. Despite how eloquent he could be on the rare times when he decided to compose a piece of writing, Frank did not like to prepare speeches and preferred to talk extemporaneously, counting on his warmth, amiability, and sincerity to get him by. He seemed without guile, and he knew that he could communicate earnestness, which on the occasion of a memorial service would often suffice, even if it was accompanied by some hesitation and rambling.

Frank was particularly shaken by Lewis's death, and despite how sensitive he was to anti-Semitism and how frequently he tended to make oblique references to his Jewish heritage, mostly connected to anxiety and worry, he never felt particularly comfortable in a synagogue, particularly not on the pulpit. He began his eulogy by saying that he had always expected that since Peter Lewis was several years younger, Lewis would be speaking at Frank's funeral, not the other way around. "So I'm not prepared," Frank said. Lewis, he was sure, would have been ready with a speech for his service. He spoke of the "incredible voyage" the two had taken together, under Lewis's patronage, in designing his house, which was never built, and the buildings for Case Western Reserve and Princeton, which were, and in working together on various ventures for the Guggenheim. "I loved the guy, so this is very emotional for me," Frank said, but he never managed to get much beyond praising Lewis as a patron who believed in him, and as a consequence had an impact on the future of architecture. Unlike his written tribute to Ken Price, his remarks at Peter Lewis's service never quite captured the essence of Lewis's quirky, passionate, mercurial, and determined personality. Frank's close relationship with Lewis was marked by an unusual combination of love, awe, common identity, and deep competitiveness, and it was as if Frank had never, in the end, fully sorted all of that out.

Frank's sadness at the loss of his friends never turned to despair. As always, his work sustained him, and the feeling that he still had a large social and professional circle; if death had taken some of its members, it seemed as if new ones were always being added. And there were always a few things he would turn to in the rare moments when he needed a break from architecture. He and Berta began to attend the Los Angeles Philharmonic with more regularity, making use of their seats right next to Deborah Borda, the orchestra's executive director and their close friend. The success of the architecture made it easier for Frank to focus on the music—he no longer worried about what was wrong with the building, or wondered what people were thinking of it.

Often he and Berta would go backstage afterward to visit with Gustavo Dudamel. When friends of Frank like Emanuel Ax, the pianist, were in town to play with the orchestra, Frank and Berta would join Borda and Dudamel in a postconcert supper at Patina, the restaurant on the ground floor of the Walt Disney Concert Hall. Musicians had come to take the position in Frank's life that hockey players once occupied, as the people who were masters of a realm of activity that he loved and wanted to feel connected to. He could admire his musician friends, like his hockey friends, without feeling competitive with them. They, in turn, admired him as an important architect, and he saw none of the envy that was sometimes directed at him by other architects.

In the summer of 2012, music and architecture came together in a new way, when Frank and Berta agreed to host the cellist Yo-Yo Ma at their house in Santa Monica in a small benefit concert for the Obama presidential campaign. The cost of admission was a minimum contribution of $10,000. Frank was excited about the event, and managed to dissuade the Obama campaign coordinators from their original plan of putting up a tent in his backyard. Frank wanted the concert to be inside the house. He was eager to see how the living room, with its slatted wood ceiling, would work acoustically, as well as how it would look when much of his furniture was removed and replaced with folding chairs. In 2012 he was feeling particularly enthusiastic about Obama—it would be another year before Obama would appoint Bruce Cole, an avowed opponent of Frank's design, to the Eisenhower Memorial Commission, and Frank would feel let down, if not betrayed.

After cocktails in the backyard, seventy people managed to squeeze into the living room, most in white folding chairs arranged roughly in a semicircle, with three of Frank's fish lamps and one of Ed Ruscha's famous silkscreens of the Hollywood sign in the background. There were no political speeches. Frank didn't want them, and besides, everyone in the room was already backing Obama. Instead, Frank stood up and said to the audience, "I tried to replicate Disney Hall for you—well, here he is," and then invited Ma to take a seat in the center of the semicircle. Ma, like Frank one of the few people in his field to have become at once a serious artist and a popular celebrity, seemed entranced with his surroundings. "So this is liquid architecture? Frozen music? It is such an honor to be in your home," he said to Frank and Berta. "I thought that Bach would be appropriate," Ma went on. "He was one of the great architects of music. I thought I would play the Third Suite—he wrote six—since we hope we are midway through [Obama's presidency] so I picked a middle number."

He then proceeded to play the Bach, and the acoustics were as good, if not better, than Frank had hoped. The sound was crisp, yet resonant, and Bach, whom Frank had loved since he had heard Greg Walsh play what he liked to call "the "Gehry Variations" six decades earlier, seemed to echo many aspects of Frank's architecture: complex, but not discordant, its rich structure always visible yet always in the service of comfort and sensuousness. In his conversations with Barbara Isenberg for her book, Frank had compared his design process in the Atlantic Yards project to Bach: "I look at it like composing a Brandenburg concerto, which has a coda but layering. It builds up notes as it goes, and then it shifts into another octave. It adds different instruments and changes the character as it unfolds." As Ma played, Frank sat in the second row, next to Deborah Borda, listening intently with a peaceful smile on his face. He had lived in the house for thirty-four years, and that night, hearing Yo-Yo Ma, he was experiencing it as never before.

Frank began 2013 with a bronchial infection that led him to cancel trips to Europe and Asia. It frightened him. At eighty-three, anything more than a slight cold could instill a fear that he might be at the beginning of a permanent decline. It turned out to be no more than a brief illness, and by late January his strong constitution had bounced back sufficiently for him to be able to plan a surprise birthday party for Berta, who would turn seventy on January 31. To keep her suspicions at bay, Frank scheduled a family dinner for that night, which fell on a Thursday, and arranged for Berta's sister to fly up from Panama to join them. Two nights later, her birthday over and done with, Berta agreed to a request from her sons that she and Frank come to a new restaurant they said they had discovered in Santa Monica. When they arrived at the restaurant, they were greeted by a crowd of the people Berta loved best: her family, Frank's sister, Doreen; his former brother-in-law Richard Snyder; and longtime Gehry standbys like Gere Kavanagh, the writer Joseph Morgenstern, Richard and Edina Weinstein, and Bobby and Malissa Shriver. Sid Felsen and Joni Weil, the owners of the lithography studio Gemini G.E.L., were there, and so were

Ed Moses, Ed Ruscha, and Chuck Arnoldi from the old artists' contingent. As was often the case at intimate Gehry social events, there were relatively few architects—Greg Lynn and his wife, the architectural historian Sylvia Lavin, and Craig Hodgetts and his wife and partner, Ming Fung, were among the few, as well as Greg Walsh, who remained a part of the extended family. A Latin band played live jazz, and Sam and Alejandro toasted their mother. "Thanks for making us," Alejandro said. "And thanks for managing your husband."

The party was every bit as celebratory as the one Berta had given for Frank's eightieth, but altogether different. Berta's party was spirited, but small and private, while Frank's was an over-the-top celebration of his public identity. If the contrast between the two events underscored the extent to which Frank and Berta wanted different things, it demonstrated even more their strength as a couple. As party planners no less than in so many other things, they were both skilled at knowing exactly what the other wanted, in taking charge to make sure that it happened, and in having no inclination to be judgmental about how different their desires were.

Berta had nothing to do with the planning for Frank's next major birthday, his eighty-fifth, which was marked in February 2014 at the Guggenheim in Bilbao. Frank thought it would be good to take a family trip back to the museum, and late in 2013 he told Juan Ignacio Vidarte, the former Bilbao government official who had played a critical role in the establishment of the museum and had worked for the Guggenheim since the time of construction,* that he was turning eighty-five and that he wanted to celebrate next February 28 in Bilbao with his family. Vidarte offered to arrange a dinner. "He said he didn't want anything fancy," Vidarte said. But Vidarte and his colleagues in Bilbao thought otherwise. "Everyone said that if he does this, we should make it a tribute to him and show the gratitude of the city and the Basque country," Vidarte said. And then, at home watching television on New Year's Eve, Vidarte saw Daniel Barenboim conducting the Vienna Philharmonic, and recalled how much Frank had come to like and admire Barenboim and the West-Eastern Divan Orchestra that he had created with a roster of Arab and Israeli musicians playing together. "I know of their connection, and I thought it would be a wonderful surprise for Frank," Vidarte said. He contacted Barenboim, who could not bring his orchestra, but said he was free to come himself and play a recital in Frank's honor. Barenboim played a Schubert piano

---

* See chapter 14.

Frank talks to Daniel Barenboim (*back to camera, foreground*) at his eighty-fifth birthday party at the Guggenheim Bilbao in 2014. Juan Ignacio Vidarte is to the right.

sonata before an invited audience of four hundred in the Guggenheim auditorium, which was followed by a dinner in the museum rotunda. "I know Frank wanted something more subdued, but it was very moving for all of us," Vidarte said, and Frank was overwhelmed. "Barenboim played for my bday in museum. I cried," he e-mailed from Bilbao. For his eighty-fifth birthday, he had it both ways. He was able to enjoy the good feeling that came from sincerely asking for something modest, and then he could enjoy just as much the elaborate celebration that had been planned by people who knew not to take his request for modesty too seriously.

One of the things that Vidarte and his colleagues arranged in Bilbao was a video tribute from several of Frank's professional colleagues, including Peter Eisenman, Norman Foster, Rafael Moneo, Jacques Herzog, and Álvaro Siza, as well as artists like Anish Kapoor, James Rosenquist, Claes Oldenburg (who, as an inside joke, was filmed holding a pair of binoculars), Jenny Holzer, and Marina Abramović. The architects, not surprisingly, were respectful, if a bit guarded. Herzog toasted Frank with wine from the Marqués de Riscal vineyard in Spain, for which Frank had designed an inn. Eisenman said he liked to think of himself and Frank as two race cars, and "no matter how fast my race car goes, there's always another one in front of me, kicking up dirt," he said. The artists were a bit more effusive. "Thank you for making museums new and improved, and for enhancing the experience of thousands and thousands of museum visitors," Jenny Holzer said. Carmen Jimenez, the Guggenheim's curator, hailed Frank for creating "a milestone in world history" at Bilbao. And Anish Kapoor addressed Frank by saying, "Dear Frank, for all these years we've watched you play—play seriously, but play. Eighty-five, and playing. I say that's the secret of a good life." It was clear that the seventeen years since the museum's opening had done nothing to dim its value for Bilbao and the Basque region, or its meaning as a work of architecture, and that the Basques were as proud of the building as they had been when the world turned to it with excitement in 1997. Frank's eighty-fifth birthday was in every way a triumphant return to the place of one of his greatest achievements. He went back to Los Angeles joyful and rejuvenated.

Daily life still brought its pleasures and its challenges, however. Frank and Berta continued to live in the house in Santa Monica, and although they had created a small studio in their former garage as a potential place for live-in help should they ever feel it was called for, they had yet to concede that they needed any more than part-time cleaning and gardening help. Frank drove himself to work in his Audi S6, a supercharged car that he received first as a loan under a program to put prominent tastemakers and trendsetters behind the wheel of Audis, an effort that clearly worked in his case, since he liked the car enough to have bought it from the company when the loan period ended. Berta drove herself to and from the office in her BMW—like most Los Angeles families, they could not imagine having less than a car per person.

Frank did concede in 2012 that he was no longer comfortable driving any distance at night, and when they went to a dinner party or downtown to Walt Disney Hall, they hired a car and driver. They went out to dinner most nights, often at Vicente's, an exuberant Italian restaurant nearby in Brentwood, or the Pacific Dining Car, the staid, wood-paneled steakhouse near their house in Santa Monica where they had hosted the memorial luncheon for Leslie. It was as far from Frank's design sensibility as any restaurant in Los Angeles, but had the virtues of being unusually quiet, handy, and of serving trustworthy food. They did much of their entertaining at the two restaurants.

Or they ate take-out food at home. One night in the summer of 2014, Frank and Berta were entertaining a friend with take-out sushi from their favorite place in Venice when, in the middle of dinner, the alarm system in the house began to chirp, at first intermittently, and then so continually that conversation became difficult. Frank called the alarm company and tried to explain the problem, and waited on hold for several minutes. It was late on a Friday night, and there was no assistant, no housekeeper or secretary to handle the problem for him. He waited and waited, and when an operator finally came on the line, he pleaded with her to send a repairman. "We are just an elderly couple, living alone here," he said. "Can't you do something? We have nowhere to go, and we can't sleep here with this." The operator told him that she would try but made no guarantee. After a half hour, it was clear that Frank had failed in his attempt to convince the alarm company that he and Berta were old and bereft and that the problem constituted an emergency. So he walked around the outside of his house, climbed into the crawl space underneath the superstructure, found the alarm wires, and disconnected the system. He was nowhere near as helpless as he had said.

Happy as he and Berta continued to be in the house in Santa Monica, Frank had never been able to shake himself fully of the desire to design another house for themselves after abandoning the Venice project. Bruce Ratner had arranged for him to have an apartment on the fifty-first floor of the 8 Spruce Street building in New York to use when he was in Manhattan, and he and Berta both enjoyed spending time in the building, looking out at the view toward the Brooklyn Bridge. But that hardly sated his desire to design a freestanding house for himself again, and he continued to look at possible sites with Santa Monica real estate brokers. On January 31, 2011, he acquired for $7.3 million an old pink Spanish colonial house at 316 Adelaide Drive, overlooking Santa Monica Canyon. He had come a long way since he had to borrow money to buy the house on 22nd Street, on the other side of town. This house, purchased through a limited liability corporation called Adelaide Properties LLC, was on the best street in the best neighborhood in Santa Monica, close to the ocean but quiet and private. The annual tax bill was $65,800 per year.

The house, which was constructed in 1919, had been significantly altered in 1980, with many of its historic elements removed. Frank was not interested in using the existing house as a starting point, as he had done with his previous house; he saw the place as a teardown, and wanted to work with an open site and design a completely new building. It would be relatively easy, he thought, to demolish the old building and start over; in his view there was nothing worth preserving. Santa Monica preservationists thought otherwise, and there was a brief campaign to declare the relatively unchanged north section of the house a historic landmark, which would not only have required Frank to keep it, but also would have given the city's landmarks commission the power to approve his designs for the rest of the property. Ultimately the commission, whether out of a genuine belief that the case for landmark designation was weak or because it feared an awkward contretemps when it was faced with deciding whether or not Frank was capable of creating a piece of new architecture that was in sympathy with the remnants of a Spanish colonial house, declined to grant landmark designation. Frank was free to do what he wanted.

He and Berta remained somewhat ambivalent about moving. He would, after all, be in his late eighties by the time the house was finished, an age when people, if they move at all, tend to move into assisted care facilities, not spectacularly designed custom houses. And leaving the house on 22nd Street would also push into the present the challenge of figuring out what its future should be. Still, he figured that he had little to lose: unlike the property on Harding Avenue in Venice, a new Frank Gehry house on Santa Monica's most sought-after street would be valuable under any circumstances. Unlike in Venice, he realized, he was better off going ahead with construction. He and Berta could always sell it if they decided not to move in, and might well make a profit. There was no reason to make a decision yet.

Frank turned much of the design work over to his son Sam. Not the least of the attractions of the project was that it would give Sam some significant experience in taking charge of a project, and it would allow Berta to be in effect her son's client, with Frank backing up both his wife and his son in their roles. To everyone's pleasure, the process proceeded smoothly. Sam, with Frank serving as a kind of design adviser, came up with a Gehryesque scheme that was based on large diagonal timbers that formed a framework that loosely recalled elements both of Frank's early work and of such recent projects as the underlying structure of the Fondation Louis Vuitton. Much of the building was to be made of glass, but without the curving "sails" of the Paris building or its steel trusses; this was more of a great lodge, with flat planes of glass framed in wood set at different angles, arranged in a large composition in which the pieces overlapped to form a large whole. It was clearly a grand villa, even though it was designed with only a few rooms, and there were separate quarters for visitors and, should Frank and Berta require it, for the live-in help that they had always disdained. Some aspects of the design recalled the temporary Serpentine Pavilion that had been built in Hyde Park, London, in 2008.* As a test of Sam's abilities, Frank had given him almost total responsibility for designing and overseeing the pavilion, and he was delighted with the result. Sam had earned the right to oversee the house, Frank thought. By the end of 2014, with construction well under way, he was exceptionally pleased at how it was coming along, and thoughts of selling the new house were put aside.

O ver half a century of practice Frank had disposed of almost nothing, and he had accumulated an archive that was more than voluminous. His office records filled hundreds of boxes. There were old datebooks, invitations, solicitations, calendars, letters, phone records, almost every piece of paper that had ever crossed his secretary's desk. Some were compliments, like the handwritten note from the architect Rafael Vinoly, written after his first visit to Bilbao in 2000, in which Vinoly said, "I have never seen anything so powerful, so intelligent and so embracing. You made my life better," to which Frank responded, "It is nice to get stuff like that from talented colleagues." Others were less flattering, like the letter from agents for Fossil, the watch company, who were furious that Frank, after creating preliminary sketches for watches for them, had changed his mind and decided not to go ahead with the project. They were shocked, they said: "The opportunities that you dismissed could have created a well-known, worldwide icon. . . . We do not believe that a building in Spain, no matter how famous, will place you in the same genre as perhaps Armani or Ralph Lauren." The archive also contains 1987 letters from Arthur Liman, chief counsel in the Iran-Contra hearings, and the California congressman Mel Levine thanking Frank for writing to protest the testimony of Oliver North, who was defending the illegal plan to sell arms to Iran and use the proceeds to aid rebels in Nicaragua, a political issue that, given Berta's roots in Panama, Frank and Berta viewed with particular urgency.

At the opposite end of the spectrum from politics, the archive contains a remarkable series of photographs Frank had made of industrial buildings in Los Angeles in the early 1970s, somewhat inspired by the work of his friend Ed Ruscha; the collection of images of oil derricks, factories, lumberyards,

---

* Since 2000, the Serpentine Gallery has commissioned a temporary summer pavilion from a prominent architect who had not previously built a public building in England. Other architects who have designed Serpentine pavilions include Herzog & de Meuron, Daniel Libeskind, Rem Koolhaas, Toyo Ito, Peter Zumthor, and Álvaro Siza along with Eduardo Souto de Moura.

and warehouses was a rare instance of his having documented some of his influences rather than simply absorbing them into his own architecture. Frank also saved an invitation from Graydon Carter to attend the *Vanity Fair* Oscar party in 2005; paperwork from the Screen Actors Guild indicating that his "appearance" as himself on *The Simpsons* had earned him $1,825 in 2005 and $34.22 in 2007, as well as membership in SAG; and a gracious letter he wrote in 2000 to the American Institute of Architects urging that the Institute award the Gold Medal, its highest honor, to Michael Graves. (Frank had received it the previous year, in 1999.) Although he was generally supportive of his colleagues, and often acted, like his old friend Philip Johnson, as if he saw himself as a kind of godfather, his collegial instincts failed him when he wrote to the British developer Peter Palumbo in 1987, declining Palumbo's request that he write a letter in support of his controversial project to build No. 1 Poultry, a postmodern office building by James Stirling in the City of London. "I cannot muster up the conviction to be convincing," Frank confessed to Palumbo, putting sincerity above loyalty. "I just have problems with the implication that the present must regress into the past to deal with the future. This is a very personal point of view but buried deep in my gut."

Frank also saved hundreds of pages of telephone logs, such as the one for an afternoon in April 2004 that showed calls from Eli Broad, Brad Pitt, Marshall Rose, and Michael Maltzan, as well as calls from three architecture critics, one museum director, one of his doctors, and someone asking for money. There was a letter Frank wrote to his old friend Richard Saul Wurman on July 21, 1984, turning down Wurman's request for a list of Frank's favorite things in Los Angeles for a forthcoming guide. His response, in toto, was, "As you know I work all day. I come to the office and work and I go home and spend time with my family. That's what I do, that's all I like to do. I am a driven workaholic. Help me before I self-destruct."

To Beverly Weinger Boorstein, a family court judge in Cambridge, Massachusetts, who wrote to him in July 2000 to ask if he would consider being the architect for a new building for her county's court because "it does not seem that you have yet done a 'palace of justice' [and] nothing would be more exciting than for this Commonwealth to take the lead in rethinking American courthouse design," Frank wrote, "I wish my Mother were alive so I could send her your letter. She would be so proud of me. Anyway, thanks for the inquiry. You are absolutely right. We have not yet done a Palace of Justice. The reason is that the bureaucracy that runs these things are [*sic*] terrified of people like me."

Of far more significance were the thousands of drawings, documents, and models related to the design of projects both built and unbuilt. Many projects had generated dozens of models of different sizes and scales, and there were hundreds of projects in total. While the older drawings and documents could theoretically be digitized, and the recent ones had been created in digital form to start with, the firm's models, even if they had been created from digital systems through 3-D printing technology, were physical objects that took up physical space. Simply storing them was a burden. The archive had long ago outgrown whatever storage space there was in the office.

By 2014, Frank was renting warehouse space in three different locations at a cost of slightly under a million dollars a year. Just storing the archive was a huge part of the firm's overhead. But that money was spent to limited benefit, since the archive had never been fully cataloged or organized. It was used from time to time by scholars who were documenting the firm's work, such as Mildred Friedman back in the 1980s with her early show at the Walker and an even larger exhibition of Frank's work that filled the Guggenheim Museum in New York in 2001 that Friedman directed as a guest curator,[*] and Frederic Migayrou of the Pompidou Center in Paris, who organized a comprehensive retrospective of Frank's entire career in 2014 to coincide with the opening of the Fondation Louis Vuitton. These curators were among many researchers who at various times sifted through old material and in the process helped to give the sprawling archive some degree of shape. The exhibitions and their catalogs, not to mention the other books on Frank's work that made use of the archive, were ample evidence that Frank had not been foolish in retaining as much material as he had. But he was not sure how long it could continue, especially given that the firm's high level of activity meant the volume of material in the archive

---

[*] The Guggenheim exhibition, which like the one at the Walker was designed by Frank's office, was the most serious and comprehensive review of the Gehry firm's work up to that point, and it set attendance records for the museum. It was notable not only for the models and drawings that were assembled, but for the drama of the installation. Frank suspended huge swaths of aluminum mesh, recalling his early chain link, from the skylight at the top of the Guggenheim's dome, tying them back to the ramps of Frank Lloyd Wright's rotunda. A minor historical curiosity about the exhibition is that its major corporate sponsor was Enron, which collapsed in a major accounting fraud just a few months after the exhibit. In a press release issued by the Guggenheim, Enron's chief executive officer, Jeff Skilling, praised Frank's commitment to "innovative product," calling it "a quality Enron relates to every day as we question traditional business assumptions. We are pleased to help showcase Frank Gehry's genius." Enron was doing Frank no favors by claiming to have been inspired by his creativity, since the company's "innovative product" turned out to be fraudulent accounting, and Skilling was sentenced to federal prison on a felony conviction.

was continuing to grow. Every month meant not only another storage bill to pay, but also more to store.

From time to time Frank tried to cull the vast store of material, but sometimes this only compounded the problem. At one point, convinced that the Abu Dhabi Guggenheim was not going ahead, he ordered a huge model of the interior to be thrown away, figuring there was no point in devoting storage space to an outsize model of a building that was unlikely to be built. Not long after the model was gone, the dormant project began to show renewed signs of life. If the project did go ahead, the office would just have to make another model and absorb the time and expense.

For years, Frank had been having discussions with curators, museum directors, universities, auction houses, and potential patrons about every possible scenario for the archive. Its sheer size, along with the fact that Frank did not feel he was in a position to provide a large endowment to support its maintenance, made the idea less attractive to a university that otherwise might have welcomed a treasure trove of Gehry objects. He considered selling it off in pieces, but that would flood the market with objects, reducing their value considerably. And it was not just a matter of monetary value. The scholarly value of the archive would be diminished if the various models showing different stages in the development of a project were split among many owners, making it impossible to trace the project's evolution. Many of the simple cardboard models were valuable primarily as part of a set, to demonstrate how Frank's ideas had evolved from a beginning concept to a final design. Yet showing that took a huge amount of space, which is why most museum exhibitions of Frank's work, like the major retrospectives at the Guggenheim in 2001 and the Centre Pompidou in 2014, included just a single model of each project, not a series to show how Frank's ideas had developed, step by step. For the reinstallation of the Centre Pompidou show at the Los Angeles County Museum of Art in late 2015, Frank persuaded the museum to offer somewhat more space to allow the evolution of some projects to be displayed. But even that was just a small sampling of what the archive held.

The biggest object in the archive, in a sense, was the one thing that was not stored in a warehouse: the original Santa Monica house at 1002 22nd Street. Whether or not Frank and Berta moved to the new house on Adelaide or stayed on 22nd Street, there would have to be some eventual disposition of the older house. It was neither likely nor, in Frank's view, particularly desirable to sell it to a buyer who would occupy it, even if such a buyer could be found. The house *was* Frank, in every way, and it was hard to imagine anyone else, even an admirer of the house, actually living in it. His sons felt deep affection for the house, but neither wanted to be the custodian of his childhood home; they both wanted to live in places of their own. And converting 1002 22nd Street into a house museum would take money, too, and lots of attention besides. A house, unlike boxes of drawings and shelves of models, would need ongoing maintenance, which would require both money and time.

Over the years, various friends of Frank's tried to propose solutions to the problem. Richard Koshalek laid out a plan to convert the archive into a museum and study center in 2008, suggesting that the Getty Trust provide the funding to purchase Frank's models. Under Koshalek's plan, Frank would donate his drawings, and the Museum of Contemporary Art would offer the Geffen Contemporary, where Frank's eightieth birthday party was held in 2009, as a permanent location. Frank's house in Santa Monica would also have been preserved and opened to the public as part of the plan.

Later, Richard Cohen, the real estate developer who had hired Frank to design a building in Boston back in 1985,* came up with the idea of creating a Gehry museum in the Inland Steel Building, a celebrated Chicago skyscraper of 1957 by Skidmore, Owings & Merrill that he owned. Frank particularly admired the building and since 2004 had had a small ownership stake in it, a result of his having helped some Chicago investors who he had hoped would restore the building. Instead, they sold it at a profit to Cohen, who, happy to renew his friendship with Frank, increased Frank's stake slightly and suggested that the former banking hall within the building would be a good place for a Gehry museum. Ultimately nothing came of it—perhaps just as well, since it would have been hard to explain why a famous building by another architect in a city far from Los Angeles was the logical place for the Gehry archive—but Frank did end up designing a new reception desk of glass for the Inland Steel lobby when Cohen renovated the building. And he continued to take pride in owning a small piece of a building that he considered one of the great modernist landmarks.

When the idea of creating the small museum in Chicago was put aside, Richard Cohen told Frank he would like to find another way to help with the archive. He proposed that his company acquire a warehouse in Los Angeles that could serve as a more economical holding facility than the

---

* See chapter 12.

commercial warehouses where Frank was then storing all of the archival material. Richard Koshalek had just left his most recent job as head of the Hirshhorn Museum in Washington, Frank told Cohen, and he suggested that since Koshalek was familiar with the challenges of the Gehry archive, it might be worth hiring him to work out a plan. Frank liked the idea that he could be a matchmaker, arranging what he hoped would be a mutually beneficial relationship between two friends.

It did not work out. Koshalek brought in another old Gehry friend, Richard Weinstein, and the two of them produced not the simple plan for cataloging and organizing the archive in the new warehouse space that Cohen was planning to purchase, but a more elaborate scheme for a full-fledged Frank Gehry museum. It was not what Cohen had in mind. He discharged Koshalek, putting Frank awkwardly in the middle of a dispute between two of his good friends. It was similar to the position he had been in years before when he matched another friend with substantial resources, Peter Lewis, with Tom Krens, another museum director, hoping that Lewis would be the answer to all of Krens's needs, and the two had had a bitter falling-out.* That relationship at least had lasted several years. Cohen and Koshalek managed only a few months.

Frank, eager not to lose any friendships over the issue, carefully patched things back together with Koshalek, as well as with Weinstein, assuring them that he considered the matter a business dispute between them and Richard Cohen, not anything that would affect their ongoing friendship with him. As for Cohen, he remained a loyal, if mercurial, presence in Frank's life, less a client than a mix of patron, fan, and friend. An avid sailor, he asked Frank to design a custom sailboat that would be crafted at a shipyard in Maine. At one point Cohen told Frank he planned to build the boat in duplicate—one would be for him to use on the East Coast and the other for Frank to berth in Los Angeles—and at another he said it would be a one-of-a-kind design that he would sail for a period in the East, then sail to Los Angeles through the Panama Canal. He wanted to name it *Foggy*, continuing the name of Frank's existing sailboat. The boat was to be finished in 2015, but Cohen had still not figured out a long-term plan for it, although he was telling Frank he intended to keep it at the California Yacht Club in Marina del Rey, where Frank was a member, so that Frank would have regular use of it.

Cohen continued to work with Frank on the archive question, and at

* See chapter 14.

the end of 2014 Frank was looking into to buying a warehouse in downtown Los Angeles as a storage facility, freeing Gehry Partners from the burden of ongoing rental payments. But there remained the possibility of interest from several institutions. Phyllis Lambert, the founder of the Canadian Centre for Architecture in Montreal, who had acquired the archives of many architects, including Peter Eisenman, came to see Frank in 2014 to propose that a portion of his archive go to Montreal in recognition of his Canadian birth. And the Getty Trust had made a proposal to purchase a portion of the archive, a plan that, if not a complete solution, at least provided a basis for negotiation, and the potential removal of a portion of the archive to the Getty's campus in Brentwood, next door to Santa Monica. Frank remained torn between his frustration at paying for storage and the lack of an easy solution, and his pleasure at being romanced by multiple suitors. In early 2017, he finally accepted an offer from the Getty to purchase his drawings, models, and papers covering the period of 1954 through 1988, as well as additional material involving key Los Angeles projects such as Walt Disney Concert Hall, assuring that his archive would remain in Los Angeles.

Sam Gehry's gradually increasing responsibilities, along with Edwin Chan's absence, made the question of the future of the office harder for Frank to avoid. Craig Webb was the only senior design partner who remained from the firm's earlier phases, but several younger architects, including David Nam, Anand Devarajan, and John Bowers, were taking on increasing responsibility, and Brian Aamoth and Larry Tighe were administering projects with growing self-assurance. Although Frank would grumble from time to time about each of them, he genuinely liked all of them and respected their work. His complaints, such as they were, seemed more in the category of an impatience and irritability that presented itself more frequently as he got older. He was edgier in his mid-eighties than he had been before, and he tired more quickly. And he was a bit wary, after Edwin, of allowing anyone to look like a favorite son.

Still, there were two other architects who had some special status in his mind. One, of course, was his actual son, Sam, whose growth Frank had watched at first with skepticism and later with great pleasure. Sam was low-key and relaxed, and he was careful not to act as an heir apparent. He gave every impression of having inherited his father's warmth without too much of his angst. The other was Meaghan Lloyd, who, Frank believed, could run anything. As a Yale-educated architect she had design skills that her job as Frank's chief of staff and as head of Gehry Technologies had given her few opportunities to use, but they could be invaluable if she were one of several managing partners.

Frank had given the more senior architects in the firm the status of partner, even though none of them had an ownership stake, as Jim Glymph and Randy Jefferson had. Sam, of course, would have a de facto stake once Berta inherited ownership of the firm, as Frank had specified. Frank met with the partners group several times to discuss the future, but the meetings were never conclusive. "All we decided was that we like working together," Sam Gehry said.

The truth was that the future of the firm was a subject that Frank enjoyed talking about, but not deciding. In this case a decision not only eliminated other options, which Frank was never happy to do, but it also reminded him of his mortality at a time when he was maintaining a full schedule, working every day, and traveling around the world. With his health mostly good, especially for a man in his mid-eighties, this was not a time to upset the status quo.

Early in 2014, Craig Webb approached Frank and offered to assemble a group of investors and buy Gehry Partners for $30 million. Frank had considered selling the firm a couple of times in the past to large corporations, most recently to Omnicom, a holding company that owns several advertising and communications firms, including Chiat/Day and Arnell, a branding firm then run by Frank's friend Peter Arnell, who had been a presence in Frank's life on and off since the time three decades earlier when he was operating mainly as a producer of architecture books and put together Frank's first monograph. To Arnell, who for a period in the mid-2000s was advising Frank on management issues in the firm, "Frank seemed like the king of branding." Arnell believed that corporations were only going to become more interested in connecting their images to real places in the built world, and that no one was better suited to do this than Frank. "I thought it was a natural," Arnell said. "Frank was doing furniture, industrial design, and he would have been introduced to businesses all over the world." Omnicom would have delivered to him a steady stream of corporate clients, and it would have added to its portfolio, Arnell believed, "the greatest creative mind of our time."

A deal like the sale to Omnicom would have been a way of getting a lot of cash into his family's coffers without, Frank thought, giving up control. In the end, although the chief executive of Omnicom, John Wren, met with Frank and the two men got along well, Omnicom recognized how different Frank's firm was from the businesses they operated and decided not to pursue the deal, too unsure of the economic parameters to measure architecture by and worried about the liability issues of architectural practice. It was just as well. The notion that Gehry Partners could become a division of a large corporation seemed contrary to everything Frank had ever aspired to. It was hard to believe he would have seriously considered it had it not been for his friendship with Peter Arnell, and his characteristic desire to create business partnerships with his friends. Had the Omnicom deal been consummated, it is unlikely that Frank would have been able to continue to manage the firm as he did, or that he would have been happy with a board of directors to report to, no matter how much money he had in the bank. And Omnicom had no track record of supporting creative people outside the advertising and communications fields.[*] Architecture is not a typical business, and Gehry Partners was not a typical architecture firm.

Craig Webb's offer was different: it would have put control in the hands of the next generation of architects, the generation Frank had been training. Frank declined. He said no in part, he said, because he didn't need the money, and besides, he thought the valuation was too low—just 20 percent of the amount he had been discussing with Omnicom. But Frank had also come to think that maybe it wasn't the best idea for him to make any final decision. "We all agreed that there is no Frank Gehry practice without Frank Gehry," David Nam said. "Frank *is* the office"—meaning that without Frank, it would not be the office. It would be a talented group of architects working together, but in time they would inevitably be doing different things, perhaps with a different name.

David Nam thought that one possible scenario could follow the example of Eero Saarinen, one of the few modern American architects who, like Frank, had achieved great popular success with what critics considered significant work. Saarinen died suddenly in 1961, but his practice continued to produce work of distinction under the leadership of his partners, who reorganized the office as Kevin Roche, John Dinkeloo & Associates, since Saarinen had indicated that he did not want to have his name connected to architecture that he did not design. Frank had not made up his mind about whether he wanted his name to be on an ongoing firm, at least not at

---

[*] It did not always support creative people inside advertising, either. In 2011, Omnicom fired Peter Arnell from his own company and two years later closed the Arnell Group altogether.

this stage, when the whole question of succession still felt rather abstract. What he felt strongly about, as Saarinen did, was that his colleagues should be able to stay together, and that the succeeding generation of architects would all play a role that they would have to define for themselves. What he needed to do, he felt, was to keep increasing the amount of responsibility he was giving the younger partners in carrying out new jobs. Frank was proud of how Sam had handled Gehry Partners' presentation for a shelter for battered children in Watts, one of the firm's newest pro bono projects, and of how Anand was working with the clients for the new mixed-use project on Sunset Boulevard. But Frank had no intention of going anywhere, and so it would be a big mistake, he thought, to anoint any one of the younger group as the leader or to prescribe a structure going forward. They were all good people, they had pretty much committed to remaining, and Frank felt confident that somehow they would figure it out together.

21

In Paris, Looking Back and Looking Forward

The Fondation Louis Vuitton was finished in the autumn of 2014, and its opening in late October was celebrated with both the pomp befitting a major French cultural institution and the glamour of a splashy fashion debut. The battle over whether the building was appropriate for the Bois de Boulogne was largely, if not entirely, forgotten, although the decision by LVMH to place an immense, shiny version of the famous LV monogram, like a gargantuan jeweled brooch, over the front entrance served as a clear reminder that whatever the cultural benefits of the project, it was very much a commercially sponsored enterprise. Frank, like the critics who complained about the monogram, had no choice but to live with it. The good news was that the addition of this piece of bling did not affect the power of his architecture. The building itself was constructed largely without compromise, save for a few awkward interior details, mainly where some of the supporting steel trusses connected to interior walls. If there was anything to be criticized about the museum, it was that the circulation around the galleries and the various terraces and roof decks that surrounded them could be confusing. But it was a benign kind of confusion, more the sense of being unsure what the clearest route to the next enticing space or view platform would be, not the anxiety-provoking confusion of feeling lost in a maze. Staircases, escalators, and elevators were never too far away.

Frank spent a week in Paris, and the opening had the air of a state visit. He and Berta, along with Sam and his wife, Joyce; Alejandro and his wife, Carrie; Frank's sister, Doreen; and several other members of the Gehry entourage, including Meaghan Lloyd, Larry Ruvo, and his wife; and Larry Field, his companion, and his daughter, all stayed at the George V, where

Frank held court in the lobby, often meeting journalists for back-to-back interviews. He started out the visit with a press conference and tour of the museum, followed by multiple private interviews, keeping to a schedule that would have exhausted a younger man. He seemed this time to have a larger reservoir of patience than usual, and the flashes of testy behavior that he had demonstrated in the past year were absent. He was more like the Frank of years ago, when he courted the press so successfully, charming journalists with his low-key, aw-shucks manner. He was too energized to snap at anyone in Paris, and he certainly could not deny that he was getting the recognition he sought. When he interrupted an interview in the lobby of the George V after he saw the musician Pharrell Williams walking by with his entourage, it seemed at first like another instance of his attraction to the famous that friends had teased him about for decades. "Hey, Pharrell," Frank said, jumping up to greet Williams. "Frank Gehry." But Williams, who had been given a private tour of the Fondation Louis Vuitton the day before, acted as if Frank, not he, was the major celebrity. "Your building was incredible," he told Frank. "Going through it, it felt like walking through your mind."

The museum's formal opening was on Monday night. But there were special events in Frank's honor leading up to it. On Saturday morning, Bernard Arnault asked Frank to walk him through the large retrospective exhibition of his career that had just opened at the Centre Pompidou to coincide with the completion of the building. Frank found the experience difficult, not because of Arnault, but because the last thing he felt like doing at that point was looking back, especially at projects that for one reason or another had never gone ahead. His happiness at his achievement in Paris, however well founded, was not strong enough to overcome the insecurities that he felt looking backward. "Seeing all my old stuff freaked me out, all those old hurts from my past," he said. "It brought up a lot of feelings—why didn't I do this, why didn't I do that." And he went on to recount some of the slights that the early projects brought back to him.

That evening, Arnault and his family held an intimate, private dinner at the restaurant at the Fondation Louis Vuitton to give the Arnaults a chance to sample the chef's cooking before the opening. Frank was the guest of honor, and he brought along several of his friends who had flown over for the celebration, including the actress Catherine Keener and his lawyer, Patricia Glaser. There were fifteen people in all, and before and after dinner they walked around the empty building, taking photographs—even Arnault acted like a tourist, snapping a picture of the building with his

Bernard Arnault, Frank, and French president François Hollande at the dedication of the Fondation Louis Vuitton, October 20, 2014

phone and then asking his sons to pose in front of the building with Frank. The group walked through the museum shop, examining a $3,775 purse Frank had designed for Louis Vuitton that resembled a twisted cube,* and then they explored the gallery that contained an exhibition about the building, curated by Frédéric Migayrou in tandem with the larger exhibition at the Pompidou. Migayrou, following Frank's wishes, had included multiple models of the Fondation Louis Vuitton to show the evolution of the design, a curatorial luxury that was not available in the more limited space of the Pompidou.

The next night, Larry Ruvo hosted a dinner at L'Atelier de Joël Robuchon on the Champs-Élysées for Frank and his family and a few other guests, including the musician Herbie Hancock, with a tasting menu so elaborate that the meal stretched from 8:30 until midnight. Frank and

---

* Part of a commemoration of the new building that also included shop windows with curving ribbons of metal designed by Frank, the purse was one of several bags LVMH commissioned to encourage designers to create new objects with its famous LV logo. In addition to Frank, there were pieces by Karl Lagerfeld, Cindy Sherman, Christian Louboutin, Rei Kawakubo, and Marc Newson.

Berta had a quiet lunch the following day with Victoria and Si Newhouse, who had also traveled to Paris for the opening. The official events began that evening at seven o'clock with a dedication ceremony that included remarks from Arnault, Frank, and François Hollande, the president of France.

Frank, who almost never wore a shirt with a collar, let alone a tie, was dressed in a dark suit, a white shirt, and a light blue tie. "It was an incredible honor to be asked to play with M. Arnault," he said, standing beside Arnault and Hollande at the podium. The casualness of Frank's favorite verb was in contrast to the solemnity of the occasion, but it was the architect at his most endearing. "You all know M. Arnault as a great businessman, but it was great to be able to play with him intuitively, because he is also an artist. Thank you, thank you, thank you." Hollande hailed Frank: "Frank Gehry, vous aimez la France," he said. And he called the building "un palais de crystal pour le culture, un bâtiment unique, un miracle de l'intelligence, de la création, de technologie." Hollande went on to connect the building to the history of Paris, and to place it in the company of the Eiffel Tower.

The dedication ceremony was followed by a dinner for four hundred guests who were served chestnut soup with white truffles, veal, and caramelized pear, with Le Petit Cheval 2005 and Château d'Yquem 2011, both vineyards owned by Arnault. The beau monde of both the art and the fashion worlds was there, including Anna Wintour, Karl Lagerfeld, Jeff Koons, Larry Gagosian, Arne Glimcher, Glenn Lowry, and Michael Govan. Frank had brought over most of the partners from the office as well as his family and friends, so his entourage in the end numbered several dozen.

They did not get back to the George V until after 1 a.m., and stayed up talking in the bar for two more hours. Frank realized that however long his career continued, he might not have an event of this kind again, and he was clearly prepared to make the most of it. He was feeling genuinely celebratory, but he was suspicious of his own feelings, and his propensity to worry ran deep enough that at least some of the time in Paris he worried about why he wasn't enjoying himself more. "I wish I could enjoy it like you're supposed to," he said. "I wish I could be that guy—at least for an hour. I wish I could live in the place people are making for me. I want to be popular, but I don't trust it."

The honors continued the next day, when Frank and his family were invited to lunch at the Élysée Palace, where President Hollande presented him with a medal signifying that he was now a Commander of the Legion of Honor. The two men talked for two hours, in English, and Frank was impressed that Hollande had learned a great deal about his background, even mentioning that he knew Frank had spent some of his youth in the tiny town of Timmins. They talked as much about politics as architecture, and Frank was gratified that Hollande expressed concern about anti-Semitism in Europe. The French president also told Frank that he had noticed that in a recent book Hillary Clinton had used his architecture as a metaphor for a more nimble and creative foreign policy.* Frank liked Hollande, and said he found him "not so pretentious—no bullshit." The only guest Frank invited to the luncheon with the president other than members of his family was Mark Biass, who he realized would take special pride in being received at the Élysée Palace. After the event, as Frank's car was driving out of the palace courtyard, he saw Biass walking away, a small, solitary figure in a raincoat. He asked the driver to stop, jumped out of the car, ran over to Biass and embraced him.

Frank could not keep himself from thinking back to his first trip to France, with Anita, and how little he knew then about the city, and about European architecture in general. He remembered Mark Biass taking him to Notre Dame as soon as he arrived, and hearing Gregorian chants as he walked into his first Gothic cathedral and began to think for the first time about how structure could be both heavy and full of drama. He knew how important France was to him, since it was where he began to see architecture with a whole different sense of historical depth and breadth, and where he experienced not only the power of Romanesque and Gothic cathedrals, but the lyricism of Le Corbusier's chapel at Ronchamp, which continued to move him. And now he could repay his debt to France. He had designed the most important new building in the country and had been honored by its president.

He was also honored by the critics, or at least most of them. Oddly, several English critics seemed not to like the building: Rowan Moore, in *The Observer*, commented that the building would have been better without the glass sails, and Oliver Wainwright, in *The Guardian*, called it "a

---

* The reference is on page 33 of Clinton's memoir *Hard Choices*, where, using architecture as a metaphor for international relations, she wrote: "I came to liken the old architecture to the Parthenon in Greece, with clean lines and clear rules. The pillars holding it up— a handful of big institutions, alliances, and treaties—were remarkably sturdy. But time takes its toll, even on the greatest of edifices, and now we needed a new architecture for a new world, more in the spirit of Frank Gehry than formal Greek classicism." Frank was so pleased that for several weeks he kept a copy of Clinton's book on the coffee table in his office.

crazed indulgence of over-engineering." Ellis Woodman in *Architectural Review* called the building "as spatially and structurally profligate as any I know," with a floor plan "so disaggregated as to challenge description," noting the confusing internal circulation that was surely the building's weakest aspect. Frank, ever sensitive, seemed to focus more on the negative reviews than the many positive ones, like Joseph Giovannini's in *The New York Times*, which referred to the building as "a Cubist sailboat" that was the "culmination" of Frank's career, or Chistopher Hawthorne's in the *Los Angeles Times*, who said the Fondation Louis Vuitton was "brilliant, a late career triumph," though he also questioned whether the building could be considered the self-indulgent act of a billionaire wanting a "personal museum for the new gilded age." The art historian Irving Lavin, no stranger to the connection between patronage and architecture, was not troubled by the notion that the building had been commissioned and paid for by Arnault, and found only pleasure in its excesses. Writing in the catalog published for the exhibition on the building, he said that "two great themes of Gehry's lifework, the fish and the sailing boat, converge in a single creature, the Louis Vuitton Museum. The fusion is a mythic creature that supersedes architecture itself. The visitor is transported into a delirious domain of endless wonderment, where every step is a new, dizzying environment."

It seemed as if critics were divided between those who, like Irving Lavin and Joseph Giovannini, saw the building as the culmination of Frank's career, and those who thought it was all simply too much, a building that when looked at in comparison to Frank's earlier work seemed to add bombast more than fresh ideas, rather like late Picasso or late Frank Lloyd Wright. Martin Filler, writing in *The New York Review of Books*, paid Frank the compliment of comparing his influence and his stature with that of Mies van der Rohe, but found the building in Paris "notably lacking in repose," and took a particular dislike to the exposed structure, which he thought it was altogether wrong to reveal.

Yet the notion of making the innards visible goes back to Frank's earliest work, and is in many ways altogether consistent with it. The Fondation Louis Vuitton, for all its spectacular effect, feels in some places like a pure, polished object and in others like a work that is still under construction; the juxtaposition of its sleek surfaces with raw structure harkens back to Frank's earliest houses, and to his love of the unfinished. The "iceberg" gallery sections evoke the compositions of unevenly stacked boxes of many of his earlier projects. Despite the large scale, the flamboyant form, and the grandiose ambitions of the Fondation Louis Vuitton, it is no exaggeration to say that in its design Frank managed to wrap early and middle Gehry inside late Gehry, at once looking back on his career and moving it forward. The exhibition at the Pompidou organized by Frédéric Migayrou was not the only retrospective of Frank's work that appeared in Paris in the fall of 2014: Frank had designed another one himself, in the form of this building.

From Paris, Frank and his family continued on to Spain, where he was scheduled to receive another honor, the 2014 Prince of Asturias Award for the Arts, presented by King Felipe VI in Oviedo. When the Gehrys arrived the day before the presentation, Frank was exhausted, and thought he had a few hours to nap before his first obligation. He undressed and climbed into bed. Twenty minutes later, he was awakened by a telephone call telling him he was expected at a press conference. He had no choice but to get dressed again and show up, nap or no nap.

The first reporter asked him what his response was to charges that his buildings were more in the line of dazzling spectacles than functional architecture. This time, he was too tired to be polite. He extended his middle finger. There was an awkward silence, and then another reporter asked whether "emblematic" buildings would continue to be a feature of cities. Frank replied with only slightly more patience than he had shown to the previous questioner. "In this world we are living in, 98 percent of everything that is built and constructed today is pure shit," he said. "There's no sense of design, no respect for humanity or for anything else. Once in a while, however, a group of people do something special. Very few, but God, leave us alone. We are dedicated to our work. . . . I work with clients who respect the art of architecture. Therefore, please don't ask questions as stupid as that one."[*]

Someone caught Frank's raised finger in a photo, and soon it spread across the Internet. So did his words. He later apologized for his rudeness, claiming fatigue, but he saw no reason to disavow his statement. After all, he believed that most buildings *were* terrible, and that most people were in

---

[*] Frank was quoted in the Spanish newspaper *El Mundo* as saying that "98 percent of everything that is built and designed today is pure shit," and his use of the word "designed" made him sound as if he were trying to condemn his fellow architects rather than to denounce the poor level of the built environment put up by nonarchitects, which he said was his intention. He believed he had been deliberately misquoted.

denial of the mediocrity around them. "It's why I did the chain-link thing," he said.

It was a trivial incident, funny more than scandalous, and mainly a reminder that Frank's celebrity had reached a point where his every gesture would be noticed, and sometimes blown out of proportion. Lost in the discussion were the questions that he was trying, through his exhaustion, to communicate: How much should architecture be considered a humane pursuit, an artistic enterprise, a cultural event, as opposed to a practical work of construction? And even when architecture is pursued with the highest aims, how much impact can it have?

Those were the things that mattered to him. Architecture had a responsibility to keep you out of the rain, but it served little purpose if that was all it did, Frank believed. If it could keep you out of the rain and inspire emotion at the same time, then it amounted to something. If more people would look at buildings that way, he thought, they would be less tolerant of what was around them, and more willing to demand something better. Frank had never been good at separating his architecture from people's emotional responses to it, and much of his own emotional connection to his work derived from his desire to have it please others. Sometimes that was what seemed to matter to him most of all. Philip Johnson saw this when he was talking about Frank to Sydney Pollack and said, "In fact, he enjoys more the fact that you enjoy it and I enjoy it than he does enjoying it himself."

Frank was hardly an ascetic, working solely to please others. While the desire to prove his worth to his doubting father remained with him throughout his life, motivating him long after Irving was gone, his creative ambition was rooted in far more than his need for approval. But he craved approval nevertheless. He was no Howard Roark; he cared passionately about what people thought, and for all that he has been considered controversial, he was always more eager to satisfy than he was to scandalize. For Frank Gehry, the shock of the new has never by itself been enough. He has always wanted the surprise to contain, to at least some degree, pleasure and fulfillment.

Frank, saw himself, in part, as a missionary for emotional engagement. "I was looking for a way to express feeling in three-dimensional objects," he told Sydney Pollack about Bilbao, but he could have been referring to all of his work, from the early houses to the concert halls, museums, and public buildings he did in mid- and late career. Everything he designed, from Tiffany jewelry to chairs, as well as his teaching, was directed toward the goal of encouraging the same kind of emotional engagement with architecture and design that people expect to have with art. But that no more makes Frank Gehry an artist instead of an architect than the ability to make meaningful spaces within a work of sculpture makes Richard Serra an architect instead of an artist. Gehry's retort, "No, I'm an architect," has always been correct. He appropriates the techniques of art, but he always uses them to architectural ends: to solve the fundamental architectural problems of creating objects that function well for a particular purpose, are well constructed, and have a meaningful relationship to the world around them. His journey has always been guided by intuition more than by data, and despite the critical role digital software plays in his work, his architecture has never been driven by technology. Technology for him has always been a means, not an end, a way of getting ideas out of his head and into the built world. The starting point is always inside his head, in an imagination that was always seeking to push on, to find some new way of making space, some new way of making shapes.

That new way has always been his own, and he never envisioned it as a system, or as a model for what all architecture should be: he would be the first to agree that the solution to the problems of contemporary architecture is not for everyone to start designing as he does. The most commonly heard criticism of the distinctive, one-of-a-kind buildings Gehry generally designs is that they make poor models, and that a city made up of Gehryesque architecture would be chaos. It would indeed, because it was never conceived as a prescription for what all architecture should be. The success of Gehry's sculptural architecture depends, at least to a certain extent, on other architects not doing the same thing. His buildings are many things, but prototypes they are not. They are works of architecture created for pleasure and for thought as well as for use.

Frank's obsession with making the new has often invited another misunderstanding, which is that he is indifferent, even hostile, toward what has come before. In fact, the opposite is true: his architecture is based on a deep knowledge, not to say love, of the architecture of the past, and he has not so much broken with the past as found a new and different way of expressing continuity with it. Not for nothing is Igor Stravinsky's *Poetics of Music*, based on the composer's Charles Eliot Norton Lectures at Harvard, one of his favorite books, since Stravinsky makes clear how much his work—like Gehry's often taken as representing a rejection of all that preceded it—owes to the past and how little he saw his music as revolutionary. "I hold that it was wrong to have considered me a revolutionary,"

Stravinsky wrote. "To speak of revolution is to speak of a temporary chaos. Now art is the contrary of chaos. . . . Let us understand each other: I am the first to recognize that daring is the motive force of the finest and greatest acts; which is all the more reason for not putting it unthinkingly at the service of disorder and base cravings in a desire to cause sensation at any price. I approve of daring; I set no limits to it. But likewise there are no limits to the mischief wrought by arbitrary acts."

Great art, Stravinsky was saying, is not arbitrary; it emerges out of knowledge and discipline, and of new—daring—ways to work within the constraints of reality to make new kinds of order. Stravinsky, whose work was often misunderstood as cacophonous, denounced cacophony; Frank, often misunderstood as creating capricious form to incite chaos—as his opponents on the Eisenhower Memorial accused him of doing[*]—never had much patience for architecture that emerges out of personal impulses more than as a response to the constraints of a program and a site. What he always sought was not freedom from constraints but new ways to respond to them. His work, in Michael Sorkin's words, seeks not "an alternative system" but "the breath of new life injected into old forms," acknowledging with Stravinsky that "tradition is carried forward in order to produce something new."

Like the fashion designer Alexander McQueen, who said, "You've got to know the rules to break them. That's what I'm here for, to demolish the rules but keep the tradition," Frank Gehry wants his work to invigorate tradition, not destroy it. To be new, Frank has always felt, is not to deny the old, any more than to be timeless is to deny the new. The greatest of all art is both anchored in its time and able to transcend it; as Max Raphael observed in his writing on prehistoric cave paintings, "the work of art closest to perfection is both most profoundly determined by its time and goes furthest beyond it into timelessness."

Stravinsky offers another insight into Gehry's sensibility when he defines music as "nothing more than a succession of impulses that converge towards a definite point of repose"; Gehry, too, has always sought to achieve a certain degree of resolution, if not always easy or superficial comfort, and he has never consciously sought to make his work disquieting. If it is not serene in the traditional sense, neither does it seek to provoke discomfort, disorientation, or confusion. Like Stravinsky, he has sought to reach a traditional end by a different route: in architectural terms, this means both

---

[*] See chapters 19 and 20.

a sense of visual and sensual rightness or naturalness, the opposite of disquiet. Gehry buildings are admittedly not what would normally be called tranquil, but they possess the ability to evoke the same sense of well-being.

Gehry's work is traditional in another way as well, in that he uses concrete, physical form to create meaningful sensation, which once was taken for granted as the only way to create any kind of architectural experience, but in the age of digital technology and virtual space no longer is. To the extent that he relies on the crafting of real physical materials to make real physical spaces that are one-of-a-kind, and not on the use of digital technology to evoke the images of physical things to make virtual space or to create a physical form that can be replicated an infinite number of times, Gehry is as old-fashioned an architect as Stravinsky was an old-fashioned composer, or Rauschenberg an old-fashioned artist. He has never sought to use technology to create the illusion of something that does not exist in the physical world. He creates buildings that are real physical presences, and that use the ancient architectural tools of proportion, light, materials, scale, and space to create the sensations that raise them to the level of art.

"The faculty of creating is never given to us all by itself. It always goes hand in hand with the gift of observation," Stravinsky wrote, connecting his sensibility in a further way to Frank's, "and the true creator may be recognized by his ability always to find about him, in the commonest and humblest thing, items worthy of note. He does not have to concern himself with a beautiful landscape, he does not need to surround himself with rare and precious objects. He does not have to put forth in search of discoveries: they are always within his reach. He will only have to cast a glance about him. Familiar things, things that are everywhere, attract his attention."

And so the surroundings of his buildings, different though they may be from what he is designing, never fail to influence him and shape what he is doing: the bridge and the river at Bilbao, the Woolworth Building near 8 Spruce Street in Lower Manhattan, Pariser Platz in Berlin. Most of all, of course, it was Los Angeles, and its rough landscape of expedience, its landscape of cars and warehouses and factories and signs and bungalows, that attracted Frank's attention and inspired him to create new spaces and new shapes, teasing out of the seeming chaos of the city new forms that possess the undeniable power of the profound. What those spaces and shapes mean is not for him to say. If architecture, like music, offers some inherent formal cues—certain kinds of spaces are, by nature, exclamatory and exuberant, while others are more somber and brooding, just as certain tempos and keys are in music—these cues do not define the meaning of the work or determine how we will react to it. As with the greatest music, literature, or painting, Gehry's architecture can inspire myriad associations and feelings, and the greatest gift it confers is not in the specifics of what it evokes, but in the depth, sureness, and subtlety of how it affects us. In fact, for all the strength of Gehry's form making, he does not force us to see the world as he does. His buildings transcend his own story, just as the work of any great artist, composer, writer, or filmmaker transcends his or her story. All artistic works emerge from their creators' lives, but the greatest of them possess an inherent power that leads us to turn inward, and to make of these works experiences of our own. Gehry's architecture invites interpretations that are as revelatory of our own lives and feelings as they are to those of Frank Gehry.

Once, after one of Frank's buildings was finished, he was asked to talk about his design process and where his ideas came from. He told lots of anecdotes, but he said that in the end, it all came down to the way in which clients, constraints, his knowledge, and his intuition all came together. And it was not something he could predict; all he knew was that it could not be reduced to a formula, and he had never believed that his work could be described in terms of a precise theory. To choose to create was, to him, to accept the notion that you did not know where the process would take you. Far from being troubled by this, he had always felt liberated by it.

"On a building, I don't know where I'm going when I start," he said. "If I knew where I was going, I wouldn't go there, that's for sure."

Acknowledgments

No book is the work of just one person, and that is particularly true of a book such as this one. I have spent my life writing about architecture, but writing about someone's work is not the same as writing about his life, and I have been learning the craft of biography as I have progressed through my research on Frank Gehry. So it feels right to acknowledge a certain debt to other biographers. I have learned much both from writers of the past like Lord David Cecil and biographers of our time, like Robert Caro, Jean Strouse, Richard Ellmann, David McCullough, Maynard Solomon, Walter Isaacson, Adam Begley, Ron Chernow, Stacy Schiff, and Mark Stevens and Annalyn Swan.

My greatest debt, of course, is to this book's subject, who has given of his time and energy with extraordinary generosity and goodwill, all the more noteworthy because it had been agreed that he could have no editorial control over the text. This biography is "authorized" in the sense that Frank Gehry has cooperated with me in my research, but it has not been written subject to his approval or review.

As I said at the beginning of this book, Frank Gehry and I have been talking on and off for more than four decades, but when I embarked on this project it seemed important to try to give our conversations less randomness, and to review the events of his life in sequence from his childhood through to the present. For the first time, I recorded our sessions together. It is not always easy to struggle through the haze of memory, particularly when the recollections are not all happy ones, and I cannot express my gratitude deeply enough to Frank Gehry for his willingness to embark on this long process, and then to clear his overcrowded schedule whenever I made my way to his home base in Los Angeles. Over the years we met for countless hours in his office, at his home, in restaurants, and on airplanes, sometimes with family members and colleagues, but most often just the two of us. One conversation took place on his sailboat, *Foggy*, captained by the architect Greg Lynn, as we traveled from Marina del Rey to Malibu and back again. Another took place in the lobby of the George V hotel in Paris. And much as I like the lively buzz of many of Los Angeles's trendy restaurants, I have come, like Gehry, to value the peace and quiet, if not the décor, of the Pacific Dining Car, the old-fashioned place not far from his house in Santa Monica where we have talked over more break-fasts, lunches, and dinners than I could count. Gehry's warmth was always present, and so, I should say, was his wit. It may have been during one of those conversations that he told me he had come up with a perfect title for this book: "You should call it *Goldberger on Goldberg*," he said.

Our conversations always had substance to them, although I am struck, looking back at the transcripts, by how rarely I succeeded in my intention of having our interviews proceed in orderly fashion through his life. And there is a reason for this. Like many people who succeed in working actively into old age, Frank Gehry lives very much in the present, and talks most comfortably about what he is doing right now—or, more to the point, what he hopes to be doing next week, next month, and next year. Looking back is not his favorite thing to do. As a result, almost every one of our meetings began with a lively discussion about what was occupying his mind at the moment, and only after he had "warmed up," so to speak, did he begin to delve into his memory. I mention this only because it revealed something essential about him: that while he is proud of his life and his accomplishments, he is driven by what comes next, and that he has no desire to live in the past.

The people closest to him have been equally generous in sharing both their time and their thoughts. I owe a deep debt to Berta Gehry, who has responded to every request with the easy grace she is known for. Alejandro and Samuel Gehry, and their wives, Carrie and Joyce, have been consistently warm and helpful, as has Doreen Gehry Nelson, who offered great insight into her parents and grandparents as well as important recollections spanning all of the family's decades in Los Angeles. Early on in this project, Doreen hosted me for a wonderful dinner at her home, where we pored over old family photo albums. When we discovered we would both be in Paris for the opening of the Fondation Louis Vuitton in 2014, she brought an antique locket of her mother's containing childhood photographs of her and her brother, which she had just discovered, all the way across the world to show me.

Richard Snyder, Frank's former brother-in-law, erstwhile lawyer, and now close friend, and Paul Vincent Wiseman have been extraordinarily generous and candid with their insights, and not the least of the pleasures of this project is the friendship that has grown between us. I consider it a privilege to have come to know them both. It is telling that Gehry wanted me to speak with his first wife, Richard Snyder's sister, saying that "you shouldn't hear that story only from my side," and I regret that Anita Brenner declined my request to talk about her ex-husband. Thanks to Richard Snyder's help, I believe the story of their marriage is told fairly.

Frank Gehry's office has been as helpful as his family. Meaghan Lloyd has helped in innumerable ways through the entire history of this project, and I am deeply grateful to her for her logistical help, her sharp insights, and her warm demeanor. Stephanie Pizziorni, Samantha Messick, Diana Ward, and Amy Achorn, his assistants, have responded to my frequent requests with courtesy and promptness, as have Joyce Shin and Jill Auerbach, who helped navigate through the sprawling Gehry office archives and photo files. Many of Gehry's present and former architectural colleagues have helped in other ways, including making time to talk about their experiences with him: my thanks to Craig Webb, Edwin Chan, Michelle Kaufmann, David Nam, Paul Lubowicki, Brian Aamoth, Anand Devarajan, Jim Glymph, Randy Jefferson, John Clagett, John Bowers, Laurence Tighe, Tensho Takemori, Dennis Shelden, Jennifer Ehrman, and Michael Maltzan. Gregory Walsh is more than a former colleague—he has been a part of Frank Gehry's life for more than sixty years—and he, too, has been unfailingly generous with his recollections.

The line between Frank Gehry's personal and professional lives has sometimes blurred to the point of invisibility, which suits him. Some of my most important conversations have been with people with whom he has both a professional and a personal connection, most significantly the late Peter Lewis, at whose New York apartment I spent a wonderful afternoon in 2012, as he recounted the story of his unbuilt house and his other Gehry projects; and Thomas Krens, with whom I've met both in New York and in his extraordinary house in Williamstown to talk about how he and Gehry came together to create the Guggenheim in Bilbao, which could be a book in itself. An evening with Deborah Borda would be a pleasure under any circumstances; talking about Frank Gehry over good wine made it even better. So, too, with lunch at Vitra's campus outside Basel, where Rolf Fehlbaum and I spent a memorable afternoon at the Vitra Design Museum and surrounding buildings. Cindy Pritzker graciously hosted me in Chicago to talk about one of her favorite subjects, Frank Gehry, and Michael Tilson Thomas kindly welcomed me to his study in the Gehry-designed New World Symphony Center in Miami Beach where we spoke for several hours about his architect. Larry Field, Larry Ruvo, Richard Koshalek, Richard Weinstein, Richard Cohen, Richard Saul Wurman, Peter Arnell, Marshall Rose, Bruce Ratner, Victoria and Si Newhouse, Elyse and the late Stanley Grinstein, Sidney Felsen and Joni Moisen Weil, Irving and Marilyn Lavin, Juan Ignacio Vidarte, Mark Biass, Gere Kavanagh, and Martin and the late Mildred Friedman are other Gehry friends whose relationships with him began professionally and became warmly personal, and each of them has shared important recollections and insights, as has Greg Lynn, both a fellow architect and a sailing companion. I have learned a great deal from either casual conversations or more formal interviews with Eli Broad, Norman Lear, Bernard Arnhault, Jean-Paul Claverie, Babs Altoon Thompson, Thomas Hines, Nancy Wexler, Ginny Mancini, Michael Govan, Gail Harrity, Nan Peletz, Alan Heller, Adam Flatto, David Weinreb, Nick Vanderboom, John Burnham, Paul Allen, Stephanie Barron, Barbara Guggenheim, Anna Gangbar, Hartley Gaylord, Michele de Milly, Philippa Polskin, Matthew Teitelbaum, Dominic Loscalzo, Rocco Siciliano, Al Trevino, Jack Brogan, Rick Salomon, Barry Diller, and Carol Burnett.

I have benefited greatly from conversations with architects and with other critics about Gehry, whether or not they were in the context of formal interviews for this book. My thanks to Christopher Hawthorne, the late Ada Louise Huxtable, Michael Sorkin, Nicolai Ouroussoff, Alexander Garvin, Olivier Boissière, David Childs, Eric Owen Moss, Moshe Safdie, Mark Rakatansky, Aaron Betsky, Stanley Tigerman, Margaret McCurry, Jaquelin T. Robertson, Robert A. M. Stern, Thomas Phifer, Paul Masi, Vincent Scully, and the late Philip Johnson. Barbara Isenberg has been most generous in agreeing to allow me to use material from her excellent *Conversations with Frank Gehry*, and Ultan Guilfoyle, who produced the late Sydney Pollack's film *Sketches of Frank Gehry*, has provided full transcripts of the interviews that were edited for the film as well as recollections of the process of making the film, and I am very grateful to him.

The artists who have been so important a part of Frank Gehry's life have also been helpful to this project. I am particularly grateful to Ed Moses, Peter Alexander, Chuck Arnoldi, Tony Berlant, Laddie Dill, Ed Ruscha, and Billy Al Bengston, all key members of the Los Angeles artists' group of the 1960s. They each spoke at length to me about Gehry, as did the New York artist James Rosenquist. I am grateful to them all, as I am to Hunter Drohojowka-Philp, author of *Rebels in Paradise: The Los Angeles Art Scene and the 1960s*, who kindly shared her notes on Frank Gehry. My thanks also must go to the archivists and librarians at the University of Southern California, Harvard University, and the Getty Research Institute, all of whom provided key early assistance.

As a writer based in New York, it would have seemed logical for me to have moved to Los Angeles for several months to work on this project. I chose instead to shuttle back and forth, not so much because I wanted the research on this book to enrich American Airlines—though it certainly did—as because the dozens of interviews I held with Frank Gehry needed to be spaced out, for the benefit of both his schedule and his sanity. I did not want either of us to grow tired of the other. Lacking a place of my own in Los Angeles, I sometimes stayed in hotels, but often took advantage of the hospitality of friends, and it is a special pleasure to thank them: Robert Bookman; Tobias Meyer and Mark Fletcher, whose extraordinary Buff & Hensman house was a perfect place in which to think about the architecture of Los Angeles; and, most of all, Martha De Laurentiis and Randy Sherman, whose warm hospitality in Benedict Canyon seemed never to dim, despite how often I took advantage of it. I owe them a special debt of gratitude.

Back on the East Coast, thanks go also to my friends Charles Kaiser, Steven Rattner, Clifford Ross, Joel Fleishman, Dan Rabinowitz, and Pamela and Peter Flaherty, people with no direct connection either to Frank Gehry or to my research, but with whom I have had memorable conversations that have helped me focus my thoughts during the years this book was in preparation.

I t was my extreme good fortune to have encountered Patrick Corrigan in 2010 as a student in my seminar on architecture criticism at Parsons The New School for Design. When he received his master of architecture degree in 2011, he forwent the opportunity to begin his architecture career right away and agreed to work with me on research for this book. From late 2011 until the fall of 2014, when the call of his profession became too strong to resist, he has been a welcome constant in this project, and has assembled information, organized files, done picture research, and in some cases conducted interviews, all with the utmost professionalism. His knowledge and his judgment have been essential to this book, and they have made him not just a researcher but also an astute reader and perceptive critic. His contributions have been invaluable. By now, Patrick surely knows as much about Frank Gehry as I do. I can truly say that this is in many ways his book as well as mine.

I was fortunate to have Ann Close as my editor many years ago on another project, and her gentle wisdom and knowing eye, so welcome then, have been even more important to this book. It is a joy to be working with her again, as well as with her incomparable assistant, Annie Eggers, who helped organize many of the final details, as did Alex Tonnetti. I am also grateful to Iris Weinstein for her handsome design of the interior of this book. And it was a special privilege to have Peter Mendelsund, whose work I have long admired, design the cover.

Amanda Urban, my agent, has helped me with many projects over the years, but none so much as this one, and I am grateful to her, as always, for her active and supportive engagement. She encouraged me to take on this project, and her enthusiasm for it has remained all the way through.

I am lucky enough to have a family that not only surrounds me with love, but also with genuine interest in what I do, and they inspire me with their own creativity. My son Adam Hirsh, his wife, Delphine, and our grandchildren, Thibeaux and Josephine, as residents of Los Angeles have been particularly close to this project, and they have kept tabs on its progress as I made regular appearances at their house during all of my research trips, and made me feel even more welcome in California. My sons, Ben Goldberger and Alex Goldberger, both journalists, and my daughter-in-law, Melissa Rothberg, have helped me focus and refine ideas throughout, as has Carolyna De Laurentiis. Ben and Alex are grown and out of the house and have not noticed my frequent absences, but my wife, Susan Solomon, has, and it is she who has borne the brunt of this project, having given up much time that we might have spent together so that I could see one more Gehry building, talk to one more Gehry client, or have one more conversation with the book's subject. Instead of complaining, she has read the manuscript, made critical suggestions, and helped me to shape it from the beginning.

It is with pleasure and gratitude that I dedicate this book to her.

Notes

1. NIGHT OF THE SUPERMOON

5   "Therefore it seems fair to conclude": Matt Tyrnauer, "Architecture in the Age of Gehry," *Vanity Fair*, August 2010.

8   "It's very important for Frank": Babs Thompson, interview with the author, July 10, 2013.

9   "his gentle, humble ways": Peter Alexander, interview with the author, December 12, 2011.

10   "there are some artists": Barbara Isenberg, *Conversations with Frank Gehry* (New York: Alfred A. Knopf, 2009), 56.

11   "I think Frank is the foremost artist": Billy Al Bengston, interview with the author, June 13, 2013.

11   "Success is much harder": Frank Gehry made this comment frequently in passing to the author, although it does not appear in any of the formal interviews for this book.

13   "Frank, why are you wasting your time": Joshua Olsen, *Better Places, Better Lives: A Biography of James Rouse* (Washington, DC: Urban Land Institute, 2004), 266.

13   "I'm a do-gooder": Paul Goldberger, "The House as Art," *New York Times Magazine*, March 12, 1995, 44.

15   "He came and said": Bruce Ratner, interview with the author, November 26, 2013.

18   "One of the things about my life": Bruce Ratner, observed by the author, March 19, 2011.

19   "This is not far from where": Frank Gehry, observed by the author, March 19, 2011.

2. CANADA

21   in the early 1930s: James Lemon, *Toronto Since 1918: An Illustrated History* (Toronto: James Lorimer & Co., 1985), 197.

21   "for Toronto the City of Churches": Ernest Hemingway, *Selected Letters, 1917–1961*, ed. Carlos Baker (New York: Scribner, 1981), 84, 88, 95.

21   In 1923, for example: Lemon, *Toronto*, 53.

21   Toronto's Jewish population: Gerald Tulchinsky, *Branching Out: The Transformation of the Canadian Jewish Community* (Toronto: Stoddart Publishing Co., 1998), 17.

22   In 1920, the city's aldermen: Lemon, *Toronto*, 53.

23   The Kensington Market: Ibid., 51.

23   "But she went along": Frank Gehry, interview with the author, July 14, 2011.

24   When Samuel was in the store: Doreen Nelson, interview with the author, January 14, 2012.

24   She was skilled: Barbara Isenberg, *Conversations with Frank Gehry* (New York: Alfred A. Knopf, 2009), 15.

24   The windows were covered: Frank Gehry, interview with the author, July 14, 2011.

25   "he was crazy about her": Doreen Nelson, interview with the author, January 14, 2012.

25   "kind of a diamond in the rough": Isenberg, *Conversations*, 17.

25   Thelma, who had never: Frank Gehry, interview with the author, November 18, 2014.

26   a "safe haven": Isenberg, *Conversations*, 16.

26   He would recall sometimes: Ibid., 14.

26   Later he would help: Ibid.

26   "There were round pieces": Frank Gehry, interview with the author, July 14, 2011.

27   "the most fun I ever had": Isenberg, *Conversations*, 16.

27   "I used to go in there": Frank Gehry, interview with the author, July 14, 2011.

27   "to feign anti-intellectualism": Frank Gehry, interview with the author, March 12, 2012.

28   "summer resort": Isenberg, *Conversations*, 14.

28   "about the importance": Ibid.

28   "into the old arguments": Frank Gehry, interview with the author, July 14, 2011.

28   "one of the most important things": Frank Gehry, interview with the author, January 29, 2012.

28   "hills and blue and sea": Frank Gehry, interview with the author, July 14, 2011.

29   "loved to play with stuff": Doreen Nelson, interview with the author, January 14, 2012.

29   "I don't know where he got": Frank Gehry, interview with the author, August 9, 2012.

30   "reminded him of the old country": Doreen Nelson, interview with the author, January 14, 2012.

30   "the gambling business": Frank Gehry, interview with the author, March, 12, 2012.

30   "Growing up in Timmins": Anna Gangbar, interview with Patrick Corrigan, October 11, 2012.

31   "It was mostly Poles": Frank Gehry, interview with the author, August 7, 2012.

31   "They saw me being beat up": Frank Gehry, interview with the author, January 29, 2012.

32   "I loved taking the train": Ibid.

32   "My father drove his car": Frank Gehry, interview with the author, August 7, 2012.

33   "He'd walk in": Frank Gehry, interview with the author, July 14, 2011.

33   "stupid" and "a dreamer": Ibid.

33   "talked about her refined English background": Ibid.

33 "Goldberg family was crazy": Doreen Nelson, interview with the author, January 28, 2012.

33 There were limited opportunities: Frank Gehry, interview with the author, June 20, 2011.

34 "I always felt cheated": Frank Gehry, interview with the author, August 7, 2012.

34 "gold in the hand": Frank Gehry, interview with the author, July 14, 2011.

34 "super Jews": Frank Gehry, interview with the author, June 20, 2011.

34 "Solly and I were bonkers": Frank Gehry, interview with the author, August 7, 2012.

35 "there ain't no God": Frank Gehry, interview with the author, June 20, 2011.

36 "a big industrial building": Frank Gehry, interview with the author, July 14, 2011.

36 Years later he would recall: Frank Gehry, interview with the author, August 7, 2012.

36 "He was like me": Ibid.

37 "wanted to get closer": Frank Gehry, interview with the author, June 20, 2011.

37 has a childhood memory: Doreen Nelson, interview with the author, January 14, 2012.

37 "He used to talk": Frank Gehry, interview with the author, November 12, 2012.

37 "a big nose": Frank Gehry, interview with the author, July 14, 2011.

37 "want to crawl under the table": Frank Gehry, interview with the author, June 20, 2011.

38 "I would go": Frank Gehry, interview with the author, August 7, 2012.

39 "It was designing these little cottages": Frank Gehry, interview with the author, June 20, 2011.

39 "Timmins is very northern": Frank Gehry, interviews with the author, July 14, 2011, and June 20, 2011.

39 "Frank, this ain't for you": Frank Gehry, interview with the author, August 8, 2012.

40 "coming apart": Frank Gehry, interview with the author, June 20, 2011.

40 "beat the shit out of him": Doreen Nelson, interview with the author, January 28, 2012.

40 "My relationship with my father": Doreen Nelson, interview with the author, January 14, 2012.

40 "Underneath all this craziness": Doreen Nelson, interview with the author, January 28, 2012.

40 Doreen said much later: Doreen Nelson, interview with the author, January 14, 2012.

40 "couldn't contain himself": Frank Gehry, interview with the author, July 14, 2011.

41 "He was having business setbacks": Frank Gehry, interview with the author, June 20, 2011.

41 "a heavy burden": Frank Gehry, interview with the author, June 20, 2011.

41 "My dad was forty-seven years old": Isenberg, *Conversations*, 18.

41 Still, Irving did not want: Frank Gehry, interview with the author, August 8, 2012.

3. TO LIFE IN THE SUN

43 "It was sunny and warm": Barbara Isenberg, *Conversations with Frank Gehry* (New York: Alfred A. Knopf, 2009), 18.

44   479 new defense plants: Arthur C. Verge, "The Impact of the Second World War on Los Angeles," *Pacific Historical Review* 63, no. 30 (August 1994): 294.

44   Employment in the region: Ibid., 293.

44   Local shipyards: Ibid., 303–4.

44   Its large tracts: Ibid., 292.

45   The government's decision: Ibid., 313.

47   "two rooms": Doreen Nelson, interview with the author, January 14, 2012.

48   "She cooked as if": Ibid.

48   "was a comedown": Frank Gehry, interview with the author, July 14, 2011.

48   Irving tried to find: Frank Gehry, interview with the author, August 9, 2012.

48   He enjoyed talking: Ibid.

49   "It couldn't have been": Hartley Gaylord, interview with Patrick Corrigan, November 13, 2012.

49   "My father was very personable": Isenberg, *Conversations*, 18.

49   Uncle Harry: Hartley Gaylord, interview with Patrick Corrigan, November 13, 2012.

49   He drove a black Plymouth convertible: Doreen Nelson, interview with the author, January 28, 2012, and Hartley Gaylord, interview with Patrick Corrigan, November 13, 2012.

50   Frank was skillful: Isenberg, *Conversations*, 19.

50   "I really worked hard": Ibid., 20.

50   "sweet and cuddly": Frank Gehry, interview with the author, July 14, 2011.

50   which impressed Irving and Thelma: Isenberg, *Conversations*, 20.

50   One night not long afterward: Frank Gehry, interview with the author, July 14, 2011.

50   "clean jewelry and fix watches": Isenberg, *Conversations*, 19.

50   "I was handy": Frank Gehry, interview with the author, August 9, 2012.

50   "I loved the old Victorian houses": Isenberg, *Conversations*, 19.

50   Frank didn't receive money: Frank Gehry, interview with the author, August 9, 2012.

51   The plane was based: Frank Gehry, interview with the author, June 20, 2011.

51   "I didn't know what I wanted to be": Frank Gehry, interview with the author, August 9, 2012.

51   Not long after his arrival: Isenberg, *Conversations*, 20–21.

51   "professional practice for novices": Frank Gehry, interview with the author, July 14, 2011.

51   "was the thing": Frank Gehry, interview with the author, January 29, 2012.

52   "the right age": Frank Gehry, interview with the author, July 14, 2011.

52   "They kept pushing me": Ibid.

53   "Her mother was pushing": Frank Gehry, interview with the author, January 29, 2012.

53   Anita and her father: Richard Snyder, interview with the author, August 1, 2012.

53   "brilliant": Frank Gehry, interview with the author, January 29, 2012.

53   "they had a television": Ibid.

53   Michael Tilson Thomas: Michael Tilson Thomas, interview with the author, January 30, 2014.

54   Richard Snyder recalled seeing: Richard Snyder, interview with the author, May 22, 2012.

54   "Once, I remember": Isenberg, *Conversations*, 21.

55   "There was Soriano": Ibid., 22.

55   "He was a kind of a prima donna": Frank Gehry, interview with the author, November 12, 2012.

55   "pushing steel around": Isenberg, *Conversations*, 22.

55   "I knew every building": Frank Gehry, interview with the author, November 12, 2012.

56   "Schindler was interesting": Isenberg, *Conversations*, 23.

56   "I think they thought about him": Frank Gehry, interview with the author, July 14, 2011.

56   "very full of himself": Isenberg, *Conversations*, 23.

56   Frank remembered watching Neutra: Frank Gehry, interview with the author, July 14, 2011.

4. BECOMING AN ARCHITECT

58   "I adored that woman": Frank Gehry, interview with the author, July 14, 2011.

58   Doreen has a recollection: Doreen Nelson, interview with the author, January 28, 2012.

58   "We just innocently called her": Frank Gehry, interview with the author, January 29, 2012.

59   Thelma had been doing well: Frank Gehry, interviews with the author, July 14, 2011, and January 29, 2012.

59   "We'd go there": Sandra Gaylord, interview with Patrick Corrigan, November 13, 2012.

60   "My mother used to say": Doreen Nelson, interview with the author, January 28, 2012.

60   Irving was working: 1952 Form 1040, in Doreen Nelson records.

60   He could be jovial: Hartley Gaylord, interview with Patrick Corrigan, November 13, 2012, and Frank Gehry, interview with the author, July 14, 2011.

60   "it was really depressing": Doreen Nelson, interview with the author, January 28, 2012.

60   "was taking three shots of insulin a day": Ibid.

60   "It was unconscionable": Frank Gehry, interview with the authror, August 12, 2014.

60   "He was cared for": Doreen Nelson, interview with the author, January 28, 2012.

61   "the first time somebody said nice things": Barbara Isenberg, *Conversations with Frank Gehry* (New York: Alfred A. Knopf, 2009), 22.

62   "They gave us little buildings": Frank Gehry, interview with the author, November 12, 2012.

62   "It could be anti-Semitism": Ibid.

63   "crappy slides of Chartres": Frank Gehry, interview with the author, March 12, 2012.

64   "I hated the Farnsworth House then": Frank Gehry, interview with the author, August 9, 2012.

64   "The only humanistic thing": Ibid.

64   "I couldn't relate to it": Frank Gehry, interview with the author, November 12, 2012.

65   "was one of the good ones": Greg Walsh, interview with the author, January 28, 2012.
65   "was actually the only person": Ibid.
65   "Greg and I bonded": Frank Gehry, interview with the author, July 14, 2011.
65   Frank recalled going: Frank Gehry, interview with the author, January 10, 2013.
66   "I was always going": Frank Gehry, interview with the author, January 4, 2013.
66   "Greg glommed on to me": Frank Gehry, interview with the author, November 12, 2012.
66   "Greg was like my other brother": Doreen Nelson, interview with the author, January 14, 2012.
66   "Frank chose Schindler": Greg Walsh, "Recollections of Frank Gehry," unpublished manuscript, 2012.
67   "seminal": Ibid.
67   "Cal Straub was my third-year professor": Frank Gehry, interview with the author, January 4, 2013.
67   "an ideal, kind of Garden City type thing": Greg Walsh, interview with the author, January 28, 2012.
68   "He called me in one day": Frank Gehry, interview with the author, November 12, 2012.
68   "I think all of us students": Walsh, "Recollections."
68   "I recall the two of us": Ibid.
68   "reshape it into something": Ibid.
69   "wasn't in on the poetry": Frank Gehry, interview with the author, November 12, 2012.
69   "became my closest": Frank Gehry, interview with the author, July 14, 2011.
69   "being harassed": Ibid.
70   "Frank, you know the road": Frank Gehry, interview with the author, November 12, 2012.
71   Eventually Frank was asked to leave: Frank Gehry, interview with the author, January 29, 2012.
71   "I knew what they were doing": Frank Gehry, interview with the author, November 12, 2012.
72   "Thelma was bouncy": Richard Snyder, interview with the author, August 1, 2012.
72   "He always loved fish": Ibid.
72   They stayed at the Desert Hot Springs Motel: Frank Gehry, interview with the author, January 29, 2012.
73   "cynical and disillusioned": Greg Walsh, interview with the author, January 28, 2012.
73   "I could never tell": Frank Gehry, interview with the author, November 12, 2012.
73   "His rigorous, logical approach": Walsh, "Recollections."
74   "I remember we were all excited": Frank Gehry, interview with Patrick Corrigan, September 28, 2012.
75   He remembered that the architect William Pereira: Ibid.
75   "He and Greg must have spent nights": Doreen Nelson, interview with the author, January 14, 2012.
76   There was nothing wrong: Doreen Nelson, interview with the author, January 28, 2012.

76 "I didn't want to do it": Frank Gehry, interview with the author, January 29, 2012.
76 "She was adamant": Ibid.
76 "If you knew Anita": Frank Gehry, interview with the author, July 14, 2011.
76 "placating her endlessly": Frank Gehry, interview with the author, January 29, 2012.
77 The change became final: Frank Gehry, interview with the author, July 14, 2011.
78 "furious with me": Frank Gehry, interview with the author, January 29, 2012.
78 "So there were a whole group": Frank Gehry, interview with the author, July 14, 2011.
78 "And he got up to leave": Frank Gehry, interview with the author, January 29, 2012.
79 "'We've made a terrible mistake'": Frank Gehry, interview with the author, November 12, 2012.
79 Later, Frank thought: Frank Gehry, interview with the author, August 12, 2014.
79 "He looked at my leg": Isenberg, *Conversations*, 29.

5. DEALING WITH AUTHORITY

81 "done to her": Frank Gehry, interview with the author, November 12, 2012.
81 "Anita was difficult": Frank Gehry, interview with the author, January, 29, 2012.
81 "My mother tried": Richard Snyder, interview with the author, August 1, 2012.
82 The tensions were palpable: Frank Gehry, interview with the author, January, 29, 2012.
82 "So there I was": Barbara Isenberg, *Conversations with Frank Gehry* (New York: Alfred A. Knopf, 2009), 30.
83 "Don't worry about it": Ibid., 33.
83 "they're processing orders": Frank Gehry, interview with the author, January 11, 2013.
83 "When he told me he was going": Isenberg, *Conversations*, 33.
83 "Okay, what the fuck else": Frank Gehry, interview with the author, November 12, 2012.
83 "go out and measure bridges": Isenberg, *Conversations*, 34.
84 "I had the most beautiful graphics": Frank Gehry, interview with the author, January 11, 2013.
84 "Well, you're a good": Isenberg, *Conversations*, 35.
84 "All the liberal organizations": Frank Gehry, interview with the author, January 11, 2013.
84 "And I said": Frank Gehry, interview with the author, July 14, 2011.
84 "I was into Frank Lloyd Wright": Frank Gehry, interview with the author, January 11, 2013, and Isenberg, *Conversations*, 36.
85 "And it turns out": Frank Gehry, interview with the author, January 11, 2013.
85 "I went back": Isenberg, *Conversations*, 37.
86 "Mine looked a lot like": Ibid., 38.
86 "Frank may have had better ideas": Dominick Loscalzo, interview with the author, June 7, 2012.
86 "George Nelson had a chair": Ibid.
87 Among the local architects: Isenberg, *Conversations*, 45.
87 "air-conditioning was at a premium": Richard Snyder, interview with the author, August 2, 2012.

87   "They also knew I wasn't interested": Isenberg, *Conversations*, 40.

87   They encouraged him to return: Frank Gehry, interview with the author, November 12, 2012.

88   "I was going to Harvard": Mark Biass, interview with the author, April 20, 2013.

89   "It wasn't easy": Isenberg, *Conversations*, 41.

89   "I was devastated": Frank Gehry, interview with the author, January 11, 2013.

90   "You don't want": Frank Gehry, interview with the author, January 29, 2012.

91   "I approached it": Isenberg, *Conversations*, 42.

91   "Mr. Gehry": Ibid.

92   "I looked at him": Frank Gehry, interview with the author, January 29, 2012.

92   "Professor Sert": Isenberg, *Conversations*, 42.

92   "He said, 'That's the only way'": Isenberg, *Conversations*, 43.

92   To support his family: Frank Gehry, interview with the author, January 11, 2012.

93   "Margaret Mead was there": Frank Gehry, interview with the author, January 29, 2012.

93   "A very difficult program": Mark Biass, interview with the author, April 20, 2013.

93   "Sert just adored him": Frank Gehry, interview with the author, January 11, 2013.

94   "Corb was very present": Isenberg, *Conversations*, 43.

94   "Before Harvard": Ibid., 43–44.

94   "I knew these weren't paintings": Ibid., 44–45.

94   But some conversations: Frank Gehry, interview with the author, January 11, 2013.

6. DISCOVERING EUROPE

96   "I found that offensive": Frank Gehry, interviews with the author, November 12, 2012, and January 29, 2012.

98   "They made it very theatrical": Frank Gehry, interview with the author, July 14, 2011.

98   "I didn't like it": Frank Gehry, interview with the author, January 11, 2013.

103 "an urban planning disaster": Robert Campbell, "Charles River Park at 35," *Boston Globe*, May 26, 1995.

103 "that huge monster": Frank Gehry, interview with the author, January 4, 2013.

103 "I loved doing housing": Barbara Isenberg, *Conversations with Frank Gehry* (New York: Alfred A. Knopf, 2009), 48.

104 "I knew it was fucking up my marriage": Frank Gehry, interview with the author, January 4, 2013.

104 Bella Snyder saw how unhappy: Frank Gehry, interview with the author, November 11, 2012.

104 "It became obvious": Isenberg, *Conversations*, 47.

104 "I had a mind of my own": Ibid.

104 "In hindsight I think": John Pastier, "Q&A: Gehry at 80," *Architect's Newspaper*, March 24, 2009.

107 "cowboy contractor": Mildred Friedman, *Frank Gehry: The Houses* (New York: Rizzoli, 2009), 103.

107 He looked beyond Los Angeles: Frank Gehry, interview with the author, January 4, 2013.

107 "There was a beauty": Ibid.

107 "was interesting to me": Ibid.

108 "I liked the matter-of-factness": Frank Gehry, interview with the author, March 13, 2015.

108 "was begging me": Frank Gehry, interview with the author, January 4, 2013.

108 "Frank wrote me": Mark Biass, interview with the author, April 20, 2013.

108 "It seemed like it would be a way": Isenberg, *Conversations*, 47.

108 "I walked in to Rudi": Frank Gehry, interview with the author, July 14, 2011.

109 "Three months before": Frank Gehry, interview with the author, January 4, 2013.

109 "Well, you never did": Ibid.

110 "I had two kids": Ibid.

110 "enamored with America": Ibid.

111 "Bonjour, monsieur!": Ibid.

111 Remondet's office produced: Audouin Dollfus, *The Great Refractor of Meudon Observatory* (New York: Springer, 2013).

112 Mark Biass took it upon himself: Frank Gehry, interview with the author, October 21, 2014.

112 "We tried to visit Paris": Mark Biass, interview with the author, April 20, 2013.

112 "I came from the West Coast aesthetic": Frank Gehry, interview with the author, July 14, 2011.

112 "I was enough of a modernist": Ibid.

113 "I became more Eurocentric": Ibid.

113 Mark recalled that his wife: Mark Biass, interview with the author, April 20, 2013.

114 "We'd meet them": Frank Gehry, interview with the author, July 14, 2011.

114 "So Frank told me": Mark Biass, interview with the author, April 20, 2013.

114 "He said, 'Show me Paris'": Frank Gehry, interview with the author, July 14, 2011.

115 "He said, 'I'm opening an office'": Ibid.

7. RESTART IN LOS ANGELES

116 "gave me the confidence": Barbara Isenberg, *Conversations with Frank Gehry* (New York: Alfred A. Knopf, 2009), 49.

117 "he could sell a building": Doreen Nelson, interview with the author, January 28, 2012.

117 "I think my father": Richard Snyder, interview with the author, August 1, 2012.

117 Frank and Anita eventually bought: Frank Gehry, interview with the author, January, 29, 2012.

117 "a pretty steady stream of projects": Isenberg, *Conversations*, 50.

117 "could take on a multistory building": Ibid., 49.

117 "we kind of cobbled together a living": Frank Gehry, interview with the author, May 18, 2013.

118 "I was shy": Ibid.

119 "I don't think Frank knew": Doreen Nelson, interview with the author, January 28, 2012.

122 "I like elements which are hybrid": Robert Venturi, *Complexity and Contradiction in Architecture* (New York: Museum of Modern Art, 1966), 16.

123 "She thought it was derivative": Frank Gehry, interview with the author, May 18, 2013.

123 There may also have been tension: Ibid.

127   Whatever the circumstances: Ibid.
128   "deft authority": Reyner Banham, *Los Angeles: The Architecture of Four Ecologies* (Berkeley: University of California Press, 1971), 180.
129   "Is this reparations": Richard Snyder, interview with the author, August 1, 2012.
130   "When I went to the project": Isenberg, *Conversations*, 56.
131   "When Frank first came to my studio": Ed Moses, interview with the author, December 13, 2011.
132   "Kienholz and Hopps": Hunter Drohojowska-Philp, *Rebels in Paradise: The Los Angeles Art Scene and the 1960s* (New York: Henry Holt, 2011), 30.
132   "I don't think we had the pressure": Chuck Arnoldi, interview with the author, December 13, 2011.
133   "Who is this little putz": Ed Moses, interview with the author, December 13, 2011.
133   "He was like, 'Gee whiz'": Ed Ruscha, interview with the author, December 13, 2011.
133   "Frank had an insatiable appetite": "Frank Gehry and the Los Angeles Art Scene," panel discussion at the Getty Center, Los Angeles, December 13, 2011, with Frank Gehry, Peter Alexander, Chuck Arnoldi, Tony Berlant, Billy Al Bengston, and Ed Moses, attended by the author.
133   "It wasn't two separate acts": Isenberg, *Conversations*, 57–58.
134   "So you were looking at the studs": Ibid., 59.
135   "I asked them to take me": Aram Moshayedi, "Decorative Arts: Billy Al Bengston and Frank Gehry Discuss Their Collaboration at LACMA," *East of Borneo*, February 4, 2014.
135   "He started yelling at me": Ibid.
136   Wexler met Altoon: Ed Moses, interview with the author, December 13, 2011.
136   "because, like a lot of people": All quotations in this paragraph from Marlo Thomas, *The Right Words at the Right Time* (New York: Atria Books, 2002), 109–11.
137   "Nothing was the same after that": Ibid.
137   "he lacked a lot of confidence": Milton Wexler in *Sketches of Frank Gehry*, directed by Sydney Pollack, Sony Pictures Classics, 2006.
139   "Milton gave Frank a second childhood": Nan Peletz, interview with the author, September 4, 2014.
139   "I held away from her": Frank Gehry, interview with the author, January 10, 2013.
139   "Milton said, 'Look'": Frank Gehry, interview with the author, June 6, 2013 (second interview).
139   Then he went straight: Babs Thompson, interview with the author, July 10, 2013.
140   "not in some sad-sack": Frank Gehry, interview with the author, May, 18, 2013.
140   she also told Richard Snyder: Richard Snyder, interview with the author, May 22, 2012.
140   She told Frank's mother: Doreen Nelson, interview with the author, January 14, 2012.

8. INDEPENDENCE

141   "He had to go someplace": Doreen Nelson, interview with the author, January 28, 2012.

143   "madly in love": Frank Gehry, interview with Hunter Drohojowska-Philp, September 28, 2007.

144   "I went to the ranch": Ibid.

144   In 1973, long after: "Stars in Burro Race Highlight 'Day in the Country' Benefit," *Los Angeles Times*, November 7, 1973.

144   The hay barn: Frank Gehry, interview with Hunter Drohojowska-Philp, September 28, 2007.

146   "We were all scratching": Billy Al Bengston, interview with the author, June 13, 2013.

146   "I think it was all held together": Barbara Isenberg, *Conversations with Frank Gehry* (New York: Alfred A. Knopf, 2009), 57.

147   "I said, 'Babs'": Frank Gehry, interview with Hunter Drohojowska-Philp, September 28, 2007.

147   "When sixty-five came and went": Babs Thompson, interview with the author, July 10, 2013.

148   "memory lane": Ibid.

148   "We were screaming and hollering": Frank Gehry, interview with the author, May 18, 2013.

149   "It's too soon": Babs Thompson, interview with the author, July 10, 2013.

150   "I didn't know I was being interviewed": Frank Gehry, interview with the author, January 4, 2013.

150   "a do-gooder like me": Joshua Olsen, *Better Places, Better Lives: A Biography of James Rouse* (Washington, DC: Urban Land Institute, 2004), 189.

150   "I said, 'Look'": Frank Gehry, interview with the author, January 4, 2013.

150   "It's Mort Hoppenfeld": Ibid.

151   "an unqualified architectural and acoustic success": Harold Schonberg, "Hurtling from Famine to Feast," *New York Times*, July 23, 1967.

152   "Esther Williams and Fernando Lamas": Isenberg, *Conversations*, 53.

152   "Thank God": Frank Gehry, interview with the author, January 4, 2013.

154   "The usual store": "Things to Come . . . Now," *Furnishings Daily*, July 2, 1968.

154   "experiment, change and refine": *Stores: The Retail Management Magazine*, December 1971, 5.

155   For a long time: Frank Gehry, interview with the author, August 12, 2014.

155   "The sails": Frank Gehry quoted in Alex Browne, "Love for Sail," *New York Times*, April 16, 2009.

155   "egged me on": Frank Gehry, interview with the author, May 18, 2013.

156   "support mechanism": Billy Al Bengston, interview with the author, June 13, 2013.

157   The first step: Esther McCoy, "Report from Malibu Hills," *Progressive Architecture*, December 1974, 40.

157   "a labor of love for him": Marshall Berges, "Ron Davis: He Plays Tricks with Dimensions," *Los Angeles Times Home*, August 17, 1975.

158   "He decided he wanted rooms": Paul Goldberger, "Design Notebook: Inglorious Urban Entries," *New York Times*, March 24, 1977, C14.

158   "a big barn we could play with": Paul Goldberger, "Studied Slapdash," *New York Times Magazine*, January 18, 1976, 49.

160   "while Gehry has designed": Ibid., 50.

9. EASING THE EDGES

162   "Architects mostly practice": Frank Gehry in *Designers West*, May 1969, 31.

163   "Buildings are less permanent": Ibid.

163   "We thrash around": Ibid.

163   "Suppose we separate a unit": Ibid.

164   "The value system": Ibid.

165   "I suggest that we are really involved": Ibid.

166   "When I was doing houses": Barbara Isenberg, *Conversations with Frank Gehry* (New York: Alfred A. Knopf, 2009), 6.

167   The optimistic start: *Kid City*, directed by Jon Boorstin, produced by the University of Southern California, 1972.

168   "Ron Davis thought": Frank Gehry, interview with the author, January 18, 2014.

170   "I thought, That's beautiful": Isenberg, *Conversations*, 189–90.

171   He later gave it to his friend: Frank Gehry, interview with the author, January 17, 2014.

172   Frank then formed a company: Jack Brogan, interview with the author, January 16, 2014.

173   *House & Garden* published: *House & Garden*, August 1972, 34–35.

173   "the most astonishing furniture": Dan MacMasters, "Easy Edges: Why Didn't Somebody Think of This Before?," *Los Angeles Time Home Magazine*, April 30, 1972, 13.

173   "strong, graphic shapes": Norma Skurka "Paper Furniture for Penny Pinchers," *New York Times Magazine*, April 9, 1972.

174   "Tell me about these guys": Frank Gehry, interview with the author, January 17, 2014.

175   "He called me": Ibid.

175   But that would not be so easy: Jack Brogan, interview with the author, January 16, 2014.

179   Concord is surrounded: Peter Arnell and Ted Bickford, eds., *Frank Gehry: Buildings and Projects* (New York: Rizzoli, 1985), 84.

179   "I kept looking at it": Ibid., 98.

179   "Funny you asked": Ibid.

181   "realized I was a total nut": Frank Gehry, interview with the author, June 20, 2011.

182   Thelma Gehry: Doreen Nelson, interview with the author, January 28, 2012.

182   "an indignity we had to suffer": Frank Gehry, interview with the author, January 18, 2014.

183   "It was devastating": Ibid.

183   "You'd better fucking get in here": Ibid.

184   "I'm intense about my work": Arnell and Bickford, *Frank Gehry*, xiv.

184   "If you really want to understand it all": Frank Gehry, interview with the author, January 18, 2014.

184   "were wined and dined": Ed Moses, interview with the author, December 13, 2012.

186   "was hysterical": Doreen Nelson, interview with the author, January 28, 2012.

10. A HOUSE IN SANTA MONICA

190 "The site was a parking lot": Peter Arnell and Ted Bickford, eds., *Frank Gehry: Buildings and Projects* (New York: Rizzoli, 1985), 154.

190 "everybody hates it": Frank Gehry, interview with the author, January 4, 2013.

191 "I see I've converted you": Ibid.

191 "You could call the chain-link guys": Barbara Isenberg, *Conversations with Frank Gehry* (New York: Alfred A. Knopf, 2009), 61.

191 "I love the way it looked": Frank Gehry, interview with the author, January 18, 2014.

192 "He thought I was expressing anger": Ibid.

192 "I confronted him": Ibid.

193 "You know, when you-know-who": Berta Gehry, interview with the author, December 28, 2014.

193 "My mother said": Doreen Nelson, interview with the author, January 14, 2012.

194 "The first moment I went through it": Berta Gehry, interview with Mildred Friedman in *Frank Gehry: The Houses* (New York: Rizzoli, 2009), 65.

194 "pink asbestos shingles": Friedman, *Frank Gehry: The Houses*, 64.

195 "I wasn't trying": Arnell and Bickford, *Frank Gehry*, 134.

195 "Frank and I have in common": Berta Gehry, interview with Mildred Friedman in *Frank Gehry: The Houses*, 65, 68.

196 "sketching with wood": Arnell and Bickford, *Frank Gehry*, 128.

197 "I said, 'I really like that'": Paul Lubowicki, interview with Mildred Friedman in *Frank Gehry: The Houses*, 61.

197 "a way for Frank": Ibid., 61–62.

199 "employed an original vocabulary": Herbert Muschamp, "A Masterpiece for Now," *New York Times Magazine*, September 7, 1997, 54.

200 "In this world": *Frank O. Gehry/Kurt W. Forster: Art and Architecture in Discussion*, ed. Christina Bechtler (Ostfildern-Rutt: Cantz Verlag, 1999), 20.

201 "It seems to me": Charles Moore, *The City Observed: Los Angeles* (New York: Random House, 1984), 162.

201 "It looks like a Tijuana sausage factory": Alex Hoyt, "AIA 25-Year Award," *Architect*, May 2012, 208.

201 "has put his money and talent": John Dreyfuss, "Gehry's Artful House Offends, Baffles, Angers His Neighbors," *Los Angeles Times*, July 23, 1978.

201 "There's a smugness": Frank Gehry, interview with Mildred Friedman in *Frank Gehry: The Houses*, 64–65.

202 "My attitude is": Ibid., 65.

202 "a major work of architecture": Joseph Morgenstern, *New York Times Magazine*, May 17, 1979, 48.

203 "I never had a bad play date": Alejo Gehry, interview with the author, June 23, 2014.

203 "I remember going": Sam Gehry, interview with the author, June 25, 2014.

203 "He didn't like it": Isenberg, *Conversations*, 67.

204 "You're mad at me": Frank Gehry, interview with the author, May 8, 2015.

206 "I would bring ideas": Jane Spiller, interview with Mildred Friedman in *Frank Gehry: The Houses*, 159–60.

207   "Frank was the architect": Chuck Arnoldi, interview with Mildred Friedman in *Frank Gehry: The Houses,* 167.

208   he never made any money from it: Frank Gehry, interview with the author, March 13, 2015. Gehry gave up his fees in exchange for a share of the profits, but according to his recollection the houses were sold at a loss.

208   "Frank, you don't like": Joshua Olsen, *Better Places, Better Lives: A Biography of James Rouse* (Washington, DC: Urban Land Institute, 2004), 266.

11. FISH AND OTHER SHAPES

211   "immediately struck": Thom Mayne, "Architecture 1979," in *A Confederacy of Heretics,* ed. Todd Gannon and Ewan Branda (Los Angeles: J. Paul Getty Museum, 2013), 208.

211   "Frank and I have a lot of common ground": Frank Gehry, Introduction to *Franklin D. Israel* (New York: Rizzoli, 1993), 10–11.

212   "Many of them": John Dreyfuss, *Los Angeles Times,* October 11, 1979, reprinted in *A Confederacy of Heretics,* 35.

214   "When Frank Gehry": Craig Hodgetts and Robert Mangurian, "Architect's Statement," in *A Confederacy of Heretics,* 85.

216   "In the end": Germano Celant, "Strada Novissima," *Artforum,* December 1980.

216   "was decorative": Barbara Isenberg, *Conversations with Frank Gehry* (New York: Alfred A. Knopf, 2009), 127.

217   At a lecture at UCLA: Frank Gehry, interview with the author, October 19, 2013. In the absence of a transcript, he described what he recalled saying at the UCLA lecture.

217   "a complete vocabulary": Isenberg, *Conversations,* 129.

220   "So each guy had to have a sketch": Frank Gehry, interview with author, October 19, 2013.

221   "We made a still life": Ibid.

223   "was gutsy": Frank Gehry, interview with the author, April 23, 2014.

224   "I decided I could have": Ibid.

225   "twist and turn": Henry N. Cobb, foreword to *The Architecture of Frank Gehry* (Minneapolis: Walker Art Center / New York: Rizzoli, 1986).

225   "a Monopoly house": Frank Gehry, interview with the author, April 23, 2014.

227   "I was always looking": Frank Gehry, interview with the author, December 28, 2014.

228   "undoubtedly the most menacing library": Mike Davis, *City of Quartz* (London: Verso, 1990), 239.

229   "he would take to subtracting": John Clagett, notes sent to the author, May 14, 2013.

230   "It's my Jewish guilt": Frank Gehry, interview with the author, May 5, 2014.

230   "a forceful reassembly": Leon Whiteson, "Frank Gehry's Buildings Invent Their Own Order," *Los Angeles Herald-Examiner,* July 29, 1984.

233   It would be difficult: Isenberg, *Conversations,* 110.

233   "I looked at them": Ibid.

12. ONTO THE WORLD STAGE

236   "We wanted to make something": Julie Lazar, "Interview: Frank Gehry," *Available Light,* Los Angeles Museum of Contemporary Art, 1983.

237 "I was interested in inaugurating": *The Architecture of Frank Gehry*, 103.

237 "Gehry rushes in": Mildred Friedman, "Fast Food," in *The Architecture of Frank Gehry*, 108.

239 "primarily because of the architecture": Richard Cohen, interview with the author, June 9, 2014.

241 "I didn't want to mess": Janelle Zara, "All Grown Up, Frank Gehry's Morandi-Inspired Kiddie Playhouse Leaves Home for College," *Blouin Artinfo*, September 30, 2011, available at http://www.blouinartinfo.com/news/story/749201/all-grown-up-frank-gehrys-morandi-inspired-kiddie-playhouse.

242 He finished the design: *The Architecture of Frank Gehry*, 201.

243 Yet Frank was so angry: Connie Bruck, "The Art of the Billionaire," *New Yorker*, December 6, 2010.

244 "I had looked at a lot of his work": Mildred Friedman, interview with the author, June 18, 2012.

245 "frequently depressed": Thomas Hines, "Heavy Metal: The Education of F.O.G.," in *The Architecture of Frank Gehry*, 11.

246 "Alejo assuring us": Coosje van Bruggen, "Leaps into the Unknown," in *The Architecture of Frank Gehry*, 123.

246 "they are working on the same issues": Ibid.

247 "was too 'arty'": Ibid.

250 "We didn't have a million": Frank Gehry, interview with the author, May 6, 2014.

250 "He said, 'Come on, Gehry'": Ibid.

250 "That's great": Ibid.

253 "I came from a very simple background": Rolf Fehlbaum, interview with the author, October 19, 2012.

253 "Frank is not greedy": Ibid.

254 "For me, it was a defining experience": "The Client as Curator," interview with Rolf Fehlbaum in *The Vitra Campus*, Vitra Design Museum, 2014.

256 "sense of dislocation": Mark Wigley, "Deconstructivist Architecture," in *Deconstructivist Architecture* (New York: Museum of Modern Art, 1988).

257 "Frank, you've won": Frank Gehry, interview with the author, June 20, 2014.

257 "Since I was a Japanophile already": Ibid.

258 "I realize I will have to work harder": Ibid.

258 "I am obsessed with architecture": Frank Gehry, Pritzker Prize acceptance speech, May 18, 1989.

13. WALT DISNEY CONCERT HALL: FIRST MOVEMENT

261 "one of the finest in the world": Lillian Disney quoted in Ted Vollmer, "For Disney Concert Hall: Take the $50-Million Gift, County Advised," *Los Angeles Times*, June 12, 1987.

261 Mrs. Disney agreed: Richard Koshalek and Dana Hutt, "The Impossible Becomes Possible: The Making of Walt Disney Concert Hall," in *Symphony: Frank Gehry's Walt Disney Concert Hall*, ed. Garrett White and Gloria Gerace (New York: Harry N. Abrams, 2003), 38.

261 Nicholas took on the task: Ibid., 40.

262 "You can't pick Frank Gehry": Ibid., 41.

262 "It can't be Frank Gehry": Richard Koshalek, interview with the author, June 23, 2014.

262   "Walt Disney would not have wanted": Frank Gehry, interview with the author, June 22, 2014.

262   Just after they had chosen: Richard Weinstein's recollection is cited as the source in Koshalek and Hutt, "The Impossible Becomes Possible," 42.

262   "They were scared to death": Richard Koshalek, interview with the author, June 23, 2014.

263   "They asked us to waive the right": Richard Weinstein, interview with the author, Febuary 2, 2012.

263   "There was criticism": Ibid.

264   "Come to lunch": Frank Gehry, interview with the author, June 22, 2014.

264   "zillions of tiny people": Koshalek and Hutt, "The Impossible Becomes Possible," 44.

264   "a living room for the city": Frank Gehry, interview with the author, June 22, 2014.

265   "the only one I'd really want to see": Koshalek and Hutt, "The Impossible Becomes Possible," 48.

265   "Mrs. Disney said": Richard Koshalek, interview with the author, June 23, 2014.

265   "I need you back here": Frank Gehry, interview with the author, June 22, 2014.

266   "I can't work with you": Jim Glymph, interview with the author, June 20, 2014.

266   "Let's try again": Ibid.

267   "his buildings had to work better": Ibid.

268   "architects don't build buildings": Gregg Pasquarelli, remark made in unrecorded panel discussion with the author at NYC AIA, May 16, 2014.

269   "that got Frank's attention": Jim Glymph, interview with the author, 1998.

269   "The ground rule": Ibid.

270   "I think we did fifty or sixty": Michael Maltzan, interview with the author, June 25, 2014.

270   As Frank became more comfortable: Michael Webb, "A Barge with Billowing Sails," in *Symphony*, 121–22.

270   Michael Maltzan remembered: Michael Maltzan, interview with the author, June 25, 2014.

271   "If you throw enough money at it": Diane Haithman and Carla Rivera, "Disney Site in Danger of Lease Default, County Warns," *Los Angeles Times*, December 21, 1994.

271   "virtually useless": Koshalek and Hutt, "The Impossible Becomes Possible," 50.

272   "It was harder to get him excited": Michael Maltzan, interview with the author, June 25, 2014.

272   Wurman, who had settled: Richard Saul Wurman, interview with the author, September 22, 2014.

273   When Disney Hall stopped: Larry Gordon, "Gehry Tries to Rebuild Image After Disney Hall," *Los Angeles Times*, May 30, 1996.

273   "huge and voluminous figures": Irving Lavin and Marilyn Lavin, interview with the author, October 21, 2014.

274   "Gehry and Eisenman are unmatched": Philip Johnson, "Introduction," in *Peter Eisenman and Frank Gehry* (New York: Rizzoli, 1991).

276   Not the least of the pleasures: Frank Gehry, interview with the author, August 12, 2014.

277   "What garden party?": Frank Gehry, interview with the author, July 14, 2011.

278   Thelma Gehry was buried: Frank Gehry, interview with the author, April 23, 2014.

278   Sam, who was fifteen: Ibid.

278   It was a moment: Ibid.

279   Sam remembered thinking: Sam Gehry, interview with the author, June 25, 2014.

279   "Don't do that all day": Alejo Gehry, interview with the author, June 24, 2014.

279   He really wanted: Alejo Gehry, interview with the author, October 19, 2014.

279   Alejo, who was dyslexic: Alejo Gehry, interview with the author, June 23, 2014.

280   "He swindled me": Sam Gehry, interview with the author, June 25, 2014.

281   "So I got to know": Berta Gehry, interview with the author, December 28, 2014.

282   He was the center: Frank Gehry, interview with the author, August 12, 2014.

282   She once drew: Gehry family papers, courtesy of Doreen Nelson.

282   "My mom ran the house": Alejo Gehry, interview with the author, June 23, 2014.

283   "a rising star": Peter Lewis unpublished memoir, chapter 25, "Adventures with Frank Gehry, 1984–2010."

283   "iconoclasts, analysands": Ibid.

284   "Like some fervent groupie": Ibid.

285   "Frank was getting more and more famous": Peter Lewis, interview with the author, April 25, 2012.

285   "Probably about fifty million dollars": This is how Gehry recollected the conversation with Lewis in an interview with the author on March 13, 2015, which was after Lewis's death. Lewis did not mention it in interviews with the author, and it is contradicted by Lewis's statement that he had envisioned $40 million as the maximum cost he would accept.

285   "I'm a do-gooder": Frank Gehry quoted in Paul Goldberger, "Houses as Art," *New York Times Magazine*, March 12, 1995.

286   "For Christ's sake": Peter Lewis, interview with the author, April 25, 2012.

286   "That's crazy": Lewis, "Adventures with Frank Gehry."

286   a revised and simplified version: Frank Gehry, interview with the author, March 13, 2015.

287   "Gehry schooled himself": Lewis, "Adventures with Frank Gehry."

14. THE GUGGENHEIM AND BILBAO

291   "How do you make": Mildred Friedman, ed., *Gehry Talks: Architecture and Process* (New York: Rizzoli, 1999), 140.

291   "Frank would just do a sketch": Michelle Kaufmann, interview with the author, March 20, 2014.

293   "Our challenge": Juan Ignacio Vidarte, interview with the author, May 16, 2014.

294   "the apotheosis of the stand-alone building": Tom Krens, quoted in Coosje van Bruggen, *Frank O. Gehry: Guggenheim Museum Bilbao* (New York: Guggenheim / Harry N. Abrams, 1997), 96.

294   "The relationship I had": Tom Krens, interview with the author, May 15, 2014.

294   purchased for $22 million: Ibid.

295   It was also Krens: Frank Gehry, interview with the author, August 12, 2014.

295   "had only one criterion": Tom Krens, interview with the author, May 15, 2014.

297   "offer an architectural context": Victoria Newhouse, *Towards a New Museum* (New York: Monacelli Press, 2006), 254–56.

298   "But we all thought": Juan Ignacio Vidarte, interview with the author, May 16, 2014.

298   "like wallpaper": Randy Jefferson, interview with the author, June 25 2014.

299   "helped the contractors": Juan Ignacio Vidarte, interview with the author, May 16, 2014.

299   In fact, it was $3 million: Meaghan Lloyd, letter to the editor, *Providence Journal*, September 18, 2012.

301   "the genius idea": Sverre Fehn, Pritzker Prize acceptance speech, May 31, 1997; transcript available at http://www.pritzkerprize.com/1997/ceremony.

301   "the greatest building of our time": Matt Tyrnauer, "Architecture in the Age of Gehry," *Vanity Fair*, August 2010.

301   "The word is out": Herbert Muschamp, "A Masterpiece for Now," *New York Times Magazine*, September 7, 1997, 54.

301   "the reincarnation": Ibid., 82.

303   "This is Uncle Rick": Alejo Gehry, interview with the author, June 24, 2014.

303   Projections had been: Leslie Crawford, "Guggenheim, Bilbao and the 'Hot Banana,'" *Financial Times*, September 4, 2001.

303   According to *Forbes*: Martin Bailey "The Bilbao Effect," *Forbes*, February 2, 2002.

304   "we recovered our self-esteem": Crawford, "Guggenheim, Bilbao and the 'Hot Banana.'"

304   In 2012: "The Bilbao Effect," *Economist*, December 21, 2013.

305   "When I saw Bilbao": Barbara Isenberg, "Frank Gehry Weighs in on Guggenheim Bilbao Nod," *Huffington Post*, July 3, 2010.

305   "Before Bilbao": Michelle Kaufmann, interview with the author, March 20, 2014.

305   The acclaim of Bilbao: Ibid.

306   "I think I've found my architect": Frank Gehry, interview with the author, May 18, 2014.

306   "The way I think about it": Frank Gehry, interview with the author, May 6, 2014.

307   "titanium cloud": David Dunlap, "Guggenheim Drops Plan for East River Museum," *New York Times*, December 31, 2002.

308   According to *Vanity Fair*: Vicky Ward, "A House Divided," *Vanity Fair*, August 2005.

15. WALT DISNEY CONCERT HALL: SECOND MOVEMENT

314   "People didn't believe": Eli Broad, interview with the author, April 18, 2012.

314   "As our hockey game intensified": Richard J. Riordan, *The Mayor* (Franklin, TN: Post Hill Press, 2014), 171.

315   "Build It and They Will Come": Advertisement, *Los Angeles Times*, March 4, 1997.

316   "because of past history": Calvin Tomkins, "The Maverick" (profile of Frank Gehry), *New Yorker*, July 7, 1997.

316   First he stalked out: Connie Bruck, "The Art of the Billionaire" (profile of Eli Broad), *New Yorker*, December 6, 2010.

316   Then he decided: Tomkins, "The Maverick."

316   "Some people have": Frank Gehry, letter to Eli Broad, published in *Los Angeles Times*, May 30, 1997.

316 "They don't want to listen": Joseph Giovannini, "Disney Hall and Gehry in Deal," *New York Times*, August 7, 1997.

317 She recalled that her father: Frank Gehry, interview with the author, January 11, 2013.

317 Miller told the concert hall committee: Ibid.

317 "We promised Los Angeles": Giovannini, "Disney Hall and Gehry in Deal."

320 "that no matter how spectacular": Michael Webb, "A Barge with Billowing Sails," in *Symphony: Frank Gehry's Walt Disney Concert Hall*, ed. Garrett White and Gloria Gerace (New York: Harry N. Abrams, 2003), 117.

321 "I thought it was the most amazing thing": Deborah Borda, interview with the author, June 22, 2014.

322 "I said to Frank": Ibid.

323 "If you have been playing": Ibid.

323 "You've all heard": Bob Colacello, "Eli Broad's Big Picture," *Vanity Fair*, December 2006.

324 "Disney Hall is the most gallant building": Herbert Muschamp, "A Moon Place for the Hollywood Dream," *New York Times*, October 23, 2003.

324 "in richness of sound": Alex Ross, "Kingdom Come," *New Yorker*, November 17, 2003.

326 "His music is very organic": Paul Allen, interview with the author, September 5, 2014.

326 "swoopy" form: Paul Goldberger, "Architect of Dreams," *Vanity Fair*, June 2000.

326 For his part: Paul Allen, interview with the author, September 5, 2014.

327 "I was always the liberal": Goldberger, "Architect of Dreams."

327 "It was guitar strings": Ibid.

328 Jim Glymph remembered: Jim Glymph, interview with the author, June 20, 2014.

328 "something that crawled out of the sea": Herbert Muschamp, "The Library That Puts on Fishnets and Hits the Disco," *New York Times*, May 16, 2004.

328 "capture the exuberance": Paul Allen, interview with the author, September 5, 2014.

328 "They were suspicious by nature": Edited transcript of talk, "Reflections on Designing and Architectural Practice," given by Frank Gehry at a symposium in Cleveland in 2002 held to mark the opening of the Peter B. Lewis Building at Case Western Reserve University. The proceedings of the symposium were published as *Managing as Designing*, ed. Richard J. Boland Jr. and Fred Collopy (Stanford, CA: Stanford University Press, 2004).

329 "I got a lot of hate mail": Ibid.

329 "a metaphor for the freedom": Robert Campbell, "Dizzying Heights," *Boston Globe*, April 25, 2004.

330 "She said, 'I just love it'": Irving and Marilyn Lavin, interview with the author, June 19, 2012.

331 "no obvious purpose": John Silber, *Architecture of the Absurd: How "Genius" Disfigured a Practical Art* (New York: Quantuck Lane Press, 2007), 75.

334 He saw it as a chance to demonstrate: Gehry spoke about his plans for the Philadelphia Museum of Art in a video interview prepared in connection with a 2014 exhibition on his designs, available on the museum's Web site at http://www.philamuseum.org/exhibitions/2014/809.html. He confirmed his view of the

project as the complement to Bilbao in an e-mail to the author on March 19, 2015.

335   "I didn't understand": Cindy Pritzker, interview with the author, May 10, 2012.
335   "So one of them said": Ibid.
336   "It was a very simple model": Ibid.
336   "We all said, 'Yes'": Ibid.
337   "I know your work": Frank Gehry, interview with the author, March 13, 2015.
337   "Tom got up and spoke": Cindy Pritzker, interview with the author, May 10, 2012.

16. NEW YORK: TRIALS AND TRIUMPHS

338   "was so eager to know": David Childs, interview with the author, February 12, 2013.
339   "That made us all the more eager": Victoria Newhouse and S. I. Newhouse, interview with the author, July 1, 2014.
340   "On one of our visits": Ibid.
345   "a space that is so magnificent": Deborah Solomon, "Questions for Frank Gehry," *New York Times Magazine*, January 5, 2003.
345   "a building that could be spiritual": Ibid.
345   "demeaning": Ibid.
347   Instead, late in the summer of 2014: Robin Pogrebin, "Arts Center at Ground Zero Shelves Gehry Design," *New York Times*, September 3, 2014.
349   "I thought, wow": Gere Kavanagh, interview with the author, February 3, 2013.
351   "It's a woman thing": Frank Gehry, interview with the author, August 13, 2014.
351   "I said, 'Leslie'": Ibid.
351   "I did what a father does": Ibid.
351   Anita met Sam and Alejo: Sam Gehry, interview with the author, June 25, 2014.
352   "We got stoned": Alejo Gehry, interview with the author, June 24, 2014.
353   "I still love you": Frank Gehry, interview with the author, December 27, 2014.
355   "I've been struggling to understand": Jonathan Lethem, "Brooklyn's Trojan Horse," *Slate*, June 19, 2006.
355   "It's fair to ask": Nicolai Ouroussoff, "Skyline for Sale," *New York Times*, June 4, 2006.
355   "There was no way": Bruce Ratner, interview with the author, November 26, 2013.
356   "I said, 'Let's go around the table'": Ibid.
356   "I'm passionate about the challenge": Frank Gehry, interview with the author, March 20, 2011.
357   "understood how to get to an essence": Ibid.
358   "I woke up and thought": Ibid.
360   Six subcontractors bid: Ibid.

17. FRANK AT EIGHTY

362   "One thing that nobody knows": Jori Finkel, "Museum Directors Hated Bilbao: Interview with Frank Gehry," *Art Newspaper*, October 2014.
369   "I found her sitting alone": Frank Gehry, interview with the author, August 14, 2014.

369   "He said, 'How are you doing'": Meaghan Lloyd, interview with the author, August 13, 2014.

369   "figured it out at the eleventh hour": Frank Gehry, interview with the author, August 14, 2014.

369   "He said, 'You won't like it'": Meaghan Lloyd, interview with the author, August 13, 2014.

369   Despite Frank's warning: Frank Gehry, interview with the author, August 14, 2014.

371   They were traveling: Meaghan Lloyd, interview with the author, August 13, 2014.

372   "How about the TC": Berta Gehry, interview with the author, September 19, 2012.

372   "That was kindergarten stuff": Ibid.

372   The actress Sally Kellerman: All quotes from Paul Goldberger, "Old and New: Gehry at Eighty," in "Talk of the Town," *New Yorker*, March 16, 2009.

374   And Serra was so intrigued: Michelle Kaufmann, interview with the author, March 20, 2014.

375   "Now we have architects": Calvin Tomkins, "Man of Steel," *New Yorker*, August 5, 2002.

375   "talked to each other": Ibid.

377   Frank felt that despite the attention: Frank Gehry, interview with the author, March 13, 2015.

378   "It has haunted me": Frank Gehry, interview with Fareed Zakaria on GPS, CNN, September 4, 2011.

379   "Let's get out of here": Michelle Kaufmann, interview with the author, March 20, 2014.

379   At the first showing: Lisa Rochon, interview with the author, August 1, 2012.

18. THE LEGACY OF TECHNOLOGY

380   "the bleeding-heart Canadian nebbish": Michael Sorkin, "Animating Space," in *Some Assembly Required* (Minneapolis: University of Minnesota Press, 2001), 98.

382   "He said, 'Are you crazy?'": Frank Gehry, interview with the author, October 19, 2014.

383   "We *were* Frank Gehry": Randy Jefferson, interview with the author, May 5, 2014.

383   "I want to say something": Frank Gehry, "Reflections on Designing and Architectural Practice," lecture from 2002, published in *Managing as Designing*, ed. Richard J. Boland Jr. and Fred Collopy (Stanford, CA: Stanford Business Press, 2004).

384   "I also insisted": Ibid.

384   "there is no way": Ibid.

384   "A serious CEO": Ibid.

386   "re-empower the architect": Frank Gehry, interview with the author, March 13, 2015.

387   "We are way ahead": Ibid.

387   "was not just an architectural point": Dennis Shelden, interview with the author, March 18, 2015.

387   "The success of Bilbao": Jim Glymph, interview with the author, June 20, 2014.

388   a forty-four-foot fiberglass-hulled Beneteau First: Frank Gehry, interview with the author, August 12, 2014.

389   "Why do people go": All quotes from an unrecorded meeting of the Gehry Technology architectural advisory board at 7 World Trade Center in New York on October 17, 2011, attended by the author.

390   Myers's priority: Frank Gehry, interview with the author, March 13, 2015.

392   "I never thought": Edwin Chan, interview with the author, April 25, 2014.

392   "the development of the architecture": Ibid.

392   "someone to play off of": Frank Gehry, interview with the author, April 25, 2014.

392   "Edwin was like family": Frank Gehry, interview with the author, June 20, 2014.

393   His intended few years: Edwin Chan, interview with the author, April 25, 2014.

395   "I've been reluctant": Frank Gehry, interview with the author, June 20, 2014.

19. FROM DWIGHT EISENHOWER TO LOUIS VUITTON

399   "an iceberg wrapped in a cloud": Jean-Paul Claverie, interview with the author, May 21, 2014.

399   The engineering: Graphic and sidebar text in Cathleen McGuigan, "Sacré Bleu! Fondation Louis Vuitton Paris," *Architectural Record*, October 2014.

401   "individualistic, uncouth Philistines": Henri Samuel, "World's Top Architect Frank Gehry Brands Paris Residents 'Philistines' After Planning Permission Revoked," *Telegraph*, February 6, 2011.

401   he also claimed not to have made: Frank Gehry, interview with the author, March 13, 2015.

401   "outraged by the selfishness": John Lichfield, "Parisian Residents Halt Gehry Building," *Independent*, February 7, 2011.

402   "I've got to package": Larry Ruvo quoted in Matt Jacobs, "The Rise of the Ruvo," *Vegas Seven*, April 24–30, 2014.

402   "Listen, I'm not doing a building": Quotes and anecdote from Jacobs, "The Rise of the Ruvo," and Frank Gehry, interview with the author, August 14, 2014.

405   "And Frank says": Michael Tilson Thomas, interview with the author, January 30, 2014.

405   "He said, 'In terms'": Ibid.

406   "I said, 'Okay'": Ibid.

406   "We'll put the juice on the inside": Ibid.

408   "My first thing": Frank Gehry, interview with the author, August 13, 2014.

409   "a kind of think tank": Diane Solway, "The Insider," W, September 2012.

410   "Why would someone of your reputation": Frank Gehry, interview with the author, January 4, 2013.

412   "finished ahead of schedule": Mark Zuckerberg, Facebook posting, April 6, 2015, 5:07 p.m.

413   "I fell in love with him": Frank Gehry quoted in Paul Goldberger, "A Monumental Conflict," *Vanity Fair*, August 2012.

416   "has managed to achieve": Jeffrey Frank, "Rescuing the Eisenhower Memorial," *New Yorker*, March 25, 2013.

416   "a roofless classical temple": Witold Rybczynski, "I Like Ike (and His Memorial)," *New York Times*, March 22, 2012.

417   "The commission persevered": "Another Battle for Eisenhower," editorial, *New York Times*, November 3, 2014.

20. AN ARCHIVE AND A LEGACY

418 "I don't know what's going to happen": Observed by the author, February 12, 2015.

419 "his avant-garde prior works": National Civic Art Society, *Report on Frank Gehry's Eisenhower Memorial*, February 2012.

422 "It knocked our socks off": Frank Gehry, interview with the author, January 19, 2015.

422 "I'm not involved in the politics": Ibid.

423 "filled the stage with huge icebergs": Zachary Woolfe, "Mozart's 'Don,' in a Lunar Landscape, Haunts Gehry's Hall in Los Angeles," *New York Times*, May 27, 2012.

424 "I have a personal affinity": Frank Gehry, "I Can't Imagine Living in a Place Without a Ken Price," in *Ken Price* (Los Angeles: Los Angeles County Museum of Art, 2012).

427 "So this is liquid": Observed by the author, August 6, 2012.

427 "I look at it like composing": Barbara Isenberg, *Conversations with Frank Gehry* (New York: Alfred A. Knopf, 2009), 208.

428 "He said he didn't want anything fancy": All quotes from Juan Ignacio Vidarte, interview with the author, May 16, 2014.

428 Barenboim played: Frank Gehry, e-mail to the author, March 1, 2014.

431 "We are just an elderly couple": Frank Gehry, observed by the author, June 20, 2014.

431 On January 31, 2011: Report on 316 Adelaide Drive, from propertyshark.com.

438 At one point Cohen told Frank: Frank Gehry, interview with the author, November 17, 2014.

440 "All we decided": Sam Gehry, interview with the author, August 14, 2014.

440 "Frank seemed like the king": Peter Arnell, interview with the author, December 18, 2014.

440 A deal like the sale: Frank Gehry, interview with the author, June 24, 2014.

441 He said no in part: Frank Gehry, interview with the author, August 14, 2014.

441 just 20 percent: Frank Gehry, interview with the author, June 24, 2014.

441 "We all agreed": David Nam, interview with the author, August 14, 2014.

21. IN PARIS, LOOKING BACK AND LOOKING FORWARD

444 "Seeing all my old stuff": Frank Gehry, interview with the author, October 18, 2014.

446 "I wish I could enjoy it": Ibid.

447 "not so pretentious": Frank Gehry, interview with the author, October 21, 2014.

447 Rowan Moore: Rowan Moore, "Everything and the Bling from Frank Gehry," *Observer*, October 19, 2014.

447 "a crazed indulgence": Oliver Wainwright, "Frank Gehry's Fondation Louis Vuitton Shows He Doesn't Know Where to Stop," *Guardian*, October 21, 2014.

448 "as spatially and structurally profligate": Ellis Woodman, "Carte Blanche: Fondation Louis Vuitton, Paris, France, by Gehry Partners," *Architectural Review*, October 27, 2014.

448 "a Cubist sailboat": Joseph Giovannini, "An Architect's Big Parisian Moment," *New York Times*, October 20, 2014.

448   "brilliant, a late career triumph": Christopher Hawthorne, "Gehry's Louis Vuitton Museum Is a Triumph, but to What End?," *Los Angeles Times*, October 17, 2014.

448   "two great themes": Irving Lavin, "La Magie de FOG: Le Bâtiment le Plus Complexe Jamais Construit," in catalog *Frank Gehry: La Fondation Louis Vuitton* (2014).

448   "notably lacking in repose": Martin Filler, "Frank Gehry in Paris," *New York Review of Books*, January 8, 2015.

450   "It's why I did the chain-link thing": Frank Gehry, interview with the author, November 17, 2014.

450   "In fact, he enjoys": Philip Johnson, in *Sketches of Frank Gehry*, directed by Sydney Pollack, Sony Pictures Classics, 2006.

450   "I was looking for a way": Frank Gehry, in *Sketches of Frank Gehry*.

451   "I hold that it was wrong": Igor Stravinsky, *Poetics of Music in the Form of Six Lessons* (Cambridge, MA: Harvard University Press, 1942), 9–11.

452   "an alternative system": Michael Sorkin, *Some Assembly Required* (Minneapolis: University of Minnesota Press, 2001), 100.

452   "tradition is carried forward": Stravinsky, *Poetics of Music*, 57.

452   "You've got to know the rules": Alexander McQueen, quoted in wall label, *Alexander McQueen: Savage Beauty*, exhibition at the Victoria and Albert Museum, London, 2015.

452   "the work of art closest to perfection": Max Raphael, *Prehistoric Cave Paintings* (New York: Pantheon, 1945), 17.

452   "nothing more than a succession": Stravinsky, *Poetics of Music*, 35.

453   "The faculty of creating": Ibid., 54.

454   "On a building": Gehry has made this comment in various forms multiple times over the years. The idea is most clearly stated in his talk from 2002, "Reflections on Designing and Architectural Practice," published in *Managing as Designing*, ed. Richard J. Boland Jr. and Fred Collopy (Stanford, CA: Stanford Business Press, 2004).

Selected Bibliography

Arnell, Peter, and Ted Bickford, eds. *Frank Gehry: Buildings and Projects.* New York: Rizzoli, 1985.

Banham, Reyner. *Los Angeles: The Architecture of Four Ecologies.* Berkeley: University of California Press, 1971.

Barron, Stephanie, and Lauren Bergman. *Ken Price Sculpture: A Retrospective.* New York: Prestel USA, 2012.

Bechtler, Cristina, ed. *Frank O. Gehry/Kurt W. Forster: Art and Architecture in Discussion.* Ostfildern, Germany: Hatje Cantz Verlag, 1999.

Begiristain Mitxelena, Iñaki. *Building Time: The Relatus in Frank Gehry's Architecture.* Reno: University of Nevada Press, 2014.

Bletter, Rosemarie Haag. *The Architecture of Frank Gehry.* New York: Rizzoli, 1986.

Boissière, Olivier, and Martin Filler. *The Vitra Design Museum.* New York: Rizzoli, 1990.

Boland, Richard J., Jr., and Fred Collopy, eds. *Managing as Designing.* Stanford, CA: Stanford University Press, 2004.

Caughey, John, and LaRee Caughey. *Los Angeles: Biography of a City.* Berkeley: University of California Press, 1977.

Celant, Germano. *Frank O. Gehry Since 1997.* New York: Skira Rizzoli, 2010.

———, ed. *Il Corso del Coltello (The Course of the Knife).* New York: Rizzoli, 1986.

Dal Co, Francesco, and Kurt W. Forster. *Frank O. Gehry: The Complete Works.* New York: Monacelli Press, 1998.

Davis, Mike. *City of Quartz.* London: Verso, 1990.

De Wit, Wim, and Christopher James Alexander, eds. *Overdrive: L.A. Constructs the Future, 1940–1990.* Los Angeles: Getty Research Institute, 2013.

Dollfus, Audouin. *The Great Refractor of Meudon Observatory.* New York: Springer, 2013.

Drohojowska-Philp, Hunter. *Rebels in Paradise: The Los Angeles Art Scene and the 1960s.* New York: Henry Holt, 2011.

Ferguson, Russell, ed. *At the End of the Century: One Hundred Years of Architecture.* Los Angeles and New York: Museum of Contemporary Art / Harry N. Abrams, 1998.

Filler, Martin. *Makers of Modern Architecture: From Frank Lloyd Wright to Frank Gehry.* New York: New York Review of Books, 2007.

FOG: Flowing in All Directions. Los Angeles: Circa Publishing / Museum of Contemporary Art, 2003.

Foster, Hal. *Design and Crime and Other Diatribes.* London: Verso, 2002.

Frank Gehry, 1987–2003. Madrid: El Croquis, 2006.

Frank Gehry, GA Document 130. Tokyo: ADA Edita, 2014.

Frank Gehry: New Bentwood Furniture Designs. Montreal: Montreal Museum of Decorative Arts, 1992.

Frank Gehry: Recent Projects. Tokyo: ADA Edita, 2011.

Frank Gehry: Toronto. Toronto: Art Gallery of Toronto, 2006.

Frank O. Gehry: Design and Architecture. Weil am Rhein, Germany: Vitra Design Museum, 1996.

Frank O. Gehry: European Projects. Berlin: Aedes Gallery, 1994.

Friedman, Mildred. *Frank Gehry: The Houses.* New York: Rizzoli, 2009.

——. *Gehry Talks: Architecture + Process.* New York: Rizzoli, 1999; rev. ed., New York: Universe, 2002.

Fulford, Robert. *Frank Gehry in Toronto: Transforming the Art Gallery of Ontario.* New York: Merrell, 2009.

Futagawa, Yukio. *GA Architect 10: Frank Gehry.* Tokyo: ADA Edita, 1993.

——. *GA Document: Frank O. Gehry 13 Projects After Bilbao.* Tokyo: ADA Edita, 2002.

Gannon, Todd, and Ewan Branda, eds. *A Confederacy of Heretics.* Los Angeles: J. Paul Getty Museum, 2013.

Garcetti, Gil. *Iron: Erecting the Walt Disney Concert Hall.* South Pasadena, CA: Balcony Press, 2002.

Gilbert-Rolfe, Jeremy. *Frank Gehry: The City and Music.* Amsterdam: G+B Arts International, 2001.

Goldberger, Paul. *Building Up and Tearing Down: Reflections on the Age of Architecture.* New York: Monacelli Press, 2009.

——. *Frank Gehry at Gemini.* Los Angeles: Gemini G.E.L., 2000.

——. *Frank Gehry Fish Lamps.* New York: Gagosian Gallery, 2014.

——. *Why Architecture Matters.* New Haven, CT: Yale University Press, 2009.

Goldberger, Paul, and Frank Gehry. *Frank Gehry IAC Building.* New York: Georgetown Company, 2009.

Hines, Thomas S. *Architecture of the Sun: Los Angeles Modernism, 1940–1970.* New York: Rizzoli, 2010.

Huxtable, Ada Louise. *On Architecture: Collected Reflections on a Century of Change.* New York: Walker & Co., 2008.

Isenberg, Barbara. *Conversations with Frank Gehry.* New York: Alfred A. Knopf, 2009.

Israel, Franklin D. *Franklin D. Israel: Buildings and Projects.* New York: Rizzoli, 1992.

Janmohamed, Hanif, and James Glymph. *Confluences: The Design and Realization of Frank Gehry's Walt Disney Concert Hall.* Los Angeles: Gehry Technologies, 2004.

Jencks, Charles. *The New Moderns.* New York: Rizzoli, 1990.

Joyce, Nancy E. *Building Stata: The Design and Construction of Frank O. Gehry's Stata Center at MIT.* Cambridge, MA: MIT Press, 2004.

Kamin, Blair. *Terror and Wonder: Architecture in a Tumultuous Age.* Chicago: University of Chicago Press, 2010.

Kaplan, Wendy, ed. *California Design: Living in a Modern Way.* Cambridge, MA: MIT Press, 2011.

Kornblau, Gary, ed. *Frank Gehry Designs the Lou Ruvo Brain Institute, Las Vegas.* Bright City Books, 2006.

Lavin, Sylvia, ed. *Everything Loose Will Land: 1970s Art and Architecture in Los Angeles.* Nuremberg: Moderne Kunst Nürnberg, 2014.

Lemon, James. *Toronto Since 1918: An Illustrated History.* Toronto: James Lorimer & Co., 1985.

Lindsey, Bruce. *Digital Gehry.* Boston: Birkhäuser, 2002.

Lubell, Sam, and Douglas Woods. *Julius Shulman Los Angeles.* New York: Rizzoli, 2011.

Lynn, Greg, ed. *Archaeology of the Digital.* Berlin: Canadian Centre for Architecture/ Sternberg Press, 2013.

Meyer, Esther Da Costa. *Frank Gehry: On Line.* New Haven, CT: Yale University Press, 2008.

Migayrou, Frédéric. *Frank Gehry.* Paris: Centre Georges Pompidou, 2014.

Moore, Charles, with Peter Becker and Regula Campbell. *The City Observed: Los Angeles.* New York: Random House, 1984.

Morgan, Susan, ed. *Piecing Together Los Angeles: An Esther McCoy Reader.* Valencia, CA: East of Borneo Books, 2012.

Mount, Christopher, and Jeffrey Deitch. *A New Sculpturalism: Contemporary Architecture from Southern California.* New York: Skira Rizzoli, 2013.

Muschamp, Herbert. *Hearts of the City: The Selected Writings of Herbert Muschamp.* New York: Alfred A. Knopf, 2009.

Nero, Irene. *Transformations in Architecture: Frank Gehry's Techno-Morphism at the Guggenheim Bilbao.* Lambert Academic Publishing, 2009.

Newhouse, Victoria. *Sight and Sound: The Architecture and Acoustics of New Opera Houses and Concert Halls.* New York: Monacelli Press, 2012.

———. *Towards a New Museum.* New York: Monacelli Press, 1998; expanded ed., 2006.

Novartis Campus—Fabrikstrasse 15, Frank O. Gehry. Basel: Christoph Merian Verlag, 2010.

Olsen, Joshua. *Better Places, Better Lives: A Biography of James Rouse.* Washington, DC: Urban Land Institute, 2004.

Peabody, Rebecca, and Andrew Perchuk, eds. *Pacific Standard Time: Los Angeles Art, 1945–80.* Los Angeles: Getty Research Institute, 2011.

Peter Eisenman and Frank Gehry. New York: Rizzoli, 1991.

Ragheb, J. Fiona, ed. *Frank Gehry, Architect.* New York: Guggenheim Museum Publications, 2001.

Rappolt, Mark, and Robert Violette, eds. *Gehry Draws.* Cambridge, MA: MIT Press, 2004.

Robertson, Colin M., ed. *Modernist Maverick: The Architecture of William L. Pereira.* Reno: Nevada Museum of Art, 2013.

Robertson, Jacquelin, intro. *The Charlottesville Tapes.* New York: Rizzoli, 1985.

Roccati, Anne-Line, ed. *The Fondation Louis Vuitton by Frank Gehry: A Building for the Twenty-First Century.* Paris: Flammarion, 2014.

Silber, John. *The Architecture of the Absurd: How "Genius" Disfigured a Practical Art.* New York: Quantuck Lane Press, 2007.

Sims, Peter. *Little Bets: How Breakthrough Ideas Emerge from Small Discoveries.* New York: Free Press, 2011.

Sorkin, Michael. *Some Assembly Required.* Minneapolis: University of Minnesota Press, 2001.

Steele, James. *California Aerospace Museum: Frank Gehry, Architecture in Detail.* London: Phaidon Press, 1992.

Stravinsky, Igor. *Poetics of Music in the Form of Six Lessons.* Cambridge, MA: Harvard University Press, 1942.

Street-Porter, Tim. *L.A. Modern.* New York: Rizzoli, 2008.

Symphony: Frank Gehry's Walt Disney Concert Hall. Los Angeles: Los Angeles Philharmonic / New York: Harry N. Abrams, 2003.

Tigerman, Stanley, intro. *The Chicago Tapes.* New York: Rizzoli, 1987.

Tulchinsky, Gerald. *Branching Out: The Transformation of the Canadian Jewish Community.* Toronto: Stoddart Publishing Co., 1998.

Van Bruggen, Coosje. *Frank O. Gehry: Guggenheim Museum Bilbao.* New York: Guggenheim Museum Publications, 1997.

Venturi, Robert. *Complexity and Contradiction in Architecture.* New York: Museum of Modern Art, 1966.

Weisman Art Museum: Frank Gehry Designs the Building. Minneapolis: University of Minnesota Press, 2004.

CHILDREN'S BOOKS ABOUT FRANK GEHRY

Bodden, Valerie. *Xtraordinary Artists: Frank Gehry.* Mankato, MN: Creative Co., 2008.

Chollet, Laurence B. *The Essential Frank O. Gehry.* New York: Harry N. Abrams, 2001.

Greenberg, Jan, and Sandra Jordan. *Frank O. Gehry: Outside In.* London: Dorling Kindersley, 2000.

Johnson, Jinny, and Roland Lewis. *Frank Gehry in Pop-up.* San Diego: Thunder Bay Press, 2007.

Lazo, Caroline Evensen. *Frank Gehry.* Minneapolis: Twenty-First Century Books, 2005.

Miller, Jason. *Frank Gehry.* New York: MetroBooks, 2002.

Poulakidas, Georgene. *The Guggenheim Museum Bilbao: Transforming a City.* New York: Children's Press, 2004.

Stungo, Naomi, *Frank Gehry.* London: Carlton Books, 2000.

Index

Page numbers in *italics* refer to illustrations.

Illustration Credits

Grateful acknowledgment is made to the following for permission to reprint photographs:

PHOTOGRAPHS IN TEXT

Ave Pildas: 215

DBox/OTTO: 359

Facebook: 411

Forest City Ratner: 4, 18

Frank Gehry and Ed Moses: 185

Gehry Partners: 22, 24, 27, 35, 55, 77, 97, 106 (photograph by Greg Walsh), 121, 145, 158, 167, 198, 221 (photograph by Greg Walsh), 240, 247, 263, 274, 279, 281, 295, 296, 313, 318, 320, 325, 327, 332, 341, 350, 366, 370, 373, 393, 400, 414, 421, 429

The IAC Building: 347

Iwan Baan: 406

The Guggenheim: 299, 300, 429

Michael Moran/OTTO: 126

Olivier Boissiere: 143

Paul Goldberger: 445

The Simpsons® & © 2005 Twentieth Century Fox Film Corporation. All Rights Reserved: 378

Squire Haskins: 213

Thomas Mayer: 254

Tim Street-Porter/OTTO: 199

Todd Eberle: 373

INSERT

Frank Gehry. Source: Gehry Partners

Fish lamp. Source: Fred Hoffman

Easy Edges. Source: © Bettina Mathiessen

Ron Davis house. Source: Gehry Partners

Loyola Law School campus. Source: Gehry Partners

Guggenheim Bilbao, rear façade. Source: Guggenheim

Guggenheim Bilbao, main façade. Source: Guggenheim

Museum of Biodiversity. Photographer: Fernando Alda. Source: Biomuseo de Panama

Walt Disney Concert Hall. Source: Gehry Partners

Walt Disney Concert Hall interior. Source: Gehry Partners

Fondation Louis Vuitton (all three photos). Source: Fondation Luis Vuitton

Exhibits at Los Angeles County Museum of Art. Source: Frederick Nilsen

Aboard *Foggy*. Source: Richard Snyder

513